Gaming for Classroom-Based Learning:
Digital Role Playing as a Motivator of Study

Youngkyun Baek
Korea National University of Education, Republic of Korea

Information Science REFERENCE
INFORMATION SCIENCE REFERENCE
Hershey · New York

Director of Editorial Content: Kristin Klinger
Director of Book Publications: Julia Mosemann
Acquisitions Editor: Lindsay Johnston
Development Editor: Beth Ardner
Typesetter: Gregory Snader
Production Editor: Jamie Snavely
Cover Design: Lisa Tosheff
Printed at: Yurchak Printing Inc.

Published in the United States of America by
Information Science Reference (an imprint of IGI Global)
701 E. Chocolate Avenue
Hershey PA 17033
Tel: 717-533-8845
Fax: 717-533-8661
E-mail: cust@igi-global.com
Web site: http://www.igi-global.com/reference

Library of Congress Cataloging-in-Publication Data

Gaming for classroom-based learning : digital role playing as a motivator of study / Youngkyun Baek, editor.
p. cm.
Includes bibliographical references and index.
ISBN 978-1-61520-713-8 (hardcover) -- ISBN 978-1-61520-714-5 (ebook) 1. Educational games. 2. Motivation in education. I. Baek, Youngkyun. LB1029.G3G355 2010
371.33'7--dc22
2009039677

British Cataloguing in Publication Data
A Cataloguing in Publication record for this book is available from the British Library.

Table of Contents

Section 2
Cases of Gaming Use in Teaching and Learning

Section 3
Use of Gaming in Virtual Worlds

Detailed Table of Contents

Section 1
Gaming Relevant to Classroom Teaching and Learning

Section One, "Gaming Relevant to Classroom Teaching and Learning," introduces ideas of how to bring digital games effectively into classroom. The first section, consisting of five chapters, attempts to implement results in achieving learning objectives by effectively using games in the classroom. Teachers and parents need to agree on games' positive functions toward students' learning, decide and select good educational games relevant to content and tasks in the classroom, and disseminate their acquired knowledge into the teaching field. Section One opens with a chapter by O'Brien. In "A Taxonomy of Educational Games," he proposes a taxonomy of digital games in education based on the cognitive functions and skills players engage. Price and Moore suggest a new theoretical approach based on situated learning, the experiential learning cycle of Kolb, and the ARCS model of Keller in "The Design and Development of Educational Immersive Environments: From Theory to Classroom Deployment." Third section of this section opens with McNamara, Jackson, and Graesser introducing "Intelligent Tutoring and Games (ITaG)." Their point of view is that game-based learning improves students' motivation with the instructional system. Aremu provides support for the effectiveness of the use of digital games in the classroom and presents teacher perceptions on how to use a computer game in the classroom in "Using 'TRIRACE©' in the Classroom - with Nigerian Teachers – Perception on Modes and Effectiveness." Finally, in Gibson's chapter "Bridging Informal and Formal Learning Experiences with Participatory Media," the author uses the game-based learning to illustrate the framework of the participatory media bridge between informal and formal education.

This chapter proposes a taxonomy of digital games in education based on the cognitive functions and skills players engage. The theoretical basis for the taxonomy was drawn from Gagné's Five Categories of Learning Outcomes, Bloom's Taxonomy of Educational Objectives, and Jonassen's Typology of Problem Solving. The links between these theories and the educational games taxonomy will allow educators and researchers to understand games in light of their educational affordances. Instructional design based on these theories can more effectively integrate games into the classroom.

This chapter starts from a review of current educational issues and moves to an evaluation of educational theory and instructional design principles. Their proposed and developed "Educational Immersive Environments" may embrace both the technology and the authors' approach to develop their own learning resources. They suggest a new theoretical approach based on situated learning, the experiential learning cycle of Kolb, and the ARCS model of Keller.

This chapter approaches gaming's effectiveness from the game design side. The authors' point of view is that game-based learning improves students' motivation with the instructional system. They describe a conceptual framework that provides a guide to how adding game-based features and components may improve the effectiveness of ITS learning environments by improving students' motivation to engage with the system. ITS researchers have begun to incorporate game-based elements within learning systems. They provide insight into how elements within each category may affect various types of motivation.

This chapter provides support for the effectiveness of the use of digital games in the classroom and presents teacher perceptions on how to use a computer game in the classroom. The author also recommends that teacher preferences should be integrated into the design of games as well as training on the integration of games in the classroom and teacher training should place an emphasis on practical sessions of game playing in the curriculum so as to develop teachers' competence and confidence in the use of games. This would go a long way in ensuring that teachers implement educational games in their classroom.

Arizona State University, USAIn this chapter, the author describes the architecture of participatory media and the transition in formal education needed to mine the spare time and effort of learners. According to Gibson, teachers who are trained to travel both ways on this bridge can be highly effective in creating new learning experiences that function as spreadable media appropriated by teens and others in a myriad of new ways in the emerging participatory culture of schools of the future. The author uses the game-based learning framework of The Global Challenge Award program in order to illustrate the framework of the participatory media bridge between informal and formal education.

Section 2
Cases of Gaming Use in Teaching and Learning

Section Two, "Cases of Gaming Use in Teaching and Learning," consists of six chapters, discusses effective ways to use gaming in the classrooms of various subject areas and school levels. The first part of this section starts with a chapter by Katzlinger. "Technology Enhanced Language Learning in Early Childhood-Competencies for Early Childhood Teachers" deals with a training curriculum for kindergarten teachers to introduce a learning game for technology-enhanced language learning in early childhood, and demonstrate how kindergarten teachers can launch the game in their classes. Following that, Graham and his colleagues explore a case study of interactive fiction in an elementary classroom, and suggest that the process of creating a text-based game helped improve literary and social skills amongst the students in "The Haunted School on Horror Hill: A Case Study of Interactive Fiction in an Elementary Classroom." The section continues with Kim, who uses multiplayer English teaching online games and finds that elementary students' online game experiences increased self-efficacy in the chapter "Use of Interactive Online Games in Teaching English as a Foreign Language." Sauvé also uses online games to stimulate learning based on the findings of STIs in online games in "Using Educational Online Game to Stimulate Learning." Martins cover the question of how teachers can bring the realities of decision-making and action into the curriculum in his chapter, "The Experience of an Online Management Simulation Game to Foster Collaboration and Teamwork." Finally, VanFossen, Friedman, and Hartshorne answer the question of the potential of massively multi-player online role-playing games (MMORPGs) meeting content standards in social studies in "Exploring Guild Participation in MMORPGs and Civic Leadership."

This chapter deals with a training curriculum for kindergarten teachers to introduce a learning game for technology-enhanced language learning in early childhood and how kindergarten teachers can launch the game in their classes. The game helps children to become familiar with the German language as a mother tongue or as a second language. The game "Schlaumäuse" was developed to enhance the children's language learning. Children between the ages of four to eight are the target group of this software. The different activities in the story of the game encourage the children's phases of language learning like structure of syllables, phoneme, rhymes or phonological features.

In this chapter authors considers that games help students to gain a real 'feel' for collaboration, managerial decision-making and teamwork, and describing how a web-based competitive management game helps to achieve business decision-making. Overall, the simulation game course was seen as a better vehicle in helping students make career preparations, achieve educational goals, and utilize time. He notes:

This chapter reflects on the concept of educational simulations and games and aims at describing how a web-based competitive management game helped to achieve that. The authors discuss their objectives and those of the game and outline their reasons for choosing it. They describe the context at ISCAL and the game's main features, showing how it is played over a semester. The authors consider, as online simulation facilitators of what is predominantly a student-led learning process, that the game helps students to gain a real 'feel' for collaboration, managerial decision-making and teamwork. The results of the authors' empirical study show that students perceive the simulation course as superior to the lecture-centered method. On the overall dimensions, the simulation course was seen as a better vehicle in helping students make career preparations, achieve educational goals, and utilize time.

Section 3
Use of Gaming in Virtual Worlds

Section Three, "Use of Gaming in Virtual Worlds," discusses the usage of the virtual world in the learning and teaching environment with focuses on the engagement in social learning, socialization, and meta-learning, thereby helping students to acquire social skills. In first part of this section Kaplan-Rakowski and Loh provide an overview of the modification process to create new resources within a virtual environment. Bauer introduces new tools in order to match virtual worlds to reality and determined the solutions delivered needed to provide task-oriented functionality. Next, Ferry and his colleagues summarize six years of research in the virtual learning environment of ClassSim provide an effective way of introducing pre-service teachers to their future work in classrooms. In Chaka's chapter, the author answers the question: how do virtual games enable gamers to engage in social learning, situated learning, and problem based learning on the one hand, and in meta-gaming, meta-literacies, and multi-tasking, on the other hand? Finally, Toro-Troconis and her colleague explore the elements associated with game-based learning in Second Life.

Preface

Can a game motivate students to learn effectively? Can it improve one's knowledge and skill as a motivator of study? As part of an international dialog between researchers in educational technology, this key question and many more related to it have led to this new collection of ideas, research, and reflections by researchers looking for answers.

The word "gaming" is included in the title of this book to ensure readers know we are talking about the heart of playing games and its role in classroom-based learning. Thus, this book is intended primarily for classroom teachers as well as pre-service teachers who are looking into games with an eye to their potential for improving teaching and learning. If this is you, then welcome to an emerging community!

The authors here approach their work variously as experimental, development-based, philosophical, conceptual and pragmatic, and sometimes in several configurations of these perspectives. Hopefully, this means you will find several chapters here that are to your immediate liking and others that will appeal to you in time. Perhaps a few chapters will not be exactly what you are looking for now, but we trust they will all guide you to think further about the issues, lead you to deeper levels of research, and help link you with active researchers in this emerging field.

An edited collection of different authors presents a challenge, an opportunity, and a diversity of viewpoints, opinions, and research perspectives. This book is expected to repay your time spent in browsing and sampling its many offerings and will serve you as a reference for future forays into its subject: gaming for classroom-based learning that seeks to motivate teaching and learning for game players.

GAMING RELEVANT TO CLASSROOM TEACHING AND LEARNING

Is a game a learning tool which can be adopted in classroom teaching and learning? Or is it a systematic learning environment? In the perspective that learning is an ongoing process, contexts where gaming for classroom-based learning happens can be established as a dynamic learning environment through the various, frequent, and prompt interactions between players and the systematic environment of a game.

Digital games have often been categorized as harmful media by both parents and educators. This is partly due to their understanding that students are spending their time on gaming just for fun. They also think that study and fun cannot coexist and that study requires deliberate hard, not fun. They often misunderstand games' value for education. This is partly caused by their perception of many diverse types of games in the same way.

Learning components, rules, strategies, scaffolding, feedback, controls and management, and collaborative work among players are all incorporated in the interactions of digital games. In order to effectively use games in the classroom, teachers and parents need to agree on games' positive functions toward students' learning, decide and select good educational games relevant to content and tasks in the classroom, and disseminate their acquired knowledge into the teaching field. Many chapters in this book attempt to implement results in achieving learning objectives. Those chapters are deemed to refresh possibilities and affirmation in gaming for classroom-based learning fields.

Dan O'Brien proposes a taxonomy of digital games in education based on the cognitive functions and skills players engage. The theoretical basis for the taxonomy was drawn from Gagné's Five Categories of Learning Outcomes, Bloom's Taxonomy of Educational Objectives, and Jonassen's Typology of Problem Solving. The links between these theories and the educational games taxonomy will allow educators and researchers to understand games in light of their educational affordances. Instructional design based on these theories can more effectively integrate games into the classroom.

In designing effective gaming environments, one perspective is that teachers and students can both utilize gaming activities in classroom practice and curriculum development. Collin Price and Moore's expectation is that the expectation of utilizing new digital technologies in learning contexts by both teachers and students may change classroom practice and inform curriculum developments. They start from a review of current educational issues and move to an evaluation of educational theory and instructional design principles. Their proposed and developed "Educational Immersive Environments" may embrace both the technology and outheir approach to develop their own learning resources. They suggest a new theoretical approach based on situated learning, the experiential learning cycle of Kolb, and the ARCS model of Keller. Another perspective is manifested in Danielle McNamara, Tanner Jackson, and Art Graesser's chapter. They approach gaming's effectiveness from the game design side. Their point of view is that game-based learning improves students' motivation with the instructional system. They describe a conceptual framework that provides a guide to how adding game-based features and components may improve the effectiveness of ITS learning environments by improving students' motivation to engage with the system. ITS researchers have begun to incorporate game-based elements within learning systems. They provide insight into how elements within each category may affect various types of motivation.

We cannot deny that teachers are a critical factor in a game-based learning system, even though students have initial control for their gaming activities. Thus teachers' perceptions are critical to the success or failure of integrating digital games, as indicated by Ayotola Aremu. He goes on:

If teachers' attitudes are negative and they do not have a say in how to use the innovation, then no matter how well a game has been packaged, it would not be effective (Aremu, 2004). One way to ensure positive teachers' attitudes is to involve them, right from the teacher training period, in design, validation, and implementation.

He provides support for the effectiveness of the use of digital games in the classroom and presents teacher perceptions on how to use a computer game in the classroom. He also recommends that teacher preferences should be integrated into the design of games as well as training on the integration of games in the classroom and teacher training should place an emphasis on practical sessions of game playing in the curriculum so as to develop teachers' competence and confidence in the use of games. This would go a long way in ensuring that teachers implement educational games in their classroom.

Educational games, especially off-the-shelf games, necessitate a redesign of curriculum activities to fit into classrooms. David Gibson describes the architecture of participatory media and the transition in formal education needed to mine the spare time and effort of learners. According to Gibson, teachers who are trained to travel both ways on this bridge can be highly effective in creating new learning experiences that function as spreadable media appropriated by teens and others in a myriad of new ways in the emerging participatory culture of schools of the future. He uses the game-based learning framework of The Global Challenge Award program in order to illustrate the framework of the participatory media bridge between informal and formal education.

CASES OF GAMING USE IN TEACHING AND LEARNING

Many teachers, educators, and researchers are searching effective ways to use gaming in the classrooms of various subject areas and school levels. Elizabeth Katzlinger deals with a training curriculum for kindergarten teachers to introduce a learning game for technology-enhanced language learning in early childhood and how kindergarten teachers can launch the game in their classes. The game consisted of observation and experiment with the language, e.g., to write characters and listen to them. The children can choose where they want to learn and the speed of learning in the game. Avatars explain the game and give hints and positive feedback to the player. In the teacher training course, there is time to play the game in the same way the children play it. Additionally there is time for pedagogical reflection about the learning game and how it can be used with children. Shawn Graham did a case study of interactive fiction in an elementary classroom and suggests that the process of creating a text-based game helped improve literary and social skills amongst the students.

This concept of interactive fiction points to the literary aspirations of the best of the new creators – that the computer would merely provide the setting (the simulated world); the game playing would in fact be an act of writing. By performing the game, the player – the reader – creates her own narrative, her own story, which (in the best works) only happens once.

Hoe Kyeung Kim uses multiplayer English teaching online games and finds that elementary students' online game experiences increased self-efficacy. Interestingly, students with low social-affective values showed more improvement than those with high social-affective values in both self-efficacy and performance scores. On gaming tasks, six interactive games focus on identifying alphabet phonics. These interactive online games use jigsaw puzzles and picture matching activity formats. As for learning tasks, students read level-appropriate E-books and animation books, take quizzes on three language skills (reading, writing, and listening), and complete given tasks.

Louise Sauvé shows that the on-line game STIs: Stopping the transmission, supported learning in terms of structuring of knowledge and integration of information for youth between the ages of 14 and 15also uses online games to stimulate learning based on the findings of STIs in online games: Stopping the transmission, supporting learning in terms of the structuring of knowledge, and the integration of information for youth between the ages of 14 and 15. The games have positive results on the way learners mentally build schemas. This helps the learner with problem solving, visualizing concepts, and establishing links. Therefore, "the game allows the learner to integrate new materials and new concepts in a more intuitive manner and also helps the learner organize previously acquired information in a more comprehensive manner".

How do teachers bring the realities of decision-making and action into the curriculum? Hélder Fanha Martins considers that games help students to gain a real 'feel' for collaboration, managerial decision-making and teamwork, and describing how a web-based competitive management game helps to achieve business decision-making. Overall, the simulation game course was seen as a better vehicle in helping students make career preparations, achieve educational goals, and utilize time. He notes:

The most obvious advantage of using simulations is the ability to replicate real-world environments. Additional advantages include the ability of participants to actively engage in the learning process, develop critical thinking skills, become team players, captivate a competitive spirit, interconnect decision making, risk taking and management of operation, and just as important, have fun.

Adam Friedman, Richard Hartshorne, and Phillip VanFossen answer the question of the potential of massively multi-player online role-playing games (MMORPGs) meeting content standards in social studies. They attempt to describe the degree to which guild leaders and members in World of Warcraft engaged in civic gaming experiences and to explore the relationship between civic participation and leadership in the virtual world of WoW and the world outside the game. They concluded that both guild leaders and guild members tended to be politically moderate on both social and fiscal issues.

USE OF GAMING IN VIRTUAL WORLDS

Teaching and learning in virtual worlds has recently become an increasing topic of study in many research journals. More and more schools are building their classrooms and campuses in virtual worlds. Also, researchers have shown their interest in using virtual classrooms for their own purposes. This increase in popularity arises from the fact that virtual worlds offer an opportunity for people to interact in a way that conveys a sense of presence lacking in other media. Tele-presence, based on the vividness of increased reality and interactive roles of multi-users, appears to be a characteristic of virtual worlds. Gaming in virtual worlds includes massively multiplayer online role-playing games (MMORPG) such as Everquest Online Adventures (EQOA) and MUD (Multi-User Dungeons) such as Dungeon-Dragon. This type of virtual gaming enables gamers to engage in social learning, socialization, and meta-learning, thereby helping them to acquire social skills.

Virtual worlds, by their very nature, facilitate meta-gaming, multi-skills, and multi-literacy for their residents. Modding and rezzing, creating new resources in computer games and virtual worlds by modification is a popular pastime activity of the new generation of learners.

Regina Kaplan-Rakowski and Christian Sebastian Loh provide an overview of the modification process to create new resources within a virtual environment. Readers can understand the potential of these activities for education, and to possibly integrate some of them into school curricula. However, gaming for classroom-based learning should mesh with classroom environments. Brian Bauer introduces new tools, a Virtual Corporate Environment Business Tool box in order to match virtual worlds to reality and determined that although users were open minded to trying virtual worlds and other types of immersive technologies, the solutions delivered needed to provide task-oriented functionality. Educators have "a vision for what they hope will happen in a virtual world, but quite often the vision does not mesh with reality."

Brian Ferry, Lisa Kervin, and Lisa Carrington summarize six years of research that has consistently found that games and simulations in the virtual learning environment of ClassSim provide an effective way of introducing pre-service teachers to their future work in classrooms. They used various methodologies during their studies with ClassSim such as semi-structured interviews, observations and the collection and analysis of artifacts; surveys of users; group interviews after initial and final use of ClassSim; and analysis of users' logs. They report that through engagement with the VLE and their field experience, a number of pre-service teachers incorporated teaching terminology into their everyday language.

How do virtual games enable gamers to engage in social learning, situated learning, and problem based learning on the one hand, and in meta-gaming, meta-literacies, and multi-tasking, on the other hand? Chaka Chaka takes notice of meta-gaming, meta-literacies, and multi-tasking through five case studies involving five virtual games: Everquest Online Adventures; NUCLEO; Homicide; Mad City Mystery; and Lineage. Five case studies show how virtual games help leverage multi-skills and multi-literacies for gamers and illustrate how virtual gaming serves as an ideal platform for harnessing 21st-century skills.

Teachers and educators need to explore the benefits of applying game-based learning in virtual worlds. Maria Toro-Troconis and Martyn Partridge explore the elements associated with game-based learning in Second Life, focusing on the design process. They say:

We attempt to explore the elements associated with game-based learning in Multi-User Virtual Environments, focusing on the design process and how effective game-based learning activities can be achieved following pedagogic frameworks. We view learning in games as a form of "experiential learning" reflected in the design and development of the Imperial College virtual hospital explained in this chapter.

The preceding chapters imply that gaming for classroom-based learning is best when social interactive play such as self-organization, instrumental coordination, and sociability occurs. Players in virtual worlds can manipulate concrete objects in the world enjoyably, exercising immersive explorations to the new world which has been hidden to them. Especially in virtual gaming and simulation, they assemble several objects and create new objects as they see fit. These activities allow players to analyze, evaluate, and synthesize given data, objects, or facts. They have an opportunity to explore whatever ideas they have in mind. Thus, virtual gaming adds much more self-directive activities and live experiences for classroom-based learning.

EPILOGUE

Gaming can be a motivator for classroom-based learning. Learners, who are active players, are apt to fall into playing and learning simultaneously. In addition to the obvious traits of fun and immersion, challenge, curiosity, control, fantasy, collaboration, and competition are some of the main elements which attract the attention of players. The external structure and genre of games are sufficient enough to endow players with fun and immersion. However, games for classroom-based learning should match content with learning objectives and guarantee the effectiveness of the game. This point leaves a concern that games for classroom-based learning should include motivating elements while they also contain learning content.

Gaming use in the classroom serves as edutainment insofar that play a natural human instinct. As such, teachers in classrooms let learners play and arrive at the terminal behavior by their own will. Gaming needs to accompany the spontaneous activity of learners. It should not serve as another constraint or pressure to them. Thus, gaming for classroom-based learning needs to relate the activities of players to their current environment.

Another aspect for gaming in the classroom is that it promotes experiential learning. Experience, according to Dewey, is a process, not an outcome. Experience is a whole process of humans adapting to their surroundings. It comprises both behavior and thinking. Therefore, gaming for classroom-based learning must give actions as well as reflections based on social interactions.

For the last aspect, learners in 21st century are living in digital age where learning happens anywhere, anytime. Learning is ubiquitous and goes beyond classrooms in this open society. To be sure, gaming and games, if educationally designed and offered at low cost, can contribute to youngsters' learning.

The final chapter explores the internal structures of games and activities of players learning with games with a view to discovering what kinds of application types and game activities are meaningful in classroom settings. It presents obstacles and solutions for using games in classrooms and finally suggests an instructional design process for teaching with games in classroom settings.

Section 1
Gaming Relevant to Classroom Teaching and Learning

Chapter 1
A Taxonomy of Educational Games

Dan O'Brien
University of Illinois, USA

ABSTRACT

Digital games are a relatively new tool for educators, who often misunderstand their value for education. This is partly since they perceive many very different types of games in the same way. The authors propose a taxonomy of digital games in education based on the features that are relevant to instructional design and educational research. The taxonomy outlines four genres into which games fall, depending on the cognitive functions and skills they engage. The theoretical basis for the taxonomy the authors develop draws from R. M. Gagne's Five Categories of Learning Outcomes, Bloom's Taxonomy of Educational Objectives, and D. H. Jonassen's Typology of Problem Solving. The links between these theories and the educational games taxonomy will allow educators and researchers to understand games in the light of their educational affordances. Instructional design based on these theories can more effectively integrate games into the classroom.

INTRODUCTION

The adoption of digital games in the classroom has met with mixed responses. Educators who are familiar with digital games are often eager to introduce them into instruction, since the power of games to motivate students to engage in an activity is well known (Gee, 2005; Martens, Gulikers, & Bastiaens, 2004). Researchers have also described videogames as a foundation for designed educational experiences (Squire, 2006), ideological contexts for interaction (Young, Schrader, & Zheng, 2006), third spaces in which highly complex, social networks develop (Steinkuehler, 2006) and venues in which authentic mentoring and literacy practices abound (Schrader, Lawless, & McCreery, 2009; Schrader & McCreery, 2007; Schrader & Lawless, in press). However, some stakeholders in the education of young people do not share this enthusiasm, and feel digital games in the classroom might be, among other things,

DOI: 10.4018/978-1-61520-713-8.ch001

a distraction from learning, a waste of time, a tool for teachers to control behavior, or even an immoral influence (Baek, 2008; Kutner, 2008). This apprehension may be somewhat alleviated if digital games themselves are more easily understood, their various applications were more apparent, and their educational affordances were more obvious.

One step in making computer games more understood by educators is to explicate their value for education. If educators and other adults who are unfamiliar with games were able to learn about them in relation to their educational affordances, it might make using games in the classroom easier for educators, more effective for enhancing learning, and even more motivating for students. We propose a taxonomy of computer games that describes the genres into which educational games fit, together with the aspects of these types that apply to their use in educational settings. By organizing and categorizing educational computer games, we hope to aid educators in their research about both computer games as a domain of knowledge and individual games with which they may come into contact. Additionally, since the technology and, indeed, the names of computer games is constantly changing it is futile to describe individual games and their educational applications. More effective is this development of a taxonomy of game types so that specific games may be recognized more readily for their content, structure, and educational affordances.

It is our hope that our taxonomy will assist educators who wish to use educational games, regardless of their knowledge or understanding of them, to make salient instructional design decisions based on sound educational objectives. We further hope our taxonomy will scaffold research on educational games to promote their use in the classroom. This line of research may well evaluate the specific educational affordances of the game genres outlined in our taxonomy. Such findings may lead to the refinement or extension of this taxonomy, hopefully to the betterment of educational games research.

BACKGROUND

Educational vs. Commercial Games

Although many commercial games have educational affordances, the motive of the companies developing them is largely profit. This leads to the entertainment and marketability value of games taking precedence over the educational value. If the profitability of a game is of primary importance, we must question whether it has even come close to meeting its *potential* educational value. Four common features of commercial games can add to their entertainment value and marketability, but are either not desirable in an educational game or must be minimized: chance, critical competition, inappropriate material, and advertising. By "chance," we mean any aspect of a game in which chance has a major effect on a player's success. This is particularly important when the success of the students' learning experience hinges on their success in the game. Although it is true games of chance are, for many, highly engaging and highly entertaining, we know them to be highly addictive (Clarke, Lawrence, Astley-Jones, & Gray, 2009). Second is the level of competition between players. Although competition can engage players, students may become frustrated when another player is foiling their attempts to advance in the game, inhibiting their level of engagement. Further, the research reports that boys and girls do not demonstrate the same preference for competition. Although the data refer to older games, Kafai (1996) reported that on average more girls than boys prefer cooperative or single player games.

The content of games also calls some issues into question. Inappropriate material includes any references to illegal or immoral behavior, as perceived by the standards of the community. There seems no reason, objectively, to consider such material in direct opposition to the educational affordances of a game. However, the level of distraction it creates and, more to the point, the inability to promote a game for use in schools with such material makes it detrimental to educational games. Similarly, advertising within digital games has become more commonplace in recent years (Yang & Wang, 2008). It may not directly detract from the educational affordances of the game, and can make the development of a game much more cost-effective. However, a powerful capital interest having a stake in the success of a game may very well compromise its educational value in the interest of marketability. A consideration of the effect of these features will narrow the scope of what we consider educational games, but will enhance our understanding of them.

While there has been a good deal of research examining computer games and their educational affordances (Rice, 2007), much of this research and much of the curricula involving educational games has been developed with a particular game as a starting point (Childress & Braswell, 2006; Delwiche, 2006; Hamalainen, 2008). This is usually because the researcher chooses one game because it is relatively inexpensive, applies to the curricular domain under study, is appropriate for the grade level, or satisfies some other convenience. The curriculum is then developed "backwards." Specifically, classroom experiences are built around the game first and then educational objectives selected based on what is deemed possible to achieve using the game in question. This is understandable, since the primary question for games researchers during the field's infancy has been to establish that games can be used to educate at all (Huang & Cappel, 2005; Rosas, Nussbaum, Cumsille, Marianov, Correa, & Flores, et al., 2003; Steinkuehler, 2004). With that established, educators can reverse the direction of study. The educational objectives that are under study can be the starting point, and the type of game that will enhance the achievement of them can be determined. It is at this point that a taxonomy of educational games becomes valuable.

Although the commercial game industry has its own categorizations of games (Kremeier, 2002), there have been few attempts at developing an organizational system for educational games with the intent of furthering the educational use of games. Amory, in his development of the Game Object Model II (2006), outlines a design framework for games based on Object-Oriented Programming. He bases his theory less on the intent to use games in the classroom as on the intent to classify games themselves. Björk, Lundgren, and Holopainen (2003) established a description of games themselves that is instructional in the basic nature of games. However, these models are somewhat finely detailed for the purposes of the average teacher (and, indeed, the average educational researcher). Additionally, Björk et al. are researchers connected with the commercial industry, and their intent was a more thorough understanding of games as products, rather than educational tools. Lee, Ko, Song, Kwon, Lee, and Nam, et al. (2007), focusing on excessive game play and internet addiction, categorized games into "genres", predicated primarily on their commercial classification. Rice (2007) made some connections between games and higher-order thinking skills, but from a highly interpretive perspective. Squire (2006) categorized games according to the linkage between the context and the game play, but not according to problem solving affordances. Gee (2005) makes a clear description of how "good" games include appropriate problem solving opportunities, but not detailing which types of games present which types of problem solving. Examples of game classification such as these reveal the need for a taxonomy that focuses on the problem-solving application of certain game genres in an educational setting by educators, who may not be aware of the basic nature of games.

THE EDUCATIONAL GAMES TAXONOMY

The theoretical basis for the taxonomy we develop in this chapter is a combination of R. M. Gagne's Five Categories of Learning Outcomes (1974), Bloom's Taxonomy of Educational Objectives (1956), and D.H. Jonassen's Typology of Problem Solving (2000). Gagne's Five Categories, as a canonical organization of the major outcomes of education, outline the overall capabilities each game genre generally engages. Although various authors have critiqued and/or revised Bloom's original work in various ways (Anderson and Krathwohl, 2001; Furst, 1981; Ormell, 1974), his taxonomy remains a major directive for instructional design. Bloom's Taxonomy provides reasoning for deciding which genres are suitable for developing cognitive skills of varying levels. Finally, Jonassen's Typology gives specific information about a game player's problem solving behavior. The intent is that all educators (e.g., researchers, instructional designers, teachers, etc.) will be capable of designing instruction by first determining the learning outcome the students should achieve, based on the learning standards (Wiggins, 1992). This will lead to the selection of one or more levels of educational objectives. Then, one or more problem-solving types that will assist in attaining these objectives can be selected. At this point, our taxonomy can aid the educator in choosing an appropriate game genre and thus a particular game. Admittedly, this process is not necessarily linear or prescribed. However, the sequence follows a logic that can serve as a starting point in any design process involving educational games.

The taxonomy of educational games separates games into four categories or genres. Although there are a multitude of types of games defined by the game-play experience (i.e., first-person shooters, flight simulators, sports games), these characteristics are not always useful in education. Therefore, for the purposes of instructional design and educational research, it is most valuable to identify games according to their educational affordances. Of the possible educational objectives for which educators might use games, they lend themselves most readily to the teaching of cognitive skills. Thus, these genres describe games according to the varieties of cognitive skills employed.

Genres

For many years, society has considered video games as a single concept, often disparagingly. Those not familiar with them bemoan games as the downfall of today's youth and the antithesis of academic development and focus on school (Bartholow, Sestir, & Davis, 2005). It is true that many people play games to the detriment of maintaining a balance of interests and activities, and some games lend themselves to this type of obsession. However, understanding how some types of games are different from others can aid the understanding of how and when games can be beneficial for learning. Thus, in our taxonomy (Table 1), we propose describing games according to the following genres, with the caveat that although most games can be classified fairly clearly into one genre, any game may include features of multiple genres. The names given to these genres are similar to the genres described for commercial games. However, we based our choice for each on the educational nature of the games within it, as an indicator of their particular educational applications. Additionally, the higher-level genres very often include game play within one or more of the lower genres as part of the complexity of their features. Thus, rather than an absolute taxonomy such as is found in the natural sciences, this is meant as a descriptive classification system such as is found in the social sciences.

First of these genres is *linear* games, which are often described as "arcade" games. These are the most common type of game, and the most popular (Gee, 2003). Somewhat more advanced than these

Table 1. The taxonomy of educational games

Game Genre	Linear	Competitive	Strategic	Role-Playing
Description	Success requires linear logic	Success requires linear logic, plus anticipating actions of other players	Success requires strategic planning and management of a complex system	Success requires developing and maintaining a profile of probabilities within a complex environment
Examples	Puzzles, jump-and-run, first-person shooters	Sports, combat	War and management	Large, online multiplayer environments
		Attitudes	Attitudes	Attitudes
		Cognitive Strategy	Cognitive Strategy	Cognitive Strategy
Gagne's Learning Outcomes	Intellectual Skill	Intellectual Skill	Intellectual Skill	Intellectual Skill
	Verbal Information	Verbal Information	Verbal Information	Verbal Information
	Motor Skill	Motor Skill	Motor Skill	Motor Skill
				Evaluation
			Synthesis	Synthesis
			Analysis	Analysis
Bloom's Educational Objectives		Application	Application	Application
	Comprehension	Comprehension	Comprehension	Comprehension
	Knowledge	Knowledge	Knowledge	Knowledge
	Psychomotor	Psychomotor	Psychomotor	Psychomotor
				Dilemma
				Case Analysis
			Design	Design
		Strategic performance	Strategic performance	Strategic performance
			Diagnosis-Solution	Diagnosis-Solution
			Trouble-shooting	Trouble-shooting
	Decision-making	Decision-making	Decision-making	Decision-making
	Rule-Using	Rule-Using	Rule-Using	Rule-Using
Jonassen's Problem Solving Types	Story	Story	Story	Story
	Algorithmic	Algorithmic	Algorithmic	Algorithmic
	Logical	Logical	Logical	Logical

are *competitive* games, including sports games and simple fighting or combat games. Also frequently competitive, but using much more advanced forms of cognition are *strategic games*, which are often complex war games or games involving the management of a system. At the top end of our spectrum are *role-playing games*, or *RPGs*. These are variations on the board games developed in the 1970's. Each player creates a unique profile of probabilities that determines their success, and enhances those probabilities throughout the game. These genres do not describe games according to what the player sees, but rather what the player *does*, or more specifically how they *think*. There are varieties of graphic interfaces possible for any genre of game, and so games that are very similar in appearance may be in very different genres. Some very simple puzzle games use complex 3d graphics and a high aesthetic, whereas some very complex problem solving games use a very simple, plain interface or perhaps are even text-based. Thus, many games that appear to be very different may be classified in comparable ways. Specifically, the cognitive skills required by them and their educational affordances may be very similar.

Linear Games

Linear games are those that use linear logic, although the actions employed in playing them may not be linear. Like simple algebraic problems, the variables involved in the problem are clear. Although they may be difficult games, the steps necessary to succeed are sequential. These games require only knowledge of information and well-structured problem solving, and so most of their value in education is exposure to content. However, this type of content interaction is reminiscent of traditional drill-and-practice learning, and research has shown they mostly have the same amount of value in education (Rosas et al., 2003). From a play-based perspective, these are often puzzle games, shooting games, or what are often termed "jump-and-run" games in which the player moves through the game collecting objects and avoiding obstacles or what are described in game parlance as *non-player characters*, or *NPCs*. NPCs are entities in a game that are not like simple obstacles, because they act in response to the player's actions (a falling rock is an obstacle; a rock-monster that chases you is an NPC). These are extremely popular games because they are usually very straightforward in their rules and are often very repetitive. Often they require very little complex problem solving ability while requiring highly developed fine-motor skills. The actions required to win are clear, the learning curve is low and there is frequent payoff for effort in the form of points scored or encouraging feedback. Many of these games have a very simple aesthetic, such as the enormously popular Tetris™ where the focus is on the logic of the problem rather than the experience of play. However, these games can also be, on the surface, very complex games using intricate 3d graphics and involved storylines, such as first-person shooters. Yet when examined for the type of problems solved within them, they may require the same cognitive skills as something like Tetris™. In the first-person shooter style of game, the player sees the world through the eyes of a character in a three-dimensional environment while attempting to traverse the environment and usually shooting or otherwise overcoming the various obstacles or NPCs preventing such progress. Although, to the casual observer, this is a very different style of game than Tetris™, the types of problems the player solves are very much the same. Although people can play together in linear games by collaborating simultaneously to succeed or by comparing their levels of success, the difference between linear games and competitive games comes when there are other players, either real or computer-controlled, which are not only blocking the player's attempts at completing the game but are simultaneously attempting to win the game themselves.

Competitive Games

Competitive games, like linear games, often require well-developed fine-motor skills, require linear logic to solve the problems presented in them, and vary widely in their aesthetic features. However, whereas in linear games there may be NPCs that foil the player's attempts at success, competitive games, as their name suggests, include other players that are also playing the same game either competitively or collaboratively. A player can be controlled by either a human being or the computer, using AI software that simulates the actions of a real player (Björk & Holopainen, 2003), or a combination of both. These players are known commonly as *bots*, short for "robots". In some games, human players can adjust the ability levels of bots to fine-tune the difficulty level of the game. This can be a significant feature for adequately challenging students (Wang & Reeves,

2007). This genre includes games that simulate real-world sports, competitive versions of the first-person shooter games described above, and their ancestor, Pong™. A comparison between Pong™ and another early game, Breakout™, since these™, since these games were absolutely minimalist and similar in their design, serves as a pristine example of the difference between linear and competitive games. In Breakout™, the player moved a rectangle or "paddle" back and forth across the bottom of the screen in order to hit a ball (or rather, a small square) around the inside of a three-sided rectangle, knocking out bricks from the opposite side and keeping the ball from moving past the paddle. In Pong™, the player used a paddle on the side of the screen to hit the ball, but attempted to hit the ball *past another player*. Although these games were very similar, the difference is telling: the addition of the opponent causes the players to move from solving a simple problem in dynamic plane geometry (in order to determine where the ball will travel so that it might be hit) to anticipating the movements of another player (and/or bot) and attempting to exploit those predictions. When a player moves between competing with players and working on their own within the same game, it can become unclear whether the game is a linear or competitive game. Although bots can act somewhat predictably depending on the sophistication of their AI software, human players are highly unpredictable and make very simple logic problems terribly difficult to solve, even when they are on the player's side. In fact, the attempt to predict the actions of other people in games has led to the development of one of the most complex fields of mathematics, known as *game theory* (Kuhn, 2003). The techniques of this field can often clarify how others will act in a competitive or collaborative situation, but its complexities are beyond the scope of this chapter. Of note, however, is game theory's ability to determine the possible actions of a player who may choose to work *either* in cooperatively or competitively with oneself. These situations and other factors separate competitive games from the next genre: strategic games.

Strategic Games

Strategic games involve managing a complex system, often in the form of a city, a country, a business, or some other organization. The strategic aspect of these games is in the management of resources, cost/benefit ratios, return-on-investments, and military planning and anticipating the same strategies for any opposing players. In this genre, players learn domain-specific content knowledge, and begin to apply that knowledge to complex problem solving in an authentic context, adding value to the learning experience (Artino, 2008). Aspects of the linear and competitive genres come into play in these games, and so strategic games also require fine-motor skills. If the system being managed is not very complex, there can be some apparent overlap between this genre and the previous two. However, in this genre, fine-motor skills usually become much less critical for success. The player spends a great deal of time planning and organizing, either before taking action in the game or during game-play. These games often become highly complex, involving the simultaneous management of several sub-systems. Each individual game may be played with a random set of initial conditions, forcing players to use unique strategies with each game. For example, a game in which the player rules a country may involve the management of food production for a growing population, the building of a military force to protect that population, and defending against invasions from neighboring countries. Meanwhile, other players or bots control these neighboring countries, and so the most important strategy is to understand ones opponent well-enough to anticipate their actions and reactions. Thus, it is with strategic games that communication and socialization becomes a much more critical aspect of multiplayer games. Players may form alliances, and so need to collaborate on strategy, economics, and military movements. They may compete, and so need to negotiate, cajole, or misinform their opponents. Strategic games are much more involved than our previous two genres, and players may find themselves in the role of military general, CEO, or emperor. However, the role of the player in these games is straightforward: the player is in charge of the entire system, and their decisions about how to manage that system are the rule of law. Collaborations with other players are tenuous, as the length of play in any one game is usually no more than a few hours. However, as we shall see in our last genre, when the length of game play stretches to days, weeks, or years, the player's involvement, the role they play, and their socialization in the game become far more complex.

Role-Playing Games

In computer-based RPGs, players create unique characters at the start of the game comprised of *abilities*. Each of these abilities is a score or percentage, which indicates the level of that ability the character possesses. With character creation, there are only a certain number of points to distribute amongst the various abilities. Thus, an increase in one ability usually means a reduction in another. During game play, a character will be more successful in situations that call upon their higher-level abilities. Once the player creates a character, the player must succeed at various challenges in order to improve their character's abilities and advance in the game. This can be done through allotment of points or, in some games, through in-game currency systems, in which players "buy" items to improve their abilities. Indeed, many players derive enjoyment primarily from investing in these virtual markets, or running virtual businesses within the game. Such play would fall more into the strategic genre, depending the level of commitment to these alternate activities. As the player improves certain abilities, they often become more highly specialized in their chosen role, and thus become even better suited for specific situations. Conversely, players may manage their character to balance abilities, allowing them to suit a variety of roles. If a situation requires abilities that are weak in that player's character, they can collaborate with players whose characters are strong in the required ability. Strategically formed groups of characters can adapt to a variety of situations, with each player fulfilling a particular role in the group, hence the name. Players become highly involved in the development and refinement of their characters in an environment that is persistent over weeks, months, and years (Steinkuehler, 2004). Players may also develop more than one character, changing roles as required by the situation.

This need for collaboration in RPGs significantly increases the level of socialization used in them. Players are in constant communication to manage groups, direct action, plan strategy, etc. They communicate through many forms of communication such as in-game text and voice chat, email, and discussion forums, extending the social sphere beyond the game itself (Schraeder, Lawless, and McCreery, 2009). These players engage voluntarily in highly collaborative, ill-structured problem solving, also known as *computer-supported collaborative learning* (Kapur & Kinzer, 2007). Additionally, the extended length of play and socialization results in players developing long-term relationships and, thus, more subtle interactions. In most RPGs, players form extended groups in the form of clubs, guilds or leagues. Players also assume leadership and management roles within these groups, assembling and scheduling smaller groups to tackle particular challenges. All of these interactions lead to players engaging in problem solving which imitates or even replicates that found in "real life".

EDUCATIONAL THEORIES IN THE TAXONOMY

In progression through these genres, it seems apparent that not only does game play itself change, but the cognitive processes of the player change significantly as well. When considered in the light of current educational theory, a linking pattern appears between types of problem solving and educational affordances, and the levels of game genres described herein. First, Gagne and Briggs (1974) categorized five Categories of Learning Outcomes, organizing the various skills acquired through educational experience. These types of skills translate to the skills required for success in the several genres in the taxonomy. Bloom's Taxonomy of Educational Objectives (1956) describes increasingly advanced levels of cognitive skills that students develop. As the cognitive complexity of a game increases, so do the cognitive abilities exercised by the player. David Jonassen's Typology of Problem Solving (2000) delineates categories of problems according to, in part, how well they are structured. The genres in our taxonomy encompass increasingly ill-structured problem types as described by Jonassen. Designers of instructional activities involving games can exploit this linking pattern to make informed decisions about what type of game, or even what particular game, is most suitable for their objectives. Depending on the objective, designers may consider these theories and the taxonomy separately or in conjunction with each other. A better understanding of this pattern will aid educational policy makers, educational researchers, instructional designers, game designers, teachers, parents, and students to embrace games in curriculum and instruction.

Gagné's Five Categories of Learning Outcomes

Robert M. Gagne, in his *Principles of Instructional Design* (1974), describes five outcome areas toward which educators can direct instruction: *intellectual skills*, *cognitive strategies*, *verbal information*, *motor skills*, and *attitudes* (Table 1). Intellectual skill is the ability to manipulate knowledge through cognitive operations. Cognitive strategies are akin to metacognitive abilities, monitoring a learner's behavior. Verbal information, although the name is misleading, is the ability to retain, recall, and communicate facts. Motor skills are abilities in physical control and expression. Attitudes, although also a cognitive ability, are the learner's ability to choose from among a group of options due to personal preference rather than logic. Instructional designers must decide, ahead of the design process, into which of these categories their learning objectives fall, and how to weight the focus of those categories. Most of the genres in our taxonomy can target all of these objectives in one way or another, but the focus on which of these skills is more engaged changes. With this in mind, the choice of an appropriate genre of educational game can be more obvious.

Linear games, even though they may often be difficult, as we shall see, use a very simple logic. Thus, the skills needed to succeed in them do not tend to engage higher order thinking skills. Under Gagne's outcomes, these games mostly teach the use of motor skills, verbal information, and intellectual skills. Players are required to move objects around the screen in response to stimuli, often very quickly and accurately. To understand the stimuli, they must acquire verbal information about the game's elements and be able to recall it at will. In doing so, they develop their intellectual skills as they learn the rules and patterns that govern the behavior of the game elements. These games can be highly complex as well, increasing the use of verbal information and intellectual skills and downplaying the need for acute motor skills. Although these games may seem to have limited use in education, their low learning curve and the ability to adopt them for many different curricular areas may make them the most prevalent genre as games become ubiquitous in the classroom.

The same learning objectives are obtainable through competitive games; however, the specific skills acquired can be much different. Since players are now trying to solve linear logic problems in spite of another player doing the same thing, the logic required can change rapidly. The verbal information the player must master includes not only the rules and features of the game elements, but also certain features of the opponent and their possible behavior. This type of information can be much more tenuous and difficult to grasp. Additionally, the intellectual skill needed to predict another player or bot's behavior is much more advanced than simply understanding the predictable actions of NPCs. Even the motor skills required by competitive games are more difficult to master since a player must track and counteract the movements of opponents. Although these games are primarily multiplayer extensions of linear games, there is an argument to be made that they may become more like strategic games if players develop more acute understanding of strategy and the ability to monitor their own learning of that strategy. In addition, players have choices about whether they play more offensively, defensively, and what strategies suit them outside of the strategy's efficacy. Thus, when players interact in these games, they may begin to develop the attitudes or preferences they have for the type of play in which they engage. However, players develop these last two skills more thoroughly as game play becomes more involved.

In strategic games, players begin to plan and organize much more than in the previous two genres. Although they use motor skills to execute actions, these skills are not critical in many strategic games. Additionally, students develop some attitudes in their game play about preferred methods and styles of play. However, Gagne's other three objectives are far more heavily engaged in these games. Strategic games often require knowledge of a great deal of information to determine how game elements act or interact, and this knowledge must be readily accessible to the player. If this knowledge is available, the player uses intellectual skill to plan and execute strategy. Here, cognitive strategies themselves come into play when the player monitors and adjusts their thinking and learning to be more successful. In strategic games, these skills work together continually to allow the player to adapt to the changing conditions of the game. However, in order for all of Gagne's objectives to be attainable through game play, the game must engage the player in many different ways, motivating them to invest themselves more fully. The fourth genre, RPGs, satisfy this requirement, engaging players even when they are not avid game players (Smyth, 2007).

RPGs are highly complex. They include the development of unique character identities, a diverse in-game social structure, a wide variety of obstacles and NPCs, engrossing competition, active virtual economies, and strategic planning and organization, both on large and small scales and over the short and long term. This complexity creates the possibility to engage players in a wide range of educational experiences, such that educators can address all of Gagne's learning objectives. The complex organization in these games can require comprehensive knowledge of verbal information and the intellectual skill to manipulate that information. When players become highly engaged in this complex play, they must activate cognitive strategies to improve their application and understanding of that manipulation. The investment in their character increases their investment in success in the game, and they invest more time learning and developing their own ability to improve (Yee, 2006). This investment in the metacognition of learning is one of the most difficult learning objectives to achieve, and the most valuable. When students are engaged in improvement, learning follows. It is up to the instructional designer to harness that engagement such that all students can achieve that outcome.

Bloom's Taxonomy of Educational Objectives

Bloom's well-known and widely used Taxonomy of Educational Objectives (Table 1) (Bloom, 1956) is descriptive of the increasingly complex content learning which occurs through the four genres in our taxonomy. Bloom described three domains of objectives: *psychomotor*, *affective*, and *cognitive*. Most educational games exercise all of these domains in some way. The psychomotor domain is always engaged in playing digital games, to a greater or lesser extent depending on the game's design. Educational games also engage the affective domain, but to a greater extent at the higher levels of our taxonomy. However, our focus in the description of the educational games taxonomy is on Bloom's cognitive domain and the subcategories therein. The focus in most good instructional design is within this domain (Gagne & Briggs, 1974), and cognitive development is the area where games have the most potential for educational application. Educators can use all types of games to teach at the knowledge level, through engaging exposure to content. Players also practice comprehension in any of the genres, as games allow for authentic use of facts and concepts to enhance understanding. At the levels of application and analysis, we start to see where linear, competition, and role-playing games become more useful for authentically teaching content knowledge, as games may simulate authentic situations where players may apply and analyze knowledge. At the highest two levels of the genre, where players begin using more complex problem solving skills, there comes the ability to exercise the synthesis of knowledge to form unique solutions to problems. Finally, only in the RPG genre are students usually able to practice evaluation by forming unique opinions about the value and meaning of content knowledge. It is the unique nature of each genre that denotes its applicability to Bloom's Taxonomy.

Knowledge and Comprehension

Games at all levels of the taxonomy suit the teaching of content at the levels of knowledge and comprehension as long as they are engaging. Indeed, the high motivation games induce can make learning at these levels much more enjoyable. Linear games, as with most classroom instruction, present students with clear, logical steps to perform in recalling and understanding knowledge. Competitive games, if played against real people instead of bots, make learning a social event, and thus more engaging (Cole & Griffiths, 2007). In strategic games, often many factors change simultaneously, so there is often a dramatic increase in the need to recall significant amounts of detailed information in order to manage systems in the game. RPGs magnify this aspect, as not only do players manage many systems, but also they are often changing from system to system, or managing many systems simultaneously. RPGs may address the knowledge and comprehension levels of facts most readily: in some RPGs, players have developed searchable online databases full of information about game elements such as obstacles, NPCs, and rewards (Gee, 2003). In an information-rich society, students must often learn to manage large amounts of data, and RPGs have begun to give them an engaging way to practice that skill. However, the value of games comes when students need to use knowledge authentically.

Application

In Bloom's Taxonomy, the application level of learning requires making use of knowledge in contexts unlike those in which the learner acquires the knowledge. Linear and competitive games can require the application of knowledge, but they tend to be limited in the variety of novel situations that they produce. Their repetitive nature allows for ample practice of knowledge application, but players quickly master the limited use of knowledge required to play them. Thus, when the objective is for students to apply knowledge with practiced aptitude, linear or competitive games may provide the most suitable format for honing those skills. In strategic games and RPGs, however, there is a significant increase in the need for players to apply knowledge in novel situations. These games present a multitude of unique challenges, and often require players to have considerable content knowledge to be successful. Players must also manage this significant amount of data, such as the specific capacities of game elements, geographical and mapping data, and the hierarchical structure of organizations. Although these games are usually themed around fictional contexts, instructional designers can construct games at these levels to reflect the desired educational content domain. Thus, the variety of situational contexts these games create would allow for extensive novel application of the content knowledge. For example, in a strategic war game, a player may apply knowledge of European geography to plan various military offensives. In a fantasy RPG, the knowledge of a healer's (one who assists other characters) weakness in combat is applied to compensate with the strength of a warrior (who can protect the healer) or avoid dangerous situations. If students must demonstrate the application of knowledge in a great variety of contexts, strategic or role-playing games may create a more suitably authentic environment. The games in these two genres are also the most suitable for the highest levels of Bloom's Taxonomy.

Analysis and Synthesis

Linear and competitive games rarely require much thinking at this level. Any in-depth analysis of the structure of these games does not prove valuable when the player cannot affect that structure. Also, if the acquired knowledge can be synthesized to create new knowledge, there are rarely opportunities to apply that new knowledge, since the player is usually already provided with the knowledge needed to solve the game's problems. In strategic games and RPGs, players must not only master their command of the applicable factual knowledge in the game's content domain. They must also clearly understand the rules and variables of the game, and use that knowledge to adapt to changes. Thus, their command of knowledge must be at the analysis level to separate the component elements of their knowledge so that they can understand the relationships between these elements, and thus the systems the game requires them to manage. Additionally, as the player begins to command more and more complex systems, interact with other players in more complex ways, and, in RPGs, develop a more complex profile, they are required to synthesize their knowledge to develop original thinking about their game play. To become very successful in these games, players must thoroughly understand the organization of the knowledge they have developed through the game, and express their understanding of that knowledge in a way that is understandable to other players. In RPGs, they may even develop critiques of their own and other players' understanding.

Evaluation

RPGs provide the most authentic environments for simulating real world, ill-structured problem solving (Steinkuehler & Chmiel, 2006). Based on subtle probabilities, they provide players with endless variations and outcomes to which they must constantly adapt. Additionally, the rules, the objectives, and the criteria for success are not always clear. The inclusion of hundreds or even thousands of players and the development of complex communication networks make them highly social "third spaces" and thus even more authentic environments (Steinkuehler & Williams, 2006). With this social engagement and authenticity comes a responsibility for the players to develop much of the structure of the game, and to maintain a cohesive, functioning social system. Thus, players in these games often engage in heated debates, both in game and in message forums, about their own and each other's actions, behavior, beliefs, policies, and procedures (Steinkuehler & Chmiel, 2006). This demonstration of the evaluation level of Bloom's Taxonomy is possibly the most valuable feature of RPGs, as it creates an opportunity for social cognition. By giving players an environment in which they can engage socially while simultaneously working together to solve problems, RPGs foster natural curiosity and intellectual engagement.

Bloom's Taxonomy has provided, for many years, a solid foundation for instructional designers to outline the knowledge-centered objectives of curriculum, instruction, and assessment. However, in recent years, there has been a movement away from the focus on the understanding of content knowledge, as described by Bloom, and toward the development of the cognitive skills necessary for real world problem solving (Fernandes & Simon, 1999). The play of games is based on the solving of problems. Thus, although games provide many ways in which students may be engaged in their development of knowledge, in the next section we shall see they are far more valuable in their ability to develop students' problem solving skills.

Jonassen's Typology of Problem Solving

David H. Jonassen, in his 2004 *Typology of Problem Solving*, outlined specific problem types that fit into the linking pattern of the educational games taxonomy. In his typology, Jonassen describes many facets of problems, including their *abstractness, dynamicity, complexity*, and *structuredness*. Of particular concern for the taxonomy is the structuredness of problems. Briefly, however, there are connections with Jonassen's other facets as well. Abstractness (also referred to as domain, or context, specificity) is the degree to which a problem is situated in the context in which it is being solved. One of the advantages of digital games is the ability to create and control the domain in which problems occur. This ability has led, in the higher levels of the taxonomy, to the creation of games in what Gee (2003) describes as *semiotic domains*. These domains embody the authentic types of problems that engage higher order problem solving skills. Dynamicity refers to the problem's tendency to change even as one solves it, and can contribute to a problem's difficulty. The problem solver's ability to adapt to these changes can be one of the most difficult aspects of problem solving to assess (Schacter, Herl, Chung, Dennis, & O'Neil, 1999), but digital games may provide a way of monitoring a player's adaptations. Complexity contains a number of aspects of the problem:

Problem complexity is determined by the number of issues, functions, or variables involved in the problem; the degree of connectivity among those variables; the type of functional relationships among those properties; and the stability among the properties of the problem over time. (Funke, as cited in Jonassen, 2004, pp. 67-68)

Complexity also contributes to the difficulty of a problem. All of the types of problems Jonassen describes can vary in complexity, depending on the above conditions. Similarly, games in any of the genres in the taxonomy can and do vary in their complexity. Although the different genres engage different functions of cognition, games within each genre can be more or less difficult depending on the complexity of the problems the player is solving. Thus, linear games may follow a very straightforward logic, but have many variables and require careful thinking to solve. Conversely, RPGs may be very simple and easy to play, while using the same probabilities and organization of their more difficult counterparts. Educational game designers may manipulate dynamicity and complexity as a way to customize a game for a particular subject area or grade level. However, of Jonassen's facets of the various problem types, the most critical to educational games is a problem's structuredness.

This facet follows most clearly the linking pattern in the taxonomy.

Structuredness refers to whether a problem is more "well-structured," having a clear set of "rules and principles" for solution, or more "ill-structured", having more "uncertainty about which concepts, rules, and principles are necessary for the solution" (Jonassen, 2000). Jonassen's problem types separate roughly into two groups based on their structuredness, with some variability (Table 1). Additionally, there is a drop-off in structuredness between the two lower and the two higher genres. This change in structuredness links these problem types closely with the genres in the taxonomy, with the problem types encountered in the higher genres decreasing in structuredness. Thus, the taxonomy can provide instructional designers with a plan for integrating games by examination of the problem types encountered in the curriculum.

Problem Solving in Linear Games

The games in the linear genre, with their clear logic problems, only lend themselves to the some of the well-structured problem types in Jonassen's typology. Although very often the actions required by these games test fine-motor skills, success requires the straightforward thinking of logical, algorithmic and story problems. In fact, the spatial representation in these games, whether two-dimensional or three-dimensional, is also usually linear, requiring a player to follow a more or less straight line, hence the term "linear". These spaces are often maze-like, with one point of entry and one exit point. The players may spend a great deal of time exploring the various areas of the maze, but, ultimately, success will depend on whether they can follow the route to the exit. There are only obstacles and NPCs to deal with in these games, which require one of a few possible actions (run from the monster, fight it, or hide) and there is always one best answer in any given situation (if the monster is too big, run or hide; if it's small enough, fight). However, these games can present somewhat more complex problem types. Rule-using problems can arise as players are required to recall and comprehend larger sets of more complex rules, and to apply those rules to situations appropriately (what type of monster is attacking determines what type of weapon to use). Additionally, some more complex linear games include decision-making problems, as players have more options for action and must weigh those options and test them in trials (if the fire sword does not kill the dragon, try the ice sword). Thus, these games are excellent tools for students to practice curricular objectives such as mathematics, grammar rules, and simple cause and effect relationships. However, these well-structured problem types become more authentic when someone (or something) is trying to stop you from solving them.

Problem Solving in Competitive Games

Competitive games are closely related to linear games, and so many of the same problem types occur in them. Problems encountered in these games, although involving opponents, are still very straightforward, and much of the discussion about linear games above applies to competitive games. Indeed, the competition aspect of these games is often less in trying to stop one's opponent from solving the game's problems and more in trying to solve the problems first. However, particularly when the opponents are humans rather than bots, the nature of rule-using and decision-making problems in these games can change dramatically. The rules involved in competing with other people can be very straightforward (stop them from winning a race, kill the dragon first), but the dynamicity of these rules can be extremely high. Humans, and even bots, are very unpredictable, and so players are required to change which rules apply as situations change quickly and dramatically. With decision-making problems, players must consider not only possible actions, but must test theories about those actions and then adapt those theories based on outcomes. When solving these problems in real-time, combined with the unpredictability of the opponent, they become strategic performance problems. As the number of opponents increases and players begin working in teams, competitive games can involve very complex strategies and tactics. Those strategies may be clear, but whether or not teammates will agree with them or apply them can vary. Additionally, teams usually include members who take on somewhat different roles, i.e. offensive positions, defensive positions, assignments to specific areas, or varying leadership roles. At this point, the more ill-structured nature of strategic performance problems becomes significant. This lends these games to instructional objectives such as history and politics. However, although the leaders of such groups may begin to grapple with the trouble-shooting and diagnosis-solution problems common to managing systems, their lack of control over teams in this genre precludes them from truly encountering those types of problems. When players can affect more control over systems, these types of problems become prevalent.

Problem Solving in Strategic Games

Strategic games can seem to be very well-structured forms of games. Indeed, much of the problem solving required by them is at the lower levels of Jonassen's typology, but in much more complex form. Managing systems such as businesses or countries involves large numbers of variables that players must organize into finite problems to solve. In fact, it is typical of strategic games that they often involve very simple logic problems to perform routine maintenance and repair of the system (which are often, in more poorly designed games, somewhat tedious). However, success in these games requires much higher-level cognition. These logic problems interconnect, with the outcome of one affecting the variables of another. The player frequently must solve rule-using and decision-making problems, managing large numbers of variables and needing to consider many possible courses of action. The complexity of the systems under control (and the length of time usually required to play these games) brings into play trouble-shooting and diagnosis-solution problems, when players must develop the system, observe its operation, find faults in it, and work to correct those faults. This genre also presents very ill-structured problems. Especially when playing competitively, players must manage a system in an environment and against an opponent, all of which are in constant flux. Strategic performance problems, as one might expect, describe the primary type of problem solving in these games. Players must integrate many objectives at once, and must balance the needs of these objectives evenly to attain success. These games, less frequently, can present design problems, when the system involved is intended to produce a particular product, such as with manufacturing simulation games. With the inclusion of these problem types, these games become suitable for simulations in domains such as the natural and physical sciences, business, and politics. Although strategic games can replicate much of the problem solving of real-world systems management, they fail to engage players in forms of problem solving which, although the most ill-structured and vexing, are also the most authentic.

Problem Solving in Role-Playing Games

Role-playing games, particularly the more complex of them, have emerged with some of the most engaging and rich game play experiences to date. By creating experiences in which players can take on unique identities they develop over time, RPGs allow players to invest themselves in ways unseen in other game types (Smyth, 2007). Since many of these games involve huge numbers of players, complex social networks develop within them, creating the opportunity for computer-supported collaborative learning, discussed above. RPGs are not only ill-structured problem solving games; many are virtual gaming environments in which players may encounter individual problems of many types, often working to solve them simultaneously. As a player begins to develop and enhance the role of their character, they become involved in sub-games of all three previous genres. Individual sessions of play may involve overcoming obstacles or NPCs to obtain a reward, such as in linear games. Indeed, often the most common actions of players in RPGs are linear sub-games. In these linear sub-games, they may also compete against other players alone or in teams, organizing and planning tactics. Individual players may strategically manage systems such as in-game businesses using the currency system, in which they gather resources to produce items for other players, bartering or dealing to maximize profits. They may also form larger groups of players, or "guilds" in which they lead, manage and schedule the play of other players. Design problems become highly prevalent in RPGs, as players develop or "design" their characters throughout the course of the game. The design of a character involves the consideration of a number of factors, such as the weighting of abilities for different situations, the management of resources, and the role the character must play in conjunction with other characters. Thus, this integration of the lower genres within RPGs includes the problem solving types found in those games. However, the value of the RPG as an environment rather than a singular game is in the way players must learn to cope with unknown elements when solving problems.

The two final problem types RPGs may engage are not possible within the other genres, namely case analysis problems and dilemmas. Case analysis problems typically occur in the real world in various business and educational environments in which specific hypothetical situations are analyzed to understand various possible courses of action. In RPGs, players often engage in case analysis either casually when trying to plan ahead, or in discussion with other players in-game or in discussion forums (Steinkuehler & Chmiel, 2006). This type of problem solving is highly ill-structured, with no clear reasoning that should be followed, no obvious steps that should be taken, and even no assurance that there is a solution (Jonassen, 2004). These problems, like the complex environments of RPGs, often involve multiple domains of knowledge and are approached using a variety of techniques, none of which is clearly the best. Case analysis problems have traditionally been used mostly in higher education settings, and professional ones at that (Artino, 2008). The ability to present case analysis problems to students in secondary or, even, elementary settings through engaging digital games may open up new avenues for instructional design. However, RPGs also have the ability to extend problem solving to less discrete educational domains, such as social, moral, and ethical development.

The last problem type includes social, moral, ethical, and many other types of dilemmas. These problems are the most complex and ill-structured in Jonassen's typology, affecting many people in critical ways but with no solution that can "... meet the needs of the majority of the people or escape the prospects of catastrophe" (Jonassen, 2000). In RPGs, players face mostly less complex dilemmas when they weigh the advantages and disadvantages of social interactions and involvement, such as who to befriend in-game or thinking about their own motivation for playing (Cole & Griffiths, 2007). But the environment of RPGs can create more complex dilemmas, especially as players become more heavily invested in the game, and they must make choices about what direction they want to develop their skills and how best to spend their time playing or in game-related activity. RPGs have the potential for instructional design that simulates complex, real-world dilemmas. Dilemmas are highly context-dependent (Jonassen, 2004), and so the development of games for practice in grappling with dilemmas can align with real-world domains. As RPGs become even more complex and include larger numbers of variables, larger numbers of players, and simulate more real-world problems, they may become invaluable in teaching problem solving at this level.

FUTURE RESEARCH DIRECTIONS

Research on educational games has taken a turn away from merely attempting to show the possibility of using games in the classroom and toward the specific steps necessary to integrate them effectively into curricula. With the development of this taxonomy, we hope to assist both the research of this research and the integration process by educators working in the field. The future of instructional design hinges on the development of well-established theory in order to focus design on the intended outcomes of instruction rather than a desired classroom activity. Since using games in the classroom has been seen in recent years as a desirable activity from the standpoint of researchers and educators, it is our hope that a connection can be made between instructional outcomes and the educational games that best suit them. Additionally, educational research in the area of games and problem solving has been sparse, and by laying the groundwork for research in the joint study of these domains we may further the understanding of their intersection.

We have developed our taxonomy with the intent to tease out the linking pattern between the genres of games we describe and established educational theory. This taxonomy should allow instructional designers who intend to use games in the classroom better to understand which types of games are suitable for which educational objectives. If the objective is to teach pure factual content, linear games may be most suitable. However, as is usually the case, students more readily understand content in a social, interactive context, and thus competitive games may be more suitable. As the objectives move from content knowledge to the application of content in novel situations, instructional designers may use strategic games to create dynamic environments. Finally, when the learning objectives entail authentic, complex, ill-structured problem solving, role-playing games in complex, social, online environments allow students to replicate much of the authenticity of real-world problems. It is our intent that further research, review, and development of this taxonomy will more clearly refine the relationships in this pattern. We expect there may be additional theories to incorporate or exchange for those we have included. In addition, there may be games that do not fit in any of these genres, and that require further examination of their educational affordances for inclusion and expansion of this taxonomy.

CONCLUSION

This chapter discussed the need for a comprehensive organization of educational games. Previous research has focused either on individual games for classroom use, or has been focused on classifying games for their features rather than for their applicability to education. We established that revealing connections between games and established educational theory would allow instructional designers and educational researchers to choose games for their educational affordances, and to understand the nature of games. We described the taxonomy of four genres, categorized according to their educational affordances. If instructional designers consider the discussed theories and the linking pattern with the genres in the taxonomy, this may lead to a more logical and effective design process. This, in turn, can lead to incorporating games in the classroom with specific intent and with greater success.

REFERENCES

Amory, A. (2007). Game object model version II: a theoretical framework for educational game development. *Etr&D-Educational Technology Research and Development, 55*(1), 51–77. doi:10.1007/s11423-006-9001-x

Anderson, L. W., & Krathwohl, D. R. (Eds.). (2001). A taxonomy for learning, teaching and Assessing: A Revision of Bloom's Taxonomy of Educational Objectives: Complete Ed. New York: Longman.

Artino, A. R., Jr. (2008). *A brief analysis of research on problem-based learning*. Online submission. Retrieved April 12, 2009, from http://eric.ed.gov/ERICWebPortal/contentdelivery/servlet/ERICServlet?accno=ED501593

Baek, Y. K. (2008). What hinders teachers in using computer and video games in the classroom? exploring factors inhibiting the uptake of computer and video games. *Cyberpsychology & Behavior, 11*(6), 665–671. doi:10.1089/cpb.2008.0127

Bartholow, B. D., Sestir, M. A., & Davis, E. B. (2005). Correlates and consequences of exposure to video game violence: hostile personality, empathy, and aggressive behavior. *Personality and Social Psychology Bulletin, 31*(11), 1573–1586. doi:10.1177/0146167205277205

Björk, S., & Holopainen, J. (2004 October). Describing games: an interaction-centric structural framework. In M. Copier & J. Raessens (Eds.), *Level Up – CD-ROM Proceedings of Digital Games Research Conference2003*. Retrieved from http://www.playresearch.com/publications/2003/structuralframework.pdf

Bloom, B., & Krathwohl, D. R. (1956). *Taxonomy of educational objectives: the classification of educational goals, by a Committee of College and University Examiners. Handbook 1: Cognitive Domain*. New York: Longmans, Green.

Childress, M. D., & Braswell, R. (2006). Using massively multiplayer online role-playing games for online learning. *Distance Education, 27*(2), 187–196. doi:10.1080/01587910600789522

Clark, L., Lawrence, A. J., Astley-Jones, F., & Gray, N. (2009). Gambling near-misses enhance motivation to gamble and recruit win-related brain circuitry. *Neuron, 61*(3), 481–490. doi:10.1016/j.neuron.2008.12.031

Cole, H., & Griffiths, M. D. (2007). Social interactions in massively multiplayer online role-playing gamers. *Cyberpsychology & Behavior, 10*(4), 575–583. doi:10.1089/cpb.2007.9988

Delwiche, A. (2006). Massively multiplayer online games (MMOS)) in the new media classroom. *Educational Technology & Society, 9*(3), 160–172.

Fernandes, R., & Simon, H. A. (1999). A study of how individuals solve complex and ill-structured problems. *Policy Sciences, 32*(3), 225–244. doi:10.1023/A:1004668303848

Gagne, R. M., & Briggs, L. J. (1974). *Principles of instructional design*. New York: Holt, Rinehart, and Winston, Inc.

Gee, J. P. (2003). *What video games have to teach us about learning and literacy*. New York: Palgrave/Macmillan.

Gee, J. P. (2005). Learning by design: good video games as learning machines. *e-learning, 2*(1), 5–16. doi:10.2304/elea.2005.2.1.5

Hamalainen, R. (2008). Designing and evaluating collaboration in a virtual game environment for vocational learning. *Computers & Education, 50*(1), 98–109. doi:10.1016/j.compedu.2006.04.001

Huang, Z. Y., & Cappel, J. J. (2005). Assessment of a web-based learning game in an information systems course. *Journal of Computer Information Systems, 45*(4), 42–49.

Jonassen, D. H. (1997). Instructional design model for well-structured and ill-structured problem-solving learning outcomes. *Educational Technology Research and Development, 45*(1), 65–95. doi:10.1007/BF02299613

Jonassen, D. H. (2000). Toward a design theory of problem solving. *Etr&D-Educational Technology Research and Development, 48*(4), 63–85. doi:10.1007/BF02300500

Jonassen, D. H. (2004). *Learning to solve problems: an instructional design guide*. San Francisco: Pfeiffer.

Kafai, Y. B. (1996). Electronic play worlds: gender differences in children's construction of video games. In Kafai, Y., & Resnick, M. (Eds.), *Constructivism in practice: Designing, thinking, and learning in a digital world* (pp. 97–123). Mahwah, NJ: Erlbaum.

Kreimeier, B. (2002, March 13). The Case for Game Design Patterns. *Gamasutra.* Retrieved April 12, 2009, from http://www.gamasutra.com/features/20020313/kreimeier_03.htm

Kuhn, H. W. (2003). *Lectures on the theory of games*. Princeton, NJ: Princeton University Press.

Kutner, L. A., Olson, C. K., Warner, D. E., & Hertzog, S. M. (2008). Parents' and sons' perspectives on video game play - a qualitative study. *Journal of Adolescent Research, 23*(1), 76–96. doi:10.1177/0743558407310721

Lee, M. S., Ko, Y. H., Song, H. S., Kwon, K. H., Lee, H. S., & Nam, M. (2007). Characteristics of internet use in relation to game genre in korean adolescents. *Cyberpsychology & Behavior, 10*(2), 278–285. doi:10.1089/cpb.2006.9958

Martens, R. L., Gulikers, J., & Bastiaens, T. (2004). The impact of intrinsic motivation on e-learning in authentic computer tasks. *Journal of Computer Assisted Learning, 20*(5), 368–376. doi:10.1111/j.1365-2729.2004.00096.x

Rice, J. W. (2007). Assessing higher order thinking in video games. *Journal of Technology and Teacher Education, 15*(1), 87–100.

Rosas, R., Nussbaum, M., Cumsille, P., Marianov, V., Correa, M., & Flores, P. (2003). Beyond Nintendo: design and assessment of educational video games for first and second grade students. *Computers & Education, 40*(1), 2. doi:10.1016/S0360-1315(02)00099-4

Schacter, J., Herl, H. E., Chung, G. K. W. K., Dennis, R. A., & O'Neil, H. F. (1999). Computer-based performance assessments: a solution to the narrow measurement and reporting of problem-solving. *Computers in Human Behavior, 15*(3-4), 403–418. doi:10.1016/S0747-5632(99)00029-1

Schrader, P. G., & Lawless, K. A. (in press). The hidden literacies of massively multiplayer online games. In Pullen, D. L., Baguley, M., & Gitsaki, C. (Eds.), *Technoliteracy, Discourse and Social Practice: Frameworks and Applications in the Digital Age*. Hershey, PA: Information Science Reference.

Schrader, P. G., Lawless, K. A., & McCreery, M. (2009). Intertextuality in massively multiplayer online games. In Ferdig, R. E. (Ed.), *Handbook of Research on Effective Electronic Gaming in Education* (*Vol. 3*, pp. 791–807). Hershey, PA: Information Science Reference.

Schrader, P. G., & McCreery, M. (2007). The acquisition of skill and expertise in massively multiplayer online games. *Educational Technology Research & Development, 56*(5-6), 557–574. Retrieved October 10, 2007, from http://www.springerlink.com/content/n2496u376825u512/

Smyth, J. M. (2007). Beyond self-selection in video game play: an experimental examination of the consequences of massively multiplayer online role-playing game play. *Cyberpsychology & Behavior, 10*, 717–721. doi:10.1089/cpb.2007.9963

Squire, K. D. (2006). From content to context: videogames as designed experience. *Educational Researcher*, *35*(8), 19–29. doi:10.3102/0013189X035008019

Steinkuehler, C., & Chmiel, M. (2006). Fostering scientific habits of mind in the context of online play. In S. A. Barab, K. E. Hay, N. B. Songer & D. T. Hickey (Eds.), *Proceedings of the International Conference of the Learning Sciences* (pp. 723-729). Mahwah, NJ: Erlbaum.

Steinkuehler, C., & Williams, D. (2006). Where everybody knows your (screen) name: online games as third places. *Journal of Computer-Mediated Communication*, *11*(4), 26. doi:10.1111/j.1083-6101.2006.00300.x

Steinkuehler, C. A. (2004). Learning in massively multiplayer online games. In Y. B. Kafai, W. A. Sandoval, N. Enyedy, A. S. Nixon, & F. Herrera (Eds.), *Proceedings of the Sixth International Conference of the Learning Sciences* (pp.521–528). Mahwah, NJ: Erlbaum.

Top of Form

Wang, S. K., & Reeves, T. C. (2007). The effects of a web-based learning environment on student motivation in a high school earth science course. *Educational Technology Research and Development*, *55*(2), 169–192. doi:10.1007/s11423-006-9016-3

Wiggins, G. (1992). Creating tests worth taking. *Educational Leadership*, *49*(8), 26–33.

Yang, H. L., & Wang, C. S. (2008). Product placement of computer games in cyberspace. *Cyberpsychology & Behavior*, *11*(4), 399–404. doi:10.1089/cpb.2007.0099

Yee, N. (2006). Motivations for play in online games. *Cyberpsychology & Behavior*, *9*(6), 772–775. doi:10.1089/cpb.2006.9.772

Young, M. F., Schrader, P. G., & Zheng, D. P. (2006). MMOGs as Learning environments: an ecological journey into Quest Atlantis and the Sims Online. *Innovate, 2*(4). Retrieved March 20, 2006, http://www.innovateonline.info/index.php?view=article&id=66

ADDITIONAL READING

Akl, E. A., Sackett, K., Pretorius, R., Erdley, S., Bhoopathi, P. S., & Mustafa, R. (2008). Educational games for health professionals. *Cochrane Database of Systematic Reviews*, 1.

Amory, A., Naicker, K., Vincent, J., & Adams, C. (1999). The use of computer games as an educational tool: identification of appropriate game types and game elements. *British Journal of Educational Technology*, *30*(4), 311–321. doi:10.1111/1467-8535.00121

Araki, M., & Carliner, S. (2008). What the literature says about using game worlds and social worlds in cyberspace for communicating technical and educational content. *Technical Communication*, *55*(3), 251–260.

Barlett, C. P., Harris, R. J., & Bruey, C. (2008). The effect of the amount of blood in a violent video game on aggression, hostility, and arousal. *Journal of Experimental Social Psychology*, *44*(3), 539–546. doi:10.1016/j.jesp.2007.10.003

Becker, K. (2007). Digital game-based learning once removed: teaching teachers. *British Journal of Educational Technology*, *38*(3), 478–488. doi:10.1111/j.1467-8535.2007.00711.x

Bellotti, F., Ferretti, E., & De Gloria, A. (2005). Discovering the European heritage through the ChiKho educational web game. In Proceedings of Intelligent Technologies for Interactive Entertainment (LNCS 3814, pp. 13-22).

Bergeron, B. P. (2008). Learning & retention in adaptive serious games. *Studies in Health Technology and Informatics*, *132*, 26–30.

Brezinka, V. (2008). Treasure hunt - a serious game to support psychotherapeutic treatment of children. *Studies in Health Technology and Informatics*, *136*, 71–76.

Burgess, M. C. R., Stermer, S. P., & Burgess, S. R. (2007). Sex, lies, and video games: the portrayal of male and female characters on video game covers. *Sex Roles*, *57*(5-6), 419–433. doi:10.1007/s11199-007-9250-0

Carnagey, N. L., Anderson, C. A., & Bushman, B. J. (2007). The effect of video game violence on physiological desensitization to real-life violence. *Journal of Experimental Social Psychology*, *43*(3), 489–496. doi:10.1016/j.jesp.2006.05.003

Chang, J. H., & Zhang, H. X. (2008). Analyzing online game players: from materialism and motivation to attitude. *Cyberpsychology & Behavior*, *11*(6), 711–714. doi:10.1089/cpb.2007.0147

Chen, L. S. L. (2008). Subjective well-being: evidence from the different personality traits of online game teenager players. *Cyberpsychology & Behavior*, *11*(5), 579–581. doi:10.1089/cpb.2007.0192

Chen, L. S. L., Tu, H. H. J., & Wang, E. S. T. (2008). Personality traits and life satisfaction among online game players. *Cyberpsychology & Behavior*, *11*(2), 145–149. doi:10.1089/cpb.2007.0023

Colwell, J. (2007). Needs met through computer game play among adolescents. *Personality and Individual Differences*, *43*, 2072–2082. doi:10.1016/j.paid.2007.06.021

Cummings, H. M., & Vandewater, E. A. (2007). Relation of adolescent video game play to time spent in other activities. *Archives of Pediatrics & Adolescent Medicine*, *161*(7), 684–689. doi:10.1001/archpedi.161.7.684

Dworak, M., Schierl, T., Bruns, T., & Struder, H. K. (2007). Impact of singular excessive computer game and television exposure on sleep patterns and memory performance of school-aged children. *Pediatrics*, *120*, 978–985. doi:10.1542/peds.2007-0476

Evreinova, T. V., Evreinov, G., & Raisamo, R. (2008). Non-visual game design and training in gameplay skill acquisition - a puzzle game case study. *Interacting with Computers*, *20*(3), 386–405. doi:10.1016/j.intcom.2008.02.008

Feng, J., Spence, I., & Pratt, J. (2007). Playing an action video game reduces gender differences in spatial cognition. *Psychological Science*, *18*, 850–855. doi:10.1111/j.1467-9280.2007.01990.x

Frey, A., Hartig, J., Ketzel, A., Zinkernagel, A., & Moosbrugger, H. (2007). The use of virtual environments based on a modification of the computer game quake iii arena (r) in psychological experimenting. *Computers in Human Behavior*, *23*(4), 2026–2039. doi:10.1016/j.chb.2006.02.010

Furst, E. J. (1981). Bloom's Taxonomy of educational objectives for the cognitive domain: philosophical and educational issues. *Review of Educational Research*, *51*(4), 441–453.

Gunter, G. A., Kenny, R. F., & Vick, E. H. (2008). Taking educational games seriously: using the retain model to design endogenous fantasy into standalone educational games. *Etr&D-Educational Technology Research and Development*, *56*(5-6), 511–537. doi:10.1007/s11423-007-9073-2

Hayes, E. (2008). Game content creation and it proficiency: an exploratory study. *Computers & Education*, *51*(1), 97–108. doi:10.1016/j.compedu.2007.04.002

Hobbs, L. J., & Yan, Z. (2008). Cracking the walnut: using a computer game to impact cognition, emotion, and behavior of highly aggressive fifth grade students. *Computers in Human Behavior*, *24*(2), 421–438. doi:10.1016/j.chb.2007.01.031

Ingram, C., Ray, K., Landeen, J., & Keane, D. R. (1998). Evaluation of an educational game for health sciences students. *The Journal of Nursing Education, 37*(6), 240–246.

Jannink, M. J. A., Van Der Wilden, G. J., Navis, D. W., Visser, G., Gussinklo, J., & Ijzerman, M. (2008). A Low-cost video game applied for training of upper extremity function in children with cerebral palsy: a pilot study. *Cyberpsychology & Behavior, 11*(1), 27–32. doi:10.1089/cpb.2007.0014

Jimison, H. B., Pavel, M., Bissell, P., & McKanna, J. (2007). A framework for cognitive monitoring using computer game interactions. *Studies in Health Technology and Informatics, 129*(2), 1073–1077.

Kao, J. J., & Chen, Y. J. (1996). An educational water quality management game. *Water Science and Technology, 34*(12), 205–211. doi:10.1016/S0273-1223(96)00871-2

Katsionis, G., & Virvou, M. (2008). Personalised e-learning through an educational virtual reality game using web services. *Multimedia Tools and Applications, 39*(1), 47–71. doi:10.1007/s11042-007-0155-2

Kim, E. J., Namkoong, K., Ku, T., & Kim, S. J. (2008). The relationship between online game addiction and aggression, self-control and narcissistic personality traits. *European Psychiatry, 23*(3), 212–218. doi:10.1016/j.eurpsy.2007.10.010

Kinzie, M. B., & Joseph, D. R. D. (2008). Gender differences in game activity preferences of middle school children: implications for educational game design. *Etr&D-Educational Technology Research and Development, 56*(5-6), 643–663. doi:10.1007/s11423-007-9076-z

Klimmt, C., Hartmann, T., & Frey, A. (2007) Effectance and control as determinants of video game enjoyment. *Cyberpsychology & Behavior, 10*(6), 845–847. doi:10.1089/cpb.2007.9942

Martinez-Ortiz, I., Moreno-Ger, P., Sierra, J. L., & Fernandez-Manjon, B. (2006). *Production and deployment of educational videogames as assessable learning objects.*

Monteiro, S. S., Rebello, S. M., & Schall, V. T. (1991). Zigzaids--an educational game about aids for children. *Hygie, 10*(4), 32–35.

Moreno-Ger, P., Burgos, D., Martinez-Ortiz, I., Sierra, J. L., & Fernandez-Manjon, B. (2008). Educational game design for online education. *Computers in Human Behavior, 24*(6), 2530–2540. doi:10.1016/j.chb.2008.03.012

Ormell, C. P. (1974). Bloom's Taxonomy and the objectives of education. *Educational Research, 17*, 3–18. doi:10.1080/0013188740170101

Peters, C. S., & Malesky, L. A. (2008). Problematic usage among highly-engaged players of massively multiplayer online role playing games. *Cyberpsychology & Behavior, 11*(4), 481–484. doi:10.1089/cpb.2007.0140

Rehm, M. (2008). She is just stupid - analyzing user-agent interactions in emotional game situations. *Interacting with Computers, 20*(3), 311–325. doi:10.1016/j.intcom.2008.02.005

Schafer, L., Stauber, A., & Bokan, B. (2004). StoryNet: an educational game for social skills. *Technologies for Interactive Digital Storytelling and Entertainment, 3105*, 148–157.

Spector, J. M., & Ross, S. M. (2008). Special thematic issue on game-based learning INTRODUCTION. *Etr&D-Educational Technology Research and Development, 56*(5-6), 509–510. doi:10.1007/s11423-008-9096-3

Sun, D. L., Ma, N., Bao, M., Chen, X. C., & Zhang, D. R. (2008). Computer games: a double-edged sword? *Cyberpsychology & Behavior, 11*(5), 545–548. doi:10.1089/cpb.2007.0145

Wang, T. H. (2008). Web-based quiz-game-like formative assessment: development and evaluation. *Computers & Education*, *51*(3), 1247–1263. doi:10.1016/j.compedu.2007.11.011

KEY TERMS AND DEFINITIONS

Abstractness: The dependency of the problem on the nature of its domain.

Competitive Games: Success requires linear logic, plus the anticipation of an opponent's actions.

Complexity: The number variables and the level of detail in their relationships.

Dynamicity: The degree to which a problem changes over time.

Linear Games: Success requires linear logic and movement from a starting point to an ending point.

Non-Player Characters: Entities that react to a player's actions.

Role-Playing Games: Success requires developing and maintaining a profile of probabilities within a complex environment.

Semiotic Domains: Complex, interdisciplinary domains capable of engaging higher-order thinking skills.

Strategic Games: Success requires strategic planning and management of a complex system

Structuredness: The amount of structure the problem contains as presented.

Chapter 2
The Design and Development of Educational Immersive Environments:
From Theory to Classroom Deployment

Collin B. Price
University of Worcester, UK

J.S. Moore
University of Worcester, UK

ABSTRACT

Computer game technology is poised to make a significant impact on the way our youngsters will learn. Our youngsters are 'Digital Natives', immersed in digital technologies, especially computer games. They expect to utilize these technologies in learning contexts. This expectation, and our response as educators, may change classroom practice and inform curriculum developments. This chapter approaches these issues 'head on'. Starting from a review of the current educational issues, an evaluation of educational theory and instructional design principles, a new theoretical approach to the construction of "Educational Immersive Environments" (EIEs) is proposed. Elements of this approach are applied to development of an EIE to support Literacy Education in UK Primary Schools. An evaluation of a trial within a UK Primary School is discussed. Conclusions from both the theoretical development and the evaluation suggest how future teacher-practitioners may embrace both the technology and our approach to develop their own learning resources.

INTRODUCTION

The design and development of computer games for education and training has become a hot topic in multidisciplinary research involving elements from education, computing, art and design. The fruits of this research are now starting to penetrate the classroom, as serious computer games based educational material is developed. This in turn will inform classroom practice and eventually national policy. Like many educational innovations, the proposed use of computer games may be traced to the availability of a new and cost-effective technology (such as the introduction of interactive white-

DOI: 10.4018/978-1-61520-713-8.ch002

boards), but in this case the context is much more complex and involves many factors.

First there is the cultural context of our digital age, where our youth has grown up immersed in digital technologies, especially computer games. These 'Digital Natives' (Prensky, 2001) expect to play computer games. This expectation when coupled with the findings the JISC report (JISC, 2004), which suggests that learning should be congruent with the cultural context and also with Prensky's description of today's learners as 'engage me or enrage me' (Prensky, 2005), leads to the conclusion that our digital natives will *expect* computer game technology to appear in some form on the school curriculum. In this chapter we argue that this technology should be harnessed to produce 'Educational Immersive Environments' (EIEs), learning resources which use computer games technology, but which are based on sound pedagogical principles and may be used in all school classes from physics to literacy (Price, 2008; Moore and Price, 2009).

A second factor has been the falling recruitment in 'Science Technology Engineering Mathematics' (STEM) subject courses. This is especially true of physics education which is seen to be in a state of crisis due to lack of interest in these subjects (Smithers & Robinson, 2005; 2006). The Institute of Physics has called for 'an increasing number of young people who should be enthused by physics' (IOP, 2001). What better motivation than virtual experiments investigated within an EIE? A third factor is the drop in literacy standards in UK primary schools (Frean & Woolcock, 2007; Paton, 2007). This has resulted in a call for an examination of teaching standards in education and a call for new forms of expression in the classroom in order to prepare our Digital Natives for the knowledge-based 21st century (Dede 1995).

Against this backdrop, research has suggested that computer games may be used to address these issues (FAS, 2006; Gee, 2003; Price, 2006). Indeed it is suggested that computer game technology may be transformed into a new educational technology which, when grounded in educational theory such as *experiential learning* may equip our Digital Natives with skills required in the contemporary world (FAS, 2006). The design of any EIE must start from sound educational theories as well as being informed by content specified by the curriculum (Tang et al., 2007). Often in the past, educational materials have been driven by technology, with learning approaches adjusted to the technology.

The history of computer games in training and education can be traced back to the 'America's Army' games; the first 'AA-Soldiers' game was aimed to combat falling recruitment, the second 'AA-Operations' game was developed as a training resource (Zyda et al., 2003; Zyda et al., 2005). These are examples of 'Serious Games' which combine various aspects of education and simulation. Other examples include 'Foodforce', 'Stone City' and 'VR Therapy for Spider Phobia'. Some early educational games were produced as part of Becta's 'Computer Games in Education' project and MITs 'Games-to-teach' project. A more recent educational game is Disney's 'Hot Shot Business', a game designed to teach children of ages 9-13 how to run a business. Links to these games are provided at the end of this chapter.

This chapter aims to provide teacher-practitioners with theory and skills to help them appreciate the usefulness of EIEs, and also to consider authoring their own material. In the first section this chapter explores how a successful EIE may be designed using (i) educational theory, (ii) instructional design principles, (iii) approaches to game design. Some novel theoretical approaches are suggested in (iv) where an integration of various theories and approaches is provided, to construct a unified theory of EIE design. The second section contains a case study where this approach has been applied to the production of an EIE for Primary School Literacy learning according to the UK curriculum requirements. This section explores (i) how to work with teachers to develop an EIE, (ii) how to apply theories and principles to construct an effective EIE, and ends with (iii) a full evaluation of the materials deployed within a local primary school.

GROUNDING THEORY

The design of EIE content and approaches must be grounded in theory. This is fundamental. The Constructivist paradigm (Bruner, 1966) has much to offer here. Many other theories such as Gardner's 'multiple intelligence', (see Becker, 2005). Maslow's 'hierarchy of [learner] needs' (Maslow, 1943), Gagne's 'conditions of learning' (Gagne, 1977) and Keller's 'ARC theory' of motivation (Keller, 1987) all have their place. There is one systems-based complete model of learning which is relevant to some extent. This is Anderson's 'General Learning Model' (GLM), see Buckley & Anderson (2006). While this is distilled from studies and theories of aggression, it provides a useful synthesis of various approaches. At the time of writing there has been no thorough empirical research into the validity of theories presented below nor of the effectiveness of EIEs in improving learning.

Education Theory

Constructivism aligns well with the nature and affordances of computer game technology and this theory is useful in informing the design of EIEs. In the 'Constructivist' learning paradigm, proposed by Bruner (1966), learning is seen as an *active* process where learners build upon their *past experiences* and *knowledge* to advance their understanding of a subject. Constructivism asserts three basic dimensions: (i) Situated Learning. Here learners are placed in an authentic context (one which is based on a real world, professional, scenario), and learning is obtained through interaction with this context. (ii) Cognitive challenge or puzzlement where problems and finding solutions motivate the learner. (iii) Collaboration where inter-learner discourse and dialogue provide a peer-review process of checking and validating understanding (Savery & Duffy, 1995). Constructivist EIEs empower students with control over their learning, providing *choice* of what they learn, and how they learn (through multiple representations); these EIEs make learning directly relevant to real life scenarios and encourage social, collaborative and interactive learning (Honebein, 1996). Within such a system, learners build personal hypotheses concerning the ontology of the experienced world and identify a suitable epistemology on how to engage with this world. The need to engage with the real world has been coined 'Epistemic Learning' where participation in a community of professional practice justifies the assertion of collaborative rather than individual learning (Lave & Wenger, 1991). This can be viewed as a strong blend of Situated Learning and Collaboration.

The *dynamics* of the learning process is an important concept. The learning process for a single learner is often modeled using the 'Experiential Learning Cycle' of Kolb (1984) which outlines a cyclical dynamic of direct experience, personal reflection, the situation of this reflection within existing theory, and the formation of a plan to inform the subsequent direct experience. The interactivity and dynamics of computer game technology support this experiential learning cycle; this cycle is found in most computer games, not solely in crafted EIEs (Gee 2003). Kolb's Cycle has been used to design EIEs for secondary physics education, where the learner cycles between four rooms of first *concrete experience* where the learner observes the phenomena resulting from a particular experiment, second, *reflective observation* where data associated with the experiment are selected, third, *abstract conceptualization* where the data is analyzed and the learner forms a hypothesis to explain the chosen experimental data and fourth, *active experimentation* where the learner tests the hypothesis through a modification of the experiment (Price, 2009; Price, 2008). Price models the dynamics of collaborative learning as a coupling of each individual's Kolb Cycle.

Learning *dynamics* occurs on a number of differing time scales. The Kolb cycle moves on a short time scale, in almost 'real time' as the learner engages with the EIE. On the other hand *adaptation* of the EIE to the learner's state of progression occurs on a longer time scale. For example, as the learner becomes more familiar with the EIE content, the 'fun factor' programmed into the EIE can be reduced. Initially a high 'fun factor' may be used to elicit motivation, but once this is obtained, more abstract or challenging content may be introduced, (Appelman & Goldsworthy, 1999). Adaptation may also be programmed on this longer time-scale as a response to individual learners' performance. Additional help or extension material may be offered to the weaker or stronger learner (Burgos & Specht, 2006).

It is clear that EIEs may have some solid pedagogical advantages. These include: (i) The realization of deep learning through arousal of curiosity (Gee, 2003). (ii) The acquisition of cognitive skills not realised in a traditional educational setting, *ibid.* (iii) Promotion of a problem-solving approach (Khoo & Gentile, 2007), (iv) Enabling peer-review through collaboration (Hamalainen, 2008), (v) Real-time feedback of success and failure, to remove misunderstanding (Laughlin et al., 2007).

Through a study of the literature, elements of Constructivism which may usefully inform the design of EIEs emerge (Honebein, 1996). These elements have been used to aid in the construction of the case study reported below. Constructivist EIEs should (i) allow the learner to take responsibility for their own learning, (ii) present multiple perspectives about the material to the learner, (iii) make the learner aware of their own learning process, (iv) be relevant, based on real-world scenarios, (v) be highly interactive, (vi) should encourage collaboration, (vii) use various modes of representation (e.g., text, visuals and audio material), (viii) be cognitively challenging using puzzles and conflicts. Perhaps the last point is the most significant and follows from Piaget's model of cognitive dissonance (see Gredler, 1992).

Instructional Design Principles

Instructional design principles focus on elements of instruction which may be best deployed to achieve intended learning outcomes. They complement educational theory which may be considered as an ontological substrate, whilst instructional design focuses on designing educational *processes* which transform educational theory into practice. Kurt Squire (2006) commented, in the discussion of how one should design EIEs, '... this shifts the question from one of delivering content to one of designing experience'. Delivering content is an arrow pointing at the learner where the content informs the learner. Experience is a *process* where the content informs the learner, but the learner can select the content, through choice.

The design of instructional materials has been influenced greatly by Gagne (1977) and Keller (1987). Gagne's nine 'events of instruction' have been used in the production of the EIE discussed in the case study below. These are (i) Gaining attention, (ii) Informing the Objective, (iii) Stimulating Recall of prerequisite learned capabilities, (iv) Presenting the stimulus material, (v) Provision of learning guidance, (vi) Eliciting performance (practice), (vii) Providing feedback, (viii) Assessing the performance, (ix) Enhancing retention and transfer (generalization). Keller (1987) developed an alternative model of motivational design, the 'ARCS' model which proposed four steps: **At**tention, **R**elevance, **C**onfidence and **S**atisfaction. These steps were intended to motivate learners to engage with and to maintain the learning process. To gain the learner's *attention*, a fact could be introduced to challenge or contradict previous experience, or perhaps humour or some exciting visual could be introduced. To be *relevant*, the learner needs to be shown how each activity draws upon previous experiences. The learner should be presented with clearly defined goals and if possible, these should support the learner's interest. Strategies to build up *confidence* could be simple, such as stating clear and appealing learning goals or taking learners through stages of difficulty. Challenges should be balanced against ability, so that learning becomes neither a bore nor impossibility. With increasing confidence, learners will develop autonomy in their learning. To achieve *satisfaction*, the learner could acquire a new skill and then transfer it to a new context. Also rewards should be given with immediate task-related feedback, as well as unexpected rewards.

More recently, Gunter et al., (2006) have suggested that deployment of instructional theories enhance learning achievement and motivation. They considered instructional approaches alongside game design principles, and concluded that these approaches and principles should be applied together. Constructivist researchers also contribute here: Jonassen (1999) provides a constructivist design framework, Hanaffin and Land (1997) provide examples of how constructivist theory can be applied to instructional design. Perhaps the most fundamental work is due to Malone (1980) who investigated how to make computer games immersive, captivating and enjoyable for young children. More recently Becta (2001) have proposed several factors which aim to increase engagement. The work of Csikszentmihalhi (1992) forges a connection between motivation theory and instructional design principles. Here the concept of 'flow' is introduced. This is a dynamic state where challenges and frustration are in equilibrium, where obstacles vanish from view. As learner skills increase so does the balance. Learners in this state of flow are consumed by the activity *for its own sake* and not by a desire to achieve a separate motivational reward.

Game Design Principles

Since computer game technology is a new *phenomenon* of expression, interaction and engagement, there is not yet a sufficient body of data to establish a *theory* of computer games to inform the design and development of these games. Therefore computer games are designed and developed according to 'principles' (as well as market considerations). Salen and Zimmerman (2003) capture the essential principles of computer game design: (i) *Rules*. These define the *process* of the game, especially the nature of interactions within the game, (ii) *Play*. In-game activities define the experience of the player (Crawford 2003), (iii) *Culture*. The game visuals, objects, sounds and music, and the behaviour of the NPCs all serve to establish 'beliefs' and 'norms' within the game.

Transferring these principles over to EIEs requires some effort. Merely adding educational content to a 'game' will not normally produce a viable EIE. Units of educational activity ('lessons', 'modules of instruction') are aligned with *Learning Outcomes* specified by the course or the curriculum. These may be best aligned with 'rules' of game-play. If this is done then play will realize educational *processes* as challenges or problem-solving activities. Learning activities crafted into an EIE to develop cognitive skills and the formation of new concepts, may be aligned with 'play'. Here through 'play' the learner may appreciate correlations between cause (the learner's actions) and effect (results of these actions). Concerning 'culture', one expects educational games to *bury* the educational process to some extent, behind a cloak of fun and motivation where the learner learns without being aware of the learning process. At first sight this does not agree with the constructivist paradigm, but it's a question of *time scale*. While having fun performing activities and completing tasks the learner is not aware of the learning process. Yet in moments of reflection (which may be built into the EIE as dedicated areas), the learner will be encouraged to reflect on these activities and tasks and so on their learning. As noted by Malone and Lepper (1987) cultural beliefs and norms should be recast as learning objectives rather than through play, which should be fun and may involve a fantasy context.

Lepper and Malone (1987) suggest four factors to inform game design. (i) Games must introduce challenges in a way that the learner feels continually challenged, where the difficulty of challenge increases with the learner skill. This corresponds to the notion of 'flow'. (ii) Games must arouse cognitive and sensory curiosity. There must be sufficiently rich and powerful visual semiotics, audio information and interactions. (iii) Games should impart a feeling of 'being in control' by providing immediate (or delayed) causal feedback. (iv) Games should use fantasy to stimulate the learner.

Towards a Unified Theory of EIE Design

In this section a number of new theoretical directions are explored. These are then combined with theories and principles discussed above to achieve a synthesis which we propose as the basis for a sound design and development approach. This synthesis is based upon the unifying mathematical theory of self-organizing systems where structures spontaneously emerge without engineering, following interactions within the system. In the context of EIEs, we introduce the concept of 'Self-Organizing EIEs' (SOEIEs) which organize themselves according to learner activities. But first, some preparatory ground must be explored! A game designer must juggle various aspects of a game such as the spatial arrangement of rooms or an external terrain, the flow of the game through time, the level and nature of interaction with game elements, a narrative or storyline. The fundamental question for the game designer is how to construct a believable interesting game, which to some extend mimics the real physical world, in the same sense that 'science fiction' is not science, but close enough to be believable. The question for the EIE designer is the same, but with the additional quest to produce an authentic learning experience.

The abstract concept of **metaphor** may be useful here, since metaphor often bridges the gap between the real and unreal. In particular the power of the spatial metaphor has previously been identified by Lakoff (1987).

Metaphor of Space. In constructing physics educational materials, we have used the metaphor of space. First the 'knowledge structures' of the expert teacher are constructed as *concept maps* where the various concepts identified with a particular domain of physics are drawn as boxes. The relationships between these concepts are drawn as arcs between relevant boxes, resulting in a network of related boxes which also displays a hierarchical organization (Price 2009). Concept maps were introduced by Novak while studying children's development of science knowledge (Novak and Musonda, 1991). They form a graphical representation of concepts and their relationships in a hierarchy. This network is then used to define the *topology* of the EIE, e.g., concept boxes are transformed into rooms and relationships between these are transformed into passageways. As the learners move through such an EIE they are effectively traversing the knowledge structure of the expert teacher. Concept maps are not static, but like neural networks they are plastic, where the strengths of the relationships may change in time as the learner progresses. New concepts may be added and existing ones removed. An established map may be re-configured by interactions with the environment through events of puzzlement, challenge and conflict. Such events are common in computer games (Ulrich 1997). Another useful spatial metaphor is the 'magic circle' metaphor proposed by Salen and Zimmerman (2003). This 'magic circle' space is a finite bounded place, but contains unbounded infinite possibilities which produce a sense of flow and suspension of disbelief. Within this place, learning objectives and motivational elements are closely woven together. It is here that Prensky's 'learning by stealth' may actually occur.

Metaphor of the WWW. This is closely linked with spatial metaphor and *topology*. The WWW has a structure where some 18 or 19 clicks can navigate from any page to all other pages on the web! While the surfer may not be aware of this topology, navigational tools are easily understood and used to journey the web. It has been suggested that use of hypertext in obtaining knowledge engages the learner in constructivist principles (Jonassen & Wang 1993). This metaphor can be usefully applied to constructing EIEs where learners move between rooms or areas not using passageways or paths but by using *teleporters* which are metaphorical hyperlinks. Here, areas of learning contain activities but also related hyperlinks *(teleporters)* to other areas. The EIE can be constructed as a web of learning activities providing a high level of learner choice, and a familiar navigational structure.

Metaphor of Embodiment. Dreyfus (2004) has expressed concern with existence in various cyberspaces such as the WWW and *Second Life*. He asserts that without bodily engagement ('embodiment') with phenomena we cannot understand their relevance or meaning. Yet computer games and EIEs appear to work differently, through their enormous immersive pull. Benyon (2005) suggests that games and EIEs achieve this by being authentic, by providing learner identification with the EIE's 'Non-Player-Characters' (NPCs), due to their adaptability and by providing narrative and flow. Embodiment can result from encountering situations that foster invention and creativity. This is the 'Cognitive Apprenticeship' metaphor of Collins (1991). Through modeling of real processes and expert activities, learners become aware of how experts solve problems, generate novel solutions and generate new artifacts such as knowledge. This modeling is characterized by making knowledge explicit (articulation) and forming and testing hypotheses (exploration). However embodiment also recognizes the need for the learner to have an impact on the environment, the EIE reacts, responds and adapts to the learner's actions. A theoretical basis for embodiment is provided by Varela et al. (1991).

Metaphor of Systems. Systems comprise components and relationships between these; systems theory describes how the components interact. There are two poles: at one end is the theory of 'Hard Systems', (based upon a mathematical description of an underlying ontology comprising components and interactions), to 'Soft Systems', (based upon human perceptions of that ontology). Systems theory can be applied to the work of Sfard (2008) who notes that students today, are encouraged to choose their own learning trajectories rather than converge to teacher-defined goals. She describes this as a shift from the 'acquisitional' to the 'participatory' metaphor. Students no longer have a conversation with the world, but rather with others' perceptions of the world. Here language is fundamental, where learning becomes a process of modifying and extending one's capacity for discourse. Sfard goes on to posit that there are two levels of learning, the object-level and the meta-level, both of which are necessary for a learner to progress from novice to expert. At the object level, learners will discuss material within a provided linguistic field, and within this linguistic field, they will be able to progress in learning and come to understand associated concepts. Since a field exists *a priori*, there is no need for a teacher to be present. However, the situation jumps dramatically when further material is introduced which requires a different linguistic field. Since this new linguistic field lies outside the learners' experience, and therefore cannot be learned autonomously it must be taught. This is a meta-level of learning where a new vocabulary must be introduced (by the teacher) in order to establish an expanded space of discourse. In this shift the 'acquisitional' to the 'participatory' metaphor, Sfard is in fact using the Systems theory metaphor, where this shift may be viewed as a movement from the 'hard' to the 'soft' systems approach.

The question of the **content** of the EIE has aroused some interest in the literature. This has been referred to by Gee as 'a central paradox of learning' (Gee 2004). Gee asserts that the learner should not be thrown into a complex learning scenario, but also that the scenario itself needs to be built up over time. This paradox can be simply reduced to a conflict of two time scales, the short time scale of the learner and the long time scale of the learning scenario. This is reminiscent of Sfard where the object-level is associated with the short time scale and the meta-level is associated with the long time scale. This relates back to the work of Ausubel (1968) who recognized the importance of previous knowledge. Aldritch (2004) provides an initial classification of content into (i) linear, such as experienced in a traditional PowerPoint presentation, (ii) cyclical which seems to imply learning by 'drill and fill', or (iii) open-ended where activities have no 'right answer'. He argues that EIEs should combine a mix of these. The authors propose a different analysis and resulting classification. As previously mentioned, EIEs, by being programmable in nature are able to adapt to a situation, whether this is the current learning status of the learner, or the learning outcomes defined by the teacher.

In an attempt to effect a synopsis of current thought, and to extend this into future development, we propose a theory of EIE design based on the 'Complex Dynamical Systems' (CDS) approach. This approach is based upon a mathematical description of the dynamic evolution of properties of abstract objects and abstract interactions over time. It is usually described by systems of non-linear ordinary differential equations which describe the properties of these objects as these properties evolve over time due to their interactions. CDS have been extensively researched in a number of domains such as theoretical physics, mathematical biophysics and chemical thermodynamics. Here we introduce this matter into the study of EIEs. We do not propose to assert mathematical models explicitly, but rather to use the concepts and theories and experimental results from CDS to inform the design of EIEs.

There are several characteristics of CDS. (i) They are not engineered to produce a particular behaviour, but are constructed according to a system of fundamental elements and their interactions. (ii) The CDS behaviour *emerges* from this system specification. (iii) These systems are *self-organizing* where interesting spatial and temporal structures appear without having been specified (iv) This emerging behaviour is observed as *patterns* in space and time. (v) Typical patterns which emerge in **time** can be classified as *cyclical* where a particular series of states is repeated, or as *chaotic* where there is no obvious sequence, or as *static* where there is no temporal change. (vi) Typical patterns which emerge in **space** can be classified as *homogeneous* where there is no spatial structure, *patterned* where there is a regular spatial structure, or *clustered* where there is a structure which is not regular and not random, (see Strogatz, 2004).

We propose to use Self Organizing principles to design EIEs where structure and behaviour emerge in response to the learners' activities. In terms of designing these 'Self-Organizing EIEs' (SOEIEs), this theory first tells us *what not to do*. We must not (i) Prescribe a sequence of learning activities (ii) Define 'rooms' or 'places' where learners engage. According to our theory, a sequence of learning activities (drawn from a space of all sequences) will emerge according to the learners' interactions with each other and with the system. Also, the places of interaction will emerge, according to the learners' interactions. In other words, the learners will construct their learning environment, over time, according to their interaction with the environment. This is *self-organization*. This theory assumes that the EIE starts as an amorphous but pregnant domain; it has no structure but is highly generative. It is the interaction with the learners that engages with this pregnancy and converts the amorphous into a structure which provides learning outcomes best attuned to the learners, as a consequence of their continued interactions. As learners continually engage with the SOEIE, the emergent structure is strengthened and refined.

How do we design SOEIEs? The EIE is programmed to learn from learner activity and therefore self-organize. For example connections between learning areas could be strengthened or weakened according to learner engagement. If a learner assessed an activity to be interesting, its accessibility would be enhanced. If learners engage with a particular activity, then the activity could replicate (spawn) similar activities. If activities were under-used, then access to them would be reduced and eventually they would delete themselves. Of course as the learner progresses the SOEIE will become aware of this progression and will spawn new (or re-spawn deleted) activities. This will raise the level of learning. Following Sfard, this requires "teacher instruction" which will be achieved using NPCs. Many possible techniques of interaction will be programmed; their deployment will follow according to the degree of their use. How could Self-Organizing EIEs develop structures which support learning theories and design principles?

Concerning **Constructivist theories,** *situated learning* can be obtained by programming NPCs to behave like experts. This can be achieved by supplementing the current NPC 'Rule Based System' AI approaches with Artificial Neural Networks (ANNs). The NPC will demonstrate expertise supporting situated learning. A Self-Organizing environment provides the ultimate in *cognitive challenge* where there is initially little information about the structure of the environment; the learners' actions uncover the slowly changing ontology of their environment. The feedback of effects to the learners occurs on a short time scale while the environment generates its structure and reveals this to the learner on a longer time scale. *Collaboration* can be obtained by allowing several learners to enter the EIE as a group and engage in discourse and dialogue with each other and the intelligent NPCs.

Concerning **Experiential Learning**, the emergence of the classical experiential learning structures necessitates multiple activities which provide feedback on a short time scale. Each activity provides many learner choices (inputs, parameters) and associated outputs to allow the learner to construct and challenge alternative hypotheses. This will lead to the emergence of forms of Experiential Learning Cycles. The success of this emergence is predicated only on the learner's natural curiosity and their capability for rational thought.

Concerning **Instructional Design,** the SOEIE will commence in a high dimensionality learning space which through the self-organization process will crystallize into an acceptable number of recognizable activities. Initially the learner will find *attention-gaining* stimuli but as they progress they will gain *confidence* as the *relevance* of the space emerges. The initial high level of motivation will promote discovery and understanding, then its character will change as the EIE emerges, to promote learner progression.

Concerning **Game Design Principles,** initially there will be no *game rules*, only a large number of interesting activities to perform. The game rules will emerge and be discovered as the EIE crystallizes in response to player activity. Also, *game play* will emerge as the learners create their own game. The *game culture* will evolve as elements are added or deleted to the game and as interconnection weights are changed. Of course the emergence of game rules can be seen as an *interpretation* of the behaviour of the Self-Organizing EIE, but their emergence could be used as a validity check on the correctness of the EIE.

In summary, we propose a Self-Organizing systems approach to the development of EIEs which support principles of constructivist learning and approaches from instructional design. These SOEIEs learn from the learners and adapt to their level of learning.

A CASE STUDY: PRIMARY LITERACY EDUCATION

This case study discusses a project which was designed and developed as an EIE supporting Primary Literacy learning for children of ages 7-11 within the UK system. The theme was a classroom activity based upon an approach to literacy learning known as 'VCOP' (Vocabulary, Connectives, Openers and Punctuation). These are fundamental elements of reading and writing taught separately, and are brought together in a creative class activity called 'Big Writing'. In this synoptic activity, the classroom is filled with music, contains a burning candle (on which the silent pupils may focus while reflecting) and the pupils are asked to write a story using VCOP.

The EIE constructed to support this approach was informed by (i) the requirements of the curriculum and the needs of the teacher-practitioners in the classroom, (ii) educational theory, principles of instructional design, and consideration of game design principles, (iii) the technology available (game engine) and the ability to extend the game engine affordances through programming.

The Development Process

The UK National Curriculum Order defines what must be taught at each key stage. To support teachers, the Department for Education and Skills has produced the Primary National Strategy Framework (PNSF), a complex document which contains details of learning outcomes to be achieved at all stages. Following the agreement to work with the local Primary School, a 'demonstrator' EIE was created based on elements of the PNSF and presented to a group of around 8 teachers. Feedback (collected through a formal questionnaire and audio recording) proved crucial to the development of the project. Teachers requested not to use the PNSF, (as ample resources exist), but rather to embrace the VCOP methodology which lacks resources. Other technical feedback was used to construct the first VCOP prototype. This prototype was presented to teachers and feedback from this presentation indicated that the prototype could indeed support their classroom activities. Further technical detail was provided and used in the development process. The second prototype was constructed and vetted by the key stakeholder who agreed that it was of high quality and safe to be used with school children. This EIE was deployed in the school, and following a period of pupil familiarization, formal observations of the pupils commenced. Some glitches emerged which were corrected and a third prototype delivered, based on the pupils' feedback. This developmental process highlights a close collaboration between the teacher-practitioner-experts, the pupils and the EIE development team, which ensured that the final prototype was fit for purpose.

Design and Construction of the EIE

The VCOP EIE has been informed by the theory and principles discussed above. As mentioned, the 'VCOP' method required four rooms. The *topology* of these rooms was informed the teacher in order to guide pupils between various combinations of rooms. For example, some pupils would be required to visit the 'V' and 'C' rooms; others would visit 'V', 'C' and 'P' rooms during the course of a particular lesson. A programmable topology was therefore chosen; all rooms are connected to a central 'atrium', and doors from the atrium to each room could be configured to be open or closed according to the teacher's specified lesson. Once the topology of the rooms was established, the *geometry* was chosen. Since the pupils were dealing with history and culture, the geometry of a Roman Villa was chosen. The topology and geometry are shown in Figures 1 and 2.

This initial structure was extended by attaching additional rooms to the primary VCOP rooms which provided supporting activities, and separate 'Library' and 'Big Writing' rooms. Finally a 'Castle Map' was created, which is an autonomous fun EIE, intended as a motivating final reward for the pupils progressing through the VCOP rooms. It may be useful to take a walk through this EIE. The associated web-pages provide various movies, from the point of view of the teacher and the pupils (see end of Chapter). First, the learner enters the EIE and logs in (establishing a personal file which

Figure 1. Shows the topology of the EIE. Rooms are clustered around a central atrium. Solid lines indicate passageways between the rooms, dashed lines indicate teleporters.

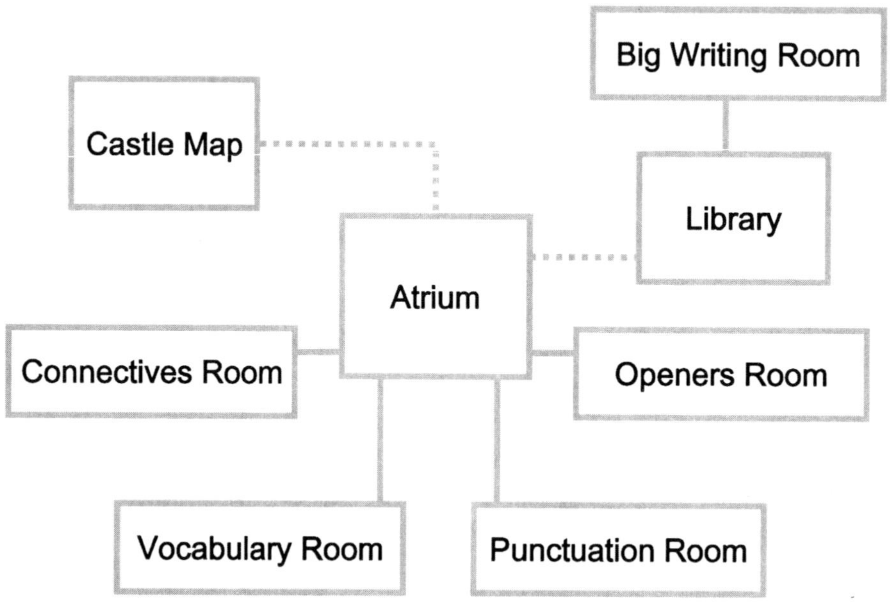

records their activity). They are asked to choose a 'lesson', which is a configuration of VCOP activities defined by their teacher (via a 'Teacher Portal' login). On starting the EIE, the learner is immediately approached by an NPC who offers instructions to go to a particular room, such as the 'Vocabulary Room'. Here, there is an activity where the learner receives an audio instruction to spell a word which appears on a banner. Following a time delay the word disappears and a dialogue box opens up, then the learner must type in the remembered word. This activity cycles through a word list (constructed by the teacher) or the learner may choose to quit. Then the learner enters the adjacent room which contains some ten words on banners. The learner must pick these words up using a cross-hair and mouse and deposit them on a board in the correct sequence to make up a sentence. Incorrectly placed words fly back into the room. In the 'Punctuation, Openers and Connectives' rooms a similar method of interaction is used to complete groups of sentences. Learners may access the 'Library' at any time using a teleporter located at the end of the atrium. They are informed about this by a large bright sign, and by an NPC who tells them how to get to the 'Library'. Following some time in the 'Library', learners have the opportunity to enter the 'Big Writing' room where they are able to write a story using the material they have learned, together with other resources provided in this room and from other 'information rooms', which they can teleport to for specific help. Since this classroom activity occurs at the end of the week, it seemed appropriate to place it at the end of the 'Library'.

A number of interactive approaches were designed and programmed. These included (i) in-play dialogue boxes to provide hints and collect input (such as words to test spelling), (ii) a text-to-speech facility where input words could be replayed as computer-generated speech, (iii) a cross-hair which could be used to select items (such as the correct punctuation to complete a sentence, or items to be picked up). Attention was given to how best present *information* to the learners, in particular *instructions* concerning each activity or task. The methods used (in order of decreasing significance, starting with the most significant) were (i) the use of a programmed NPC to approach the learner and give the instruction using recorded speech, (ii) pages of text containing instructions which emerged out of the floor, (iii) static instructions attached to the walls of the rooms. Other features were employed such as (i) music triggered on entering a room, e.g., the 'Big Writing' room, the 'silent-e' song which was triggered in the 'Jolly Phonics' area, (ii) programmed dynamic fire in the 'Castle Map' which could be extinguished by the learners, (iii) sounds e.g., the sounds of fireworks or cheering crowds.

Following this brief sketch on the EIE structure and affordances, it is necessary to reflect on how the learning tasks and activities were constructed according to the Constructivist Paradigm (see Table 1).

Figure 2. Two views are shown of the EIE. In (a) an overview of the central atrium surrounded by the 'VCOP rooms', and supporting rooms is shown. The close-up (b) shows more detail of the atrium, the learner starting position (the 'police box') and shows the information available to the learner on the 'heads up display'. This comprises the learner's current score, and a clock which counts down from 10 minutes which is the duration of the lesson.

Table 1. A mapping of constructivist principles onto EIE design showing how each principle is used in the design detail.

Constructivist Principle	Embodiment in the EIE
The learner is allowed to take responsibility for their own learning.	(i) Choice of which activities to perform, (ii) choice of the order of activities, (ii) choice to repeat a task or quit the task.
The learner is presented with multiple perspectives on the material.	(i) Various ways of input into the system, such as selection of words by the cross-hair, the use of a dialogue box.
The learner becomes aware of the learning process.	(i) Immediate feedback through response to learner input, (ii) staged feedback through a fireworks display on increasing the score by 10, (iii) access to the *fun area* 'Castle Map' when the score reaches 20.
Relevance of the learning context, based on real-world scenarios.	(i) Roman Villa context supports curriculum, (ii) fire-fighting as a critical process.
The learner is cognitively challenged, e.g., using puzzles and conflicts.	(i) How to find buckets of water to put out the fire in the 'Castle Map', (ii) How to get 20 points as quickly as possible to get to the *fun-area* 'Castle Map'
There is a high level of interactivity.	(i) Selection of words and other objects (such as newspapers) using the cross-hair, (ii) Inputting text through dialogue boxes, (iii) Running away from the NPC who wants to provide instruction, (iv) triggering information sheets which emerge from the floor, (v) triggering music and sounds, (vi) receiving feedback from the 'score' and the 'time count-down' on the HUD.
Collaboration is encouraged.	The EIE can be used in a 'multi-player' and hence collaborative mode. This fell outside the remit of this project. However, collaboration was fundamental in the *use* of this EIE where pupils worked in pairs.
There are various modes of rich representation (e.g., text, visuals and audio material).	(i) The visual semiotics of this EIE were designed to provide an appealing experience which was neither figurative nor cartoon, but 'semi-realistic'. (ii) A combination of text (words on banners), visuals (icons corresponding to those words) and audio materials (words spoken) was used.

This table was kept to hand during the design and development of the EIE and took on the nature of a 'working document'. A second 'working document' was Gagne's nine events of instruction (see Table 2). The Gagne approach to instructional design was adopted as it was judged to be the most comprehensive, and most strongly aligned with both game design principles and also the affordances of our chosen game engine.

EVALUATION

The prototype EIE was donated to a local primary school on a mid-range computer system (Pentium 4 2Ghz CPU 512 Meg RAM). The system was located in a 'break-out' area which pupils could access in their free time, as well as during scheduled time-slots for formal evaluations. The evaluations involved the researcher conducting a classical 'observation' of the pupils' interaction with the EIE. Pupils worked in pairs, audio and video recordings were made of their time spent within the EIE. A range of pupils was selected (by the ICT Coordinator) including children of ages 7-11 (years 3-6 in the UK system). A total of 11 pairs were presented. The researcher also recorded pupil activity according to various factors; (i) understanding of and ability to use various components of the HCI, (ii) response to instructions, (iii) ability to navigate within the space-time of the EIE, (iv) appreciation of the learning tasks provided, (v) expression of enjoyment or motivation (vi) understanding of subject detail (e.g. use of capital letters in a sentence).

The evaluation procedure was primarily based on individual pairs' observation records, supplemented with information from audio and video recordings and of the individual pairs log files. First an analysis of the *sequence* of progression

Table 2. A mapping of Gagne's nine instructional events onto the design of the EIE showing how each event has been realized within the EIE

Gagne's Event	Realization in the EIE
Gaining attention	(i) Compelling visuals e.g. cheering crowd scene, flashing arrows, (ii) NPC instructor who uses human voice. (iii) Sound icons (e.g. loudspeakers and sound box instructors).
Informing the Objective	(i) Score indicates number of correct answers. The score does not decrement if the answer is wrong. (ii) Timer decrements showing how much time remains. This creates a sense of a goal and increases excitement as learners try to beat the clock. (iii) Explicit instructions via static instructions sheet which emerge from the floor. (iv) Implicit signs including constrained pathways. (v) 'Distant' animations e.g. fire in castle map.
Stimulating recall of prerequisite learned capabilities	(i) Consistent use of interface components e.g. crosshairs, menus, floor targets which become familiar throughout the lessons. (ii) Need to remember facts such as spelling a word which has been visualized then hidden.
Presenting the stimulus material	(i) Firework display when score increments by 10. (ii) A score of 20 releases a 'flash screen' informing the learner that they may enter the *fun-area;* the 'Castle Map' Stimulates motivation as learners become are aware of an ultimate goal.
Provision of learning guidance	Learners learn how to play this EIE by investigation and exploration, in which the EIE becomes an implicit 'tutor'. The VCOP environment is spatially intuitive, allowing freedom of choice of tasks and also whether or not to complete each task.
Eliciting performance (practice)	Heightened interactivity, compared with 2D multimedia "point and click" applications giving the player greater *control* compared. Engagements with certain interactivities within each of the VCOP rooms build and call upon previous knowledge and understanding of previous activities. This enables them to progress through the lessons in a non –linear way.
Providing feedback	There are a multitude of feedback elements which operate on several *time scales.* (i) The learner is given immediate feedback on a task and is invited to repeat or quit. The HUD provides a subtle feedback mechanism where the timer counts down from 10 minutes and the learner score increases (but never decreases on an incorrect response)
Assessing performance	The accumulative performance of the learner as they work through the various VCOP rooms is set against their timing and score. This is recorded in a log file available to the teacher.
Enhancing retention and transfer (generalization)	(i) The simple and familiar HCI enables the learners to retain and generalize their learning experiences, since they are not distracted by the technology. (ii) The EIE context implies transfer, since it refers to existing classroom-based activities (VCOP, Big Writing, study of Roman History).

through various activities was made. This is important given the degree of choice available in the EIE; how did the learners use this choice factor? Second, a series of more than 60 questions were formulated through a reading of individual observation records. These questions were then applied to all observation records; the answers provided support of the proposed theories (or not) and also guidelines to inform future EIE design. Concerning constructivism, there were many examples of providing *cognitive challenges*. One pair fell into a moat and had to work out how to escape. All pairs reflected *collaboratively* (through discussion) on which answer to a particular question was correct. They shared discovered information, (e.g. the need for capitalization in spelling) learned skills and agreed on tasks. There was also *collaboration* 'on the playground' where pupils shared information about the EIE with their peers. The EIE contained a high level of *interactivity* which was mastered by most pupils. Interestingly 12 pairs visited the library, a highly interactive space, while only 6 pairs completed all VCOP rooms where the interactivity was lower. Learning was judged to be relevant *based on real-world scenarios*. This was evidenced by the amusement shown on encountering non real-world elements such as flying submarines. Three pairs displayed *curiosity* by running off the beaten track to explore the exterior terrain in sequences not intended by the designer, (e.g.

moving directly to the library, ignoring VCOP). One pair had discovered the 'fly cheat' (by their own research) and used this to fly around the EIE in a spree of discovery. Concerning instructional design, the *stimulus material* worked well but not always. This sometimes failed in *attention gaining*; some pairs ignored instructional text and even flashing arrows. Only 4 pairs engaged with pop-up information panels, yet 8 pairs learned to stand on floor targets. There was often a lack of response to *learning guidance*, e.g. only 5 pairs listened to instructions given by NPCs. Consequently the learners missed some important information such as the score to unlock the Castle Map, or indeed the existence of this map! Pupils were attempting to discover what to do (the 'game rules') by 'playing the game'; this did not always work. The provision of *feedback* worked well. The learners appreciated the reward system, (displayed score and fireworks on a score of 10), as well as effects consequent on their actions, such as words which moved onto a whiteboard, spoken text, doors which opened and closed. Interestingly where feedback was not provided, such as the number of buckets collected in the Castle Map, learners did not keep a tally on this number. The EIE was successful in *stimulating recall* of facts learned within the game. Examples are, where to use capital letters, how to use the cross-hair, and the purpose of floor targets. They also learned to associate the NPC as a source of instruction. In the VCOP rooms, all instructor NPCs were female, and all 11 pairs soon made this association. Learners carried this association into the Castle Map where the instructor NPC was male; consequently 6 pairs ignored him completely. All learners expressed *satisfaction* in using this EIE and displayed high levels of motivation evidenced by spending their free time in the EIE and showing a drive to complete all tasks.

There was no gender issues, both girls and boys engaged with equal enthusiasm, though girls were more willing to complete the VCOP lessons. Not a single girl questioned that her avatar was actually a boy! One pair of girls wished to be able to choose male or female NPCs and one pair of girls wished to be able to 'dress' the NPCs!

DISCUSSION

The EIE has been a great success as evaluated by the pupils and teachers in the school. Its presence in the school spread like wild fire and pupils were frequently using the EIE during their free time. However, we must reflect on the more negative aspects of the evaluation to inform how to create better EIEs. There are a number of issues. (i) Information Flow. More thought needs to be given on how to improve communication of information to the learners through NPCs and other interactive elements. An explicit approach could be taken, e.g., by providing the learners with a small paper guidebook, or the flow of information could be enhanced implicitly, by increasing the opportunity to gain information, through repeated exposure, or pausing the learner until the information has been read. (ii) Separation of learning areas (VCOP) from the fun area (the 'Castle Map'). This was an explicit design feature, intended to motivate the learners to complete the VCOP lessons. However the small number of pairs who completed VCOP is worrying. Perhaps the existence of the 'Castle' caused them to abandon the VCOP lessons too early? Interestingly, one pair who successfully completed VCOP, (and amassed a score of 76), were *unaware* of the existence of the 'Castle'. We could conclude that the separate 'Castle' may hinder learning or actually reduce motivation to learn, and that a future EIE should integrate fun and learning within the same space. (iii) Choice and Exploration. The current EIE restricted choice based on the teacher's lesson plan. It may be more appropriate to remove this restriction by abandoning separate learning rooms and allowing the learners to choose their own path through the VCOP activities. This retains the *topological* structure of the EIE while modifying its geometrical form. The teacher would make suggestions to the pupils on which areas are more appropriate for the individual's progress, but ultimately the pupils would choose. (iv) Thought needs to be given on the provision of *learning guidance*. There was clear a conflict between the freedom of the EIE design which elicited *curiosity*, and the need to temporarily constrain the learners to give them guidance.

FUTURE RESEARCH DIRECTIONS

This research is currently being extended in two directions. First the VCOP EIE is being refined, based on continuing feedback. A further study is planned to evaluate the effectiveness of this EIE as a classroom activity, and to quantify the *transference* of learning from within the EIE to traditional classroom activities. Second, additional EIEs are in development to address the STEM (Science, Technology Engineering and Mathematics) disciplines, which are crucial in supporting the research and manufacturing base of our economy.

CONCLUSION

This chapter has attempted to engage teacher-practitioners as well as researchers in issues concerned with the design and development of Educational Immersive Environments. We have stressed the need for engagement with many aspects; educational theories, instructional design and game design principles, and the need to work closely with teachers and pupils in the production of EIEs. We started this chapter with reference to our "Digital Native" youth, their interests and needs. While we truly believe in the need to develop EIEs for the classroom; we also acknowledge a concern. Our "Digital Natives" may be moving into an uncharted space of engagement with digital technologies "for its own sake" without reason or purpose. We therefore suggest that EIEs may actually provide our youth with a 'rescue lifeboat' to re-engage with the real human world of society, interaction, sport and existence.

ACKNOWLEDGMENT

We should like to express sincere thanks to the teachers and pupils at Cherry Orchard Primary School, Worcester, UK, and especially to the ICT Coordinator Mr. Mark Miles. Many thanks, to the Head Teacher Jeremy Harwood for supporting this project. Finally thanks to the University of Worcester for providing help and resources.

REFERENCES

Aldrich, C. (2004). *Simulations and the future of learning*. San Francisco: Pfeiffer.

Appelman, R., & Goldsworthy, R. (1999). *The Juncture of Game & Instructional Design: Can Fun be Learning?* Paper presented at the Association for Educational Communications and Technology, Houston, TX.

Ausubel, D. P. (1968). *Educational Psychology: A Cognitive View*. New York: Holt, Rinehart & Winston.

Becker, K. (2005). How Are Games Educational? Learning Theories Embodied in Games. *Proceedings of DIGRA 2005 Conference: Changing Views – Worlds in Play.*

Becta. (2001). *Computer Games in Education Project: Findings Report*. Retrieved July 2008, from http://partners.becta.org.uk/index.php?section=rh&rid=13595

Benyon, D., Turner, P., & Turner, S. (2005). *Designing Interactive Systems*. Harlow, UK: Addison Wesley.

Bruner, J. S. (1966). *Toward a Theory of Instruction*. Oxford, UK: Oxford University Press.

Buckley, K. E., & Anderson, C. A. (2006). A Theoretical Model of the Effects and Consequences of Playing Video Games. In Vonderer, P., & Bryant, J. (Eds.), *Playing Video Games - Motives, Responses, and Consequences* (pp. 363–378). Mahwah, NJ: LEA.

Burgos, D., & Specht, M. (2006). Adaptive e-learning methods and IMS Learning Design. An integrated approach. In Proceedings of ICALT2006, Kerkrade, Holland.

Collins, A. (1991). Cognitive apprenticeship and instructional technology. In Idol, L., & Jones, B. F. (Eds.), *Educational values and cognitive instructions: Implications for reform*. Hillsdale, NJ: Erlbaum.

Crawford, C. (2003). *Chris Crawford on Game Design*. Carmel, IN: New Riders Publishing.

Csikszentmihalyi, M. (1992). *Flow: the Psychology of Happiness*. London: Random House.

Dede, C. (1995). 21st Century. In *Committee on Science and Committee on Economics and Educational Opportunities* (pp. 1–10). Testimony to the U.S Congress, House of Representatives, Joint Hearing on Educational Technology in the.

Dreyfus, H. (2004). *A Phenomenoloy of Skill Acquisition as the basis for a Merleau-Pontian Non-representationalist Cognitive Science*. Retrieved May 2006 from http://socrates.berkeley.edu/~hdreyfus/html/papers.html

FAS. (2006). Harnessing the power of video games for learning. In *Summit on Educational Games 2006*. Retrieved July 2008, from http://fas.org/gamesummit/Resources/Summit%20on%20Educational%20Games.pdf

Frean, A., & Woolcock, N. (2007, December 6). Overhaul of primary schools as progress in 3Rs grinds to a halt. *Times Online*. Retrieved December 2007, from http://www.timesonline.co.uk/tol/life_and_style/education/article3007334.ece

Gagne, R. (1977). *The Conditions of Learning*. New York: Holt.

Gee, J. P. (2003). *What Video Games Have to Teach Us About Learning and Literacy*. New York: Palgrave Macmillan.

Gee, J. P. (2004). *Game-Like Learning: An Example of situation Learning and Implications for Opportunity to Learn*. Retrieved May 2008, from http://www.academiccolab.org/ resources/documents/Game-Like%20Learning.rev.pdf

Gredler, M. (1992). *Designing and Evaluating Games and Simulations – a Process Approach*. London: Kogan Page.

Gunter, G., Kenny, R., & Vick, E. H. (2006). *A Case for a Formal Design Paradigm for Serious Games*. Retrieved May 2008, from http://www.units.muohio.edu/codeconference/ papers/papers/Gunter%20Kenny%20Vick%20 paper.pdf

Hamalainen, R. (2008). Designing and evaluating collaboration in a virtual game environment for vocational learning. *Computers & Education, 50*(1), 98–109. doi:10.1016/j.compedu.2006.04.001

Hannafin, M. J., & Land, S. M. (1997). The foundations and assumptions of technology-enhanced student-centered learning environments. *Instructional Science, 25*, 167–202. doi:10.1023/A:1002997414652

Honebein, P. C. (1996). Seven goals for the design of constructivist learning environments. In Wilson, B. G. (Ed.), *Constructivist Learning Environments: Case Studies in Instructional Design*. Englewood Cliffs, NJ: Educational Technology Publications.

IOP. (2001). *Physics-Building a flourishing Future. Report of the Inquiry into Undergraduate Phyiscs*. Institute of Physics, London. Retrieved August 29, 2006, from http://policy.iop.org/UPI/index.html

JISC. (2004). Effective Practice with e-Learning - A good practice guide in designing for learning. Retrieved Sept. 2008, from http://www.jisc.ac.uk/elearning_pedagogy.html

Jonassen, D. H. (1999). Designing constructivist learning environments. In Reigeluth, C. M. (Ed.), *Instructional Design Theories and Models: Their Current State of the Art*. Mahwah, NJ: Lawrence Erlbaum Associates.

Jonassen, D. H., & Wang, S. (1993). Acquiring Structural Knowledge from Semantically Structured Hypertext. *Journal of Computer-Based Instruction*, *20*(1).

Keller, J. M. (1987). Development and use of the ARCS model of motivational design. *Journal of Instructional Development*, *10*(3), 2–10. doi:10.1007/BF02905780

Keller, J. M. (1987). Development and use of theARCS model of motivational design. *Journal of Instructional Development*, *10*(3), 2–10. doi:10.1007/BF02905780

Khoo, A., & Gentile, D. A. (2007). Problem based Learning in the World of Digital Games. In Tan, O.-S. (Ed.), *Problem-based Learning in eLearning Breakthroughs* (pp. 97–129). Singapore: Thompson Learning.

Kolb, D. A. (1984). *Experiential Learning*. Englewood Cliffs, NJ: Prentice-Hall.

Lakoff, G. (1987). *Women, Fire and Dangerous Things: What Categories reveal about the Mind*. Chicago: Il., University of Chicago Press.

Laughlin, D., Roper, M., & Howell, K. (2007). NASA eEducation Roadmap: Research Challenges in the Design of Massively Multiplayer Games for Education & Training. Retrieved Nov. 2008, from http://www.fas.org/programs/ltp/publications/roadmaps/_docs/NASA%20eEducation%20Roadmap.pdf

Lave, J., & Wenger, E. (1991). *Situated Learning. Legitimate Peripheral Participation*. Cambridge: University of Cambridge.

Lepper, M. R., & Malone, T. W. (1987). Intrinsic motivation and instructional effectiveness in computer-based education. In Snow, R., & Farr, M. (Eds.), *Aptitude, Learning and Instruction, III: Cognitive and Affective Process Analysis*. Hillside, NJ: Lawrence Erlbaum Associates.

Malone, T. (1980). *What makes things fun to learn? A study of intrinsically motivating computer games*. Technical Report CIS-7, Xerox Parc.

Malone, T. W., & Lepper, M. R. (1987). Making Learning Fun: A Taxonomy of Intrinsic Motivations for Learning. In Snow, R. E., & Farr, M. J. (Eds.), *Aptitude, Learning and Instruction* (*Vol. 3*). Lawrence Erlbaum Associates.

Maslow, A. (1943). A theory of human motivation. *Psychological Review*, *50*, 370–396. doi:10.1037/h0054346

Moore, J. S., & Price, C. B. (2009) Development of an Educational Immersive Environment for Primary School Literacy Education (To appear, *European Conference on Games Based Learning*, 2009).

Novak, J. D., & Musonda, D. (1991). A twelve-year longitudinal study of science concept learning. *American Educational Research Journal*, *28*(1).

Paton, G. (2007) England slides down world literacy league http://www.telegraph.co.uk/news/main.jhtml?xml=/news/2007/11/29/nliterate129.xml (accessed Jan. 2009)

Prensky, M. (2001). Digital natives, digital immigrants. *Horizon, 9*(5). http://www.marcprensky.com/writing/Prensky%20-%20Digital%20Natives,%20Digital%20Immigrants%20-%20Part1.pdf accessed Jan. 2009.

Prensky, M. (2005). Engage me or Enrage me What today's learners demand. *EDUCAUSE Review, 40*(5), 60–65.

Price, C. B. (2006). A Crisis in Physics Education: Games to the Rescue! (2006) *ITALICS* 5(3), http://www.ics.heacademy.ac.uk/italics/vol5iss3.htm (accessed Jan. 2009)

Price, C. B. (2008). Learning Physics with the Unreal Tournament engine. *Physics Education, 43*(3). doi:10.1088/0031-9120/43/3/006

Price, C. B. (2009). The Path from Pedagogy to Technology: Establishing a Theoretical Basis for the Development of Educational Game Environments. In Conolly, T., Stansfield, M., & Boyle, L. (Eds.), *Games-Based Learning Advancements for Multi-Sensory Human Computer Interfaces: Techniques and Effective Practices. Information Science Reference, Salen, K., & Zimmerman, E. (2003). Rules of Play: Game Design Fundamentals.* Cambridge, MA: The MIT Press.

Savery, J. R., & Duffy, T. M. (1995). Problem based learning: an instructional model and its constructivist framework. *Educational Technology, 35*, 31–38.

Sfard, A. (2008). *Thinking as Communicating: Human development, the growth of discourses and mathematizing*. Cambridge: CUP. doi:10.1017/CBO9780511499944

Smithers, A., & Robinson, P. (2005). *Physics in Schools and Colleges: Teacher Deployment and Student Outcomes*. Buckingham, UK: Carmichael Press, University of Buckingham.

Smithers, A., & Robinson, P. (2006). *Physics in Schools and Universities: Patterns and Policies*. Buckingham, UK: Carmichael Press, University of Buckingham.

Squire, K. (2006). From Content to Context: Videogames as Designed Experience. *Educational Researcher, 35*(8), 19–29. doi:10.3102/0013189X035008019

Strogatz, S. (2004). *Sync: The Emerging Science of Spontaneous Order*. New York: Hyperion.

Tang, S., Hanneghan, M., & El-Rhalibi, A. (2007). *Pedagogy Elements, Components and Structures for Serious Games Authoring Environment.* Paper presented at the 5th International Game Design and Technology Workshop (GDTW 2007), Liverpool, UK.

Ulrich, M. (1997). Links Between Experiential Learning and Simulation & Gaming. In J. Geurts, C. Joldersma, & E. Roelofs (Eds.), *Gaming/Simulation for Policy Development and Organizational Change.* Proceedings of the 28th Annual International Conference of the International Simulation and Gaming Association (ISAGA) July 1997, Tilburg, the Netherlands (pp. 269-275).

Varela, F., Thompson, E., & Rosch, E. (1991). *The embodied mind*. Cambridge, MA: The MIT Press.

Zyda, M., Hiles, J., Mayberry, A., Wardynski, C., Capps, M., & Osborm, M. (2003). *Entertainment R&D for Defense*. IEEE Comp.Graphics and Applications.

Zyda, M., Mayberry, A., McCree, J., & Davis, M. (2005). From Viz-Sim to VR to Games: How We Built a Hit Game-Based Simulation. In Rouse, W. B., & Boff, K. R. (Eds.), *Organizational Simulation: From Modeling & Simulation to Games & Entertainment*. New York: Wiley Press.

ADDITIONAL READING

America's Army. (n.d.). Retrieved April 2009, from http://www.americasarmy.com

Becta's Computer Games in Education project. (n.d.). Retrieved April 2009, from http://partners.becta.org.uk/index.php?section=rh&&catcode=&rid=13588

FoodForce. (n.d.). Retrieved April 2009, from http://www.food-force.com

Hot Shot Business. (n.d.). Retrieved April 2009, from http://www.hotshotbusiness.com

Materials to support this chapter are available at the authors' website: http://www.worc.ac.uk/departs/bm_it/colin/Resources/ClassroomGames/

MIT. (n.d.). *Game-to-Teach*. Retrieved April 2009, from http://www.educationarcade.org/gtt/home.html

Stone City. (n.d.). Retrieved April 2009, from http://www.persuasivegames.com/games/game.aspx?game=coldstone

KEY TERMS AND DEFINITIONS

Computer Game: Commercial software which creates a 2D or 3D world which is designed to elicit fun for the player.

Serious Game: A computer 'game' designed with the explicit intention of providing education or training.

Immersive Environment: A 3D world created using computer game technology, but not according to game design principles. Such an environment may be used for simulation or visualization purposes.

Educational Immersive Environment: An Immersive Environment constructed using learning theories and instructional design principles.

Constructivism: A learning theory which asserts that it is individual experiences which allow us to learn, to generate knowledge and meaning. Associated with Dewey and Piaget

Instructional Design: Principles which focus on elements of instruction to achieve intended learning outcomes. These principles have been influenced by Gagne and Keller.

Computer Game Design: These are principles but not theories which are used by commercial computer game companies to produce viable games.

Map: Refers to a small computer game or part of a computer game containing a number of objects and interactions.

Chapter 3
Intelligent Tutoring and Games (ITaG)

Danielle S. McNamara
University of Memphis, USA

G. Tanner Jackson
University of Memphis, USA

Art Graesser
University of Memphis, USA

ABSTRACT

Intelligent Tutoring Systems (ITSs) have been producing consistent learning gains for decades. The authors describe here a conceptual framework that provides a guide to how adding game-based features and components may improve the effectiveness of ITS learning environments by improving students' motivation to engage with the system. A problem consistently faced by ITS researchers is the gap between liking and learning. ITSs effectively produce learning gains, but students often dislike interacting with the system. A potential solution to this problem lies in games. ITS researchers have begun to incorporate game-based elements within learning systems. This chapter aims to describe some of those elements, categorize them within functional groups, and provide insight into how elements within each category may affect various types of motivation.

INTRODUCTION

Many contend that the future of affordable, high-quality education lies in harnessing the potentials of computer technologies. While implementing computer technologies in schools has had both failings and challenges (Dynarski et al., 2007), significant progress in the quality of education to some extent depends on our ability to leverage the many advantages of computer technologies. Recent advances in computer technologies include interactive tutors that can mimic very closely the best features of human one-on-one tutoring. Intelligent Tutoring Systems (ITSs) afford adaptive, one-on-one tutoring to individual students in the classroom and have demonstrated remarkable success in helping students learn challenging content and strategies (Woolf, 2009). Nonetheless, we propose that a new generation of learning technologies will emerge from hybrid systems that combine ITS and

DOI: 10.4018/978-1-61520-713-8.ch003

game-based principles. Whereas ITS principles maximize learning, game technologies maximize motivation. Hence, serious games can be expected to optimize learning with the incorporation of ITS principles, and ITSs should be rendered more engaging to the student by incorporating inherently motivating game components. We call this combination of best practices, *Intelligent Tutoring and Games* (ITaG). In this chapter, we focus on the potential benefits of integrating game-based features into existing ITSs. For this purpose, we propose a conceptual framework that can be used to guide the integration of games into ITSs.

BACKGROUND

Game Research

Game research is booming. In 2007, industries such as music and movies saw either negative or stagnant growth (-10.0% and +1.8% respectively), but the gaming industry reported dramatic growth (+28.4%; Combs, 2008). It is arguably the fastest growing area of learning research in the 21st century, and spans multiple disciplines, including: computer, education, and social sciences.

There are numerous goals of game research. One area has examined whether, how, and what students learn from entertainment games (e.g., SimCity, World of Warcraft). A second area concentrates on the development of serious games and evaluates the degree to which these games both engage learners and help them learn. A third area of research focuses on identifying the features of games that best promote learning in the context of serious games.

In this chapter, we propose two additional areas of research that have yet to be extensively promoted in the literature. The first is to examine the benefits of adding ITS or learning principles to serious games. Learning principles would include notions such as the importance of generating information, paraphrasing, summarizing, explaining, observing and evaluating examples, modeling-scaffolding-fading, cognitive disequilibrium, practicing skills, and receiving feedback (as well as principles on how to schedule feedback). For example, research has indicated that various forms of instructional support can facilitate learning from games (Moreno & Mayer, 2005; Rieber, 2005; Shaffer, 2007; Swaak & de Jong, 2001), including guidance, tutors, explanations on feedback, and prompted reflection. The second relatively new area of research under focus in this chapter is on the benefits of incorporating game-based principles into established ITSs. Together, these two areas of research form the essence of ITaG, the optimal fusion of principles of learning and motivation for creating games that are enhanced with learning and game principles. The ultimate goal is to better understand the features of ITSs and games that can be most effectively merged within a learning environment (i.e., optimizing learning, motivation, and engagement).

Goals for Learning Technologies

Educational problems in the United States are readily apparent. These problems are manifested in national and international tests of reading, science, and math. Students in the United States score lower on measures of reading comprehension than students in many other countries (Snow, 2002). A staggering 26% of 8th grade students cannot read even at the basic level (Donahue et al., 2003). Test scores indicate that our students' reading comprehension scores have not improved in over a decade. In 1992, U.S. 8th graders scored an average of 260 (out of 500), whereas in 2007 U.S. 8th graders scored an average of 263 (Snyder, 2009). Our record on science achievement is even worse. In 1996, U.S. 12th graders scored an average of 150 (out of 500) but in 2005, U.S. 12th graders scored an average of 147 (Snyder, 2009). The NAEP scores in 2000 and 2005 (National Center for Education Statistics, 2001, 2006) have generally declined; indeed, at grade 12, the percentage of students *below* basic level proficiency in science increased from 43% in 1996 to 48% in 2000 and 46% in 2005. This means that almost 50 percent of students in the United States do not have basic knowledge and skills in science. According to the PISA (2006) report, U.S. students scored below the average international science literacy score, and the United States. ranked 25th out of 30 developed countries in science literacy. The same PISA report reported that math scores for U.S. students were in the bottom 20% of all participating countries.

It is clear that student achievement must improve. But what can be or should be expected from the student? Our goal is to develop adaptive, engaging technologies that scaffold the student toward both basic and deep levels of understanding of the content domain. Certainly, the ultimate goal of education is for the student to develop a deep, conceptual understanding of the content. Deep knowledge requires inferences, an understanding of complex mechanisms, and the ability to apply knowledge to new situations (Bereiter & Bird, 1985; Bloom, 1956; Bransford et al., 2000; Graesser, Leon, & Otero, 2002; Kintsch, 1998). However, we also recognize that the first step toward deep understanding is an understanding of the simple ideas, basic facts, properties, and even definitions. The advantage of adaptive ITSs is that they can recognize the needs of the student, and move the student toward deeper, contextualized representations of the content and skills.

The development of deep knowledge requires time and practice. The mastery of content and learning strategies that will generalize to multiple contexts and tasks does not happen in hours. Proficiency in content and strategies requires multiple sessions, across months of time. However, over time, ITSs can become boring and tedious to students, particularly for those who most need such tutoring. Hence, game-based principles offer a means of enhancing ITSs so they can be more appealing to students and engage them more frequently and seriously. The central hypothesis is that ITSs will be more engaging to the student, and thereby more effective in promoting learning, by incorporating motivational components that sustain concentration for long periods of time (Graesser, Chipman, Leeming, & Biedenbach, 2009; Moreno & Mayer, 2005). Our long-term research goal is to examine the benefits of incorporating game-based components within established tutoring systems to improve motivational aspects.

Intelligent Tutoring Systems

ITSs can be distinguished from more conventional Computer-based Training (CBT) systems by the intelligence of the computational mechanisms that track the student's performance and adaptively respond (Graesser & King, 2008; Shute & Psotka, 1996; Woolf, 2009). In a typical CBT system, the learner (1) studies material presented in a lesson, (2) is tested with a multiple-choice test or another objective test, (3) gets feedback on the test performance, (4) restudies the material if the performance is below threshold, and (5) finally progresses to a new topic. Such systems are moderately effective, demonstrating effect sizes of 0.39 sigma compared to classroom instruction (Dodds & Fletcher, 2004). However, CBTs often consist of *page-turning, tell and test* content presentation, which is more conducive to instruction of declarative and shallow knowledge than deep knowledge (Bereiter & Scardamalia, 1985; Bransford et al., 2000). CBT also does not adapt training to the abilities of the student at a fine-grained level that is often incorporated in more advanced ITS learning environments. Because ITSs provide more scaffolding and guidance to the student, they are often more appropriate for less skilled students (McNamara & Shapiro, 2005) as well as students lacking self-regulatory learning skills (Azevedo, 2005).

The added intelligence of ITSs has produced some notable successes. Meta-analyses indicate that ITSs fare well compared to classroom instruction and other control comparisons with average effect sizes around 1 standard deviation (i.e., 1 sigma) (Corbett, 2001; Dodds & Fletcher, 2004; Fletcher, 2003; Wisher & Fletcher, 2004). Successful systems have been developed for mathematically well-formed topics, including algebra, geometry, programming languages (the Cognitive Tutors, Anderson et al., 1995; Koedinger et al., 1997), physics (Andes, Atlas, and Why/Atlas, VanLehn, et al., 2005; VanLehn, et al., 2007), electronics (Lesgold, Lajoie, Brunzo, & Eggman, 1992), and information technology (Mitrovic et al., 2004). These systems show impressive learning gains, particularly for deeper levels of comprehension.

More recent ITSs have been extended to knowledge domains that are less mathematically precise and well-structured. These include *the Intelligent Essay Assessor* (Foltz et al., 2000), *e-Rater* (Burstein, 2003), *Summary Street* (Kintsch et al., 2007), *AutoTutor* (Graesser, Chipman, et al., 2005; Graesser, Lu, et al., 2004; VanLehn et al., 2007) and *iSTART* (McNamara Levinstein, & Boonthum, 2004; McNamara, O'Reilly, et al., 2007). Many of these ITSs depend on natural language understanding and assessment for fast and accurate interpretation of human language so that the systems can respond intelligently in natural language. They function by interpreting the meaning of student input, assessing the extent to which it manifests learning, and generating suitable feedback. Thus, sophisticated algorithms and approaches are required to accurately assess student input and provide appropriate real-time feedback (Graesser, Jackson, et al., 2007; McNamara, Boonthum, et al., 2007; Rus, McCarthy, McNamara, & Graesser, 2008).

While CBTs and ITSs have shown considerable success, a problem arises when the student is required to use the systems over long periods of time. The novelty of an ITS and the interactive components are quite engaging when they are used for short periods of time (e.g., hours), but can become monotonous and even annoying when a student is required to interact with an ITS for weeks or months. Simply put, CBTs and ITSs are often far from fun.

MAIN FOCUS OF THE CHAPTER

Motivation

Within the current context we use the term motivation in a broader sense that incorporates emotions and social parameters in addition to traditional attributes of motivation. Our goal is to increase students' motivation to engage with learning systems. While it is not a main focus of this paper, it is important to note that researchers frequently distinguish between two sources of motivation: extrinsic and intrinsic. Extrinsic motivation is typically viewed as performing a given task in order to receive some external award/reward (e.g., a toy, a good grade, a compliment, etc). Extrinsic motivation is relatively facile to implement within a learning environment, and often succeeds in inducing students to perform well on an assigned task. However, approaches focusing on increasing extrinsic motivation have also been linked to decreased interest in the target activity (Morgan, 1984). Thus, extrinsic motivators can work, but they may have a cost. In contrast, intrinsic motivation is conceptualized as performing a given task because of an inherent personal interest in that activity (e.g., reading a book that interests you, working on a hobby, etc.). Intrinsic motivation is particularly difficult to manipulate within a learning environment, but is typically related to increased on-task performance and long-term retention (Tobias, 1994). These two types of motivation will likely play important roles within and between game elements, and are intertwined with specific constructs related to motivation, on which we focus here. These include *self-regulation, self-efficacy, interest,* and *engagement.*

Self-regulation refers to student initiated processes of monitoring, regulating, and controlling their cognition, motivation, and behavior (Greene

& Azevedo, 2007). Many researchers have focused on the metacognitive process of students monitoring their own successes and weaknesses during the learning process (e.g., Pintrich, 2000; Winne, 2001; Winne & Hadwin, 2008; Zimmerman & Schunk, 2001). Theories of self-regulation assume that good students regulate key cognitive, metacognitive, motivational, social, and affective processes. Self-regulation involves actively seeking a coherent understanding of a topic by using strategies and goals, regulating and monitoring cognitive processes, behavior, and motivation, and then modifying behavior to achieve learning goals (Boekaerts, Pintrich, & Zeider, 2000; Pintrich, 2000; Zimmerman & Schunk, 2001).

Self-efficacy regards the learner's sense of success and achievement (Bandura, 2000; Pajares, 1996). Lepper and colleagues (Lepper, Drake, & O'Donnell-Johnson, 1997; Lepper & Wolverton, 2002) argue that tutoring systems should attempt to build self efficacy and empowerment, particularly when a student is struggling or is unsuccessful in the learning task.

Interest refers to the degree to which underlying needs or desires of learners are energized (Alexander et al., 1997). *Individual interest* is characterized by a desire to develop competence or a personal investment in a particular topic or domain. *Situational interest* is transitory, pertaining to the specific events and contexts (Alexander et al., 1997; Hidi, 1990; Murphy & Alexander, 2000; Schiefele, 1991). For the latter, while the nature of the content may play an important role, how the content is framed is more important in driving interest. For example, framing the content within a game can be used as a spring board to capture the interest of the student.

Engagement is another important construct related to both motivation and learning. Assumedly, when students are not engaged, they are bored or inattentive, neither being conducive to learning. For example, Craig et al. (2004) found that increased levels of boredom while students learned about computer literacy topics with an ITS negatively correlated with learning (r = -0.39) whereas *flow* (i.e., high engagement; Csikszentmihaly, 1990) was positively correlated with learning (r = 0.29). Bored learners are also more likely to strategically bypass the system (Rodrigo et al., 2007). Furthermore, boredom may trigger a vicious cycle that prevents students from actively reengaging in constructive learning processes (D'Mello, Taylor, & Graesser, 2007).

Game-Based Features

Serious games are educational games designed with the goal of helping students learn about subject matter content, problem solving strategies, and cognitive or social skills. Instead of learning about biology by conventional means, the learner plays a game that successfully integrates the game with curriculum. All games have rules, actions of the player, uncertainty, and feedback on outcomes. Many games have points, rewards, competition, and levels of privilege that are linked to success. And, many games are set in the context of narrative or fantasy. Further, some claim that enjoyment forms the core of the entertainment process, including the experience of games (e.g., Vorderer, Klimmt, & Ritterfeld, 2004).

Aside from the essence of games, there is the question of what renders games successful psychologically. Indeed, one important question about serious games is how the features of games are systematically aligned with features of pedagogy and curriculum (Fletcher & Tobias, 2007; Gee, 2003; Gredler, 1996, 2004; O'Neil, Wainess, & Baker, 2005; Rieber, 1996; Shaffer, 2004; Van Eck, 2007). O'Neil et al. presented a mapping of game features to Kirkpatrick's (1994) four levels of evaluating training and to Baker and Mayer's (1999) five major families of cognitive demands. Likewise, Van Eck analyzed how Gagné et al.'s (2005) principles of instructional design map onto particular features of games. Along these lines, numerous theoretical analyses of games, game taxonomies, and game features have been proposed by game designers (Gredler, 1996, 2004; Salen & Zimmerman, 2004) and researchers (Gee, 2003; Malone & Lepper, 1987; O'Neil et al., 2005; Rieber, 2005; Shaffer, 2004; Van Eck, 2007; Vorderer & Bryant, 2006). Indeed, there are several discussions of game features and taxonomies discussed in this volume.

Our goal is to identify broad categories of game features that can potentially be used to inform modifications of ITS technologies. Based on the literature, we propose a framework that classifies game-based features into five broad categories, including feedback, incentives, task difficulty, control, and environment. In Table 1, we present example game-based features for each of the categories and the motivational constructs that can be expected to be affected by adding such a feature to an ITS. We expect that each of these features affect motivation (positively or negatively), but particular aspects of motivation may be more or less affected.

Feedback

Feedback is an important feature common to both ITS and game technologies. There is abundant literature in the cognitive area on the effects of feedback structure, schedule, and delivery-method. Providing students with accurate, intelligent, and motivating feedback is a critical aspect of learning environments and is vital to the learning process (Anderson, Conrad, & Corbett, 1989; Anderson, Corbett, Koedinger, & Pelletier 1995; Azevedo, & Bernard, 1995; Graesser, Person, & Magliano, 1995; Merrill, Reiser, Ranney, & Trafton, 1992; Moreno & Mayer, 2005). This literature suggests several aspects of feedback that may influence the learning process, including: timing, content, control, and delivery-method of the feedback. For example, it may be optimal in some systems to provide an intermediate rate of feedback that allows time for the user to catch their own mistake, but not so much time that a misconception can form, which is harder to remediate. Additionally, the literature suggests that the content of the feedback should (depending on the nature of the material) include noting that an error occurred as well as an explanation of what a correct behavior could have entailed. Prior research has shown mixed effectiveness concerning the delivery method of feedback, such as whether the feedback is in a visual or auditory modality. The discrepancies are possibly due to differences in system goals and to the complexity of the learning environment.

Feedback on performance can be conveyed in various forms, including immediate corrections, delayed corrections, explanations, level of mastery achieved on specific content, paths or actions taken by the system, progress bars, cumulative points, levels, and *skillometers* (i.e., progress bars, or *thermometers*, representing the acquisition of skills). These forms of feedback can be broadly categorized as information-based, consequence-based, and point-based feedback. Information-based feedback takes the form of providing specific feedback on the accuracy and quality of answers and actions within the ITS or game. Consequence-based feedback occurs when the system reacts to the user's responses or actions by changing the system path. For example, when a student answers incorrectly in an ITS, the student may be redirected into remediation. When a player is killed in a game, the game ends. This is the ultimate form of feedback.

Both information-based and consequence-based feedbacks are common to most ITSs. By contrast, point-based feedback is a feature more characteristic of games and less common in ITSs. Point-based feedback can be conveyed in the form of cumulative points, progress bars, and levels. All of these are based directly or indirectly on the accuracy or the quality of responses and actions by the user or player. They differ in their specificity and detail. A progress bar is a means of conveying performance schematically (e.g., shaded progress bar, skillometer), without the specificity of points. Likewise, the use of levels (e.g., Level 1 vs. Level 3; Novice vs. Expert) is less

Table 1. Categories of game-based features, their function, and the motivational construct expected to be most influenced by adding the feature to an ITS

Category	Enhancement Features	Function	Motivational Construct
Feedback	Verbal information, consequences, points, progress bar, skillometer, levels	Information regarding the accuracy or quality of responses is provided to the student	self-regulation, self-efficacy
	Competition	Information is provided on performance relative to others	self-regulation, self-efficacy, interest, engagement
Incentives	Points, levels, skill bar	Student acquires points or advances in levels by completing tasks successfully	self-regulation, self-efficacy, engagement
	Mini-games, exchange or modify avatar or environment	Student provided with motivational hooks (e.g., play game, change features of environment)	self-efficacy, interest, engagement
Task Difficulty	Tasks or materials vary in difficulty, task requirements gradually increase in mini-games	ZPD: Task or material is appropriately challenging and scaffolded according to Zone of Proximal Development (ZPD)	self-efficacy, engagement
	Tasks or materials vary in difficulty	Backsliding: Student is given easier task after failure	self-efficacy
	Tasks or materials vary in difficulty; feedback varies according to performance history	Empowerment: Task is conveyed as difficult, but is below ZPD	self-efficacy
Control	Choosing rewards: mini-game, character, color	Student controls aspects of environment	self-regulation, self-efficacy, interest, engagement
	Levels, points, tasks, materials (e.g., texts), rewards (change agent/color)	Student sets goals or subgoals to complete	self-regulation, self-efficacy, interest, engagement
Environment	Game-like environment, changeable colors, icons, aesthetically pleasing backgrounds	ITS is set in a (more) appealing environment	interest, engagement
	Animated agents or avatars	Animated agents improved/incorporated	interest, engagement
	Multi-media: mini-games, graphics, video, simulations,	Simulations and other multimedia improved/incorporated	interest, engagement
	Narrative, immersive environment, fantasy	Game revolves within a narrative or immerses the learner within an environment simulating the real world or depicting fantasy	interest, engagement

specific than points (though levels may be based on points) and conveys feedback on performance across a longer time-span, rather than conveying feedback on immediate performance.

We expect point-based feedback features to facilitate self-regulation and self-efficacy in computer-based learning environments (Anderson et al., 1995; Corbett & Anderson, 1990; Foltz et al., 2000; Jackson & Graesser, 2007; Schunk & Pajares, 2001; Shute, 2006). Points provide direct and quantifiable feedback to the user on performance, complements any verbal feedback provided, and affords regulating and monitoring performance more accurately. For example, a student can discern that a score of 50 is clearly better than a score of 30, whereas any accompanying verbal feedback may not indicate such a measurable difference (by contrast, its purpose is to provide information on how to improve the student response that received only 30 points).

Points can provide a turn-by-turn indicator of student performance, but they can also provide a global indicator of performance quality over an extended period of time (thus providing both local and global feedback). These kind of performance-contingent rewards have been shown to produce a corresponding increase in self-efficacy and motivation (Schunk & Pajares, 2001). Schunk and colleagues have also demonstrated that there is an associated increase in student self-efficacy and motivation to continue improving performance by providing feedback on the overall progress through learning.

Feedback can be further exploited as a form of competition. Many games display feedback in the context of others' performance. The player may be told the number of points earned relative to the highest scorer. Or the player may be compared to other players within a certain regional area or age range. Many players are highly motivated by competition, and are further driven by having a goal to beat others. Thus, when conveyed as a competition, we can expect feedback to affect many if not all aspects of motivation.

Incentives

Incentives are performance-contingent rewards that primarily target extrinsic motivation in a learning environment. Incentives can maintain student interest and help to prolong engagement with the environment (Graesser, Chipman, Leeming, & Biedenbach, 2009; Moreno & Mayer, 2005). Generally, incentives should be contingent on some aspect of task performance. In the context of entertainment games, the player may earn points, and those points can be traded for such things as powers, tools, skills, or weapons. Adapting this to the context of an ITS, the student may earn points while completing a task, and those points can be similarly traded for a variety of objects, choices, or actions. For example, the student may be given options such as changing the avatar, changing color schemas (e.g., the background color), adding features to an avatar (e.g., buying new clothes), or playing a mini-game.

Within the context of an ITS, mini-games may provide an optimal form of providing incentives to learners. Mini-games are short 5-15 minute dynamic games. They may be purely for entertainment (e.g., off-road racing or tower defense) or optimally they present educational content (a mini serious game or puzzle game). The former serve primarily as extrinsic reinforcers, as they are unrelated to the content and run the risk of sacrificing time on task. Entertainment that is deeply integrated with the content is preferable. Mini-serious games (i.e., those tightly integrated with the domain content) still provide an incentive within the ITS, but also provide a greater variety of learning contexts to the student. This combination allows the mini-games to serve as performance-contingent rewards as well as a chance to frame content within a positive engaging environment (which should hopefully increase interest in the content itself). Given that many ITSs are complete entities with a set structure, one of the most promising means of adding game-based features to ITSs may be to add mini-games that reinforce the content in the ITS and are earned by accruing points in the context of the ITS. The student is thereby given the incentive to earn points within the ITS, and is provided with a greater variety of learning contexts through the mini-games.

Notably, we have distinguished between points as a means of feedback and points as a means of providing incentives. Feedback can be provided for the sole purpose of giving information regarding performance, and as we discussed earlier, we expect that adding such a feature should affect self-regulation and self-efficacy. Feedback can also have the added consequence of providing an incentive (if that is built into the system). If the points allow the student to obtain something, then they also provide incentives. With that added benefit, we expect feedback systems such as points to affect engagement as well as self-regulation and self-efficacy. We expect that engagement will be affected because the points then have an extrinsic value in addition to the intrinsic value as feedback.

The use of points and the option to trade the points for a utility both provide incentives to the player. However, they are expected to influence different aspects of motivation. We expect that providing incentives in the form of rewards that can be chosen by the student will affect self-efficacy, interest, and engagement. We expect self-efficacy to be affected because the student has been afforded the power to make choices and to do something different on the basis of performance. Thus, the reward is an external evidence of performance. We expect interest in the domain material or activity to be increased when students engage in educational activities that are more fun, such as the mini-games. That is, if a student interacts with specific science content in a fun, engaging, and meaningful way, then we would anticipate that the student would have a corresponding increase of interest in that science content. By contrast, we would not necessarily expect a student's interest in the domain content to be affected by student actions that involve superficial modifications of the environment (e.g., changing the avatar, changing the color of the background, etc.). However we might expect that engagement will be influenced through these superficial environmental changes because the student has an external reward and evidence for having performed well. Also, increased engagement may result from their novelty and the change in tasks. Additionally, there are some social dynamics to consider as well because peers (e.g., in the same classroom) can notice and remark that the changes have been made to the student's interface; such peer acknowledgement can provide some additional motivation to do well.

Task Difficulty

Varying the difficulty of the task, and matching the difficulty of the task to the learner is a characteristic of both ITSs and games. Nonetheless, we include this category in the list because the specific manipulations of task difficulty that we discuss seem to have strong associations with games. Indeed, Malone and Lepper (1987) identified *challenge* as a crucial feature of successful video games. Many argue that successful games have *optimal levels of challenge*. Game developers have argued that a good game is at the *zone of proximal development* (ZPD) or at the brink of zones of ability, cognition, and emotion (Conati, 2002; Mallone & Lepper, 1987; Rieber, 1996). A moderately challenging game sustains engagement by providing accomplishment while maintaining effort. Success in the game environment breeds self-efficacy, which is highly correlated with interest in games (Zimmerman & Kitsantas, 1997) as well as tutorial environments (Lepper et al., 1990).

We include three subcategories of task difficulty. We view these modifications of task difficulty as means of allowing a system to engage in the ZPD expansion cycle. The first step in this cycle is to use the student's zone of proximal development (ZPD) to help select tasks or materials that provide an achievable amount of challenge for the student. The process of overcoming this challenge is expected to provide a boost to self-efficacy, extend the application of student knowledge, and prevent boredom from a task that is too easy. Thus, we expect that maintaining the student at the ZPD should affect both self-efficacy and engagement.

The second step occurs if a student is unable to overcome this new challenge. If the task or material proves to be too difficult for the student, then backsliding can be implemented. The requirements of the task would be lowered to an achievable level, along with increased scaffolding. Reducing the amount of failure by adapting the task difficulty is expected to help the student to maintain a sufficient level of self-efficacy.

The third step may be implemented shortly after backsliding and adapting to the student's ability level. In this step, the system would attempt to empower the student through feedback strategies and thereby restore the student's sense of self-efficacy. Once a student has regained a stable performance level, this cycle would begin again as the system attempts to expand the student's ZPD.

Control

The amount of control that a student has in any learning environment is an important issue. For example, an internal locus of control has been found to help students progress through tasks more quickly and accurately (Corbett & Anderson, 2001). However, while many learners prefer to have some degree of control over their learning environment, less skilled or low ability learners are often unable to make choices that optimize learning (McNamara & Shapiro, 2005). They often lack the self-regulatory skills necessary to make choices regarding learning tasks, and thus need to be provided with sufficient guidance within the learning system. However, game-based features may offer a means of providing a sense of control by the learner, without allowing them to make choices on what and how they learn the serious content.

Game designers frequently include multiple features that encourage user personalization and control. Allowing users to control particular aspects of the learning environment provides opportunities for students to become invested in that environment and to identify themselves with some aspect of the experience. This investment of "self" may carry over into other dimensions of the learning environment, leading hopefully to enhanced learning and retention of the content (Cordova & Lepper, 1996).

Table 1 shows two types of control. The first is affording control over aspects of the environment. For example, the student may be allowed to change the color schemes, the background, the avatar, a task, or a mini-game. Such choices may be open to the student to choose at any time. However, we expect that the time to make choices should be limited to prevent them from perseverating on trivial aspects of the environment. Also, some students become irritated by a large menu of options that form barriers to progressing to the core activities. In an ITS or ITaG, the opportunities for students to make choices should ideally be dependent on their performance within the ITS system.

The second source of control included in Table 1 addresses the student's setting of personal goals or subgoals. For example, if points or levels are included in the system, the student may set the goal of achieving a targeted number of points or reaching the top level in the system. Likewise, the student may have the goal of being able to play a mini-game and perform at a certain level in the game, or they may want to change features of the avatar or other aspects of the environment. Expecting students to naturally set explicit learning goals is somewhat unrealistic (e.g., the goal to learn as much as possible about academic topic X). It may also be difficult for students to set an explicit learning goal if they do not possess sufficient domain knowledge, whereas the concepts of points and levels are domain independent and readily prolific in today's society. Although intrinsic goals and rewards are far more important to motivation (Gottfried, Fleming, & Gottfried, 2001), many students lack intrinsic motivation to learn the content in an ITS (Azevedo & Cromley, 2004). Hence, within the context of an ITS or ITaG, it seems more reasonable to expect students to set and achieve tangible game-based goals, such as obtaining a certain number of points or reaching a certain level. By imposing this game-based feature, the student's overt goal is to achieve points, but the student is induced to learn the target material or skills in order to reach those goals. Such extrinsic motivators in the context of a learning environment, particularly when combined with components that improve engagement with the material, are expected to increase motivation to perform well and learn the material.

We expect that adding a sense of control over the environment could potentially affect a wide range of motivational constructs. Given a goal or subgoal, the student is more likely to monitor performance (increasing self-regulation) and have a greater sense of self-efficacy when the choices are earned. Interest is likely to increase because of the investment in the learning environment. We expect the student to be more engaged in the learning activities because performance has an intrinsic value.

Environment

The game environment is what is most apparent to both the players and researchers. Many popular entertainment games are set in colorful, semi-realistic settings. Some of these games include avatars as well as simulation. Games are sometimes embedded in a story narrative with characters, settings, conflict, competition, action episodes, and outcomes. Some games allow the learner to explore hypothetical worlds and eventualities.

We have listed four aspects of the learning environment that are characteristic of games. The first regards ***aesthetics***. An ITS may be rendered more aesthetically pleasing by using rich 3-d visualization, incorporating sophisticated high-end graphics or images, using professional voice-overs, including recognizable icons to convey information, or improving the layout and structure of the user interface. These modifications could potentially affect interest and engagement, but probably to a lesser extent than the gameplay features and options. While the aesthetics of a game are most obvious, some doubt that they are the most crucial aspects for a learning environment.

The second aspect of the environment regards the use of ***avatars*** or pedagogical agents. Animated agents have become more commonly incorporated in learning technologies over the last decade (Atkinson, 2002; Baylor & Kim, 2005; Biswas et al., 2005; Cole et al., 2003; Johnson, 2001; Lester et al., 2001; Moreno & Mayer, 2004; Reeves & Nass, 1996). They appear to captivate students' interest (Atkinson, 2002; Reeves & Nass, 1996) and may affect learning (Graesser et al., 2003; Moreno & Mayer, 2004).

Avatars are useful for many reasons. Individual agents and groups of agents can be carefully choreographed to mimic virtually any activity or social situation: reading and learning strategies, curiosity, inquiry learning, negotiation, interrogation, arguments, empathetic support, helping, and so on. One important pedagogical utility is the modelling of appropriate learning strategies. This is important because students rarely observe other students exhibiting good learning strategies in the classroom. Agents can enact these strategies overtly by thinking aloud while they do so (McNamara et al., 2004). Avatars can interact with students and help them learn by providing hints, clues, feedback or instruction, by modelling good pedagogy, or by holding a conversation. Avatars can also take on different roles: mentors, tutors, peers, players in multiparty games, or avatars in the virtual worlds. They can express themselves with speech, facial expressions, gesture, posture, and other embodied actions. Indeed, several researchers (e.g., Johnson et al., 2003; Shaw et al., 2004) have developed avatars' social skills so that they can convey emotions and attitudes (expressiveness), show sensitivity to the learners' motivational and emotional states (empathy), and understand when and how to interact in socially appropriate ways (politeness).

Many ITSs such as AutoTutor and iSTART use avatars to present information and to engage the learner. AutoTutor has a *talking head* that interacts with a student, whereas iSTART uses full-body animated agents with various gestures (McNamara et al., 2004). Text-to-speech synthesizers allow agents to respond in human-like speech. Nonetheless, while avatars and speech engines may be characteristic features of some ITSs, many if not most ITSs do not incorporate them, and those that do may benefit from improving the avatars (or their voices).

The benefits or effects of an avatar will depend on how they are used. For example, if they are used to interact with the student, by stimulating responses, providing answers, giving explanations, or discussing reasons, then they will likely have a direct influence on the learning process. Indeed, implementing these kinds of sophisticated learning principles is the purpose of avatars used in AutoTutor and iSTART. By contrast, if avatars are used simply to convey information and provide some novel aesthetic value, then they may have less of a prolonged impact on interest and engagement by the learner.

A third feature that is characteristic of games is the use of ***multimedia***. Material can be delivered in different presentation modes (verbal, pictorial), sensory modalities (auditory, visual), and delivery media (text, video, simulations). The impact of different forms of multimedia has been extensively investigated by Mayer and his colleagues (Mayer, 2005). There is an extensive literature on the impact of multimedia on learning that is beyond the scope of this chapter to cover. From the standpoint of ITSs, it is important to align the multimedia facilities to the particular substantive content that helps learning. This is a nontrivial challenge because the available research on systems as advanced as animation and simulation technologies has revealed disappointing learning gains (Ainsworth, 2008). Even interactive simulations, where learners manipulate features of a microworld and observe what happens, have small influences on learners because the vast majority of learners have no systematic strategies on what to manipulate (Jackson, Olney, Graesser, & Kim, 2006). The hope is that the game environments will be insightfully designed to seduce learners to manipulate interesting parameters that lead to deep learning.

Finally, the use of ***narrative***, often included in both immersive and epistemic environments, is a feature that is uniquely characteristic of games, and is infrequently used in ITSs. Unlike text or film, incorporating narrative within games provides the distinct ability for story plans to be co-constructed between the player and the game system (with or without other players) and also makes it possible to experience hundreds of game threads instead of a single linear plotline (Gee, 2004; Van Eck, 2007; Young, 2006). Narrative has the added advantage of being comprehended quickly and remembered well compared with other genres (Bruner, 1986; Graesser, Singer, & Trabasso, 1994; Graesser & Ottati, 1995; Read & Miller, 1995; Schank & Abelson, 1995). Some games design narratives that completely immerse the player into a fantasy world (Malone & Lepper, 1987; Shaffer, 2007). For example, an epistemic game requires the user to play a specified role and engage in behaviors associated with an expert in a certain field (e.g., you are a doctor and have to examine a fake patient presenting with a specific set of symptoms). Narrative and immersive games allow the learner to explore hypothetical worlds and eventualities in a safe and secure manner, rather than being constrained to a single situation model or reluctant to perform actions due to real world consequences. Uncertainty in a narrative can also build suspense, one of the prominent features that sustain one's attention (Cheong & Young, 2006; Vorderer, Wulff, & Friedrichsen, 1996).

While narrative, epistemic, and immersive environments may be an important and effective aspect of games, they may also be the most difficult aspects to combine within an existing ITS. That is, ITSs tend to have an obvious learning structure, so imposing a narrative on top of an existing ITS structure may be artificial, if not impossible. However, if the learning environment is in the initial development stages, and the developer of an ITaG intends to incorporate both ITS and game principles, then the use of narrative, fantasy, episteme, and immersion are certainly features to consider incorporating (e.g., Millis, Cai, Graesser, Halpern, & Wallace, 2009).

SOLUTIONS AND RECOMMENDATIONS

Serious games presumably should captivate the attention, motivation, and learning activities of students more so than traditional environments such as ITSs. However, we do not know which components of games are most critical and effective in order to capitalize on the seductive aspects of games for learning. While it is generally assumed that games are more engaging and potentially *could* lead to better or more sustained learning (Gee, 2004; Steinkuehler, 2006; Vorderer & Bryant, 2006; Van Eck, 2007), there has been too little research thus far examining the effectiveness of gaming environments in comparison to more traditional ITS environments (O'Neil & Fisher, 2004; O'Neil & Perez, 2003; O'Neil, Wainess, & Baker, 2005). Furthermore, there is a lack of research that examines the effectiveness of the two approaches to promoting learning. We suspect that learning environments that incorporate game-based features are more likely to capture students' attention and to increase their motivation to participate over the long-term. On the other side, learning principles, such as those incorporated in current ITSs will increase gains in terms of learning and skill acquisition. As such, ITaGs can be expected to maximize the benefits of both worlds.

FUTURE RESEARCH DIRECTIONS

We do not expect that the list of features that we have provided is complete, nor exhaustive. We hope that this list can provide a springboard for ideas on how game-based features may be related to various aspects of motivation and what aspects of learning and motivation may be affected by game-based features. For example, does the presence of a personalized avatar increase interest, engagement, or investment within the environment? Or does it detract from the interaction as some form of "seductive detail" (Garner, Alexander, Gillingham, & Brown, 1991; Garner, Gillingham & White, 1989)? What types of rewards or incentives are sought most often by students? That is, are there differences between rewards that provide control over the environment, that customize their identity, or that provide entertainment? Do the educational mini-games contribute to any changes in learning, interest, and motivation of the content itself, or do they simply serve as a distraction and a change of tasks? What is the role of aesthetics and eye-candy to motivating learners? Addressing and answering such questions using ITaGs will further advance our understanding of the effects of game-based features as well as the effects of motivation during learning.

A further consideration addresses the effects of game components in combination versus individually. We suspect that many game components may result in interactive effects, such that they produce one pattern in isolation and another in combination with other features. For example, points may need to be paired with levels or rewards in order to provide more meaningful game-play. Along these lines, research has shown that adding game-like features in isolation (without context) provides no benefits to either learning or motivation (Jackson & Graesser, 2007). Simply adding points or levels to an ITS will likely not result in any significant learning changes, nor will it improve motivation. In order to be effective, these game features must be fully integrated within a coherent system, and must serve some purpose. This "purpose" could be as simple as using points to compare performance between students (competition), or it could require a combination of multiple features, such as redeeming points to modify a personal avatar.

CONCLUSION

In this chapter, we have focused on outlining how features of games might be incorporated with an existing ITS, and how those features can be expected to affect the motivation of the learner. We have discussed motivation in terms of four related constructs: self-regulation, self-efficacy, interest, and engagement. We did so in order to be more precise about which aspects of motivation are more likely to be affected by particular game features, and implicitly, which are not. However, we expect this list to change as research further investigates this issue and as researchers further consider these issues and this framework. We expect that there may be other constructs related to motivation that emerge as critical to game-based research, and we expect our understanding of these constructs to mature with further research.

The game elements discussed within this chapter will likely have varying ties to both extrinsic and intrinsic motivation. For example, spending points to change environmental elements, and other non-content related actions will likely serve as extrinsic motivators (which should increase interest in the environment itself, but not increase interest in the target activity). On the other hand, playing content-related mini-games, using labeled levels as symbols of success, and other performance-contingent rewards is more likely to positively influence intrinsic motivation within the content area. The included game features were in part selected to establish a balance between intrinsic and extrinsic motivating factors, however our goal here was to address more specific and malleable motivational components that have been positively linked to learning.

One of our implicit assumptions is that the incorporation of game-based elements into an ITS is unlikely to *directly* influence learning. We assume that ITS pedagogical principles are more likely to directly affect learning, whereas game-based features are more directly tied to the motivation of the learner, and the drive to engage with the system. If these game features increase long-term interest and interaction within the environment, and the environment consistently produces learning gains, then we can expect for students' knowledge and skill mastery to increase in the target domain. Increases in domain knowledge and skill mastery have been shown to have a corresponding increase in interest for that material (i.e., an increase in intrinsic interest for the content; Tobias, 1994). The hope is that these game features will encourage students to continue interacting with the ITaG in a positive (and effortful) way, which should consequently increase overall learning from the system. Hence, we are implying within this framework that researchers may not expect to see *direct* benefits on learning from ITaGs. Nonetheless, we do expect to observe *indirect* benefits. When learners are more willing to engage with the system, and for longer periods of time, then we can expect learning benefits to increase. Notably, however, learning principles such as inducing explanations, reasons, and generated responses by the student are most important to the learning process itself. Teasing out these effects will be challenging. But, hopefully, future research will shed light on which aspects of learning environments affect learning, and which affect motivation, as well as how to improve both without sacrificing the other.

The list of features we have provided does not include all possible game-based features, and we expect future research to provide additional evidence that will inform what is affected by game-based features and how. Nonetheless, our hope is that the ITaG framework will inspire researchers to vary certain aspects of learning environments and examine which aspects of motivation are enhanced, as well as to examine the potential learning benefits evoked by ITaGs. Ultimately, we expect hybrid ITaG learning environments to dramatically impact, if not revolutionize the effectiveness of computer-based training as well as further our understanding of the complex motivational aspects of learning environments and their interplay with learning. In sum, developing systems that exploit the best practices of games and ITSs is expected to significantly enhance learning systems, as well as our understanding of learning environments.

REFERENCES

Ainsworth, S. (2008). How do animations influence learning? In Robinson, D., & Schraw, G. (Eds.), *Current Perspectives on Cognition, Learning, and Instruction: Recent Innovations in Educational Technology that Facilitate Student Learning* (pp. 37–67). Charlotte, NC: Information Age Publishing.

Alexander, P. A., Murphy, P. K., Woods, B. S., Duhon, K. E., & Parker, D. (1997). College instruction and concomitant changes in students' knowledge, interest, and strategy use: A study of domain learning. *Contemporary Educational Psychology*, *22*, 125–146. doi:10.1006/ceps.1997.0927

Anderson, J. R., Conrad, F. G., & Corbett, A. T. (1989). Skill acquisition and the LISP tutor. *Cognitive Science*, *13*, 467–505.

Anderson, J. R., Corbett, A. T., Koedinger, K., & Pelletier, R. (1995). Cognitive tutors: Lessons learned. *Journal of the Learning Sciences*, *4*, 167–207. doi:10.1207/s15327809jls0402_2

Atkinson, R. (2002). Optimizing learning from example using animated pedagogical agents. *Journal of Educational Psychology*, *94*, 416–427. doi:10.1037/0022-0663.94.2.416

Azevedo, R. (2005). Using hypermedia as a metacognitive tool for enhancing student learning? The role of self-regulated learning. *Educational Psychologist*, *40*, 199–209. doi:10.1207/s15326985ep4004_2

Azevedo, R., & Bernard, R. M. (1995). A meta-analysis of the effect of feedback in computer-based instruction. *Journal of Educational Computing Research*, *13*, 109–125.

Azevedo, R., & Cromley, J. G. (2004). Does training on self-regulated learning facilitate students' learning with hypermedia? *Journal of Educational Psychology*, *96*, 523–535. doi:10.1037/0022-0663.96.3.523

Baker, E. L., & Mayer, R. E. (1999). Computer-based assessment of problem solving. *Computers in Human Behavior*, *15*, 269–282. doi:10.1016/S0747-5632(99)00023-0

Bandura, A. (2000). Self-efficacy: The foundation of agency. In Perig, W., & Grob, A. (Eds.), *Control of human behavior, mental processes, and consciousness: Essays in honor of the 60th birthday of August Flammer* (pp. 17–33). Mahwah, NJ: Erlbaum.

Baylor, A. L., & Kim, Y. (2005). Simulating instructional roles through pedagogical agents. *International Journal of Artificial Intelligence in Education*, *15*, 95–115.

Bereiter, C., & Bird, M. (1985). Use of thinking aloud in identification and teaching of reading comprehension strategies. *Cognition and Instruction*, *2*, 131–156. doi:10.1207/s1532690xci0202_2

Bereiter, C., & Scardamalia, M. (1985). Cognitive coping strategies and the problem of 'inert knowledge. In Chipman, S. F., Segal, J. W., & Glaser, R. (Eds.), *Thinking and learning skills: Current research and open questions* (pp. 65–80). Hillsdale, NJ: Lawrence Erlbaum Associates.

Biswas, G., Leelawong, K., Belynne, K., & Adebiyi, B. (2005). Case studies in learning by teaching behavioral differences in directed versus guided learning. In *Proceedings of the 27th Annual Conference of the Cognitive Science Society*, Stresa, Italy (pp. 828-833).

Bloom, B. S. (1956). *Taxonomy of educational objectives: The classification of educational goals, Handbook 1: Cognitive domain*. New York: McKay.

Boekaerts, M., Pintrich, P., & Zeidner, M. (2000). *Handbook of self-regulation*. San Diego, CA: Academic Press.

Bransford, J. D., Brown, A. L., & Cocking, R. R. (2000). *How people learn*. Washington, DC: National Academy Press.

Bruner, J. (1986). *Actual minds, possible words*. Cambridge, MA: Harvard University.

Burstein, J. (2003). The *e-rater* scoring engine: Automated essay scoring with natural language processing. In Shermis, M. D., & Burstein, J. (Eds.), *Automated essay scoring: A cross-disciplinary perspective* (pp. 113–124). Hillsdale, NJ: Erlbaum.

Cheong, Y., & Young, R. M. (2006). A Computational model of Narrative Generation for Suspense. *Proceedings of AAAI 2006 Workshop on Computational Aesthetics*.

Cole, R. V. S., Pellom, B., Hacioglu, K., Ma, J., Movellan, J., & Schwartz, S. (2003). Perceptive animated interfaces: first steps toward a new paradigm for human-computer interaction. *Proceedings of the IEEEE: Special Issue on Human-Computer Multimodal Interface, 91*(9), 1391–1405.

Combs, S. (2008). Current trends in the media industry: File production, television commercials and video games. *The Current and Potential Economic and Fiscal Impacts of Texas' Moving Media Industry*. Texas Controller of Public Account report.

Conati, C. (2002). Probabilistic assessment of user's emotions in educational games. *Journal of Applied Artificial Intelligence, 16*, 555–575. doi:10.1080/08839510290030390

Corbett, A. T. (2001). Cognitive computer tutors: Solving the two-sigma problem. *User modeling: Proceedings of the 8th International Conference* (pp. 137-147). Berlin: Springer.

Corbett, A. T., & Anderson, J. R. (1990). The effect of feedback control on learning to program with the lisp tutor. In *Proceedings of the Twelfth Annual Conference of the Cognitive Science Society* (pp. 796-803). Austin, TX: Cognitive Society.

Corbett, A. T., & Anderson, J. R. (2001). Locus of feedback control in computer-based tutoring: Impact on learning rate, achievement and attitudes. In *Conference on Human Factors in Computing Systems* (pp. 245-252). New York: ACM Press.

Cordova, D. I., & Lepper, M. R. (1996). Intrinsic motivation and the process of learning: Beneficial effects of contextualization, personalization, and choice. *Journal of Educational Psychology, 88*, 715–730. doi:10.1037/0022-0663.88.4.715

Craig, S., Graesser, A. C., Sullins, J., & Gholson, B. (2004). Affect and learning: An exploratory look into the role of affect in learning. *Journal of Educational Media, 29*, 241–250.

Csikszentmihaly, M. (1990). *Flow, the psychology of optimal experience*. New York: Harper Collins.

D'Mello, S. K., Taylor, R., & Graesser, A. C. (2007). Monitoring affective trajectories during complex learning. In D. S. McNamara & J. G. Trafton (Eds.), *Proceedings of the 29th Annual Cognitive Science Society* (pp. 203-208). Austin, TX: Cognitive Science Society.

Dodds, P., & Fletcher, J. D. (2004). Opportunities for new 'smart' learning environments enabled by next-generation web capabilities. *Journal of Educational Multimedia and Hypermedia, 13*, 391–404.

Donahue, D., Daane, M., & Grigg, W. (2003). *The Nation's Report Card: Reading Highlights 2003 (NCES 2004-452). U.S. Department of Education, National Center for Education Statistics*. Washington, DC: U.S. Government Printing Office.

Dynarski, M., Agodini, R., Heaviside, S., Novak, T., Carey, N., & Campuzano, L. (2007). *Effectiveness of reading and mathematics software products: Findings from the first student cohort*. Washington, DC: U.S. Department of Education, Institute of Education Sciences.

Fletcher, J. D. (2003). Evidence for learning from technology-assisted instruction. In O'Neil, H. F. Jr, & Perez, R. (Eds.), *Technology applications in education: A learning view* (pp. 79–99). Hillsdale, NJ: Lawrence Erlbaum Associates.

Fletcher, J. D., & Tobias, S. (2007). What research has to say about designing computer games for learning. *Educational Technology Magazine*, *47*, 20–29.

Foltz, P. W., Gilliam, S., & Kendall, S. (2000). Supporting content-based feedback in online writing evaluation with LSA. *Interactive Learning Environments*, *8*, 111–129. doi:10.1076/1049-4820(200008)8:2;1-B;FT111

Gagné, R. M., Wager, W. W., Golas, K. C., & Keller, J. M. (2005). *Principles of Instructional Design* (5th ed.). Orlando, FL: Harcourt Brace.

Garner, R., Alexander, P. A., Gillingham, M. G., & Brown, R. (1991). Interest and learning from text. *American Educational Research Journal*, *28*, 643–659.

Garner, R., Gillingham, M., & White, C. (1989). Effects of seductive details on macroprocessing and microprocessing in adults and children. *Cognition and Instruction*, *6*, 41–57. doi:10.1207/s1532690xci0601_2

Gee, J. P. (2003). *What video games have to teach us about learning and literacy*. New York: Palgrave MacMillian.

Gee, J. P. (2004). *What videogames have to teach us about learning and literacy*. New York: Palgrave-MacMillan.

Gottfried, A. E., Fleming, J. S., & Gottfried, A. W. (2001). Continuity of academic intrinsic motivation from childhood through late adolescence: A longitudinal study. *Journal of Educational Psychology*, *93*, 3–13. doi:10.1037/0022-0663.93.1.3

Graesser, A. C., Chipman, P., Haynes, B. C., & Olney, A. (2005). AutoTutor: An intelligent tutoring system with mixed-initiative dialogue. *IEEE Transactions on Education*, *48*, 612–618. doi:10.1109/TE.2005.856149

Graesser, A. C., Chipman, P., Leeming, F., & Biedenbach, S. (2009). Deep learning and emotion in serious games. In Ritterfield, U., Cody, M., & Vorderer, P. (Eds.), *Serious games: Mechanisms and effects* (pp. 81–100). Mahwah, NJ: Routledge, Taylor, and Francis.

Graesser, A. C., Jackson, G. T., Mathews, E. C., Mitchell, H. H., Olney, A., Ventura, M., Chipman, P., Franceschetti, D., Hu, X., Louwerse, M. M., Person, N. K., & TRG. (2003). Why AutoTutor: A test of learning gains from a physics tutor with natural language dialogue. In R. Alterman & D. Hirsh (Eds.), *Proceedings of the 25th Annual Conference of the Cognitive Science Society* (pp. 1–6). Mahwah, NJ: Erlbaum.

Graesser, A. C., Jackson, G. T., & McDaniel, B. (2007). AutoTutor holds conversations with learners that are responsive to their cognitive and emotional states. *Educational Technology*, *47*, 19–22.

Graesser, A. C., & King, B. (2008). Technology-based training. In Blascovich, J. J., & Hartel, C. H. (Eds.), *Human behavior in military contexts* (pp. 127–149). Washington, DC: National Academy of Sciences.

Graesser, A. C., Leon, J. A., & Otero, J. C. (2002). Introduction to the psychology of science text comprehension. In Otero, J., Leon, J. A., & Graesser, A. C. (Eds.), *The psychology of science text comprehension* (pp. 1–5). Mahwah, NJ: Erlbaum.

Graesser, A. C., Lu, S., Jackson, G. T., Mitchell, H., Ventura, M., Olney, A., & Louwerse, M. M. (2004). AutoTutor: A tutor with dialogue in natural language. *Behavior Research Methods, Instruments, & Computers*, *36*, 180–193.

Graesser, A. C., & Ottati, V. (1995). Why stories? Some evidence, questions, and challenges. In R. S. Wyer Jr. (Ed.), Knowledge and memory: The real story. Vol. 8, Advances in social cognition (pp. 121-132). Hillsdale, NJ: Lawrence Erlbaum Associates, Inc.

Graesser, A. C., Person, N. K., & Magliano, J. P. (1995). Collaborative dialogue patterns in naturalistic one-on-one tutoring. *Applied Cognitive Psychology*, *9*, 495–522. doi:10.1002/acp.2350090604

Graesser, A. C., Singer, M., & Trabasso, T. (1994). Constructing inferences during narrative text comprehension. *Psychological Review*, *101*, 371–395. doi:10.1037/0033-295X.101.3.371

Gredler, M. E. (1996). Educational games and simulations: a technology in search of a research paradigm. In Jonassen, D. H. (Ed.), *Handbook of research for educational communications and technology* (pp. 521–540). New York: Simon & Schuster Macmillan.

Gredler, M. E. (2004). Games and simulations and their relationships to learning. In Jonassen, D. H. (Ed.), *Handbook of research on educational communications and technology* (pp. 571–582). Mahwah, NJ: Lawrence Erlbaum Associates.

Greene, J. A., & Azevedo, R. (2007). Adolescents' use of self-regulatory processes and their relation to qualitative mental model shifts while using hypermedia. *Journal of Educational Computing Research*, *36*, 125–148. doi:10.2190/G7M1-2734-3JRR-8033

Hidi, S. (1990). Interest and its contribution as a mental resource for learning. *Review of Educational Research*, *60*, 549–571.

Jackson, G. T., & Graesser, A. C. (2007). Content Matters: An investigation of feedback categories within an ITS. In Luckin, R., Koedinger, K., & Greer, J. (Eds.), *Artificial Intelligence in Education: Building technology rich learning contexts that work* (pp. 127–134). Amsterdam, The Netherlands: IOS Press.

Jackson, G. T., Olney, A., Graesser, A. C., & Kim, H. J. (2006). AutoTutor 3-D Simulations: Analyzing user's actions and learning trends. In R. Son (Ed.), *Proceedings of the 28th Annual Meetings of the Cognitive Science Society* (pp. 1557-1562). Mahwah, NJ: Erlbaum.

Johnson, W. L. (2001). Pedagogical Agent Research at CARTE. *AI Magazine*, *22*, 85–94.

Johnson, W. L., Kole, S., Shaw, E., & Pain, H. (2003). Socially intelligent learner-agent interaction tactics. *Proceedings of the 11th International-Conference on Artificial Intelligence in Education (AIED)*. Amsterdam: IOS Press.

Kintsch, E., Caccamise, D., Franzke, M., Johnson, N., & Dooley, S. (2007). Summary street: LSA-based software for comprehension and writing. In Landauer, T., McNamara, D. S., Dennis, S., & Kintsch, W. (Eds.), *Handbook of latent semantic analysis*. Mahwah, NJ: Erlbaum.

Kintsch, W. (1998). *Comprehension: A paradigm for cognition*. Cambridge, MA: Cambridge University Press.

Kirkpatrick, D. L. (1994). *Evaluating training programs: The four levels*. San Francisco: Berrett-Koehler.

Koedinger, K. R., Anderson, J. R., Hadley, W. H., & Mark, M. A. (1997). Intelligent tutoring goes to school in the big city. *International Journal of Artificial Intelligence in Education*, *8*, 30–43.

Lepper, M. R., Aspinwall, L. G., Mumme, D. L., & Chabay, R. W. (1990). Self-perception and social-perception processes in tutoring: Subtle social control strategies of expert tutors. In Olson, J. M., & Zanna, M. P. (Eds.), *Self-inference processes: The Ontario symposium* (pp. 217–237). Hillsdale, NJ: Erlbaum.

Lepper, M. R., Drake, M., & O'Donnell-Johnson, T. (1997). Scaffolding techniques of expert human tutors. In Hogan, K., & Pressley, M. (Eds.), *Scaffolding student learning: Instructional approaches and issues. Advances in learning and teaching* (pp. 108–144). Cambridge, MA: Brookline Books.

Lepper, M. R., & Woolverton, M. (2002). The wisdom of practice: Lessons learned from the study of highly effective tutors. In Aronson, J. (Ed.), *Improving academic achievement: Impact of psychological factors on education* (pp. 135–158). San Diego, CA: Academic Press. doi:10.1016/B978-012064455-1/50010-5

Lesgold, A., Lajoie, S., Bunzo, M., & Eggan, G. (1992). SHERLOCK: A Coached Practice Environment for an Electronics Troubleshooting Job. In Larkin, J. H., & Chabay, R. W. (Eds.), *Computer assisted instruction and intelligent tutoring systems* (pp. 201–238). Hillsdale, NJ: Lawrence Erlbaum.

Lester, J., Callaway, C., Gregoire, J., Stelling, G., Towns, S., & Zettlemoyer, L. (2001). Animated Pedagogical Agents in Knowledge-Based Learning Environments. In Forbus, K., & Feltovich, P. (Eds.), *Smart machines in education: The coming revolution in educational technology* (pp. 269–298). Menlo Park, NJ: AAAI/MIT Press.

Malone, T., & Lepper, M. (1987). Making learning fun: A taxonomy of intrinsic motivations of learning. In R. E. Snow & M. J. Farr (Eds.), Aptitude, learning, and instruction: Vol. 3. Cognition and affective process analyses (pp. 223-253). Hillsdale, NJ: Lawrence Erlbaum.

Mayer, R. E. (2005). *Multimedia Learning*. Cambridge, MA: Cambridge University Press.

McNamara, D. S., Boonthum, C., Levinstein, I. B., & Millis, K. (2007). Evaluating self-explanations in iSTART: Comparing word-based and LSA analysis. In Landauer, T., McNamara, D. S., Dennis, S., & Kintsch, W. (Eds.), *Handbook of latent semantic analysis* (pp. 227–242). Mahwah, NJ: Erlbaum.

McNamara, D. S., Levinstein, I. B., & Boonthum, C. (2004). iSTART: Interactive strategy trainer for active reading and thinking. *Behavior Research Methods, Instruments, & Computers, 36*, 222–233.

McNamara, D. S., O'Reilly, T., Rowe, M., Boonthum, C., & Levinstein, I. B. (2007). iSTART: A web-based tutor that teaches self-explanation and metacognitive reading strategies. In D. S. McNamara (Ed.), Reading comprehension strategies: Theories, interventions, and technologies (pp. 397-421). Mahwah, NJ: Erlbaum.

McNamara, D. S., & Shapiro, A. M. (2005). Multimedia and hypermedia solutions for promoting metacognitive engagement, coherence, and learning. *Journal of Educational Computing Research, 33*, 1–29. doi:10.2190/7N6R-PCJL-UMHK-RYPJ

Merrill, D. C., Reiser, B. J., Ranney, M., & Trafton, J. G. (1992). Effective tutoring techniques: a comparison of human tutors and intelligent tutoring systems. *Journal of the Learning Sciences, 2*, 277–306. doi:10.1207/s15327809jls0203_2

Millis, K., Cai, Z., Graesser, A., Halpern, D., & Wallace, P. (2009). Learning scientific inquiry by asking questions in an educational game. In T. Bastiaens et al. (Eds.), *Proceedings of World Conference on E-Learning in Corporate, Government, Healthcare, and Higher Education* (pp. 2951-2956). Chesapeake, VA: AACE.

Mitrovic, A., Suraweera, P., Martin, B., & Weerasinghe, A. (2004). DB-suite: Experiences with three intelligent web-based database tutors. *Journal of Interactive Learning Research, 15*, 409–432.

Moreno, R., & Mayer, R. E. (2004). Personalized messages that promote science learning in virtual environments. *Journal of Educational Psychology, 96*, 165–173. doi:10.1037/0022-0663.96.1.165

Moreno, R., & Mayer, R. E. (2005). Role of guidance, reflection, and interactivity in an agent-based multimedia game. *Journal of Educational Psychology, 97*, 117–128. doi:10.1037/0022-0663.97.1.117

Morgan, M. (1984). Reward-induced decrements and increments in intrinsic motivation. *Review of Educational Research*, *54*, 5–30.

Murphy, K. P., & Alexander, P. A. (2000). A motivated exploration of motivation terminology. *Contemporary Educational Psychology*, *25*, 3–53. doi:10.1006/ceps.1999.1019

National Center for Education Statistics. (2001). *The nation's report card: Science highlights 2000 (NCES 2002-452). U.S. Department of Education, National Center for Education Statistics*. Washington, DC: U.S. Government Printing Office.

National Center for Education Statistics. (2006). *The nation's report card: Science highlights 2005 (NCES 2006-466) U.S. Department of Education, National Center for Education Statistics*. Washington, DC: U.S. Government Printing Office.

O'Neil, H. F., & Fisher, Y. C. (2004). A technology to support leader development: Computer games. In Day, D. V., Zaccaro, S. J., & Halpin, S. M. (Eds.), *Leader development for transforming organizations* (pp. 99–121). Mahwah, NJ: Lawrence Erlbaum Associates.

O'Neil, H. F., & Perez, R. (2003). *Technology Applications in Education: A Learning View*. Hillsdale, NJ: Lawrence Erlbaum Associates.

O'Neil, H. F., Wainess, R., & Baker, E. L. (2005). Classification of learning outcomes: Evidence from the computer games literature. *Curriculum Journal*, *16*, 455–474. doi:10.1080/09585170500384529

Pajares, F. (1996). Self-efficacy beliefs in academic settings. *Review of Educational Research*, *66*, 543–578.

Pintrich, P. R. (2000). Multiple goals, multiple pathways: The role of goal orientation in learning and achievement. *Journal of Educational Psychology*, *92*, 544–555. doi:10.1037/0022-0663.92.3.544

PISA. (2006). Science competencies for tomorrow's world: volume 1 Analysis. New York: OECD publishing.

Read, S. J., & Miller, L. C. (1995). Stories are fundamental to meaning and memory: For social creatures, could it be otherwise. In Wyer, R. S., Abelson, R. P., & Schank, R. C. (Eds.), *Knowledge and Memory: The Real Story* (pp. 139–152). Hillsale, NJ: Erlbaum.

Reeves, B., & Nass, C. (1996). *The media equation: How people treat computers, television, and new media like real people and places*. New York: Cambridge University Press.

Rieber, L. P. (1996). Seriously considering play: Designing interactive learning environments based on the blending of microworlds, simulations, and games. *Educational Technology Research and Development*, *2*, 43–58. doi:10.1007/BF02300540

Rieber, L. P. (2005). Multimedia learning in games, simulations and microworlds. In Mayer, R. E. (Ed.), *The Cambridge Handbook of Multimedia Learning*. New York: Cambridge University Press.

Rodrigo, M. M. T., Baker, R. S. J. D., Lagud, M. C. V., Lim, S. A. L., Macapanpan, A. F., Pascua, S. A. M. S., et al. (2007). Affect and usage choices in simulation problem solving environments. In R. Luckin, K. R. Koedinger & J. Greer (Eds.), *Proceedings of the 13th International Conference on Artificial Intelligence in Education* (pp. 145-152). Amsterdam: IOS Press.

Rus, V., McCarthy, P. M., McNamara, D. S., & Graesser, A. C. (2008). A study of textual entailment. *International Journal of Artificial Intelligence Tools*, *17*, 659–685. doi:10.1142/S0218213008004096

Salen, K., & Zimmerman, E. (2005). *The game design reader*. Cambridge, MA: MIT Press.

Schank, R. C., & Abelson, R. P. (1995). Knowledge and memory: The real story. In Wyer, R. S. (Ed.), *Knowledge and memory: The real story* (pp. 1–85). Hillsdale, NJ: Lawrence Erlbaum Associates.

Schiefele, U. (1991). Interest, learning, and motivation. *Educational Psychologist, 26*, 299–323. doi:10.1207/s15326985ep2603&4_5

Schunk, D. H., & Pajares, F. (2001). The development of academic self-efficacy. In Wigfield, A., & Eccles, J. (Eds.), *Development of achievement motivation*. San Diego, CA: American Press.

Shaffer, D. W. (2004). When computer-supported collaboration means computer-supported competition: Professional mediation as a model for collaborative learning. *Journal of Interactive Learning Research, 15*, 101–115.

Shaffer, D. W. (2007). *How computer games help children learn*. New York: Palgrave.

Shaw, E., LaBore, C., Chiu, Y. C., & Johnson, W. L. (2004). Animating 2D Digital Puppets with Limited Autonomy. *Proc. of the Smart Graphics 4th Int'l Symposium, SG 2004*.

Shute, V. (2006). *Focus on formative feedback*. Unpublished manuscript. Princeton, NJ: Educational Testing Service.

Shute, V., & Psotka, J. (1996). Intelligent tutoring systems: Past, present, and future. In Jonassen, D. H. (Ed.), *Handbook of research for educational communications and technology* (pp. 570–600). New York: Macmillan Library Reference USA.

Snow, C. E. (2002). *Reading for understanding: Toward an R&D program in reading comprehension*. Santa Monica, CA: Rand Education.

Snyder, T. D. (2009). *Mini-Digest of Education Statistics, 2008 (NCES 2009-021). National Center for Education Statistics, Institute of Education Sciences, U.* Washington, DC: S. Department of Education.

Steinkuehler, C. A. (2006). Why game (culture) studies now? *Games and Culture, 1*, 1–6. doi:10.1177/1555412005281911

Swaak, J., & de Jong, T. (2001). Discovery simulations and the assessment of intuitive knowledge. *Journal of Computer Assisted Learning, 17*, 284. doi:10.1046/j.0266-4909.2001.00183.x

Tobias, S. (1994). Interest, prior knowledge, and learning. *Review of Educational Research, 64*, 37–54.

Van Eck, R. (2007). Building Intelligent Learning Games. In Gibson, D., Aldrich, C., & Prensky, M. (Eds.), *Games and Simulations in Online Learning Research & Development Frameworks*. Hershey, PA: Idea Group.

Van Lehn, K., Graesser, A. C., Jackson, G. T., Jordan, P., Olney, A., & Rose, C. P. (2007). When are tutorial dialogues more effective than reading? *Cognitive Science Journal, 31*, 3–62.

Van Lehn, K., Lynch, C., Schulze, K., Shapiro, J. A., Shelby, R., & Taylor, L. (2005). The Andes Physics Tutoring System: Lessons Learned. *International Journal of Artificial Intelligence in Education, 15*, 147–204.

Vorderer, P., & Bryant, J. (2006). *Playing computer games – Motives, responses, and consequences*. Mahwah, NJ: Lawrence Erlbaum Associates.

Vorderer, P., Klimmt, C., & Ritterfeld, U. (2004). Enjoyment: At the heart of media entertainment. *Communication Theory, 14*, 388–408. doi:10.1111/j.1468-2885.2004.tb00321.x

Vorderer, P., Wulff, H. J., & Friedrichsen, M. (1996). *Suspense: Conceptualizations, theoretical analyses, and empirical explorations*. Mahwah, NJ: Erlbaum.

Winne, P. H. (2001). Self-regulated learning viewed from models of information processing. In Zimmerman, B. J., & Schunk, D. H. (Eds.), *Self-regulated learning and academic achievement: Theoretical perspectives*. Mahwah, NJ: Erlbaum.

Winne, P. H., & Hadwin, A. F. (2008). The weave of motivation and self-regulated learning. In Schunk, D. H., & Zimmerman, B. J. (Eds.), *Motivation and self-regulated learning: Theory, research, and applications* (pp. 297–314). Mahwah, NJ: Lawrence Erlbaum Associates.

Wisher, R. A., & Fletcher, J. D. (2004). The case for advanced distributed learning, information, and security. *International Journal (Toronto, Ont.)*, *14*, 17–25.

Woolf, B. P. (2009). *Building intelligent interactive tutors*. Burlington, MA: Morgan Kaufmann Publishers.

Young, R. M. (2006). *Story and discourse: A bipartite model of narrative generation in virtual worlds*. Interaction Studies.

Zimmerman, B. J., & Kitsantas, A. (1997). Developmental phases in self-regulation: Shifting from process goals to outcome goals. *Journal of Educational Psychology*, *89*, 29–36. doi:10.1037/0022-0663.89.1.29

Zimmerman, B. J., & Schunk, D. H. (2001). Reflections on theories of self- regulated learning and academic achievement. In Zimmerman, B. J., & Schunk, D. H. (Eds.), *Self-regulated learning and academic achievement: Theoretical perspectives* (pp. 289–307). Mahwah, NJ: Erlbaum.

Chapter 4
Using 'TRIRACE©' in the Classroom:
Perception on Modes and Effectiveness

Ayotola Aremu
University of Ibadan, Nigeria

ABSTRACT

Teachers are a critical factor in the educational system; they are vital to the success or otherwise of any innovation (such as computer games) in the school system. Their perceptions are critical to the success or failure of integrating computer games (Can & Cagiltay 2006). If teachers' attitudes are negative and they do not have a say in how to use the innovation, then no matter how well a game has been packaged, it would not be effective (Aremu, 2004). One way to ensure positive teachers' attitudes is to involve them, right from the teacher training period, in design, validation and implementation. This is the rationale behind the study which would be presented in this chapter. The goals of this chapter are therefore to firstly, provide support for the effectiveness of the use of computer games in the classroom and secondly, present teacher perceptions on how to use a computer game in the classroom.

INTRODUCTION

'TRIRACE©' is a board game on triangles. It was designed to meet the objectives of one of the topics in the Nigerian primary Mathematics curriculum focused on types and properties of triangles. The nature of the topic is such that pupils have to learn the various characteristics of triangles and be able to differentiate them when seen or described. This at most times have been found to need a lot of drill and practice, thus the reason for the board game. 'TRIRACE©' is a typical board game with 'start' and 'finish' positions. The successful use of the board game with Nigerian primary pupils (n=6) and the attendant effectiveness of the game based strategy on achievement of pupils showed that games could actually make learning easier, more interesting and motivating (Aremu 1998). Based on this success and the increasing access of the Nigerian primary school pupils to computers, which has resulted in great levels of interest in computer use, the board game was transformed into a computer game with

DOI: 10.4018/978-1-61520-713-8.ch004

slight changes made to the game to accommodate the computer format. Using such a game successfully in the classroom is contingent upon teacher's acceptance of the game. Teacher's acceptance is based on their attitudes and predispositions. The latter can however be modified if the teachers are involved in the process of design, validation and/or process of implementation. In a country like Nigeria where the market for locally made computer packages for learning and particularly, computer games is still very scanty, it becomes imperative for game and other software designers to ensure teacher acceptability.

Thus in this chapter we shall be looking at what pre-service teachers are saying about computer games. This is done by exposing the teacher to the use and application of TRIRACE©. This way their perceptions are now based on their use of this game. This is very important because not many teachers have yet had the opportunity to interact with computer games. The format of the game is very simple and easy to interact with. This is so since this would make it easier for first time users of educational games to manipulate and easily understand. For this country this is such a pioneering work which would assist curriculum planners, teachers and other stakeholders to make decisions concerning the use of games in the classroom.

The purpose of the study which is the basis of this chapter was to show what pre-service teachers' perceptions are about integrating such computer games into the classroom.

In the study

- The teachers evaluated the 'TRIRACE©' for effectiveness, content accuracy, suitability, etc.
- The teachers were also exposed to two (2) video recordings of life lectures in which students were using the computer game in the classroom. The teachers perceptions on the possibilities and problems associated with each format were expressed.
- Recommendations were made based on the perception of teachers about what would be the best formats for integrating computer games in Nigerian classrooms.

In this chapter therefore, attempts would be made to give convincing proof about the effectiveness of the use of games in the classroom and also to provide teacher perceptions of using computer games in the classroom based on a study carried out with teachers. From the latter, suggestions on classroom integration of computer games based on what teachers are saying would be provided.

BACKGROUND

A lot of reasons have been highlighted for the inclusion of computers generally into teaching and learning systems. One of the reasons is the increase in knowledge as well as complexity of such knowledge. Today's pupils are inundated with a lot of information which they may not be able to cope with except they resort to the use of computers. (Birgin et al,2009; Alkan, 1995). Furthermore in many developed countries lack of adequate number of teachers has made computers more popular for teaching.

However this popularity has been enhanced by the fact that researches have shown the effectiveness of computer assisted learning in learning various subjects and at virtually all levels of education-whether formal or informal. (Tutak & Birgin, 2008,; Liao, 2007; Basturk, 2005; Vale &Leder, 2004).

Studies, though few in Nigeria has also supported the efficacy of using various modes of computer assisted learning in teaching and learning processes. (Udousoro,2000; Egunjobi, 2002; Ibode, 2004; Aremu & Adefelu, 2005; Aleburu, 2008). It is therefore imperative that computers be seen as a necessary tool for learning in this fast paced age.

Games are defined as a form of fun and play. This usually leads to enjoyment and pleasure for all involved. They have goals, rules and conditions for winning. These characteristics of games give structure to the users and more importantly motivates them to learn (Prensky, 2001). Generally the use of task based games have been seen to contribute to the achievement of learning goals, these goals include personal and social development (interest in learning, maintaining attention, group work), language and literacy (use talk to organize, sequence and clarify thinking and so on), mathematical development, creative development, knowledge and understanding of the world and physical development (TEEM, 2002). Furthermore, TEEM (2002, pp.4) explains that *'games provide a forum in which learning arises as a result of tasks stimulated by the content of the game'*. In addition to this, knowledge and skills are also developed as a result of playing of games and according to Graeme (2003) games are educational. He went on to explain that the attributes of games such as; being entertaining though challenging, relaxing though purposeful, providing opportunities for socializing, allowing competition in a non aggressive and secure environment, they requiring exercise of knowledge and mental skills are probably what accounts for why board games are considered to be likely candidates as learning tools. These attributes are even more pronounced in computer based games because the latter involves more interaction and a fascinating play environment.

Games provide learning opportunities for children. While playing games, children have to operate within rules, think logically especially while planning their next move in a game, take turns, think under stress, learn to be gracious winners and gracious losers, learn how to manange disappointment, set aside their frustration to begin play again and be decisive in risk taking. All these are intended outcomes of any learning programme. Studies show that playing games have a lot to do with developing mathematics skills. For example, problem solving skills, (Kraus, 1982), and multiplication skills (Aremu, 2008).

Technology has provided the 21st century learner with a lot of things to be engaged with. It could be watching videos, capturing scenes and events, downloading and playing music and also playing computer games. All the aforementioned has to do with fun and entertainment which the students enjoy. Thus it becomes difficult for learning processes that are devoid of these fun based technologies to catch and sustain their attention in their learning process. When, however these technologies are integrated in the learning process, the attention of the learners could become highly focused.

This has been emphasized by Grabe and Grabe (2007). They explained that *'the extended focus on interactive digital entertainment in combination with preference for fast paced television has created a strong preference for these styles of interaction and presentation that may have resulted from brain restructuring'* (Grabe & Grabe, 2007 pp. 134). The consequence of this is that students would prefer learning that is presented in such a manner and could actually believe that the more traditional modes of learning is incompatible with how their brain works. This is one more reason why educators cannot shy away from using technology such as computer games in the classroom.

Computer games have the ability to voluntarily engage students for long periods of time, motivate learners to collaborate, scaffold the development of complex motor skills, rules, and facts. They could also help to activate existing knowledge and arouse student interest in the content that would be learnt following the use of the games. (Gee, 2003; Grabe & Grabe, 2007). When students use games to learn according to Prensky (2005) and Batson and Feinberg (2006) they are active, they see and do as opposed to the traditional way of just listening and reading. This leads to students being motivated to retain the information being presented through the game. It has also being discovered that games benefit students classified as poor performers apart from the general gains for all other category of students (Mayer, 2001; Virvou, Katsionis, & Manos 2005).

Conventry Evening telegraph (2002) explains recent research confirms that computer games offer significant educational value and do not have a bad effect on children DISTIL interactive (2009) has said that Digital Games-based Learning (DGBL) is being adopted by many organizations because games provide a safe environment in which to fail and can give learners incremental challenges and control over their progress. According to them the learning that comes from the games is informal and implicit. The players do not think about what ways they are acquiring their learning content, so learning is non-threatening. Furthermore, since they simply react to the game they are not conscious that they are in a process of learning. This goes a long way to help. Game based learning is interactive and engaging, learners are usually in control, they make learning fun, and games provide a safe environment for learning (DISTIL interactive, 2009; NESTA, 2004; TEEM, 2002; Facer, 2001; BECTA, 2001). The summary of all this research is that games and game based learning should be promoted in the learning environment. Furthermore, it could be beneficial that school subjects which students find naturally difficult, for which they develop negative attitudes and which they do not enjoy, arebe presented using games or the learning could be supported by the integration of games into the learning environment. Such a subject that could highly benefit from games is Mathematics (Kraus, 1982; Basturk, 2005; Aremu, 2008; Birgin, Çathoğlu, Coştu, & Aydin 2009). Traditionally mathematics has been viewed as a difficult subject. This has been worsened by the way teachers have taught the subject over the years. There has been a disconnect from reality with the emphasis on numbers and computation. This has become quite abstract for learners. While not saying that the computational processes and the drill and practice should be removed, it would be advantageous to both learners and teachers if mathematics content is designed and delivered within the game framework.

The integration of games call for a lot of systematic design and planning. There are issues of design, development, production, trial testing and so on. Other chapters in this book describes these methods in detail. There are also issues of acceptance and curriculum integration. These can only be effectively done when teachers are involved in the whole process. Teachers are key drivers who play crucial roles in technology integration in schools, what they believe about the usefulness of innovations like games, what they believe about their abilities to use them and what they believe about the integration and effectiveness of such innovations go a long way in determining whether the implementation is going to be successful or not. This is based in the Social cognitive theory of Bandura. According to Bandura(1986), a person's belief in performing a behaviour or a task can lead to the successful completion of the task. Therefore it is important to find out the views of computer game end users' (especially teachers), in order to ensure a successful integration in the classroom.

When educational materials are produced for the classroom, the teacher is encumbered with the task of choosing and adapting them to the classroom environment. This may not be too easy if they do not get involved in the whole cycle of design and development. Thus there is a great need for teacher involvement.

WHAT ARE THE FORMS THAT TEACHER INVOLVEMENT SHOULD TAKE?

Mainly the teacher education curriculum should ensure trainee teachers are exposed to design, development and evaluation of games, not leaving out also, the effective integration of such into the classroom. This will eliminate the problem of traditional inertia (that is sticking to the conventional way of doing things), low self efficacy and negative perceptions about games in learning. The latter is a factor which may hinder teachers from fully exploring the potentials of computer based games. Evaluation of software particularly games is something every teacher must be involved in doing right from the pre-service training period. When teachers evaluate software they can make decisions about format as well as content and process of learning. They are also able to give and recommend to students materials that are non-offensive, outdated or biased. Furthermore, the process would enable them to provide objective data regarding the effectiveness of the multimedia software before purchase (Herring, Notar & Wilson 2005). Doing all these during training provides a solid foundation for the teachers and a guarantee for their use latter.

When teachers also evaluate game software it helps them to think about suitable learning formats for integrating the games. The involvement of teachers in game evaluation is synonymous to their role in traditional textbook selection. If teachers are involved in the former, there is the guarantee that they would use the materials later in the school. Evaluation of game software by teachers could contribute to verify that relevant aspects of the rationale have been taken into consideration and implemented adequately. This is especially important because most software design is not done by teachers but professional game designers. Furthermore, it will allow teachers choose games that add value rather than those that are just entertaining, matching appropriate levels of challenge to varying ability levels to ensure progress.

METHODOLOGY

Research Questions

The research questions that guided the study reported in this chapter are

1. What are the teacher perceptions of computer games?
2. What are the teacher perceptions of TRIRACE©?
3. What is the preference of these teachers in terms of learning formats for computer game integration in the classroom?

Selection of Subjects for the study

A group of 200level pre-service teachers were selected in the College of Primary Education having Mathematics as one of their teaching subjects. Although there are many Colleges of Education in the country the chosen college is the only College of Primary Education in Nigeria. The college prepares teachers specifically for the primary school level, thus the choice. Students undergo a 3-year training to obtain the National Certificate of Education (N.C.E). Out of the 100 students who offer mathematics as one of their teaching subjects at this level, 50 participated in the study. Out of the 50, only 45 were able to complete the necessary documents and information requested for the study.

Instruments

The following are the instruments used in the study

a. TRIRACE©

This is a computer game fashioned after a conventional board game. The objective of the game is to be the first to get to the finish. Players proceed from start by clicking on game cards during their turn. Whatever is on the game card dictates were to drag your play piece/ icon (which is either a square or a circle). The players have an opportunity to identify the various types of triangles as they play and also match properties to the different triangles. The board has been divided into sections and each section has one type of triangle. The game cards contain either the name of a triangle, the property of a triangle,

Figure 1. First player interface/introductory screen. ©[2005] [ABC Eduplay Consult.] used with permission.

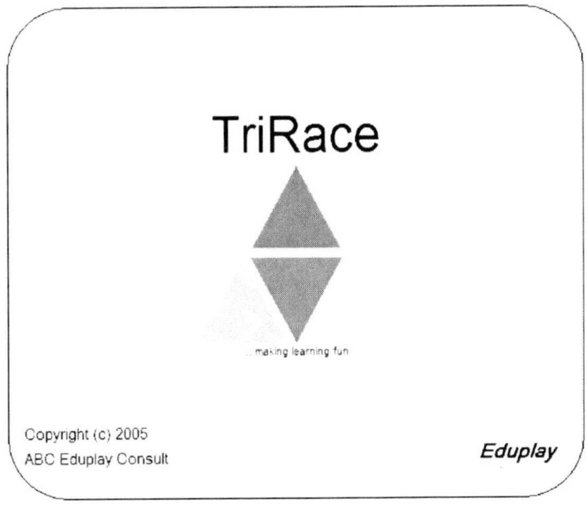

miss a turn or go to start. Players have to drag their play piece to the section that has the indicated triangle on the board. If dragged to a section that does not match what is on the card, the computer automatically returns the play piece to its former position. Another rule is that the play piece must be dragged to the nearest section that has the triangle that matches the description on the card.

More fun is created with the 'miss your turn' and 'go to start' cards. If a player picks any of these cards, the computer automatically implements it at a click of the mouse. The game can be played by 2 people who choose a play piece/icon each. Playing the games in pairs could help especially the pupils who are of low ability. Pupils of higher ability can correct and thereby assist one another It could also be played by an individual, in this case the pupil has more opportunities to practice the properties of triangles.

b. Teachers' perception of the use of educational computer games (Can and Cagiltay 2006)

This tool was developed by Gulfidan Can (Can and Cagiltay 2006). It consists of 2 parts, with a total of 58 questions. The first part deals with demographic and computer game playing characteristics of the participants. It also has the questions on the general perception toward playing computer games. The second part investigates the perceptions regarding the use of computer games with educational features in education. The questionnaire is a 4-point Likert scale; this according to the authors was preferred over a 5-point scale because of a high number of neutral responses in their pilot study. The internal consistency estimate of the reliability analysis for the questionnaire was calculated and the overall coefficient –alpha value was 0.87.

In this study, this questionnaire was used to collect information on the participants' perception of educational games. In addition, a section with questions on preferred learning formats was added to find out from the participants learning formats that are most preferable for using computer games. The questionnaire were filled by the pre-service teachers after they had had about an hour playing the game and looking at the 2 video recordings of primary school pupils playing the game. The first recording was of 15 pupils individually receiving teacher-led, computer based, animated instruction on triangles before using the games singly. The second recording was of 30 pupils working on the games in pairs after they had done some peer tutoring. This latter group worked in pairs.

Figure 2. Play interface/board showing various parts of the board. ©[2005] [ABC Eduplay Consult.] Used with permission

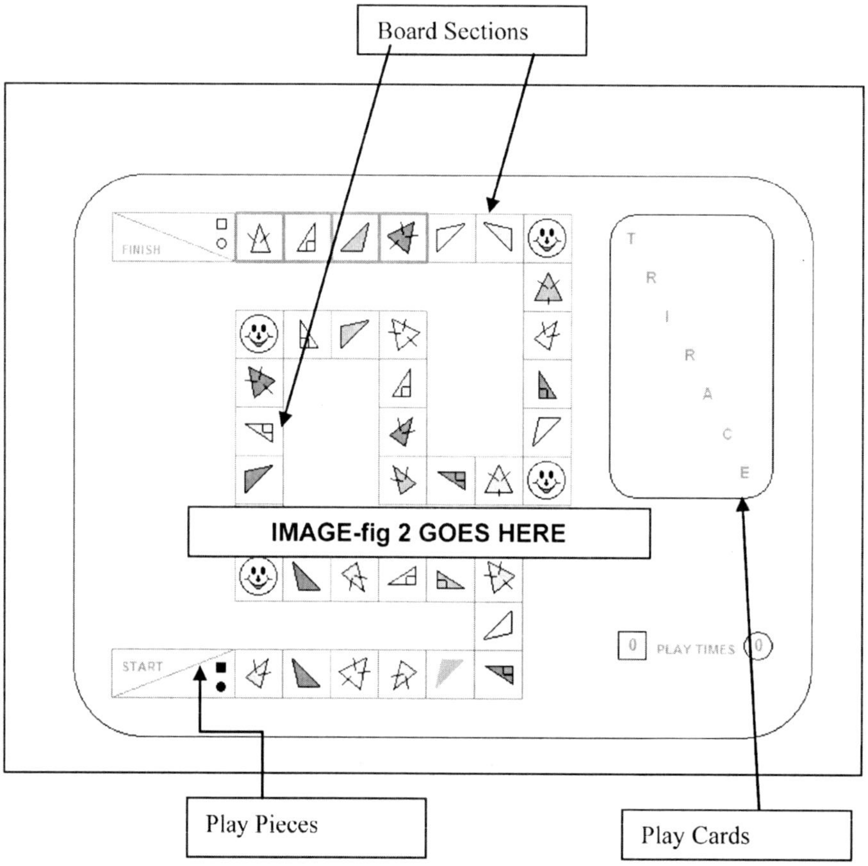

c. Evaluating Multimedia software form (Herring, Donna F and Notar Charles 2005)

This is a tool developed by Herring, Donna F and Notar Charles (available at http://www.jsu.edu/dept/ edprof/dherring). The authors designed the form to engage pre-service teachers in the selection of materials for development of instructional activities that can be used in multidisciplinary environments. The form is diagnostic and predictive. The authors having considered that most forms they had encountered concentrated on the technology and mechanics and did not look at pedagogy and content decided to design a form that met the requirements of some balance between mechanics, content and pedagogy that is user friendly. This was the reason for the choice of this instrument in this study. According to Tergan (1998) a comprehensive approach to software evaluation should include checking both quality as well as predictive power of combinations of design features on learning efficacy. This condition is satisfied by the chosen tool. In the development/validation of the tool, the authors reported that, the students gave 90% good or excellent rating to 3 out of the 5 items on the software evaluation form: completeness, logical sequence and rating scale. In this study this form was used by pre-service teachers to evaluate the game TRIRACE©. This form was filled by the participants after they had been introduced to the game and they had had about an hour of game play.

RESULTS AND DISCUSSION

The results are discussed guided by the research questions

Research Question 1

What are the teacher perceptions of computer games?

The following table shows the teacher perceptions of computer games.

The data as analysed show that the teachers are favorably disposed to using computer games. The Questionnaire has 3 parts, general perception about playing games on the computer, perception about computer games with educational features, and perception about how computer games could be effective. The teachers were positive about most of the questions.

For the discussion following, the percentages for Strongly Agree responses and Agree responses were added together as percentage of agreement while the percentages for Strongly disagree and Disagree responses were added together to give the percentage of disagreement.

Almost all of the pre-service teachers agreed that playing computer games develops skills and knowledge (92.6%agreement) and despite the fact that it requires so much engagement time (75.6% agreement), it stimulates learning (79% agreement). They did not think that playing computer games impacts social life negatively (78.9% agreement), rather it develops social skills (91.4% agreement). Furthermore the students were positive about games fulfilling all the goals of learning (cognitive 94.8%, psychomotor 78.9%, and affective 94.7% agreement). Having a positive disposition like this would most probably help pre-service teachers to integrate computer games into learning when they have their own classroom. Contrary to Can and Cagiltay (2006), almost all the pre-service teachers 83.7% said it was not time wasting. This is most probably because they were exposed to games in mathematics and they knew the challenges involved in teaching the subject. Thus any additional time invested to promote learning in the subject cannot be seen as waste.

The pre-service teachers were positive about games with educational features being applicable at all levels - 89.4% (though contrary to the study of Can and Cagiltay, 2006). This is in line with an earlier question that games are suitable for only children. 84.2% disagreed about the latter, this most likely could have been because they had benefitted from playing the game and they are adults. However a little less than these agreed that it could be used for all subject matters (73.7%). It may not be too obvious if games can be used for all subjects especially if these pre-service teachers have not been exposed to games in all subject areas. This could have been the reason for some of them feeling that it could not be used for all subjects.

It may seem quite contradictory that a high percentage of students agreed that games are effective both in the co-operative and competitive learning environment (81.6% and 97.4%respectively). One would have expected that with a high percentage of agreement in one, there would be a low percentage in the other since they are not complementary. On the other hand, this could actually mean that they believed that games can bring about learning goals whether there is a competitive environment or cooperative environment. The fact that they agreed to a high extent that games are effective as teaching aids, rewards, main instructional tools and so on show that they probably would be willing to explore the use of games in the various settings.

RESEARCH QUESTION 2

What are the teachers' perceptions of TRIRACE©?

To answer the research Question 2, the tool designed by Herring and Notar (2005) was used. It is an online tool. However for this study the tool was distributed in paper form and students rating were tallied based on the rating scale provided.

Table 1. Teachers' perception of the use of educational computer games(percentages in bracket)

A	GENERAL						
No	**Statement-**	**SA**	**A**	**D**	**SD**	**MEAN**	**Standard Deviation**
1	Playing computer games requires so much of engagement time	17 (37.8)	17 (37.8)	- (0.0)	4 (8.9)	3.24	.91
2	Playing computer games is suitable for every age group	17 (44.7)	13 (34.2)	- (0.0)	8 (17.8)	3.03	1.15
3	Playing computer games helps in developing some useful knowledge and skills	20 (52.6)	18 (40.0)	- (0.0)	- (0.0)	3.53	0.51
4	Girls and boys prefer playing different types of computer games	17 (44.7)	17 (44.7)	2 (5.3)	2 (5.3)	3.29	0.80
5	Playing computer games leads to addiction	8 (21.1)	21 (55.3)	4 (10.5)	5 (13.2)	2.84	0.92
6	Playing computer games stimulates curiosity in learning something	12 (31.6)	18 (47.4)	4 (10.5)	4 (10.5)	3.00	0.93
7	When computer games are played with a group, this helps development of social skills	17 (44.7)	21 (46.7)	- (0.0)	- (0.0)	3.45	0.50
8	playing violent games affect people negatively	8 (4.1)	17 (44.7)	9 (23.7)	4 (10.5)	2.76	0.91
9	Playing computer games affects the social life of people negatively	2 (5.3)	6 (15.8)	20 (52.6)	10 (26.3)	2.00	0.81
10	Playing computer games is a waste of time	2 (5.3)	2 (5.3)	20 (52.6)	14 (31.1)	1.79	0.78
11	Playing computer games is an important leisure time activity	14 (36.8)	24 (63.2)	- (0.0)	- (0.0)	3.37	0.49
12	Playing computer games is suitable for only children(primary and secondary level)	- (0.0)	6 (15.8)	14 (36.8)	18 (47.4)	1.68	0.74
	GRAND MEAN	**2.83**					
B	**Computer games with educational features:**						
No	**Statement-**	**SA**	**A**	**D**	**SD**	**MEAN**	**Standard Deviation**
1	can be applicable to all grade levels	14 (36.8)	20 (52.6)	- (0.0)	4 (10.5)	3.16	0.89
2	can be applicable to all subject matters	6 (15.8)	22 (57.9)	7 (18.4)	3 (7.9)	2.82	0.80
3	can be used in accordance with the goals of schools' curriculum plans	16 (42.1)	20 (52.6)	2 (5.3)	- (0.0)	3.37	0.59
4	can be used without causing any problem with the school's curriculum plans in terms of classroom management	9 (23.7)	21 (55.3)	6 (15.8)	2 (5.3)	2.97	0.79
5	can help student's fulfill cognitive learning goals which are defined in the schools' curriculum plans	18 (47.4)	18 (47.4)	- (0.0)	2 (5.3)	3.37	0.75
6	can help student's fulfill psychomotor learning goals which are defined in the schools' curriculum plans	17 (44.7)	13 (34.2)	6 (15.8)	- (0.0)	2.97	1.26
7	can help student's fulfill affective learning goals which are defined in the schools' curriculum plans	17 (44.7)	19 (50.0)	- (0.0)	- (0.0)	3.29	0.93
	WEIGHTED AVERAGE	**3.14**					

continued on following page

Table 1. continued

A	GENERAL						
No	**Statement-**	**SA**	**A**	**D**	**SD**	**MEAN**	**Standard Deviation**
C	**Computer games with educational features can be effective in learning:**						
No	**Statement**	**SA**	**A**	**D**	**SD**	**MEAN**	**Standard Deviation**
1	when used as a teaching aid in courses	21 (55.3)	14 (36.8)	1 (2.6)	2 (5.3)	3.37	0.97
2	when used as a reward in courses	8 (21.1)	23 (60.5)	3 (7.9)	6 (15.8)	2.92	0.85
3	when used during free times in courses	11 (28.9)	17 (44.7)	1 (2.6)	6 (15.8)	2.82	1.11
4	when used as a main instructional tool in courses	13 (34.2)	20 (52.6)	1 (2.6)	4 (10.5)	3.11	0.89
5	when they provide cooperative learning environment	12 (31.6)	21 (55.3)	3 (7.9)	2 (5.3)	3.13	0.77
6	when they provide competitive learning environment	13 (34.2)	18 (47.4)	1 (2.6)	4 (10.5)	2.95	1.14
7	when goal is specified in a game	13 34.2)	24 (63.2)	1 (2.6)	- (0.0)	3.32	0.53
8	when students are allowed to choose their own goals	8 (21.1)	19 (50.0)	5 (13.2)	6 (15.8)	2.76	0.97
9	When goal is not specified in a game	4 (10.5)	10 (26.3)	13 (34.2)	11 (28.9)	2.18	0.98
10	When they are based on realistic goals	14 (36.8)	19 (50.0)	3 (7.9)	2 (5.3)	3.18	0.80
11	When they are based on fantasy goals	8 (21.1)	23 (60.5)	3 (7.9)	4 (10.5)	2.92	0.85
	WEIGHTED AVERAGE	**2.97**					

(SA-Strongly agree, A-Agree, D-Disagree, SD-Strongly Disagree)

Table 2. Pre-service Teacher perception of Trirace for teaching

SCORE	JUDGEMENT	FREQUENCY	%
0-19	Unacceptable, unworthy for use or purchase	-	0.0
20-24	Poor, significantly below standards of quality	-	0.0
25-29	Fair, undistinguished, average	10	22.2
30-35	Good, fulfills most standards	21	46.7
36-40	Excellent, highest possible	14	31.1
	TOTAL	45	100

The result is as shown in Table 2. The results show that 46.7% rated the Trirace game as good while 31.1% rated it as excellent. The implication of this is that the students found the game fascinating. This could actually be because most of the students only been playing entertainment and other types of games and not educational games. Thus Trirace could be a novelty to them. This is attested to by the answers to a general question posed to the pre-service teachers during the study. Out of the valid 38 responses for that question (whether they had seen computer games used in the classroom for learning), 24 indicated that they had never seen computer games used in the classroom before, though all of them indicated that they played computer games.

The inference that can be drawn from this is that, the students were able to see a possibility of using computer games in the class, thus expanding their knowledge about computer based tools available for teaching and learning. This hopefully would have an impact on their practice in future.

RESEARCH QUESTION 3

What is the preference of these teachers in terms of learning formats for computer game integration in the classroom?

7 of the pre-service teachers did not respond to this section out of the 45 pre-service students, only 38 responses were analysed in this section.

To provide answers for which type of learning formats would be the preference of the teachers, Data was generated and presented in Table 3. The table shows some interesting things. One of it is the crucial presence of the teacher. 68.4% wanted teacher instruction of a concept before a game is used and 63.2% have a preference for a teacher led instruction rather than computer led instruction before using games. This could be because being teachers in training and having had some experiences in the classroom, they must believe that the teacher is indispensable. This may be an ego boosting issue and it could also be because a life teacher seems more comforting than a mechanical one (the computer). The latter does not exhibit passion and care as the former would. The implication of this is that if games must be produced and used for educational purposes, then it should be designed in such a way as to incorporate teacher input. This means that the teacher should not be completely replaced in the instructional process involving games.

Other results indicate that the computer laboratories are preferable than any other format for playing games. One may not know the reason for this, however it can be posited that the classroom teacher may not feel too competent about having pupils play games in the classroom. The environment of the computer laboratories would offer a more secure place to learn for the teacher because he/she would have the assistance of the technically competent personnel to handle any technical problems/issues arising. The implication of this however is that teachers who feel incompetent may not actually want to implement games in the classroom. One of the questions posed to the pre-service teachers after the study was for them to list some of the obstacles to their implementing games in the classroom in the future, the responses show that the most frequently cited obstacle is the technical know-how of the teacher. This confirms the responses that they preferred such games to be played in the computer laboratories, since they may not feel too confident about their computer handling capabilities.

With respect to when computer games should be used, the pre-service teachers responses were varied, 28.9% said during class as the teacher teaches, 31.6% said after class when the teacher has taught and 31.6% said during free period after the class. This does not really show any particular trend. In fact, the 28.9% who said it should be as teacher teaches contradicts the earlier discussion that they preferred the laboratories. However, one very interesting thing to note is that only 5.3% indicated that it could be used as homework. The

Table 3. Teacher preference of learning formats

What learning formats do you think would be best when using educational games		
	FREQUENCY	VALID %
working individually	0	0.0
working individually after teacher instruction	26	68.4
Working in pairs	0	0
Working in groups	12	31.6
TOTAL	38	100
Which learning environments would you prefer for playing educational games		
No indication	1	2.6
in the classroom with many computers and all students using them at the same time	11	28.9
in the computer laboratory	26	68.4
in the classroom with 2-3 computers and students taking turns to use it	0	0.0
TOTAL	38	100
If students are to work in groups to play computer games, which type of pairing do you think would be appropriate?		
No indication	1	2.6
girls only and boys only group	7	18.4
mixed girls and boys group	16	42.1
same ability groups	0	0
different ability groups	14	36.8
TOTAL	38	100
When should computer games be used		
No indication	1	2.6
during class as the teacher teaches that concept	11	28.9
after class when the teacher has taught the concept	12	31.6
as homework after the concept has been taught	2	5.3
during free periods after the concept as been taught	12	31.6
TOTAL	38	100
Which would you prefer		
No indication	1	2.6
computer led instruction and then computer game	13	34.2
teacher led instruction and then computer game	24	63.2
TOTAL	38	100

most probable reason for this is the fact that they may feel that pupils need more serious homework and games were just mere play. If this is so, then it may mean that these pre-service teachers still actually harbor the feeling that games are not serious learning tools. On another wise, it may be because many pupils do not have access to such facilities at home, thus this option may not seem feasible. Finally in terms of grouping for games, the teachers preferred mixed ability groups and also mixed gender groups. The reasons for this may be rooted in researches that have proved that mixed ability and gender groupings have been more effective for learning than others.

IMPLICATIONS AND CONCLUSION

The results and ensuing discussions, raise some issues which is presented below.

Game Design and Classroom Integration

Evidence from the results suggests that teachers believe they are indispensable in the classroom. The implication of this is that any game design that excludes the role of the teacher, whether as facilitator, guide or provider of instruction may not be acceptable in the classroom. Since it is the teachers that would implement the games in the classroom then it is necessary that they see themselves as part of the game process and not that they are being eliminated. One of the ways to include the teacher is that they should provide initial instruction on the concept that is to be learnt before the game is introduced. Another way is to provide for flexibility in the instructions for using games in such a way that allow for teacher decisions about, how to use, when to use, for how long and so on. This could help the teachers have a sense of being part of the whole process. The only caution is that the games should be prepared such that replicable assistance can be given to pupils who use them which would not be biased in any way by teacher competence. This has implications for teacher training.

Teacher Training and Games

The need to expose teachers to games that are educational is very glaring in the study. This becomes more important when it is being suggested that teachers be part of the learning provided by the games. Teachers must be trained in the art of evaluating computer games, using and integrating them in the classroom. One of the obstacles of the use of games as identified by the pre-service teachers in this study is the lack of technical knowhow. This can hinder to a great extent the use of games in the classroom. Therefore it would be needful to train teachers on things like installation, characteristics and troubleshooting on a general basis. Teachers need to feel competent enough to use games. This can come by integrating practical sessions of game playing into the training curriculum, all throughout the training period. This will provide the pre-service teachers opportunity to play games as often as possible. The various content areas/ subjects can be the springboard for such practical interactions with computer games. Such training can also extend to classroom administration in a game based environment for learning. All these would equip the teachers both cognitively and psychologically and would enhance their competence for the future use of games.

Perception of Games and TRIRACE (c)

The results of the study have shown that students perceived positively the impact of games on learning. Furthermore, it showed that the game used as the basis of this study was evaluated as being very good. This shows that no matter how simple a game is, the fact that it has the characteristics of games make it motivating and quite effective for instruction. The implication of this for beginners in game design for educational purposes is that they could actually start from simple formats. In a developing country like Nigeria, where the awareness of game use is the class is just being created, it may not be advisable to start with games with complicated formats or games that resemble already existing entertainment games. There could be a blockage in accepting the former, the reason being that most people, particularly parents of school age children are not positively disposed to use of toys and games in the school which are not particularly focused on teaching a concept (Aremu and Ekine 2003). Thus the advice is that games should be simple for a start and when it has been acceptable the more complicated formats could be introduced.

FUTURE RESEARCH DIRECTIONS

From the foregoing, it is quite clear that the issue of what teachers perceive as the best format for use of games is very important. This is an area of research that could be ongoing particularly because there are different types of games and they could be used in different settings. Thus future research should build on this investigating perceptions at all levels of teacher training (degree, in-service, professional development) on a consistent basis. One vital area of research that has emerged from this study is designing interventions for training of teachers on the use and integration of games. The preferred learning modes and strategies for computer use could be the basis for such an intervention. Gender, learning styles, and subject specialization could also be investigated as moderating variables. Outcomes of such researches would provide data to plan curriculum in teacher education with respect to computer game use and integration in classrooms.

CONCLUSION

This chapter has tried to establish the efficacy of using games in the classroom. From various researches, it has been able to show that there is a lot to gain from integrating games as a learning technology tool in the classroom for teaching content and topics particularly that learners perceive as difficult. Furthermore in this chapter, the role of teachers as the key personnel in implementing a game based classroom was emphasized and thus the need to find out how teachers perceived game use in the classroom and their preferred learning formats for using games in the classroom were investigated. To be able to accomplish this, a study was carried out and presented in the chapter. The results of the study and consequently the implications of the findings are also presented.

In conclusion, from the analysis of data collected it is recommended that teacher preferences should be integrated into design of games as well as training on the integration of games in the classroom. This would go a long way in ensuring that teachers implement educational games in their classroom. Some of the teacher preferences include teacher led instruction before playing of games, games being used in the computer laboratories, mixed ability and gender grouping for games and so on. It is also recommended that teacher training should lay emphasis on practical sessions of game playing in the curriculum so as to develop the competence and confidence of teachers in the use of games.

REFERENCES

Aleburu, J. O. (2008). *Design and utilization of ICT-based instructional delivery system and students' learning outcomes in computer application course in Colleges of Education in Lagos.* Unpublished Ph.D. dissertation, University of Ibadan, Nigeria.

Alkan, C. (1995). Eğtim teknolojisi. Ankara, Atilla: Kitapevi.

Aremu, A. (2004). Knowledge of the Educational Implications of Computer Games by some student Teachers in Southwest Nigeria. *The Nigerian Journal of Guidance & Counselling, 9*(1), 16–24.

Aremu, A. (2008). Why are games effective? A look at the interaction patterns in a game based Mathematics classroom in Nigeria. In Gómez Chova, L., Martí Belenguer, D., & Candel Torres, I. (Eds.), *INTED 2008 conference proceedings*. Valencia, Spain: International Association of Technology, Education and Development IATED.

Aremu, A. (2008b). The Acquisition of Environmental Knowledge through the Development of Games in a Higher Degree Course in Nigeria. *The International Journal of Learning, 15*(5), 299–306.

Aremu, A., & Adefelu, J. A. (2005). Computer Assisted Instruction and Achievement of Girls in Integrated Science. *African Development Review, 1*(1&2), 34–37.

Aremu, A., & Ekine, F. (2003, October). *Parental Perception of The Educational Values of Toys in school processes*. Paper presented at the 2nd National Conference of the Active Learning and Leisure Libraries. Stellenbosch, Cape Town, South Africa.

Bandura, A. (1986). *Social Foundations of Thought and Action.: A Social cognitive Theory*. Englewood Cliffs, NJ: Prentice Hall.

Bastruk, R. (2005). The effectiveness of Computer-assisted Instruction in teaching Introductory Statistics. *Educational Technology & Society, 8*(2), 170–178.

Batson, L., & Feinberg, S. (2006). Game Designs that Enhance Motivation and Learning for Teenagers. *Electronic Journal for the Integration of Technology in Education, 5*, 34–43.

Birgin, O., Çathoğlu, H., Coştu, S., & Aydin, S. (2009). The investigation of the views of student mathematics teachers towards computer assisted mathematics instruction. *Procedia Social and Behavioural Sciences, 1*, 676–680. doi:10.1016/j.sbspro.2009.01.118

British Educational Communications and Technology Agency (BECTA). (2001). *Computer Games in Education Project*. Retrieved December 30, 2008, from http://www.becta.org.uk

Can, G., & Cagiltay, K. (2006). Turkish Prospective Teachers' Perceptions Regarding the Use of Computer Games with Educational Features. *Educational Technology & Society, 9*(1), 308–321.

Coventry Evening Telegraph. (2002). *Computer games can help children develop*. Retrieved March 26, 2009, from http://www.highbeam.com/doc/1G1-84164174.html

Egunjobi, A. O. (2002). *The Relative Effectiveness of Computer assisted Instructional modes on student's learning outcomes in Geography*. Unpublished Ph.D. dissertation, University of Ibadan, Nigeria.

Facer, K. (2001). *Children's Out of School Uses of Computers. A Report for the InterActive Education Project*. Retrieved December 30, 2008, from http://www.interactiveeducation.ac.uk/school.pdf

Gee, J. P. (2003). *What video games have to teach us about learning and literacy*. New York: Palgrave Macmillan.

Grabe, M., & Grabe, C. (2007). *Integrating Technology for meaningful Learning*. Boston: Houghton Mifflin Company.

Graeme, D. (2003). *Board Games for learning*. Retrieved September 22, 2007, from http://magazines.fasfind.com/wwwtools/magazines.cfm?rid=210

Herring, D. F., Notar, C., & Wilson, J. (2005). Multimedia software evaluation form for teachers. *Education*. Retrieved March 26, 2009, from http://www.highbeam.com/doc/1G1-136846796.html

Ibode, O. F. (2004). *Relative effects of Computer-Assisted and Video tape Instruction methods on students' achievement in and attitude to English Language*. Unpublished Ph.D Dissertation. Institute of Education, University of Ibadan, Nigeria.

Interactive, D. I. S. T. I. L. (2009). *Learning with Digital Game Based Learning (DGBL)*. Retrieved July 19, 2008, from http://www.distilinteractive.com/approach/learning_with_dgbl.php

Kraus, W. H. (1982). The Use of Problem-Solving Heuristics in the Playing of Games involving Mathematics. *Journal for Research in Mathematics Education, 13*(3), 172–182. doi:10.2307/748554

Liao, Y. C. (2007). Effects of computer-assisted instruction on student's achievement in Taiwan: A meta analysis. *Computers & Education, 48*(2), 216–233. doi:10.1016/j.compedu.2004.12.005

Mayer, R. E. (2001). *Multimedia Learning*. New York: Cambridge University Press.

National Endowment for Science. Technology and the Arts (NESTA) Futurelab. (2004). *Literature Review in Games and Learning*. Retrieved December 30, 2008, from http://www.futurelab.org.uk/resources/publications_reports_articles/literature_reviews/Literature_Review378

Prensky, M. (2001). *Digital Game based Learning*. Boston: McGraw-Hill.

Prensky, M. (2005). Engage me or enrage me: What today's learners demand. *EDUCAUSE Review, 40*(5), 61–65.

TEEM. (2002). *Report on the Educational Use of Games – An Exploration by TEEM of the contribution which games can make to the education process*. Retrieved December 28, 2008, from http://www.teem.org.uk/publications/teem_gamesined_full.pdf.

Tergan, S.-O. (1998). Checklists for the evaluation of educational software: Critical review and prospects. *Innovations in Education and Training International.* Retrieved March 26, 2009 from http://www.highbeam.com/doc/1P3-29781007.html

Tutak, T., & Birgin, O. (2008). The effect of computer assisted instruction on the students' achievement in geometry. *International Educational Technology Conference Proceedings* (pp.1062-1065). Ankara, Turkey: Nobel Yayin Dağtum

Udousoro, U. J. (2000). *The relative effect of computer and text- assisted programmed instruction on student's learning outcomes in mathematics*. Unpublished Ph.D. Dissertation. University of Ibadan,Nigeria.

Vale, C. M., & Leder, G. C. (2004). Student Views of Computer-Based Mathematics in the Middle Years: Does Gender Make a Difference? *Educational Studies in Mathematics, 56*(2/3), 287–312. doi:10.1023/B:EDUC.0000040411.94890.56

Virvou, M., Katsionis, G., & Manos, K. (2005). Combining Software Games with Education: Evaluation of its Educational Effectiveness. *Educational Technology & Society, 8*(2), 54–65.

ADDITIONAL READING

Bethke, E. (2003). *Game Development and Production*. Davie, FL: Worldwide Publishing Inc.

British Educational Communications and Technology Agency (BECTA). (2001). *Computer Games in Education Project* [online]. Retrieved July 4, 2007, from http://partners.becta.org.uk/index.php?section=rh&rid=11207

Fullerton, T., Swain, C., & Hoffman, S. (2004). *Game design Workshop- Designing, Prototyping and Playtesting*. San Francisco: CMP Books.

Garris, R., Ahlers, R., & Driskell, J. E. (2002). Games, motivation and learning. *Simulation & Gaming, An Interdisciplinary Journal of Theory. Practice and Research, 33*(4), 43–56.

Grabe, M., & Grabe, C. (2007). *Integrating Technology for meaningful Learning*. Boston: Houghton Mifflin Company.

Janodia, M. D., Sreedhar, D., Ligade, V., Pise, A., & Udupa, N. (2008). Importance of Management Games in Classroom learning - A perspective. *Pharmaceutical Reviews, 6*(1). Retrieved May 15, 2009, from http://www.pharmainfo.net/reviews/importance-management-games-classroom-learning-perspective

Ketamo, H. (2003). An Adaptive Geometry Game for Handheld Devices. *Educational Technology & Society, 6*(1), 83–95.

Ketamo, H., & Suominen, M. (2005). *AnimalClass*. Retrieved March 30, 2007, from http://amc.pori.tut.fi/game/

Kiili, K. (2005). Digital Game-based Learning: Towards an Experiential Gaming Model. *The Internet and Higher Education, 8*(1), 13–24. doi:10.1016/j.iheduc.2004.12.001

Kiili, K. (2007). Foundation for Problem-Based Gaming. *British Journal of Educational Technology – Special issue on Game-Based Learning, 38*(3), 394-404.

Kirriemuir, J., & McFarlane, A. (2004). *Literature Review in Games and Learning*. Bristol, UK: Futurelab.

Machado, M. L. M., de Souza, D. G., Dandolini, G. A., de Souza, J. A., & Silveira, R. A. (2004). Implementing a Pedagogical Game: an Approach Using Multiagents Systems. In *Proceedings of the IADIS International Conference e-Society* (pp. 292-298). Madrid, Spain: IADIS press.

Magnussen, R. (2005). Learning Games as a Platform for Simulated Science Practice. In *Proceedings of DiGRA 2005 Conference: Changing Views – Worlds in Play.*

Malone, T. (1980). *What Makes Things to Learn? A Study of Intrinsically Motivating Computer Games*. Palo Alto, CA: Xerox.

Mitchell, A., & Savill-Smith, C. (2004). *The use of computer and video games for learning: A review of the literature*. London: Learning and Skills Development Agency.

Moreno-Ger, P., Martinez-Ortiz, I., & Fernández-Manjón, B. (2005). The <E-GAME> Project: Facilitating the Development of Educational Adventure Games. In *proceedings of the IADIS International Conference on Cognition and Exploratory Learning in Digital Age* (CELDA 2005) (pp. 353-358). Madrid, Spain: IADIS press.

Morrison, G. R., & Lowther, D. L. (2005). Integrating Computer Technology into the classroom-3ed. Upper Saddle River, NJ: Pearson Prentice Hall.

National Library of Singapore – NLB. (2006). *The mystery of the missing book – a virtual game*. Retrieved May 15, 2009, from http://exhibitions.nlb.gov.sg/virtual_games/

Prensky, M. (2001). *Digital game-based learning*. New York: McGraw-Hill.

Quinn, C. N. (1994). Designing educational computer games. In Beattie, K., McNaught, C., & Wills, S. (Eds.), *Interactive multimedia in university education: Designing for change in teaching and learning* (pp. 45–57). Amsterdam: Elsevier.

Roblyer, M. D. (2006). *Integrating Educational Technology into Teaching*. Upper Saddle River, NJ: Pearson Prentice Hall.

Ruben, B. (1999). Simulation, games and experience- based learning: The quest for a new paradigm for teaching and learning. *Simulation & Gaming, 30*(4), 8–12. doi:10.1177/104687819903000409

Salen, K., & Zimmerman, E. (2004). *Rules of Play: Game Design Fundamentals*. Cambridge, MA: The MIT Press.

Ulicsak, M., Facer, K., & Sandford, R. (2007). Issues impacting games based learning in formal secondary education. *International Journal on Advanced Technology for Learning (ATL)*, 4(3). Retrieved June 4, 2007, from http://futurelab.org.uk/resources/publications_reports_articles/external_publications/External_Publication294

Uzun, L. (2009). An Evaluative Checklist for Computer Games used for Foreign Language Vocabulary Learning and Practice: VocaWord Sample. *Novitas-ROYAL, 3*(1), 45–59.

Van Lent, M., & Swartout, W. (2007). Games: Once More, with Feeling. *IEEE Computer, 40*(8), 98–100.

KEY TERMS AND DEFINITIONS

Games: These are play activities that involve contestants who compete or co-operate in groups or pairs to compete, under some rules to achieve the objective of the game which would make them win.

Educational Games: These are games that have educational content. As contestants play, thet are engaged in the learning of some concept, fact, ideae.t.c.

Computer Games: These are games that can be played only on the computer.

Board Games: These are traditional games that have a gameboard with game pieces that represent the players. the players move their game pieces on the board from one point to the other based on the rules of the game.

Perception: This is belief or understanding about something or someone.

Perception of Games: This is belief about games and what they can do/achieve.

Effectiveness: How useful, how helpful or how valuable a thing is.

Mode of Game Use: Methods(form or style) by which games can be used in the classroom.

Classroom Integration: A systematic way of how an idea or resource is incorporated or added into the classroom practice.

Chapter 5
Bridging Informal and Formal Learning:
Experiences with Participatory Media

David Gibson
Arizona State University, USA

ABSTRACT

What is "one wikipedia's" worth of time and effort outside of school? About 100 million hours of free labor, which illustrates one of the features of participatory media. How can formal education take advantage of the new digital media, Web 2.0 and the like? This chapter describes the architecture of participatory media and the transition in formal education needed to mine the spare time and effort of learners. Bringing participatory media into formal education necessitates a redesign of learning institutions as well as the art of teaching. At the same time, as unobtrusive performance assessment improves and becomes available, new information can enhance formal education by making clear the educative value of digital experiences outside of school. Teachers who are trained to travel both ways on the bridge can be highly effective in creating new learning experiences that function as spreadable media appropriated by teens and others in a myriad of new ways in the emerging participatory culture of schools of the future. The game-based learning framework of The Global Challenge Award program is used to illustrate the framework of the participatory media bridge between informal and formal education.

INTRODUCTION

The trend in Web-based software toward participatory media that is exemplified in Web sites such as YouTube, Facebook and Wikipedia, is a result of the "cognitive surplus" (Shirky, 2008b) plus the social networking of participants. That surplus is in turn, based on people's informal free time, which in today's youth culture, is increasingly spent playing games and creating personalized content on the Web. Clay Shirky's "back of the envelope" calculation, which he worked out with Martin Wattenberg at IBM, is that all of Wikipedia — "the whole project--every page, every edit, every talk page, every line of code, in every language that Wikipedia exists in [about 190] — represents something like the accu-

DOI: 10.4018/978-1-61520-713-8.ch005

mulation of 100 million hours of human thought" (Shirky, 2008a). In contrast, the time people spend watching television consumes 2000 "Wikipedia projects" per year in the U.S. alone! Therefore, only a small a fraction of the informal cognitive surplus is involved in creating and sustaining the world's largest encyclopedia (and with only eight employees) (Perrien, 2008). How much of this cognitive potential are formal educators tapping?

Unfortunately, formal educational environments pose several barriers to the use of participatory media in schools. The hallmarks of the new technology—active creation of personalized online content and fluid communication networks—don't fit well with a traditional school's authoritative control of learning objectives, chronic lack of time, inadequate access to high-end technology, and the limited range of effective use of technology found in most classrooms (NCES, 2000; Tomorrow, 2001). For example, the 2007 findings of Project Tomorrow's annual "Speak Up" survey of students, teachers, parents and administrators notes that during school, students in grades 6-12 are using technology for these top 5 activities:

- Writing assignments (74%)
- Onlinc rcscarch (72%)
- Checking assignments or grades online (58%)
- Creating slideshows, videos, web pages for schoolwork (57%)
- Email or IM with classmates about assignments (44%)

Meanwhile, outside of school, it is a completely different story. The first national survey on "Teens, Video Games and Civics" by the Pew Research Center (Pew, 2008) finds that virtually all American teens play digital games - at least half on any given day - and those experiences are rich and varied, with a significant amount of social interaction and potential for civic engagement. Students in the Speak Up survey (Tomorrow, 2007) report on their regular use outside of school:

- Gaming – over 64% of students in grades K-12 play online and/or electronics based games regularly
- Download music – This #1 activity by middle and high school students mirrors increases in MP3 usage
- Social networking - 40% of middle school students and 67% of high school students have a personal website (Facebook, MySpace, Xanga) – most popular activity on that website: emailing with friends
- Communications (email, IM, text messaging) – while over 50% of all high school students use these tools regularly, girls' use outpaces boy's use by an average of 12 percentage points

Let's not forget that mobile devices outnumber computers 3:1 today (Perrien, 2008) and most students have one or more of these devices. The broad surveys such as the Pew study and the annual "Speak Up" data collection haven't begun to ask about mobile devices yet!

These broad survey sources provide evidence that Gcn-Y studcnts arc producing content and using graphically rich social media in their lives outside of school, but their teachers are for the most part unaware of and not tapping into or using this activity to advance learning. For example, the #1 use of technology by teachers (51%) is assigning homework or practice work. Teachers in the "Speak Up" survey report this about their use of technology:

- 93% use email to communicate with colleagues or parents (only 34% email with students!)
- 59% create a Powerpoint presentation
- 35% create or listen to podcasts or videos
- only 21% maintain a personal website like MySpace or Facebook

Table 1. Changing tools and methods from web 1.0 to 2.0

From Publishing	To Participation
Institutional Web sites	Personal Sites, Facebook, Blogs
Documentation / APIs	Patterns / tutorials
Books and articles	Wikis / forums
Encyclopedia	Wikipedia
Directories with indexes	Meta-tagging, folksonomies, tag clouds
Centrally controlled downloads	Peer to peer networks

There is an obvious disconnect between what students are doing with technology outside of school and what teachers ask them to do during school. Students are participatory users of media, but teachers have not yet caught on, nor are they using media effectively to promote learning. The premise of this chapter is that if teachers knew how (and had the tools) to tap participatory media in ways that engage learners, they could motivate students and expand the time spent interacting with educative media both in and out of school.

To address the gap between the youth culture's practices with technology and today's teaching practices, teacher educators and a new generation of teachers now have an opportunity to work together to study and develop new knowledge and methods for using participatory media and informal learning approaches in schools. The focus of this chapter is to provide two frameworks for educators to help guide thinking, research and practice that can build bridges between formal classrooms and informal Web-based learning spaces. The frameworks can be summarized as the "architecture of participation and production" and "what teachers need to know" to use the architecture.

THE ARCHITECTURE OF PARTICIPATION AND PRODUCTION

What do video-sharing sites, wikis, blogs, and folksonomies have in common? An architecture of participation. Participatory applications have increased as the Web has moved from storage to sharing, from publishing to participation (Perrien, 2008). Web 1.0 was about connecting machines. Web-based languages and media production methods began converging toward an operating system that is now largely independent of hardware platform, is highly mobile, rich with graphics and sound, and always online. The media convergence has led to Web 2.0, which connects people and their creations with each other across the globe.

Web 1.0 was characterized by publishing (mostly text) from authoritative sources. In that era, "authoritative" meant those institutions with the means to produce and control distribution of media to masses of people: magazines, newspapers, book publishers, television studios, government agencies, higher education institutions. With Web 2.0 the source of authority moved to the masses, what Davidson and Goldberg (Davidson & Goldberg, 2009) call "collective credibility," as the example of Wikipedia illustrates. The transition of authority underway in Web 2.0 is thus one of authorship, which entails several new tools and methods of production and the control of ideas and media, which are now in everyone's hands, turning each of us into a source of information (Table 1).

For example, blogs, which date from about 1998 and began as "web diaries and journals," are now indexed as a group of newsfeeds in the active blogosphere, the collective community of all blogs. Technorati (http://technorati.com) tracks 113 million blogs daily and counts a blog's authority in terms of links that represent how many other sites look for its content. The site's "State of the Blogoshpere 2008" notes "bloggers have been at it an average of three years and are collectively creating close to one million posts every day. Blogs have representation in top-10 web site lists across all key categories, and have become integral to the media ecosystem" (Technorati, 2008). The shift in perceived authority toward individuals is evidenced by the fact that one third of all bloggers have been approached by companies to be "brand advocates."

A second example of the transition from publishing to participation is represented by a wiki, a database of pages that visitors can edit, which allows the accumulation and organization of a knowledge base by participants. They have become so popular as repositories of knowledge that one search engine provides searches across all wikis (http://www.wiki.com/). The role of individual authors contributing to globally accessible data repositories has led to Wikipedia, the largest ever encyclopedia of the world's knowledge, created by the cognitive surplus. What could educational appropriation of this method lead to? Collaboratively written books (e.g. Wikibooks: http://en.wikiversity.org/wiki/Wikiversity:Main_Page), and a wiki-school-college-university system (e.g. Wikiversity: http://en.wikiversity.org/wiki/Wikiversity:Main_Page) are two possibilities.

A third example of the transition to productivity-centered participation is social bookmarking. These applications help users add metadata to shared content in the form of keywords. Collaborative tagging of web resources can be applied to web sites (e.g. Delicious: http://delicious.com/), pictures (Flickr: http://www.flickr.com/), videos (YouTube: http://www.youtube.com), encyclopedia articles (Wikipedia Categories: http://en.wikipedia.org/wiki/Special:Categories) and other media elements.

With these new ways of making and sharing things, Web 2.0 applications allow users to belong to new kinds of global communities where they can create a wide variety of expressive media, collaborate with others in making things, and distribute and recycle content to a worldwide audience.

These hallmarks of the "participatory culture" (Jenkins, Purushotma, Clinton, Weigel, & Robison, n.d.) entail new media literacy skills (Table 2) and new forms of knowledge production. In the same way that a change in environment creates new niches for life to evolve, the transformation to participatory culture is a game-changer for learning and educational institutions. The transformation is giving rise to new species of performance and performers on the global stage.

THE TRANSITION FROM FORMAL TO INFORMAL LEARNING

The transition from publishing to participation heralds changes in learning opportunities that are impacting schooling, education, and the preparation and improvement of teachers. Offsite training workshops are less vital if you can find out exactly what you need today, right when you need it. Teachers are less the source of knowledge than the guide to critical thinking and use of information, tools, and global access. Students are less the passive recipients of a system and more like active consumers and creators of knowledge who form networks of colleagues without concern for classroom walls and time schedules. These fundamental shifts signal the rise of informal learning over, into and integrated with formal educational settings of training centers, colleges, schools and classrooms.

Informal learning is characterized, among things, by free choice and self-directed use of resources to acquire new knowledge and skills independently from instructor-led programs. A good example is early language learning in the home. As Dewey pointed out in "Experience and Education" (Dewey, 1938) how a baby learns to

Table 2. New media literacy skills (Jenkins et al., n.d.)

Play	Experimenting with one's surroundings as a form of problem-solving
Performance	Adopting alternative identities for the purpose of improvisation and discovery
Simulation	Interpreting and constructing dynamic models of real-world processes
Appropriation	Meaningfully sampling and remixing media content
Multitasking	Scanning one's environment and shifting focus as needed to salient details.
Distributed Cognition	Interacting meaningfully with tools that expand mental capacities
Collective Intelligence	Pooling knowledge and comparing notes with others toward a common goal
Judgment	Evaluating the reliability and credibility of different information sources
Transmedia Navigation	Following the flow of stories and information across multiple modalities
Networking	Searching for, synthesizing, and disseminating information
Negotiation	Traveling across diverse communities, discerning and respecting multiple perspectives, and grasping and following alternative norms.

speak can teach us much about learning environments and the nature of human experience. A baby acquires language in order to get her needs (and eventually intentions) met within a responsive social environment (e.g. a cry gets caring attention). Cries soon become labels such as "ma ma" and "ba ba" and soon a self-reinforcing cycle of learning takes hold that shapes the continuity of past experience and provides a stage for present experience. In this environment, play is a critical component of exploration and is, in a sense, the original pedagogy. Because digital media has made the transition to participation, it strongly supports self-guided inquiry, expression and social networks allowing new forms of free choice play leading to self-directed learning.

The wider world, including everyday experiences with digital media, provides the informal setting for the majority of learning, not the formal settings of classrooms. Traditional school programs have understood this and structured homework, individual reading, laboratory experiences, off-campus trips, and so forth, to enhance formal learning. Now, with web-based digital media, many new avenues are opening up to bridge between formal and informal learning, but teachers need to learn how to use the bridges. They also need to make fundamental changes in their teaching assumptions and methods in order to unleash the power of their students' (and other people's) cognitive surplus, for example, by utilizing the time a learner spends outside of the classroom as well as by integrating the wider world into the classroom via digital media based interactions, tools and processes.

Unfortunately, during the formal school day there are barriers to both teachers and students in utilizing Web 2.0 tools and processes. In a study of barriers to informal learning by teachers (Lohnman, 2000), four issues were surfaced: lack of time for learning, lack of proximity to learning resources, lack of meaningful rewards for learning, and limited decision-making power in school management. Much the same could be said for students, whose time is used up shuffling from class to class, and in sitting quietly listening (teachers often hope), remaining inactive for most of the day. Students cannot use cell phones, PDAs and computers routinely in classes. Imagine trying to get work done in any environment other than school without constant access to these basic tools of communication and information. Students are not usually rewarded for independent thinking and action (e.g. for using Web 2.0 for self-directed exploration and play during classes), and students have limited decision-making power about what and when they study. To reverse the direction of analysis, barriers are also found when learning does take place outside the school or workday. It is difficult to account for time, document the use of resources for learning, garner or request consideration for accomplishments if not specifically requested by an instructor, and make decisions about how to connect informal learning into sequences leading to verifiable outcomes and certifications.

To begin to intuit how to directly address these kinds of barriers, it is helpful to see an example of new ways of organizing learning for both teachers and students. Then we can consider ways to build and strengthen the bridge to digital media learning.

AN EXAMPLE: THE GLOBAL CHALLENGE AWARD

The Global Challenge Award (GCA) is a digital media and learning program that aims to give students the tools and confidence to collaboratively solve complex problems (Gibson & Grasso, 2007). As an informal, online competition, it provides an example of the integration of Web 2.0 tools and methods into a digital learning experience. Students from anywhere in the world self-select to participate: they then choose among several tracks of competition to best fit their desires, intentions and commitment level. Each track requires the formation of a global team of four students, two from the home country and two from elsewhere. Each track is structured as a grand challenge game, with rules and a scoring guide for team products and processes that all focus on global warming and the future of energy. An expert external panel scores the team submissions and awards and recognition are granted in the form of scholarships, travel stipends, letters and certificates of recognition and permanent recognition on a web site. Simply put, the students are challenged to "Save the World On Your Way to College."

The GCA exemplifies the characteristics of informal learning in a game-based digital media context (Table 3) and because it concentrates on a large, ill-structured problem in a global context, it helps students acquire and use 21st Century knowledge and skills such as those outlined by the National Academy of Engineering (NAE, 2004) for engineers of the future (Table 4). To explain these foundations in more depth, the GCA program can be analyzed as a type of alternate reality game that helps fulfill the vision for the future workforce.

In alternate reality games (ARG), players interact with each other, the real world (including its technology), and a game master or set of rules to tell a story or play out a narrative. According to Sean Stewart, the lead writer of the online Web mystery "The Beast" that helped establish the genre, "Building an ARG is like running a role-playing game in your kitchen for 2 million of your closest friends. Like a role-playing game, we get players to actually enter the world of our story and interact with it, both online and in the real world." (Stewart, 2008). According to Jane McGonigal (McGonigal, 2008), who is "trying to make the real world more like games," alternate reality games help create a new form of personal capital – happiness - by providing:

1. Satisfying work to do
2. The experience of being good at something
3. Time spent with people you like
4. The chance to be a part of something bigger.

The unique vocabulary of alternate reality games, which has been evolving since 2001 (Dena, 2008), colorfully describes its key characteristics to include a puppetmaster (game staff), the curtain (separation of game players and game staff), rabbitholes (the starting prompt or context that kicks off a game), trailheads (signposts and clues to players), and a TINAG "this is not a game" aesthetic, (the verisimilitude, authenticity or epistemic reality of the game). The Global Chal-

Table 3. GCA game-based elements

Game Elements	GCA Elements
Puppetmaster (game staff)	GCA Staff (Program Director, Curriculum Writer, Mentors, Judges)
Curtain (separation of players and staff)	External Judges and the Web site itself
Rabbitholes (prompts, context, starters)	The premise "Save the world on your way to college?" that leads students into the game
Trailheads	Team challenges and explorations along with rules and scoring guides
TINAG (authenticity)	Global warming is real, solutions are needed; while playful and competitive, this is clearly "not just a game"
Computational Interface	Integrated application: social networking, Web pages with links to games and simulations, electronic portfolio
Computational Resources	Games, simulations, computational science tools embedded in self directed explorations
Fun & Attractiveness	Teams and individuals are in control
Playful Effort	No punishments, no formal assessments; incentive-driven
Motivating Stimuli	Open outlines for product elements, more than one solution, past solutions available, transparency & objectivity
Constant Feedback	Scoreboard changes daily, peer feedback, responsive help
Reflection	Final products, awards, sharing, winners

lenge Award takes inspiration from this approach and enhances it with other key features of digital game-based learning (Prensky, 2001) in particular:

1. Fun and attractiveness to players
2. The sense of playful rather than laborious effort
3. Stimuli that motivate repeated efforts
4. Constant visible improvement of knowledge and skills
5. Reflection on what has been learned.

A guiding vision for GCA includes working with others to create a World Game of the future in which digital media learning is preeminent (Gibson & Grasso, 2008). The intro to such a world will feel more like a movie than a textbook:

- Stacey hops into her Explorer Capsule for an unguided exploration of Earth. From her vantage point, flying high in the stratosphere or skimming Earth's surface, she stops wherever she wishes to observe an animal, chat with a friend, or simply enjoy the view. She notices the weather patterns in the Caribbean, watches melting glaciers over Greenland, sees people and machines scurrying across war-torn regions, and begins to appreciate some of the complexities our world faces.
- While flying over New Zealand, Stacey notices bands of wild horses running across the open landscape. She is a horse lover, so she takes a closer look. She lands in the middle of a large field busy with soldiers in training maneuvers and overhears them complaining. "Those Kaimanawa mares are interfering with our war games. They need to be controlled! Get someone on this or kill 'em!" shouts an officer. Near the edge of the field, Stacey sees two Department of Conservation ecologists looking up from their survey of plant species, making notes, and pointing. Drawing near, she overhears them say, "The horses have damaged these native plants to the brink of extinction." Stacey has never seen plants like this before; she wonders, "What are they?"
- She clicks on and becomes one of the horses! Her actions are now defined and

Table 4. Attributes of the engineer of 2020

Attributes of the Engineer of 2020	**Global Challenge Award Processes**
Strong analytic skills	Students must demonstrate their understanding of the science, technology, engineering and mathematics contents that are critical to their solution to global warming and the future of energy. STEM Explorations designed by scientists guide students to develop and use analytic skills to understand the causes and impacts in the complex systems involved in climate change and energy. A scoring tool is used by the students as well as by external judges to rate the demonstration of their analytic skills in their solutions.
Practical ingenuity	The team's solution must be innovative; it must utilize leading edge science and technology and demonstrate an innovative approach to any outstanding STEM challenges that would need to be solved or addressed in order for their solution to be feasible and globally scalable.
Creativity	Teams go through an initial phase of generating potential solutions as well as rating and justifying their team decisions. Documentation of these decisions is scored as an integral part of their final solution. See "Patent office ideas from the 2006-2007 Global Challenge" (Table 2) for a list of creative ideas by the international teams of high school students.
Communication	Students use telecommunications as they undertake their global teamwork. Students regularly use online chats and "voice-over-Internet" phone and video conference calls. An online electronic portfolio provides each team with a private space for documents, receiving feedback from mentors, and self-scoring using the guiding "Business Plan" rubric. Team advisors and project staff monitor semi-private student communications in the "eFolio" electronic portfolio. Teams are encouraged to submit transcripts of their communications as evidence of global teamwork.
Business and management	The long-term challenge (5 to 8 months depending on when the team forms) is the production of an innovative and comprehensive "Business Plan" (BP) for a globally significant solution to the challenge of climate change and the future of energy. The format is a modified version of a full scale BP and incorporates innovative several features that address content knowledge and teamwork. A detailed scoring guide allows the teams to work iteratively on their solution and receive feedback from people outside the team on the major elements of the BP: Table of Contents 1. Executive Summary 2. Industry Analysis 3. Product Description & Technical Analysis 4. Market Analysis 5. Manufacturing and Operations 6. Financial & Political Feasibility 7. Key Personnel 8. Bibliography 9. Appendix
Leadership	One of the barriers of global teamwork in an all-volunteer team is the various levels of team member commitment, access to communications, and persistence on a long-term project. Successful teams all develop internal leadership solutions to these issues.
High ethical standards	In the final solution, teams are scored high for honest team-appraisal sections that reflect on the problems and adjustments the team made along the way. Good documentation of references are essential for a high scoring solution. Innovative ideas can come from a synthesis of pre-existing technologies put together in a new way, so teams are encouraged to use acceptable practices for acknowledging prior work. Students also each make a personal statement about their role in the teamwork process, which is included in the final solution as documentation of global teamwork.
Professionalism	A resident scientist and group of undergraduate engineering students provide additional contact points, subject area expertise and team support to the international teams.

continued on following page

Table 4. continued

Dynamism, agility, resilience, and flexibility	Several rapidly changing conditions test the students' adaptability. School schedules around the world are not coordinated, so sometimes students are on vacation or between school years in the middle of the long-term project of their team. Time differences make synchronous communications difficult. Students do not use asynchronous communication tools in their normal "school life," so communications are halting, passive, and sparse unless strongly encouraged. Decision-making in a dispersed team with such barriers takes much longer than students are used to in "school project teams." These sorts of challenges require a dynamic change in practices. For example, students need support in learning to propose an idea to the group, when feedback might be sparse and cultural communication difficulties impede progress. In worst-case scenarios, teams might need to re-configure around one or two highly invested members. The project encourages every student with an interest to be resilient and persist through all the changes while staying focused on their interest, their core idea, and the prospects of completing "the toughest assignment you'll ever give yourself in high school."
Lifelong learners	Since the entire project depends on student initiative and self-directed learning, life-long learning capacities are provided as scaffolds for learning (e.g. self-scoring, seeking objective observer and expert advice, self and team monitoring in relationship to a suggested schedule, self-paced and self-leveled online learning modules). Structuring the production of evidence for scoring also rewards students for using lifelong learning practices.

constrained by Kaimanawa horse behavior. Other horses are in the field with her and she senses that other online users have transformed into horses too and joined in. The herd is disturbed and running. Stacey forms an impromptu international team with students from China and Korea who are playing as other horses. She goes where they go, eats what they eat, and talks to them about those strange plants.

- Stacey is beginning to understand that there is a dynamic conflict between human, animal, and plant life in this virtual environment that could involve her in any role—even as a plant! As she tries out each role, she is using technology, learning new science concepts and solving problems. Noticing a nearby sign that reads "Mission," she clicks on it and reads:

The International Council on Global Challenges seeks to resolve the issue of the feral Kaimanawa horses in New Zealand. Your help is requested. To be successful, you must within 5 days:

1. Explain to the Council whether and why you believe the Kaimanawa wild horses should be saved.
2. Design a management plan that preserves the wild horse population while addressing societal and environmental concerns.

Would you accept this mission? If you did, would your instructor (and classroom friends, and school or college department) help you, take part and enjoy the experience? To imagine so will require a new bridge connecting formal and informal learning.

BUILDING A BRIDGE TO DIGITAL MEDIA LEARNING

Imagine a bridge from formal education systems to Web 2.0 tools and methods, which a classroom teacher can cross as easily and fluently as they now do with a blackboard and lecture notes. Let's call this the "formal to informal" pathway. Teachers on this pathway, who are largely in control of the formal learning environment, need to reach out, embrace and utilize tools such as games, simulations, other participatory media and informal methods, to help their students acquire 21st Century knowledge and skills.

Two general directions of research on the "formal to informal" pathway focus on changing schools (e.g. definitions of content, patterns of time utilization, student groupings and teaching assignments) and teaching (e.g. releasing control to students, shifting into guidance roles, becoming experience designers who integrate games, simulations, and Web 2.0 tools and methods).

REDESIGNING LEARNING INSTITUTIONS

The authors of "The Future of Thinking: Learning Institutions in a Digital Age" offer ten principles for institutional redesign (Davidson & Goldberg, 2009).

- **Self-Learning.** Today's learners create their own paths to understanding.
- **Horizontal structures.** Not top-down curriculum, but collaboratively peer-driven.
- **Collective credibility.** Knowledge authority is crowd-sourced.
- **De-centered pedagogy.** Uses inductive and collective skepticism and assessment.
- **Networked learning.** Built on cooperative interactions, with mutual benefits.
- **Open source.** Creation and distribution of knowledge is freely shared.
- **Connected interactivity.** Working in isolation is unnecessary.
- **Lifelong learning.** Continuous change entails continuous adaptation.
- **Mobilizing networks.** New schools mobilize flexibility, interactivity, outcomes.
- **Flexible scalability and simulation.** Student grouped for small and extended projects

These principles challenge many of the notions of bricks and mortar institutions, the centering of pedagogy in expertise and cultural authority, and the predisposition to view learning, knowledge and performance only through the lens of the individual. At the same time, schools still have important roles to play as gathering sites for people to meet and work together, as centers of resources for learning, and environments that embody the goals of developing literacy, numeracy and citizenship required by society. So work must begin in earnest to redesign schools for the new realities of digital media in learning in order to be seen as part of the continuum of lifelong learning paths, and not an irrelevant temporary way-stop during the journey.

Formal education will not be able to address these principles without making significant changes in and reinvestments of its resources. However, as Web 2.0 and the participatory culture influence the formal system, we may begin to see a continuum from informal to formal as well as promising routes for building bridges between them. One important point of contact for the transformation will be the classroom, where individual teachers can redesign learning experiences to take maximal advantage of the new media skills in an expanded context for learning, and reinvent themselves as teachers.

REDESIGNING TEACHING

What could the future of learning look like in a formal K12 classroom? As a starting point, it might be helpful to ask whether a daily lesson plan contains any of the four main informal uses of technology that teens say they use every day.

1. **Fun and engaging.** Does the lesson plan have a game or simulation that is fun to play with?
2. **Sound.** Does it involve listening to music and other sounds during the activity or as central to it?

3. **Involve their friends.** Does it engage them in using their social networks to display themselves to others and note their successes and observations?
4. **Sharing ideas and media "finds."** Does it entail the use of synchronous communication software, passing messages, and getting in touch with others during the experience?

In addition to these four criteria, is the activity itself voluntary at its core or have significant freedom of choice? Can the social pressure of friends be the focal point of the strain between cultural transmission and individual freedom of expression, not the "assignment" or "teacher demand?" To what extent can the student determine the time, level of interaction, and the nature and quality of the product?

RETURNING ACROSS THE SAME BRIDGE

Traveling in the other direction on the bridge, along the "informal to formal" pathway, the informal tools, methods and content of digital media need to be useful to a classroom teacher while also leveraging the hallmarks for student participation: personalized creation of content and fluid social relevance. Teacher educators and future teachers could work together and with others to unobtrusively bring formal education practices into participatory media.

What does this look like?

Research on the "informal to formal" pathway in needed in several areas. The focus, instead of concentrating on changing teaching, classrooms or schools, would make the cognitive surplus products of informal learning a natural result of a self-fulfilling activity that contains evidence of what students gain in terms of knowledge and skills (Gibson, 2008).

While working on design projects within this branch, future teachers can build a special kind of knowledge that enables observation of the technologically enriched enactment of 21st-century skills.

WHAT TEACHERS NEED TO KNOW TO TRAVEL BOTH WAYS ON THE BRIDGE

Punya Mishra and Matthew Koehler have outlined a new way of thinking about technology-savvy teachers (Mishra & Koehler, 2006) that explores the intersection of knowledge about using various technologies (T), knowledge about how to teach - pedagogy (P) and knowledge of a specific discipline's content (C). From a learner's perspective, "T" is primarily about some particular mediational technology (a game, a simulation, a social network personal page); "P" is about its educative interactional affordances (e.g. fun and challenge, personal expression, acquiring skills and following curiosity); "C" is about what one learns (e.g. how to succeed in a particular setting, how to make something cool happen that amazes your friends, how to use the "cheat code" for solving a problem, which might be the periodic table of elements or a specific mathematical formula).

Glenn Bull, a founder of the Society for Information Technology and Teacher Education as well as a convener of the National Technology Leadership Summit is fond of saying that a few people got together a bought a vowel "A" to make the model memorable, at least a more pronounceable mouthful. The emergent intersection - TPACK - is about effectively bringing these aspects all together for learning. I have argued elsewhere that TPACK might be a useful framework for thinking about not only the teacher's level of skill, but also the affordances of a particular learning experience (Gibson, 2008). TPACK, interpreted as a teacher's skill, requires "a form of expertise different from, and greater than, the knowledge of a disciplinary expert (say a mathematician or a historian), a technology expert (a computer scientist) and a pedagogical expert (an experienced educator)" (TPACK, 2008). Interpreted as a property of a learning experience, the teacher's level of TPACK is entailed by any experience she designs and manages and that in turn constrains what students can learn from the experience.

Developing TPACK in future teachers includes modeling the use of technology in teaching content, helping them use ready-made technologies, and providing guidelines for appropriate and effective use of technology. By seeing models, reflecting on guidelines, and practicing new techniques, a teacher's tech-savvy skill (TPACK) grows.

A teacher's level or maturity of TPACK (what the teacher knows and knows how to do) becomes embedded in a learning environment and educational experience created by the teacher. This well-known property of designed artifacts is what allows performance assessment of student products to provide evidence of what students know and can do. When the "student" is a "teacher" we can thus focus on the degree and complexity of "TPACK embedding" into that person's designed products such as new lesson plans that integrate technology, new media products such as videos and web sites, and the integrated use of participatory media (e.g. games, simulations, blogs, wikis) as part of the learning experience (Gibson, 2008). To illustrate, let's consider a design project involving a rich participatory media – making a game or simulation. Imagine this complex assessment prompt in a pre-service teacher education program: *"Show an example of a game or simulation you have made to teach a concept."*

Engagement in a design project is complex and time-consuming; it powerfully situates a developing teacher's learning in a socially meaningful context that increases personal motivation and relevance. The knowledge and skills needed to design an online-course, an educational film, or an interactive, participatory game or web site include planning, communication, a specific content, an imaginative approach, symbolic reasoning, specific technical skills, and a sense of how people learn. The extent to which the designed product acts as a learning experience that engages students in a content area, with an appropriate use of technology embedded in an effective educative process, is a sign of the sophistication of that teacher's TPACK.

One of the geniuses of any design project is that the creator actively learns while making something for an audience. When the end product of the design project is a game or simulation, not only does the creator benefit, some audience also benefits from a highly interactive "epistemic" experience (Shaffer, 2007), affording the possibility of higher levels of knowledge building for both the creator and audience. This is less true for less interactive design projects. The audience of a typical film for example, watches the "C"ontent compared to the creator who searched, acquired, manipulated, enhanced and contextualized it. If "P" occurs it usually resides outside of the film watching experience, so the audience gets only a fraction of the integration that was the essence of the lived experience for the creator. The power of epistemic experience is realized by most creators in well-designed technology-enhanced design projects, but is best offered to and consumed by audiences through more participatory media (e.g. games, simulations, social networks, and video sharing sites).

Producing a game or simulation that "teaches something" requires a highly complex integration of technology, pedagogy, and content that must in turn be presented to an audience as an interactive experience. In particular, the requirement for audience interactivity in a game or simulation raises the bar for embedding TPACK into the product, because it captures the design team's (or individual's) level of sophistication in enlisting "T," "P" and "C" as essential elements of the activity's success.

The game or simulation design project example, as any participatory media design project would do (e.g. using a social network to form a community identity, or a blog to create peer review) illustrates how the two-way bridge metaphor requires thinking about TPACK as both a professional practice knowledge base (e.g., a teacher's level of TPACK) and a characteristic of an educative experience (e.g., the combined effect of a TPACK-planned experience on a learner). This way of thinking helps us remember that teaching with an overhead projector is different than with iMovie, a blog, or a video mash-up site, and at the same time, the student experience is co-constrained by both the emergent product of the teacher's knowledge and the affordances of the experience. A bad lesson with a game is no better than a bad one with a PowerPoint slide show if the teacher does not possess appropriate TPACK skill.

The dual role interpretation of TPACK as both a teacher skill and a specific characteristic of a learning experience provide a theoretical framework for how knowledge and practice is embedded in highly interactive digital teaching materials, including games and simulations. In quite ordinary terms, the student experiences some technologies that have particular affordances for inquiry and expression (T), the experience is organized to produce some effect on the student (P), and the effects have emotional, intellectual, and social content (C). In turn, the level of the teacher's awareness and skill in understanding and leveraging the TPACK intersection for stimulating inquiry and expression, social learning, and personal meaning greatly impacts the student learning experience and achievement.

THE ROLE OF GAMES AND SIMULATIONS IN BUILDING THE BRIDGE

Recall from above that over 64% of students in grades K-12 play online or electronics based games regularly and over half of all teens are playing on any given day. These facts should be enough to warrant serious consideration of the use of games and simulations as a digital media bridge between formal and informal education. But there are other compelling reasons as well.

Large-scale digital games and simulations are becoming increasingly integrated, rich media contexts with multiple layers of interaction (e.g., stunning graphical displays, data-rich environments, networks of players, ad hoc guilds, cheat sheet wikis, after-markets, and virtual-world entrepreneurs). Research communities now emerging are beginning to analyze and identify the criteria for successful social playability at the intersection of games with other ubiquitous media to find elements underlying successful social games and media services such as Flickr and Facebook (Mayra, 2008).

At the same time, digital game-based learning research, still in its infancy, has indicated that a wide range of competencies and habits of mind are engaged during game-play (Aldrich, 2005; Galarneau & Zibit, 2006; Gee, 2004; Prensky, 2002; Shaffer, 2007; Squire & Jenkins, 2003). The knowledge and skills entailed in game-based informal learning environments include some of the most difficult to measure and document, but they are at the same time, universally heralded as crucial to the success of formal education. A nation's global competitiveness in the 21st century, according to the emerging consensus, will depend on capabilities such as creativity, innovation, global awareness, critical thinking, problems solving, collaboration, initiative, self-direction, flexibility, and adaptability (P2CS, 2008).

The strands we've been discussing - participatory media, informal learning, and 21st Century skills - merge at the center of the TPACK of games and simulations. Participatory media are part of the new "T" of games; informal learning is an underutilized "P;" and 21st-century skills are more complex than traditional "C." For example, playing most complex networked-based video games involves forming and managing collaborative teams, setting and reaching one's own agenda including long term and intermediate goals, and acquiring sets of adaptable skills and a knowledge base that makes one fit for high performance in the game's space. What a teacher wouldn't give to get this much accomplished within a course!

At the intersection of digital media, pedagogy, and content knowledge we reach and can foster the newly transformed participatory culture, with self-direction and creative global leadership skills emerging from play. At the intersection also sits the agenda for teacher development in digital media learning, especially through games and simulations, in both the sense of how teachers select and use it, and the entailed content and pedagogy of the technology. Schools of education are well situated to help build the two-way bridge from informal to formal education by developing and nurturing the expertise needed to enhance formal education goals with new game-based informal digital media tools, methods and content.

CONCLUSION

Since the bulk of student life experience is and will remain outside of schools, participatory media in informal learning settings hold a vast untapped potential for enhancing the goals of formal education. A one-way bridge that brings participatory media into formal education could dramatically improve classroom experiences and outcomes. A two-way bridge that also brings unobtrusive performance assessment information into formal education from participatory media can link informal learning to valued formal outcomes and enhance education by making clear the educative value of digital experiences outside of school. Teachers who are trained to travel both ways on the bridge can be highly effective in creating learning experiences as spreadable media that is appropriated by teens and others in a myriad of new ways in the emerging participatory culture of schools of the future.

REFERENCES

P2CS. (2008). *Partnership for 21st Century Skills*. Retrieved September 9, 2008, from http://www.21stcenturyskills.org/

Davidson, C., & Goldberg, D. (2009). *The Future of Learning Institutions in a Digital Age*. Chicago, IL: John D. & Catherine T. MacArthur Foundation.

Dena, C. (2008). *ARG Stats*. Retrieved November 9, 2008, from http://www.christydena.com/online-essays/arg-stats/

Dewey, J. (1938). *Experience and education*. New York: The Macmillan Company.

Gibson, D. (2008). Make it a two-way connection: A response to Connecting informal and formal learning experiences in gthe age of participatory media. *Contemporary Issues in Technology & Teacher Education, 8*(4).

Gibson, D., & Grasso, S. (2007 November). The global challenge: Saving the earth on their way to college. *Leading and Learning with Technology*, 12-16.

Gibson, D., & Grasso, S. (2008). An enterprise simulation platform for education: Building a world game for pre-college students with Microsoft ESP. *Innovate, 4*(6).

Jenkins, H., Purushotma, R., Clinton, K., Weigel, M., & Robison, A. (n.d.). Confronting the challenges of participatory culture: Media education for the 21st Century [Electronic Version]. *New Media Literacies Project*, 72. Retrieved April 5, 2009, from http://www.newmedialiteracies.org/files/working/NMLWhitePaper.pdf

Lohnman, M. C. (2000). Environmental inhibitors to informal learning in the workplace: a case study of public school teachers. *Adult Education Quarterly, 50*(2), 83–101. doi:10.1177/07417130022086928

Mayra, F. (2008). *Games & Social Media - SoPlay*. Retrieved September 9, 2008, from http://www.sombiz.net/content/games-social-media-soplay

McGonigal, J. (2008). Alternate Realities: Jane McGonigal Keynote. *South by Southwest World*. Retrieved from http://www.slideshare.net/avant-game/alternate-realities-jane-mcgonigal-keynote-sxsw-2008

Mishra, P., & Koehler, M. (2006). Technological pedagogical content knowledge: A new framework for teacher knowledge. *Teachers College Record*, *108*(6), 1017–1054. doi:10.1111/j.1467-9620.2006.00684.x

NAE. (2004). *The Engineer of 2020*. Retrieved from http://www.nap.edu/catalog/10999.html

Perrien, C. (2008). *Web 2.0: from publishing to participation*. Retrieved January 20, 2009, from http://www.issi.at/index.php?id=5

Pew. (2008). Teens, Video Games and Civics. *Pew Internet and American Life Project*. Retrieved January 20, 2009, from http://www.pewinternet.org/PPF/r/263/report_display.asp

Prensky, M. (2001). *Digital game-based learning*. New York: McGraw-Hill.

Shaffer, D. (2007). *Epistemic games*. Innovate.

Shirky, C. (2008a). *Gin, Television, and Social Surplus*. Retrieved January 20, 2009, from http://www.shirky.com/herecomeseverybody/2008/04/looking-for-the-mouse.html

Shirky, C. (2008b). *Here comes everybody: The power of organizing without organizations*. New York: Penguin Press.

Stewart, S. (2008). *Alternate reality games*. Retrieved from http://www.seanstewart.org/interactive/args/

Technorati. (2008). *State of the Blogosphere 2008*. Retrieved April 5, 2009, from http://technorati.com/blogging/state-of-the-blogosphere/

Tomorrow Project. (2007). *Speak Up Survey 2007*. Retrieved January 20, 2009, from http://www.tomorrow.org/speakup/speakup_reports.html

TPCK. (2008). *TPCK - Technological Pedagogical Content Knowledge*. Retrieved September 9, 2008, from http://www.tpck.org/tpck/index.php?title=Main_Page

KEYWORDS AND DEFINITIONS

Participatory Media: An approach to digital media in which users are creators of content and social groups emerge from the active participation of many people, making possible "many-to-many" fluid relationships between knowledge, consumers, creators, and interactivity.

Cognitive Surplus: Clay Shirky's phrase that represents where socially produced media such as YouTube arise from the free time and voluntary actions of masses of active participants.

Blogosphere: The indexed totality of all web logs or "blogs," estimated in 2009 to be over 113 million sites, with over 1 million new postings each day. Bloggers represent a shift in perceived authority toward individuals, which is evidenced by the fact that one third of all bloggers have been approached by companies to be "brand advocates."

Social Bookmarking: Collaborative tagging of web resources made possible by applications that help users add metadata to shared content in the form of keywords.

New Media Literacy Skills: Henry Jenkins and others define a new set of interactive capabilities and propensities that are being fostered throughout the culture due to pervasive digital media, including learning through play and experimentation, adopting new identities for improvisation and discovery, using dynamic models, sampling and remixing of content, scanning the environment and shifting focus, co-construction, expanded mental models, following narratives across media, networking and negotiation across diverse communities.

Alternate Reality Games: A form of gaming in which players interact with each other, the real world (including its technology), and a game master or set of rules to tell a story or play out a narrative.

Section 2
Cases of Gaming Use in Teaching and Learning

Chapter 6
Technology Enhanced Language Learning in Early Childhood:
Competencies for Early Childhood Teachers

Elisabeth Katzlinger
Johannes Kepler University Linz, Austria

ABSTRACT

This chapter deals with a training curriculum for kindergarten teachers to introduce a learning game for technology-enhanced language learning in early childhood and how kindergarten teachers can launch the game in their classes. The game helps children to become familiar with the German language as a mother tongue or as a second language. The game "Schlaumäuse" was developed to enhance the children's language learning. Children between the ages of four to eight are the target group of this software. The different activities in the game's story encourage the children's phases of language learning like structure of syllables, phoneme, rhymes or phonological features.

INTRODUCTION

Language development is a process that starts early in human life, when a person begins to acquire language by learning it as it is spoken and by mimicry. Children's language development moves from simplicity to complexity. Infants start without language. Yet by four months of age, babies can read lips and discriminate speech sounds. Between the ages of three and six years the children´s language becomes more complex and the children learn to use the rules of grammar correctly.

DOI: 10.4018/978-1-61520-713-8.ch006

This "emergent literacy" period is a good time for children to learn a second language. Language is broken into two categories: words and grammar. Children develop these two components at different times and in different areas of the brain. During this period of development, the plasticity of the brain provides an excellent opportunity to teach the child a second language, since the brain is already wired for language acquisition (Wasserman, 2007). Whereas the earlier concept of 'reading readiness' suggested that there was a discrete maturational point in time when children were ready to learn to read and write, emergent literacy instead proposes that there is a smooth and continuous progression in children's literacy development between the early behaviors children display when interacting with print materials, and those displayed later once children can read independently (Parette, Hourcade, Dinelli & Boeckmann, 2009). According to the emergent view, the skills of reading and writing develop both concurrently and interrelatedly in young children, rather than sequentially. Therefore, early childhood teachers should seek to create a learning environment that integrates both reading and writing.

The creation of the learning environment for language development is essential part of the work of the early childhood teachers. They need to offer learning experiences that surround young learners with meaningful and interactive literacy-based activities in order to support second language development (Akcan, 2005). Early childhood educational games, including digital games, provide an important new opportunity for structuring learning experiences.

Game-based learning is a promising new approach to educating young children that combines information technology and new media. Game designers have developed rich, media-specific methods for engaging and retaining the interest of players. The idea to associate game dynamics with learning content is not new, as every game teaches something, but digital games offer new affordances for learning such as individualized learning sequences, responsive practice sessions, social as well as independent gaming, and new forms of unobtrusive assessment.

The task of the kindergarten teacher is to design a learning environment that fits the interests, strengths and needs of children. However, during their pre-service education, and in their professional life, they have little involvement with Information and Communication Technology (ICT). That's why the curriculum contains the topic ICT in the kindergarten (not only for language learning). Our experience with a technology-training program shows that kindergarten teachers need assistance in introducing games in their group. The potentials of new media are another highlight of the training. The training provides a place where teachers exchange their points of view about this particular language game as well as other ICT in the kindergarten.

THE GAME: "SCHLAUMÄUSE – KINDER ENTDECKEN DIE SPRACHE"

The game "Schlaumäuse – Kinder entdecken die Sprache" [Children explore language] (Kochan & Schröter, 2006) is a learning game intended to help children to improve their use of the German language as a mother tongue or as a second language. Kochan and Schröter developed the game at the Technical University Berlin in the Computer Learning Workshop. The first kindergarten classrooms that adopted the game were located in social hot spots where there were a large number of children with German as a second language. For most of the children, the computer in these initial kindergarten classes was the only contact with ICT.

The population of children in early childhood settings is becoming increasingly culturally and linguistically diverse, and these changes in demographics have warranted teachers becoming more culturally responsive and better prepared to work with different groups of children and families. This phenomenon can be observed as a characteristic of developed countries, especially in urban areas (Lim, 2009). The learning game is a possibility to bring children together with diverse language acquisition.

In the game "Schlaumäuse," the children get to know not only the spoken language but also the written language. Young children are interested in letters, reading and writing long before they go to school. This natural interest in written language is sparked by the game. Letter knowledge is indisputably one of the basic foundations for the acquisition of reading and spelling skills in alphabetic orthographies (Byrne, 1998; Ehri, 1998). The recognition of letters has repeatedly been found to be one of the best predictors for reading and spelling acquisition later in school across alphabets and educational systems (Levin, 2007). Currently, many researchers and educators believe that letter knowledge should be enhanced in kindergarten, prior to entry into school where children are taught formally to read and spell. However, no agreement exists about how this enhancement should be accomplished in terms of timing and sequencing.

Levin, Shatil-Carmon & Asif-Rave (2006) reviewed curricula for kindergartners in North America (e.g., California State Board of Education) and in the United Kingdom. These reviews have indicated that children are expected to recognize letters, name all or most of them, and become familiar with the sounds of some of them prior to school entry. In the United Kingdom, teaching about letters starts in prekindergarten with their sounds. Letter names are not formally introduced prior to first grade (Caravolas & Hume, 2001).

The children learn a language not only by observation, but also by experimenting with the language. In this way they find the rules of the grammar and learn new words. In the learning game "Schlaumäuse," there are many possibilities to experiment with letters, syllables and words.

At the same time, playing the game engages the children in using and learning about technology. The children learn to work with the PC, the keyboard and the mouse. They also learn to use the tools of the game such as a question mark for help, a loudspeaker icon for listening to words or a stethoscope for listening to single characters. In one part of the game, the Writing Workshop, the children use word processing tools (figure 1) such as different types and font sizes and they can format and print their written words. In the Writing Workshop, they also produce their first written works, and with the loudspeaker tool. The player can hear what he or she has written. The game's affordances motivate the children to experiment with letters and words.

Pedagogical Principles of the Game "Schlaumäuse"

The children can play the game alone or in a group. Our observations in the kindergarten have shown that the children like to play together in a group. One child uses the keyboard and the mouse and the other children assist. The children interact around the game, communicating about which part of the game they should play next or deciding the best way to solve the quest of the game. Some children, especially the younger ones, prefer to observe their friends playing the game. With their observations these children learn how to play the game while learning German.

After signing on with his or her name the player starts the game at the central playground (figure 2). This is the starting point of all activities of the learning game. In the central playground the child can choose an activity, for instance the audio cube, a memory with rhymes or the magic booth, where the child can conjure new words with different initial sounds.

In every activity of the game the player has to perform a task and trains another field of language learning. The main figures in the game (Lolly and Pop) explain the tasks of the game. These characters tell the player what to do. The figures act cooperatively with the player and help if there is something wrong. They give hints on how to solve the problem. The hints become more detailed and after a certain number of wrong trials they give the child the right answer or solution. They express the feedback to the player positively. If a child performs a task he or she gets a piece of cheese. With eight pieces of cheese the child can go to a party to dress up or to take a picture.

The children seek their own path through the different activities of the learning game. He or she can choose the place to learn as well as the speed of learning in the game. From the central playground the child can also make the choice of which tasks to play. The child is placed in the role of "I want ..." instead "I have to do ..." The

Figure 1. Schlaumäuse writing workshop

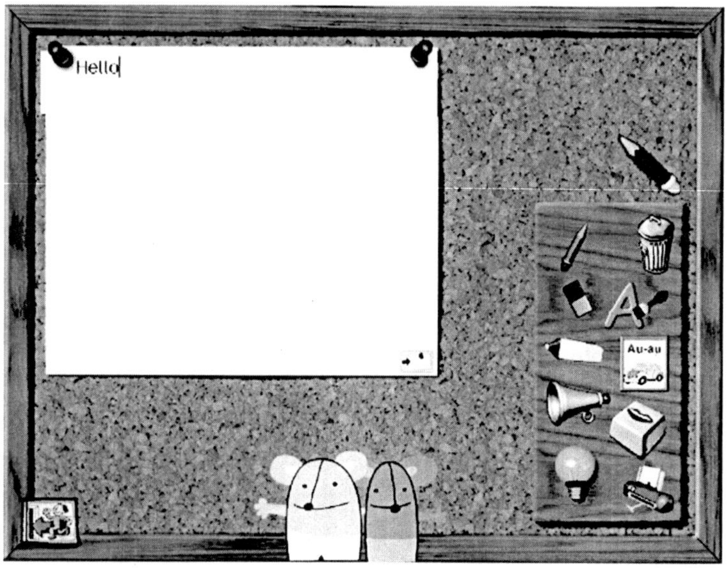

children choose the activities of the game that fit their ability. If a task is too difficult, their interest wanders and they play another part of the game. On the other hand, tasks that raise no challenge for a child are not interesting. Because of this freedom of decision, the children are neither under- nor over-challenged.

Younger children learn language as a medium of communication by using it through a purposeful, real, here and now experience. The intention of the children is to use language for their personal aims; they want to communicate with the people around them. Therefore they have to use language in a correct way; otherwise the child will be misunderstood. In the game the children can experiment with the language, for instance to write characters and listen to them. The mistakes that the children make provide many new chances for learning more about the language.

The children build their own theories about the rules of the language. The player can experiment with the spoken and the written language. The game corrects them in an appropriate way. The spoken language of the game is very clear and in correct pronunciation.

The Learning Fields of the Game

The activities of the game train different fields of language learning. In the process of language acquisition children develop both language production and language perception (Leuckefeld, 2006). The game environment helps children learn both structures of language step by step. In addition, the abilities acquired by the children become more complex and extensive with time and practice.

- **Spoken language use**: Spoken language can be trained by everyday vocabulary and terminology of word fields like body parts, traffic signs or fruits. In one part of the game, the child works on everyday language. The child hears commands to do something in the game for instance “take the green brush and paint the brown chair!” The player gets direct feedback about his or her action. If the command is misunderstood a friendly voice corrects the action. In this way the children learn the words and their meaning in everyday language. They hear, act and get a meaningful interaction.

Figure 2. Schlaumäuse central playground with Lolly and Pop

- **Phonemic awareness** (the recognition of sound): In another learning field the children learn phonological features with syllables and rhymes. They build words with two or three syllables by choosing the right syllables out of a group and arranging the syllables in the right order (figure 3: seesaw). If they cannot read the syllables they can still listen to them. In another challenge the player is a magician and conjures rhyming words.
- **Reading**: The children also learn to read words and sentences in the game. They have to combine a spoken word with a written one. In another task the player has to read and complete a sentence.
- **Alphabetic Principles**: In the Writing Workshop the player can write characters and words, then with the loudspeaker tool the child can listen to what was written. The learners thus begin to understand the correspondence between printed symbols and their associated sounds (phonemes).
- **Orthography**: Another part of the game trains the orthographic writing of words, with a task that requires the creation of letters and words.

The Computer as Learning Environment

The computer has special potential for language learning, which is used in Schlaumäuse:

- Memorizing spoken language is fostered by constant repetition of the words. The children can listen to the speech as often as they like. The computer is more patient in reading repeatedly than a grown-up can be. The articulation and pronunciation of the voice output in the learning game is very clear, consistent and grammatically correct.
- The children can also hear the silent scripts. The speech capabilities of the program allow young readers to access written work both visually and aurally. The player can listen to single characters, syllables or words and sentences.

Figure 3. Schlaumäuse seesaw

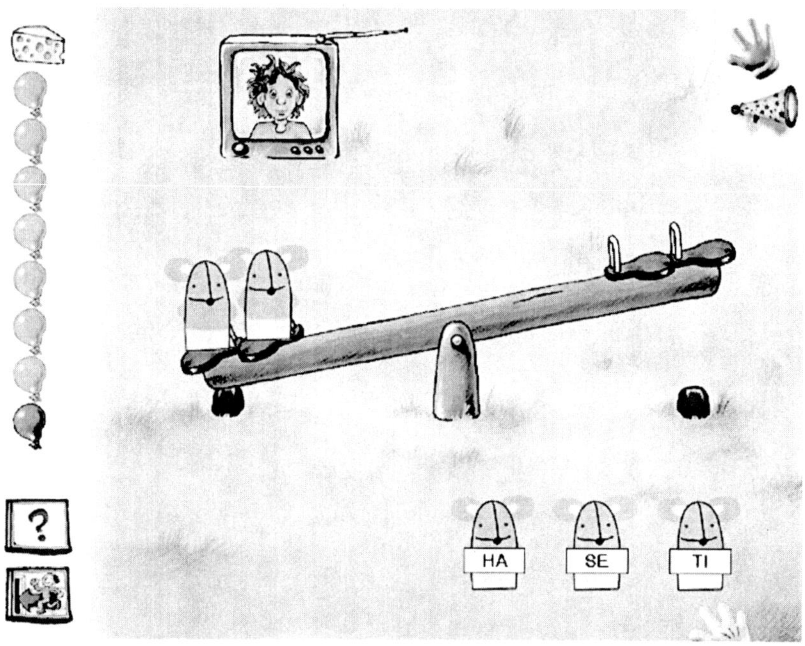

- Typing a character is easier for a child than writing a character with a pencil. In addition, it is easier to read typed letters than handwritten ones. The typed words can be printed and taken home to the child´s parents.
- The children can experiment with the text; they can delete, copy or insert new letters and words into the text and see what's happening with the words. They discover, for example, that the meaning of a word alters even if only one letter is changed.

PREPARATION PROGRAM FOR EARLY CHILDHOOD TEACHERS

The starting point for the development of the training program for kindergarten teachers has been the result of the research project "Blended Learning in the Kindergarten" (Pils & Pils, 2005). This project has shown that kindergarten teachers have little involvement with ICT during their preservice education and in their professional life. So the Schlaumäuse competence center was established to create a training program for early childhood teachers with the main focus on language learning with the Schlaumäuse learning game. A second focus is on technology enhanced learning in the Kindergarten in general (Schlaumäuse, 2009).

So the training program has been designed as one-day training in a group of eight to twelve learners. Kindergarten teachers with a class of children are the main target group of the program. Speech therapists and primary school teachers are welcome to the training, too. The training program is an elective course of the professional training of the kindergarten teachers offered by the institution of education. The size of the learning group is determined by the number of computers for the practical work with the learning game and the chance of exchange of experiences with the learning game and ICT in the kindergarten.

Traditionally, educators of young children have sought to promote social development by providing activities that encourage children to interact with one another and with adults. In all areas of development, children learn best through hands-on, real world interactions. However, the acceptance of technology enhanced learning in early childhood depends, amongst other things, on the technical background of the kindergarten teachers and given the traditional standards of preparation, there is often a prejudice against ICT in the kindergarten to avoid computer or game addiction (Bergmann & Hüther, 2006). Therefore one of the targets of the program is to get the kindergarten teachers familiar with ICT. We next recount the main line of the concerns and how we address them.

Levin and Rosenquest (2001) argue that early years educators should be concerned about the harmful effects of electronic toys and suggest that we "need to begin to develop strategies for stemming the tide as these toys flood homes and classrooms" (Levin et al, 2001, p. 245). They present a series of arguments to support their case, which focus on the supposed potential of electronic toys to create children who will become used to playthings which have pre-programmed responses and limited options, luring them away from more open-ended, non-electronic (and thus, they argue, more creative) toys (Levin et al, 2001). However we are living in a rapidly changing "landscape of communication" (Kress, 1998, p. 3). There is no doubt that technological developments in the latter part of the twentieth century have led to a paradigm shift in which familiarity with electronic and digital equipment is essential for successful engagement in both employment and leisure activities (Marsh, 2002).

In terms of social development, children need concrete experiences with peers and adults in order to learn (1) to differentiate themselves from others, (2) the social expectations that others hold, (3) how to resolve conflicts, and (4) how to participate as a member of a community. In her research Becigalupa (2005) found out that the interactions of the children while playing video games do not necessarily lead to the development of important social skills because the nature of the games preclude meaningful interactions and because the games distract all of the children from more beneficial activities.

Stephen, McPake, Plowman, and Berch-Heyman (2008) found in their work that most children were acquiring competencies with a range of technologies at home and that they enjoyed using both ICT and toys that are more traditional. The data gathered directly from the children endorsed this picture. The children sorted activities into 'happy day' and 'sad day' lists. Their choices suggest that the children enjoy physical activities outside and new technologies indoors. About half of the children selected swimming and playing in a garden or playground slide as activities, which would make them happy. Over two-thirds of the children placed the computer on the 'happy side' and over half made the same decision about television. Children like to play both traditional and electronic games.

Pedagogical questions such as these are part of the training program especially since they influence the way ICT is integrated into the classroom and how Schlaumäuse is used with children. Our trainers bring into the course their pedagogical experience with ICT in the kindergarten, with the message that technology enhanced learning changes the role of the kindergarten teacher: She or he has to arrange the basic conditions and to be the troubleshooter, if the children have problems with the PC or the software.

PRINCIPLES OF THE TRAINING PROGRAM

The main target of the training program is to develop the competences of the kindergarten teachers to improve their performance in both language teaching and ICT. The competences are a combination of knowledge, skills and attitudes for performing in the specific role of an early childhood educator. The process of competence development is a lifelong series of doing and reflecting. And it requires a special environment. The training program contains both doing and reflecting in a self-determined way.

In its most basic form learning is a self-regulated process powered by an individual's inborn motivation to assimilate and accommodate experiences (Piaget, 1992). This motivation is influenced by the individual's perceptions and beliefs about the value of the experience. Thus, the type of experiences to which the individual is exposed is a critical factor in learning. Learners should be provided opportunities to make choices and develop ownership of their own learning. Instruction should be organized to promote critical thinking (Malone, 2008). In this spirit, learners in the training program can choose in the second part of the training program which way they would prefer to learn about the game. The trainers are in the role of a respondent and a discussion partner.

Two trainers always attend the course. One of the trainers comes from the university and has the theoretical background about technology-enhanced learning. The other trainer is a kindergarten teacher, who has experience working with the children using the software. The connection between theory and practice is one of the bases of the training program.

The kindergarten teachers work in a familiar surrounding with the computer and with the learning game. In their everyday professional life in kindergarten they often have no time to work with a game. In the training, however, there is time to play the game in the same way the children play it. Additionally there is also time for reflection about the learning game and how it can be used with groups of children.

To support the children's language acquisition the kindergarten teacher has to know the part of the game with which the children can learn. The participants in the course create a pedagogical reflection about the different learning areas of the game.

The possibility for exchange of experiences and the building of networks is another basis of the training program. After the course the kindergarten teachers come together in meetings to discuss their experiences with the learning game. They also discuss technology-enhanced learning in the early childhood in general. Another form of communication is a discussion forum open for teachers who work with the Schlaumäuse learning game.

CURRICULUM OF THE TRAINING PROGRAM

Table 1 gives an overview to the curriculum of the training program. It is designed for an one-day training in groups of eight to twelve.

The curriculum of the schools providing vocational education of the kindergarten teachers does not contain any ICT. In Austria the prospective teachers attend vocational school between fourteen and nineteen and start afterward directly into their professional life. So, during their education and in their professional life, they have only little involvement with information technology. Thus, the curriculum contains technology education for the teachers. The goal of targeting this topic in the lesson is to enhance the computer literacy of the early-childhood educators (not only for language learning). One of the experiences of the training program is that about half of the teachers have only very limited knowledge of ICT.

The potentials of new media are another highlight of the training. The advantage of the media in the "Schlaumäuse" game is that the silent scripts can be heard. On the other hand memorizing the spoken language is fostered by constant repetition of the words. The teachers learn about the potentials of the new media for educational purposes.

In our training curriculum the kindergarten teachers get their hands on the game in a familiar situation and can learn to play the game in the way a child does. The learners play the different levels to get familiar with the progression of the game. The different levels of the learning game are suit-

Table 1. Curriculum of the training program: overview

Topic	Content, questions and tasks
Come together and warming up	What are the experiences with learning games? Do you use a computer in the kindergarten?
Computer in the kindergarten	Pedagogical consideration; experiences in the classes; technical hints.
Language development	Main steps on the way of language acquisition and first steps in writing.
Project "Schlaumäuse"	Targets of the project; outcomes of the studies.
The learning game "Schlaumäuse - Kinder entdecken Sprache"	Overview over the software, figures of and their role in the game; learning fields of language.
Hands on	"Play the game like a child!" Look for different ways and levels!
Analysis of the different activities in the game	Work in pairs and present the results!
Language development and specific activities of the game	Discussion; ideas, how to adopt the game in the class.
Networking	Further activities and meetings.

able for different phases of language acquisition. In the work with the children the teachers have to decide which part of the game is adequate for each child.

The next step of the training is to analyze the game according to the different phases of the language learning that are encouraged by the different parts of it. Consequently, the game can be applied to assist children in their specific development of their language learning. The pedagogical analysis of the learning game is the most important part of the curriculum. The learners work together in groups. Each group discusses and analyzes a learning field of the game. By this the learners can reflect on their own experience with the game. In the group they learn from each another and hear the opinions of the other members of the group. Each group presents their results of the discussion to the other groups. With this teaching method all participants can learn about the whole game.

The experience with our training program shows that the kindergarten teachers need assistance in introducing the game to their class of children. The training is a place where they exchange their points of view about the learning game and ICT in the kindergarten. In our training we have realized that the models of how to work with the computer and the learning game in the children's group are very different: from open access for most of the day to very restricted access only for a short period at a particular time.

The last part of the training is reserved for further activities. The early childhood teachers, who work with the Schlaumäuse learning game, work together in a community. They are very interested in the experiences of the other teachers about how to work with the game in the children's group. For further activities other learning games are fascinating. The work with ICT and new media is another absorbing topic for the kindergarten teachers.

IMPLEMENTATION

The Schlaumäuse competence center in Austria started its work in September of 2006. The training program began four months later. The number of participants of the training in this evaluation was 52. The evaluation methods included a group discussion at the end of the training day and a questionnaire with open questions. The participants in the trainings were mostly kindergarten teachers, with a few preschool teachers or speech therapists also attending. The feedback has been used to improve the content and the organization of the training and to develop new ideas for future activities of the competence center.

CONCLUSION

In the Schlaumäuse competence center one of the goals is to bring a language learning game to the kindergarten classes in Austria. To achieve this goal it is important not only to distribute the software but also to train the kindergarten teachers and to support them in their efforts to integrate the game in their everyday pedagogical life in the kindergarten. The positive experiences of other pedagogues in the kindergarten facilitate this introduction.

The kindergarten teachers in our training program generally accepted ICT in the kindergarten. However, they reported some discussions about this topic in their organizations in which not all colleagues accepted the computer as a meaningful learning medium for the children. In this atmosphere it is important to help the kindergarten teachers with positive examples.

As a result of the project, we discovered that the kindergarten teachers need some technology education to become competent using the ICT and the learning game. Participants with little technical expertise are more doubtful about the adoption of the game for their pedagogical work. If there are technical problems with the computer the teachers are frustrated very quickly. Therefore a basic competence in ICT is essential for a meaningful application of the learning game.

The high quality of the Schlaumäuse software initiates the discussion about the learning game in kindergarten. The pedagogical and the linguistic concept of the game is very sophisticated and this is important for work with young children.

To achieve a sustainable success with the Schlaumäuse learning game the training curriculum remains central. The constructive learning atmosphere is one of the supporting pillars of the acceptance of the learning game. The connection of theory and practical experience is the other. The feedback of the participants of the training confirms this statement about the curriculum.

FUTURE RESEARCH DIRECTIONS

The work in the Schlaumäuse competence center is ongoing. The kindergarten teachers are very interested in the trainings; the feedback of the trainings is very positive. Another focus of the work of the competence center is to support the communication and networking of the kindergarten teachers with ICT but this is a difficult task.

The future research activities analyze the different ways of adoption of the learning game to the children's groups and the factors for successfully in bringing the learning game to the children in a positive way. Another research project deals with the question how the learning game improves the media and ICT literacy of the children.

REFERENCES

Akcan, S. (2005). Supporting Oral Second Language Use: A Learning Experience in a First Grade German Immersion Class. *Early Childhood Education Journal*, *32*(6), 359–364. doi:10.1007/s10643-005-0005-7

Bacigalupa, C. (2005, August). The Use of Video Games by Kindergartners in a Family Child Care Setting. *Early Childhood Education Journal*, *33*(1), 25–30. doi:10.1007/s10643-005-0016-4

Bergmann, W., & Hüther, G. (2006). *Computersüchtig. Kinder im Sog der modernen Medien*. Düsseldorf: Walter Verlag.

Byrne, B. (1998). *The foundations of literacy: The child's acquisition of the alphabetic principle*. Hove, UK: Psychology Press.

California State Board of Education. (n.d.). *Kindergarten English-language arts content standards*. Retrieved June 19, 2009, from http://www.cde.ca.gov/be/st/ss/documents/elacontent-stnds.pdf

Caravolas, M., Hulme, C., & Snowling, M. G. (2001). The foundations of spelling ability: Evidence from a 3-year longitudinal study. *Journal of Memory and Language*, *45*, 751–774. doi:10.1006/jmla.2000.2785

Ehri, L. (1998). Learning to read and learning to spell are one and the same, almost. In Perfetti, C., Rieben, L., & Fayol, M. (Eds.), *Learning to spell* (pp. 237–269). Mahwah, NJ: Lawrence Erlbaum.

KidSmart. (2007). Retrieved March 13, 2009, from http://www.kidsmartearlylearning.org/

Kochan, B., & Schröter, E. (2006). Abschlussbericht über die Studie zur Microsoft Bildungsinitiative. *Schlaumäuse – Kinder entdecken Sprache*. ComputerLernWerkstatt an der Technischen Universität Berlin. Retrieved March 13, 2009, from http://www.schlaumaeuse.de/Informationen/Seiten/Mediathek.aspx

Kress, G. (1998). *Before Writing: rethinking the paths to literacy*. London: Routledge.

Leuckefeld, K. (2006). Der Erwerb sprachlicher Strukturen. In K. Jampert, K. Leuckefeld, A. Zehnbauer, & P. Best (Eds.), Sprachliche Förderung in der Kita. Wie viel Sprache steckt in Musik, Bewegung, Naturwissenschaften und Medien? (pp. 28-48). Berlin: Verlag das netz, Weimar.

Levin, D. E., & Rosenquest, B. (2001). The Increasing Role of Electronic Toys in the Lives of Infants and Toddlers: should we be concerned? *Contemporary Issues in Early Childhood*, *2*(2), 242–246. doi:10.2304/ciec.2001.2.2.9

Levin, I. (2007). The role of Hebrew letter names in early literacy: The case of multiphonemic acrophonic names. *Journal of Experimental Child Psychology*, *98*, 193–216.

Levin, I., Shatil-Carmon, S., & Asif-Rave, O. (2006). Learning of letter names and sounds and their contribution to word recognition. *Journal of Experimental Child Psychology*, *93*, 139–165. doi:10.1016/j.jecp.2005.08.002

Lim, C.-I., Maxwell, K. L., Able-Boone, H., & Zimmer, C. R. (2009). Cultural and linguistic diversity in early childhood teacher preparation: The impact of contextual characteristics on coursework and practica. *Early Childhood Research Quarterly*, *24*, 64–76. doi:10.1016/j.ecresq.2008.10.003

Malone, M. D. (2008). The Efficacy of Personal Learning Plans in Early Childhood Teacher Preparation. *Early Childhood Education Journal*, *36*, 47–56. doi:10.1007/s10643-008-0238-3

Marsch, J. (2002). Electronic Toys: why should we be concerned? A Response to Levin & Rosenquest (2001). *Contemporary Issues in Early Childhood*, *3*(1), 132–138. doi:10.2304/ciec.2002.3.1.3

Parette, H. P., Hourcade, J. J., Dinelli, J. M., & Boeckmann, N. M. (2009). Using Clicker 5 to Enhance Emergent Literacy in Young Learners. *Early Childhood Education Journal*, *36*, 355–363. doi:10.1007/s10643-008-0288-6

Piaget, J. (1992). *Einführung in die genetische Erkenntnistheorie* (5th ed.). Frankfurt am Main: Suhrkamp Taschenbuch Wissenschaft.

Pils, E., & Pils, M. (2005). Blended Learning im Kindergarten. In Auinger, A. (Ed.), *Oesterreichische Computer GesellschaftWorkshop-Proceedings der 5. fachübergreifenden Konferenz Mensch und Computer 2005* (*Vol. 197*, pp. 119–126).

Schlaumäuse. (2009). *Österrreichisches Schlaumäuse-Kompetenzzentrum*. Retrieved March 13, 2009, from http://www.idv.edu/schlau/schlau1.ssi

Stephen, C., McPake, J., Plowman, L., & Berch-Heyman, S. (2008). Learning from the children: exploring preschool children's encounters with ICT at home. *Journal of Early Childhood Research*, *6*, 99–117. doi:10.1177/1476718X08088673

Wasserman, L. H. (2007, June). The Correlation Between Brain Development, Language Acquisition, and Cognition. *Early Childhood Education Journal*, *34*(6), 415–418. doi:10.1007/s10643-007-0155-x

ADDITIONAL READING

Fthenakis, W. (2004). *Frühpädagogik international: Bildungsqualität im Blickpunkt*. Wiesbaden: VS Verlag.

Grüninger, C., & Lindemann, F. (2000). Vorschulkinder und Medien: Eine Untersuchung zum Medienkonsum von drei- bis sechsjährigen Kindern unter besonderer Berücksichtigung des Fernsehens. Wiesbaden: Leske + Budrich.

Holland, V. M. (2007). *The Path of Speech Technologies in Computer Assisted Language Learning: From Research Toward Practice*. New York: Routledge.

Kochan, B., & Schröter, E. (2006). *Abschlussbericht über die Studie zur Microsoft Bildungsinitiative "Schlaumäuse – Kinder entdecken Sprache."* ComputerLernWerkstatt an der Technischen Universität Berlin.

Saracho, O. N., & Spodek, B. (2008). *Contemporary perspectives on science and technology in early childhood education*. Charlotte, NC: Information Age Publishing.

Chapter 7
The Haunted School on Horror Hill:
A Case Study of Interactive Fiction in an Elementary Classroom

Kevin Kee
Brock University, Canada

Tamara Vaughan
The Western Quebec School Board, Canada

Shawn Graham
Grand Canyon University, USA

ABSTRACT

As gaming technology for personal computers has advanced over the last two decades, the text-adventures that predominated in the 1980s ceased to be commercially viable. However, the easy availability of powerful authoring systems developed by enthusiasts and distributed free over the Internet has led to a renaissance in text-adventures, now called "Interactive Fiction." The educational potential in playing these text-based games and simulations was recognised when they were first popular; the new authoring systems now allow educators to explore the educational potential of creating these works. The authors present here a case-study using the ADRIFT authoring system to create a work of interactive fiction in a split grade 4/5 class (9 and 10 year-olds) in Quebec. They find that the process of creating the game helped improve literary and social skills amongst the students.

INTRODUCTION

Advocates for so-called "serious games"[1], computer games that are played for purposes other than fun have made the case that computer gaming presents a novel way for students to learn (Chen and Michael, 2005). Not only do these games engage multiple learning styles (visual, auditory, kinaesthetic, and reading), but they also set the student up to participate in multiple cycles of "cognitive disequilibrium", in which the student forms a hypothesis (i.e., "what

DOI: 10.4018/978-1-61520-713-8.ch007

happens if...”), tests it, and revises (i.e., “oops, I lost the game when I did that–better try something else!”) (cf. Van Eck, 2006, p. 20).

We present here a case study in which we employed a specific genre of computer gaming (“interactive fiction” or “text adventure”) in an experiment to see whether it could enhance the literacy skills of students in a grade 4/5 split class (9 – 10 year olds). Text-adventure games were prominent in the 1980s, a time when computer graphics hardware and software were rather rudimentary. In this case study, the students created a text-adventure game and played it with younger students. The creation and playing of the game had enormous positive benefits for increased literacy skill. It also had the pleasant side effect of fostering class unity and improving the social skills of the students as they worked together to create the game.

We found five major benefits to incorporating interactive fiction in this classroom:

1. It increases student engagement with the lesson.
2. It meets the needs of various learning styles or “multiple intelligences”.
3. It provides opportunities for students to become leaders in the classroom.
4. It allows all learners to contribute and experience success
5. It allows students to take ownership of their learning.

It is important to note here that we did not simply load a work of interactive fiction onto a school”s computer lab computers and say, “Go play”. The role of the teacher in using interactive fiction is crucial. To understand the benefits and possibilities of using interactive fiction in the classroom, we must first understand what interactive fiction, and its predecessor, the text-adventure, is.

THE PREHISTORY OF COMPUTER GAMES

Text-adventure computer games had their origins in the 1975 main-frame computer game *Colossal Cave* (Montfort, 2003, p. 85-93), also known as *Adventure*. *Colossal Cave* was a room-by-room description of a cave system near the author’s home in Kentucky. In its earliest forms, a player could only move through the rooms using the cardinal directions, or by typing “up” or “down”. It was not so much a game as a *simulation* of a particular environment, albeit one described in text. When *Colossal Cave* began to be widely distributed, other programmers added characters into it. The ability to pick up or use particular objects, in particular ways, was added. Perhaps the earliest non-player character to gain fame in the computer gaming world was the “Thief”, who would follow the player around, occasionally pick-pocketing items from the player, just when the player needed them most.

As text adventures grew more complex and more popular, they became increasingly sophisticated. They could accept a wider vocabulary of words, and syntax that was more complicated. The computer “parser”, the interface between the player and the world being simulated, also grew more sophisticated in its interactions with the player. Typing “go north and get the hammer” might be met with the response “I can’t go north, and anyway, what do you want with a hammer?”. Notice the “I”. In the game, other non-player characters always interacted with “you”: “The thief tells you, ‘I only need a few more coins and I can retire!’ But when the player tried to do something that the game did not allow, this omnipresent “I” would come to the fore. It was as if the parser was a kind of homunculus in the player’s head, at least when the player was embodied in the world. This shifting viewpoint within the fiction, though complex, is a useful jumping-off point for discussing point-of-view and narrative structure in fiction more generally, because it confronts the student with the problem of determining "Who is doing the action?"

FROM TEXT ADVENTURES TO INTERACTIVE FICTION

With the collapse of Infocom, the main publisher of these kinds of games, text adventures steadily declined in popularity and commercial viability in the 1990s.[2] The collapse, however, corresponded with the dawn of the World Wide Web, which allowed enthusiastic gamers to connect, swap games, types, and strategies. This nascent community also fostered a number of individuals who did not want just to *play* text adventures; they wanted to *write* them. Talented programmers opened up the world of interactive fiction to the masses by creating a kind of word-processor programme for writing text-adventures; to play or read a work of interactive fiction requires another piece of software, an interpreter (often called a z-machine, after the interpreter used and developed by Infocom).

Thus was born the Interactive Fiction Competition.[3] In a sense, the lack of a commercial interest in text adventures allowed the writers of text games to broaden their horizons, and to experiment and push the format. Indeed, the phrase "text adventure" has now largely been superseded by "interactive fiction". This new concept points to the literary aspirations of the best of the new creators – that the computer would merely provide the setting (the simulated world); the playing of the game would in fact be an act of *writing*. By performing the game, the player – the reader – creates her own narrative, her own story, which (in the best works) only happens once. The winner of the 2006 competition, *Galatea*, by Emily Short,[4] would not be recognizable to the players of *Colossal Cave* or *Adventure*; in *Galatea* all of the action takes place in a single room in a museum after a reception. The reader – the player – is admiring a statue of Galatea when the statue suddenly comes to life. The story emerges from the dialogue between the reader and Galatea. Depending on the kinds of questions and comments made by the player, very different trajectories may be charted. No more puzzles, thieves, or cave-trolls. Galatea is a very different creation, a work of interactive literature. Interactive Fiction may be gaining academic respectability as an area worthy of literary criticism. A group blog, "Grand Text Auto", devoted to "computer narrative, games, poetry, and art" is written by prominent "new media" academics and frequently highlights innovations (both technological and literary) in the genre.[5] A recent Ph.D. thesis studied interactive fiction in terms of its literary qualities, including its use of language structures, its narrative structures, and its "filmic representations" (Douglass, 2007).[6]

The interactivity inherent to this genre of game and literature is especially attractive to students. Students are used to playing computer games. In many games today, the player can go almost anywhere within the simulated world; in the jargon, these are games "without rails". Similarly, these students grew up immersed in the Internet, where anything is just a click away. Television similarly panders to shortened attention spans through its multiplicity of channels. It is not surprising then that some of our students have difficulty focusing on a book for longer than five minutes at a time. What does a book offer? It offers a simulated world, in text, on the page. However, with the exception of the "Choose your own adventure!" books (cf. Packard, 1987), there is only one start point, and one finish point, and the reader is at the mercy of the author. Books are "on rails". Interactive fiction overcomes what, to some of our students, would appear to be the shortcomings of the traditional book.

INTERACTIVE FICTION IN THE CLASSROOM

In its first great hay-day in the 1980s, interactive fiction was *the* computer game that everyone was playing. Early enthusiasts for the power of computer mediated game-based learning immediately latched onto the possibilities offered by the new medium. A study published in 1986 explored whether or not the "quests" offered by the text-adventures then commercially available would foster engagement with written texts, i.e., whether playing a game would turn reluctant readers into voracious ones (Lancy and Hayes, 1986). These investigators were interested in creating an anthology of games to target particular reading or grade levels. Lancy and Hayes write,

We believe that students are more likely to become fluent readers if they are exposed to "real" texts written for real purposes and that are highly motivating and interesting to children. We believe that interactive fiction could offer students who are reluctant readers a new motivation and interest to use their reading ability for personal satisfaction (p. 8).

Puzzles are a hallmark of interactive fiction. For Lancy and Hayes, it is the number, quality, and quantity of puzzles that really drive the engagement with the texts. Later researchers call this "flow" (Csikszentmihalyi, 1991), where the challenges of the game are just a little bit beyond the player's ability, but not so far as to discourage her from playing. It is the flow that drew the students into the games in 1986, causing them to read for hours at a time (Lancy and Hayes, 1986). If the puzzles were too difficult, the player would quit the game in disgust. However, if they were able to solve the puzzle, the "buzz" at driving the story forward would keep them enthralled with the game/story (Lancy and Hayes, 1986 found it helped to have a facilitator on hand who could offer hints to get through the toughest puzzles).

From the point of view of developing literacy skills, one of the aspects of these games that caught the attention of the early researchers was the extremely structured relationship between the player and the computer parser. That is, the more complicated the game, the more complicated the sentences that a player could type in and that the computer could understand. These researchers felt this constrained the student players and forced them to clarify their thoughts and to learn to communicate effectively, although it could be a source of frustration for the players (pp. 5-6). In a later article, Lancy and Hayes suggest different models for incorporating interactive fiction into the classroom, including using various programmes for *writing* interactive fiction, as part of creative writing classes (Lancy and Hayes, 1988, p. 46).

In the 1980s, it was easy enough to persuade students to play (and read) interactive fiction, as it was the dominant gaming paradigm on the computers available in classrooms. After this first wave of enthusiasm, and with the emergence of better and faster graphics-rendering, text-adventures became passé. However, as text-adventures became the purview of a dedicated group of enthusiasts, and the literary qualities of the best work became better known, better and easier tools for creating interactive fiction became easily and freely accessible. Today's students might be too sophisticated for playing a text-adventure; but with modern gaming comes the "modding ethos", the desire to modify and change the games. This creative urge is what we hoped to channel in our case study using interactive fiction for developing literacy skills.

WRITING INTERACTIVE FICTION

In the same way a person might use a word-processor to write a novel, and some word-processors are more powerful/more user-friendly than others, there are a number of programmes available (with similar levels of ease of use) for generating interactive fiction,[7] for reading or playing on a number of devices. These authoring systems let the writer focus on the story and its branching structure without having to worry about operating systems, or other technical problems.

The three most common authoring systems are Inform (Nelson, 2008),[8] TADS (Text Adventure Development System) (Roberts, 2006),[9] and ADRIFT (Adventure Development and Runner Interactive Fiction Toolkit) (Wild, 2008).[10] The three are distinguished by how they approach the task of modeling a world, and agency within that world (both the agency of the player, and the agency of non-player characters within the game). Inform uses a powerful interpreter to parse written text to create the game. In Inform, one could write,

The Kitchen is a room north of the Library. "The smell of rancid bacon stains everything in this kitchen, which, by the look of it, has not been cleaned in some time."

The authoring system will understand that the Kitchen and the Library are places to which the player may go. The first time the player arrives in the Kitchen, the parser will display the description. This system similarly interprets player commands, and understands what to do as the situation within the game changes. Writing an interactive fiction in Inform is very close to writing a story in a word processor. TADS, on the other hand, is much more like a computer programming language (indeed, TADS is built on the C+ language). Its input looks like this:

```
Startroom: room
Sdesc = "In the kitchen"
Ldesc = "The smell of rancid
bacon stains everything in this
kitchen, which, by the look of
it, has not been cleaned in some
time."
South = Library
```

Of these three systems, ADRIFT is probably the easiest one in which a beginner might generate a playable fiction. ADRIFT is a Windows-based menu- and icon-driven program. Adding a room or location to the game is achieved simply by clicking on the "add room" button, filling in the description, and clicking on the other locations to create links between them. Adding objects or other characters is similarly menu-driven.

In our case study, we explored both Inform and ADRIFT, with the intention of getting the students to do the actual programming themselves. While Inform certainly lends itself to what is more recognisable as writing, we felt that ADRIFT was more suitable for the students to use in this first experiment, given the level of literacy skills in the group.

YOU ARE STANDING IN THE HALLWAY. THERE IS A CLASSROOM DOOR BEFORE YOU. THERE IS A KEY HERE.

Our case study was lead in the classroom by Tamara Vaughan, a grade 4/5 teacher at St. John's Elementary School, in Campbell's Bay, Quebec, a rural community approximately 80 kilometres north-west of Ottawa, Ontario. Tamara has developed a specialization in the use of technology in the classroom and in distance learning. Before the first session, we prepared a "starter game" to model what interactive fiction was (or could be), and to get the students used to the idea. We told the students, "we're going to be making a video game" (to great cheers) "and it's going to be a text adventure" (to great moans). Upon further querying, it became apparent that the students did not know what a text adventure was (it was almost as if they had a conditioned response to the word "text" (it must be awful, whatever it is!). The classroom that we were in was equipped with a "Smart Board",[11] a digital white board onto which the teacher, Tamara, could project the "starter game". The setting for the starter game (or starter story) was in that class's room. When the students

Figure 1. A game being made in ADRIFT

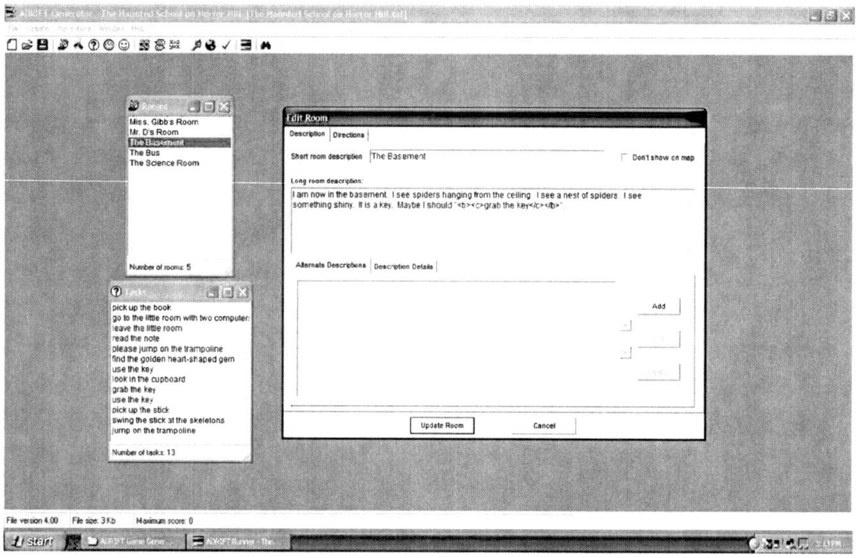

read the text aloud, and discovered that the setting for the story was *in their own room*, they became excited. Their interest was heightened when the teacher selected students to go up to the board and type in commands. These students enjoyed using the Smart Board, so the selection of students was a useful management technique for the teacher. As different students tried to input commands, others in the class would offer suggestions, or corrections. In short order the whole class was deeply engrossed in the game.

The experience with the starter game illustrates the power of games-for-learning. The students would engage with the material, try different approaches, and modify their actions based on what they had learned. Being able to understand the situation presented by the game successfully and to discover an appropriate response gave the students a sense of accomplishment. Just as important, failure to type in the correct response was not viewed as a failure, but as part of the process of winnowing out options. The teacher had the students break into groups to write possible endings for the starter story. Then, using the ADRIFT game generator, the teacher and students were able to incorporate the new endings, allowing the students to play them quite soon after they were written. As a class, they voted for the endings that they liked best.

In the next session, the teacher told the class that the game that they would be making would be for a class of younger students (a split grade 2/3 class of seven- to eight-year-olds, who required simple or small words). This had the advantage of giving the grade 4/5 students, many of whom often felt marginalized, a sense of confidence and importance: they were helping the teachers "teach the smaller kids". The grade 4/5 students with lower levels of literacy (as determined by standardised testing) did not feel embarrassed because they were working with younger children who were even weaker readers and writers. The teacher organized the class into groups of four or five students and each student was assigned a role within the group (timekeeper, task master, writer, scene setter). The only boundaries set for the story was that it had to take place within the school or its grounds, and it had to consider the reading abilities of the audience (i.e., the younger children). Each group worked on a particular room for some aspect of the adventure. They answered such questions as "What does the room look like?"

Figure 2. "The Haunted School on Horror Hill", early play-through

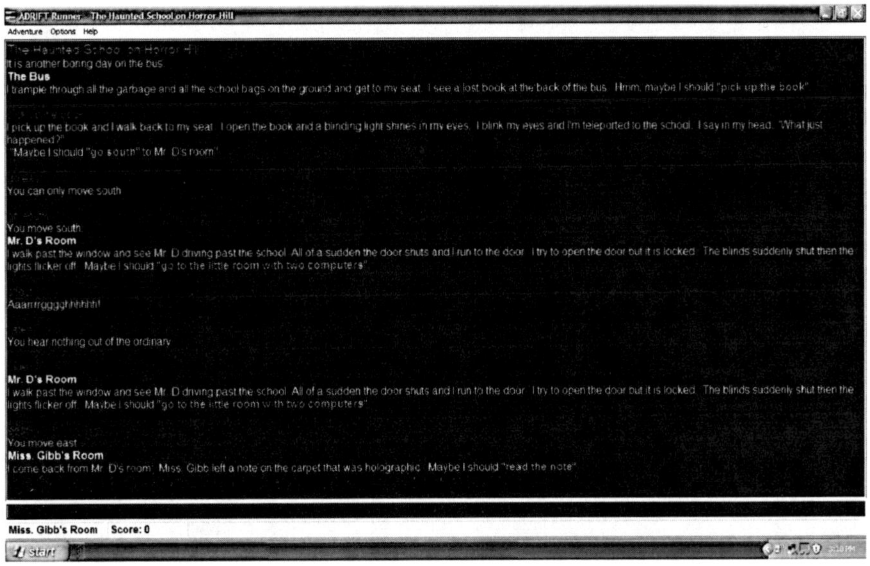

"What will happen in this room?" etc. This collaborative work was done with pencil and paper, followed by students" swapping their work with each other for editing.

In most cases, the editing process substantially improved the descriptions of each room (although one group, upon receiving the edited version of their room, proceeded to erase the changes in an effort to return their story to its original state). The students reported that they found it easier to pick up spelling and grammatical errors when working as a group. The weaker students found that they learned from the stronger students without feeling inadequate, since the task and the group made the process safe. The class as a whole took the editing process seriously, because they knew that anything they did would be visible to the children in grade 2/3.

As a class, they discussed what they thought should be allowed to happen in the story. They held a secret ballot, with the winning ideas forming the meta-structure of the story. This allowed the teacher to discuss the mechanics of fiction (plotting, characterizations, and voice) with a group that had never before been able to maintain such a discussion. In a nice touch, the winning plot was interactive itself: a student finds an unusual book on the school bus, starts to read it, and discovers himself becoming part of its story.

The students then connected the different rooms using the ADRIFT software. The class then played the completed game so that the students could see where they needed to edit the language to make the flow of the story feel more natural. In order to present the game to the younger students, the class decided that when the story progressed to a room that a particular group had made, that group would become responsible for the presentation. This had the added benefit of improving the student's public speaking skills. At this point, the students became concerned that their story did not have a suitable title. Again, secret balloting was used to select from competing ideas. Each student recorded his or her idea for a title on a piece of paper, and the teacher read each title aloud. Then, on another piece of paper, the students recorded three choices. The one with the majority won. The process was democratic, but more remarkable was that the class voted for the title written by a girl whose verbal contributions in class were often shouted down with "stupid!" or "nobody likes you so we don't want to hear you". The winning choice: *The Haunted School on Horror Hill.*

The day came to present the interactive story to the grade 2/3 class. The teacher again made the presentation using a Smart Board. Each group selected a presenter, and a person to type the younger students' responses on the computer. The presenter became a teacher responsible for explaining how the software worked and how to interact with the game's parser. The typist was responsible for typing *exactly* what the younger students requested (including spelling mistakes). The younger students were amazed at what the older students had created. They even rewarded them with a spontaneous round of applause. The older students were proud of their creation, requesting copies on CD-ROM so that they could teach their parents to play.

BENEFITS

In terms of literacy benefits, the game/story/interactive fiction makes a virtue out of what is often a frustrating aspect of the computer: it responds to exactly what you have typed or commanded, and not what you intended. The story cannot progress if even one letter is mistyped (although it can be programmed to respond with helpful hints when common mistakes are made). This requires that students take their time and repeatedly spell high frequency words perfectly. In addition, playing the game is fun so reading, which for many of these students is a very frustrating, unrewarding experience, became fun. Creating and playing the game placed the students in a leadership role. Students wanted to help each other within the group setting, so that they could complete the story and play the game. The stronger students helped the weaker students to spot and understand errors of grammar. When presenting and playing the game, the older students helped the younger students to understand the story and move the narrative forward. They also helped the younger students to read each section and spell words correctly.

DRAWBACKS

For this project, a facilitator managed the programming tasks, while the teacher managed the student side. The immediate drawback to incorporating interactive fiction into the classroom is that, despite the advent of ADRIFT or Inform, learning how to create a working game is a laborious process. On the other hand, it took us approximately four or five hours of working with the programme to create the simple "starter" game – learning how to create a PowerPoint presentation, or Word document, would take a similar amount of time. Moreover, the community of writers and creators of interactive fiction are supportive, for the most part, and willing to offer tips and to get the novice up to speed (many websites may be found at *The Brass Lantern*).[12] Also, many works are available with their source version (not just the playable/readable version) on the Internet at the *Interactive Fiction Archive*,[13] so it is possible to see how the creator put the game together and how to mimic or alter the original work.

The most significant issue we encountered was keeping the students focused and on-task. We found that blocks of 30 to 45 minutes at a time worked best. The project took about three weeks of class time, for an hour and a half each morning. *The Haunted School on Horror Hill* required another four or five hours to stitch together the students' work. More advanced classes might want to pass the majority of this stage on to the students themselves.

THE QUEBEC EDUCATION PROGRAM AND CROSS-CURRICULAR COMPETENCIES

Our work here is applicable to almost any classroom, a hypothesis that we will test when we use interactive fiction in a grade 10 (15- to 16-year-olds) "History of Quebec and Canada" class to teach historical literacy and how to evaluate historical documents. However, we undertook this project in the context of the Quebec Education Program (QEP) (Government of Quebec, Ministry of Education).[14] The QEP requires that learners meet certain goals that map across different curricula. A class project should therefore meet the goals of different subject domains. Of the official "Cross-Curricular Competencies", this interactive fiction project met the following:

Cross-curricular competency #3: To exercise critical judgement

- To articulate and communicate his/her viewpoint
- To justify his/her position with reasons and arguments
    - (When working in a group, students were encouraged to be articulate and to be concise to help other group members understand their point of view.)
    - (Students had to convince their group members that their ideas were important through justifying why these ideas should be used in their group's room.)

Cross-curricular competency #4: To use creativity

- To become actively involved in the process
    - (Students were excited about the project, thus this was never a difficult task to achieve.)
- To accept risks and unknowns
    - (Most students in this class did not like to take risks. Through working in groups, the responsibility was shared so students found it easier to take risks.)
- To persevere in exploring
    - (These students tended to give up when answers were not readily in front of them. The knowledge that someone else was relying on their work pushed students to persevere.)
- To be receptive to new ideas and ways of doing things
    - (Students were very open to this project because they have experience with video games.)

Cross-curricular competency #6: To use information and communications technologies (ICT)

- To explore the potential of ICT for a given task
    - (Through creating their text adventure, students in the 4/5 class were able to explore the possible uses of ADRIFT interactive fiction software.)
    - (Students came up with endless suggestions for creating stories later.)

Cross-curricular competency #8: To cooperate with others

- To participate actively in classroom and school activities with a cooperative attitude
- To plan and carry out a task with others
- To carry out the task according to the procedure agreed on by the team
    - (The very nature of this project demanded that students become active participants, that they work together to plan out their group's chapter, and that they stick to their assigned task.)

Cross-curricular competency #9: To communicate appropriately

- To consider the purpose of the communication and identify the recipients
- To explore ideas related to the situation
  - (As a group, the students decided they wanted to present to the grade 2/3 class.)
  - (Students created and presented the story according to the learning abilities of the grade 2/3 class.)

CONCLUSION

The use of interactive fiction resulted in a substantial difference in the literacy and social skills of this class of students. During this project, we scraped the surface of what could be accomplished in terms of narrative complexity, branching structure, and indeed, in the representation of a game on the computer.

Our experience should demonstrate the potential of using the conventions of computer games to enhance the learning of our students. In using a game technology that the commercial world now regards as obsolete, we were able to concentrate on the substance of the learning in a novel and engaging way that resonated with our students. As one of the students said about regular computer games after the project was over, "y'know, sometimes, graphics get in the way".

REFERENCES

Chen, S., & Michael, D. (2005). Proof of Learning: Assessment in Serious Games. *Gamasutra.* Retrieved December 20, 2008, from http://www.gamasutra.com/features/20051019/chen_01.shtml

Csikszentmihalyi, M. (1991). *Flow: The Psychology of Optimal Experience.* New York: Harper Perennial.

Douglass, J. (2007). *Command lines: Aesthetics and technique in interactive fiction and new media.* Dissertation, University of California, Santa Barbara.

Government of Quebec, Ministry of Education. (2001) *Quebec Education Program: Approved Version.* Retrieved March 27, 2009 from http://www.mels.gouv.qc.ca/DGFJ/dp/programme_de_formation/primaire/ educprg2001h.htm

Lancy, D. F., & Hayes, B. L. (1986). Building an Anthology of "Interactive Fiction." *Report: ED275991.*

Lancy, D. F., & Hayes, B. L. (1988). Interactive Fiction and the Reluctant Reader. *English Journal, 77*(7), 42-66. Retrieved March 26, 2009, from http://www.jstor.org/stable/818936

Montfort, N. (2003). *Twisty Little Passages: An Approach to Interactive Fiction.* Cambridge, MA: MIT Press.

Nelson, G. (2008). *Inform 7 – A Design System for Interactive Fiction Based on Natural Language.* Retrieved from http://www.inform-fiction.org/I7/Welcome.html

Packard, E. B. (1987, October). Interactive Fiction for Children: Boon or Bane? *School Library Journal*, , 40–41.

Roberts, M. J. (2006) *TADS – Text Adventure Development System.* Retrieved March 27, 2009, from http://www.tads.org

Van Eck, R. (2006, March/April). Digital Game-Based Learning: It's Not Just the Digital Natives Who Are Restless. *EDUCAUSE Review, 41*(2), 16–30.

Wild, C. (2008). *ADRIFT – Adventure Development and Runner – Interactive Fiction Toolkit.* Retrieved from http://www.adrift.org.uk

ADDITIONAL READING

Blogs and online magazines that frequently cover the educational potentials and pitfalls of interactive fiction (and video games more generally) include:

On the evolution of the genre and its literary possibilities: Douglass, J. (2007). *Command Lines: Aesthetics and technique in interactive fiction and new media*. Dissertation. University of California, Santa Barbara, CA. Retrieved from http://jeremydouglass.com/dissertation.html

Grand Text Auto. (n.d.). Retrieved from http://grandtextauto.org

Montfort, N. (2003). *Twisty Little Passages: An Approach to Interactive Fiction*. Cambridge, MA: MIT Press.

On writing interactive fiction: Nelson, G. (2001). The Craft of Adventure. In *The Inform Designer's Manual, 4th Edition (Inform 6)*. Retrieved from www.inform-fiction.org/manual/html/ch8.html

Short, E. (n.d.). *Writing IF*. Retrieved from http://emshort.wordpress.com/writing-if

The Escapist. (n.d.). Retrieved from http://escapistmagazine.com

OTHER THOUGHT-PROVOKING WORKS

Baltra, A. (1990). Language Learning through Computer Adventure Games. *Simulation & Gaming*, *21*(4), 445–452. doi:10.1177/104687819002100408

Blanchard, J. S., & Mason, G. E. (1985). Using Computers in Content Area Reading Instruction. *Journal of Reading*, *29*(2), 112–117.

Clement, J. (1994). Fiction interactive et modernité [Interactive fiction and modernity]. *Littérature*, (96), 19-36.

Howell, G., & Douglas, J. Y. (1990). The Evolution of Interactive Fiction. *Computer Assisted Language Learning*, *2*, 93–109. doi:10.1080/0958822900020108

Marcus, S. (1985 November). Computers in Thinking, Writing, and Literature. *Report: ED266468.*

McVicker, J. (1992). Several Approaches to Computer-Based Reading Study. *CAELL Journal*, *3*(4), 2–11.

Newman, J. M. (1988). Online: Write Your Own Adventure. *Language Arts*, 65.

Niesz, A. J., & Holland, N. N. (1984). Interactive Fiction. *Critical Inquiry Chicago*, *11*(1), 110–129. doi:10.1086/448277

Pea, R. D., & Kurland, D. M. (1987). Chapter 7: Cognitive Technologies for Writing. *Review of Research in Education*, *14*(1), 277–326. doi:10.3102/0091732X014001277

Sampson, F. (1987). Interactive Fiction: An Experience of the "Writers in Education" Scheme. *Children's Literature in Education*, 18.

Tavinor, G. (2005). Videogames and Interactive Fiction. *Philosophy and Literature*, *29*(1), 24–40. doi:10.1353/phl.2005.0015

Thomas, S. (2006). Pervasive learning games: Explorations of hybrid educational gamescapes. *Simulation & Gaming*, *37*(1), 41–55. doi:10.1177/1046878105282274

KEY TERMS AND DEFINITIONS

Authoring System: A computer program used to create a work of interactive fiction.

Games Off Rails *or* **Open-World Games:** Games where the player may explore any aspect of the game world, without guidance by the game designer.

Games on Rails: Games where the sequence of interactions is plotted out precisely by the game designer.

Interactive Fiction: Often used interchangeably with 'text adventure', it refers more broadly to works of computer simulation delivered via written prose that may or may not contain 'adventuring' components.

Interpreter: A computer program used to interact with a work of interactive fiction.

Parser: The game entity that describes the world of the interactive fiction to the player; most often encountered explicitly by the player when the player gives an instruction not understood by the game: "I don't know how to x,y,z!".

Text Adventure: A computer simulation delivered via written prose, a kind of interactive fiction, where the "interactor controls a player character who sets out on out-of-the-ordinary undertakings involving risk or danger" (Montfort, 2003, p.6)

Chapter 8
Use of Interactive Online Games in Teaching English as a Foreign Language

Hoe Kyeung Kim
Cleveland State University, USA

ABSTRACT

The purpose of this study is to examine how the use of multiplayer English teaching online games influences students' self-efficacy and their English performance scores. The participants of this study were sixty elementary students in Korea. They were selected based on the scores on the social-affective value test and then divided into two groups-high and low groups. During five weeks, the participants played with an English teaching online game two hours per week. The students' self-efficacy scores were collected before and after they played the online game. Their English performance scores on the online game were collected to compare the two groups. The findings indicated that their online game experience increased self-efficacy. Interestingly, students with low social-affective values showed more improvement than those with high social-affective values in both self-efficacy and performance scores.

INTRODUCTION

Today many young people spend much of their time on computers and online games. With this trend, online gaming has attracted the interest of educators and researchers (Godwin-Jones, 2005). A growing number of educators and researchers believe that the use of online games can induce student motivation and engagement in their learning process. For instance, online games promote students' socializing skills (Shimai, Masuda & Kishimoto, 1990; Steinkuehler, 2006) and language skills (Meskill, 2005) through collaboration among multi-players. In spite of its popularity among young learners, there is little empirical study done on the educational benefits of online games in language education.

One of the difficulties that English as a foreign language (EFL) learners face is limited opportunities to use and practice the target language. Interaction and communication is a key requirement for learning a language. In an EFL setting, lack of interaction often fails to promote student engage-

DOI: 10.4018/978-1-61520-713-8.ch008

ment and their self-efficacy in communicating in the target language. As multiplayer games promote learners' collaboration and their application of learned knowledge in real-world settings (DeKanter, 2004), the use of interactive games will benefit EFL students in learning English. There is a need for examining whether the use of interactive online games improves EFL students' self-efficacy and their English skills and whether the experience of online games relates to students' social-affective values.

LITERATURE REVIEW

In the current study, I define social-affective values as self-esteem, self-efficacy, risk taking, anxiety and extroversion/introversion. The interactive online game used in this study is one of the English teaching online games where multiple players participate in a given cyberspace simultaneously.

INTERACTIVE GAMES AND EFL LANGUAGE LEARNING

Meaningful and authentic interaction is an essential element in language learning (Ellis, 1985; Gass, 1997; Gass, MacKey & Pica, 1998; Hall & Verplaetse, 2000). Input, interaction and the creation of output in authentic contexts should be a major component of activities in a second or foreign language context. An assumption underlying the use of interactive games in language education is that they will create an environment for promoting this type of interaction among students and will provide an opportunity to apply their language knowledge into a real situation. As language knowledge includes two categories, organizational knowledge and pragmatic knowledge (Bachman, 1990), the major aim of the use of technology in language education is to generate many different environments for interaction and the negotiation of meaning. In the case of EFL settings where students lack an opportunity to practice their target language, the potential advantage of using online games is great.

Multiplayer online games can promote student motivation, increase communication, and encourage collaboration among participating students. Brown (2007) stated that computers can provide a convenient venue to practice the target language, support multimodal practices (auditory, visual and written), and promote the fun factor. Although interactive online games could offer many useful tools for language learning and teaching, most of studies related to online games have focused on vocabulary teaching (e.g., Huyen & Nga, 2003; Yip & Kwan, 2006). Especially in EFL settings, multiplayer English teaching online games which promote interaction and communication will provide meaningful and authentic learning tasks for EFL learners. As Sharrock and Watson (1987) stated, simulation and gaming could provide practice of real-world communication that EFL classes are lacking.

The use of interactive games has an impact on the meaning of interactivity for learning (DeKanter, 2004). He explained that the elements of interactive game playing-- that is, adaptivity, competition and communication-- overlap with the traits of successful students. After investigating the use of educational games, Wood (2001) concluded that students paid more attention to learning materials that use game-like formats than traditional learning materials such as textbooks.

SELF-EFFICACY AND SOCIAL-AFFECTIVE FACTORS IN LANGUAGE LEARNING

In language education, it is important to understand how language learners feel and how they respond to learning a target language. A large number of variables are involved in the affective domain during the language learning process. The affective domain refers to how students' social and emotional personality traits affect their language learning. Brown (2007) said the self-efficacy and social-affective factors are closely related to student motivation. Among other factors, student motivation is one of the strongest indicators of language success.

Task-based activities have been popular by language educators because they promote student motivation through authentic interaction. Language tasks are activities that involve individual learners in using the target language for the purpose of achieving a particular goal or objective in a particular situation (Bachman & Palmer, 1996). The tasks-based learning promotes conversational adjustments and interactional modifications on the part of the learners, which advance learners' language acquisition. In EFL settings, the task-based approach has been welcomed to language teaching for its usefulness as it focuses on authentic use of the target language.

Bandura (1977) stated that self-efficacy measures in academic areas operate on the belief that learners can successfully accomplish a performance to produce a desired outcome. If a learner feels a high sense of self-efficacy in language learning, he or she may be devoted to achieving success in learning the target language. In other words, students are actively engaged in their learning activities as they increase self-efficacy. Thus, it is important to develop high levels of self-efficacy in language learners during the process of language learning.

Equally important as self-efficacy, creating an environment where learners feel comfortable as they learn a foreign language is critical. As Dufeu (1994) argued, learners need to feel accepted and encouraged to participate in the learning process. He adds that it is also important for learners to take risks without feeling embarrassed. Heyde's (1979) study on self-esteem and oral production task also reported a strong correlation between task self-esteem and production measure. However, being willing to take a risk in learning a foreign language is a necessity trait. Considering the importance of interaction in language learning, those students who are reserved and afraid to make mistakes do not have the ideal attitude of the successful language learner. The fact that self-esteem is closely connected to a risk-taking factor seems to be somewhat conflicting. Students who have high self-esteem do not want to take risks and lose face. Therefore, in this paper, task self-esteem, would refer to learners' self-evaluation of a particular skill or a class or learning activity (Brown, 2007).

ONLINE GAMES, SELF-EFFICACY, AND SOCIAL-AFFECTIVE FACTORS

In the past, the most popular hypothesis regarding online games was that online games have a negative influence on children's social skills (Lee & Peng, 2006). The negative image was associated with online game playing because children who play games mostly played alone at home. However, a study in Japan reported that children who played games developed higher sociability than children who were non-players (Shimai, Masuda, & Kishimoto, 1990). Following this finding, Durkin and Barber (2002) reported that compared to low players, non-players did not score high on any measure of self-esteem and academic performance. A moderate amount of game playing is beneficial to academic performance. Lee and Peng (2006) explained that playing games improved students' sociability because it allowed students to exchange their gaming experience with peers both face-to-face and through the Internet.

In general, educational benefits of computer games are immersion, flow and intrinsic motivation (Lee & Peng, 2006). Although the effectiveness of computer games needs to be discussed with a specific target subject, there is general consensus, that is, students playing online games tend to exhibit their active engagement and satisfaction. In particular, introverted students seem to favor online learning. Roberts, Smith, and

Pollock (2000) found that shy students reported decreased inhibition and less shyness in the online environment. Overbaugh and Lin (2004) compared student achievement in both face-to-face and online environments and reported that introverted students performed better in online environments than extroverted students. The implication of these studies is that low social-affective students may benefit from the online learning environment.

Many games and simulations are designed to create low anxiety environments that foster positive affective learning atmospheres and allow players to try new behavioral patterns with a minimum of stress. For instance, avatar-mediated plays and role-playing games can promise the anonymity of players. Roed (2003) suggested that virtual environments might constitute a more relaxed and stress-free atmosphere than classroom settings. The low level of inhibition and anxiety in virtual environments is beneficial for language learners. It is believed that educational online games might provide a setting where both introverted and extroverted students might benefit from playing games while they are interacting with the peers to accomplish the given tasks.

RESEARCH HYPOTHESES

In this current study, the impact of online game on learners' self-efficacy and language learning was examined. The following three hypotheses were developed based on the research question.

- **Hypothesis 1:** There is a difference in the impact of online game on high and low social-affective students' self-efficacy.
- **Hypothesis 1a:** There is a difference in the impact of online gaming on high and low social-affective students' task self-esteem values
- **Hypothesis 1b:** There is a difference in the impact of online gaming on high and low social-affective students' risk-taking values.
- **Hypothesis 2:** There is a difference in the impact of online gaming on high and low social-affective students' English performance scores.

METHODOLOGY

A t-test was conducted to compare a difference of the impact of online gaming on high and low social-affective students' self-efficacy and English performance scores.

Participants

Sixty participants were selected from a pool of 102 students in the 6th grade in Korea based on their social-affective test scores. They were categorized as high (n=30) or low (n=30) social-affective based on the test scores. Both groups of students had never played Norischool (Educational multiplayer English teaching online game) previously.

All 60 students received training on basic computer skills and basic operational skills for Norischool, such as how to navigate Norischool, how to play games and how to gain points from the tasks. After completing the training, all participants played with Norischool for two hours per week for over five weeks.

Instrumentation

This study used the modified version (Shin, 2007) of Social-Affective Value Test (SAVT) developed by the Korean Testing Center. The 30 item test consisted of three parts: collaboration, communication, and flexibility. The alpha reliability was highly acceptable (Cronbach α= .89) and the reliability of the modified test for the current study was high (Cronbach α= .82).

A self-efficacy test developed by Kim, Hyun and Han (2008) was conducted two times. The 20-item test consisted of three parts: task self-esteem, self-regulatory and risk-taking. The reliability of the test is very high (Cronbach α= .97).

The performance scores were recorded by Learning Management System (LMS) and accumulations of the participants' points earned through completing learning tasks were reported to the students. In this study, students' final performance scores were used as a measure of English performance skills. Each student's final score was a compilation of task accomplishments, quizzes scores, and numbers of completed learning activities.

Once students logged into the site, they selected their online characters (avatar) and completed given tasks. Each participant's performance scores over five weeks were recorded on LMS.

Norischool

Norischool is one of the educational online games designed for teaching English. It was developed in 2005 by a Korean company in the format of a multiplayer online role-playing game. The major target groups for this online game are elementary and middle school students (6-14 years) in Korea. The primary purpose of this educational game is to help Korean students learn English through online games.

Students are required to login to its homepage before playing the game. After login to the website, each player creates his/her avatar and assigns it a name. Using a computer keyboard, students can move around their avatars and chat with other players. The first time user friendly tutorial on JAVA explains how to play the game in detail.

There are two different tasks given to all players: gaming tasks and learning tasks. On gaming tasks, students have to fight against monsters, compete with other team players and complete given tasks. Students compete and cooperate with other players in order to complete these various given tasks. As for learning tasks, students read level-appropriate E-books and animation books, take quizzes on three language skills (reading, writing and listening), and complete given tasks.

At each level, students need to earn enough points in both learning and gaming tasks to move up to the next level. As they move up to the next level, their avatars grow. In addition, students can earn Alphie (similar to tokens) when they complete each task. In each task, students are rewarded in various ways: improving their English skills, earning Alphie, and accumulating points. Alphie is used as a token for purchasing virtual objects or items and trading virtual items with other players. Through this various tasks, students become more engaged in the game and interact more frequently with other players.

1. Gaming Elements

Norischool incorporates many elements from adventure games. Once students create their avatars in the virtual worlds, they navigate to complete their given tasks. Using a dialogue window, students communicate with other players and exchange objects to complete their tasks.

One of the game tasks is to fight against monsters. Students need to collaborate with other players to achieve the goal of chasing the target objects. The communication that players are engaging in is goal oriented and authentic. When they complete the task, they receive full points to move up to the next level.

In addition to the main games, there are six interactive games focusing on identifying alphabet phonics. These interactive online games are using jigsaw, puzzle, and picture matching activity formats. The main purpose of these games is to enhance student motivation and reinforce language knowledge they learn.

2. English Learning Elements

The major educational features of this online game are its emphasis on collaboration among participants and various rewards to the players. It attempts

Figure 1. Communication with other players' avatars

to encourage both high and low social-affective learners to participate in tasks using interactive features. It provides various types of positive feedback whenever the players complete tasks.

Students are required to read both E-books and animation books based on their level. After reading both books for each level, they take English quizzes on reading, writing and listening skills to earn points. There are six different levels and 83 learning units. A total number of the target vocabulary is 2,500 with 188 different topics. Each unit usually consists of one or two pairs of E-Books and animation books.

E-Books are audio picture books on the topic of phonics and basic vocabulary for different subject areas such as social studies, math and science. Each E-book allows students to control their learning pace using stop or skip buttons. Each book consists of three parts: looking at the picture and listening to the words carefully; understanding the picture and repeating the words; and recalling the picture and repeating the words. One E-book introduces about six new vocabulary words. Each vocabulary word is introduced with authentic pictures and pronounced twice. Also, the target vocabulary words are introduced in a complete sentence.

Figure 2. Collaboration with other players to fight against monsters

Figure 3. An example of an animation book

With input-enhanced features, certain consonants or vowels are emphasized. Students are able to identify and understand the target vocabulary as well as to produce it within a context.

Coupled with E-book, each animation book tries to reinforce certain consonants or vowels that students learn in E-books. After completing an E-book, students can expand their vocabulary with reading a paired Animation book. Like E-books, Animation books are designed for students to keep their own pace using stop and move buttons. These Animation books provide audio sound and offer both Korean and English subtitles. Each Animation book starts with a short story and followed by a chant with a focus on a target word or sound.

After reading both E-books and animation books, students take English quizzes on the materials they read to earn a point. English quizzes have six levels and consisted of reading, writing and listening parts. The format of test items is multiple choices. English quizzes have a multiplayer format so, at maximum usage, eight students can play a quiz simultaneously. When the students are playing with other peers or competing with other players, they receive double points. This multiplayer playing format is used to add fun to learning and to enhance student motivation.

Student learning activities and points are all recorded on My Record through LMS. Students can access My Record where they can view their attendance records, performance records, and a list of their incorrect answers on English quizzes. At any stage, students can check the points they earned and monitor their own progress. The educational components of Norischool are summarized in Table 1.

The gaming elements and the learning elements in Norischool are distinctive. Gaming elements include use of virtual reality, use of avatars, level advancement features, flexibility and interactivity. Learning elements are English immersive environments, level appropriate materials, self-motivated learning, engagement enhancement through collaboration and competition, and self-evaluation through LMS.

Data Collection and Analysis

The participants in both groups took self-efficacy pencil and paper survey before and after they played with the online game. The pre- and post-test scores were compared to examine the impact of

Table 1. The educational components of Norischool (Kim, Hyun, & Han, 2008)

Components	Types of activities
English learning environments	-Communicate in English -Read level-appropriate animation books and E-books -Take English quizzes on reading, writing and listening skills
Level-appropriate materials	-Offer various proficiency levels to learners -Provide both English and Korean subtitles
Self-motivated learning	-Select the tutor's questions and respond with answer
Enhanced interactions	-Communicate with other players in English and video-chat in cyberspace -Induce students' collaboration and competition with other players in solving English quizzes
Learning Management System (LMS)	-Take English quizzes to meet the minimum requirement -Keep record of attendance and quiz scores

their online gaming experiences. Also their scores on LMS were collected to examine the impact of online gaming. All the collected data was analyzed using SPSS (Version 12.0).

Results

Hypothesis 1: There is a difference in the impact of online game on high and low social-affective students' self-efficacy.

An independent t-test analysis of pre-and post-test of self-efficacy scores showed a significant difference both high and low social affective groups (see Table 2). On the pre-test, high social affective group students showed higher self-efficacy than low group students. There was a significant difference between two groups ($t(58)=6.55$, $p<.01$) on the self-efficacy pre-test. On the variables of task self-esteem and risk-taking, high group showed higher task self-esteem and risk-taking values than low group. The mean scores of high group were 3.63 and 3.78 while those scores of low group were 2.85 and 2.81 respectively. On the self-efficacy post-test that were conducted after playing the online game for five weeks, there was a significant difference between high and low social-affective students ($t(58)= 4.31$, $p<.01$). After playing with online games, high group students still showed high self-efficacy than low group students. The mean score of high

Figure 4. An example of learning management system.

Table 2. Participants' mean scores on the self-efficacy survey

Variables		Social-affective values	N	M	SD	*t*	*p*
Task self-esteem	Pre	High group	30	3.63	.67	5.04	***
		Low group	30	2.85	.53		
	Post	High group	30	4.02	.54	2.94	*
		Low group	30	3.49	.50		
Risk-taking	Pre	High group	30	3.78	.61	5.94	***
		Low group	30	2.81	.65		
	Post	High group	30	4.04	.48	3.88	***
		Low group	30	3.57	.46		
Self-efficacy	Pre	High group	30	3.60	.54	6.55	***
		Low group	30	2.68	.57		
	Post	High group	30	4.00	.48	4.31	***
		Low group	30	3.50	.43		

Note: *p<.05, ***p<.01

group on self-efficacy was 4.0 while that of low group was 3.5.

Hypothesis 1a: There is a difference in the impact of online gaming on high and low social-affective students' task self-esteem values. On the variables of task self-esteem, there was a significant difference between high and low groups (t(58)=2.27, p<.05). Interestingly, the low group showed more improvement than the high group did.

Hypothesis 1b: There is a difference in the impact of online gaming on high and low social-affective students' risk-taking values. There was a significant difference between two groups on risk-taking (t(58)=2.97, p<.01). Similar to task self-esteem, the low group showed more improvement than the high group did.

On the variables of task self-esteem and risk-taking, the mean scores of high group on the post were 4.02 and 4.04 while those scores of low group were 3.49 and 3.57. The effect of online game playing was tested by comparing the pretest and posttest score changes for both high and low groups (see Table 3). Based on the impact of online game playing, there was a significant difference between high and low groups on self-efficacy test scores (t(58)=3.17, p<.01). The score difference of the low group was bigger than that of the high

Table 3. Score changes between self-efficacy pre- and post- surveys

Variables	Social-affective values	N	M	SD	*t*	P
Task self-esteem	High group	30	.37	.48	2.27	*
	Low group	30	.77	.82		
Risk-taking	High group	30	.26	.62	2.97	***
	Low group	30	.76	.68		
Self-efficacy	High group	30	.39	.30	3.17	***
	Low group	30	.78	.63		

Note: *p<.05, ***p<.01

Table 4. Performance scores between high and low social-affective students

Social-affective values	N	M	SD	*T*	*P*
High group	30	5.06	2.98	2.92	***
Low group	30	6.92	1.80		

Note: ***p<.01

group. There was greater impact of online game playing on students in the low group than those in the high group.

Hypothesis 2: There is a difference in the impact of online gaming on high and low social-affective students' English performance scores. The effect of online game playing was shown in Table 4. On the final performance scores, students with low social-affective values scored higher than those with high social-affective values. There was a significant difference between the two groups (p<.01).

DISCUSSION

As shown in the results, there were significant differences between students reporting high and low social-affective on the self-efficacy pre-and post-surveys. Interestingly, the impact of online gaming was higher for students reporting low social-affective scores. The performance scores showed that the students in the low-score group performed better in English tasks than those in the high-score group.

Students' Self-Efficacy

When the two groups were compared on their self-efficacy scores, there were differences between pre-and post-test scores. Post-test scores were higher than pre-test scores in both groups. On the pre-test, high-scored group students scored higher than low-scored group students and the same pattern showed on the post-test. These results were expected because online games promote student interaction and motivate students to participate in their learning tasks. The increased scores from pre-test to post-test in both groups confirm the benefits of online games in improving students' self-efficacy.

Changes of Self-Efficacy Pre-and Post-Survey

The interesting finding in the results is the change in the low-score group. There was a significant change in low group students. This finding confirms the argument regarding the benefits of multiplayer online games: that is, online games provide introverted learners with an opportunity to interact and collaborate with other players by decreasing inhibition (Roberts, Smith & Pollock, 2000). In the case of shy and introverted learners, the anonymity of online settings and interactive features of online games foster their participation. As a result, the impact of online games on students with low social-affective values is greater than on students in the high group.

English Performance Scores

The students with low social-affective values scored higher than those with high social-affective values on English performance scores. As shown in Table 4, there was a significant difference between the two groups. Notably, the low group students outperformed their peers in English quizzes and learning tasks. It seems that shy and introverted students felt more comfortable in participating in online games.

CONCLUSION

The findings of the current study suggest three things. First, multiplayer online games improve elementary students' self-efficacy, especially task self-esteem and risk-taking factors. Considering the fact that self-efficacy is closely related to student motivation, the benefit of interactive online games in teaching language is promising. Without a doubt, English teaching online games featuring multiplayer mode can be a valuable tool for EFL students who often lack an opportunity to practice English in an authentic situation. Multiplayer online games which create authentic communication advance student engagement and motivation.

Second, students with low social-affective values benefit more from playing with online games in improving self-efficacy than their peers. As Roberts, Smith and Pollock (2000) argued, online game features (such as the use of an avatar) could make students feel comfortable and decrease inhibition. The bigger increase among low social-affective students on self-efficacy confirms that shy and introverted students favor online learning environments. It is important in language education to create a relaxed learning environment where communication is more meaning-focused than form-focused. In EFL settings, the use of multiplayer online games is a useful supplementary learning tool.

Third, low social-affective students perform better in English quizzes than high social-affective students. The performance score is an accumulated point that students earned from their tasks and English quizzes. The difference between the two groups is mainly due to their scores on English quizzes. One of the attributing factors in their better performance is the improvement of self-efficacy among low social-affective students. As Brown (2007) stated, self-esteem and language success are factors that interact. He further argued that language teaching needs to consider both language performance and learners' affective factors. The results of the current study suggest that the use of multiplayer interactive online games serve as a positive language learning tool.

FUTURE RESEARCH DIRECTIONS

Based on the findings, there are two suggestions for future study. Due to the concern from parents, there was a time limit on using online games for students. The parents did not allow their children to play with online games for more than five weeks. In the current study, students' performance scores on the English teaching online game, instead of their scores on standardized language proficiency tests, are compared to examine the impact of online game playing on student language learning. However, to understand the benefit of educational games better, there is a need for a longitudinal study on the impact of educational online games on student learning. Second, there is a need to explore the relationship between students' use of online games and their scores on a language proficiency test.

REFERENCES

Bachman, L. (1990). *Fundamental considerations in language testing*. New York: Oxford University Press.

Bachman, L., & Palmer, A. (1996). *Language teaching in practice*. New York: Oxford University Press.

Bandura, A. (1997). *Self-efficacy: The exercise of control*. New York: W.H. Freeman.

Brown, D. (2007). *Principles of Language Learning and Teaching* (5th ed.). New York: Pearson Longman.

DeKanter, N. (2004). Gaming redefines interactivity for learning. *TechTrends*, *29*(3), 26–31. doi:10.1007/BF02763644

Dufeu, B. (1994). *Teaching myself.* Oxford: Oxford University Press.

Durkin, K., & Barber, B. (2002). Not so doomed: Computer game play and positive adolescent development. *Journal of Applied Developmental Psychology, 23*, 373–392. doi:10.1016/S0193-3973(02)00124-7

Ellis, R. (1985). Teacher-pupil interaction in second-language development. In Gass, S. M., & Madden, C. (Eds.), *Input in second language acquisition* (pp. 69–85). Rowley, MA: Newbury House.

Gass, S. M. (1997). *Input, interaction and the second language learners*. Mahwah, NJ: Lawrence Erlbaum Associates.

Gass, S. M., Mackey, A., & Pica, T. (1998). The role of input and interaction in second language acquisition: Introduction to the special issue. *Modern Language Journal, 82*(3), 299–305.

Godwin-Jones, B. (2005). Skype and podcasting: Disruptive technologies for language learning. *Language Learning & Technology, 9*(3), 9–12.

Hall, J. K., & Verplaetse, L. S. (2000). Language learning through classroom interaction. In Hall, J. K., & Verplatse, L. S. (Eds.), *Second and foreign language learning through classroom interaction* (pp. 1–20). Mahwah, NJ: Lawrence Erlbaum.

Heyde, A. (1979). *The relationship between self-esteem and the oral production of a second language.* Unpublished doctoral dissertation, University of Michigan, MI.

Kim, B., Hyun, E., & Han, S. (2008). A Study on the effects of students' sociality level on self-efficacy and academic achievement in on-line game-based Learning. *Journal of Learner-Centered Curriculum and Instruction, 8*(2), 49–75.

Lee, K. M., & Peng, W. (2006). What do we know about social and psychological effects of computer games? A comprehensive review of the current literature. In Vorderer, P., & Bryant, J. (Eds.), *Playing video games, motives, responses, and consequences* (pp. 327–345). Hillsdale, NJ: Lawrence Erlbaum.

Meskill, C. (2005). Triadic Scaffolds: Tools for Teaching English Language Learners with Computers. *Language Learning & Technology, 8*(4), 46–59.

Nguyen, T. T. H., & Khuat, T. T. N. (2003). The effectiveness of learning vocabulary through games, *Asian EFL Journal Quarterly,* 5(4). Retrieved April 25, 2009, from http://www.asian-efl-journal.com/dec_03_vn.pdf

Nuyen, N. T. T., & Nga, K. T. T. 2003. The effectiveness of learning vocabulary through games. *Asian EFL Journal* 5. Retrieved April 20, 2009 from http://www.asian-efl-journal.com/dec_03_sub.Vn.html

Overbaugh, R. C., & Lin, S. (2004). Student characteristics, sense of community, and cognitive achievement in web-based and lab-based learning environments. *Journal of Research on Technology in Education, 39*(2), 205–223.

Roberts, L. D., Smith, L. M., & Pollock, C. M. (2000). U r a lot bolder on the net. In Ray Crozier, W. (Ed.), *Shyness: Development, consolidation and change*. New York: Routledge.

Roed, J. (2003). Language learner behavior in a virtual environment. *Computer Assisted Language Learning, 16*, 155–172. doi:10.1076/call.16.2.155.15880

Sharrock, W. W., & Watson, D. R. (1987). Power and realism in simulations and gaming: Some pedagogic and analytic observations. In Crookall, D., Greenblat, C., Coote, A., Klabbers, J., & Watson, D. (Eds.), *Simulation-gaming in the late 1980's* (pp. 35–42). Oxford, UK: Pergamon.

Shimai, S., Masuda, K., & Kishimoto, Y. (1990). Influence of TV games on physical and psychological development of Japanese kindergarten children. *Perceptual and Motor Skills*, *70*, 771–776. doi:10.2466/PMS.70.3.771-776

Shin, B. (2007). *The effect of the interaction patterns on the task commitment according to sociality level of the students in Educational game*. Unpublished master's thesis. Korea National University of Education.

Steinkuehler, C. (2006). Games as a highly visible medium for the study of distributed, situated cognition. In S.A. Barab, K.E. Hay, N.B. Songer, & D.T. Hickey (Eds.), *Proceedings of the International Conference of the Learning Sciences* (pp. 1048-1049). Mahwah, NJ: Erlbuam.

Wood, D. (2001). In search of fluency: What is it and how can we teach it? *Canadian Modern Language Review*, *57*, 573–589.

Yip, F. W. M., & Kwan, A. C. M. (2006). Online vocabulary games as a tool for teaching and learning English vocabulary. *Educational Media International*, *43*(3), 233–249. doi:10.1080/09523980600641445

ADDITIONAL READING

Chapelle, C. (2005). Computer-assisted language learning. In Hinkel, E. (Ed.), *Handbook of research in.*

García-Carbonell, A., Rising, B., Montero, B., & Watts, F. (2001). Simulation/Gaming and the Acquisition of Communicative Competence in Another Language. *Simulation & Gaming*, *32*(4), 481–491. doi:10.1177/104687810103200405

Godwin-Jones, R. (2005). Emerging Technologies. Messaging, Gaming, Peer-to-peer sharing: Language

(n.d.). Learning strategies & tools for the millennial generation. *Language Learning & Technology*, *9*(1), 17–22.

second language teaching and learning. (pp. 743-755). Mahwah, NJ: Lawrence Erlbaum Associates.

KEY TERMS AND DEFINITIONS

Communicative Language Learning and Teaching: A language teaching methodology that stresses student-to-student interaction, authentic use of a target language, and implementation of task-based activities.

ESL/EFL: ESL refers to English learned as a second language, and EFL refers to English learned as a foreign language. In most cases, EFL settings lack input of the target language.

Game-Based Language Learning: Game-based language learning supports student motivation and an authentic use of language through simulations or playing real-life situations.

Introversion: This term describes the dimension of personality which has been examined as a contributing factor in language learning and teaching. Introverted people are relatively quiet and tend to avoid taking risks.

Multiplayer Online Game: Typically video games that are capable of supporting multiple players simultaneously.

Self-Efficacy: One's beliefs in his/her own capabilities to successfully perform an activity or a task.

Task-Based Instruction: This approach uses learning activities to encourage students to engage in their own learning and to increase their motivation.

Chapter 9
Using an Educational Online Game to Stimulate Learning

Louise Sauvé
Télé-université /SAVIE, Canada

ABSTRACT

Digital games are increasingly being seen as effective learning resources. This is especially true because of how society is being transformed by the technological revolution, with adolescents as the key players in this transformation. In order to diversify teaching methods, schools in Quebec have been experimenting with educational games. This chapter reports on research that was based on a single group, pretest-posttest design. The findings showed that the online game STIs: Stopping the transmission, supported learning in terms of structuring of knowledge and integration of information for youth between the ages of 14 and 15. Several recommendations for further research have been made in the discussion.

INTRODUCTION

Educational professionals and theorists have mixed feelings as to the effectiveness of games as learning tools: games are very much used in primary schools, but secondary schools, colleges and universities have resisted their use. It appears that few of these institutions are exploring the educational potential of games. In many countries, the educational potential of computer games has been ignored (Piette, 2005; Prensky, 2006). In Europe, a study led by the European Union demonstrated a gap between the use of Internet at home and at school (Union européenne en éducation des médias, 2006). Many of the important uses for young people exist outside of school. For example, basics are learned mostly through self-teaching and learning with peers. These are important uses made available by educational online games.

The border between the *virtual world* of gaming and the *real world* of learning is still not clearly defined. According to Lisowki (2007), playing games and learning are two activities that make almost identical intellectual demands. The main difference lies in the context and environment in which the activity takes place. Educational games

DOI: 10.4018/978-1-61520-713-8.ch009

may provide a bridge between the virtual and real worlds to promote learning. But what do we mean by the term educational games?

A game is a fictitious, whimsical or artificial situation in which one or many players are put in a position of competition. Sometimes players square off against one another and at other times they are on the same side and are pitted against other teams. The game is governed by rules which structure their actions in view of a learning objective (educational game) and a purpose determined by the game such as to win or to take revenge. The notion of 'artificial' refers to a fictional activity with no referent in reality (e.g., Tic Tac Toe, Bingo) or one that is outside of the norms of reality. By placing oneself in a fictional situation, a player (or players) can experience fun by playing out imaginary and sometimes unrealistic situations (Sauvé and Chamberland, 2006).

In the context of this study, funded by the Social Sciences and Humanities Research Council (SSHRC, 2003-2008), we examined the impact of educational online games on cognitive learning. Based on modified rules from the board game Parcheesi, *STIs: Stopping the transmission* was developed as a method of health education for secondary school students between the ages of 14 and 15. In this game we aimed to create an online environment in which the player entered and progressed through the game by attaining the desired learning outcomes.

This chapter presents the results of the study involving secondary students in Quebec. They experimented with the educational online game on sexually transmitted infections. The first part of the chapter, discusses the place and the role of online games in schools. In the second part, the theoretical framework describes the type of cognitive learning that the educational game can encourage as it pertains to the structuring and integration of knowledge. The third part describes the pre-test and post-test research design used on a single group, the target population, the variables being studied, the measurement instruments, the variables of analysis, the educational game, and the successive steps in the experiment. In the fourth part, the results of the analysis starts with a presentation of the sampling, then moves on to the results in connection with the specific objectives of our study selected for this chapter in order to determine: (1) the students' knowledge in the use of computers and the Internet as well as their perceptions of the importance of Information and Communication Technologies (ICT) and games in their learning process; (2) the degree of structuring of knowledge about sexually transmitted infections (STI), (3) the degree of integration of information on sexually transmitted infections and (4) if there is a difference in terms of learning through games according to gender. In the fifth and last part, a few recommendations are formulated in the discussion.

PROBLEM

The invention of the Internet and the growing possibilities available through the use of computers (including video games) provide many opportunities for society and for learning. However, some people worry about the potential negative effects on the social development of an individual that a phenomenon such as this might have. Nevertheless, no one can ignore the existence of the 'digital natives', represented by children and adolescents of today. This game culture fundamentally shapes their way of learning and behaving. Young people prefer experimenting and playing as ways of learning. Asakawa and Gilbert (2003), Bain and Newton (2003) and Prensky (2006) suggest that "the game generation" has developed a new cognitive style characterized by multitasked learning, which is usually not paid much attention to during the learning process, and a way of learning which relies on exploration and discovery.

Several recent studies show that games have positive influences on learning, particularly on the structuring of knowledge (Evreinova, Evreinova

& Raisamo, 2006; Lennon & Coombs, 2006; Shaftel, Pass & Schnabel, 2005) and the integration of information (Haas et al, 2006; Padgett et al, 2005; Purushotma, 2005).

Building on the findings of Moisy (2004) and Guillot (2004), who is also interested in computer assisted psychotherapy, takes note that video games or digital games can be used within a context of relational help and have positive results on mental health and on learning. Hingston et al. (2006) argue that the use of educational games which exploit current technological possibilities accommodate different types of learners and encourage interaction with the educational materials.

However, other studies (e.g. Baldaro et al, 2004; Barab et al., 2005) note a negative result or limited impact theses games have on cognitive and affective learning. Shreve (2005) is an enthusiast when it comes to the introduction of educational computer games in the classroom but emphasizes the difficulties associated with their use. For example, it is difficult to follow the progress of multiple learners in a game while they are all using one assigned computer (the teacher then has difficulty controlling the group) and the games do not always adequately respond to the educational objectives determined by teachers.

Rassin, Gutman and Silner (2004), in an experiment with digital games for helping children prepare for a medical operation, show certain negative aspects of games, including the violence that certain games develop in children or the physical inactivity found in certain players. Virvou, Katsionis and Manos (2005), Shreve (2005) and Kelly (2005), who have developed educational software, have noted that many digital educational games created in the past were either not particularly fun or not very educational.

Cuban (2001) notes, based on varied research sources, that specialists in the domain of child development do not agree with the use of information and communication technologies (ICT) and consequently on the use of educational computer games. Their agreement on the use of these technologies is highly conditional (several "ifs" and many precautions are included). Finally however, Fournier, Vincent and Brougère (2004) do believe that it is possible to learn while playing.

Our systematic analysis of the literature on the impact of games on learning (Sauvé et al, 2008) supports his comments. Issues such as methodological weaknesses and problems with the definitions of concepts and operational variables do not currently permit us to clearly identify the real efficacy that games have on learning. The study described in this chapter aimed to assess the efficacy of a game, conceived by teachers and health practitioners for prevention and promotion of health, in terms of knowledge acquisition among students aged 14 to 15. It tried to answer the following question: What type of cognitive learning resulted from use of an online educational game?

In more specific terms, this chapter will present certain results of our research, particularly those that had as an objective to determine: (1) students' knowledge of the use of computers and the Internet and their perceptions on the importance of ICT and games in the learning process; (2) the type of learning promoted by an online educational game in terms of structuring knowledge; (3) the integration of information, and (4) whether there is a difference in terms of learning through games according to gender.

THE THEORETICAL FRAMEWORK

In this section, we will first examine how games can promote the structuring of knowledge. Then, we will identify how games allow for the integration of information. The choice of these two aspects of cognitive learning is based on the scope of studies done in the recent years on the subject and the generally positive results that have emerged (Sauvé, Kaufman & Renaud, 2007).

Educational effectiveness is defined by positive consequences from the use of a game on participant knowledge, attitudes or psychomotor skills.

It takes into account the relationship between the results of using a game for learning and the initially-stated objectives (Blouin & Bergeron, 1997).

As for *learning*, our definition corresponds to most dictionary definitions; the acquisition of knowledge or skills with the help of experience, practice or study. Learning outcomes are measured in terms of the knowledge, attitudes and skills acquired by students as a result of learning.

The Structuring of Knowledge

Structuring of knowledge refers to the construction and organization of knowledge, schemas (mental models), or representations by the learner in order to understand a concept or a given situation. Studies have shown that games (i.e., computer, video, serious, classic) reinforce or improve the structuring of knowledge. Some studies conclude that games have positive results on the "structuring of knowledge" (e.g. Evreinova, Evreinova & Raisamo, 2006; Lieberman, 1998, 2001; Lennon & Coombs, 2006; Mondozzi & Harper, 2001; Rosas et al, 2003). They mention specifically that the participation of the learner in the game improves or reinforces their knowledge of the subject matter at hand. Other authors (e.g. Fukuchi et al, 2000; Miller, Lehman & Koedinger, 2000; Mondozzi & Harper, 2001) reiterate this conclusion based on comparative experiments (pre-tests and post-tests on the game's subject of focus). Starting with results from previous studies (Blum & Yocom, 1996; De la Cruz, Cage & Lian, 2000; Holton et al, 2001). Shaftel, Pass and Schnabel (2005) obtained positive results when they tested with a mathematics game. Ravenscroft (2007), testing in the domain of secondary school kinematics instruction, also determined that an educational game allowed students to improve their understanding of the concepts being taught. In most cases, authors note that the games they used with their students helped assimilate the information being learned.

Other studies (e.g. Gee, 2003; Steinman & Blastos, 2002); show that games have positive results on the way learners build mental schemas. This helps the learner with cognitive skills such as problem solving, visualizing concepts, and establishing links. Therefore, the game allows the learner to integrate new materials and new concepts in a more intuitive manner and also helps the learner organize previously acquired information in a more comprehensive manner. While examining the structuring of mathematical knowledge Shaftel, Pass and Shnabel (2005, p. 32) stated that games "can provide an environment to come into contact with incorrect solutions, which are nevertheless meaningful steps in gathering elements of mathematical knowledge." Lastly, certain authors (e.g. Asakawa & Gilbert, 2003; De Grandmont, 2005) mentioned that games develop the structuring of knowledge, without defining the concept, nor presenting experiment results.

To confirm that the *STIs: Stopping the transmission* game results in knowledge structuring, we established some indicators of analysis based on the links that the learner is able to establish between elements and concepts or schemas according to Andrieu and Bourgeois (2003). We defined the following indicators:

- The capacity to call upon prior knowledge, or establish a link (sequential or chronological) between prior knowledge and information acquired during the learning process;
- The capacity to locate key elements of the subject under study, as in identifying theoretical or declaratory knowledge of a given subject and to put it in logical order. This link corresponds to a hypothetical relationship between several elements of the same contents;
- An increased awareness of the differences and similarities between the various elements of the subject being studied, establishing a link based on the principle of

contradiction. This link comes into play in the operations of distinction, selection, sorting and classification;

- The capacity to establish links across concepts, as in developing a cause-and-effect link between two or more ideas or concepts. This can also work in the other direction, starting with the result and discovering and establishing the cause;
- The capacity to establish an analogy or comparison between two additional pieces of information, either contradictory or complementary, in order to gain understanding.

In our study, the students will be asked throughout the game to respond to questions and learning activities about STIs. The objective is to structure their knowledge.

Integration of Information

Several studies confirm that games have a positive impact on the integration of information. Certain authors (e.g. Barnett et al, 2005; Green, 2002; Higgins & Barkley, 2004; Krajewsky & Piroli, 2002; Moyer & Bolyard, 2003) define the integration of information in learners as the capacity to develop links in an intuitive or non-intuitive manner thanks to the game. Therefore the game supports the development of the capacity to transpose knowledge acquired in other contexts. Other authors (e.g. De Grandmont, 2005; Markey, Power & Booker, 2003; Ravenscroft & Matheson, 2002; Silverman et al, 2002; Vandeventer & White, 2002) attribute the integration of information to a general increase in the learner's knowledge. They discuss the notion of assimilation or consolidation of knowledge based on statistics and results obtained from testing students after learning through the game in a scholastic setting (e.g. Baker, Navarro & Van der Hoek,2004; Hamalainen et al, 2006; Morris, Fritz & Buck,2004; Padgett, Strickland & Coles, 2005; Virvou, Katsionis & Manos,2005; Ward & O'Brien, 2005) or a particular subject matter (e.g. Haas et al, 2006; Jensen, Sims & Reventos,2004; Moreno & Duran, 2004; Purushotma, 2005) (mathematics, French, medicine) without explicitly defining the indicators for measuring the degree of information integration.

We noted that the majority of studies discussing the effectiveness of games on the integration of information did not define or hardly defined indicators to measure the development of information integration. Only two articles developed the subject further; Wissman and Tankel (2001) mentioned the capacity for appropriation as being an element of measurement of information integration; Sauvé, Renaud and Hanca (2008) used the degree of acquisition of declaratory knowledge to measure the level of integration of information from a game among students at the secondary level. As for retention, no authors mentioned this aspect in their studies.

Under such conditions it is difficult to determine whether games do lead to information integration and various authors deal with this in different ways. Taking into account this methodological weakness, we have retained one indicator of the effectiveness for analysis in our study. The indicator selected was the capacity for the learner to apply his or her declarative knowledge in a given context. By declarative knowledge we mean "knowledge which allows a person to assimilate ideas and facts in a particular domain" (Brien, 1994, p. 207). In our study, the students will apply concepts, indicative propositions, the sum of interrelated propositions and metacognitive knowledge pertaining to STIs through different situations which will allow them to integrate information acquired while playing the game. We formulated the following question: Does the *STIs: Stopping the transmission* game aid secondary school students to integrate information on sexually transmitted infections?

In order to ensure that the learner structures his or her knowledge and integrates information, Frété (2002) states that games offer a question and response structure which encourages drill and practice, as well as association questions accompanied by a reward system. Detective games, mystery solving games and adventure games are particularly effective. In the case of this study, a board game based on Parcheesi using different types of question and response structures was used.

Accounting for the Gender Variable in Online Educational Games

Playing games is the most common activity for 6 to 13 year olds using a computer (Kirriemuir & McFarlane, 2004). The differences between girls and boys, in terms of involvement in games and what this says about them is, according to Frété (2002), the most highly debated topic for researchers examining games as learning tools. Gros (2003) states that computer games are designed for boys between the ages of 8 and 14. Research shows that the majority of young gamers are at the elementary school level and early secondary levels after which numbers decline (Kirriemuir & McFarlane, 2004; McFarlane et al, 2002; Williamson & Facer, 2004). However, this tendency is contradicted by other studies (ESA, 2004) which show that the average age of the majority of computer gamers is 29 years old.

Boys and girls enjoy playing computer games equally (Mitchell & Savill-Smith, 2004). Studies show that boys are more interested in learning when they are involved in a game (ESA 2004; Roberts et al, 1999; Subrahmanyam et al, 2001). In Quebec, an inquiry clearly revealed that male adolescents aged 12 to 17 in Quebec are significantly more involved in online games (70.7%) than female adolescents (40.6%) (Lamy, 2004). The difference between boys and girls in gaming seems more pronounced after the age of 13 (Gros, 2003).

Many studies have come to the conclusion that girls and boys have different interests and preferences. Kafai (2001) states that boys emphasize competition when they play educational games while girls focus on the learning objectives to be attained. Girls prefer games that require cooperation while boys prefer games that emphasize competition (Cassell & Jenkins, 1998). Girls enjoy playing educational games while boys generally prefer realistic games with violent themes (Cesarone, 1998). Girls prefer games that allow them to recreate common family-life themes while boys prefer fantasy games (Gros, 2003; Subrahmanyam & Greenfield, 1998; Vail, 1997). Girls appreciate sharing information and boys prefer reaching goals to demonstrate mastery and accomplishment (Ching et al, 2000, cited in Blumberg & Sokol, 2004). Boys play computer games more than girls do and are more confident using technology in general (Jenson & De Castell, 2006). Considering that schools are integrating technology into the learning environment, what effect will the introduction of computer games in secondary schools have on learning for boys and girls?

THE METHODOLOGICAL FRAMEWORK

The methodological approach used in the research was a single group, pretest-posttest design, which allowed us to measure whether the game *STIs: Stopping the transmission* promoted learning by identifying learners' prior knowledge before the game and then comparing this to any knowledge developed during the game. The target population, the variables in the study, the four measuring instruments and their methods of analysis, the educational game as well as the process of the experiment will be described in detail below.

Target Population

We chose to sample groups totaling 160 students at the grade 9 level because of how difficult it is to experiment in schools. The sample was drawn from school class groups, and all students from each class group were invited to participate. All participants in this experiment knew they were involved in this research process and signed a consent form to confirm that they agreed to participate in the experiment.

Concepts and Variables Studied

In order to reach the research objectives, the main concepts used were defined and associated with evaluation indicators which allowed us to devise research instruments. Let's take a closer look.

To respond to the first objective of the study, "evaluating the students' knowledge of the use of computers and the Internet as well as their perceptions of the importance of ICT and games in their learning process", four variables were identified: (1) the degree of familiarity in the use of a computer and the Internet, (2) the perceptions on the integration of ICT's in learning, (3) the degree of use of educational games on paper, CD-Rom or online in learning and (4) what their attitude is towards the use of games in learning.

To meet the second objective of the study "evaluating the type of learning developed by online educational games in terms of structured knowledge, five indicators were used: (1) the capacity to call upon prior knowledge; (2) identification of key terms in the subject being studied; (3) increase in understanding of the differences and similarities between various elements of the subject studied; (4) the creation of links between concepts, and (5) the creation of the analogy or comparisons between two pieces of information. To verify if these indicators had an effect on learning, 24 statements relating to the subject were developed. The statement from the questionnaire "True or False - Condylomas, Chlamydia, gonorrhea, hepatitis B, genital herpes, syphilis, crab louses and HIV are sexually transmitted infections. " is the example of prior knowledge.

To meet the third objective of the study, "evaluating the type of learning developed by an online educational game in terms of integration of information", one indicator was used, the student's capacity to apply declarative knowledge in a given context. To verify if the indicator has an impact on learning, five statements relating to the subject were developed. For example, "True of False. Abnormal leakage from the vagina or penis since my last sexual encounter is a symptom that tells me it is urgent to have a screening test done."

To meet the fourth objective of the study, "identifying any differences in learning between genders using the *STIs: Stopping the transmission* game", we compared the data from boys and girls from the first three objectives to identify any differences.

Measurement Instruments

Four measurement instruments were used at different points in this experiment. **Before beginning** the *STIs: Stopping the transmission* game experiment, two questionnaires were given to the students:

- The *Questionnaire on ICT and GAME competencies* was divided into three parts. The first part dealt with socio-demographic and academic demographics. The second part consisted of seven statements accompanied by a rating scale or multiple choice questions concerning the student's knowledge of games and Internet use as learning methods. The third part consisted of eleven statements with a rating scale to determine students' perceptions of the importance of ICTs and games in learning.
- The *Questionnaire on STIs knowledge* was administered the week before the game was played. The objective was to determine what prior knowledge the students had concerning STIs. Twenty-seven statements were used to measure the impact of the game on knowledge structuring and the integration of information. The multiple choice questions determined (1) prior knowledge; (2) key points of the subject at hand; (3) understanding of differences

and similarities; (4) the capacity to establish conceptual links; (5) analogies, and finally (6) the capacity to apply declarative knowledge in a given context.

During the game experiment, which took place during two consecutive sessions of approximately one and a half hours each, the students were invited to play the game in groups of three on a single computer. They were given instructions on how to access the game. Certain player actions were recorded in real time by the tracking system integrated in the game, namely, the duration of the game, the number of questions answered correctly, the number of questions answered incorrectly, the number of games completed in the class, etc.

After experimenting with the *STIs: Stopping the transmission* game, the *Questionnaire on STIs knowledge* was given immediately after the end of the game after the second session. The objective was to measure how the game contributed to the furthering of knowledge about STIs. This questionnaire consisted of the same number of questions as the pre-test and the wording of the questions was the same. The order of the questions was modified so that students could not rely on remembering the pre-test.

The quantitative data were organized using different descriptive analysis techniques (frequency, average, percentage, etc.). The results were interpreted in order to draw conclusions concerning the impact of the *STIs: Stopping the transmission* game on the structuring of knowledge and the integration of information.

The Game - STIs: Stopping the Transmission

This game was created for prevention and promotion of health and sexually transmitted infections (STIs), focusing on informing 14 to 15 year olds (Cantin, Delage, Sauvé, Renaud & Gauvin, 2006). The game (Figure 1) was created based on the Generic educational game shell of the Parcheesi

Figure 1. Game board STIs: Stopping the transmission

board game. Generic Educational Game Shell (GEGS) is used as an online design environment that allows teachers and trainers to create games by providing all the tools needed to: (1) set the game parameters; (2) create instructions and rules that direct player actions; (3) create pedagogical material; (4) set the criteria that determine the end of the game and the winner, and (5) detail the tools required for revision and evaluation of the game, in order to ensure that the game is updated regularly and that learning is maximized.

Once the game has been created, two game modes are possible: single computer or network game. By definition, the single computer game mode requires only one computer. This mode however, allows multiple people to play together, taking turns using the same keyboard. The network game mode is used when players are in different locations. They each use their own computer.

The game content was developed in collaboration with two doctors, experts in game techno-pedagogy and teachers and subsequently validated by experts working in the school system. Seventy-nine questions were integrated into the game mechanism. The questions were placed into 4 activity categories as follows: (1) transmission of STIs (18 questions); (2) prevalence of STIs (11 questions); (3) STIs prevention (34 questions), and (4) STIs treatments (16 questions).

The development of cognitive questions took several forms: questions requiring a yes-no answer, true or false questions, multiple choice questions (with 2, 3, or 4 choices), fill-in-the-blank questions, sequence-based questions, short answer questions and open questions requiring longer answers or performance (e.g. role playing). Every question, whether it be a short-answer or open-ended question; allows the insertion of video clips,

Figure 2. Example of questions asked in the game

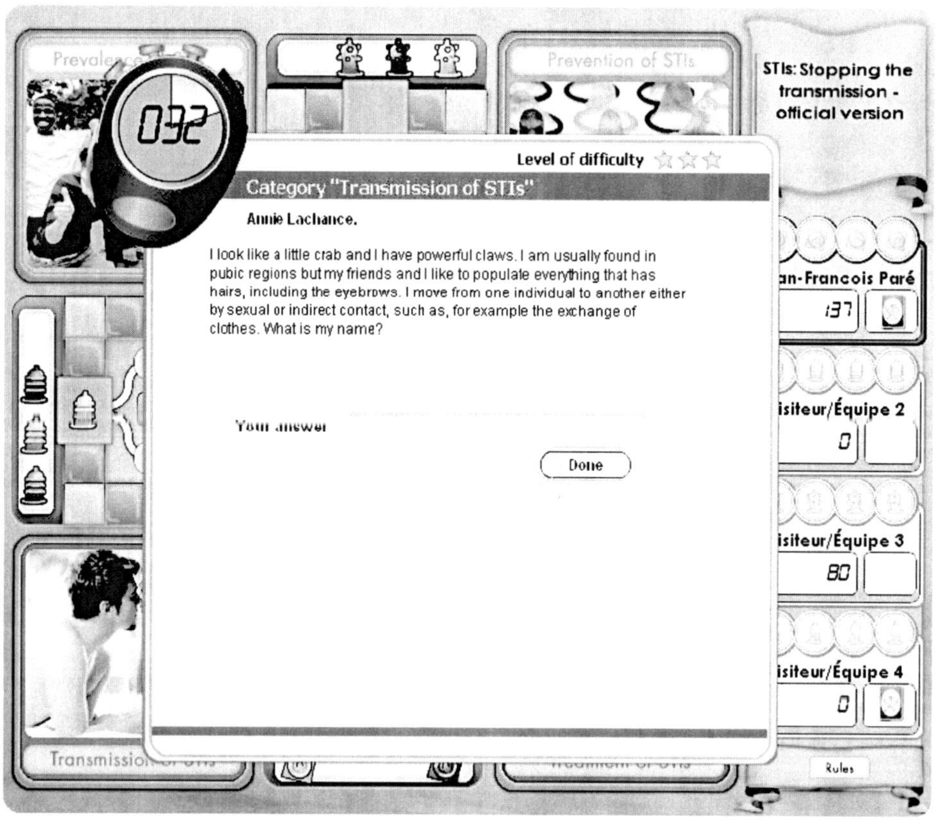

images and sounds either in the question or in the answer(s) or feedback Figure 2 provides examples of questions from the game.

The *STIs: Stopping the transmission* game integrates feedback mechanisms by providing the following elements:

- For every learning activity or question there is a feedback mechanism according to whether the question was answered correctly or incorrectly;
- For every player's move the computer displays instructions or game rules;
- For every navigational error, the computer displays a message to correct or reorient the user.

In terms of challenge and competition among players, the game uses *Chance* cards and rules that make it more difficult to win the game.

Let's take a look at how the game progresses online.

1. Each team clicks the dice in a random order to determine who will start the game. The team that rolls the highest number starts the game.
2. A team must obtain a double (1-1, 2-2, 3-3, 4-4, 5-5, 6-6) in order to move one of its four pieces to the *Start* square. The team clicks the piece it wishes to move first (the blue or red one for example). Once the piece has been moved to the *Start* square, the team must *immediately* respond to a learning activity in the category corresponding to the color of the piece:
    - If a team succeeds in *the first activity* when its piece is in the *Start* square, it rolls the dice and the team's piece moves along the fast track and advances the number of squares determined by the last roll of the dice.
    - If the team does not succeed in *the first activity*, the piece stays on the *Start* square and the team waits for the next turn to try again.
    - If on the following turn, the team does succeed in *the second activity* when its piece is in the *Start* square, this piece moves along the regular track.

    If the team does not succeed in *the second activity*, the piece stays in the *Start* square and waits for the next turn until it succeeds.

3. Once a team has managed to move a piece, turns will consist of the following:
    - The team responds to a learning activity corresponding to the color of the piece it has moved in the previous turn.
    - If the team succeeds in the activity within the allotted time for the question, the team clicks on the dice and the piece of their choice moves along the number of squares determined by the last roll. The team can also decide to free a new piece if the results obtained allow it. Two pieces of the same team cannot be placed on the same square; this means that a team with a piece on the *Start* square will not be able to free any new pieces until this first one has been moved.
    - If the team fails an activity, it cannot click the dice and must wait until it has correctly answered a question in this same category in the following turn before clicking the dice.
    - Once one of these possible outcomes has taken place, it is the following team's turn.
4. When a team moves a piece (on the fast track or regular track) and this team lands on a *Start* square, it most answer a learning activity, *even if* the piece passes the square. Success in the learning activity determines the track that the piece will *follow*, whether

on the current turn or the next. If the *team* *su*cceeds in the activity, the piece will continue on the fast track. If the team fails, the piece will move along the regular track. The same rule applies if the team's piece arrives by an exact number on the *Start* square. In the case of a success, the team does not *click* the dice but its piece will access the fast track during the next turn, even if the team chooses to move another piece on its turn after succeeding in a learning activity.

When a piece crosses the *Start* square before heading to the centre of the board, the team must once again respond to a learning activity. If it fails, the piece stays where it is and the team will have to answer the next learning activity correctly before heading to the centre of the board. If the team succeeds in the activity and the piece's travel was obstructed by the *Start* square, the piece is free to continue its trajectory towards the centre of the board.

5. Each team that succeeds in a learning activity gains points. The point system varies according to the time taken to complete the activity.
6. A piece that stops in a square already occupied by an other piece sends this piece back to the *Start* square. If the *Start* square is already occupied by a piece, that piece is sent back to the personal space.
7. Pieces may land in the centre of the board only if the exact number of squares between it and the finish is the number obtained in the roll. The centre counts as one square. Once the piece has arrived in the centre, the piece is taken off the board and that team is awarded 200 points.
8. When a team has rolled the dice and obtained a number greater than the number of squares between a piece and the final square, there are two options:
    - Leave the piece where it is until the exact number needed is obtained and click another piece to move it along the track according to the number obtained.
    - Move the piece ahead to the centre and then back the remaining number of squares according to the number obtained in the roll. For example: if a player's piece is two squares from the centre and the team rolls a 5, this piece moves forward 3 squares and then back 2.
    - The piece that moves back along the central track cannot go back further than the first square on of the central track. If the piece lands on this square while moving backwards and is still required to move further, it begins to move back to towards the centre of the board again.
9. When a team draws a Team card, all the teams in the game participate. The first team to complete the activity successfully gains extra points. If this team has a piece in the *Start* square, it moves directly to the fast track. The team that drew the *Team* card does not miss a turn. This team responds to a new learning activity immediately after participating in the *Team* card with the other teams.
10. When a team draws a *Chance* card, the following actions are possible:
    - Free Start. This card allows the team to put a piece (of their choice) on the Start square. This means the team must complete immediately a learning activity. If the team's Start square is already occupied by one of their pieces or if all their pieces are active, the team can keep the Chance card in their bank and use it at any time to place a piece in the Start square.

- Exact Roll. This card allows a team to move a piece (any piece in play, except one from the Start square) to the centre of the board. If the team has only one piece in play and it is on the Start square, then the team can bank the card to be used later.
- Back to Start. This card sends a piece back to the Start square. If the square is already occupied by another piece, this piece is sent back to the personal space of the team it belongs to. If the team only has one piece in play when it picks the card and this piece is on the Start square, the card is banked and the piece must turn around the first time it is moved (it will be moved to the Start square). If the piece is eaten before the Back to Start card can be used, the card is deleted.
- Access to the Fast Track. This card allows a team to move the piece that made them pick a card from the regular track to the fast track without completing a learning activity when it comes up to the Start square.
- A maximum of two Chance cards can be banked per team. If one team has two Chance cards in the bank, each new card selected replaces the oldest card in the bank.

11. The game ends:
    - Once a team has retired all 4 pieces and correctly answered the final learning activity. If a team draws a Team card for the final learning activity, it wins only if it succeeds in the activity. If the team does not answer correctly, it must wait until the following turn to complete a new learning activity and win the game.
    - Once the allotted time has run out. The team with the highest score wins.

ANALYSIS OF RESULTS

The experiment, conducted on secondary school students, took place from November 2006 to February 2007. The sampling for our quantitative research was comprised of five groups of students from secondary 3, for a total of 173 students broken down as follows: 54.9% were boys and 45.1% were girls. Among these 173 students, 110 (63.6%) were 14 years old and 63 (36.4%) were 15 years old. All students signed the consent form. The results will be presented in function of the specific objectives of the study.

Students' Familiarity With Computer Use, Internet Use and Their Perceptions of the Importance of ICTs and Learning Games

The students who participated in the experiment were generally quite familiar with the use of computers and Internet. They were not nervous about using either. They reported that they use traditional games (on paper) more often than they use CD-ROM games or online games. They mostly showed a positive or neutral attitude towards using games for learning. A small percentage of the students (7 out of 173) said they were against using games as learning tools.

Boys and girls had similar experience levels with the use of different types of educational games at school. Boys demonstrated a more positive attitude however, than girls towards the use of games for learning.

All the students had computers at home except for one male student. Less than two thirds of the students used their computers to play games online and very few of them spent more than 13 hours per week playing computer games. Boys played online games more often than girls.

Participants considered these games as faster and better ways to learn. The boys, who were more used to playing games, showed more enthusiasm than the girls for the use of Internet and games in learning.

Table 1. Degree of learning through games as a function of study variables for the structuring of knowledge

Variables Studied	%
Prior knowledge	11.19
Key elements of the subject studied	8.28
Understanding of differences and similarities	24.50
The activities in the game allowed me to establish conceptual links	3.14
Establish analogies	17.88
Average rate of learning	13.00

Structuring of Knowledge Concerning Sexually Transmitted Infections Using the *Stis: Stopping the Transmission* Game

To respond to the specific research objective (i.e., to measure the type of learning that educational online games encourage in terms of structuring of knowledge), learning content about STIs was integrated into the online game. The contents were created so that they solicit prior knowledge, facilitate the identification of key points in the subject matter, help the player understand differences and similarities in key points of the subject matter and allow the player to find conceptual links and analogies, twenty-two statements from the pre and post-test questionnaire measured the possible changes in knowledge according to the indicators which establish the process that structures knowledge. The calculation for this result is established by taking the posttest score and subtracting the pretest score then dividing by the total.

The results in Table 1 indicate that generally the activities in *STIs: Stopping the transmission* improved the structuring of knowledge for the subject of sexually transmitted infections. The activities based on understanding differences (24.5%) and developing analogies (17.8%) were most successful in structuring knowledge.

Activities associated with using prior knowledge (11.19%) and identification of key points (8.28%) demonstrated a smaller increase in the participants' knowledge. Finally, the activities associated with the capacity to establish conceptual links (3.14%) developed the participants' knowledge the least.

Integration of Information in the Domain of Sexually Transmitted Infections Through the Use of the *STIs: Stopping the Transmission* Game

To respond to the specific study objective (i.e., to measure the type of learning an online, educational game fosters in terms of information integration), learning content on STIs were integrated into the online game. This content was created so that it would develop the students' capacity to apply declarative knowledge in a given context. Five statements from the pre and post-test measured the possible changes in information integration, taking into account the retained indicator. The calculation for this result is established by taking the posttest score and subtracting the pretest score then dividing by the total.

The results in Table 2 show that respondents improved in all questions in terms of integration of information: from 2.90% to 14.90%.

The Difference in Learning According to Gender

The crossing of the variables of the structuring of knowledge with the gender variable enabled

Table 2. Degree of learning through games as a function of study variables for the information integration

Information integration	Learning		
	Before %	After %	Difference %
Abnormal leakage from the vagina or penis since my last sexual encounter is symptoms that tell me it is urgent to have a screening test done. (V)	61.10	76.00	14.90
Anyone under the age of 10 is protected from sexually transmitted infections during their first sexual encounter. (F)	10.80	13.20	4.00
Getting condoms is simply a matter of purchasing them at a convenience store or drug store. (V)	78.40	85.60	7.20
It is easy to tell if someone has a sexually transmittable infection because many symptoms are very apparent. (F)	69.50	76.60	7.10
An screening test should only be taken when symptoms of a sexually transmitted infection are felt. (F)	79.00	81.90	2.90
Average	59.76	66.66	7.22

us to note in Table 3 that the boys increased their knowledge more than the girls, following their participation in the game.

The integration of knowledge in a given context in function of the gender variable, the boys learned more than the girls and this applies to all the questions. This data is shown in Table 4.

Solutions and Recommendations

Results show that the students were representative of the digital native because they show a high level of familiarity with computers. The boys and girls had similar experiences with the use of different types of educational games at school. However, the boys played online games more often than girls. Boys also showed a more positive attitude than girls towards the use of the Internet and games for learning. This attitude seems to have influenced their cognitive learning because the boys showed better results than the girls in terms of both the structuring of knowledge and the integration of information.

As far as the structuring of knowledge is concerned, the learners showed that they developed their knowledge of the five variables being studied and more precisely, the understanding of differences and similarities. Taking into account the positive results obtained with the students, we recommend following up on the research in order to validate and generalize the indicators for measuring the efficacy of games on learning

Table 3. Degree of learning by gender: structuring of knowledge

Structuring of Knowledge	Degree of Learning	
Variables Studied	Girls %	Boys %
Prior knowledge	7.30	11.19
Key elements of the subject studied	5.17	8.28
Understanding of differences and similarities	6.37	12.25
The activities in the game allowed me to establish conceptual links	1.90%	3.14
Establish analogies	9.78	17.88
Average	6.10	10.55

Table 4. Degree of learning by gender: integration of information

Integration of information	Degree of Learning	
	Girls %	Boys %
Abnormal leakage from the vagina or penis since my last sexual encounter is symptoms that tell me it is urgent to have a screening test done. (V)	12.8	16.90
Anyone under the age of 10 is protected from sexually transmitted infections during their first sexual encounter. (F)	1.30	5.70
Getting condoms is simply a matter of purchasing them at a convenience store or drug store. (V)	3.80	10.10
It is easy to tell is someone has a sexually transmittable infection because many symptoms are very apparent. (F)	0.90	16.80
A screening test should only be taken when symptoms of a sexually transmitted infection are felt. (F)	2.10	9.00
Average	4.18	11.70

and on structuring of knowledge. To this end, we propose that the questions integrated into the educational online game that will be the focus of the study should include the following elements:

- **Prior knowledge**: these questions will allow the learner to create links (sequential or chronological ones) between information acquired before learning and information acquired while learning.
- **Key points of the subject being studied**: these questions will allow the learner to identify the theoretical knowledge or declarative knowledge on a given subject to order them logically according to the topic.
- **Discriminatory links**: these questions will help learners distinguish, select, draw out or classify information in order to develop their organizational, methodological and conceptual abilities.
- **Causal conceptual links**: these questions will allow learners to determine if there is a cause and effect between two ideas, knowledge, or concepts. The questions can also start with the effect and work towards the cause.
- **Analogous links**: these questions will allow learners to establish a comparison between two elements of the same nature or multiple elements of the same or similar nature in order to understand the meaning.

In terms of integration of information, learners demonstrated that they had developed their knowledge in light of the variable being studied: the capacity to apply declarative knowledge in a given context. In spite of positive results on the variable retained, it is recommended to continue the research analysis which treats some indicators in order to identify other indicators of analysis likely to measure the real efficacy of the game on this aspect.

In terms of gender, the results allow us to reaffirm that there is a difference in terms of learning. Boys learn more than girls when using games to learn.

CONCLUSION

Thanks to rapid advancements in Web technology, possibilities for online games are growing. More and more researchers are working to show that games can be effective learning tools. We have to note that the methodological gaps and the lack of indicators of analysis do not enable us to compare emerging results and clarify the real efficacy of games on learning. Taking into account the ever-growing popularity of computer games with the digital generation, we created and carried out an experiment involving an educational game on the prevention and treatment of sexually transmitted diseases designed for 14-15 year olds.

We first verified whether the teenagers (boys and girls) that participated in this experiment exemplified the typical profile of a young adolescent of the digital native. The learners did exemplify the typical profile of the digital generation through their use of the Internet and games in learning. They showed a high level of familiarity with ICT and they were not nervous or timid about using them.

Next, the positive results showing the effectiveness of the *STIs: Stopping the transmission* game in structuring knowledge and information integration about STIs in secondary students supports the conclusions drawn by ESA (2004). If educational online games are used with adolescents, their chances of learning will increase.

Finally, while remaining aware that there are limitations to this study, it is essential to reiterate the importance of defining the indicators of analysis that positively impact in educational games. The standardization of these definitions and the way in which they are used will allow new research to conclude whether games demonstrate a real impact on learning.

Future Research

A new study is currently underway, funded by the Social Sciences and Humanities Research Council (SSHRC, 2008-2011). The objective of this study is to measure the effectiveness of online games for secondary school students in cognitive learning (structuring of knowledge) and affective learning (changing attitudes and behaviours). A new online game, Asthma: 1, 2, 3 ...Breathe!, has been developed using the educational games generic shell of the Parcheesi board game. The game's learning content was created with the help of doctors, was edited by experts and was tested by a small sample of the target audience.

REFERENCES

Andrieu, B., & Bourgeois, I. (2003). Interaction enseignant-élèves au cours des TPE, les dynamiques du processus de structuration des connaissances [Teacher-student interaction during independent study projects: Dynamics in the process of structuring knowledge]. In C. Larcher & A. Crindal (Eds.), Structuration des connaissances et nouveaux dispositifs d'enseignement (pp. 40-45). Paris: Institut national de recherche pédagogique.

Asakawa, T., & Gilbert, N. (2003). Synthesizing Experiences: Lessons To Be Learned from Internet-Mediated Simulation Games. *Simulation & Gaming, 34*(1), 10–22. doi:10.1177/1046878102250455

Bain, C., & Newton, C. (2003). Art Games: Pre-Service Art Educators Construct Learning Experiences for the Elementary Art Classroom. *Art Education, 56*(5), 33–40.

Baker, A., Oh Navarro, E., & Van Der Hoek, A. (2004). An experimental card game for teaching software engineering processes. *Journal of Systems and Software, 75*, 3–16. doi:10.1016/j.jss.2004.02.033

Baldaro, B., Tuozzi, G., Codispoti, M., & Montebarocci, O. (2004). Aggressive and non-violent videogames: short-term psychological and cardiovascular effects on habitual players. *Stress and Health, 20*, 203–208. doi:10.1002/smi.1015

Barab, S., Thomas, M., Dodge, T., Carteaux, R., & Tuzun, H. (2005). Making Learning Fun: Quest Atlantis, A Game Without Guns. *ETR&D-Educational Technology Research and Development, 53*(1), 86–107. doi:10.1007/BF02504859

Barnett, D. J., Everly, G. S. Jr, Parker, C. L., & Links, J. M. (2005). Applying educational gaming to public health workforce emergency preparedness. *American Journal of Preventive Medicine, 28*(4), 490–495. doi:10.1016/j.amepre.2005.01.001

Blouin, M., & Bergeron, C. (1997). Dictionnaire de la réadaptation, tome 2: termes d'intervention et d'aides techniques. Québec: Les Publications du Québec.

Blum, H. T., & Yocom, D. J. (1996). A fun alternative: Using instructional games to foster student learning. *Teaching Exceptional Children, 29*(2), 80–63.

Blumberg, F. C., & Sokol, L. M. (2004). Boys and girls use of cognitive strategy when learning to play video games. *The Journal of General Psychology, 131*(2), 151–158. doi:10.3200/GENP.131.2.151-158

Brien, R. (1994). *Science cognitive et formation*. Québec, Canada: Presses de l'Université du Québec.

Cantin, F., Delage, M., Sauvé, L., Renaud, L., & Gauvin, M. (2006). *Le jeu ITS: Stopper la transmission [STIs: Stopping the transmission Game]*. Québec: SAVIE - Carrefour Virtuel de Jeux Éducatifs. Retrieved from http://www.savie.qc.ca/CarrefourJeux2/Site/Jeux/ Parchesi/infoParchesi.Asp?NoPartie=255.

Cassell, J., & Jenkins, H. (Eds.). (1998). *From Barbie to Mortal Kombat*. Boston: The MIT Press.

Cesarone, B. (1998). *Video Games: Research, ratings, recommendations*. Chiago: ERIC Clearinghouse on Elementary and Early Childhood Education.

Cuban, L. (2001). *Oversold and overused: computers in the classroom*. Cambridge, MA: Harvard University Press.

De Grandmont, N. (2005) *Pédagogie du jeu... philosophie du ludique* [Game pedagogy... ludic philosophy]. Retrieved from http://cf.geocities.com/ndegrandmont/index.htm.

De la Cruz, R. E., Cage, C. E., & Lian, M.-G. J. (2000). Let's play mancala and sungka! *Teaching Exceptional Children, 32*(2), 38–42.

Entertainment Software (ESA). (2004). *ESA'S 2004 Essentials facts about the computer and video game industry*. Retrieved April 9, 2005, from http://www.theesa.com/files/EFBrochure.pdf

Evreinova, T., Evreinova, G, & Raisamo, R. (2006). An alternative approach to strengthening tactile memory for sensory disabled people. *Universal Access in the Information Society*, 1-10.

Fournier, M., Vincent, S., Brougère, G. et al. (2004). À quoi sert le jeu? [What use are games?] *Sciences humaines*, 152, 19-45.

Frété, C. (2002). *Le potentiel du jeu vidéo pour l'éducation. Mémoire de maîtrise. Université de Genève Faculté de Psychologie et des Sciences de l'Education, TECFA*. Technologies de la Formation et de l'Apprentissage.

Fukuchi, S. G., Offutt, L. A., Sacks, J., & Mann, B. D. (2000). Teaching a Multidisciplinary Approach to Cancer Treatment during Surgical Clerkship via an Interactive Board Game, Association for Surgical Education. *American Journal of Surgery, 179*, 337–340. doi:10.1016/S0002-9610(00)00339-1

Gee, J. P. (2003). *What video games have to teach us about learning*. New York: Palgrave.

Green, D. A. (2002). Last one standing: creative, cooperative problem solving. *Teaching Children Mathematics, 9*(3), 134–139.

Gros, B. (2003 July). The impact of digital games in education. *First Monday, 8*(7). Retrieved February 19, 2005, from http://www.firstmonday.dk/issues/ issue8_7/xyzgros/

Guillot, B. (2004). La psychothérapie assistée par ordinateur PsyaO. *Adolescence*, *22*(1), 53–58.

Haas, J. P., Quiros, D., Hyman, S. R., & Larson, E. L. (2006). Use of an Innovative Game To Teach and Reinforce Hand Hygiene Compliance among Healthcare Workers. *American Journal of Infection Control*, *34*(5), E52–E53. doi:10.1016/j.ajic.2006.05.109

Hamalainen, R., Manninen, T., Jarvela, S., & Hakkinen, P. (2006). Learning to collaborate: Designing collaboration in a 3-D game environment. *The Internet and Higher Education*, *9*(1), 47–61. doi:10.1016/j.iheduc.2005.12.004

Higgins, M. M., & Barkley, M. C. (2004). Improving effectiveness of nutrition education resources for older adults. *Journal of Nutrition for the Elderly*, *23*(3), 19–54. doi:10.1300/J052v23n03_03

Hingston, P., Combes, B., & Masek, M. (2006). Teaching an undergraduate AI course with Games and simulation. *Lecture Notes in Computer Science*, *3942*, 494–506. doi:10.1007/11736639_61

Holton, D., Ahmed, A., Williams, H., & Hill, C. (2001). On the importance of mathematical play. *International Journal of Mathematical Education in Science and Technology*, *32*, 401–415. doi:10.1080/00207390010022158

Jensen, J., Sims, J., & Reventos, L. (2004). Jeux vidéo: la nouvelle pop culture. *Courrier international*, 709, 40-46.

Jenson, J., & De Castell, S. (2006). You're going to die: gender, performance and digital game play. In V. Uskov (Eds.), *Proceedings of the International conference on computer and advanced technology in Education,* Lima, Peru.

Kafai, Y. B. (2001). *The Educational Potential of Electronic Games: From Games–To–Teach to Games–To–Learn.* Presented in the Playing by the Rules Conference, Chicago, October 26.-27. Retrieved November 5, 2004, from http://culturalpolicy.uchicago.edu/conf2001/papers/kafai.html

Kelly, H. (2005). Games, Cookies, and the Future of Education. *Issues in Science and Technology*, *21*(4), 33–40.

Kirriemur, J., & McFarlane, C. A. (2004). *Literature Review in Games and Learning, A Report for NESTA Futurelab*. Retrieved November 5, 2004, from http://www.nestafuturelab.org/ research/ reviews/08_01.htm

Krajewsky, P. R., & Piroli, V. B. (2002). Something Old, Something New, Something Borrowed, Something Blue: Active Learning in the Classroom. *Journal of Library Administration*, *36*(1-2), 177–194.

Lamy, C. (2004). NetAdos 2004 - Sondage réalisé auprès des ados québécois & de leurs parents [Poll of Québécois adolescents and their parents]. Québec: CEFRIO. Retrieved October 6, 2007, from http://www.cefrio.qc.ca/rapports/NetAdos_2004_rapport.pdf.

Lennon, J. L., & Coombs, D. W. (2006). Child-invented health education games: A case study for dengue fever. *Simulation & Gaming*, *37*(1), 88–97. doi:10.1177/1046878105285550

Lieberman, D. A. (1998). *Health education video games for children and adolescents: Theory, design, and research findings.* Paper presented at the annual meeting of the International Communication Association, Jerusalem.

Lieberman, D. A. (2001). Management of chronic pediatric diseases with interactive health games: theory and research findings. *The Journal of Ambulatory Care Management*, *24*(1), 26–38.

Lisowski, M. (2007). Le jeu: gadget ou innovation pédagogique? *Inffo Flash, 708, 16 au 30 septembre.* Retrieved February 2, 2008, from http://www.centre-inffo.fr/Le-jeu-gadget-ou-innovation.html

Macfarlane, A., Sparrowhawk, A., & Heald, Y. (2002). *Report on the educational use of video games: An exploration by TEEM (Teachers Evaluating Educational Multimedia) of the contribution which games can make to the education process.* Retrieved August 23, 2003, from http://www.teem.org.uk/publications/ teem_gamesined_full.pdf

Markey, C., Power, D., & Booker, G. (2003). Using structured games to teach early fraction concepts to students who are deaf or hard of hearing. [from http://www.gallaudet.edu/~ossweb/annals/]. *American Annals of the Deaf, 148*(3), 251–258. Retrieved November 5, 2004. doi:10.1353/aad.2003.0021

Miller, C. S., Lehman, J. F., & Koedinger, K. R. (1999). Goals and Learning in Microworlds. *Cognitive Science, 23*(3), 305–336.

Mitchell, A., & Savill-Smith, C. (2004). *The use of computer and video games for learning. A review of the literature. Learning and skills development Agency*. Ultralab. Retrieved November 5, 2004, from http://www.lsda.org.uk/files/PDF/1529.pdf

Moisy, M. (2004). EN-JEUX. *Adolescence, 22*(1), 77–89.

Mondozzi, M. A., & Harper, M. A. (2001). In search of effective education in burn and fire prevention. *The Journal of Burn Care & Rehabilitation, 22*(4), 277–281. doi:10.1097/00004630-200107000-00006

Moreno, R., & Duran, R. (2004). Do multiple representations need explanations? The role of verbal guidance and individual differences in multimedia mathematics learning. *Journal of Educational Psychology, 96*(3), 492–503. doi:10.1037/0022-0663.96.3.492

Morris, P. E., Fritz, C. O., & Buck, S. (2004). The Name Game: Acceptability, Bonus Information and Group Size. *Applied Cognitive Psychology, 18*, 89–104. doi:10.1002/acp.948

Moyer, P. S., & Bolyard, J. J. (2003). Classify and Capture: Using Venn Diagrams and Tangrams To Develop Abilities in Mathematical Reasoning and Proof. *Mathematics Teaching in the Middle School, 8*(6), 325–330.

Padgett, L. S., Strickland, D., & Coles, C. D. (2005, April). Case Study: Using a Virtual Reality Computer Game to Teach Fire Safety Skills to Children Diagnosed with Fetal Alcohol Syndrome. *Journal of Pediatric Psychology*, 1–6.

Piette, J. (2005). *Conférence de Jacques Piette lors du congrès de la FADBEN à Nice*. Médias communication TICE académie de Nice, avril.

Prensky, M. (2006). *Don't bother me mom – I'm learning!*St. Paul, MN: Paragon House.

Purushotma, R. (2005). Commentary: you're not studying, you're just. *Language Learning & Technology, 9*(1), 80–96.

Rassin, M., Gutman, Y., & Silner, D. (2004). Developing a computer game to prepare children for surgery. *AORN Journal, 80*(6), 1099–1102. doi:10.1016/S0001-2092(06)60689-3

Ravenscroft, A. (2007). Promoting thinking and conceptual change with digital dialogue games. *Journal of Computer Assisted Learning, 23*(6), 453–465. doi:10.1111/j.1365-2729.2007.00232.x

Ravenscroft, A., & Matheson, M. P. (2002). Developing and evaluating dialogue games for collaborative e-learning. *Journal of Computer Assisted Learning, 18*(1), 93–101. doi:10.1046/j.0266-4909.2001.00215.x

Roberts, D. F., Foehr, U. G., Rideout, V. J., & Brodie, M. (1999). *Kids and media at the new milennium: A comprehensive national analysis of children's media use*. Menlo Park, CA: Kaiser Family Foundation.

Rosas, R., Nussbaum, M., Cumsille, P., Marianov, V., Correa, M., & Flores, P. A. (2003). Beyond Nintendo: Design and Assessment of Educational Video Games for First and Second Grade Students. *Computers & Education, 40*(1), 71–94. doi:10.1016/S0360-1315(02)00099-4

Sauvé, L., & Chamberland, G. (2006). Jeux, jeux de simulation et jeux de rôle: une analyse exploratoire et pédagogique. [Games, simulation games and role-playing games: An exploratory pedogical analysis] Cours TEC 1280: Environnement d'apprentissage multimédia sur l'inforoute. Québec, Canada: Télé-université.

Sauvé, L., Kaufman, D., & Renaud, L. (2007). A Systematic Review of the Impact of Games and Simulations on Learning. In *ED-MEDIA 2007-World Conference on Educational Multimedia, Hypermedia & Telecommunications*, Vancouver, Canada, June 25-29, 10 pages.

Sauvé, L., Renaud, L., & Hanca, (2008). *Étude de cas auprès des élèves du secondaire: apprentissage des ITS à l'aide d'un jeu éducatif en ligne*. Québec, Canada: Rapport de recherche, mars.

Sauvé, L., Renaud, L., Kaufman, D., & Sibomana, F. (2008). Revue systématique des écrits (1998-2007) sur les impacts du jeu, de la simulation et du jeu de simulation sur l'apprentissage. Rapport final [Systematic review on the impact of games, simulations, and simulation games on learning: Final report]. Québec: SAGE et SAVIE, mars.

Shaftel, J., Pass, L., & Schnabel, S. (2005). Math Games for Adolescents. *Teaching Exceptional Children*, *37*(3), 27–33.

Shreve, J. (2005). Let the Games Begin. Video Games, Once Confiscated in Class, Are Now a Key Teaching Tool. If They're Done Right. *George Lucas Educational Foundation*. (Eric Document Reproduction Service No. ED 484 766).

Silverman, B. G., Holmes, J., Kimmel, S., & Branas, C. (2002). Computer games may be good for your health. *Journal of Healthcare Information Management*, *16*(2), 80–85.

Steinman, R. A., & Blastos, M. T. (2002). A trading-card game teaching about host defence. *Medical Education*, *36*(12), 1201–1208. doi:10.1046/j.1365-2923.2002.01384.x

Subrahmanyam, K., & Greenfield, P. M. (1998). Computer games for girls: What makes them play? In Cassell, J., & Jenkins, H. (Eds.), *From Barbie to Mortal Combat: Gender and computer games*. Cambridge, MA: MIT Press.

Subrahmanyam, K., Greenfield, P. M., Kraut, P. M., & Gross, E. (2001). The Impact of computer use on children's development. *Journal of Applied Developmental Psychology*, *22*, 7–30. doi:10.1016/S0193-3973(00)00063-0

Union Européenne en Éducation des médias. (2006). *The appropriation of New Media by Youth*. A European Research Project, Mediappro.

Vail, K. (1997). Girlware. *The American School Board Journal*, *184*, A18–A21.

Vandeventer, S. S., & White, J. A. (2002). Expert Behavior in Children's Video Game Play. *Simulation & Gaming*, *33*(1), 28–48. doi:10.1177/1046878102033001002

Virvou, M., Katsionis, G., & Manos, K. (2005). Combining software games with education: evaluation of its educational effectiveness. *Educational Technology & Society*, *8*(2), 54–65.

Ward, A. K., & O'Brien, H. L. (2005). A gaming adventure. *Journal for Nurses in Staff Development*, *21*(1), 37–41. doi:10.1097/00124645-200501000-00009

Williamson, B., & Facer, K. (2004). More than 'just a game': the implications for schools of children's computer games communities. *Education Communication and Information*, *4*(2/3), 255. doi:10.1080/14636310412331304708

Wissmann, J. L., & Tankel, K. (2001). Nursing student's use of a psychopharmacology game for client empowerment. *Journal of Professional Nursing*, *17*(2), 101–106. doi:10.1053/jpnu.2001.22274

ADDITIONAL READING

Dempsey, J. V., Haynes, L. L., Lucassen, B. A., & Casey, M. S. (2002). Forty Simple Computer Games and What They Could Mean to Educators. *Simulation & Gaming*, *33*(2), 157–168. doi:10.1177/1046878102332003

Lennon, J. L., & Coombs, D. W. (2007). The utility of a board game for dengue haemorrhagic fever health education. *Health Education*, *107*(3), 290–306. doi:10.1108/09654280710742582

Oblinger, D., & Oblinger, J. L. (2005). *Educating the Net Generation*. Washington, DC: Educause.

KEY TERMS AND DEFINITIONS

Game: Is a fictitious, whimsical or artificial situation in which one or more players are put in a position of competition. Sometimes players square off against one another and at other times they are on the same side and are pitted against other teams. Game is governed by rules which structure their actions in view of a learning objective (educational game) and a purpose determined by the game such as to win or to take revenge.

Generic Educational Game Shell (GEGS): Is used as an online design environment that allows teachers and trainers to create games by providing all the tools needed to: (1) set the game parameters, (2) create instructions and rules that direct player actions, (3) create pedagogical material, (4) set the criteria that determine the end of the game and the winner, and (5) detail the tools required for revision and evaluation of the game, in order to ensure that the game is updated regularly and that learning is maximized.

Effectiveness: Is defined by positive consequences from the use of a game on participant knowledge, attitudes or psychomotor skills. It takes into account the relationship between the learning results of game or simulation use and the initial objectives (Blouin & Bergeron, 1997).

Structuring of Knowledge: Refers to the construction and organization of knowledge, schemas (mental models), or representations by the learner in order to understand a concept or a given situation.

Integration of Information: Is the degree of acquisition of declaratory knowledge.

Sex (or gender): Is an array of characteristics which distinguish males from females.

Learning: Is the acquisition of knowledge or skills with the help of experience, practice or study. Learning outcomes are measured in terms of the knowledge, attitudes and skills acquired by students as a result of learning.

Chapter 10
The Experience of an Online Management Simulation Game to Foster Collaboration and Teamwork

Hélder Fanha Martins
Lisbon Polytechnic Institute, Portugal

ABSTRACT

With a new degree on Management, a new course called Management Simulation Project was created and started in the summer semester of 2006-2007 at the Lisbon School of Accountancy and Administration (ISCAL). The teaching team wanted to explore ways to bring the realities of business decision-making and action into the curriculum. This chapter reflects on the concept of educational simulations and games and aims at describing how a web-based competitive management game helped to achieve that. The authors discuss their objectives and those of the game and outline their reasons for choosing it. They describe the context at ISCAL and the game's main features, showing how it is played over a semester. The authors consider, as online simulation facilitators of what is predominantly a student-led learning process, that the game helps students to gain a real 'feel' for collaboration, managerial decision-making and teamwork. An exploratory study was carried out. A questionnaire was designed to tap students' perceptions of the effectiveness of the use of a simulation/game as a new teaching method in five areas: career preparation, traditional educational goals, use of time, involvement and satisfaction, and a set of specific skill competencies. The results of the authors' empirical study show that students perceive the simulation course as superior to the lecture-centered method. On the overall dimensions, the simulation course was seen as a better vehicle in helping students make career preparations, achieve educational goals, and utilize time. The results are presented and discussed.

DOI: 10.4018/978-1-61520-713-8.ch010

INTRODUCTION

There has been a shift in business education. "Under the new learning 'paradigm',learning is student-centered and controlled, and essentially experiential, replacing the old 'instruction paradigm' where learning is instructor- and content-centered" (Saunders 1997:98, citing Barr and Tagg). This shift emphasizes student participation and involvement in the learning process, and places lecturers in the position of acting not only as knowledge creators and disseminators, but also as learning process facilitators.

When the online business simulation game Marketplace was introduced into the curriculum, the teaching team had two objectives: first, to emphasize to students the interconnectedness of the business disciplines and, second, for them to link the content of individual management disciplines to managerial decision-making. As Chapman and Sorge (1999) point out, of particular concern in management education is development of the students' analytical, problem-solving and decision-making abilities. Students need to know not only theories and concepts but also how to apply these, and their acquired skills, to business problems. This extended web-based business simulation was chosen, set in a high-tech industry, because it requires students to tie together a series of related decisions and outcomes over time. This game gives students experience of applying new technology for group decision-making. In it, subject matter is delivered 'just-in-time', to support students' decision-making in an extended case.

The online simulation Marketplace is expected to acquaint students with the challenges of real business decisions and leadership in a complex and uncertain environment. Cadotte (1995) in advocating the use of virtual business simulations in business and management education and training stated: 'Reality simulations have unique training capabilities that foster personal transformation. Moreover, they can help students develop an almost intuitive understanding of business, including a seamless perspective of its functions and elements, and knowledge of how these elements can be coordinated to achieve a strong and profitable position in the market. Another distinctive feature of simulations is their emphasis on management – of the firm, of its strategy, and of its resources.'

This specific online management simulation was chosen because its main intended learning outcomes are the integration of knowledge and action. By the end of the game the student should be able to:

- Continuously apply strategic planning and execution skills within a rapidly changing environment;
- Demonstrate a persistent focus on bottom line profitability while simultaneously delivering customer value in running a simulated business;
- Repetitively practise budgeting and cash-flow analysis in management of an enterprise;
- Demonstrate a developed practical knowledge of marketing, accounting, finance and manufacturing functions;
- Display leadership, teamwork and interpersonal skills.

The game also fosters many key skills. By the end of the game the student should be able to demonstrate:

- Critical thinking and creativity;
- Problem solving and decision-making;
- Information and knowledge;
- Numeracy and quantitative skills;
- Effective use of information and communication technology;
- Two-way communication;
- Personal effectiveness;
- Effective performance within a team environment and the ability to recognize and utilize individuals' contributions in group processes;

- Team selection, delegation, development and management;
- Leadership and performance management;
- Ethics and value management;
- Ability to conduct research into business and management issues;
- Learning through reflection on practice and experience.

We think it is vital for students to apply their knowledge and skills to real business problems. It is well known that many employers feel that students enter the business world without some of the knowledge, skills, and experience needed to solve such problems and to function effectively (Chapman and Sorge, 1999). In computer games such as this online management simulation decisions do not occur sequentially but simultaneously and interactively, just as they do in the business world (Chapman and Sorge, 1999). The learning is focused on the application of theory, rather than the definition of business concepts, principles, and methods. This focus helps students to internalize the material they have been taught in the various modules of the course through their own experience, and to reflect on their success in both understanding and applying what they have covered (Cadotte 1995).

BACKGROUND

Chickering and Ehrmann (1996) describe how technology should be employed in ways that are consistent with the *Seven Principles of Good Practice in Undergraduate Education* created in 1987. Since the creation of these principles, technologies have become major resources for teaching and learning in higher education. In particular, the third principle, "Good Practice Uses Active Learning Techniques", encourages active learning. Technologies that encourage active learning fall into three categories: tools and resources for learning by doing, time-delayed exchange, and real-time conversation. Simulation technology is consistent with this principle by providing a tool that allows participants to learn by doing and to become active participants in the learning process.

Detweiler (2004) states "students have grown up with simulations and online collaboration, and they are ready to use them in their courses." He further concludes that simulations can be far more effective than traditional methods of teaching when teaching complex concepts.

Springer and Borthick (2004) reported that accounting students with business simulation experience outperformed students receiving only traditional principles of accounting courses on exams in financial accounting, cost accounting, and contemporary accounting information courses. The higher exam scores of each of the accounting courses revealed that students with business simulations experience had a stronger understanding of accounting concepts and procedures, and developed thinking strategies or general academic abilities faster than those students receiving only the traditional method of teaching. Blejec (2002) states that statistical simulations allow student to gain insight into specific abstract concepts such as sampling distributions and central limit theorem which otherwise might be difficult to learn through traditional learning methods, and that the use of statistical simulations facilitates the comparison of expected outcomes to actual computed results.

According to Puto (2004), simulations help students master skills such as "critical incident learning" that are not learned in generally accepted business curricula. The simulations immerse students in an intense world that replicates the actual business environment. Malik and Howard (1996) report that students have a more positive attitude toward learning when the method of learning is simulation as opposed to other teaching methods. Aldrich (2003) states that the next generation of students will increasingly ask for simulations and that educational simulation will be widely used by leading instructors within five years. Aldrich continues by adding that educational simulations "will eventually change education as much as textbooks and motion pictures."

Business Simulation Method

Cadotte (1995) compares the simulation method of teaching to the lecture/textbook method and the case study method in terms of emphasis, content, and method of learning.

The emphasis in the simulation method of teaching is placed on the business process, execution of strategy and solutions, management of tactics, and team work. This emphasis provides a more meaningful learning experience for business students as opposed to lecture/textbook methods that place emphasis only on the language and the tools of business. Though the case study method of teaching provides a textual replication of business environment by placing the emphasis on the situation analysis, problem diagnosis, problem solving, and strategic thinking, it does not allow for interactive learning on the participant's part.

Harper, Squires, and McDougall (2000) state that proponents of the constructivist approach stress the need for designers of educational software to create "open-ended exploratory authentic learning environments in which learners can develop personally meaningful and transferable knowledge and understanding." The simulation method of teaching is compatible with a constructivist view of learning. Simulations are described by Bliss and Ogborn (1989) as "programs in which the computer acts as an exploratory tool, supporting a real world activity while facilitating user understanding of the processes, which may be otherwise inaccessible, in complex dynamic systems."

Cadotte states that the instructor's role changes when moving from a traditional method of teaching to a simulation method of teaching. The instructor's role becomes a dual role of devil's advocate and coach. As the devil's advocate, the instructor challenges students to understand the dynamics of the market and the decision-making environment. As coach, the instructor helps students to develop critical thinking skills needed to be successful in business environments.

There are many advantages associated with the simulation method of teaching. The most obvious advantage of using simulations is the ability to replicate real-world environments. Additional advantages include the ability of participants to actively engage in the learning process, develop critical thinking skills, become team players, captivate a competitive spirit, interconnect decision making, risk taking and management of operation, and just as important, have fun.

One major disadvantage of business simulations, on the other hand, includes the absence of human sensitivity that is part of real business environments. The nature of simulation technology does not account for the consequences associated with making decisions that affect people in a negative way. Additional disadvantages might include high cost and extensive time associated with integrating simulations into a curriculum. However, the disadvantages of high cost can be overcome by either using free simulation software or bundling simulations with textbooks. The disadvantage of extensive time can be reduced by using simulation software that is currently on the market and by providing resources for instructors.

Early on there was great enthusiasm for the 'new' technology of instructional simulations. But beginning in the 1980s, researchers (Shirts, 1989; Greenblat, 1989, Duke & Kemeny, 1989; Shubik, 1989) tried to answer the question, "Why aren't more people using this compelling teaching method?" Most of the studies recorded in the *Journal of Simulation and Games*, measured learner outcomes with a specific emphasis on retention of content. Practitioners have underestimated the degree of entrenchment of traditional modes of instruction and student assessment did not value the type of learning offered by gaming. The learning offered by simulation/games would have to conform to the culture of existing institutions. While other kinds of learning outcomes were noted (i.e. attitude change, behavioural change and tolerance for ambiguity), the assessment of these outcomes were not usually relevant to student assessment. Institutions of mass-education still rely primarily on assessing student progress on the basis of how well content has been 'transmitted' to the student and 'retained' by them. Therefore it is not surprising that faculty did not go to the trouble of using a new, compelling teaching method when the incentives of the institutional culture principally support 'transmission of content'.

An Overview of Simulations and Games in Education

Most of the simulation/games reported in the *Journal of Simulation and Games* referred to classroom or seminar activities. Most are business simulations. However, an example of a widely used classroom simulation would be those related to sociology. For instance in *Starpower*, students were divided into socially-stratified groups and then assigned privileges based on their rank in the simulated society. This society would then test tenets of sociological theory (i.e. Would the elite willingly share their privileges? Would the lower strata be satisfied with letting the society evolve or would they be motivated to revolt?) (Dukes & Mattley, 1986). A few studies in the journal reported on simulation/games used at the high school level, most were oriented toward adult education, either in the workplace setting or at a post-secondary institution.

The development of educational simulations began in the 1950s (Faria, 1987). Computers were used even with these early simulation activities (primarily to calculate points at the end of the round, much as we would use a calculator today) (Crookall, 1986). From the 1950s to the early 1980s, the typical simulation was published in text form and instructors would refer to these manuals and then act as facilitators during the simulation (which was delivered in a workshop or seminar format). These simulations were intended to run several hours consecutively at a time (or over several days as needed). This type of time commitment was not always compatible with conventional classroom instruction (Greenblat, 1989; Shirts, 1989) and may suggest the reason why many simulations concern training for professionals and management executives. A significant number of articles in this journal describe simulations which are related to a specific job-context. Examples of the history of simulation/games include the following content topics: management training (Biggs, 1978), accounting (Sprecht & Sandlin, 1991), labour relations (Brenestuhl & Blalack, 1978), entrepreneurship training (Low et al, 1994), urban planning (Kennedy, 1973), international relations (Modelski, 1970), law (Hollander, 1977), teacher education (Tansey, 1970) and even child care (France & McClure, 1972). Another article listed over 1000 simulation games available for college and university instruction (Birnbaum, 1982). Hence simulation gaming has a substantial history and has been associated with higher education for at least four decades.

A strategy simulation game provides a *virtual* apprenticeship in decision making. Games are usually designed to describe a complex, uncertain and ambiguous environment. The student/user must successfully negotiate with and navigate this environment while engaged in solving problems (Norris & Niebuhr, 1980). As part of the process, the student may choose to approach the problem from a particular perspective. It is probable that the player will encounter other perspectives - those other of players or the biased abstractions of the game designer (as represented in the artificial intelligence of the computer program). The literature is consistent in emphasizing that the primary learning opportunity is the debriefing of learners after the game has been concluded (Gamson & Stambaugh, 1978; Petranek, 1992; Thatcher, 1990). The measured outcomes have included variables such as attitude/affect change (Orbach, 1977), behavioural change (Duke & Mattley, 1986), and tolerating ambiguity (O'Leary, 1971).

Many published studies focused on comparing simulation games to conventional instruction where the primary outcome measurement is content retention. Predictably, these studies have achieved mixed results. Some indicated no difference in content retention between the two types of instruction (Keeffe et al, 1993; Randel et al, 1992; Bredemeier and Greenblatt, 1981; Brenestuhl, 1975; Greenlaw and Wyman, 1973). Others claimed conventional instruction allowed more content retention (Boseman and Schellenberger, 1974). Others said simulation/games encouraged better learning (Page & Roberts, 1992; Stembler, 1975; Braskamp and Hodgetts, 1971). Other longitudinal studies claimed that remembering content over a period of several months was better for simulation/games (Sprecht & Sandlin, 1991). This line of inquiry suffers from the inherent complexity of simulation gaming. As a learning outcome, content retention is primarily a feat of sensory perception and memory. Simulation games also engage elements of personality (e.g., extroversion, introversion, ambition, aggressiveness, reticence, etc.), social ability (i.e. ability to assess social relationships, persuade, charm, tolerate ambiguity, etc), as well as higher forms of cognitive thinking (i.e. analysis, synthesis) (Keegan, 1994). Simulation games also invite a reflective contemplation of personal values and belief systems. While conventional instruction may intend to engage many of these same elements, it does so in an indirect manner, and ultimately changes in these elements are not measured or evaluated. Simulation games directly engage the elements of personality, social ability and value/belief systems. The debriefing process provides the opportunity to re-evaluate changes in these elements. In comparing simulation/games to conventional instruction, measuring content retention fails to acknowledge the complexity of learning outcomes for simulation/games.

Theoretical Perspectives for Teaching and Learning

In designing simulation/games for a post secondary system, professor/instructors may insist on approaching the task from their perspective as teachers. One theory suggests five possible perspectives: transmission of content, apprenticeship, developmental, nurturing, and societal reform (Pratt, 1998). Within the context of institutional education, the transmission of content is the most common form of teaching. In this perspective, the primary commitment of the teacher is to express a deep respect for the content by accurately representing the content, demonstrating an enthusiasm for the content and encouraging student/users to consider the subject. The developmental perspective is a relative newcomer to post secondary institutions and challenges many institutional constraints, in particular the requirement of evaluating student progress. The key belief of the developmental perspective is that learning depends on building effective bridges between present and desired ways of thinking. The primary challenge for the instructor is to assess the student's prior knowledge and begin instruction at this point. The end point is not a successful retention of content, but a new way of thinking about the content. Thus of all the teaching perspectives, the developmental perspective may be the most complementary to the kind of instruction offered by simulation/games.

The apprenticeship method is also a time-honoured way of providing learning opportunities. The expert is continuously present to provide guidance as needed to the apprentice, and act as mentor initiating the apprentice into a community of practice. But in the modern world, the matching of apprentices to an expert in a resource rich environment is often viewed as too expensive. Many computer technologies have attempted to recreate this relationship with the computer as 'expert' and the student as 'apprentice'—so far none has succeeded (Woolf, 1990). Most versions of computer-assisted-instruction are little more than drill and practice (Suppes, 1990). The limitations of expert systems and artificial intelligence have been described (Illovsky, 1994). Useful applications of artificial intelligence and neural networks have yet to emerge from the research laboratory. But combinations of these technologies are producing useful tools. The architecture of a computer simulation/game is usually framed around an expert system of rules. Artificial intelligence is used to animate and activate the virtual competitors who play against the end-user.

Learning through apprenticeship is an expensive, labour-intensive process. Computer simulation/games distributed through online education may represent an opportunity to realize some efficiencies. If computer simulation/games succeed in recreating the master/apprentice relationship, the professor/instructors may need to retreat from 'transmission of content' and embrace the teaching perspective of apprenticeship.

One theoretical perspective offers insight into the difficulties of categorizing the kind of learning offered by simulation/games. The instructional design of simulation games could be more aptly described by a constructivist epistemology (Jonasson et al, 1995: 11):

"*The constructivist sense of active learning is not listening and then mirroring the correct view of reality, but rather participating in and interacting with the surrounding environment in order to create a personal view of the world.*"

While constructivism makes claims for the value of this orientation, it does little to guide the designer. Two main features of constructivist instructional design require more how-to guidance: interactivity and problem solving. Designing for interactivity should include the following considerations (a) immediacy of response, (b) non-sequential access of information, (c) adaptive communication, and (d) bi-directional communication (Borsook & Higginbotham-Wheat, 1991). Designing for problem solving would focus on cognitive operations that transform the mental representation of objects, both images and concepts (Dijkstra, 1991). Declarative knowledge is developed by solving problems, and the operations must allow the learner to discover relationships between objects.

Managing complexity is the primary challenge facing learners. Learning through simulation games may provide one tool for learning to manage complexity. But the paradox is that the designing of simulation/games may have proven to be too complex. To date, there is a paucity of theoretical and practical work to guide an exploration of the design of simulation/games. Only a few articles have described the design of simulation/games and these have focused on classroom activities rather than computer software products (and certainly nothing intended for online education). Theories of instructional design are inadequate because they fail to capture the complexity of constructivist learning. Professor/instructors may need to change their teaching perspective from transmission of content to a developmental or apprenticeship perspective. From these two perspectives, professor/instructors may be more amenable to the type of learning offered by simulation/games, primarily because these two perspectives support the personal construction of meaning and are not as objectivist as the 'transmission of content' perspective. The apprenticeship model fosters the inclusion of a learner within a community of practice where situated-learning is dominated by the context. Simulation games can offer rich contextual environments. The developmental perspective intends that the learner become more aware of the process of learning rather than the product - thinking about thinking. The learner's understanding moves from Point A to Point B. The instructors' role is to assess where Point A is for each individual learner and facilitate a bridging to Point B. Simulation games offer the learner a choice of perspectives. They can choose one that is the closest match to their own worldview. They can then choose the difficulty level they are comfortable with. While engaged in the game, it is a useful strategy to intuit the intent of the designer - thinking about the designer's thinking. In this way the meta-cognitive goal of the developmental perspective is achieved.

Ultimately, it remains to be seen if the communications revolution will in some way cause a paradigm shift from an objectivist epistemology which currently governs our scientific paradigm to a paradigm which validates a more subjectivist epistemology. The institutional contexts of the education system, in both secondary and post-secondary, continue to emphasize content-retention within an objectivist epistemology. Simulation/games (and the multiple perspectives they represent) challenge objectivism. Is it possible to design simulation/games where all the competing perspectives are "correct"? As the saying goes "all models are wrong…some are useful." If the goal of higher education is to encourage students to critically evaluate the constraints of all objectivist notions and develop a greater appreciation of subjectivist influences, then learning through simulation/games provides an optimal opportunity to develop this awareness.

A Business Game at ISCAL

Given this brief review of relevant literature, we concluded that the method of gaming and simulation has distinct advantages over other interactive methods of teaching and learning, such as the use of case studies. As Saunders (1997, p.105) suggests: 'Unlike cases, simulations and games are seldom restricted by the narrative structure of prose, a point seldom noted. Most cases develop their story lines chronologically, a method which while helpful, distorts the reality of how employees actually discover problems at work and solve them. Simulations and games demonstrate a more complex business environment and show learners the effects of the decisions they make. 'Saunders also highlights disadvantages of simulations: these include the difficulty, in high-reality and complex simulations, of relating different actions and decisions taken in the game to particular outcomes. He states that 'Learners often resent the fact that their erroneous choices were not corrected by the instructor and they were left to fail, especially if their grades are based on the successful completion of the exercise. Overly complex simulations can be confusing and result in a loss of learner confidence and self-esteem' (Saunders 1997, p.106, quoting Gilley). Conversely, Saunders points out that a number of business researchers have argued that this gap in understanding the link between actions and outcomes is a common dilemma experienced in most organizations. In our own experience as facilitators, we have observed that learners may come to resent both the tutor and the simulation! In addition, the task of convincing learners that failing to solve a problem should be seen as a positive event may also prove difficult. However, as Cadotte (1995, p.3) points out: 'The instructor's role is not to provide solutions to the team's problems, but rather to raise questions and issues that have not yet been addressed. As coach, the instructor's role is to help students develop critical thinking skills.' To help the instructor/ tutor to do this, the game provides a number of useful tools. The tutor can view who is online, how much decision time each student has devoted to the game in a particular quarter and the quality of functional area decisions. Tutors can use such tools to help guide class discussions and seminar meetings with teams, or indeed may use the data to further their own knowledge about managerial decision-making. To help tutors identify key areas of performance, they can access summary results.

"Marketplace": Business Game Scenario

The students starts a new company that will enter the microcomputer business. As the executive team, the students will provide the seed capital (investment money) to start up your business. They can use this money to build a factory, open sales offices, and design brands, and will invest 1,000,000 in each of the first four quarters. An additional 5,000,000 will become available in quarter 5 from venture capitalists, for a total of 9,000,000. The executive team has the next 3 years (twelve quarters or decision periods) to get the company off the ground. Within this time frame, the team should become a self-sufficient firm, earning substantial profits from your operations. A "Balanced Scorecard" will be used to measure the firm's performance and compare the results with the competitors. The firm's performance will be based on financial results, market effectiveness, marketing performance, investments in the firm's future, human resource management, creation of wealth, asset management and manufacturing productivity.

The balanced scorecard is the most important measure of the company's total performance. It provides a single number that can be compared between companies. As such, it is the main indicator for evaluating the performance in the market. The balanced scorecard is used extensively in industry. Its popularity reflects the fact that it encourages managing executives to properly consider a host of performance criteria at the same time. The Cumulative Balanced Scorecard will be the measure used to evaluate your overall game performance at the end of the exercise. The final evaluation will be based upon an average of your balanced scorecard over the final four quarters.

The Total Business Performance indicator is a quantitative measure of the executive team's ability to effectively manage the resources of the firm. It considers both the historical performance of the firm as well as how well the firm is positioned to compete in the future. As such, it measures the action potential of the firm: Total Business Performance = Financial Performance * Market Performance * Marketing Effectiveness * Investment in Future * Wealth * Asset Management * Manufacturing Productivity.

The index employs what is called a balanced scorecard to measure the executive team's performance. The most important measure is the team's financial performance, and thus its ability to create wealth for the investors. However, the focus on current profits has caused many executives to stress the present at the expense of the future. The long-term viability of the firm requires that the executive team be good at managing not only the firm's profitability, but also its marketing activities, production operations, cash, and financial resources. The management team must also invest in the future. These expenses might depress the current financial performance, but are vital to creating new products, markets, and manufacturing capabilities.

In short, top managers must be good at managing all aspects of the firm. The balanced scorecard puts this perspective into practice. It focuses attention on multiple performance measures, and thus multiple decision areas. The Total Business Performance measure is computed by multiplying seven indicators of business performance. This model underscores the importance of all measures. This is because any strength or weakness will have a multiple effect on the final outcome, the Action Potential of the Firm.

The group will have the capability of introducing a new line of microcomputers into 20 international markets. Within the PC industry, other firms will be entering the market at the same time. The microcomputer industry is in the introductory stage of the product life cycle. There is no history and there are no established competitors. All competitors, including the students' company, will start with exactly the same resources and knowledge of the market. All manufacturers will sell through company-owned sales offices in twenty major metropolitan markets around the world and also via a web channel. The target market will be the business sector. The company will not be selling to the home market and not sell through retail stores. Thus, the business strategy will be tightly focused on direct sales to business customers.

An Exploratory Study

The teaching approach we have adopted over the past years addresses several limitations of the lecture-based method and also provides a number of other benefits. We conducted an exploratory study to examine whether students perceive these advantages because relative advantages apprehended by users ultimately determine the outcome of innovation adoption (Rogers, 1983). The benefits of the new approach were evaluated by requesting students to answer a questionnaire that gauged their perceptions. The questionnaire, adapted from Droge and Spreng (1996), was designed to tap students' perceptions of the effectiveness of a new teaching method in five areas: career preparation, traditional educational goals, use of time, involvement and satisfaction, and a set of specific skill competencies.

The population consisted of 88 students at the Lisbon School of Accountancy and Administration, which is a public higher education institution. The course was required for all the students. Among the students, 59.2% were men, and 40.8% were women. The amount of full-time work experience varied: 10.9% had 1 year of experience or less, 27.4% had 2 to 4 years, and 58.3% had 5 or more years. Each respondent had just completed the simulation course. Respondents were asked to evaluate this course and the traditional lecture-centered methods from their courses on a variety of dimensions. The lecture-centered method was verified by a survey among professors who taught the required courses. The lecture-centered approach was employed in more than 90% of all the required courses.

Following Droge and Spreng (1996), we divided measurement into the two categories of the overall measure of evaluation and the measure of specific skills. The adoption of the two categories is based on the suggestion that teaching curriculum should be assessed on two levels: broad learning objectives and specific competence skills (Duke & Reese, 1995). Duke and Reese (1995) suggested that curriculum should also be evaluated on specific competence skills required by employers. The two categories reflect this trend in curriculum assessment. The overall measure of evaluation required the students to directly compare the simulation course with the traditional lecture-centered method. On a total of 10 measures, the respondents were asked, "Which method do you think is more appropriate overall?" Students were required to evaluate on a 7 point scale, with 1 indicating the simulation method and 7 indicating the lecture-centered method, and 4 indicating that the methods were equal. The overall measure of evaluation covered four areas, which are shown in Table 1: career preparation. Traditional educational goals, use of time, and personal involvement and satisfaction. Each area contained two to four measures. The measure of specific skills incorporated 12 statements that asked the respondents to evaluate potential benefits of the two methods separately. A 7-point *disagree* (1)/ *agree (7)* scale was adopted.

The findings of two sets of evaluations, overall evaluations and evaluations of specific skills, are discussed in the following section.

On the question of "Which method do you think is better overall?" a 7-point scale was used, with 1 indicating the simulation method and 7 indicating the lecture-centered method. The results of one-sample t tests show that the means of all of the items are significantly smaller than 4 (at < 1%).

The results for the *10* items focusing on overall evaluation are presented in Table 1. These 10 items involved direct comparative evaluation of the simulation and the lecture-centered methods. As shown in Table 1, the 10 items were classified into four categories. The respondents were asked to compare the two methods on each of the 10 items on a 7-point scale (1 indicating the simulation was better, 7 indicating the lecture-centered

Table 1. Overall evaluation of simulation course over lecture-centered course

Subscales and items (Item rank)	Mean*	Standard Deviation
Career preparation		
In developing career skills	2.27	1.54
In serving as a good surrogate for real world experience (2)	1.79	1.22
Traditional educational goals		
In helping me understand the material	2.80	1.79
In achieving:"I learn a lot"	2.41	1.48
In improving my competences in this area (4)	2.33	1.42
In achieving high educational value overall	2.71	1.68
Use of time		
In making good use of class time	2.80	1.85
In achieving benefits to time ratio	2.65	1.66
Personal involvement and satisfaction		
In producing a high level of involvement (1)	1.63	1.19
In achieving overall satisfaction (3)	2.19	1.56

* One-sample t-test indicated means for each item were significantly less than 4 ($p<.01$)

method was better, and 4 indicating the methods were equal). The results of t tests show that the means of all 10 items are significantly smaller than 4 (at an alpha of .01): among the 10 items, 2 have means smaller than 2; the rest have means smaller than 3. The means of the 10 items are ranked in ascending order as follows:

1. Producing high level of involvement,
2. Serving as good surrogate for real-world experience,
3. Achieving overall satisfaction,
4. Developing career skills,
5. Improving competence,
6. Learning a lot,
7. Achieving good benefits-to-time ratio,
8. Achieving high educational value overall,
9. Making good use of class time,
10. Helping me understand the material.

As shown in Table 1, the simulation course was perceived to be most effective in the areas of personal involvement and satisfaction and in career preparation. The means of the two items related to personal involvement and satisfaction are 1.63 and 2.19 and are first and third in the positioning. The means of the two items pertaining to career preparation are 1.79 and 2.27 and are ranked second and fourth. These results are consistent with the literature that identifies career preparation and involvement as the two dimensions that benefit, in general, from experiential learning (Saunders, 1997).

Among the measures related to traditional educational goals, the item for improving competence has a mean score of 2.33 (fifth); the item pertaining to achieving educational value averages 2.71 (eighth). Both scores are significantly smaller than 4, indicating students perceived that the simulation course provided better educational value. The two items evaluating use of time cover making good use of class time and achieving good benefits-to-time ratio. The simulation course was relatively demanding in terms of workload: on average, students reported spending 8 to 12 hours per week in making decisions, with more energetic students spending 20 hours per week. In view of the time requirement, students' evaluations

Table 2. Overall evaluation of simulation course over lecture-centered course on specific skills

	Simulation		Lecture	
	Mean	Standard Deviation	Mean	Standard Deviation
Increases my competence in				
Problem solving	5.69*	1.48	3.80	1.63
Running a meeting	5.62*	1.57	2.94	1.53
Examining diverse solutions	5.91*	1.39	3.95	2.35
Thinking on my feet	5.78*	1.47	3.66	2.66
Managing operations	5.82*	1.49	3.39	1.62
Risk taking	6.02*	1.52	2.87	1.70
Team work	6.27*	3.29	3.57	1.75
Strategic planning	6.01*	1.41	3.88	1.61
Interpersonal skills	5.87*	1.48	3.58	1.67
Learning principles and concepts	5.29	1.45	5.23	1.67
Oral communication	5.58*	1.50	4.31	1.66
Written communication	4.91	1.48	4.99	1.71

*T-test for dependent samples indicated means differ significantly ($p<.01$)

were encouraging. The item measuring achieving good benefits-to-time ratio has a mean score of 2.65, indicating students' positive perception of the benefits in spite of the heavy workload. The item pertaining to making good use of class time receives a score of 2.80, reflecting students' experience with the new class format, which included team briefings, venture capital negotiations, and presentations at different stages of the game.

Evaluation of specific skills. The results of the 12 specific skills are presented in Table 2. The students evaluated the simulation and lecture-centered methods on each of the 12 skills using a 7-point *disagree/agree* scale, with 7 indicating *agree.* The results of paired sample *t* tests show the simulation course is significantly different (at .01) from the lecture-centered method for 10 of the 12 skills. The two exceptions are found in learning principles and concepts and in using written communication. For learning principles and concepts, the two methods receive mean scores of 5.29 and 5.23, respectively; for using written communication, the scores average at 4.91 and 4.99, respectively. These means are not significantly different.

One possible explanation is that both methods develop competence in these two skill areas. When the rest of the skills are analyzed, it is not surprising that the simulation is rated highly for the items related to managing businesses because the lecture-centered class would scarcely include these skills for students to practice. These items include managing operations, taking risks, using strategic planning, and examining diverse solutions. The mean differences in scores between the two methods were in the range of 2.0 to 3.0 points. Somewhat interesting were students' responses to items such as developing teamwork, developing interpersonal skills, and running a meeting. For developing teamwork, the simulation receives a mean score of 6.27 while the score of the lecture method averages 3.57. For developing interpersonal skills, the simulation has a mean of 5.87 compared with a 3.58 mean score for the lecture-centered method. The rather low ratings of the lecture approach suggest that students still receive insufficient training in these skill areas, although some professors attempt to incorporate them in their lecture classes.

The results of our empirical study show that students perceive the simulation course as superior to the lecture-centered method. On the overall dimensions, the simulation course was seen as a better vehicle in helping students make career preparations, achieve educational goals, and utilize time. It was also advantageous in providing a high level of involvement and satisfaction. In addition, the simulation course was viewed as superior in teaching specific skills ranging from managing operations and taking risks to using strategic planning and examining diverse solutions. In summary, our survey results demonstrate the relative advantage of the simulation course over the lecture method as perceived by the students. The demonstration is important because relative advantage perceived by users is a significant condition for success (Rogers, 1983).

CONCLUSION

During the game, students apply concepts relating to functions like marketing, finance, operations, human resources, etc., in an artificial business world, but they work within the real world of their teams and tutor. They gain valuable insights into the benefits and difficulties of working in multicultural teams. They reveal much of this in their final game assessment, the individual reflective essay, which gives them an opportunity to analyze retrospectively and subjectively both their own and their team's performance. They are expected to apply various organizational behavioral concepts relating to groups and teams, leadership and decision-making. Their game performance is more than adequately assessed, objectively, by the game's inbuilt Balanced Scorecard. The actual playing of the game allows students to participate in three of the four stages of Kolb's (1985) learning cycle, namely; experiencing / observing, conceptualizing/making decisions, and taking action/intervening. Whilst the students are encouraged to monitor their group processes as the game play proceeds, the exigencies of both the game play and of their other studies often prevents this. The reflective essay they have to write every week allows them to complete Kolb's cycle, by thinking/reflecting, thus closing the loop. Using this online simulation as an integral part of the Management course has been a positive experience for both students and tutors. There may be difficulties in dealing with student expectations, particularly where students expect to have a passive role as receivers of knowledge. However, we have found that in most cases the students' reflections upon their experience lead to unexpected learning and competency development. Many students tell us they are disappointed that they will not have the opportunity to play the game again. They would like to gain even more experience in this relatively safe virtual business environment.

REFERENCES

Biggs, W. D. (1978). A comparison of ranking and relational grading procedures in a general management simulation. *Simulation & Games*, *9*(2), 185–200. doi:10.1177/104687817800900204

Birnbaum, R. (1982). Games and simulations in higher education. *Simulation & Games*, *13*(1), 3–11. doi:10.1177/104687818201300101

Blejec, A. (n.d.). *Teaching statistics by using simulations on the Internet*. Retrieved August 15, 2008, from http://www.ph-ludwigsburg.de/iase/proceedings/Invited%20Papers%20refereed/Blejec.pdf

Bliss, J., & Ogborn, J. (1989). Tools for Exploratory Learning. A Research Programme. *Journal of Computer Assisted Learning*, *5*, 37–50. doi:10.1111/j.1365-2729.1989.tb00196.x

Borsook, T. K., & Higginbotham-Wheat, N. (1991). Interactivity: What is it and what can it do for computer-based instruction. *Educational Technology, 31*(10), 11–17.

Boseman, G., & Schellenberger, R. (1974). Business gaming: An empirical appraisal. *Simulation & Games, 5*(4), 383–402. doi:10.1177/104687817400500403

Braskamp, L. A., & Hodgetts, R. (1971). The Role of an Objective Evaluation Model in Simulation Gaming. *Simulation & Games, 2*(2), 197–212. doi:10.1177/003755007122005

Bredemeier, M., & Greenblat, C. (1981). The educational effectiveness of simulation games. *Simulation & Games, 12*(3), 307–332. doi:10.1177/104687818101200304

Brenenstuhl, D. (1975). Cognitive versus affective gains in computer simulations. *Simulation & Games, 6*(3), 303–311. doi:10.1177/003755007563004

Brenenstuhl, D. C., & Blalack, R. O. (1978). Role preference and vested interest in a bargaining environment. *Simulation & Games, 9*(1), 53–64. doi:10.1177/003755007891004

Cadotte, E. (1995). Business Simulations: The Next Step in Management Training. Selections, Graduate Management Admission Council, (Autumn), 8-19.

Chapman, K. J., & Sorge, C. (1999 March). Can a Simulation Help Achieve Course Objectives? An Exploratory Study Investigating Differences Among Instructional Tools. *Journal of Business Education*, 225-230.

Chickering, A. W., Ehrmann, S. E. (1996). Implementing the seven principles: Technology as lever. *AAHE Bulletin*, October, 3-6.

Crookall, D. (1986). Human and computer involvement in simulation. *Simulation & Games, 17*(3), 345–375. doi:10.1177/0037550086173005

Detweiler, R. (2004, July 9). At last, we can replace lectures. *The Chronicle Review.*

Dijkstra, S. (1991). Instructional design models and the representation of knowledge and skills. *Educational Technology, 31*(6), 19–26.

Droge, c., & Spreng, R. (1996). Enhancing involvement and skills with a student-led method of case analysis. *Journal of Marketing Education, 18, 25-34.*

Duke, C. R., & Reese, R. M. (1995). A case study in curriculum evaluation using strategic and tactical assessments. *Journal of Education for Business, 70*, 344–353.

Duke, R. D., & Kemeny, N. (1989). Keeping Score, One Score Later: Two decades of the Simulation & Games Journal. *Simulation & Games, 20*(2), 165–183. doi:10.1177/104687818902000204

Dukes, R., & Mattley, C. (1986). The effects of social structure and mobility on attitudes and behavior in a simulated society. *Simulation & Games, 17*(3), 467–484. doi:10.1177/0037550086174005

Faria, A. J. (1987). A survey of the use of business games in academia and business. *Simulation & Games, 18*(2), 207–224.

France, W., & McClure, J. (1972 June). Building a Child Care Staff Learning Game. *Simulation and Game,* 189-202.

Gamson, W., & Stambaugh, R. (1978). The model underlying Simsoc. *Simulation & Games, 9*(2), 131–157. doi:10.1177/104687817800900201

Greenblat, C. (1989). Introduction: Special Issue 20th Anniversary. *Simulation & Games, 20*(2), 123–129. doi:10.1177/104687818902000201

Greenlaw, P., & Wyman, P. (1973). The teaching effectiveness of games in collegiate business courses. *Simulation & Games, 4*(3), 259–294. doi:10.1177/003755007343001

Harper, B., Squires, D., & McDougall, A. (2000). Constructivist simulation: A new design paradigm. *Journal of Educational Multimedia and Hypermedia, 9*(2), 115–130.

Hollander, P. A. (1977). The uses of simulation in teaching law and lawyering skills. *Simulation & Games, 8*(3), 319–340. doi:10.1177/003755007783002

Illovsky, M. E. (1994). Counseling, Artificial Intelligence and Expert Systems. *Simulation & Gaming, 25*(1), 88–98. doi:10.1177/1046878194251009

Jonassen, D. (1995). Constructivism and computer-mediated communication in distance education. *American Journal of Distance Education, 9*(2), 7–26. doi:10.1080/08923649509526885

Keeffe, M. J., Dyson, D. A., & Edwards, R. R. (1993). Strategic Management Simulations: A Current Assessment. *Simulation & Games, 24*(3), 363–368. doi:10.1177/1046878193243008

Keegan, M. (1995). *Scenario educational software: Design and development of discovery learning*. Englewood Cliffs, NJ: Educational Technology Publications.

Kennedy, M. I. (1973). Theoretical Framework for the use of urban simulation games in education and urban planning. *Simulation & Games, 4*(3), 331–339. doi:10.1177/003755007343005

Kolb, D. A. (1985). *Experiential Learning: Experience as the Source of Learning and Development*. Upper Saddle River, NJ: Prentice-Hall.

Low, M., Venkataraman, S., & Zrivatsan, V. (1994). Developing and Entrepreneurship Game for Teaching and Research. *Simulation & Gaming, 25*(3), 383–401. doi:10.1177/1046878194253006

Malik, D., & Howard, B. (1996). How do we know where we're going if we don't know where we've been? A review of business simulation research. *Development in Business Simulation and Experiential Exercises, 232*, 29–53.

Milech, D., Kirsner, K., Roy, G., & Waters, B. (1993). Applications of Psychology to Computer-Based Tutoring Systems. *International Journal of Human-Computer Interaction, 5*(1), 23–40. doi:10.1080/10447319309526054

Modelski, G. (1970). Simulations, "Realities," and International Relations Theory. *Simulation & Games, 1*(2), 111–134.

Morrison, J. L., & Aldrich, A. (2003). *Simulation and the learning revolution: An interview with Clark Aldrich. Vision*. September/October.

Norris, D., & Niebuhr, R. (1980). Group variables and gaming success. *Simulation & Games, 11*(3), 301–312. doi:10.1177/104687818001100303

O'Leary, A. (1971). Attitude and personality effects of a three-day simulation. *Simulation & Games, 2*(3), 308–347.

Orbach, E. (1977). Some theoretical considerations in the evaluation of instructional simulation games. *Simulation & Games, 8*(3), 341–360. doi:10.1177/003755007783003

Page, D., & Roberts, R. M. (1992). Executive evaluation of college student learning via 'The Looking Glass Inc.' simulation. *Simulation & Gaming, 23*(4), 499–506. doi:10.1177/1046878192234010

Petranek, C. F., Corey, S., & Black, R. (1992). Three levels of learning in simulations: Participating, debriefing and journal writing. *Simulation & Gaming, 23*(2), 174–185. doi:10.1177/1046878192232005

Pratt, D. (1998). *Five perspectives on teaching in adult and higher education*. Malabar, Florida: Krieger Publishing Co.

Puto, C. (2004). The next best thing. *BizEd*, May/June, 44-49.

Raizen, S. (1994). Learning and work: The research base. In VOTEC for youth: Policy Educational Practice, Paris: OECD. pp. 69-113.

Randel, J., Morris, B. A., Wetzel, C. D., & Whitehill, B. V. (1992). The Effectiveness of Games for Educational Purposes: A Review of Recent Research. *Simulation & Gaming*, *23*(3), 261–276. doi:10.1177/1046878192233001

Rogers, E. M. (1983). *Diffusion of innovations*. New York: Free Press.

Saunders, P. M. (1997). Experiential learning, cases, and simulations in business communication. *Business Communication Quarterly*, *60*, 97–114. doi:10.1177/108056999706000108

Shirts, R. G. (1989). The second revolution. *Simulation & Games*, *20*(2), 130–143. doi:10.1177/104687818902000202

Shubik, M. (1989). Gaming: Theory and Practice, Past and Future. *Simulation & Games*, *20*(2), 184–189. doi:10.1177/104687818902000205

Sprecht, L., & Sandlin, P. (1991). The differential effects of experiential learning activities and traditional lecture classes in accounting. *Simulation & Gaming*, *22*(2), 196–210. doi:10.1177/1046878191222003

Springer, C. W., & Borthick, A. F. (2004). Business simulation to stage critical thinking in introductory accounting: Rationale, design, and implementation. *Issues in Accounting Education*, *19*(3), 277–303. doi:10.2308/iace.2004.19.3.277

Stembler, W. A. (1975). Cognitive effects of a programmed simulation. *Simulation & Games*, *6*(4), 392–403. doi:10.1177/003755007500600403

Suppes, P. (1990). Three current tutoring systems and future needs. In Frasson, C., & Gauthier, G. (Eds.), *Intelligent Tutoring Systems: At the Crossroads of Artificial Intelligence and Education* (pp. 251–265). Norwood, NJ: Ablex Publishing.

Tansey, P. J. (1970). Simulation techniques in training of teachers. *Simulation & Games*, *1*(3), 281–303. doi:10.1177/104687817000100303

Thatcher, D. (1990). Promoting learning through games and simulations. *Simulation & Gaming*, *21*(2), 196–210.

Woolf, B. (1990). 20 Years in the Trenches: What have we learned? In Frasson, C., & Gauthier, G. (Eds.), *Intelligent Tutoring Systems: At the Crossroads of Artificial Intelligence and Education* (pp. 234–250). Norwood, NJ: Ablex Publishing.

KEY TERMS AND DEFINITIONS

Active Learning: In traditional or pedagogical education, material to be learned is often transmitted to students by teachers. That is, learning is passive. In active learning, students are much more actively engaged in their own learning while educators take a more guiding role. This approach is thought to promote processing of skills/knowledge to a much deeper level than passive learning and simulation strategies are an example of this.

Balanced Scorecard: a structured measurement system based on a mix of financial and non financial measures of business performance.

Business Education: the enterprise of education directed at the study and research of the field of business. It is often or oriented toward preparing students for the practice of an occupation in business or business-related fields.

Business Simulation: A simulation used for business training in corporations and higher education. In this case, it refers to a scenario-based simulation.

Constructivism: A set of assumptions about the nature of human learning that guide constructivist learning theories and teaching methods. Constructivism values developmentally appropriate, teacher-supported learning that is initiated and directed by the student.

Decision-Making: The process of evaluating and judging information gathered and relating it to the specific requirements of the position for which the applicant is applying. In this case, it it refers to a corporate setting.

Kolb's Learning Cycle: The cycle comprises four different stages of learning from experience and can be entered at any point but all stages must be followed in sequence for successful learning to take place. The Learning Cycle suggests that it is not sufficient to have an experience in order to learn. It is necessary to reflect on the experience to make generalizations and formulate concepts which can then be applied to new situations. This learning must then be tested out in new situations. The learner must make the link between the theory and action by planning, acting out, reflecting and relating it back to the theory.

Total Business Performance Indicator: The Total Business Performance indicator is a quantitative measure of the executive team's ability to effectively manage the resources of the firm in the simulation game Markeplace. It considers both the historical performance of the firm as well as how well the firm is positioned to compete in the future. As such, it measures the action potential of the firm.

Web-Based Simulation: simulation programs over the internet, specifically through a web browser. Increasingly, the web is being looked upon as an environment for providing simulation applications, and as such, it is an emerging area of research within the simulation community.

Chapter 11
Exploring Guild Participation in MMORPGs and Civic Leadership

Adam Friedman
Wake Forest University, USA

Richard Hartshorne
University of North Carolina at Charlotte, USA

Phillip VanFossen
Purdue University, USA

ABSTRACT

This chapter reports the results of a survey study of the civic engagement and participation of guild members in the massively multi-player online role play game (MMORPG) World of Warcraft (WoW). Further, the authors explore the implications of the results of the study for K-12 social studies education. Specifically, the authors focus on the potential of MMORPGs such as WoW for meeting content standards in the social studies—in this case, the National Standards for Civics and Government--and for impacting on pre-service social studies teacher education.

INTRODUCTION

"The qualifications for self-government in society are not innate. They are the result of habit and long training." -Thomas Jefferson, 1824

Thomas Jefferson's early nineteenth century reference to the importance of preparing individuals for the awesome responsibility of citizenship is as poignant today as it was nearly two hundred years ago. The definition of citizenship is broad and its application nebulous; the dictionary defines it as "the state of being vested with the rights, privileges, and duties of a citizen," and a Google™ search of the term returns over 33 million results in a variety of categories, such as becoming a citizen, passing a naturalization test, and the philosophical definition of the term (dictionary.com, 2008, online). In twenty-first century American public schools, the curricular responsibility of preparing future citizens falls to the broad field of social studies (National Council for the Social Studies, 1994). Among the primary missions of social studies education is for students to develop the knowledge, skills, and dispositions of democratic citizenship, in which the citizens

DOI: 10.4018/978-1-61520-713-8.ch011

of tomorrow are taught "to make informed and reasoned decisions for the public good as citizens of a culturally diverse, democratic society in an interdependent world" (National Council for the Social Studies, 1994, p. 3).

Engle and Ochoa (1988) argued that in order for democracy to prosper, its citizenry must have "a willingness to be responsible for the state and to engage at all levels in decisions that chart its course" (p. 18). Civic participation in the manner which Engle and Ochoa (1988) described requires synthesis and application of ideas and concepts; both higher-order tasks. Accordingly, they argue that citizenship education should move beyond "merely knowledge of the mechanics of government," but rather, applying this knowledge (p. 17). This notion has been recognized by the National Council for the Social Studies (2001), as they put forth that "a primary goal of public education is to prepare students to be engaged and effective citizens" (online). However, an "effective citizen" can be difficult to define, complex to discern, and very challenging to teach. Therefore, in this chapter, we define an effective citizen as an individual "who has the knowledge, skills, and attitudes required to assume the 'office of citizen' in our democratic republic," and among the characteristics of this individual is that s/he "Actively participates in civic and community life" (National Council for the Social Studies, 2001, online).

In order for such citizenship education take place, however, it is necessary for social studies teachers to not only possess the qualities of a democratic citizen, but also to able to convey the importance of these characteristics to their students. Similar to Jefferson's early nineteenth century comment on citizenship, the ability to teach is not innate, therefore necessitating social studies-specific teaching methodology (commonly called 'methods' courses). The goal of these courses is multifaceted. While methods courses can be stereotypically viewed in the short term as a means to managing a secondary social studies classroom, they also offer the opportunity for future teachers to become familiar with the broad field of social studies education. Within these courses, future social studies teachers are taught pedagogical strategies within the context of content, while simultaneously becoming familiar with state and national content standards.

Familiarity with such content standards is essential because these standards spell out the knowledge, skills and dispositions needed by students in order to become effective citizens. One such example can be seen in the Center for Civic Education's (1994) *National Standards for Civics and Government* (hereafter NSCG). These standards were developed "to help schools develop competent and responsible citizens who possess a reasoned commitment to the fundamental values and principles that are essential to the preservation and improvement of American constitutional democracy," and are divided into three broad grade levels (K-4, 5-8, and 9-12) (Center for Civic Education, 1994, online). For each level, there are five essential questions as well as a number of sub-questions that provide scaffolding; an example of this is that the fifth question in the 9-12 standards, which rhetorically asks "What are the Roles of the Citizen in the American Democracy," with the first scaffolding question asking "What is citizenship," to the last being more of a higher-order application question, asking students to consider "How can citizens take part in civic life?" (Center for Civic Education, 1994, online).

While the notion of active participation in 'civic and community life' can be broad and might conjure up different images for different individuals, it is important to note that citizens in today's digital universe need not live in the same city, state, or even country to be a member of such a community. One example of this can be seen in the advent of so-called massively multiplayer online role-playing games (commonly referred to as MMORPGs). While engaged in these MMORPGs, individuals around the world can become 'citizens' of the same synthetic community. A MMORPG is a form of online computer role-playing game in which a very large number of players (in some games, upward of one hundred thousand) interact with one another in a synthetic world (Castronova, 2005). Within a particular MMORPG, a player takes on a fictional character (an in-game representation known as an *avatar*) and is responsible for nearly all of that character's actions within the synthetic world: from earning a living, to buying food and clothing, to -- most importantly -- interacting with fellow players. Perhaps most importantly, MMORPGs are 'persistent' games. That is, game play within the synthetic community continues whether any particular player is logged on or not. VanFossen, Friedman, and Hartshorne (2008) described these particular characteristics of MMORPGs as holding great potential for teaching citizenship education. For example, VanFossen, et al., noted that MMORPGs provide an opportunity to "examine citizenship education concepts such as the power of government, property rights, and consent of the governed" (p. 239).

While it is true that MMORPGs are played by a wide range of players, one stereotypical image of MMORPG players is of that of video gamers 'addicted' to game play, leaving little time for other forms of social interaction beyond the synthetic world. Indeed, Glazer (2006) reported that psychologists in the United States and Europe have begun treating Internet addicts (including MMORPG players). Further, Reynolds (2006) described the emergence of support groups for family members of these addicted online gamers. Cole and Griffiths (2007) reported that college-age students are perhaps more susceptible to this addiction with symptoms that take the form of social isolation, poor academic performance, and sleep deprivation—not the best recipe for engagement in civic society. Political scientist Joseph Kahne (2007) echoed these concerns over the potentially negative impact of such social isolation on civic engagement:

But, digital media could make us worse citizens. For example, some have worried that participation will lead to 'cyberbalkinization'--individuals might interact only with those who share their views. Or digital media might become a distraction, time spent listening to music, IMing one's friends, or playing MMORPGS, might leave little time for civic or political endeavors (n.p.).

However, some evidence also suggests that such "digital natives"[1] are in fact engaging in politics and participating in civic life. Xenos and Foot (2008) noted that in the "world of politics and public affairs on the Web in particular, the youth cohort is active and vibrant" (p. 54). The Internet, which is used by the vast majority (87%, with 51% using it daily) of teenagers, has provided the means for participating in the American democracy (Lenhart, Madden, & Hitlin, 2005) that was heretofore unavailable. Not only does the Internet make political information readily available, but through the use of blogs (and other Web 2.0 applications) as well as online videos, it also offers the opportunity to become informed about and to participate in discussions on different perspectives on a particular issue. Bennett (2008) gives an example of how youth can (and do) utilize the Internet to participate in democratic action such as contacting elected leaders to voice their opinion on fair trade (by clicking on a link from a band's Web site); precisely the democratic citizenship Engle and Ochoa (1988) advocate.

Further evidence of youth participation in civic life can be seen in the fact that Senators John McCain and Barack Obama, the Republican and Democratic nominees for the 2008 American Presidential election, both had profiles on the social networking sites Facebook© and MySpace©. The presence of these candidates on these social networks is significant because this is quickly becoming a medium by which younger citizens obtain and share political information and viewpoints. Smith and Rainie (2008) point out that "66% of internet users under the age of 30 have a social networking profile, and half of young profile owners use social networking sites to get or share information about the [2008] candidates and the campaign" (p. ii).

Despite the ubiquity of the Internet in teenagers' lives, Levin and Arafeh (2002) reported on a "substantial disconnect" between the use of the Internet in their personal lives and a lack of use in school (p. iii). Furthermore, even when the Internet is used in classrooms, it is often employed in a very low-level format, where students are engaging in little more than collecting information (VanFossen, 1999-2000, Whitworth & Berson, 2003). Finally, the reality of American schools in the 21st century is that standards and testing are increasingly important, particularly in social studies (Friedman, 2006). Within this context, Bers (2008) offers this potential method for transforming the use of technology in schools into a more higher-order thinking endeavor, while simultaneously addressing civic education:

In a test-driven educational atmosphere in which most public schools might not be able to devote resources and time to increase student's civic participation, the potential of new technologies is even greater for reaching those same students when they are outside of school and connecting to the Internet from their homes. Virtual communities, simulations, or interactive games specifically designed with civic education goals might offer a space for young people to become civically engaged—at least in the online world (p. 141).

Examining the Center for Civic Education's NSCG (1994) more closely, it is evident from the NSCG's content indicators that social studies and citizenship education involve much more than memorizing terminology, dates, people, and places. Rather, students need to be afforded opportunities to experience the activities involved in being active, engaged citizens. As previously noted, MMORPGs seem to have significant potential to improve social studies teaching and learning by providing a 'place' for just such participatory activities. However, in order to prepare teachers to integrate these emerging tools into their classrooms, it is critical that future teachers are provided effective and appropriate opportunities to explore different methods for preparing competent and responsible citizens of the future. Additionally, while students today are embracing emerging technologies, we know that this is not the case with many teachers and teacher educators (Ajjan & Hartshorne, 2008). Thus, to address these issues, it is important to examine factors that influence the integration of MMORPGs into social studies education, from the perspectives of social studies students, teachers, and teacher educators, as well as explore the effectiveness of MMORPGs in addressing the requisite knowledge, skills, and dispositions outlined in the Center for Civic Education's NSCG (1994).

Video Games and Civic Engagement

It is clear that the Internet is used by the vast majority of teenagers; "nearly every teen [97%]" spends time playing video games as well (Lenhart, Kahne, Middaugh, Macgill, and Evans, 2008, p. 7). While the specific game and genre differ from teen to teen, "73% play games on a desktop or laptop computer," and "27% play games with people who they connect with through the internet" (Lenhart, et al., 2008, p. i- iii). Significant to this current study, Lenhart, et al. (2008) proposed that video games can contain "simulations of civic or political activities, helping others, and debating ethical issues," a term they coined "civic gaming experiences" (p. vi).

For the purpose of this chapter, however, we choose to focus only on MMORPGs and their players. MMORPGs are not a unique fad in which a select niche of people participate. Indeed, more than 10 million people from around the world are participants (Woodcock, 2008a). *World of Warcraft©* holds by far the largest share in a marketplace where approximately a dozen MMORPGs account for 95% of the market share (Woodcock, 2008b).

MMORPGs are not our parents' (or, for that matter, our own) video games. Rather, many MMORPG players spend much of their waking free-time playing their 'game.' For many MMOR-

PGs this might mean joining a guild or becoming a guild leader. Within guilds, players might participate in a number of civic activities such as developing a community organization, conducting charitable events, supporting a political endeavor, or others, all the while interacting with thousands of other players role-playing similar characters and developing civic identities (VanFossen, et al., 2008). What lessons do they -- or *can* they -- learn about civic leadership and participation?

In this study, we focus on *World of Warcraft©*, or WoW. Not only does WoW holds the majority of the MMORPG market share[2], but it also has a large volume of teenage participants (MMORPGs such as WoW are used by 21% of video game playing teenagers). Further, WoW's particular structure and format make it well suited to scholarship. While participating in WoW, players "interact" as they undertake missions in which they are "adventuring together or fighting against each other in epic battles," and in so doing, "form friendships, forge alliances, and compete with enemies for power and glory" (Blizzard Entertainment, 2008a, online). More specifically, within WoW, players can join a 'guild,' which in the words of Blizzard Entertainment (2008b), "greatly enhances your gameplay experience" by making it possible to "go places and do things that players in poor guilds or no guild can't" (Blizzard Entertainment, 2008a, online). It is important to note that these guilds are not operated by Blizzard Entertainment (the proprietors of WoW), but instead by individual players themselves. This demonstrates the importance of citizenship 'skills,' as it is advantageous to be, in the words of the National Council for the Social Studies, an "engaged and effective citizen" when playing WoW (online). Moreover, the guilds can be made up of individuals from different backgrounds and cultures, much like the citizens in a democratic society. One respondent in the current study described his experience this way:

In my nearly 3.5 years of playing WoW (which is my first serious computer gaming experience) I am continuously surprised by the "type" of player I run into. My guild is nearly completely populated by people 30 and older, with kids. I can never decide if I am surprised or not with the number of very highly intelligent people I run into... My guild members have professions running from Doctoral Physicists - artists - financial managers - skilled mechanics - truck drivers - engineers - and college students.

With the proliferation of MMORPGs, a burgeoning area of research has begun to emerge, as synthetic environments such as WoW have "provided a new way for youth to create communities that extend beyond geographic boundaries" (Bers, 2008, p. 141). Raynes-Goldie and Walker (2008) studied online communities that promote civic engagement among youth, and found that "interactive Web sites and online communities" can serve as "a valuable precursor to engaging young people in their physical communities" (p. 162). Lenhart, et al. (2008) studied the video game playing habits of teenagers and their impact on civic engagement, particularly in terms of whether the "civic gaming experiences" described above occurred both within and outside of the games themselves. Among their findings were that the amount of time spent playing video games was not "related" to "interest and engagement in civic and political activity" but civic participation was related to whether the game included "civic gaming experiences" (p. 42). As Lenhart, et al. (2008) noted, individuals that have had these experiences "report much higher levels of civic and political engagement than teens who have not had these kinds of experiences" (p. 43). However, there was no difference in civic engagement among those who did and did not participate in guilds. deKanter (2007), in his small scale study (n=47) of guild leaders in WoW, found some transfer to 'real life' civic engagement: two-thirds of the respondents were registered voters -- 100% of whom had voted in the last election.

Given these findings, the underlying purpose of this chapter is to begin to determine ways in which civic leadership characteristics in a MMORPG guild might compare or transfer to those in the 'real' world outside the game. One approach by which we may study the characteristics and development of civic leaders and promoting civic engagement among these "digital natives" is through their use of, and leadership within MMORPGs, such as WoW. Additionally, we explore whether leadership experiences in the virtual world are related to those in the 'real' world. We also investigate whether participation in a synthetic community such as WoW encourages or limits civic participation in the 'real' world. Gee (2004) puts forth that "computer and video games are going to become the predominate form of popular culture interaction in our society" (p. 2). Similarly, Mitch Kapur, CEO of Linden Labs (creator of Second Life), feels that MMORPGs have "the potential to fundamentally change how humans interact" and to "accelerate the social evolution of humanity" (The Week, 2007, p. 11). Interactions in these virtual, synthetic worlds can mirror those in the 'real' world and outside society in terms of rules, laws, economic interaction, and civic engagement, thus providing a potential teaching tool by which to develop citizens in the manner Engle and Ochoa (1988) envisioned.

RESEARCH QUESTIONS

The current study was undertaken in an effort to explore and describe the degree to which guild leaders and members in a popular MMORPG engaged in civic gaming experiences and to determine the relationship -- if any -- between civic participation and leadership in the virtual world of the MMORPG and the world outside the game. Lenhart, et al. (2008) define civic gaming experiences as "experiences young people have while gaming that are similar to offline experiences in classrooms and schools that research has found promote civic and political engagement in young people" (p. 40).

In addition, the current study sought to determine if in-game leadership (e.g., guild leadership) was related to civic engagement or leadership outside the game. Our initial hypothesis was that -- because of the skills needed to be successful within the game -- guild leaders would report more civic participation and leadership outside the game than their guild member counterparts. We also proposed a second hypothesis: that both guild leaders and guild members would report more civic engagement than the general population. In an attempt to explore these hypotheses, the study investigated the following specific research questions:

1. To what degree do guild leaders and guild members engage in 'civic gaming' experiences within World of Warcraft? (Lenhart, et al., 2008).
2. Are guild leaders more likely than guild members to engage in particular types of 'out-of-game' civic engagement and to what degree of civic engagement of guild members and guild leaders differ from that of the general population?
3. What are the civic beliefs of guild leaders and guild members, and do they differ?
4. What are the political orientations of guild leaders and guild members, and do they differ?

Although not a research question per se, we were also interested in investigating the degree to which data collected from this study suggested that standards in civic education were being -- or could be -- met. Put another way, we were curious to see if, and to what degree, guild members in WoW reported engaging in game play (or learning from game play) that demonstrated indicators or benchmarks from the National Standards in Civics and Government (Center for Civic Education, 1994) had been met.

Table 1. Profile of respondents

Variable	Value	Frequency	Percent
Gender	Male	184	82.1
	Female	40	17.9
Role in World of Warcraft	Guild Leader	43	19
	Guild Member	184	81
Age	Under 15	1	0.4
	15-17	12	5.4
	18-21	17	7.6
	22-30	85	38.0
	31-45	97	43.3
	46-60	11	4.9
	Over 60	1	0.4
Highest level of education	**Guild leaders (n=43)**	**Guild members (n=184)**	
Attended high school	2.3	4.9	
High school degree	13.9	11.4	
Attended college/university	41.2	38.1	
Undergraduate degree	37.2	31.5	
Master's degree	4.7	11.4	
Ph.D. or other advanced degree	0.0	2.7	

METHODS

In an effort to answer these research questions, a questionnaire was administered during the spring of 2008. Questionnaire items focused on participant roles in WoW, guild characteristics, levels of civic participation and awareness, gameplay status, political orientations, and levels of education. Participation in the survey was completely voluntary and study respondents consisted solely of either guild members or guild leaders in WoW.

Respondents

In sum, there were 227 respondents (Table 1), including 184 males (82.1%) and 40 females (17.9%), with three respondents not indicating gender. Ages of respondents varied widely. One (0.4%) of the respondents was under 15 years of age, 12 (5.4%) were between 15 and 17 years of age, 17 (7.6%) were between 18 and 21 years of age, 85 (38.0%) were between 22 and 30 years of age, 97 (43.3%) were between the ages of 31 and 45 years of age, 11 (4.9%) were between the ages of 46 and 60, and 1 (0.4%) was over 60 years of age. Additionally, 43 (19%) of the respondents identified themselves as guild leaders in WoW, while 185 (81%) were guild members.

Instruments

The questionnaire was developed to explore parallels between civic leadership in virtual worlds and the real world. The items were adapted from an instrument used in a pilot study of guild leadership and civic skills and participation (deKanter, 2007). deKanter developed his initial pilot instrument by 'cross-walking' an instrument used to measure civic participation (Flanagan, et al., 2007) with studies of online civic engagement behavior (e.g., Steinkuehler & Williams, 2006). deKanter further modified this pilot instrument by using the civic engagement instrument developed by Kahne, Middaugh and Croddy (2005). The questionnaire used in the current study drew heavily from the civic engagement and participation subscales used in deKanter's initial pilot instrument. Finally, the current study used items drawn from the subscales Kahne and Westheimer (2006) developed in their study of high school students' civic efficacy. Kahne and Westheimer labeled these subscales "personal responsibility to help others," "commitment to community involvement," "I will volunteer," "interest in politics," "civic efficacy," "knowledge/ social capital for community development," and "leadership efficacy" (2006, p. 291).[3]

It is important to note that a number of items in the most common instruments used to measure civic engagement and civic skills (e.g., Kahne and Westheimer, 2006; Kahne, Middaugh, and Croddy, 2005) are drawn from, or parallel, indicators contained in the Center for Civic Education's (1994) *National Standards for Civics and Government* (NSCG). Because of this, these items can serve to provide a measure of the kind of civic engagement, knowledge and skills outlined by the National Standards—whether acquired in schools or not. For example Kahne and Westheimer's (2006) sub-scale "interest in politics" draws heavily on indicators contained within the NSCG Standard V.E.1 ("The relationship between politics and the attainment of individual and public goals") and Standard V.E. 3 ("Forms of political participation"). Additionally, Kahne and Westheimer's sub-scale "leadership efficacy" parallels the indicators for NSCG Standard V.E.4 ("Political leadership and careers in politics") and Standard III.E.6 ("Forming and carrying out public policy"). Because the questionnaire used in the current study draws from these sub-scales, our results can be thought of as a kind of proxy for the degree to which guild membership and game play in WoW might contribute to civic learning—the kind of civic learning the NSCG state is expected of high school graduates.

The instrument developed for the current study also contained items about guild leadership in WoW including items on leadership style and level of engagement with members of the guild. In an attempt to establish both face and content validity, final drafts of the instruments were reviewed by several veteran WoW guild leaders, whose feedback was then incorporated into the final versions. The final version of the instrument consisted of an initial branch question (guild leader/ guild member), 19 questions on guild leadership/ participation, 27 questions on civic engagement outside the game (based on Westheimer and Kahne, 2004), nine demographic questions and one open-ended item (see Appendix A).

Data Collection

The population for the current study consisted of guild leaders and guild members in WoW. The authors had hoped to utilize a contact at Blizzard Software (the owners of World of Warcraft) to post the questionnaire to Blizzard's official WoW guild leader site, but were unsuccessful. Therefore, the authors were forced to use what was a convenience sample. The authors posted invitations to participate in the survey, as well as a description of the study, on a series of WoW discussion forums frequented by both guild leaders and guild members. The use of WoW discussion boards meant that while this was a convenience sample, it was essentially a convenience sample of experts. Because the questionnaire link was posted to several discussion boards, it was impossible to know the number of potential respondents and thus we could not calculate a meaningful response rate. To increase the number of respondents, the authors offered an incentive: a drawing for a 6 month subscription to WoW (or another game) or an Amazon.com gift certificate.

Table 2. Civic gaming experiences in World of Warcraft guilds

	Guild members	Guild leaders	Teen gamers (Lenhart, et al., 2008)
Question (Lenhart, et al. items)	**'Slightly Agree' or greater**	**Slightly Agree or greater**	**"At least sometimes"**
"Players in my guild help each other learn." ("Helping or guiding other players")	92.8	100.0	76.0
"I (My guild leader) encourage(s) input from other guild members." ("Playing a game where the player helps makes decisions about how a community, city, or nation should be run"	90.9	97.9*	43.0
"When the guild leader is not online, guild members organize raids." ("Organizing game groups or guilds")	78.4	76.6	30.0

* $X^2 = 25.245; p < .001$

RESULTS

Guild Leadership and 'Civic Gaming' Experiences

As described earlier, Lenhart, et al. (2008) reported on a study that examined the relationship between teenagers' gaming experiences and their civic engagement. The current study questionnaire contained three prompts that closely resembled three of the seven civic gaming experiences (CGE) described by Lenhart, et al. (2008):

- "Helping or guiding other players"
- "Playing a game where the player helps makes decisions about how a community, city, or nation should be run"
- "Organizing game groups or guilds" (p. 40)

Table 2 reports the results of responses to these three prompts by type of guild membership. First, however, we must state clearly that while Lenhart, et al. (2008) surveyed only teenage gamers, respondents to the current study -- because it was focused on comparing guild leaders with guild members -- had a wide range of ages with only a small percentage being teen gamers. Despite this caveat, the results here are worth exploring.

Lenhart, et al., reported that 76% of teen gamers in their sample indicated helping or guiding players during game play (see Table 2). In the current study more than 90 percent of guild members (and 100 percent of guild leaders) indicated some agreement with the statement "players in my guild help each other learn." Results from the current study indicated no significant difference between guild leaders and guild members on two of the three CGE items. For example, more than seventy-five percent of both guild leaders and guild members agreed (to some degree) with the statement "When the guild leader is not online, guild members organize raids." Curiously, a significantly higher proportion of guild leaders felt they encouraged input from guild members than did the guild members themselves. These results are interesting in that these 'civic gaming experiences' parallel important concepts from civic education as outlined in the NSCG Standards (1994), including the role of informal associations (such as the guilds in WoW) in civil society. For example, Standard II.B.2 stresses that students should be able to: "describe the role of voluntary associations in performing functions usually associated with government, such as providing social welfare and education…" (p. 102).

Guild Role and Out-of-Game Civic Engagement

Yee (2006) described the potential of MMORPGs such as WoW for developing skills--such as those used in civic engagement--that can be applied in the world outside the game. According to Yee:

...a prime candidate for acquired skills is leadership skills. In emergent groups within the MMORPG environment, leaders deal with both administrative as well as higher-level strategy issues, most of which arise and have to be dealt with spontaneously. Administrative tasks include: role assignment, task delegation, crisis management, logistical planning, and how rewards are to be shared among group members.... These issues are even more salient in long-term social groups, such as guilds, which have formalized membership and rank assignments (p. 33).

Recent voting statistics show that the majority of young people of today are not civically active, at least as far as voting is concerned. The United States Census Bureau (2005) estimated that only 41.9% of 18-24 year olds voted in the November 2004 election, whereas 58.3% of the total population cast a ballot.[4] Evidence from the online world, however, paints a somewhat different picture. Yee (2006) surveyed more than 3,000 MMORPG players and found that the vast majority reported increasing their leadership skills for motivating and persuading others as well as their overall leadership skills. Several respondents in the current study echoed Yee's findings. For example, one guild leader noted:

I have ABSOLUTELY (sic) applied skills I have learned in WoW to my Real Life (sic) job. I also remain impressed by some of the skills my kids have picked up. Lessons on fiscal responsibility and politeness, not to mention repercussions of actions. Let me tell you, on-line, if you do something out of line you get peer censored RIGHT (sic) away. It is also interesting that you are in a completely non-biased environment, no one knows if you are old or young, male or female, or what you look like. You are evaluated completely on your skills.

Respondents in the current study were asked to indicate whether they had participated in a variety of civic engagement activities outside the game. Table 3 reports these results. These results suggested that guild leaders in the current study were statistically no more likely to participate in each of these activities than were guild members. For example, 88 percent of guild leaders--18 and older--indicated they were registered to vote, compared to nearly 82 percent of guild members. Seventy-four percent of the registered guild members indicated they voted in the last election compared to 75 percent of guild leaders. It is interesting to note, however, that both of these proportions were higher than for the general population. According to US Census figures for 2004, about 72 percent of all eligible adults were registered to vote with about 64 percent of these actually voting (US Census Bureau, 2005).

Table 3 also reports the degree to which guild leaders and guild members participated in a variety of civic activities from signing a petition to running for political office. Once again, no significant differences were found between the proportion of guild leaders who indicated they had participated in these activities and that of guild members. For one activity ("I have supported a political candidate--e.g., made a campaign contribution, attended a political meeting, wore a political button, put a sign in yard, etc."), it is possible to compare the current study results to national data. The National Election Survey has collected data on political activity since the 1940s and, based on the 2004 survey, about 48 percent of the American electorate had supported a political candidate. In the current survey, while only 46 percent of guild leaders had supported a political candidate, nearly 55 percent of guild members had.[5]

Table 3. Respondents' civic engagement by WoW role

Question	Percent responding 'yes'		
	Guild leaders	Guild members	General population
I am registered to vote (if 18 or older)	88.4	81.3	72.1*
If registered, voted in last election	74.4	75.8	63.8*
I have signed a petition.	74.4	72.3	
I have started a petition.	7.0	10.3	
I have run for school for political office.	23.3	23.9	
I have contacted or visited someone in government who represents my community.	53.5	38.0	
I have participated in a peaceful march or demonstration	16.3	21.7	
I have volunteered in my community.	72.1	65.2	
I have done something to help raise money for a charitable cause.	72.1	72.8	
I have worked with a group to change a policy or law in my community or state.	30.2	24.5	
I have supported a political candidate (e.g., made a campaign contribution, attended a political meeting, wore a political button, put a sign in yard, etc.)	46.5	53.5	48.0**
I have contacted a newspaper, radio, or TV talk show to express an opinion on an issue	39.5	32.8	
I have blogged or posted my opinion in a forum about a local, state, or national issue	44.2	43.3	
I have painted protest signs or slogans on walls	0.0	2.2	
I volunteer regularly within my community	34.9	22.8	
I am interested in political issues	78.6	67.2	
I often try to learn about political issues	76.7	74.4	

* Voter participation rates for the 2004 Presidential election (U.S. Census Bureau, 2005).

**Based on results from the 2004 American National Election Survey (http://www.electionstudies.org/nesguide/toptable/tab6b_1.htm).

Again, there are clear parallels between the types of civic engagement reported by guild members in the current study and those outlined in the NSCG Standards (1994). For example, Standard V.C.2 asks students to evaluate the importance of a number of civic responsibilities including:

- Being informed and attentive to public issues,
- Registering to vote and voting knowledgeably on candidates and issues,
- Serving as a juror,
- Performing public service (p. 132).

Standard V.E. 3 asks students to "evaluate, take and defend positions about the means that citizens should use to monitor and influence the formation and implementation of public policy" (p. 136). Among these are:

- "Explain what civil disobedience is, how it differs from other forms of protest, what its consequences might be, and evaluate the circumstances under which it might be justified
- Evaluate the usefulness of other forms of political participation in influencing public policy, e.g., attending political and governmental meetings, filing a legal challenge, demonstrating, contacting public officials, working in campaigns, contributing money to political parties or causes, writing letters, boycotting, community organizing, petitioning, picketing, expressing opinions

Table 4. Respondents' civic beliefs

	Percent responding 'Agree' or 'Strongly agree'	
	Guild leaders	**Guild members**
Being active in state and local issues is my responsibility	58.3	42.7
I felt I knew the major issues in the last Presidential election and where candidates stood on those issues	62.8	53.9
I think it is important to hear others' ideas even if I find their ideas very different from mine	93.0	81.5
I believe it is important to get involved in improving my community	69.7	50.3
I think it's good when people discuss the country's problems	72.1	72.2
It's good for the country that people speak up when they oppose US policies	73.8	70.8
I can learn from people with backgrounds and experiences that are different from mine	92.7	87.6
I enjoy working in groups or on projects with people whose backgrounds and experiences are different from mine	73.8	67.1

on talk shows, running for political office" (p. 136).

Civic Beliefs and Guild Roles

Table 4 reports the degree to which guild leaders and guild members held various civic beliefs. For example, a vast majority of both guild leaders and guild members thought it was important "to hear others' ideas even if I find their ideas very different from mine" and that it was "good when people discuss the country's problems." Interestingly, while less than half of the guild member respondents answered 'agree' or 'strongly agree' to the prompt "being active in state and local issues is my responsibility," nearly 60 percent of guild leaders agreed it was. This difference highlights a pattern: a greater proportion of guild leaders answered 'agree' or 'strongly agree' for each of the nine civic belief prompts. While these differences were not statistically significant, this pattern did hold throughout. This would seem to suggest that guild leaders may be more likely than guild members to participate in out-of-game civic engagement.

Political Orientation of Guild Leaders and Guild Members

The current study also investigated the self-reported political orientation of guild leaders and guild members. Yee (2007) conducted a survey of more than 30,000 MMORPG players. Among the questions he asked was where players "typically stood in terms of social issues, such as abortion, gay rights, and stem cell research" (n.p.). He found that the majority of MMORPG players tended to label themselves as 'very' or 'somewhat' liberal on these social issues, with female players rating themselves 'very liberal' more often than male players. In the current study we asked guild leaders and guild members to report their political orientation on both social issues (e.g., abortion, gun control, immigration, health care) and fiscal issues (taxation, entitlements, budget deficits, military spending). This topic also sparked an interest among several respondents to the current study. For example, one guild leader noted that s/he was "very curious to see the correlation between guild members and leaders and political ideologies and involvement in community."

Table 5. Political orientation of guild members

	Political orientation (percent responding)				
	Very conservative	Somewhat conservative	Moderate	Somewhat liberal	Very liberal
Social issues (e.g., abortion, gun control, immigration)					
Guild leaders	4.7	23.3	34.9	16.3	21.0
Guild members	10.0	13.3	31.1	31.1	14.4
Fiscal issues (e.g., taxation, entitlements, deficits, military spending)					
Guild leader	13.9	30.2	37.2	16.3	2.3
Guild members	12.3	24.0	36.3	18.4	8.9

Results from the current study indicated that both guild leaders and guild members tended to be politically moderate on both social and fiscal issues. In fact--as Table 5 reports--'moderate' was the median and modal response on social and fiscal issues for both guild leaders and guild members. Obviously, these results are different from those of Yee (2007). Results did indicate that the guild leaders who responded tended to report themselves as slightly more conservative -- although not significantly so -- - than guild members.

DISCUSSION

The current study was an attempt to describe the degree to which guild leaders and members in World of Warcraft engaged in civic gaming experiences (Lenhart, et al., 2008) and to explore the relationship between civic participation and leadership in the virtual world of WoW and the world outside the game. The study was -- for all intents and purposes -- a pilot of both the methodology and the instrument and, as with most pilot studies, the current study revealed flaws in both. Given these issues, it is important to note that the results reported here could be due to response error, sampling error or both and should be interpreted cautiously.

In spite of these caveats, however, the study did yield several interesting results. First, it was clear that there was a large degree of cooperation and civility among individuals who participated in this survey, as nearly every participant agreed (at least some degree) with the statement "players in my guild help each other learn." In terms of citizenship education, this is significant in that as the world is becoming more intertwined economically and culturally (see Friedman, 2005), it is necessary to work with others and respect and understand differences. The Partnership for 21st Century Skills (2007), which is a framework for student instruction in an increasing number of American states, calls for students to engage in activities in which they are "learning from and working collaboratively with individuals representing diverse cultures, religions and lifestyles in a spirit of mutual respect and open dialogue in personal, work and community contexts," as well as "Understanding other nations and cultures, including the use of non-English languages" (online). These results suggest that MMORPGs could be a method of fostering these kinds of skills (the emphasis on war, raids, and competition notwithstanding).

This holds particular importance for social studies teacher education. As noted above, among the goals of methods courses is to prepare future teachers for the classroom. However, in order to prepare future teachers to teach students in a rapidly changing, increasingly interconnected, technology-driven twenty-first century, it is important go above and beyond a vocational model of teacher education, and allow future teachers to ponder different resources and strategies for teaching content that may not be available in the here and now. It is for this reason that MMORPGs are appropriate for inclusion in a social studies methods course. Although for a variety of reasons their use may not be realistic in many, perhaps most, high school classrooms at this moment in time, they are nevertheless useful for achieving some of the long-term goals of a methods course. For example, one overriding objective of a methods course is to prepare professional educators who are decision makers and leaders in both their classroom and their school. A second goal is to prepare teachers who know the content standards associated with their content discipline. The use of MMORPGs has potential for satisfying both of these goals. By becoming familiar with MMORPGs within methods, if and when the possibility of integrating this technology is discussed at a department or school meeting, teachers who have had this experience in a methods course will be able to give an informed opinion, and if the decision is made to use them within their instruction, they will have been taught specific strategies. MMORPGs could also be used by classroom teachers, but the decision as to their use must be tempered in light of state standards and their associated tests, access to computing equipment, as well as acceptable use policies of their school.

Furthermore, the use of MMORPGs in the manner that was used in this study relates to national standards; for example, the Center for Civic Education (1994) describes "civil society" as "that sphere of voluntary individual, social, and economic relationships and organizations that, although limited by law, is not part of governmental institutions… provid[ing] a domain where individuals are free from unreasonable interference from government," and notes that students "should be able to explain and evaluate the argument that civil society is a prerequisite of limited government" (online). The findings of this study support this notion, as the vast majority of players agreed to some extent with the statement "players in my guild help each other learn."

It was also noteworthy that guild leaders tended to feel a greater responsibility to be civically engaged than guild members. The implication of this for citizenship education is that it is not enough to simply cover terms, dates, places, and people when teaching about how to become an effective citizen. Rather, it is important for students to actually experience being a citizen and to have opportunities to practice these skills, and one way that this could take place is through participation in a MMORPG such as WoW.

Keeping in mind the aforementioned issues with sampling, it was also interesting to note that both guild leaders and guild members reported being registered to vote (and actually voting) in higher proportions than the general population. This result, coupled with respondents' relatively high levels of reported civic engagement, seemed to counter Kahne's (2007) warning that "playing MMORPGs might leave little time for civic or political endeavors" (n.p.).

Lessons Learned

Among the most apparent outcomes of this study was the degree to which MMORPGs are truly global and that participants come from all over the world. The authors had made the tacit assumption that participants would be United States citizens and registered voters. However, as one participant noted: "Most WoW players arent (sic) from America so this survey has been completely out of my reach as a Chinese player on an EU realm…" It is possible that these players participate in the game through a different cultural and linguistic lens; thereby making the results less generalizable.

Additionally, the authors asked respondents to place themselves in only two categories: guild leader or guild member. The leadership aspect of this study would have been strengthened by including other individuals besides just the guild leader, namely guild officers. The importance of these individuals was made clear by a participant who said that "my guild's raids are led by an Officer, while the Guild Leader typically gives his input only when things are not going very well." Another participant noted that:

Next time around [it] would be good to include officers of guilds. In my experience the officers of a guild are just as important as the guild leader. I would be very interested in seeing how a successful guild (one with little turn over), compares to the education and real life experiences of those who run it.

Thus, the structure and hierarchy of guilds themselves might provide an interesting learning opportunity, as their governance could be scrutinized and viewed as a microcosm of 'real-life' government.

The findings presented in this chapter indicate that MMORPGs have the potential to both provide several pedagogical benefits in social studies education as well as serve as effective tools for preparing the young people today in becoming the citizens of tomorrow. While the use of MMORPGs in the classroom is a relatively new phenomenon, their use in social studies education has vast potential to improve teaching and learning and foster the development of active, informed democratic citizens. Thus, it is critical to understand the most effective methods of integrating MMORPGs into the teaching and learning of social studies, as well as the factors that encourage and barriers that impede their use. The results of this study can serve as a basis for modifications to existing social studies methods courses, as well as provide an opportunity for discussions of extraneous issues that might influence the effective integration of MMORPGs into the social studies classroom. Additionally, these results can be useful as an impetus for exploring innovative ways to use MMORPGs in social studies education, as well as provide a basis for beginning a dialogue between various stakeholders in the process of developing the citizens of tomorrow. While this study did have limitations, we believe that this was a positive step in discovering how the real world 'skill' of citizenship that Jefferson envisioned may be recognized and subsequently fostered, in the synthetic world of MMORPGs.

REFERENCES

Ajjan, H., & Hartshorne, R. (2008). Investigating faculty decisions to adopt Web 2.0 technologies: Theory and empirical tests. *The Internet and Higher Education*, *11*(2), 71–80. doi:10.1016/j.iheduc.2008.05.002

Bennett, W. L. (2008). Changing citizenship in the digital age. In Bennett, W. L. (Ed.), *Civic life online: Learning how digital media can engage youth* (pp. 1–24). Cambridge, MA: The MIT Press.

Bers, M. U. (2008). Civic identities, online technologies: From designing civic curriculum to supporting civic experiences. In Bennett, W. L. (Ed.), *Civic Life Online: Learning How Digital Media Can Engage Youth* (pp. 139–160). Cambridge, MA: The MIT Press.

Blizzard Entertainment. (2008a). *Intro to WoW*. Retrieved September 29, 2008 from http://www.worldofwarcraft.com/info/beginners/index.html

Blizzard Entertainment. (2008b). Joining guilds. Retrieved September 29, 2008 from http://www.worldofwarcraft.com/info/basics/joiningguilds.html

Blizzard Entertainment. (2009c). What's a guild? Retrieved April 7, 2009 from http://www.worldofwarcraft.com/info/basics/guilds.html

Blizzard Entertainment. (2009d). Create guild rules. Retrieved April 7, 2009 from http://www.worldofwarcraft.com/info/basics/guildleadership.html

Castronova, E. (2005). On the research value of large games: Natural experiments in Norrath and Camelot. *CESifo Working Paper Series No. 1621*. Retrieved June 26, 2009 from http://ssrn.com/abstract=875571

Center for Civic Education. (1994). *National standards for civics and government*. Calabasas, CA: Author.

Cole, H., & Griffiths, M. (2007). Social interactions in massively multi-player online role-playing games. *Cyberpsychology & Behavior*, *10*(4), 575–583. doi:10.1089/cpb.2007.9988

deKanter, N. (2007, July). *A guild-ed future: Lessons in leadership from massively multiplayer on-line games*. Paper presented at the 2nd James F. Ackerman Colloquium on Technology and Citizenship Education, W. Lafayette, IN.

Dictionary.com. (2008). *Citizenship* definition. Retrieved on February 8, 2008, from http://dictionary.reference.com/browse/citizenship

Engle, S., & Ochoa, A. (1988). *Education for democratic citizenship: Decision making in the social studies*. New York: Teachers College Press.

Flanagan, C. A., Syvertsen, A. K., & Stout, M. D. (2007) Civic Measurement Models: Tapping Adolescents' Civic Engagement. *Circle Working Paper 55*. Retrieved June 26, 2009 from http://www.eric.ed.gov/ERICWebPortal/contentdelivery/servlet/ERICServlet?accno=ED497602

Friedman, A. M. (2006). State standards and digital primary sources: A divergence. *Contemporary Issues in Technology & Teacher Education*, *6*(3). Retrieved from http://www.citejournal.org/vol6/iss3/socialstudies/article1.cfm.

Friedman, T. L. (2005). *The world is flat: A brief history of the twenty-first century*. New York: Farrar, Straus, and Giroux.

0

Levin, D., & Arafeh, S. (2002). *The digital disconnect: The widening gap between Internet-savvy students and their schools*. Pew Internet and American Life Project. Retrieved on February 22, 2008 from http://www.pewinternet.org/pdfs/PIP_Schools_Internet_Report.pdf

National Council for the Social Studies. (1994). *Expectations for excellence: Curriculum standards for social studies*. Washington, DC: National Council for the Social Studies.

National Council for the Social Studies. (2001). *Creating effective citizens*. Retrieved June 27, 2007, from http://www.socialstudies.org/positions/effectivecitizens/

Partnership for 21st Century Skills. (2007). *Core subjects and 21st century themes*. Retrieved October 17, 2008 from http://www.21stcenturyskills.org/route21/index.php?option=com_content&view=article&id=6&Itemid=3

Pcmag.com. (2009). *MMORPG definition*. Retrieved April 7, 2009 from http://www.pcmag.com/encyclopedia_term/0,2542,t=MMORPG&i=56863,00.asp

Prensky, M. (2001). Digital natives, digital immigrants. *Horizon*, *9*(5), 1–6. doi:10.1108/10748120110424816

Raynes-Goldie, K., & Walker, L. (2008). Our space: Online Civic engagement tools for youth. In Bennett, W. L. (Ed.), *Civic life online: Learning how digital media can engage youth* (pp. 161–188). Cambridge, MA: The MIT Press.

Reynolds, C. (2006). Videogame windows. *Maclean's*, *119*, 42.

Smith, A., & Rainie, L. (2008). *The Internet and the 2008 election*. Washington, DC: Pew Internet and American Life Project. Retrieved July 17, 2008, from http://www.pewinternet.org/pdfs/PIP_2008_election.pdf

Steinkuehler, C., & Williams, D. (2006). Where everybody knows your (screen) name: Online games as third places. *Journal of Computer-Mediated Communication, 11*(4). Retrieved June 26, 2009, from http://jcmc.indiana.edu/vol11/issue4/steinkuehler.html

The Week. (2007, February 16). Living in a virtual world. *The Week: The Best of the U.S. & International Media.*

United States Census Bureau. (2005). *Voting and registration in the election of November 2004.* Retrieved June 19, 2007, from http://www.census.gov/population/www/socdemo/voting/cps2004.html

VanFossen, P. (1999-2000). An analysis of the use of the Internet and World Wide Web by secondary social studies teachers in Indiana. *The International Journal of Social Education, 14*(2), 87–109.

VanFossen, P. J., Friedman, A. M., & Hartshorne, R. (2008). The emerging role of synthetic worlds and massively-multiplayer online role-playing games (MMORPGs) in social studies and citizenship education. In Ferdig, R. (Ed.), *Handbook of research on effective electronic gaming in education* (pp. 235–250). Hershey, PA: IGI Publishing.

Westheimer, J., & Kahne, J. (2004). What kind of citizen? The politics of educating for democracy. *American Educational Research Journal, 41*(2), 237–269. doi:10.3102/00028312041002237

Woodcock, B. S. (2008a). *MMOGCHART.COM.* Retrieved on October 2, 2008, from http://www.mmogchart.com/category/charts/

Woodcock, B. S. (2008b). *MMOG Subscriptions Market Share – April 2008.* Retrieved on October 2, 2008, from http://www.mmogchart.com/Chart7.html

Xenos, M., & Foot, K. (2008). Not your father's Internet: The generation gap in online politics. In Bennett, W. L. (Ed.), *Civic life online: Learning how digital media can engage youth* (pp. 51–70). Cambridge, MA: The MIT Press.

Yee, N. (2006). The Demographics, Motivations and Derived Experiences of Users of Massively-Multiuser Online Graphical Environments. *Presence (Cambridge, Mass.), 15*, 309–329. doi:10.1162/pres.15.3.309

Yee, N. (2007). *The Daedalus Project.* Additional player demographics. Retrieved on October 9, 2008, from http://www.nickyee.com/daedalus/archives/001556.php

ADDITIONAL READING

Aarseth, E. (2007). Game studies: The international journal of computer game research. Available: http://gamestudies.org/0601/

Alvarez, M. (2006). Second life and school: The use of virtual worlds in high school education. Available: http://www.trinity.edu/adelwich/worlds/students.html

Arnseth, H. (2006). Learning to play or playing to learn: A critical account of the models of communication informing educational research on computer gameplay. Game Studies. *The International Journal of Computer Game Research, 6*(1). Available http://gamestudies.org/0601/articles/arnseth.

Berson, I. R., & Berson, M. J. (2006). Privileges, privacy, and protection of youth bloggers in the social studies classroom. *Social Education, 70*(3), 124–128.

Bogost, I. (2006). Water cooler games – live from the serious games summit (day 1). Available: http://www.watercoolergames.org/archives/000658.shtml#swain

Castronova, E. (2004). Game development and social science. *Journal of Game Development, 1*(1), 91–94.

Castronova, E. (2005). *Synthetic worlds: The business and culture of online games*. Chicago, IL: University of Chicago Press.

Champion, E. (2008). Game-based historical learning. In Ferdig, R. (Ed.), *Handbook of research on effective electronic gaming in education* (pp. 219–234). Hershey, PA: IGI Publishing.

Clegg, A. (1991). Games and simulations in social studies education. In Shaver, O. (Ed.), *Handbook of teaching and learning in the social studies*. New York, NY: MacMillan.

Cuban, L. (2001). *Oversold and underused: Computers in the classroom*. Cambridge, MA: Harvard University Press.

de Freitas, S., & Griffiths, M. (2008). Massively multiplayer online roleplay games for learning. In Ferdig, R. (Ed.), *Handbook of research on effective electronic gaming in education* (pp. 51–66). Hershey, PA: IGI Publishing.

Dibbell, J. (2006). *Play money: Or, how I quit my day job and made millions trading virtual loot*. New York: Basic Books.

Fairfield, J. (2007). Anti-social contracts: The contractual governance of online communities. Social Science Research Network. Available: http://ssrn.com/abstract=1002997

Fulghum, R. (1988). *All I really needed to know I learned in kindergarten: Uncommon thoughts on common things*. New York: Villard Books.

Galarneau, L., & Zibit, M. (2007). Online games for 21st century skills. In Gibson, D., Aldrich, C., & Prensky, M. (Eds.), *Games and simulations in online learning: Research and development frameworks* (pp. 59–88). Arlington, VA: Information Science Publishing.

Goodlad, J. I. (1984). *A place called school: Prospects for the future*. New York: McGraw Hill.

Huizinga, J. (1944/1971). *Homo ludens*. London: Beacon Press.

Johnson, S. (2005). *Everything bad is good for you*. New York: Penguin.

Ke, F. (2008). A qualitative meta-analysis of computer games as learning tools. In Ferdig, R. (Ed.), *Handbook of research on effective electronic gaming in education* (pp. 1–32). Hershey, PA: IGI Publishing.

Kemp, J., & Livingstone, D. (2006, August). Putting a Second Life "metaverse" skin on learning management systems. In D. Livingstone & J. Kemp (eds.), Proceedings of the Second Life Education Workshop at the Second Life Community Convention (pp. 13-18). Paisley, UK: The University of Paisley.

Lastowka, G., & Hunter, D. (2006). The laws of virtual worlds. *California Law Review, 92*(1).

Locke, J. (2005). *Two treatises of government and a letter concerning toleration*. Cambridge: Cambridge University Press. (Original work published 1689)

Mason, C., Berson, M., Diem, R., Hicks, D., Lee, J., & Dralle, T. (2000). Guidelines for using technology to prepare social studies teachers. [Online serial]. *Contemporary Issues in Technology & Teacher Education, 1*(1). Available http://www.citejournal.org/vol1/iss1/currentissues/socialstudies/article1.htm.

News, B. B. C. (2005, August 25). China imposes online gaming curbs. Available: http://news.bbc.co.uk/2/hi/technology/4183340.stm

Parker, W. C., & Jarolimek, J. (1997). *Social studies in elementary education* (10th ed.). Upper Saddle River, NJ: Prentice-Hall, Inc.

Prensky, M. (2001). *Digital game-based learning*. New York: McGraw Hill.

Prensky, M. (2005). In educational games, complexity matters: mini-games are trivial – but "complex" games are not: an important way for teachers, parents, and others to look at educational computer and video games. *Educational Technology, 45*(4), 22–28.

Regan, T. (2006, June 14). What if civics class were an online game? The Christian Science Monitor. Available: http://www.csmonitor.com/2006/0614/p17s01-cogn.html

Second Life. (2007a). What is second life? Available: http://secondlife.com/whatis/

Second Life. (2007b). What is teen second life? Available: http://teen.secondlife.com/whatis?PHPSESSID=fd2f0483fa59dbc38997d0b60640 2f09

Squire, K. (2002). Cultural Framing of Computer/Video Games. Game Studies. *The International Journal of Computer Game Research, 2*(1). Available http://www.gamestudies.org/0102/squire/.

KEY TERMS AND DEFINITIONS

Social Studies: "Social studies is the integrated study of the social sciences and humanities to promote civic competence. Within the school program, social studies provides coordinated, systematic study drawing upon such disciplines as anthropology, archaeology, economics, geography, history, law, philosophy, political science, psychology, religion, and sociology, as well as appropriate content from the humanities, mathematics, and natural sciences. The primary purpose of social studies is to help young people develop the ability to make informed and reasoned decisions for the public good as citizens of a culturally diverse, democratic society in an interdependent world" (National Council for the Social Studies, 1994, p. 3). Further, "In social studies, students develop a core of basic knowledge and ways of thinking drawn from many academic disciplines, learn how to analyze their own and others' opinions on important issues, and become motivated to participate in civic and community life as active, informed citizens" (National Council for the Social Studies, 1994, p. vii). The National Council for the Social Studies (2001) also states that "the core mission of social studies education is to help students develop the knowledge, skills, and values that will enable them to become effective citizens" (online). Generally speaking, at the secondary level, a wide variety of courses fall under the umbrella of social studies. These include United States and world history, civics, government, economics, geography, sociology, psychology, and anthropology. 'Active' and 'Effective' Citizenry: Active, democratic citizenship is a broad definition, which the National Council for the Social Studies (NCSS) (1994) posits can take "diverse forms" (p. vii). This can range from individual citizens "becoming informed about issues and voting in elections" to participating in political and social movements (NCSS, 1994, p. vii). Examples of this include, but are not limited to, writing a letter to an editor, participating in a letter writing campaign, participating in a political weblog, and contacting an elected official. The National Council for the Social Studies (2001) defines an effective citizen as one who has the knowledge, skills, and attitudes required to assume the 'office of citizen' in our democratic republic" (online). NCSS defines an effective citizen as one who:

- "Embraces core democratic values and strives to live by them.
- Accepts responsibility for the well-being of oneself, one's family, and the community.
- Has knowledge of the people, history, and traditions that have shaped our local communities, our nation, and the world.
- Has knowledge of our nation's founding documents, civic institutions, and political processes.

- Is aware of issues and events that have an impact on people at local, state, national, and global levels.
- Seeks information from varied sources and perspectives to develop informed opinions and creative solutions.
- Asks meaningful questions and is able to analyze and evaluate information and ideas.
- Uses effective decision-making and problem-solving skills in public and private life.
- Has the ability to collaborate effectively as a member of a group.
- Actively participates in civic and community life." (online)

Citizenship Education: The young people of today may learn effective citizenship skills in a variety of the courses mentioned above. For example, students may learn about individuals involved in the development of the U.S. Constitution in a history course, but the application of laws and amendments in a civics or government class. NCSS (2001) states that "To accomplish this goal [of effective citizens], every student must participate in citizenship education activities each year. These activities should expand civic knowledge, develop participation skills, and support the belief that, in a democracy, the actions of each person make a difference. Throughout the curriculum and at every grade level, students should have opportunities to apply their civic knowledge, skills, and values as they work to solve real problems in their school, the community, our nation, and the world" (online).

Digital Natives: Prensky (2001b) defines "digital natives" as the first generation of students to "have spent their entire lives surrounded by and using computers, videogames, digital music players, video cams, cell phones, and all the other toys and tools of the digital age" (p. 1).

MMORPG (Massively Multi-player Online Role-Playing Game): "A role playing game on the computer played by many people. An (sic) MMORPG differs from a regular computer role playing game because its environment is perpetual. People log in, join the game, take on their role and leave whenever they wish, but the game continues" (pcmag.com, 1996-2009, online).

Guild Members: Blizzard Entertainment (2009c) defines a guild as "a group of players that join together for companionship, adventure, economic gain and more" (online).

Guild Leaders: A guild leader is simply the person in charge of a particular guild. While the specific responsibilities of guild leaders vary from guild to guild, Blizzard Entertainment (2009d) encourages guild leaders to "Come up with a list of rules for your guild. Make them available to your guild mates via a web page, if possible, or you can pass them out via email" (online). They go on to note that "Many common problems can be solved by coming up with rules and making sure everyone is aware of them."

ENDNOTES

1 Prensky (2001) terms this generation of Americans (those born in 1984 and after) as "digital natives," for whom computers and the Internet have always been part of their life, and he estimates that high school students today have spent twice as many hours engaged in video game play as reading books (p. 1).

2 Woodcock (2002-2008b) estimates that WoW has 62.2% of the market, with its closest competitor holding 7.5%.

3 Kahne and Westheimer (2006) reported Cronbach's alpha coefficients ranging from .54 to .81 for these subscales, based on a sample of approximately 23,000 students: 'personal responsibility to help others' (α=0.62), 'commitment to community involvement' (α=0.54), 'I will volunteer' (α=0.80), 'interest in politics' (α=0.81), 'civic efficacy' (α=0.66), 'knowledge/social capital for community development', and 'leadership efficacy' (α=0.78).

4 These were the last presidential election data available. The current study data were collected prior to November, 2008.

5 National Election Survey data can be found at: http://www.electionstudies.org/.

APPENDIX A

Guild Leader and Guild Member Questionnaire

1) What is your role in World of Warcraft? (Branch item)
   - Guild Leader
   - Guild Member
   - Guild Leader Items
2) How did you become a guild leader?
   - I started a guild.
   - I was appointed by a previous leader.
   - I was appointed by a select group of players.
   - I was elected by the entire guild.
3) On a six point scale (Strongly Disagree, Disagree, Slightly Disagree, Slightly Agree, Strongly Agree), please rate your agreement to the following questions:
   - My guild is like a family.
   - If there is a problem with my guild, I try to get other players to care about the problem.
   - I often express my opinions about how my guild is doing.
   - When someone in our guild does well, everyone in the guild feels good.
   - When I am not online other members frequently organize and lead raids.
   - I spend a lot of time to make the guild better.
   - I decide what raids to do without getting the opinion of other players.
   - Players in my guild help each other learn.
   - I provide strong leadership to my guild.
   - If players in my guild are unhappy, they would talk to me before switching guilds.
   - I encourage input from other guild members.
   - I know the game better than everyone in my guild.
   - If I think there is a problem with my guild I develop and propose a plan to correct it.
   - Other players often seek my advice about game-play.
   - I often propose ideas and strategies for better game-play to other members of the guild
   - Being actively involved with guild issues is my responsibility.
   - If there is a problem in my guild, I contact the concerned players to resolve the issue.
   - My advice to players is valued and respected.
   - I often think about how I can improve the guild.
4) When you communicate with your fellow members and other guild leaders about guild management, which media do you use?
   - VOIP (e.g. Skype)
   - Chat/IM/E-mail during game play
   - Chat/IM/E-mail outside of game play
   - Post to forums
5) Do you regularly blog or post to forums about other aspects of the game?
   - Yes
   - No

6) If you are 18 or older, are you a registered voter?
   - Yes
   - No
   - Under 18
7) If you are a registered voter did you vote in the last national or local election?
   - Yes
   - No
   - NA
8) Please answer Yes or No to the following questions:
   - I have signed a petition.
   - I have started a petition.
   - I have run for school or political office.
   - I have contacted or visited someone in government who represents my community.
   - I have participated in a peaceful protest march or demonstration.
   - I have volunteered in my community.
   - I have done something to help raise money for a charitable cause.
   - I have worked with a group to change a policy or law in my community or state.
   - I have supported a political candidate (e.g. campaign contribution, attended a political meeting, wore a political button, put a poster/sign in yard, etc.)
9) Approximately how often do you "get the news" (e.g. read a newspaper, watch TV news, visit a news website like CNN.com, etc.)?
   - More than once a day
   - Once a day
   - 2-3 times a week
   - Once a week
   - Rarely
10) Please answer Yes or No to the following questions:
   - I have contacted a newspaper, radio, or TV talk show to express an opinion on an issue.
   - I have blogged or posted my opinion in a forum about a local, state or national issue.
   - I have painted protest signs or slogans on walls.
   - I volunteer regularly within my community.
   - I am interested in political issues.
   - I often try to learn about current social/political issues.
11) On a six point scale (Strongly Disagree, Disagree, Slightly Disagree, Slightly Agree, Strongly Agree), please rate your agreement to the following questions:
   - Being active in state and local issues is my responsibility.
   - I felt I knew the major issues in the last presidential election and where candidates stood on those issues.
   - I think it is important to hear others' ideas even if I find their ideas very different from mine.
   - I believe it is important to get involved in improving my community.
   - I think it's good when people discuss their country's problems.
   - It's good for the country that people speak up when they oppose US policies.
   - I can learn a lot from people with backgrounds and experiences that are different from mine.

- ◦ I think it's important to hear others' ideas even if I find their ideas very different from mine.
- ◦ I enjoy working in groups or on projects with people with backgrounds and experiences that are different from mine.

12) What is your age?
- ◦ Younger than 15
- ◦ 15-17
- ◦ 18-21
- ◦ 22-30
- ◦ 31-45
- ◦ 46-60
- ◦ 60 +

13) What is your gender?
- ◦ Male
- ◦ Female

14) How old were you when you started playing on-line games?
- ◦ Younger than 15
- ◦ 15-17
- ◦ 18-21
- ◦ 22-30
- ◦ 31-45
- ◦ 46-60
- ◦ 60 +

15) On average, how many hours a week (to the nearest hour) do you play computer games?

16) How long have you been a guild leader?
- ◦ 0-3 months
- ◦ 3-6 months
- ◦ 7-12 months
- ◦ more than 12 months

17) How long did you play World of Warcraft before you became a guild leader?
- ◦ 0-3 months
- ◦ 3-6 months
- ◦ 7-12 months
- ◦ more than 12 months

18) How would you describe your political orientation on social issues (e.g. abortion, gun control, immigration, health care)?
- ◦ Very conservative
- ◦ Somewhat conservative
- ◦ Moderate
- ◦ Somewhat liberal
- ◦ Very liberal

19) How would you describe your political orientation on fiscal issues (e.g. taxation, entitlements, budget deficits, military spending)?
    - Very conservative
    - Somewhat conservative
    - Moderate
    - Somewhat liberal
    - Very liberal
20) What is your highest level of education?
    - Attended high school
    - High school degree
    - Attended college/university
    - Undergraduate degree
    - Master's Degree
    - Ph.D. or other advance degree
21) On a six point scale (Strongly Disagree, Disagree, Slightly Disagree, Slightly Agree, Strongly Agree), please rate your agreement to the following questions:
    - My guild is like a family.
    - If there is a problem with my guild, my guild leader tries to get other players to care about the problem.
    - My guild leader often expresses opinions about how my guild is doing.
    - When someone in our guild does well, everyone in the guild feels good.
    - When the guild leader is not online other members frequently organize and lead raids.
    - My guild leader spends a lot of time to make the guild better.
    - My guild leader decides what raids to do without getting the opinion of other players.
    - Players in my guild help each other learn.
    - My guild leader provides strong leadership to the guild.
    - If players in my guild are unhappy, they would talk to the guild leader before switching guilds.
    - My guild leader encourages input from other guild members.
    - My guild leader knows the game better than everyone in my guild.
    - If my guild leader thinks there is a problem with my guild, he/she develops and proposes a plan to correct it.
    - Other players often seek my advice about my guild leader's gameplay.
    - My guild leader often proposes ideas and strategies for better gameplay to other members of the guild.
    - Being actively involved with guild issues is a guild leader's responsibility.
    - If there is a problem in my guild, my guild leader contacts the concerned players to resolve the issue.
    - My guild leader's advice to players is valued and respected.
    - My guild leader is continually trying to improve the guild.
22) When you communicate with your fellow guild members, which media do you use?
    - VOIP (e.g. Skype)
    - Chat/IM/E-mail during game play
    - Chat/IM/E-mail outside of game play
    - Post to forums

23) Do you regularly blog or post to forums about other aspects of the game?
   - Yes
   - No
24) If you are 18 or older, are you a registered voter?
   - Yes
   - No
   - Under 18
25) If you are a registered voter did you vote in the last national or local election?
   - Yes
   - No
   - N/A
26) Please answer Yes or No to the following questions:
   - I have signed a petition.
   - I have started a petition.
   - I have run for school or political office.
   - I have contacted or visited someone in government who represents my community.
   - I have participated in a peaceful protest march or demonstration.
   - I have volunteered in my community.
   - I have done something to help raise money for a charitable cause.
   - I have worked with a group to change a policy or law in my community or state.
   - I have supported a political candidate (e.g. campaign contribution, attended a political meeting, wore a political button, put a poster/sign in yard, etc.)
27) Approximately how often do you "get the news" (e.g. read a newspaper, watch TV news, visit a news website like CNN.com, etc.)?
   - More than once a day
   - Once a day
   - 2-3 times a week
   - Once a week
   - Rarely
28) Please answer Yes or No to the following questions:
   - I have contacted a newspaper, radio, or TV talk show to express an opinion on an issue.
   - I have blogged or posted my opinion in a forum about a local, state or national issue.
   - I have painted protest signs or slogans on walls.
   - I volunteer regularly within my community.
   - I am interested in political issues.
   - I often try to learn about current social/political issues.
29) On a six point scale (Strongly Disagree, Disagree, Slightly Disagree, Slightly Agree, Strongly Agree), please rate your agreement to the following questions:
   - Being active in state and local issues is my responsibility.
   - I felt I knew the major issues in the last presidential election and where candidates stood on those issues.
   - I think it is important to hear others' ideas even if I find their ideas very different from mine.
   - I believe it is important to get involved in improving my community.
   - I think it's good when people discuss their country's problems.

- It's good for the country that people speak up when they oppose US policies.
- I can learn a lot from people with backgrounds and experiences that are different from mine.
- I think it's important to hear others' ideas even if I find their ideas very different from mine.
- I enjoy working in groups or on projects with people with backgrounds and experiences that are different from mine.

30) What is your age?
    - Younger than 15
    - 15-17
    - 18-21
    - 22-30
    - 31-45
    - 46-60
    - 60 +

31) What is your gender?
    - Male
    - Female

32) How old were you when you started playing on-line games?
    34) How long have you been a member of a guild?
        - 0-3 months
        - 4-6 months
        - 7-12 months
        - more than 12 months
    35) How long did you play World of Warcraft before you became a member of a guild?
        - 0-3 months
        - 4-6 months
        - 7-12 months
        - more than 12 months
    36) How would you describe your political orientation on social issues (e.g. abortion, gun control, immigration, health care)?
        - Very conservative
        - Somewhat conservative
        - Moderate
        - Somewhat liberal
        - Very liberal
    37) How would you describe your political orientation on fiscal issues (e.g. taxation, entitlements, budget deficits, military spending)?
        - Very conservative
        - Somewhat conservative
        - Moderate
        - Somewhat liberal
        - Very liberal
        - Younger than 15
        - 15-17

18-21

- 22-30
- 31-45
- 46-60
- 60 +
- 60 +

33) On average, how many hours a week (to the nearest hour) do you play computer games?

38) What is your highest level of education?
- Attended high school
- High school degree
- Attended college/university
- Undergraduate degree
- Master's Degree
- Ph.D. or other advance degree

39) If you have any comments or questions about this survey, or if you would like to learn about the results of this survey, please use the space below to contact us. Be sure you include your e-mail above so we can get back to you!

Section 3
Use of Gaming in Virtual Worlds

Chapter 12
Modding and Rezzing in Games and Virtual Environments for Education

Regina Kaplan-Rakowski
Southern Illinois University, USA

Christian Sebastian
Southern Illinois University, USA

ABSTRACT

Creating new resources in computer games and virtual worlds by modification – also known as modding and rezzing, respectively – is a popular pastime activity of the new generation of learners. Educators need to understand the potentials of these activities for education, and to possibly integrate some of them into school curricula. This chapter provides an overview of the modification process to create new resources within a virtual environment (both games and virtual worlds). It examines the differences in the modification process between game worlds and virtual worlds, and offers practical considerations for using the activities in teaching and instruction.

INTRODUCTION

In this (post-)modern age, the Internet has become a venue for self-expression. Many online "venues," such as Blogger, Twitter, Second Life (SL), World of Warcraft (WoW), and YouTube, not only allow their users to express themselves in terms of thoughts, words, and actions but their business models depend on user-created and submitted materials in order to work. Despite their claims to be "online social services," Blogger, Craig's List, and Twitter are in effect World Wide Web (WWW) environments, or "spaces" that facilitate the establishment of virtual communities and online communications among them.

Specialized environments such as SL and WoW pushed the idea of community building even further by allowing their members to interact among virtual personifications of themselves (in the form of customizable avatars) within a traversable (virtual) environment. While the idea of a traversable three dimensional (3D) Internet might appear rather innovative to most users, it was not so for computer game players, who had experienced virtual environments (albeit a much simpler version), since the days of Pong and Space Commander.

DOI: 10.4018/978-1-61520-713-8.ch012

Increasingly, social services, such as YouTube and Second Life, have become so dependent on user-created materials, without which, the continuous existence of the sites could be at stake. Not surprisingly, user-created materials were prevalent in online and console games also. For example, the award winning LittleBigPlanet (for Sony PlayStation 3) allowed players to manipulate simple geometric shapes into more complex objects, and to modify or re-use these user-created objects for the construction of new game levels as peer-to-peer challenges. Serving as a virtual canvas, the online Blueprint Creator (available at http://www.littlebigworkshop.com/en-us/Tools/Blueprint) allowed players to put down their creative thoughts before trying to design new levels within the LittleBigPlanet online world.

Unlike the majority of the digital games in which players interacted with developer-made contents, the idea of: (1) allowing players to create new contents as a new way of 'play,' and (2) reusing the created contents for play by other players, was truly revolutionary. The levels of creativity and innovation skills, as well as information and communication technology literacy shown were all part of the 21st century skills that were deemed highly desirable in tomorrow's education (Partnership for 21st Century Skills, 2006; available at http://www.21centuryskills.org). Educators and pundits alike have suggested that game modification could well become the new mode of learning in the future (see Becker & Parker, 2005; Gee, 2008; Prensky, 2001, 2008). Given the history of game modification among the gamers' community, this is not surprising at all.

GAME MODIFICATION

The origin of game modification could be traced back to 1998, when the U.S. Marines first modified a commercial off-the-shelf (COTS) video game into a training game (from Doom to MarineDoom) (McLeroy, 2008). Over the years, game modification had grown to be another reason for buying/owning video games. Over the next few years, many video game modules have been constructed and distributed by gamers through various online channels. However, not all game modules were sanctioned by the game publishers; some might even be illegal (one example being the infamous Coffee Mod of Grand Theft Auto IV).

On the other hand, many game publishers were eager to support, and even encourage, the game modification process. A publisher's expressed support of the game modification process would usually be found in the form of a game development toolkit (GDK) that was distributed together with the game. Because GDKs were game specific, anyone interested in learning the game modification process had to tackle the game (and its corresponding GDK) on a one-to-one basis. Hence, the number of game modules available could be taken as an indicator for the size of the game modification community. By far, the largest game modification community was the Neverwinter Nights group, which has made available more than 5000 game modules since the game debuted in 2002.

The game modification process was a win-win situation for many parties involved. Researchers and educators have been known to take advantage of the GDKs in creating test-beds for innovative research (Gorniak & Roy, 2005; Loh & Byun, 2009; Young & Nguyen, 2009), and in experimenting with new instructional approaches (Berger, 2006; Kafai, 2006; Squire, 2004). The game publishers benefitted directly from it because every module released by the user community would help to extend the shelf-life and sales of the product. Last but not least, gamers were delighted with the process because, not only could they customize the games to fit their gaming needs, they could further boast about their role as game designers.

Machinima

The debut of YouTube (http://www.youtube.com) in recent years has provided many independent amateur media producers with a voice. One interesting activity that had been spun off from game modification was that of digital film-making using a video game environment as a product set, or machinima – the word is a portmanteau of 'machine' and 'cinema.' By taking advantage of the real-time 3D virtual environments made possible only through video game technology (Lowood, 2008), more specifically through the GDKs, these media producers were able to tap into a near limitless number of actors and actresses without actually hiring anybody.

Since the Massive Multi-players Online Games (MMOGs) became a worldwide phenomenon in the 2000s, there have been several machinima events in which large number of gamers were mobilized to congregate at a specific time and "place" within these virtual game environments to perform, en masse, certain acts for the purpose of machinima – including group dance, and even mass suicide (for the purpose of spelling out a particular message with the virtual bodies). Other media producers have alternatively taken advantage of the fantastic settings as inspiration for storytelling and for crafting epic adventures and film series from their home computers (see http://machinima.com/series/). Annual machinima exhibitions and online repositories (such as International Machinima Expo, and Machinima.com, respectively) have been created to further promote and expand the industry. Many of these activities had been almost unthinkable before the advent of game modification.

Rezzing

Even though it was once a pastime for teenagers and casual gamers, game modification has become a means for grown-ups and professionals to advance their own personal agendas. In the last five years, the game modification process has grown beyond the confines of video games, and had spilled over into other virtual environments, including virtual worlds such as Second Life (http://www.secondlife.com), There (http://www.there.com), and Active Worlds (http://www.activeworlds.com).

In its early years, virtual worlds functioned very much like 3D chat rooms, with the exception that each user could customize their own appearance (or avatar) within the application, and create virtual models of physical objects for display or manipulation. Conceptually, the ability to create models of physical objects using predisposed geometric models was highly similar to game modification. In Second Life (SL), for example, the denizens have opted for the term 'rezzing' (SL lingo) to describe their model making efforts (Figure 1, color version available at http://www.csloh.com/research/book_chapter_images/).

Every SL account holder has the prerogative to purchase land in the virtual world and to erect buildings on it. Large corporations (such as IBM) have created virtual headquarters and offices in SL to project their business presence in the virtual world, and to facilitate meetings without the need for physical travel. Universities and colleges (such as Princeton, Harvard, and Stanford) have likewise created virtual campuses in SL, and even hosted Campus Open Days to attract potential applicants. Many denizens of SL have even made a name for themselves by selling (virtual) merchandise, handicrafts, and fashionable clothing. There is even a virtual monetary exchange created for the purpose of trading the game money (Linden dollar) with real world currencies (see http://www.lindex.com), not to mention virtual solar systems, virtual museums, etc. Once again, these types of model building (or rezzing) were unheard of before the advent of game modification.

MODIFying Games for Research, Development, and Learning

Once a non-word, the term "modding" (gamers' lingo for game modification) has increasingly been referred to in scholastic journals and gained acceptance by their international readerships. A

Figure 1. Regina creating (rezzing) a simple chair outside a restaurant.

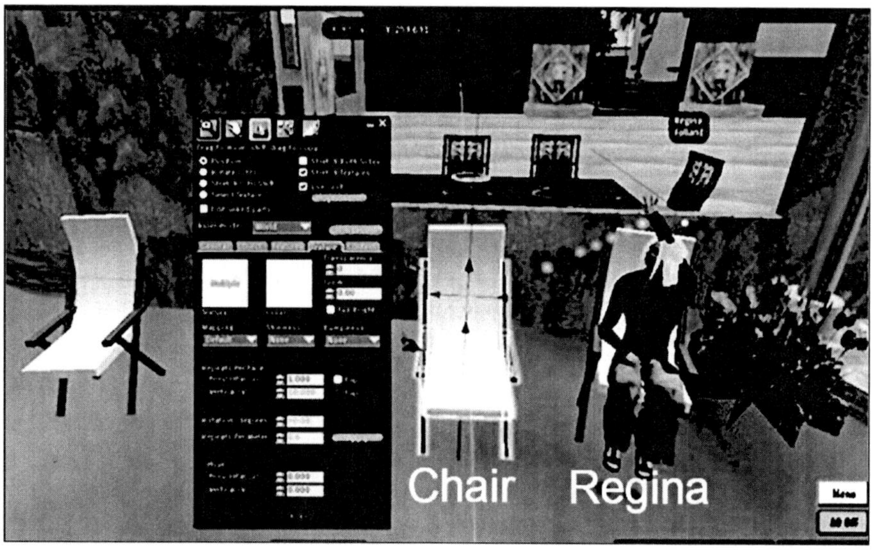

quick search using Google Scholar (http://scholar.google.com) would easily reveal thousands of articles (mostly descriptive research) about why video games should be used to support learning. No doubt, most educators would already be familiar with the thesis put forth by serious game proponents, such as Prensky (2001) and Gee (2003). Since much has been written about the potential and advantages of digital games and/or game-related activities (including game modification) for learning – ranging from motivational factors, to authentic scenario-based learning, to a safe environment for dangerous activities – they will not be repeated here. We will, instead, turn to another important issue that has seldom been addressed.

Who is Doing What? Why?

If the activities of game playing and game making are indeed good for learning, (based on the voluminous works arguing for the activity), shouldn't game modification, which is a very low cost game making process, be introduced to students and teachers as a viable classroom learning activity? Prensky (2008) argued that it would be the tech-savvy students who would master the game modding (and in turn, teach the teachers about it). As the digital natives are entering the teaching professions, we contend that they might turn the situation around, and begin to create game modules for instruction and classroom learning, and further, share the learning process with the rest of the learning community.

In just the last 5 years alone, a number of research and development works have been published that involved modding of COTS games and virtual environments. Examples include: Squire's doctoral dissertation based on Civilization III (2004), Barab and colleagues' work involving ActiveWorld (2005), Kadakia's research work using Morrowind (2005). The Neverwinter Nights game development kit (GDK) was one of the more popular GDK used by researchers and was mentioned in a number of research articles, including Gorniak and Roy (2005); Loh and Byun (2009); etc. Other educators have tested the effectiveness of instructional materials created using GDKs, for subjects such as history (Squire, 2004), narration and literacy (Robertson & Good, 2005), journalism (Paul, Hansen & Taylor, 2005), science education (Barab, Thomas, Dodge, Carteaux, & Tuzun, 2005), and economics (Carbonaro, *et al.*, 2005).

Learning to Learn

Since the mid 1980s, researchers such as Papert (1980, 1993), Kafai (1994, 1996, 1998), and Rieber (1996) have been working with children in using authoring software, such as Logo, Authorware, and Game Maker, to create games as a learning process. In other words, they regard game building (and modification) as a process of learning from a constructionist perspective. Constructionists believe that the process of learning may be defined through the very act of artifact construction (i.e., building/creating something as evidence of someone's learning).

Just like the taste and presentation of a dish directly reflects how good a chef is, the quality of the learning artifact (in this case, a playable game module instead of a dish) produced might also be used as a yardstick to measure the level of learning in the students. The learners would often go beyond the minimum requirement of learning the GDK, and in addition, engage in research about game design, scripting, programming, graphic editing, etc., in order to create a game module of which they would be proud. The quality of game modules produced could be raised even further when coupled with collaborative or competitive team works. Because the game making process might take several weeks or months to complete, this approach was best suited for after-school programs, or extra-curricular student societies.

Since game modification involves scripting and fairly complex technical skills, common wisdom suggests that a teacher who is well versed with the technical aspects of the GDK might be needed to provide guidance and assistance to the students. This might pose a problem for school teachers because many might hesitate to add to an already full plate, or to push aside anything in a tightly integrated curriculum. However, Prensky (2008) asserted that this was not a problem because many students were, in fact, more tech-savvy than their teachers. One student offered the following quip: "Don't try to use our technology, you'll only look stupid" (p.1005).

Certainly this should not be taken to mean that educators should avoid modding/rezzing (or technology), lest they appear "stupid" in the eyes of their students, should it? After all, many researchers mentioned in earlier sections had to learn how to create their unique research platforms by first learning to mod/rez, just like the rest of the gamers. As demonstrated by these researchers, both the process of modding and rezzing, as well as the product created, carried great educational potentials. In the following sections, we will examine how modding and rezzing can be used as learning processes and as tools for authoring new learning materials.

Mind Tools

The number of game authoring tools and GDKs available in the last five years has gradually increased. As more and more researchers began exploring GDKs as authoring tools to create new test-beds and environments for research, they have come to realize that GDKs can be viable tools for interactive learning development. As mentioned before, the first of its kind was MarineDoom, a game module developed by the U.S. Marines to train soldiers and marines in team work and cooperation.

From a mind tool perspective (Jonassen, 1996), GDKs for video games and the rezzing tool for SL are no different from slide presenters, Word Processors, or Web page editors, because they empower users to unlock what is in their minds and share representations of the "images/objects" with others. It is up to the researchers and educators to make use of these mind tools to author new interactive learning environments or instructional materials. Similarly, the students are free to express their mental images through storytelling using the GDKs, and to invite others to share a glimpse of their mental worlds by means of the rezzing tools.

Validating Theories

The growing trend of game modification has begun to attract the attention of researchers and educators. Besides research and development work made possible through game modification using GDKs, education researchers have also investigated the game modification process from the perspectives of contemporary learning theories. For example, using an instructivist's approach, Moshirnia (2007) conducted a study investigating the effectiveness of a modified game in helping 10th-12th graders comprehend and retain declarative knowledge of history. Findings were generally positive and showed the students to be able to retain and comprehend the learning materials. Furthermore, the students were motivated about "experiencing" the American Revolution via a Civilization IV game module.

Using a Collaborative (Social) learning approach, Steinkuehler & Johnson (2009) argued that modding demonstrates and enhances deep computer literacy "in the contemporary participatory socio-technical world" (p.55). Their analysis of World of Warcraft (WoW) modding communities led to the conclusion that modding involved a highly collaborative environment and that "the days of the lone student working on computer code in isolation are outdated" (p.63). Consequently, modding was viewed as a collaborative and negotiated authorship, whose activities were goal-driven.

In addition to the instructivist and collaborative approaches, advocates of constructivism also have shown interest in game modification. Constructivism, which inspired constructionism, promotes the idea that learners actively construct their own learning and understanding through experience and reflection on that experience. Focusing on this philosophy, Robertson and Good (2005) allowed children to build their own game modules by letting them create plots and settings, as well as narratives. The result of this experiment showed the existence of beneficial effects related to the development of narrative stills and overall literacy, which constructively speaking, the children built for themselves.

Based on the example of the above-mentioned experiment, Steiner, Kaplan & Moulthrop (2006) engaged in an analysis of the process with which their subjects created game plans and the games themselves. The focus of the analysis was on the participants' reflections on their experiences. The children made discoveries about their roles as builders and players, as well as about the differences between developers and players. These insights prompted the researchers to conclude that "both designing games and building them for themselves provide opportunities for learning problem-solving and teamwork" (p.140).

Educators should be flexible in adapting the process of modding into a learning situation. They should consider the process carefully from any number of theoretical perspectives before choosing one that is suitable for the class and the students. Learning could occur during the process of modding a game, or it could occur during the use of an educational game module. It is true that certain virtual environments may lend themselves more naturally to activities based on a particular theory of learning; and some game environments, such as first-person-shooters or war games, might be less appropriate for public school settings. But it is up to an innovative teacher to create the learning activities that best suit their students' learning abilities, based on the learning opportunities. A little creativity, coupled with the familiarity with the virtual environments, goes a long way.

VIRTUAL ENVIRONMENTS: GAME WORLDS VS. VIRTUAL WORLDS

Conceptually, a game world is a virtual environment created for one purpose: execution of the game story as conceived by the designer. When players "stepped into" the game world, they were temporarily transported into the game environment layout by the designer, to face whatever challenges were thrown at them. It would appear that the gaming activity tapped into the basic human desire to excel and overcome (both mental and physical) challenges laid before them, regardless of the form of the games: ball games, chess, maze, real-life battle, jig-saw puzzle, pen-and paper Dungeons and Dragons, obstacle course in military training, etc.

While the modification aspect might be similar, a virtual world (such as SL) does not have a grand scheme of (story) design to support its myriad activities. Despite the outward appearance of a game-like environment (i.e., buildings, roads, avatars), virtual worlds originated as 3D chat rooms and many still serve a primarily communicative purpose. However, a number of new features and plug-ins (such as video chat, and links to YouTube) that have recently been made available have transformed SL into something more.

Today, virtual worlds are less like chat rooms, but more closely resemble news centers; they have become virtual spaces for interaction with information: reading text (e.g., books and web pages), listening to sound (audio books, MP3), or both (YouTube movies, band performance, virtual dancing). With some creativity, educators can take advantage of the multimedia display capability of these virtual environments and use them for teaching and instruction. For example, educators from the University of Minnesota have designed a story world and used it to teach journalism (Wong, 2007). This is very similar in concept to the SL blog (http://blog.secondlife.com) and SL newspapers (available at http://sl-newspaper.com). Educators should be interested to find a large number of education-oriented showcases in SL [visit http://secondlife.com/showcase/education/].

In summary, a virtual world can either be an application by itself (such as Google Earth) or a shell (or container) for other systems--be it macro (e.g., solar system), micro (e.g., cells/micro-organisms), dangerous historical events (war zones), or state of mind (e.g., Virtual Hallucination Lab in SL). Apparently, the possibilities are limited only by one's creativity. As more educators embrace the virtual worlds, they can begin to approach teaching in a different way, and not be limited by contents that are too dangerous (e.g. working in a chemical plant), too complex (e.g. working in a financial market), too expensive (e.g. going abroad to speak a foreign language with native speakers), or infeasible (e.g. traveling across the solar system). Readers who are interested in learning more about virtual worlds can find a comprehensive review at http://www.virtualworldsreview.com/info/categories.shtml. As technology continues to advance, it is foreseeable that the virtual world technology would gradually be morphed into 3D Internet browsers, such as 3DXplorer (http://www.3dxplorer.com), and 3B (http://www.3b.net).

Non-Player Characters vs. Virtual People

Besides the environment factors, it is just as important to remember who really makes up the avatars of the game worlds and virtual worlds. In a pre-designed game world, most of the characters are plot-related avatars, meaning they had been placed within the game deliberately by the game designer – even when they serve only as a "filler" to make an empty village look populated. When users interact with these avatars (or non-player characters, NPCs), the purpose is to elicit information from the NPCs in order to continue on the game quests. The responses from these NPCs have all been pre-written by script/story writers. Since the responses (behaviors) of these NPCs were determined by artificial intelligence, players of video games do not need to worry at all about hurting the NPCs feelings.

This is not so for virtual worlds because most avatars (virtual people) are made up of real people logging in from some more or less remote locations. Not only are the conversations spontaneous, these virtual people may even take offense when unkind words are spoken. While there is very little story telling within the virtual worlds, it may be more difficult to elicit information from virtual people than NPCs because it calls for (real) human interaction; even when the avatar you are speaking to may not appear human.

The MMOGs can be confusing because it looks and feels like a virtual world and yet operates using game mechanics. As the name suggests, an MMOG is a game that takes place in a massive virtual world. Hence, the narratives of MMOGs are very much driven by NPCs (more specifically, the Mission/Quest givers).

However, because of the sheer number of players in MMOGs – sometimes numbering in hundreds of thousands – the virtual environments can be intimidating to new players. To help players overcome the initial navigation confusion, game publishers have implemented quest journals/logs to help players keep track of their progress, and placed floating symbols above the head of Quest Givers to distinguish them from the sea of virtual people (Karlsen, 2008). In the MMOG convention, a floating *exclamation point* [!] would indicate the availability of a new quest; and upon completion of the quest, the [!] symbol would turn into a *question mark* [?] indicating that a reward is available for collection.

PRACTICAL CONSIDERATIONS

Educators interested in implementing game and virtual world modification in their instruction need to take several considerations into account - especially considerations relating to technological requirements and the instructional design approach used in developing game modules. The technological requirements would broadly include: hardware, software, network infrastructure, high-speed Internet connection (if the server is located remotely), space to house the equipment, technical support personnel, and amount funding available. Furthermore, teacher preparation, learning to use the GDKs and the games, modification of contents, and research overhead that goes into planning and creating the narratives, are but some of the factors that needed to be considered.

Control for Undesirable Contents

Even though there are many advantages in using virtual environment for teaching and instruction, teaching and instruction using virtual environments is still not suitable for students from all age groups at this moment. Because out-of-the-box virtual environments are created by game designers and not educators, there is very little control of the contents that are in video games or virtual worlds. Besides the issues of violence and gore in video games, which frequently make headlines of news and media, a more troubling issue is the nudity and sexual content that are present in video games and virtual worlds.

Because video games are commercial products, they are created with the intention to be profitable. Since an average video game buyer is a 35-39 year-old male (ESA, 2008, 2009), it should not be surprising that a large proportion of the full-feature and more successful games were targeted at this player group. This means that many of the top quality, best-selling games (with better graphics and narratives) may have content that is not suitable for students (under 17) in public schools. Besides the usual problems about gore and violence in these online games, there also exists another controversial content that is not currently rated by the Entertainment Rating System Board (ESRB): same sex encounters. For example, *The Temple of Elemental Evil*, a game published in 2003 by Troika Games, and reputably "the first mainstream videogame to promote gay marriages" (Barton, 2004), received only a Teen rating from the ESRB (US)! Based on the ESRB rating scheme, a "Mature" rating only identify the game as containing sexual theme, but failed to distinguish between hetero- and homosexuality. This explained why some countries in the world that allowed "M" rated games, singled out and banned Mass Effects (2007) because it contained a homosexual (lesbian) romance sub-plot.

Since majority of the subscription-paying players of MMOGs (e.g., WoW) and virtual worlds (e.g., SL) are adults, they are less likely to be bothered by the use of profanity or the display of partial to full nudity. Sometimes, unsuspecting players may stumble upon "tea parties" (gathering of large group of players) with the purpose of protesting "unfair treatment" or poor maintenance practice to the authority (i.e., the game publisher/developers). While peaceful demonstration is acceptable, in their attempt to attract as much attention as possible to their plight, these "tea parties goers" would often show up in (semi-)nudity! Educators using virtual environments for teaching and instruction may, unwittingly, find themselves in the middle of a tea party (http://www.csloh.com/research/book_chapter_images/), which can result in some serious explanation to the parents or school administrators! This means that before MMOGs and virtual worlds can be considered for teaching and learning, consideration must first be given to protect educators, students, and users from other cultures (and countries) who may be offended by the depiction of violence, gore, profanity, witchcrafts, and same sex relationship/marriage.

The Need for Teacher Control

Due to the issues mentioned above, it can be seen that teacher control will remain an important contention if virtual environments are to be used more widely for teaching and instruction. Likewise, the concern for undesirable content is not merely limited to the United States but is a global concern, in particular, to the more conservative countries. Public school teachers need to protect their students and avert them from unsavory imagery and potentially harmful situations, and must have the ability to control the contents being shown in the virtual environments.

In SL, the problem can be overcome partially by purchasing private land usually in the form of islands. Since the islands can be made private (i.e., accessible only by the owners and their invited guests) or semi-private (i.e., open to visitors, but with the owner of the land retaining the rights to banish misbehaving visitors), some levels of control can be maintained. The owner may further impose what activities – which include rezzing and flying – are permissible on their properties, in an effort to reduce the amount of distractions during lessons. Nevertheless, as land ownership in SL can be a costly affair, it is questionable as to how many public school districts would be willing to fund this option in the foreseeable future.

Unfortunately, the option to purchase private land is not available in MMOGs at all. Furthermore, it is not possible to assert any form of control over the contents therein because the game servers are centrally maintained by the game publishers. Unless open source MMOG servers become available to allow for third-party content contribution, it is unclear if teacher-controlled contents will ever be possible. New business models may need to be formulated to include the option for teacher-created, or teacher-controlled, contents, with some kind of subscription scheme at the school or district level. The subscriptions may then be used by the game publishers to hire the personnel needed to create new game narratives, and provide teacher-control support.

The last viable option would be for teachers to learn how to modify COTS games and create "clean" contents that are suitable for teaching and instruction. Moreover, they should look into using only COTS games that came with dedicated servers, in order to maintain full control over user access. These school-hosted (game) servers would then serve as virtual learning environments containing teacher- or student-created interactive learning contents. Once the game modification process is under the control of teacher-designers, or teacher guided student-designers, undesirable content would become a non-issue, leaving the teachers to focus fully on teaching and instruction. Examples of COTS games that come with dedicated server services include Neverwinter Nights, Half-Life 2, and local area network (LAN) first person shooters.

Scripting (Programming)

Arguably, the most difficult task in a game modification process is that of scripting. Since NPCs were nothing more than animated 3D models, the game engines need to execute the animation only at the right moment; for example, animate a "sit" action, when the command "sit" were given. Unfortunately, game engines only communicate in programming language, and hence, scripting was needed to bridge the gap. Fortunately, game developers recognized that not everyone who is interested in game modding has a degree in Computer Science. Instead of forcing non-programmers (majority of modders) to manipulate the 3D models using programming language (such as Java or C++), game developers created scripts (simplified programming codes that resembled human language) to make life easier for the gamers/modders. The following are examples of scripts used in NWN, and SL, respectively.

Example 1 (NWN)

The following NWN script instructs an NPC object, known as "Sophia" to perform a "Sit" action on an object called CHAIR.

```
void main()
{
object oNPC =
GetObjectByTag("Sophia");
ActionSit (GetNearestObjectByTag
("CHAIR", OBJECT_SELF));
}
```

Example 2 (SL)

The SL script given below can be used to label objects with a desired text. In this case the label says "I am a floating text" with the position of this text given by the coordinates that follow.

```
{
state_entry()
{
llAllowInventoryDrop(TRUE);
llSetText("I am a floating text
", <1,1,1>, 1.5);
}
}
```

Frequency of Patch and Application Update

Another important factor for consideration when using virtual worlds for teaching and instruction can be the frequency of software update. Because of the size of the (software) program, a virtual environment application is usually divided into two portions: the server-side and client-side applications. Whenever the server-side application experiences an update, the client-side must also be updated in order to be compatible. Hence, whenever new bugs or problems arise and are fixed on the server-side application, the client-side must also be patched, or updated. At launch, the client-side would check online with the server to ensure the version number is compatible (or the same), before the client-side application would run.

Because so many people use SL, the server is under constant attack from hackers and must be updated frequently for security. Unfortunately, this means the client-side application must undergo just as many updates as the server-side: up to several times per week. Teachers who use SL for teaching and instruction until spring 2009 had to take on the additional burden to check for updates before conducting a lesson because the client-side application (so called, Second Life viewer) will not function properly until it has finished updating itself. Imagine a situation when the lesson is about to start and the teacher finds out at the last minute that SL has just released a new update which must be downloaded by every computer used in the classroom! The same situation would also apply to MMOGs.

The COTS modifiable video games (such as Neverwinter Nights and Half-Life 2) also have frequent updates, but they use a different update strategy: "pull" and not "push." This means that the update does not happen automatically (push), but is initiated on-demand by the users (pull). Hence, a teacher who discovers that an online game server needs to be updated, may do so after his/her lesson is completed, or schedule the update over the weekends, without being forced into any surprises.

Choice of Virtual Environments

Teachers who are interested in using a virtual environment for instruction need to spend time exploring the 3D modeling resources and learn how to modify the game resources using the toolkit provided. For example, if the courses were about language usage, a first person shooter game that allowed very little conversation between players and NPCs would not be useful. Likewise, virtual worlds with a futuristic setting would not be useful in teaching about the American Revolution or the Roman Empire. But above all, teachers' familiarity with the virtual worlds/video games and the development toolkit is of utmost importance because no content could be made without first learning how to use the toolkit; and not before learning how the game mechanics work.

Out of more than 30 virtual worlds available (as of 2009), each has something unique to offer. The choice of the virtual world used would depend on the themes, the budget available, the age group of the target audience, and even the speed of the Internet connection available. For example, elementary and middle school teachers could consider using Disney Toontown (http://www.toontown.com) or Teen Second Life (http://www.teensecondlife.com), which target at the respective age group. However, the authors believe that in the near future, more user-friendly GDKs will be made available to help teachers develop new virtual worlds suitable for classroom teaching and learning. Once the appropriate business model is found, game (or virtual learning) companies would begin working with school districts to create virtual environment servers for the hosting of template-based virtual interactive learning modules that are created by both teachers and students.

Instructional Development & Performance Assessment

No matter who would develop the interactive learning modules, it is crucial for some kind of instructional design underpinnings to be implemented during the development of the instructional resources or learning modules. For instance, even though Rapid Prototyping development model was originally proposed for computer application and engineering process (Dey, Abowd, & Salber, 2001; Jones & Richey, 2000), it has been successfully adapted for the development of interactive learning (game) modules by Loh and Byun (2009). Likewise, the well-known instructional design processes comprised of: Analysis, Design, Development, Implementation, Evaluation – collectively known as the ADDIE Model (Dick & Carey, 1996; Leshin, Pollock, & Reigeluth, 1992) – have also been suggested to be a possible model for serious games development (Byers, 2009).

Last but not least, assessment of what the learners do in the virtual environment is also important to educators. Although most of the research for the moment has been focused on the potential of game-like environment (e.g., Warren, 2007; Young, Schrader, & Zheng, 2006) and independent development processes (e.g., Quinn,

2005; Reese, 2007), a few researchers have begun looking into new methods of assessing learners' performance within game worlds and virtual environments (Loh, Anantachai, Byun & Lenox, 2007; Reese, 2008).

CONCLUSIONS

Virtual environments such as those commonly found in game and virtual worlds are becoming increasingly common. Many users have learned to create new content through modification using GDKs and 3D modeling tools available at a very low cost. These authoring tools allow users to quickly create a playable and traversable environment using ready-made resources, such as environmental sounds (birds chirps, water dripping, waves), 3D models (tables, containers, trees, buildings, humanoids, animals), and area templates (arctic, desserts, jungle, tundra, bottom of sea). The availability of such templates makes it easy for gamers to create virtual areas with fine details and movable props. It also lowers the technical requirements so that even teachers and students are able to learn the GDK in a short time – making the game modification process viable for classroom (and after-school) use.

Although Star Trek's Holodeck is still unattainable with today's technology, and must continue to reside in the imagination of visionaries and the silver screens (as well as in SL), the ability to create virtual environments for teaching and instruction is now possible. With some creativity and time to spare, early-adopter teachers can have a technology in their hands that will allow them to deliver classroom instruction in a whole new way that is motivating, innovative, and literally "out of this world." Instead of letting the students while away their time aimlessly on videogames, MMOGs and virtual worlds, the time has come for teachers to use the technology the students so love in a positive manner for teaching and instruction.

"Come, the game is afoot."

REFERENCES

Barab, S., Thomas, M., Dodge, T., Carteaux, R., & Tuzun, H. (2005). Making learning fun: Quest Atlantis, a game without guns. *Educational Technology Research and Development, 53*(1), 86–107. doi:10.1007/BF02504859

Barton, M. D. (2004, March). Gay characters in videogames. *Armchair Arcade*. Retrieved April 10, 2008, from http://www.armchairarcade.com/neo/node/305

Becker, K., & Parker, J. R. (2005, Oct 13-15). *All I ever needed to know about programming, I learned from re-writing classic arcade games.* Paper presented at the Future Play: The International Conference on the Future of Game Design and Technology, East Lansing, MI.

Berger, A. (2006, January 31). Neverwinter Nights in the Classroom. *University of Minnesota News*. Retrieved April 30, 2008, from http://www1.umn.edu/umnnews/Feature_Stories/22Neverwinter_Nights22_in_the_classroom.html

Byers, C. (2009). Digital simulations for improving education. In Gibson, D., & Baek, Y. K. (Eds.), *Digital simulations for improving education: Learning through artificial teaching environments*. Hershey, PA: Information Science Reference.

Carbonaro, M., Cutumisu, M., McNaughton, M., Onuczko, C., Roy, T., Schaeffer, J., et al. (2005). *Interactive story writing in the classroom: Using computer games*. Paper presented at the DiGRA 2005 Conference, Vancouver, Canada.

Dey, A. K., Abowd, G. D., & Salber, D. (2001). A conceptual framework and a toolkit for supporting the rapid prototyping of context-aware applications. *Human-Computer Interaction, 16*(2-4), 97–166. doi:10.1207/S15327051HCI16234_02

Dick, W., & Carey, L. (1996). *The systematic design of instruction* (4th ed.). New York: Harper Collins College Publishers.

ESA. (2008). *Essential facts about the computer and video game industry.* Washington, DC: Entertainment Software Association. Retrieved August 1, 2008, from http://www.theesa.com/facts/pdfs/ESA_EF_2008.pdf

ESA. (2009). *Essential facts about the computer and video game industry.* Washington, DC: Entertainment Software Association. Retrieved August 1, 2009, from http://www.theesa.com/facts/pdfs/ESA_EF_2009.pdf

Gee, J. P. (2003). *What video games have to teach us about learning and literacy* (2nd ed.). New York: Palgrave Macmillan.

Gee, J. P. (2008). Learning and Games. In Salen, K. (Ed.), *The ecology of games: Connecting youth, games, and learning* (pp. 21–40). Cambridge, MA: The MIT Press.

Gorniak, P., & Roy, D. (2005). *Speaking with your sidekick: Understanding situated speech in computer role playing games.* Paper presented at the 1st Artificial Intelligence and Interactive Digital Entertainment Conference (AIIDE). Retrieved April 10, 2008, from http://petergorniak.org/papers/AIIDE05GorniakSituatedSpeech.pdf

Jonassen, D. H. (1996). *Computers in the classroom: Mindtools for critical thinking*. Englewood Cliffs, NJ: Merrill.

Jones, T. S., & Richey, R. C. (2000). Rapid prototyping methodology in action: A developmental study. *Educational Technology Research and Development, 48*(2), 63–80. doi:10.1007/BF02313401

Kadakia, M. (2005). Increasing student engagement by using Morrowind to analyze choices and consequences. *TechTrends, 49*(5), 29–32. doi:10.1007/BF02763687

Kafai, Y. B. (1994). Electronic play worlds: Children's construction of video games. In Kafai, Y. B., & Resnick, M. (Eds.), *Constructionism in practice: Rethinking the roles of technology in learning* (pp. 97–123). Mahwah, NJ: Lawrence Erlbaum Associates.

Kafai, Y. B. (1998). Video game designs by girls and boys: Variability and consistency of gender differences. In Cassell, J., & Jenkins, H. (Eds.), *From Barbie to Mortal Kombat: Gender and computer games* (pp. 90–117). Cambridge, MA: MIT Press.

Kafai, Y. B. (2006). Playing and making games for learning: Instructionist and constructionist perspectives for game studies. *Games and Culture, 1*(1), 36–40. doi:10.1177/1555412005281767

Kafai, Y. B., & Resnick, M. (Eds.). (1996). *Constructionism in practice: Designing, thinking, and learning in a digital world.* Mahwah, NJ: Lawrence Erlbaum Associates.

Karlsen, F. (2008). Quests in context: A comparative analysis of Discworld and World of Warcraft. *Game Studies, 8*(1).

Leshin, C. B., Pollock, J., & Reigeluth, C. M. (1992). *Instructional design strategies and tactics*. Englewood Cliffs, NJ: Education Technology Publications.

Loh, C. S., Anantachai, A., Byun, J., & Lenox, J. (2007). Assessing what players learned in serious games: *in situ* data collection, information trails, and quantitative analysis. In Mehdi, Q. (Ed.), *Computer games: AI, animation, mobile, educational & serious games (CGAMES)*. Wolverhampton, UK: University of Wolverhampton.

Loh, C. S., & Byun, J. H. (2009). Modding Neverwinter Nights into serious games. In Gibson, D., & Baek, Y. K. (Eds.), *Digital simulations for improving education: Learning through artificial teaching environments* (pp. 408–426). Hershey, PA: Information Science Reference.

Lowood, H. (2008). Found technology: Players as innovators in the making of machinima. In McPherson, T. (Ed.), *Digital Youth, Innovation, and the Unexpected* (pp. 165–196). Cambridge, MA: The MIT Press.

McLeroy, C. (2008, September). History of Military Gaming. *Soldiers*, *63*, 4–6.

Moshirnia, A. (2007). The educational potential of modified video games. *Issues in Informing Science and Information Technology*, *4*, 511–521.

Papert, S. (1980). *Mindstorms*. New York: Basic Books.

Papert, S. (1993). *The Children's Machine*. New York: Basic Books.

Partnership for 21st Century Skills. (2006). *Results that matter: 21st century skills and high school reform*. Tucson, AZ: Partnership for 21st Century Skills.

Paul, N., Hansen, K., & Taylor, M. (2005). *Modding Neverwinter Nights: A simulation for reinforcing information seeking concepts for Mass Communication students*. Paper presented at the DiGRA 2005 Conference, Vancouver, Canada.

Prensky, M. (2001). *Digital game-based learning*. New York: McGraw Hill.

Prensky, M. (2008). Students as designers and creators of educational computer games: Who else? *British Journal of Educational Technology*, *39*(6), 1004–1019. doi:10.1111/j.1467-8535.2008.00823_2.x

Reese, D. D. (2007, March 23-27). *Designing Selene: Theory-based game design and data-mining*. Paper presented at the Serious Games Summit, San Francisco, CA.

Reese, D. D. (2008). Engineering instructional metaphors within virtual environments to enhance visualization. In Gilbert, J. K., Reiner, M., & Nakhleh, M. (Eds.), *Visualization: Theory and practice in science education* (*Vol. 3*, pp. 133–153). Amsterdam: Springer Netherlands. doi:10.1007/978-1-4020-5267-5_7

Rieber, L. P. (1996). Seriously considering play: Designing interactive learning environments based on the blending of microworlds, simulations, and games. *Educational Technology Research and Development*, *44*(2), 43–58. doi:10.1007/BF02300540

Robertson, J., & Good, J. (2005). Story creation in virtual game worlds. *Communications of the ACM*, *48*(1), 61–65. doi:10.1145/1039539.1039571

Squire, K. (2004). *Replaying history: Learning world history through playing Civilization III*. Unpublished Doctoral Dissertation, Indiana University, Bloomington, IN.

Steiner, B., Kaplan, N., & Moulthrop, S. (2006). *When play works: Turning game-playing into learning*. Paper presented at the 2006 Conference on Interaction Design and Children, Tampere, Finland.

Steinkuehler, C., & Johnson, B. Z. (2009). Computational Literacy in Online Games: The Social Life of Mods. *International Journal of Gaming and Computer-Mediated Simulations*, *1*(1), 53–65.

Wong, W. (2007 May). Gaming In Education. *Ed Tech Magazine*. Retrieved April 10, 2008, from http://www.edtechmag.com/higher/may-june-2007/gaming-in-education.html

Young, M., Schrader, P. G., & Zheng, D. P. (2006). MMOGs as learning environments: An ecological journey into Quest Atlantis and The Sims Online. *Innovate: Journal of Online Education*, *2*(4).

Young, M. E., & Nguyen, N. (2009). The problem of delayed causation in a video game: Constant, varied, and filled delays. *Learning and Motivation*, *40*(3), 298–312. doi:10.1016/j.lmot.2009.02.002

KEY TERMS AND DEFINITIONS

COTS Game: commercial, off-the-shelf game, made by game publishers for profit.

Game Development Kit (GDK): A toolset that is often bundled with a COTS game, usually with the sanction from the publishers, for the purpose of creating new content by the players.

Machinima: short for *machine cinema*: a movie created through screen capturing of a game mod in play, and voiced over in order to 'tell' a story.

Mod: short for game *mod*ule. A game created using GDK, requires preinstalled game engine to play.

Modding: from *mod*ifying, creating game modules (mods) with a GDK.

Rezzing: creating or making objects to appear in a virtual world, especially in Second Life.

Virtual Environment: an interactive digital environment created with computer/digital graphics, commonly found in today's video games (including Massive Multiuser online games, or MMOGs), and virtual worlds (such as Second Life).

Chapter 13
Considerations and Methodology for Designing a Virtual World:
Solution for a Large Corporation

Brian Bauer
Étape Partners, USA

ABSTRACT

This chapter centers on a publically traded Fortune 500 Pharmaceutical company based in the United States. With over 100,000 employees spread across many countries, physical separation of the workforce is an everyday reality. In the author's case, it was not the goal to attempt to unite the entire company; rather, it was the author's goal to provide a means to overcome the obstacles that present themselves when physically disparate coworkers must perform seamlessly to complete a business process. In the following case study, the author determined that although users were open minded to trying Virtual Worlds and other types of Immersive technologies, the solutions delivered needed to provide task oriented functionality that was directly in line with everyday business process. Using this basic requirement, the author developed a Virtual Corporate Environment Business Tool (VCEBT©) box. The VCEBT© philosophy is grounded on the principal that business process is accomplished by following a set of business methods each performed using a set of business tools. While it may sound like a rigid and inflexible way to describe a knowledge-worker environment, the author finds that the process-method-tools definition applies to most environments quite well. The goal is to introduce new tools that increase the effectiveness of this process in terms of its ability to meet clearly defined business objectives. The VCEBT© framework does not attempt to change people or the work that they do. VCEBT©'s do augment the business tool box, providing highly efficient tools designed to solve real world challenges that can restrict a business's ability to maximize business performance.

DOI: 10.4018/978-1-61520-713-8.ch013

INTRODUCTION

What is Virtual Reality(VR)?

Some will tell you that it is an unreal environment that has no firm connection to "real life". Merriam Webster (2009), for example, defines Virtual Reality as "an artificial environment which is experienced through sensory stimuli (as sights and sounds) provided by a computer and in which one's actions partially determine what happens in the environment". In other words, what happens there stays there, and there are no real consequences for actions. Others will tell you that if someone is fully engaged and immersed in Virtual Reality, then it *is* the only reality that is "happening" to them while they are experiencing it, In the movie " The Matrix" the subjects are forced to choose between "realities" that are both very "real". The choice between which reality to "exist" in becomes very philosophical and grounded on fuzzy concepts like faith, and beliefs. Is this a challenge that we want to confront in 2009 in the workplace? Or is there a more elegant way to introduce Immersive technologies?

According to Winifred Gallagher (2009), author of the recently published "Rapt", we constantly make decisions determining what we are going to pay attention to. Any events, experiences, and activities not within the scope of our chosen interest will not exist to us as we immerse ourselves in our selected targets of concentration and focus. What we choose to concentrate on defines our state of consciousness and becomes our Reality.

The fact that our mind and body may be "in two different places at the same time" is not a unique characteristic of Virtual Reality, and does not therefore create the need to refer to this immersive technology as "Virtual Reality". If we are deep within our own thoughts, and no longer mindful of our physical surroundings, are we in "virtual reality"? If we are reading a news article on a website, and are so engrossed that we forget that we are late for a meeting, do we say that "virtual reality" interfered with "physical reality"?

The power of "Virtual Reality" software is in its ability to emancipate the mind from the body, making physical "reality" a minor element of our Federated Reality. Federated Reality has two parts: Consciousness and Physical Existence. For our purposes, we will always need to address the requirements of Physical Existence and Consciousness. However, it is our objective to relegate Physical Existence to nothing more than a set of requirements for accessing a medium that will manipulate the Consciousness away from Physical Existence. In other words, people have bodies: eyes, hands, etc. We must build software that provides convenient physical access. But after that, the vast majority of our attention will be turned to capturing the full attention of the user. We use "federated" to mean that the two parts of Reality have a partnership, but are not so close as to be synonymous. They are individually self-sustaining. We assert that there is only one relevant reality, and it is defined as: *A context of stimulation that acutely focuses awareness and defines our state of consciousness.*

Virtual Reality as a Tool for Business

The newest VR technology provides a fully immersive 3D experience in which the user of the technology adopts the persona of a character (avatar) that exists in a software based "world" designed to have the look and feel of a physical office or learning institution. The users of Virtual Reality technology operate in the 3D space and see objects and people from the Point of View of their avatar inside the technology. Common activities inside the Virtual Reality software include:

- *Meetings*, in which a collection of avatars collocate in a virtual meeting room with the look and feel of a physical meeting. Audio is provided by integrated conference bridges

- *Instruction/Assessment*, in which teachers are able to interact with students in an authentic way. The use of avatars and realistic activity makes role-play based teaching and testing a powerful exercise in engagement
- *Learning*, game-play embedded in the Virtual Reality technology creates a framework for self-study. Study that combines an immersive environment with fun has been demonstrated to improve interest in self-study as well as data retention rates
- *Structured and Unstructured Coworker encounters*, Virtual Reality technology enables groups of people who may be physically separated to come together for formal and informal get-togethers. Frequent, and often unstructured encounters with colleagues help to recreate some of the advantage that is lost when associated coworkers become physically separated.

High quality virtual reality can be a very effective medium for gaining an employee's full attention. It is also a powerful tool that can be used for teaching and collaboration. But do we need a "world" to accomplish our business objectives? Or are we better served with a set of Business Tools that are deployed as needed in specific situations? After all, we are not trying to create the "Matrix" we are trying to achieve business results. Employees use Business Tools to accomplish tasks that are part of a process followed to achieve a result. As such, we can think of Virtual Reality as a business tool, if deployed the right way. Think of it this way: when Microsoft first created MS Word, were they attempting to change the way in which people fundamentally did their jobs? Or were they looking to create a vastly improved typewriter? More than 20 year later we might argue that Microsoft Office has fundamentally changed the way people work, but in the beginning, the goals were more modest. We believe that revolutionary change happens incrementally. Paradigm shifting tools are delivered discretely and become ubiquitous. When the timing is right, these tools can be conjoined, and we will find that the office-of-the-future exists.

The Virtual Corporate Environment (VCE) represents a collection of Business Tools (BT). VCEBT©'s are designed to help accomplish business tasks in new and more effective ways. A thoughtfully connected group of VCEBT©'s will yield a "virtual corporate world". This Case Study steps through the basic elements of how to successfully design, implement, and ensure a successful VCE.

MISSION AND OBJECTIVES

Mission

The VCE will be an environment that exists for bringing together associates who are separated not only by physical space, but by function as well. The VCE will enable both structured and casual encounters with coworkers much in the same way people would interact with each other when they work in close physical proximity. The belief is that the facilitation of more frequent and impactful encounters with coworkers will enhance working relationships and ultimately yield improved business results driven by increased productivity and efficiency.

Objectives

- Improve business results through increased efficiency and productivity
- Improve process-awareness such that work styles begin to adapt to process-oriented-results rather than functional results
- Create an environment that encourages results oriented process improvement
- Improve productivity by increasing the ease and effectiveness of associate collaboration

- To create a working process-oriented virtual environment that is modeled on physical reality, but reduces well established physical-world challenges
- To create a virtual environment that is cognizant of existing collaboration challenges, and establishes bridges to overcome these challenges
- To create a virtual environment for associate contact such that individuals may become more aware of each other's personalities and work-styles enabling coworkers to make subtle adaptations to interactions with the goal of process improvement based on more efficient personal workflows

CURRENT STATE

Why Consider a VCE?

A Virtual Corporate Environment (VCE) will help unify our client's diverse population of associates who are both physically separated and functionally discrete. Efficiency and effectiveness can be raised to levels not currently achievable in the physical space resulting in favorably impacted business results. The VCE will be an environment that exists for bringing together associates who are separated not only by physical space, but by function as well.

The VCE will enable both structured and casual encounters with coworkers much in the same way people would interact with other when they work in close physical proximity. The belief is that the facilitation of more frequent and impactful encounters with coworkers will enhance working relationships and ultimately yield improved business results driven by increased productivity and efficiency. A VCE will create a collaborative and social environment that encourages both formal and informal coworker encounters. It is anticipated that increased encounters between functional silo'd and physically separated associates will encourage communication and cross-functional awareness among individuals and groups who are all part of a cross-functional process.

Process awareness that transcends functional responsibilities is believed to be a key enabler of success when the goal is to improve a singular result. The VCE will create a platform for ensuring that all associates are well equipped with an understanding of business priority, cultural principals and process oriented objectives. It is believed that if all process contributors are fully immersed in process and not just function, the unique ability of each contributor will help to improve the quality of the end result. In today's corporate environment defined by flexible work schedules, disparate physical locations and functional alignment, providing an impactful tool that breaks through these process-challenges is essential. The VCE is such a tool.

Is the Client Audience Ready for a VCE?

An extensive polling of the target employee population yielded the following results (Figure 1).

Increase the Ease and Effectiveness of Associate Collaboration

Coworkers in the same department are two-thirds more likely to collaborate if their offices are on the same corridor than if their offices are simply on the same floor If they were not in the same department, then being on the same corridor boosted their likelihood of collaborating by over 8 times. Collaboration is about: initiating communication, conducting a conversation, and maintaining awareness of the state of the environment, task, and team. The more senses and stimuli brought into the equation, that are direct contributors to the situation, the more poised the situation becomes for impactful collaboration.

Proximity increases frequency of communication. All else being equal, people communicate most with those who are physically close by. Prox-

Figure 1. Polling results

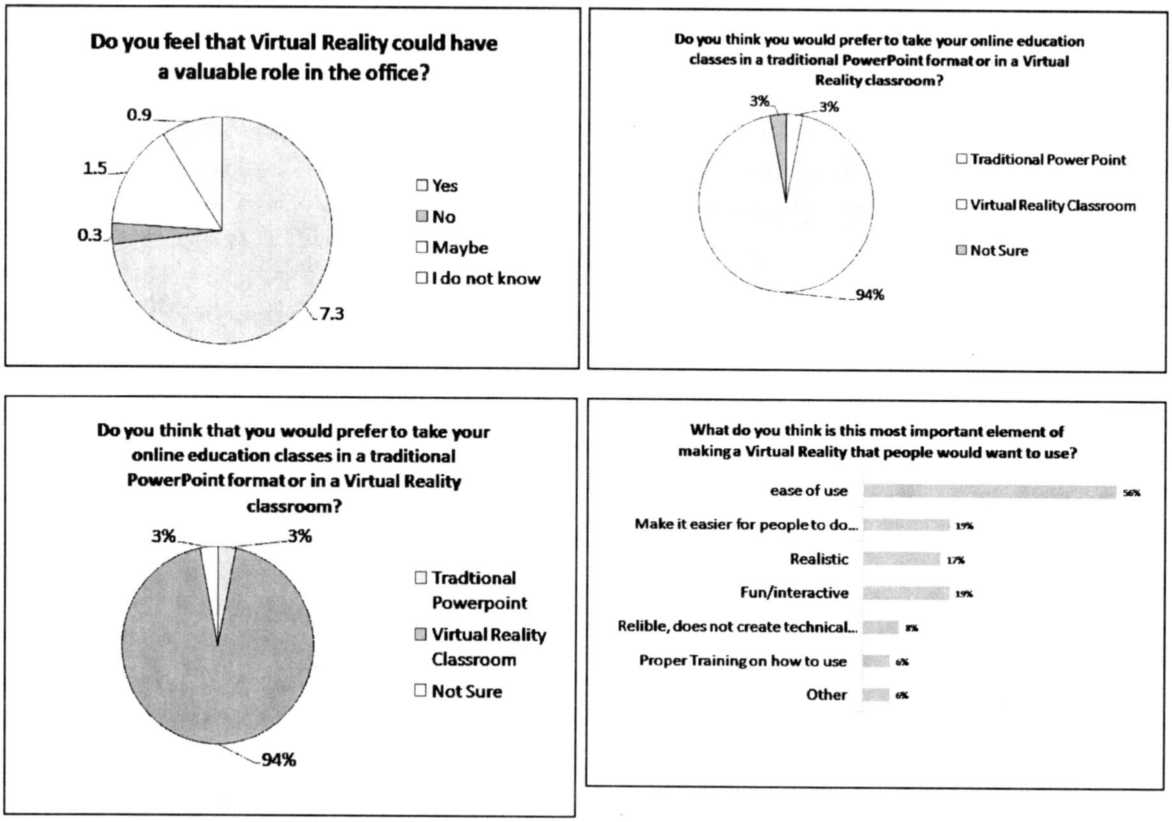

imity increases the frequency of communication by putting people who have the prerequisites for conversation in each other's presence. A VCE will seek to fabricate proximity my making a multi-sensory encounter with a remote colleague both easy to initiate and lifelike.

The magic of an office environment is contained in the atmosphere. However, even offices where the benefit of coworker proximity is ever present can lack focus. An immersive environment creates focused, situational collective knowledge. Within the constructs of well defined Process, the value of a VCE is magnified as more productive, more collaborative and more synergistic. Many of our client's team members charged with collaboration and connected by process, are also having to overcome challenges of being dis-intermediated by time, distance, and functional area. Achieving business goals that include reaching new levels of customer intimacy and customer service will require that challenges put into the path of employees be removed. The VCE embodies a methodology that targets very specific inefficiencies created by a physically disparate workforce.

Reduce Well Established Physical-World Challenges

The "Office of the Future" has been crafted in the minds of designers and scientists for decades. In almost all cases the resulting plans were exclusively physical (e.g. floor plans, etc). We now understand that the *real* "Office of the Future" is not just physical, it is a combination of location, technology and awareness that transcends physical boundaries to create a "virtual co-location".

The "Office of the Future" will consist of several nuances of what we know today but will also possess its own unique innovative ways of creating a working environment. The bindings that will create "virtual co-location" will be stronger than physical proximity due to this workforce's connection through process awareness, collaboration and tools. Due to this, workers stand a good chance at being more effective than a dysfunctional collective that happens to be physically together. Organizational capability is another edge to differentiate companies from their competition. Visionary companies translate their ideologies into tangible mechanisms aligned to send a consistent set of reinforcing signals. They impose tightness of fit, and create a sense of belonging to something special through practical, concrete items.

Client Business Objectives

Both organizational business objectives as well as financial objectives exist in the current state of the VCE acceptance process. Organizational business objects are those linked not only to the business and its product(s) but also to the development of customer relations. Customer intimacy, such as customer service and service quality for example, are great way to enhance the level of effective engagement.

Aside from the relationship of the product to the customer, objectives in respect to business performance and product quality must also be set. An objective of high productivity increased output with the same or fewer people. Similarly, the idea of a same or lower cost production of higher quality output is an objective as is the objective to reclaim "proximity driven" value lose due to FlexTime and working from home.

Lastly, an objective of partnership and collaboration is key to furthering innovation and insight that yield to business impacting actions. Education and training will also help with this.

In collaboration with organizational objectives, financial objectives should be set for several reasons. First, the objective of cost savings can only serve to be beneficial to any business. With lower production costs, organizational business objectives can also be met with lower costs. Secondly, revenue generation, for example, is a financial objective because better training yields more sales. It will also shorten the time-to-useful cycle of on-boarding. Lastly, Cost avoidance is important because more impactful training yields fewer repeats which saves money as well as resources.

VCE and Business Process Objectives

Business Processes targeted by the VCE include:

- Improve business results through increased efficiency and productivity.
- Improve process-awareness such that work styles begin to adapt to process-oriented-results rather than functional results.
- Create an environment that encourages results oriented process improvement.
- Improve productivity by increasing the ease and effectiveness of associate collaboration.
- To create a working process-oriented virtual environment that is modeled on physical reality, but reduces well established physical-world challenges.
- To create a virtual environment that is cognizant of existing collaboration challenges, and establishes bridges to overcome these challenges.
- To create a virtual environment for associate contact such that individuals may become more aware of each others personalities and work-styles enabling coworkers to make subtle adaptations to interactions with the goal of process improvement based on more efficient personal workflows.

Improve Efficiency and Productivity

If we are trying to improve knowledge worker performance, it is necessary to define it. The definition of the American Productivity and Quality Center is, "the relationship between what is put into a piece of work and what is yielded (output)" (APQC) The application of this broad definition presents a challenge since everyone defines outputs differently, especially for the "knowledge worker," whose work is characterized by intangible, ill-defined, and uncountable outputs, processes, linkage to the company's strategic objectives, performance criteria, and high independence.

As our client continues to push for more value from their assets and greater performance, there has been a surge of interest in considering the place of work, i.e., the real estate and facilities location and characteristics, as an important part of the ecology or system. This approach is especially relevant as corporations explore new workplace approaches by rethinking how, when and where people work. Planning an integrated workplace can result in solutions which change, not only the physical work setting, but the other parameters, such as behaviors, processes, and technologies. As we observe today at our client, larger corporate motivations for facilitating a physically disparate workforce present challenges that must be overcome at the Business Unit level.

Encourage Results Oriented Process Improvement that align to Business Goals

An organization's strategic goals should provide the key direction for any Business Process Improvement exercise. Alignment of function to process is another major consideration. Increased intimacy among process participants will improve alignment.

Customer Focus

Fast-changing customer needs underscore the importance of aligning business processes to achieve higher customer satisfaction. It is imperative in any BPI exercise that the "Voice of Customer" be known, and factored in, when reviewing or redesigning any process.

Establish Process Owners

For any process to be controllable, it is essential that there be clarity on who the process owners are as well as what constitutes success/failure of the process. These success/failure levels also help establish "control limits" for the process, and provide a healthy check on whether or not a process is meeting the desired customer objectives.

In an effort to increase the ease and effectiveness of associate collaboration, scientific research has been used to explain office occurrences. It has been found that physical proximity encourages collaboration. In some cases, degrees of collaboration can be multiples if offices are next to each other.

The magic of an office environment is contained in the atmosphere. However, even offices where the benefit of coworker proximity is ever present can lack focus. An immersive environment creates focused, situational collective knowledge presence that is charged with cathartic potential.

Reduce Well Established Physical-World Challenges

We now understand that the real "Office of the Future" is not just physical, it is a combination of location, technology and awareness that transcends physical boundaries to create a "virtual co-location". As well as a stronger bind than those created through physically proximity, a "virtual co-location", companies using virtual reality will differentiate themselves from their competition through their organizational capability and this will give them an edge.

Visionary companies translate their ideologies into tangible mechanisms aligned to send a consistent set of reinforcing signals. They impose tightness of fit, and create a sense of belonging to something special through practical, concrete items.

Establish Bridges to Overcome Collaboration Challenges

We can loosely define a collaborative process as integrating the communication, cooperation and coordination (3Cs) perspectives with functional, behavioral and organizational perspectives.

The dimensionality of the "collaboration matrix" does not scale, it simply needs to stretch or contract to fit an organization. For example, the Actor Network Theory (ANT) states that, entities (or, the collaborative semantic concepts) take their form and acquire their attributes as a result of their relation with other entities (within the collaborative processes) (Crawford, 2004). The relationships take their shapes at the "entity edges". In other words, people attempting to collaborate form inter-personal relationships based on their relationships with others.

These relationships are effective in direct correlation to the degree in which the "entity edges" are allowed to come into contact with each other in impactful ways (non-impactful "touches" will not shape the edges. A good collaborative process model must not focus solely on the flow and transformation of data within the system but also focus on the communication, cooperation and coordination (3Cs) among the actors

Introduction to Authentic Learning

Authentic learning typically focuses on real-world, complex problems and their solutions, using role-playing exercises, problem-based activities, case studies, and participation in virtual communities of practice. The learning environments are inherently multidisciplinary. They are "not constructed in order to teach geometry or to teach philosophy. A learning environment is similar to some 'real world' application or discipline: managing a city, building a house, flying an airplane, setting a budget, solving a crime, for example.

Educational researchers have found that students involved in authentic learning are motivated to persevere despite initial disorientation or frustration, as long as the exercise simulates what really counts—the social structure and culture that gives the discipline its meaning and relevance. The learning event essentially encourages students to compare their personal interests with those of a working disciplinary community: "Can I see myself becoming a member of this culture? What would motivate me? What would concern me? How would I work with the people around me? How would I make a difference?

Authentic learning may be more important than ever in a rapidly changing world, where the half-life of information is short and individuals can expect to progress through multiple careers. Expert thinking and complex communication will differentiate those with career-transcending skills from those who have little opportunity for advancement. It also involves the ability to identify and solve problems for which there is no routine solution. This requires pattern recognition and metacognition. Another differentiator is complex communication, such as persuading, explaining, negotiating, gaining trust, and building understanding.

Although foundational skills (reading, writing, mathematics, history, language) remain essential, a more complex set of competencies are required today. These go beyond being technically competent to being able to get things done, demonstrate ethics and integrity, and work well with others. The most important skills in new hires are quickly becoming teamwork, critical thinking/reasoning, assembling/organizing information, and innovative thinking/creativity

10 Design Elements of Authentic Learning

1. Real-world relevance: Authentic activities match the real-world tasks of professionals in practice as nearly as possible. Learning rises to the level of authenticity when it asks students to work actively with abstract concepts, facts, and formulae inside a realistic—and highly social—context mimicking "the ordinary practices of the [disciplinary] culture."
2. Ill-defined problem: Challenges cannot be solved easily by the application of an existing algorithm; instead, authentic activities are relatively undefined and open to multiple interpretations, requiring students to identify for themselves the tasks and subtasks needed to complete the major task.
3. Sustained investigation: Problems cannot be solved in a matter of minutes or even hours. Instead, authentic activities comprise complex tasks to be investigated by students over a sustained period of time, requiring significant investment of time and intellectual resources.
4. Multiple sources and perspectives: Learners are not given a list of resources. Authentic activities provide the opportunity for students to examine the task from a variety of theoretical and practical perspectives, using a variety of resources, and requires students to distinguish relevant from irrelevant information in the process.
5. Collaboration: Success is not achievable by an individual learner working alone. Authentic activities make collaboration integral to the task, both within the course and in the real world.
6. Reflection (metacognition): Authentic activities enable learners to make choices and reflect on their learning, both individually and as a team or community.
7. Interdisciplinary perspective: Relevance is not confined to a single domain or subject matter specialization. Instead, authentic activities have consequences that extend beyond a particular discipline, encouraging students to adopt diverse roles and think in interdisciplinary terms.
8. Integrated assessment: Assessment is not merely summative in authentic activities but is woven seamlessly into the major task in a manner that reflects real-world evaluation processes.
9. Polished products: Conclusions are not merely exercises or sub-steps in preparation for something else. Authentic activities culminate in the creation of a whole product, valuable in its own right.
10. Multiple interpretations and outcomes: Rather than yielding a single correct answer obtained by the application of rules and procedures, authentic activities allow for diverse interpretations and competing solutions.

Authentic Learning and the Introduction of Virtual Reality

With the help of the Internet and a variety of communication, visualization, and simulation technologies, large numbers of professionals can begin to reconstruct the past, observe phenomena using remote instruments, and make valuable connections with mentors around the world. Similarly, with access to online research communities, learners are able to gain a deeper sense of a discipline as a special "culture" shaped by specific ways of seeing and interpreting the world. They begin to grasp the subtle, interpersonal, and unwritten knowledge that members in a community of practice use (often unconsciously) on a daily basis. "Learning becomes as much social as cognitive, as much concrete as abstract, and becomes intertwined with judgment and exploration," just as it is in an actual workplace (Atwell, 2004).

Virtual Reality tools can aid in this the transformation from science to application.

A Culture of Learning

"A learning [culture] is one that is skilled at creating, acquiring, interpreting, transferring, and retaining knowledge, and at purposefully modifying its behavior to reflect new knowledge and insights."

Actionable Education

Are you more or less interested in learning about something that you can use every day, or never use? People have their own perceptions of what they can use on the job. If management and student have differing perceptions, this must be corrected.

Passive resistance in learning and development appears when there is no perceived benefit to completing the training. Can we achieve a culture of learning by, for example, counting course credits? If you believe in Transformative Learning, then the answer is no. I think we see many examples of people attending classes, getting credit, but not transforming. Is a paper-based culture is learning enough?

Transformative Learning

Transformative learning is basically the kind of learning we do as we make meaning of our lives. It's become a very popular topic in adult education because it doesn't just involve classroom learning--it involves learning about our lives. This is important because as adults, the meaning making process can change everything about how we look at work, family, and the world.

There is a set of steps that adults go through when they experience transformation and those steps are:

- Experiencing a disorienting dilemma.
- Self-examination.
- Critical assessment of assumptions.
- Recognizing that others have gone through a similar process.
- Exploring options.
- Formulating a plan of action.
- Reintegration.

Transformation is something that is usually triggered by a problem, and very often transformative experiences are painful to go through. After identifying their problem or challenge, people seem to enter a phase where they reflect critically on this--this is typically a problem that you've never experienced before, so it takes a lot of thinking and talking to others to work through. During the thinking phase, people may find that they can no longer keep their old ways of thinking and being--they are compelled to change. Finally, there is an action phase where people decide to do something. This could mean that you have to break off certain relationships that don't fit your beliefs anymore; it could mean that you decide to make a career change--action can take many forms. Also, the process itself may take a long time. You could reflect on something for years before you are ready to accept new beliefs and act on them.

Improve the Individuals' Relationship with Training

Culture within any society is made up of the attitudes, values, goals, and practices that characterize it specifically due to the people within each specific culture. Therefore, in order to change a culture, one must change the people.

Unhappy and Unmotivated individuals will not train well. In order to not only gain someone's attention but also to retain it, one must find the time to learn. In combination with time, the ability to learn is a key factor. If it seems easy, it is more than likely that the individual will have a less adverse effect to it. These will not only motivate the individual but also create an in which an entire culture is changed through the morphing of the people that make it up.

Another way to improve a relationship to learning for someone is to recognize two things. First, recognizing the barriers behind why an individual does not possess a good relationship to learning and removing them, will enable a better flow of information to the individual and ultimately enable a better association to training. Second, recognizing factors that create desires in people and using that knowledge to train individuals will also accelerate a better affiliation to training and learning. These factors could include money, responsibility, excitement, and self-worth.

Taking all these elements and implementing them will make a person want to learn.

How Do We Make Our People "Ready to Learn"

If someone is not ready to learn, the effectiveness of instruction is reduced. To increase effectiveness is to make people ready to learn. A good education and training program is holistic in approach and addresses the two important aspects that affect employee performance and productivity. First, it must equip employees with the tools of the trade. Second, it must create a workplace culture of professionalism, loyalty, and commitment, and most importantly, warm and open relationships among employees. The first aspect of education and training – skills development – is easier to accomplish than the second aspect. However, though the competency program might be appropriate, it can always be undermined by unhappy and unmotivated employees. An education and training program must be proactive and never reactive. Its main purpose is not to address employee problems that might threaten the stability of the company. Rather, it should be to transform its human resources into agents of development. Thus, its formulation is participative with ideas from management and rank in file employees incorporated in the final program.

Why Do Employees Want to Learn?

Patricia Cranton's (1994) Three Perspectives of Adult Learning suggest that actions and behaviors will be changed based on the changed perspective (Cranton, p.730).

Her first perspective, subject-oriented learning, states that the goal is to acquire content (e.g. facts, problem solving strategies, practical or technical skills). It is positivistic and most often meets the expectations of the learner and is, therefore, comfortable. The key to this step is that the expert makes the decisions, not the learner.

Her second perspective takes place when an individual expresses a need to learn, looks to the educator for fulfillment of those needs, and then proceeds to learn under the guidance of the educator. In this perspective Canton calls the consumer-oriented learning, the learner makes each decision about learning--for this reason, this kind of learning falls under constructivism.

Finally, her third perspective, emancipatory learning, is a process of freeing ourselves from forces that limit our options and our control over our lives, forces that have been taken for granted or seen as beyond our control. This kind of learning is constructivist in nature and can be transformative. At times this learning occurs independently of the educator; at other times it is fostered deliberately. Unlike the other two kinds of learning, emancipatory learning is often a difficult and painful process (Cranton, p.750)

Multiple Studies have proven that adults think in different ways and it has been deteremined that these types of learning ways can be divided into three separate learning orientations. First, goal oriented learners use education as a means of achieving some other goal. Second, activity oriented learners participate for the sake of the activity itself and the social interaction it provides. Lastly, learning oriented learners seek knowledge for its own sake (Hughes 2005).

There are generally six factors for learning participation (Abdullah et.al 2008):

1. Social Relationships: make friends and meet others.
2. External Expectations: complying with the wishes of someone else with authority.
3. Social Welfare: desire to serve others and/or community.
4. Professional Advancement: desire for job enhancement or professional advancement.
5. Escape/Stimulation: to alleviate boredom and/or to escape home or work routine.
6. Cognitive Interest: learning for the sake of learning itself.

Pedague vs. Andragogue

"I don't want education done to me..."

Andragogy, initially defined as "the art and science of helping adults learn". The term currently defines an alternative to pedagogy and refers to learner-focused education for people of all ages. The andragogic model asserts that five issues be considered and addressed in formal learning.

1. Letting learners know why something is important to learn.
2. Showing learners how to direct themselves through information.
3. Relating the topic to the learners' experiences.
4. People will not learn until they are ready and motivated to learn.
5. This often requires helping them overcome inhibitions, behaviors, and beliefs about learning.

In the information age, the implications of a move from teacher-centered to learner-centered education are many.

Postponing or suppressing this move will slow our ability to learn new technology and gain competitive advantage. For example, how can we expect to analyze and synthesize so much information if we turn to others to determine what should be learned, how it will be learned, and when it will be learned?We must take it upon ourselves to meet our learning needs and demand training providers do the same. To know our demands, we must know how we process information.

Andragogue

"Andragogy is simply another model of assumptions about learners to be used alongside the pedagogical model of assumptions, thereby providing two alternative models for testing out the assumptions as to their 'fit' with particular situations. Furthermore, the models are probably most useful when seen not as dichotomous but rather as two ends of a spectrum, with a realistic assumption in a given situation falling in between the two ends

Concept of the Learner

During the process of maturation, a person moves from dependency toward increasing self-directedness, but at different rates for different people and in different dimensions of life. Teachers have a responsibility to encourage and nurture this movement. Adults have a deep psychological need to be generally self-directing, but they may be dependent in certain temporary situations.

Role of the Learner's Experience

As people grow and develop they accumulate an increasing reservoir of experience that becomes and increasingly rich resource for learning--for themselves and for others. Furthermore, people attach more meaning to learning they gain from experience than those they acquire passively. Accordingly, the primary techniques in education are experiential ones--laboratory experiments, discussion, problem-solving cases, field experiences, etc.

Readiness to Learn

People become ready to learn something when they experience a need to learn it in order to cope more satisfyingly with real-life tasks and problems. The educator has a responsibility to create conditions and provide tools and procedures for helping learners discover their "needs to know." Learning programs should be organized around life-application categories and sequenced according to the learners' readiness to learn.

Orientation to Learning

Learners see education as a process of developing increased competence to achieve their full potential in life. They want to be able to apply whatever knowledge and skill they gain today to living more effectively tomorrow. Accordingly, learning experiences should be organized around competency-development categories. People are performance-centered in their orientation to learning.

Future State

We must paint a yellow stripe down the center of our transformational super highway. On the road to the future, we have three lanes of traffic, but everyone can still follow the road thanks to the painted lines. Our "paint" is mixed from Clear Vision/Mission and Objectives, and is applied using Branding, Marketing (gorilla and traditional) Gorilla marketing in a corporate office?? What if the Unreal villain walked the hallways, etc. Our Missions & Visions as well as our introspection tell us that we must transform and Process must permeate function.

There are three Paths of Transformation:

- Corporate
- Organizational
- Individual

CORPORATE AND ORGANIZATIONAL VISION/MISSION

Amalgamated Cultural Vision

Competitive advantage will be achieved by establishing a culture of learning comprised of scientific leaders driving innovation and excellence through essential partnerships founded on collaboration and trusted advisement

Amalgamated Mission

Unparalleled levels of scientific excellence and customer service will be delivered through harmonized frameworks of delivery founded on expert methods, tools and training

EMPLOYEE VISION AND MISSION

Personal Vision

I understand that innovation is the result of testing the boundaries of what I know, and working with others who can help me surpass these boundaries. I will challenge myself to understand the process that I am part of, and seek new ways to make valuable contributions to my organization and the products that it produces.

Personal Mission

I will exercise all available opportunities to develop my functional abilities as they pertain to the organizational framework of which I am an invaluable part. Through continued personal education and expert coaching I will achieve new levels of career fulfillment while contributing to the business objectives of my organization.

Solution

Client Research has yielded the following conclusion and requirements:

- Employee Behavior
    - The VCE must be specifically goal oriented at first (e.g. attend a meeting).
    - Employees do not have time to "hang out" or "vacation" in a Virtual World
- Employee Work-styles.
    - Our target audience is very pragmatic.
    - A VCE must offer value as a tool, not just as a toy
- Quality of Experience.
    - The experience must be high fidelity and "real".
    - The experience should not be overly-distracting(a physical meeting room is not distracting).
- Available Technology
    - Pre-built worlds concentrate on scale, not the quality of intimate experiences.
    - We don't need a World day one, we need attractive, high performing Experiences.

Uptake on 3D immersive environments in the corporate workplace will be driven by function, not frivolity.

VCE BUSINESS TOOLS

The following tool set will be supplied to the client:

- Virtual Meetings
    - Establish Proximity
    - Capture Participant Focus
    - Efficiency of Communication
- Virtual Assessments
    - Role-play based usage of subject matter
    - Allows review of ability to use information
- Virtual Teaching
    - Classroom based
- Active participation increases effectiveness
- Appeals to Authentic Learning Principals
    - Game based
- Incredibly engaging, makes them compelling to use
- Conveyance of subject matter is extremely efficient
- Virtual Chat
    - Replicates "hallway encounters" to increase collaboration
    - Increases frequency of Impactful encounters
- Virtual Simulation
    - Provides realistic encounters with people and process with opportunities to learn how to succeed
- **Virtual Games**
    - Virtual Process Orientation
- Immerses participants in a process oriented challenge that teaches the core business of the client
- Examples of success include MIT, and Volvo
    - Virtual Team Building
- Re-enforce the criticality of information sharing across functions
- Examples of success include: "Everest" from Harvard Business School*
    - Distributed Innovation and Collective intelligence
- Community based problem solving
- Eg, How do these three signals relate to each other – score points
- Examples of success include:
- Microsoft's use of Community based bug-finding
- Foldit's uses a community-based model to solve biochemical protein folding challenges
    - Cultural Indoctrination

- Re-enforce Vision, Mission, Objectives and Cultural beliefs across an organization that physically separated
- Examples of success include: Sun Microsystems, "Rise of the Shadow Specters"

Why Not a Pre-Packaged World?

Highly skilled employees functioning in a very competitive industry need professional grade tools that can provide immediate and obvious value. We can begin improving business results today by ensuring that business participants have the very best tools in the toolbox. A toolbox is stocked with individual items that have been hand selected because they are the most relevant, and the best. As an alternative(and quite likely less expensive), the toolbox can be stocked at the lowest common denominator tools to ensure that everyone has something, but quite often most people will be left wanting tools that are more specialized and precise.

Pre-packaged worlds are built using lowest common denominator technology and are quite often designed to be massively parallel, not to provide best of breed individualized experiences. However, we believe that skilled professionals need individualized experiences to enhance their everyday participation in workflow.

Hospital vs. Patient

Gaming Engines have allowed the creation of digital virtual humans with a physiology engines that include pharmaco-kinetic drug models. They're biomechanically correct. "Unlike when people are building hospitals in Second Life and everyone's rejoicing because it's an architectural walk-through, gaming engines are being used to create highly instrumented and engaging environments. You apply a bandage and stick a needle in a patient, the patient will react, from a physiological perspective, in an authentic way in terms of body size, etc.

This level of instrumentation is groundbreaking. Instructors can also control the physiology dynamically or let the physiology engine run autonomously. It can throw curveballs at medical students. While we may not be looking to build realistic bodies for our client, we are very much interested in the "art of the possible", and building professional grade tools that add value on the job.

CONCLUSION

Only a small handful of non-government companies have realized that using Serious Game technology to deliver highly focused business tools is the most direct path to success. Far more companies are still trying to understand why their Virtual World efforts are not succeeding.

The key differentiator between a VCE Business Tool(VCEBT©), and a Virtual World is that a VCEBT© targets tasks and activities that need to be performed at a point in time. First, A VCEBT© is akin to someone opening MS Word and type a letter. A Virtual World asks a user to change everything about the way they do business.

Second, focusing on key business tasks, and delivering a set of VCEBT©'s that can be added to the business toolbox is a somewhat unique approach to Immersive technologies. We are not fighting against the grain to change a person's total behavior. A collection of valuable VCEBT©'s that gain traction will create pockets of business use and this is the first priority. VCEBT©'s that are proven to be successful can be connected to form a cohesive VCE, this is the second priority.

We began this project thinking about what a "virtual world" might look like for client. We found that it would be quite feasible to build a "world", but there were significant risks. Based on our research, we found that most large (Fortune 500) companies that have used a well known virtual world provider, have achieved little or no success. Those that have achieved some success have very different parameters than our client. What seemed to be missing from many corporate initiatives into virtual worlds was a well defined set of business objectives. Everyone has a vision for what they hope will happen in a virtual world, but quite often the vision does not mesh with reality.

What we have discovered is that there are two primary reasons why our client should get involved with Virtual Reality: 1) To develop a set of readily usable business tools. 2) To become fluent in a technology that will quite likely have a very prominent role in corporate life in future years. Our belief is that the best way to future-proof our client's organization is by doing far more than experimentation in the hope of future relevance, we need to build a foundation of experience, and a track record of acceptance to provide our pathway into the future.

REFERENCES

Abdullah, M., et al. (2008). *Motivating Factors Associated with Adult Participation in Distance Learning Program*. Retrieved on August 28, 2009, from http://ccsenet.org/journal/index.php/ies/article/viewFile/629/604

APQC. (n.d.). Retrieved August 28, 2009, from http://www.apqc.org/portal/apqc/site.

Attwell. (2004). *E-Learning and Sustainability*. Retrieved on August 28, 2009, from http://lefo.net/lefo_sustainability_graham.htm.

Cranton, C. (1994). *Understanding and Promoting Transformative Learning* (pp. 3–21). San Francisco: Jossey-Bass.

Cranton, P. (1994). Self-directed and transformative instructional development. *The Journal of Higher Education*, *65*(6), 726–744. doi:10.2307/2943826

Crawford, C. (2004, July 14). *A-Ritzer-Encyclopedia*. Retrieved September 28, 2009, from http://www.sagepub.com/upm-data/5222_Ritzer__Entries_beginning_with_A__%5B1%5D.pdf.

Gallager, W. (2009). *Rapt: attention and the focused life*. New York: Penguin Publishers.

Hughes, B. (2005). Indentifying attitudes and deterring factors toward continuing education among certified athletic trainers. *The Internet Journal of Allied Health Sciences and Practice*, *3*(1). Retrieved on August 28, 2009, from http://ijahsp.nova.edu/articles/vol3num1/HUGHES.pdf

Kraut, R. E., & Fussell, S. R. (2002). Understanding effects of proximity on collaboration: Implications for technologies to support remote collaborative work. In Hinds, P. J., & Kiesler, S. (Eds.), *Distributed Work*. Cambridge, MA: The MIT Press.

Virtual reality. (2009). Merriam-Webster Online Dictionary. Retrieved August 26, 2009, from http://www.merriam-webster.com/dictionary/virtual reality

ADDITIONAL READING

Bailenson, J. (2008). The effect of interactivity on learning physical actions in virtual reality. *Media Psychology*, *11*(3), 354–376. doi:10.1080/15213260802285214

Galbraith, M. (2003). *Adult Learning Methods: A Guide for Effective Instruction*. Malabar, FL: Krieger Publishing Company.

Katsionis, G. (2008). Personalized e-learning through an educational virtual reality game using Web services. *Multimedia Tools and Applications*, *39*(1), 47–71. doi:10.1007/s11042-007-0155-2

Kausler, D. H. (1999). Adult learning and development: Perspectives from educational psychology. *Contemporary Psychology*, *44*(1), 46–47.

Knowles, M. (2005). The Adult Learner, Sixth Edition: The Definitive Classic in Adult Education and Human Resource Development. Newark, NJ: Butterworth-Heinemann.

Lee, D. (2000). Assessing adult learning preferences using the analytic hierarchy process. *International Journal of Lifelong Education, 19*(6), 548–560. doi:10.1080/02601370050209078

Lloyd, J. (2009). Equivalence of Real-World and Virtual-Reality Route Learning: A Pilot Study. *Cyberpsychology & Behavior, 12*(4), 423–427. doi:10.1089/cpb.2008.0326

Marienau, C. (2008). Educator as Designer: Balancing Multiple Teaching Perspectives in the Design of Community Based Learning for Adults. *New Directions for Adult and Continuing Education, 188*, 61–74.

Merriam, S. B. (2008). *Third Update on Adult Learning Theory*. New Directions for Adult and Continuing Education.

Merrill, B. (2001). Learning and Teaching in Universities: perspectives from adult learners and lecturers. *Teaching in Higher Education, 6*(1), 5–17. doi:10.1080/13562510020029563

Monahan, T. (2008). Virtual reality for collaborative e-learning. *Computers & Education, 50*(4), 1339–1353. doi:10.1016/j.compedu.2006.12.008

Nelken, M. (2009). Negotiating Classroom Process: Lessons from Adult Learning. *Negotiation Journal, 25*(2), 181–194. doi:10.1111/j.1571-9979.2009.00219.x

Pratt, D. (1998). *Five Perspectives on Teaching in Adult and Higher Education*. Malabar, FL: Krieger Publishing Company.

Rose, F. D. (2000). Training in Virtual Environments. *Ergonomic, 43*(4), 494–511. doi:10.1080/001401300184378

Schmidt, B. (2009). Implementing the Virtual Reality Learning Environment Second Life. *Nurse Educator, 34*(4), 152–155. doi:10.1097/NNE.0b013e3181aabbe8

Stolovitch, H. (2009). *Telling ain't training*. Alexandria, VA: ASTD Press.

Troyer, A. K. (2006). Name and Face Learning in Older Adults: Effects of Level of Processing, Self-Generation, and Intention to Learn. *The Journals of Gerontology. Series B, Psychological Sciences and Social Sciences, 61*(2), 67–74.

Wlodkowski, R. J. (2008). *Enhancing Adult Motivation to Learn: A Comprehensive Guide for Teaching All Adults*. Jossey-Bass.

Xie, B. (2007). Information Technology Education for Older Adults as a Continuing Peer-Learning Process: A Chinese Case Study. *Educational Gerontology, 35*(5), 429–450. doi:10.1080/03601270701252872

KEY TERMS AND DEFINITIONS

Physically Disparate: A situation in which employees are separated by physical distance.

Immersive Technology: Technology that enables the user to have a point of view from within a software rendering of a virtual space.

Virtual World: A virtual rendering of an environment based on Immersive Technology.

VCEBT: Virtual Corporate Environment Business Tool.

Virtual Reality: A realistic simulation of an environment by a computer system.

Federated Reality: The relationship between a person's consciousness and their physical body.

Avatar: A rendering that represents the user in a Virtual World.

VCE: Virtual Corporate Environment.

Formal Encounter: When colleagues encounter each other in a planned scenario, quite often defined by an agenda.

Informal Encounter: A chance encounter of two or more colleagues.

Proximity: How we describe the sense of "being with" a colleague.

Customer Intimacy: Having an in depth and meaningful understanding of a customer.

Flex Time: When employees do not all work the same daily hours.

BPI – Business Process Improvement: The analysis and improvement of business workflows.

Authentic Learning: Learning by doing.

Andragogy: The engagement of the Learner in the process of learning.

Serious Game: An activity that uses game play to teach important educational concepts.

Chapter 14
ClassSim:
An Approach to Educator Development Through a Simulation

Brian Ferry
University of Wollongong, Australia

Lisa Kervin
University of Wollongong, Australia

Lisa Carrington
University of Wollongong, Australia

ABSTRACT

This chapter presents one approach to educator development through games and simulations. The goal of the authors' project was to enhance pre-service teachers' ability to bridge the gap between the theory and practice of teaching. Some criteria that the authors regarded as indicators of success were the facilitation a professional dialogue, an emerging understanding of content delivery and the articulation of workplace culture in the teaching profession. The chapter describes the theory underpinning of the design and the research approaches used. In particular, the authors explain how cognitive load theory was applied to the design of the key features of this virtual learning environment. They also summarize six years of research that has consistently found that the virtual learning environment of ClassSim provides an effective way of introducing pre-service teachers to their future work in classrooms.

INTRODUCTION

As teacher educators, we are always looking for more effective and relevant ways to bridge the gap between theory and practice, to develop pedagogical content knowledge, and ultimately to enhance the development of pre-service teachers' (PSTs') professional identities so that they can be confident and effective teachers when they graduate. One approach that we have tried has been to use a virtual learning environment (VLE), known as ClassSim, as a tool to experiment with practical scenarios while providing explicit links to the theory that PSTs are exposed to during training.

ClassSim is a walk though, scenario-based simulation in which the user assumes the role of

DOI: 10.4018/978-1-61520-713-8.ch014

the classroom teacher of a class of five-year-olds during a literacy learning session. A number of virtual episodes (or lessons) are included for the user to explore and, as each episode unfolds, PSTs make a number of decisions regarding the management of the classroom and the organization of the literacy learning session. Until recently limited research has been conducted on the use of VLEs in PST education and how engagement with such environments can support the learning and development of future teachers. This project gave us an opportunity to gain some insight into PSTs' engagement with a VLE designed to assist them to make connections between the theory and practice of teaching.

The objectives of this chapter are to describe the theory that informed the design of ClassSim and to report on our research with PSTs over the past six years. In particular we draw upon cognitive load theory (CLT) to clarify how we operationalized some of the recent key recommendations of evidence-based research into the organization of instruction in order to facilitate effective learner processing of information (Pashler, et al., 2007).

BACKGROUND

Researchers report that when teachers reflect upon their role in the profession, they are not necessarily focused on what they know and what they can do (Allen, 2005; Sachs, 1999). Rather, they are more likely to question their own role within a situation. Thus, teachers appear to be more interested in understanding their immediate professional situation in connection with their previous personal and professional experiences. Instead of the question what do I know, or what can I do, for many teachers their interest is in the question who am I, what relationship do I have with the learner, what is my relationship with school administrators, and how have my personal experiences contributed to my development as a teacher. These questions demonstrate the role played by both the physical workplace and the individual's networks in the development of a teacher's professional identity.

Learning a profession means learning about the culture of the occupation and each profession has its own disposition and learnt behavior that is often referred to as the culture and practice of that profession. Teaching, as an example of such a profession, involves specific knowledge and skills related to pedagogical understandings, knowledge of workplace culture and awareness of their responsibilities within the profession. In exploring the culture and practice of teaching Sachs (1999) identifies the need for retrospective and prospective identities; retrospective identities use the past to explain the present within the profession, while prospective identities examine the future nature of the profession. We hypothesized that a VLE, such as ClassSim, affords opportunities for users to consider retrospective and prospective identities as a simulation allows users to observe and investigate what is happening at a moment in time, but it also allows the user to pause and reflect upon what has happened, with opportunity to change and redirect the future sense of story presented in the simulation. Allen (2005) asserts that such aspects of teacher professional growth are not taught, rather they are shaped by teachers' past critical incidents including the workplace and an individual's professional networks. As a result Allen's work, we also hypothesized that a VLE has the potential for PSTs to experience a series of workplace events and critical incidents that may help to shape their developing pedagogy.

Overview of Research Into the Use of Online Simulations and Games in Initial Teacher Education

Since 2000 Interactive Communication Tecvhnologies (ICT) have evolved to the point where researchers with low budgets can begin to take advantage of its potential in gaming and simulation design. Some recent examples are the work of Eckersley, Richards and Schofield (2004), Gee (2004), Gibson and Halverson (2004), Dexter (2006), and Knezek and Vandersall (2008). While much of the recent research and development work has been summarized in the publication edited by Ferdig (2009), there is still a need to develop a stronger theoretical perspective on the design of simulations and games, and this has led to some criticisms that are now outlined.

Kirschner, Sweller, and Clark (2006) argue that turning learners loose in a VLE, no matter how cleverly designed, is a poor instructional strategy. They assert that too many interventions naïvely assume that students will learn if they engage in "authentic" practices of experts in a domain; forgetting that what experts do and how experts learned to do what they do are not necessarily synonymous. Therefore, without explicit guidance, the learner is likely to wander aimlessly in a stimulating and rich digital environment finding creative but often spurious patterns, that can lead them to make false generalizations (Shaffer, 2007).

The kind of guidance that learners need will vary with the domain in which they are learning (Shaffer, 2007) and different kinds of experts develop their expertise through different kinds of guided experiences. The on-line simulation we developed created a guided experience for students beginning their careers as teachers. The goal was to develop expertise not by using the simulation as an expert, but as a novice training to be a teacher. Because direct mentoring by experts is part of any training for expertise, explicit guidance was provided. But the kind of guidance we wanted to create was to be similar to what real beginning teachers receive during quality practicum experiences, rather than the explicit commands, or random ill-structured advice, or irrelevant responses that can occur during poor practicum experiences (Ramsey, 2000).

A well-designed simulation has to do more than merely immerse a user in a virtual world; it has to teach users the rules of engagement in the virtual world. But no virtual world can accommodate every possibility. Therefore choices have to be made about the roles users play when interacting with the simulation, the norms followed, and the rules needed. We needed to provide the framework in which learners could make sense of what happens when they interact with the simulation. In addition the learners needed a framework of expert guidance that allows them to be a part of rich activities that build on their own goals, backgrounds, and interests. They also needed explicit guidance at critical times to find the underlying knowledge, skills, values, and ways of thinking in an expert (Shaffer & Gee, 2005).

When we began to develop ClassSim we wanted the VLE to make it possible for more PSTs to learn about the world of the teacher by participating in a wider range of meaningful activities than is possible with real-world experiences alone. Users would learn by doing, and emphasis would be on valuing tacit as well as abstract knowledge. However, we acknowledge that ClassSim is not the only way to accomplish these ends, but its strength lies in the cost of failure, which is lower than the real world as the 'action' takes place in a simulated world, making it possible to innovate without risk.

Theory Used to Inform the Design of ClassSim

This section explores how ideas associated with cognitive load theory informed the design of ClassSim. Cognitive science views learning as 'the active transformation of content from the environment into new knowledge and skills in memory that can be accessed when needed for the job' (Clark, 2003, p.21). Human cognitive processing involves three memory systems that interact when learning occurs. These systems are sensory memory, working memory (short-term memory) and long-term memory.

Sensory memory consists of sensory data accessed via the senses (e.g. sight, sound, smell) but it has a short-term duration. Working or short-

Figure 1. A model of human cognitive architecture (based on Bruning et al 2004, p.16)

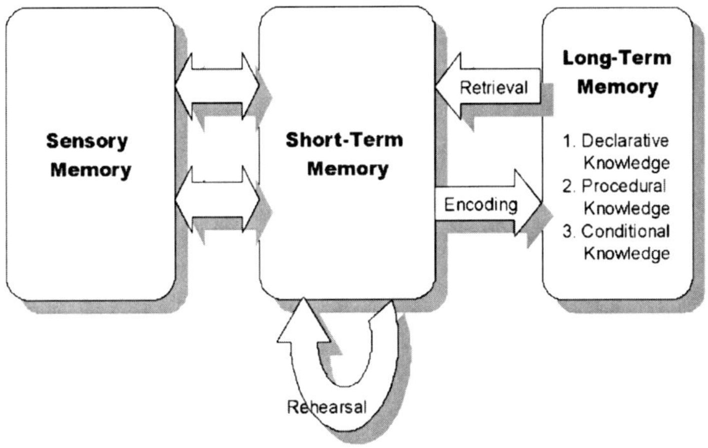

term memory (STM) is considered the centre of conscious cognition. It has a limited capacity and a brief duration. Further, it has separate areas for storing auditory and visual sensory data. By way of contrast, long-term memory (LTM) has a large capacity for storage and represents a permanent repository of knowledge that is stored in two forms: declarative (facts and concepts) and procedural (skills). However, LTM does not process knowledge, but stores it, while STM memory interacts with LTM when new knowledge is stored or existing knowledge retrieved.

Instructional content (usually in text, or audio and/or visual form) is transformed into knowledge and skills by a process that is represented in Figure 1.

Visual and auditory data enter the sensory memory where they are briefly stored. If the learner attends to these data, it is selected for transfer to working (or short-term) memory where prior knowledge is activated from long-term memory. The new content is then integrated into existing schema or knowledge structures. However, the integration of new content with existing knowledge occurs primarily in working memory that has limited capacity. Therefore, it is important to ensure that working memory is not overloaded.

The process is not complete at this stage, as the content in working memory has to be rehearsed and then encoded into long-term memory. Finally, for the new knowledge and skills to be useful, it needs to be retrieved from long-term memory back into working (short-term) memory. If the retrieval process breaks down then the new knowledge or skills will not transfer to the task at hand.

Three forms of cognitive load (intrinsic, germane and extraneous load) have been identified and while some forms are useful, others waste mental resources and overload working (short-term) memory as depicted in figure 2.

Intrinsic cognitive load "is mental work imposed by the complexity of the content" (Clark, Nguyen & Sweller, 2006, p.9) and learning tasks that involve the coordination of multiple mental and physical components fall into this category. For example, when a pre-service teacher is learning to teach, the task of teaching a lesson can seem overwhelming, as there are many interactive elements to consider. During the process of preparing a lesson, appropriate content needs to be selected to meet syllabus requirements, then the content needs to be organized into a meaningful learning sequence that will engage the targeted learners. Coupled with this is the need to efficiently organize teaching resources and

Figure 2. The various forms of cognitive load (Giumelli, 2008)

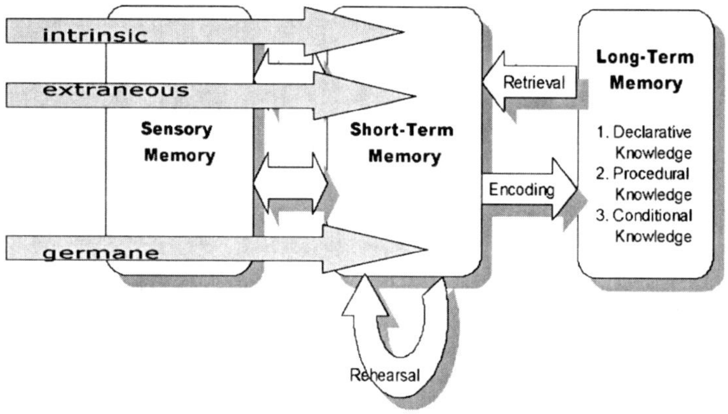

the learners. In addition, the beginning teacher needs to consider how he or she will monitor student learning and manage student behavior. Finally, the implementation of the lesson creates another layer of complexity as it usually involves making decisions, in a short time frame, about 'trouble shooting' strategies needed to correct misunderstandings, to manage resources or student behavior.

Germane cognitive load is "mental work imposed by the instructional activities that benefits the instructional goal" (Clark, Nguyen & Sweller, 2006, p.11). In the case of the situation previously described an experienced classroom teacher who is supervising the beginning teacher may provide scaffolding or explicitly model strategies that to break the tasks into more manageable elements. If the beginning teacher makes an effort to learn and apply some of the strategies demonstrated by the experienced teacher, (s)he will be more capable of dealing with many of the classroom management tasks faced, leaving room to focus his/her attention to the learning task. Over time this supervision practice, coupled with explicit feedback on lessons, builds up a set of knowledge and skills that are not only transferable from the current to future related tasks, they reduce the mental resources that the beginning teacher needs to allocate to basic classroom management so that they can focus more on student learning.

Extraneous cognitive load "imposes mental work that is irrelevant to the learning goal and consequently wastes mental resources" (Clark, Nguyen & Sweller, 2006, p.12). When a beginning teacher implements a lesson for the first time, he/she may pay too much attention to following the script of the lesson plan and to the organization and articulation of the knowledge they need to impart. Often pupil management issues arise creating a distraction that makes it difficult for the beginning teacher to maintain the flow of the lesson and this has a negative impact on pupil learning. This can be dis-heartening as the PST may have spent considerable time and effort in, learning the content, preparing the learning materials, organizing materials and writing a lesson plan. While this mental work is germane to the task and is important *prior* to the implementation of the lesson, it becomes extraneous if mental resources continue to focus on these tasks during the implementation phase of the lesson. Extraneous cognitive load could be reduced by the support strategies mentioned in the previous paragraph as well as by thoughtful preparation that focuses on a well-organised lesson plan that is easy to follow and the learning and mental rehearsal of the delivery of the subject matter. This makes it easier, during the implementation of a lesson, for the beginning teacher to rapidly retrieve relevant content and management strategies from long-term memory into working memory.

Some General Recommendations Based on This Research

The research suggests strategies that can be used to guide the design of a simulation to achieve the goals previously mentioned. The strategies are based upon the recent research of Pashler, et al. (2007) whose recommendations summarized current evidence-based research about the organization of instruction and study to improve student learning.

The seven recommendations they made were: space learning over time; interleave worked example solutions and problem-solving exercises; combine graphics with verbal descriptions; connect and integrate abstract and concrete representations of concepts; use quizzing to promote learning; help students to allocate study time efficiently; and help students build explanations by asking and answering deep questions. Many of these recommendations have been informed by studies into cognitive load and the next section describes how some of these recommendations were operationalized in ClassSim.

Operationalizing the Recommendations in ClassSim

The design of ClassSim was based upon segmenting sets of authentic classroom teaching episodes into interconnected short-term events called cycles. Sets of cycles linked in a variety of ways to form a diversity of possible teaching episodes. As a result, the way that each teaching episode unfolded was based upon the decisions that users made about the management of the classroom, of students, and of random events that occurred during each cycle.

Cycles can be experienced in one long sitting or spaced over time so a user may experience one cycle at a time and then revisit as needed (Ferry, et al., 2004, p.437). This allows learning to be spaced over time.

The incorporation of targeted students was a way of presenting a problem and provided a worked or reasoned example of a possible response (or solution). In general the targeted students represented in ClassSim are the more challenging students that teachers are often faced with in the classroom, but we were also mindful to represent a range of needs and abilities of students within a typical classroom. The student updates associated with provide examples of pupil responses to teacher pedagogy and class management decisions. These were designed to include graphics with verbal descriptions. In addition, the expert commentary provided users with an example of how experienced teachers may handle the problem they faced.

An example of a student update is shown in figure 3. The figure shows the visual feedback in terms of pupil facial expression. In addition expert commentary is provided about key dimensions of the model of quality teaching adopted by New South Wales (NSW) public schools. In NSW it was mandatory for PSTs to learn about the New South Wales Quality Teaching Model during their teacher education course. The figure also shows that links are also available to the pupil's profile, class goals and further information about the New South Wales Quality Teaching Model.

An embedded cognitive tool called the 'Thinking Space' provided a framework in which the users could reflect upon issues within the virtual classroom, articulate their rationale at decision points and identify underlying influences that affected their use of the virtual learning environment and record their professional learning as they engaged with the support material. A series of questions were added to the 'Thinking Space' and these were designed to be a quizzing cue that promoted learning of key concepts. Figure 4 shows an example of a 'Thinking Space'. The series of prompts and questions can be seen.

Thus the 'Thinking Space' and the various support materials provided were designed to help users to build explanations by asking, and supporting PSTs to answer, deep questions about a specific, virtual teaching episode that they were experiencing online.

Support materials were also used to inform and assist the PSTs in making connections between the theory and the practice of teaching as they made decisions within the simulation. The summaries included links to websites, textbook references and other literature. As such, they provided explicit examples and information that was relevant to the current scenario in ClassSim. In addition, a clock displayed the time elapsed since the lesson commenced and served as a reminder to users that they needed to use their time efficiently to complete the simulated lesson on time.

Summary of Studies Conducted With ClassSim

Over the past six years the various methodologies that we have used during our studies with ClassSim have included a comparative case study approach using data collection procedures such as semi-structured interviews, observations and the collection and analysis of artifacts; surveys of users; group interviews after initial and final use of ClassSim; and analysis of users' logs. University ethics approvals were given for these studies and at all times informed consent, confidentiality and the right to withdraw without penalty were addressed.

Our data have consistently shown that interaction with the software supported the preparation of our pre-service teachers for classroom reality. We have frequently heard participants acknowledge the complexity of the role of the teacher and the need to consider many interacting elements within the simulated environment they had not previously considered. Further, our data showed that PSTs entered actual classroom environments after using the simulation with greater awareness of the multifaceted nature of the classroom situation.

We now present a sample of our findings from a recent case study led by author Carrington with PSTs enrolled in the first year of their teacher education degree program. This is compared with PSTs enrolled in the third year of their degree program.

A comparative case study approach was adopted, utilising semi-structured interviews, observations and the collection and analysis of artefacts as data collection procedures. This design enabled the researchers to focus upon and compare two groups of pre-service teachers (first and final year students), while taking into consideration the contextual conditions (such as the participants' field experiences).

Data collection began with the use of a demographic survey of all 187 students enrolled in the first year and 150 students enrolled in the final year of a teacher education undergraduate degree program to enable purposive selection of the participants. Observations of the focus pre-service teacher participants were collected as they engaged with the software and interacted with their peers. Artefacts ('Thinking Space' entries) and semi-structured interviews occurred subsequent to interaction with ClassSim. The participants continued with their usual university coursework and field experiences, during which the researchers collected the participant reflections and conducted further semi-structured interviews. The first year pre-service teacher data were collected during the first semester of the first year, while the final year pre-service teacher data were collected during the final semester of the degree program which qualified them to be an elementary school teacher in New South Wales (NSW), Australia.

The data were coded (open and axial) and categorised according to emerging themes within data. Open coding was used to identify broad concepts such as: purpose, reflection, theory to practice connections, and design. This was followed by axial coding to explore patterns and converging trends in the data leading to possible themes including: readiness, orientation, motivation, experience and self concept

The literature suggests that a teacher's professional identity is shaped by his or her understanding of the theory of teaching/learning and unique set of life and teaching experiences. This

Figure 3. 'Student update' of Gavin

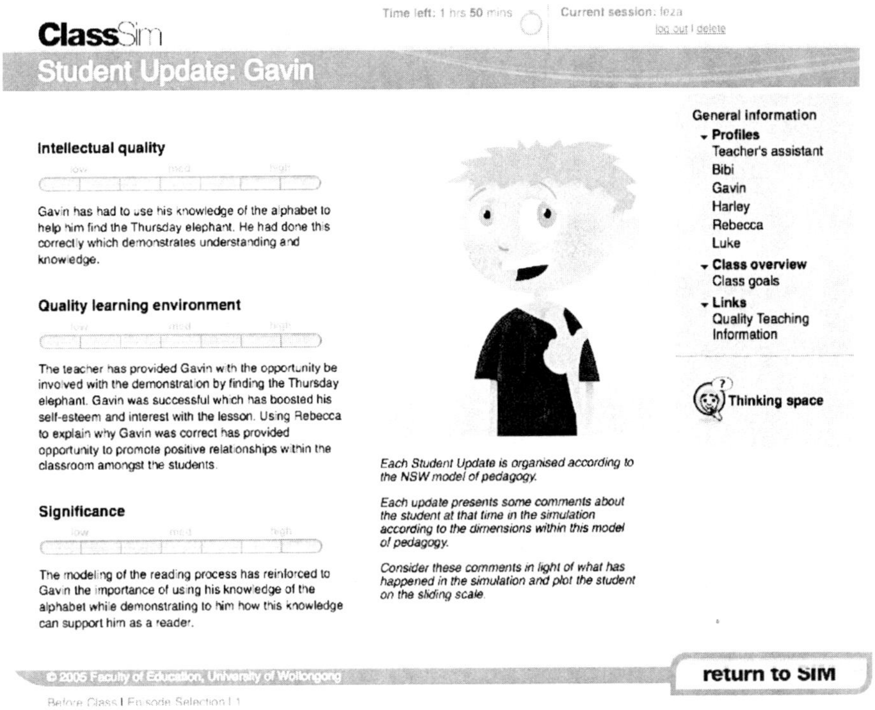

impacts a teacher's philosophical beliefs and the pedagogical approaches he or she utilize in the classroom (Allen, 2005).

Results

The results are organized under the headings of first-year pre-service teachers' results and third-year pre-service teachers' results. The findings from both groups of pre-service teachers suggest that through engagement with the VLE and other experiences, many pre-service teachers showed evidence of a developing professional identity. For example, many of the first-year pre-service teachers were about to experience their first practicum and the VLE provided affirmation of their choice of career and gave them some degree of self-efficacy. The data from the third-year pre-service teachers suggests that they were able to make stronger connections between their university coursework and their field experience than the first year pre-service teachers. We suggest that this is probably a reflection of the length of time that they have been enrolled in their degree and their more extensive classroom experience. As expected the third year pre-service teachers also showed more evidence of understanding of the overall school context.

First-Year Pre-Service Teachers' Results

During the study we explored the developing professional identity of seven, first-year pre-service teacher participants who used ClassSim. However, we acknowledge that this development occurred in conjunction with their other learning experiences. Below are some selected examples from the findings. In all cases presented in this chapter pseudonyms have been used to protect the identity of the subjects. All data is present with permission of the subjects.

Figure 4. An example of a Thinking Space

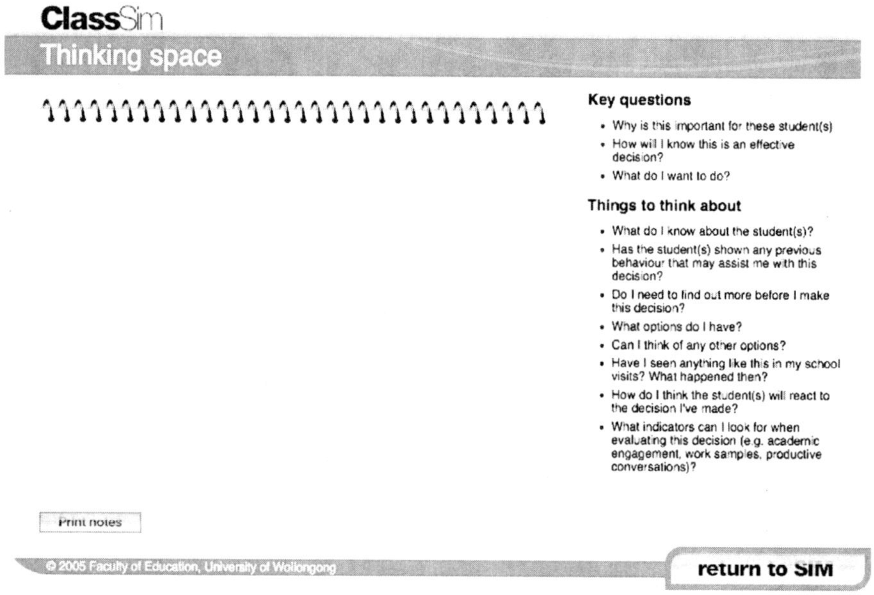

Serena's comments made during her first interview suggested that she was extremely anxious about her field experience and wondered whether or not she was capable of teaching. However, after her engagement with the VLE her anxiety level appeared to diminish to a point where she believed she was capable of teaching.

It was a lot of fun. It was a really good experience, because I actually got to see that I could actually teach, I wasn't just thinking that I might. I used to get really scared about it in my head. Like, what am I going to do if that happens? Or what am I going to do if this happens? (I_Serena_23/03)

During her second interview Serena explained that the ClassSim presented her with an opportunity to be a teacher in a classroom, rather than a student. "Before I was a student and I looked at things completely different but with the ClassSim it really was a teacher view... So it makes you think 'oh yes I'm now a uni student, I'm using a ClassSim, I see how a teacher role can be'. Then you go to prac and 'oh I'm a teacher' (I_Serena_25/07). Therefore, the findings suggest that Serena's engagement with the VLE helped her to develop a belief that she was capable of being a teacher.

Jasmine made similar comments. She explained that before engaging with the VLE she felt like a university student, and it wasn't until she was able to direct her own virtual class that she felt like a pre-service teacher. She continued by explaining that her field experience further developed her professional identity as a beginning teacher.

When I'm at uni I'm a uni student, not a pre service teacher. But with the ClassSim I actually sat down and went 'I'm actually starting to become a teacher'. And when I got to the prac I was like okay 'I'm a teacher', sort of thing. But when I first started doing a prac I thought 'oh no I'm just an observer. I'm not really supposed to be doing anything just ignore me' cause I was just a little bit shy at first, but as it got on and I did my full prac it was just like 'okay I'm a teacher'. This is a classroom listen to me (I_Jasmine_24/07).

During her engagement with ClassSim Kellie made comments in her 'Thinking Space' regarding her developing teaching beliefs. Kellie suggested that the class rules presented in the VLE were poorly worded. She explained that a certain amount of noise should be expected in a productive classroom environment and the class rules should reflect this belief.

CLASS GOALS / RULES

1. We will always work quietly.

I disagree with the above statement and the use of the word "always". Sometimes it is necessary for children to talk to the person next or across from them about the work that they are currently doing, as it helps their progression in their work.

I believe that the children need to use their "indoor voices", however at the same time work quietly (TS_Kellie_12/03).

This suggests that Kellie's teaching approach had begun to develop regarding acceptable noise levels in her classroom. It appears as though Kellie's engagement with the VLE enabled her to identify and articulate her own values and beliefs as a future teacher.

Kim made a comment in her 'Thinking Space' regarding her beliefs about rewards and punishments. Through her engagement with ClassSim she noticed that the virtual teacher often chose student Rebecca to praise for a behavior also displayed by a number of other classmates.

Using Rebecca to tell that class how to focus, I feel was slightly wrong as it makes the other kids think she is more important than they are. She could have said "now who knows how to sit when we want to learn" or similar that way it gives opportunity for students to be praised and also engage classroom discussion (TS_Kim_28/04).

Thus, it appears that Kim was able to articulate her teaching belief regarding the preferential treatment of a 'select few' students. Overall, this suggests that engagement with the VLE provided by ClassSim, and subsequent use of the 'Thinking Space', enabled Kim to experience and document her responses to a situation that resembled one in a real classroom.

During an interview Kim made comments about her field experience teacher's teaching practices. Kim explained that her field experience teacher organized the desks in rows. She said that this format did not suit her teaching philosophy. "My teacher had two lots of row for each year and this separated the class. I personally wouldn't have done it this way because I think kids work best in groups (I_Kim_25/07). This suggests that Kim was able to observe another teacher's method and explain why she would or would not use a similar strategy.

Bruce's reflections about field experience mentioned that he needed to slow down the pace of his lessons, ensure that all of the children are engaged, and increase the amount of positive reinforcement given out. "Basically, I need to slow down my lessons and keep the children focused. I suppose that was something that came through from ClassSim too – focus on engaging the kids. It was also suggested I focus on giving out more positive reinforcement, although this may not be so successful with older students. Kindergarten children loved getting stamps, stickers and house points" (FER_Bruce_18/06).

This response suggests that Bruce's field experience and engagement with the VLE helped him to identify aspects (including pace, engagement, and motivation) of his teaching which require further development. It also highlights Bruce's belief that positive reinforcement is limited to rewards of some kind, rather than through the use of praise. This may be because Bruce has yet to understand positive reinforcement can be both an intrinsic and extrinsic motivator.

Overall the findings suggest that through engagement with the VLE and other experiences, many of the first year pre-service teachers showed evidence of a developing professional identity. We now present some of the findings from the seven third year PST participants.

Third-Year Pre-Service Teachers' Results

During an interview Lauren was able to identify a teaching approach in the VLE that she did not agree with.

I guess some of the techniques she used though I didn't agree with but it wasn't, that I didn't have a better one in mind, I was just thinking I'm not comfortable with that approach but what would I do instead, I didn't know. If it was reflection, I'd say I've got a better idea that's not my style what is my style I don't know yet (I_Lauren_16/11).

Although she was unable to propose a suitable alternative to this strategy, she was certain that it did not suit her style of teaching. This suggests that Lauren's teaching philosophy was still in its emergent phase as she was unable to suggest a suitable strategy from her reservoir of pedagogical knowledge.

In his 'Thinking Space', Ross reflected upon the use of praise in his classroom to enhance to a student's self esteem and to acknowledge a contribution.

A teacher should praise students as much as possible as it allows them to feel a sense of worth within the classroom... By the teacher praising the students she is rewarding their efforts within the classroom. This is essential, as each student needs to be acknowledged in some way for contributing to class discussion (TS_Ross_21/08).

Ross' reflection indicates that he had firm beliefs in the use of praise in the classroom as advantageous to both the students' self worth and the development of a class community. In this example it appears as though Ross' engagement with the VLE may have reinforced the beliefs that he already held.

During her engagement with the VLE, Zoe reflected upon the notion of consistency in regards to behavior management. After an incident with a virtual child, she suggested that she must stay consistent in her approach to this conduct.

I would reprimand Gavin. He needs to know that his behaviour is not acceptable as much as it is difficult to keep doing. I think I would try and be consistent and reprimand him when he does something like disrupting the whole class and creating a scene because it is impacting on everyone else and everybody else needs to know that behaviour like his will not be tolerated. On the other hand, while doing this I would also try to work hard to strongly encourage him when he behaves well (TS_Zoe_18/08).

This suggests that Zoe's approach to pupil management is guided by the notion of consistency as she claims that it helps to create a balanced learning community and limits the amount of teacher bias towards students. Again it appears as though Zoe's understanding of her future role as a teaching is developing as a result of her engagement with the VLE.

After engaging with the VLE Mia commented that she did not require the support of the summary material as she believed that she possessed the knowledge about the teaching strategies and other terminology found in ClassSim.

I think by this stage I wouldn't need definitions of those words. I knew exactly what they're meaning and they're just common language. I think if I was doing first year, I would probably need the explanations, but now it's expected that you know them. Whereas when you're just starting out it's good to introduce people to the terms that they will use. So yeah, I knew exactly what was going on with that type of language that was being used and I felt comfortable to understand what was being explained within the program (I_Mia_21/08).

This suggests that Mia did not require the extra support provided in ClassSim to help her to understand and implement the various teaching strategies.

During an interview Marie was asked what she based her decisions upon when she used the VLE. She suggested that it was a combination of her university coursework and previous field experiences; however she was unable to give specific examples.

I used some things from university, ideas I've got from my prac and various things. I wasn't too worried when it came to decisions. For example, there was one choice I had to make regarding what lesson I would do first. There were a number of options so I just used my knowledge of what kind of lesson, that didn't feel was too challenging for the class. Most things I chose in the sim were based upon my previous experience in schools or from my readings, but I can't be sure exactly where I got the knowledge. I just have it (I_Marie_20/08).

In this case it appears that Marie was able to draw upon a range of previous experiences and knowledge when she used the VLE. This was interpreted as evidence of making vital connections between her university coursework (theory of teaching) and field experiences (practice of teaching). Thus Marie was able to draw upon these knowledge/skills and apply it in to the context of the VLE.

Overall, the findings suggest that through engagement with the VLE and other experiences, many of the third year pre-service teachers were able identify and articulate their emerging teaching philosophy and this may have helped in the development of their professional identity. The findings also suggest that through the engagement with the VLE and their field experience, a number of third year pre-service teachers incorporated teaching terminology into their everyday language. Another finding is that some of the third year pre-service teachers were able to make stronger connections between their university coursework and their field experience than the first year students. Thus, the interview transcripts, Thinking Space entries and other data collected all are indicators of a developing professional dialog and a developing understanding of the delivery of lessons in a school context. Further there is evidence of articulation of the role of the teacher in terms of classroom management and teaching literacy.

FUTURE RESEARCH DIRECTIONS

The research team is currently exploring two future directions. First we recently conducted a pilot study with first-time (neophyte) parents who had enrolled their children at a local school. We found that their experience in using ClassSim appeared to provide them some insights into the work of their child's teacher. Later in the year we will follow up with this group and interview the parents who used ClassSim to find out if the virtual experience with ClassSim had helped to promoted a common understanding that benefited to the parent, the teacher and the child. The outcome of this pilot study will be used to inform a larger study across a number of schools. We speculate that an online environment such as ClassSim may provide neophyte parents with insight into how schools work and relieve some of the anxiety they feel as first-time parents of school-aged children. We see this research as contributing to a future opportunity for schools to use an online, virtual learning environment to assist parents to understand the role modern schools and their teachers play in supporting the learning and development of their child. This is likely to appeal to working parents who struggle to attend school meetings. In addition, the school can ensure that they provide a virtual experience that is supportive of its mission.

Second, the authors have recently presented a panel presentation at a large international conference with a group of international collaborators from Korea and the USA. Each of these collaborators has been addressing similar problems using a variety of strategies such as second life environments and online simulations that are programmed to respond according evidence-based learner profiles and evidence-based research on classroom management and learning styles. These researchers have applied for funding to conduct an international workshop whose goal is to develop a design concept that combines our work into a simulated learning environment that can be used internationally. If successful funding is forthcoming we will develop and test this virtual learning environment in the USA, Australian and Korea. Our preliminary discussions have focused on the use of avatars and social networking to create an engaging virtual learning environment that further promotes long-term learner engagement. In this way learners would gain maximum benefit from the VLE.

CONCLUSION

The data presented during this chapter suggests that the VLE did help PSTs to develop an enhanced understanding of their future role as classroom teachers. As expected, the outcomes for the third-year PST were different than those from the first-year cohort, reflecting their different levels of experience. The design features, informed by cognitive load theory, appear to have helped the pre-service teachers achieve these outcomes. Follow-up empirical research with larger groups, changing one variable at a time, and using control and experimental groups would more clearly inform us as to which design features are the most effective in this context.

Some of the criteria for success that we set for ourselves were the facilitation a professional dialogue, an emerging understanding of content delivery and the articulation of workplace culture in the teaching profession. We feel that over the years our research over has shown that the VLE does provide a learning environment where this can occur. As a result, we feel justified in claiming that the PST use of this simulation software did enhance their development as future teachers. We believe that this is due the fact that the pre-service users felt that ClassSim was relevant to their current and future working lives. Therefore is had a relevant purpose. Furthermore, the majority of the pre-service teachers who have used ClassSim have demonstrated motivation to engage with it for sustained and frequent periods of time and to make extensive use of the resources offered within the software program.

REFERENCES

Allen, S. (2005). *The Missing Link in Alternative Certification: Teacher Identity Formation.* Retrieved January 20, 2009, from http://www.umbc.edu/llc/llcreview/2005/Vol5_No1_Fall2005.pdf#page=3

Brunning, R., Schraw, G., Norby, M., & Ronning, R. (2004). *Cognitive psychology and instruction.* Upper Saddle River, NJ: Prentice Hall.

Clark, R. (2003). *Building expertise.* Silver Spring, MD: International Society for Performance Improvement.

Clark, R., Ngyuyen, F., & Sweller, J. (2006). *Efficiency in learning: Evidence-based guidelines to manage cognitive load.* New York: John Wiley & Sons.

Dexter, S. (2006). Educational theory into practice software. In Gibson, D., Aldrich, C., & Prensky, M. (Eds.), *Games and simulations in online learning: Research & development frameworks.* Hershey, PA: Idea Group.

Eckersley, C., Richards, C., & Schofield, N. (2004). Evaluation of a Learning Object. *World Conference on Educational Multimedia, Hypermedia and Telecommunications,* 1, 3718-3720.

Ferdig, R. E. (Ed.). (2009). *Handbook of research on effective electronic gaming in education*. Hershey, PA: Idea Group.

Ferry, B., Kervin, L., Cambourne, B., Turbill, J., Hedberg, J., & Jonassen, D. (2005). Incorporating real experience into the development of a classroom-based simulation. *Journal of Learning Design, 1*(1), 22–32.

Gee, J. (2004). *What Video Games Have to Teach Us About Learning and Literacy*. New York: Palgrave Macmillan.

Gibson, D., & Halverson, B. (2004). SimSchool: Preparing tomorrow's teachers to improve student results. In *Society for Information Technology in Teacher Education Annual Conference*, March 2 – 4, 2004. Atlanta, GA: SITE.

Giumelli, K. (2008). *Cognition and learning with special needs students. Research proposal presentation*. NSW, Australia: University of Wollongong.

Kirschner, P. A., Sweller, J., & Clark, R. E. (2006). Why minimal guidance during instruction does not work: An analysis of the failure of constructivist, discovery, problem-based, experiential, and inquiry-based teaching. *Educational Psychologist, 41*(2), 75–86. doi:10.1207/s15326985ep4102_1

Knezek, G., & Vandersall, K. (2008). simMentoring Results. *simZine, 3*

Pashler, H., Bain, P. M., Bottge, B. A., Graesser, A., Koedinger, K., McDaniel, M., & Metcalke, J. (2007). *Organizing instruction and study to improve student learning. IES Practice Guide, NCER 2007-2004*. Washington, DC: US Department of Education.

Ramsey, G. (2000). *Quality Matters Revitalising teaching: Critical times, critical choices. Review of Teacher Education in NSW*. Sydney, Australia: NSW Department of Education and Training.

Sachs, J. (1999). *Teacher Professional Identity: Competing Discourses, and Competing Outcomes*. Paper Presented at the AARE Annual Conference Melbourne November 27-30

Shaffer, D. W. (2007). *How Computer Games Help Children Learn*. New York: Palgrave.

Shaffer, D. W., & Gee, J. (2005). *Before every child is left behind: How epistemic games can solve the coming crisis in education.* Department of Educational Psychology, University of Wisconsin-Madison, WI. Retrieved January 20, 2009, from http://66.102.1.104/scholar?hl=en&lr=&q=cache:TrtOVvs0SUQJ:www.discoverproject.net/greece/images/learning_crisis.pdf+shaffer++and+gee

KEY TERMS AND DEFINITIONS

A Simulation: is the imitation of some real thing, state of affairs, or process.

Online Learning: is a planned learning experience that mainly uses the Internet or computer-based tools to reach learners.

ClassSim: is is an online simulation that enables the user to assume the role of a Kindergarten teacher as they organise and implement literacy learning experiences within a virtual two- hour period.

Cognitive Load Theory: Has been designed to provide guidelines intended to assist in the presentation of information in a manner that encourages learner activities that optimize intellectual performance.

A Virtual Learning Environment (VLE): Is a computer-based system designed to support teaching and learning in an educational setting.

Pre-Service Teacher Education: Describes tertiary education courses that are design to educate future teachers.

Practicum: Supervised classroom experience.

Chapter 15
Virtual Gaming:
A Platform for Multi-Skills and Multi-Literacies for Gamers

Chaka Chaka
Walter Sisulu University, South Africa

ABSTRACT

This chapter explores how virtual gaming (VGaming) serves as an ideal platform for harnessing multi-skills and multi-literacies. It argues that VGaming provides the opportunity for gamers (learners) to engage not only in social learning, situated learning and problem based learning, but also in meta-gaming, meta-literacies, and multi-tasking. It demonstrates all this through the use of five case studies involving five virtual games: Everquest Online Adventures; NUCLEO; Homicide; Mad City Mystery; and Lineage. Most importantly, it maintains that VGaming exposes gamers to 21st century skills. Against this background, the chapter provides, first, an overview of VGaming. Second, it presents five case studies showcasing how virtual games (VGs) help leverage multi-skills and multi-literacies for gamers. In addition, it illustrates how VGs enable gamers to engage in social learning, situated learning and problem based learning on the one hand, and in meta-gaming, meta-literacies, and multi-tasking, on the other hand. Third, it argues that VGaming exposes gamers to 21st century skills. Fourth and last, the chapter outlines future trends for VGaming.

INTRODUCTION

Gaming in general is rapidly gaining currency in the learning enterprise. In particular, it is increasingly revolutionizing different spheres of learning, thereby establishing itself as one of the contemporary learning paradigms. Hence, notions like game-based learning (GBL) and digital game-based learning have emerged as some of the major paradigms characterizing the learning landscape. It is in this scenario that virtual gaming - in its various forms and models - becomes relevant. Virtual gaming (VGaming) is leveraged by various gaming technologies. Some of these technologies include computers, video players, game consoles or portable devices (e.g., *Nintendo Wii*, *Nintendo*

DOI: 10.4018/978-1-61520-713-8.ch015

DS Lite, *Xbox 360*, and *PlayStation Portable*), the Internet, and handhelds (e.g., mobile phones and personal digital assistants (PDAs)). These technologies or devices also operate as delivery or deployment platforms for VGs.

VGs can serve many purposes. For example, they can be used as learning objects within GBL. However, the primary purpose of this chapter is three-fold: to demonstrate that VGs entail social learning, situated learning and problem based learning (PBL); to explore the way in which VGs serve as a medium for promoting multi-skills (e.g., social, problem solving and scientific argumentation skills), multi-literacies, (e.g., gaming, meta-gaming, reading and writing, and scientific literacies), meta-literacies, and multi-tasking; and to emphasize that VGaming introduces gamers to 21st century skills.

Based on the above, this chapter consists of the following main parts: virtual game play: an overview; virtual games in action: what types of learning and skills are embodied in such games?; virtual gaming and 21st century skills; and future trends.

Virtual Game Play: An Overview

Virtual games (VGs) encompass, in this chapter, online, computer, simulation, video and mobile games, all of which are also regarded as digital games. In a growing body of literature and research on game-based learning (GBL), there tends to be a standard practice of classifying learning games according to the deployment devices or following the mediums or platforms on which they are offered. Here games are seen either as online-, computer-, simulation-, video- or mobile-based (see Krotoski, Ellis, Heppell, Kirriemuir & McFarlane, 2006; Mitchell & Savill-Smith, 2004; Shaffer, Squire, Halverson & Gee, 2004; Squire, 2008; Steinkuehler, 2007). Such a classification is both necessary and useful. However, this chapter chooses to use the term *virtual* as an all-encompassing term for games deployed on such devices, mediums or platforms. It does so in order to bring the disparate games under one umbrella term while allowing each game category to retain its distinct identity.

What makes the term *virtual* appropriate and all-inclusive in referring to such disparate game categories is the multiple attributes it embodies. First, *virtual* has to do with something imagined or fake - something pretending to be real. Second, it is related to an actualized reality that can be created - simulated or virtual reality - and experienced by gamers. Third, like virtual memory the word *virtual* does not have any physical placement in relation to devices, mediums or platforms (see Klastrup, 2003; Thomas & Brown, 2009). Similarly, VGs such as the ones cited above, do not have any discernible physical locations in the devices, mediums or platforms within which they are played. Fourth, the *presence* and *activation* of *virtual* is relative to that of the devices, mediums or platforms through which it occurs, failing which it ceases to be. Likewise, VGs have their presence and activation confined to that of the software packages embodying them and to that of the devices, mediums or platforms through which they are played. Without all this, their virtuality ceases to be. All of the game categories mentioned above tend to embody these virtual attributes. Hence, their being referred to collectively here as VGs.

Playing and Gaming

Two important notions related to VGs are *playing* and *gaming*. Playing is what one engages in as a source of pleasure. It is completely captivating and helps form social groupings. It involves fun, or a sense of enjoyment (Mitchell & Savill-Smith, 2004; Prensky, 2001), leading to a relaxed state of mind predisposed to further play action or risk-taking in the form of learning. Sometimes, playing embodies *free play* as when players are free to play what they want to play. Free play promotes freedom to fail, to experiment, and to assume identity; and freedom of effort and of in-

Figure 1. Three generations of games based on Egenfeldt-Nielsen(2005)

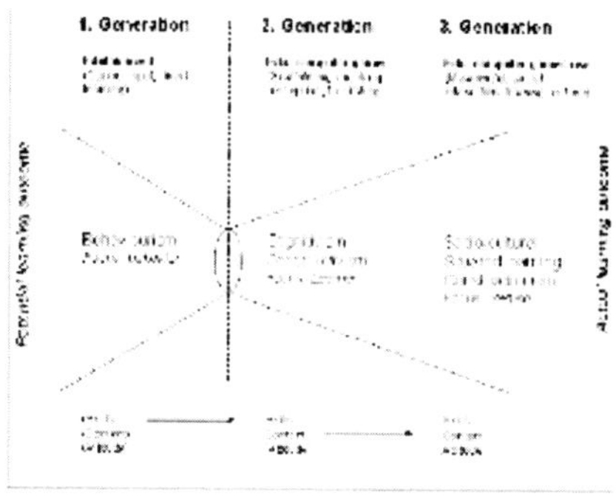

terpretation (see Klopfer, Osterweil, Salen, Haas, Groff & Roy, 2009).

In this context, gaming is a form of organized play giving rise to a heightened sense of enjoyment and excitement. It is a subset of playing (Mitchell & Savill-Smith, 2004; Prensky, 2001). Additionally, gaming helps immerse gamers in the imaginary world of gaming. Games may involve competition; they may motivate gamers through challenges, fantasies, and curiosity (Mitchell & Savill-Smith, 2004), and spur the desire to win.

Thus, unlike free play, games tend to have defined goals geared towards winning and achieving success. Moreover, they have structured rules governing playing that are applied indiscriminately to all players. All this appears, at face value, to negate the freedoms offered by free play. However, within the confined gaming space, gamers regularly display all of the freedoms characterizing free play. For example, most gamers engage in gaming bearing in mind that failure is a possibility. They also undertake gaming with the desire to experiment, to explore identities, and to interpret their game play. In the main, gaming is the sum total of activities, practices, literacies and knowledge mounted in and around a given instance of a game. It is play cutting across time, media, social spaces and networks of meanings. In this sense, it requires a sense of playfulness. Importantly, gaming allows both learning about games and learning with games to occur simultaneously (Klopfer et al., 2009). Its primary purpose in this case is to blend playing with learning and to maintain a delicate balance between the two.

Evolution of Gaming

One other significant factor about VGaming is that it has evolved within a given time span through generations of games. There are three such generations (see *Figure 1*) identified by Egenfeldt-Nielsen (2005) worth highlighting here. The 1st generation is informed by behaviorism and focuses on learner behavior. It views learning as a stimulus-response activity occurring through repetitively practicing skills-oriented tasks that require reinforcement and conditioning. Its perspective conforms to the early form of edutainment. One of its weaknesses, however, is that it does not facilitate progressive understanding of the learning material (see Egenfeldt-Nielsen, 2006).

In contrast, the 2nd generation is rooted in cognitivist-constructivism and is learner-centric. It rejects the prominence behaviorism accords to stimulus and response. Instead, it maintains that learners' cognitive structures should receive attention in educational games and that learning material and learners' cognitive abilities need to correlate. It also advocates the theory of flow in respect of learning from, especially, video games. Above all, it supports a meta-skills perspective – e.g., problem-solving, analyzing, perceiving,

Table 1. A four-theory approach based on and adapted fromKirriemuir & McFarlane (2004)

Aspect	Behaviourist Approach	CognitivistApproach	Humanist Approach	Social and SituationalApproach
View of the learning process	Change behavior	Process entirely in the head of the learner (including insight, information processing, memory, perception)	A development of personal potential	Interaction/observation in a group context, similar to an apprenticeship
Context/Site of learning	External resources and tasks matter most	Making connections in learner's head is what really matters	Emotion, attitude and thinking are important	Learning needs a relationship between people and environment
Purpose in education	Produce behavioural change in desired direction	Develop capacity and skills to learn better	Become self reliant, autonomous	Full participation in communities of practice, i.e., you graduate from apprentice to craftsman

and spatial ability - in relation to learning from VGaming (Egenfeldt-Nielsen, 2005, 2006).

For its part, the 3rd generation is informed by socio-cultural factors, situated learning and constructionism. The latter – also known as social constructivism - serves as a bridge between the 2nd and 3rd generations. In this instance, constructionists regard artifacts from within the environment as reflective of the external learning processes and as providing a platform for exploring the new learning material. This particular view is also evident in situated learning and socio-culturalism where learning is deemed to be mediated within social contexts. Furthermore, the 3rd generation views knowledge as constructed within social contexts or communities of practice. It conceives of knowledge as an interaction between culture, tools and communities. It focuses on the broader process of the educational use of computer games with the teacher facilitating computer gaming to move from simply playing to learning (Egenfeldt-Nielsen, 2005, 2006; Gros, 2007).

The three generations of games outlined above represent simultaneously learning theories that have come to influence not only game-based learning (GBL), but also the learning enterprise in general in modern times. They also correspond to Kirriemuir & McFarlane's (2004) four-theory approach to GBL that incorporates behaviourist, cognitivist, humanist, and social and situational theories. This approach is represented in *Table 1* with the latter displaying the views of learning, the context/site of learning and the purpose of learning attributed to each of these theories.

Game Genres, Gamers and Areas of Learning

Another significant factor about VGs - especially computer games - is that they display certain structural elements. Salient among these are: rules; goals and objectives; outcomes and feedback; competition/conflict/challenge/opposition; interaction; and representation or story (Mitchell & Savill-Smith, 2004). In addition to these structural elements, computer games have game types or genres as depicted in *Table 2*. Related to these game genres are categories for the educational potential video games have. There are three such categories:

- Commercial entertainment or mainstream video games: These are commercially oriented games - with a lot of appeal to youngsters - in which educational goals play a secondary role. Examples are *The Sims*, *SimCity* and *Civilization*.
- Commercial educational or edutainment video games: The primary focus of these games is on teaching players specific skills

Table 2. Game genres and their descriptions or purposes (Adapted fromClaro, 2007&Gros, 2007)

Genres	Descriptions/Purposes
Action games/Platform games	These are reaction based games
Adventure games	The player solves a number of tests or logic puzzles so as to progress through a given virtual world
Fighting games	These are games related to fighting computer controlled characters or characters controlled by other players
Puzzle games	Games in which the player solves a puzzle
Role-playing games	Here human players assume the characteristics of some person or creature
Massively multiplayer online games (MMOG's)	These are video games capable of supporting many players simultaneously
Simulations	The player has to succeed within some simplified recreation of a place or situation, e.g., a city mayor, controlling financial outlay, and building works
Sports	These are sports-based games
Strategy games	These are games intended to recreate a historical or fictional situation so as to allow the player to devise an appropriate strategy to achieve a goal

related to algebra, spelling and problem-solving. Examples are *Math Blaster*, *Castle of Dr. Brain* and *Pajama Sam*.

- Research-based educational video games: These games offer new approaches and provide guidelines for learning outcomes. Typical examples are *Phoenix Quest*, *Oregon Trail* and *Logical Journey of the Zoombinis* (Claro, 2007; Egenfeldt-Nielsen, 2006).

Furthermore, there are different types of gamers. Of these, the following six types stand out:

- Power gamers - These are hardcore video game players.
- Social gamers - These are gamers using games as a means to interact with friends.
- Leisure gamers - These are casual game players. However, they still prefer challenging titles and have keen interest in new gaming services.
- Dormant gamers - They love gaming but spare more time for family, work or school. Accordingly, they like playing with family members and friends, and prefer challenging and complex games.
- Incidental gamers - They lack motivation and play games simply out of boredom. They spend only 20 hours per month playing online games.
- Occasional gamers - They play mainly puzzle, word and board games (Klopfer et al., 2009).

Lastly, there are areas of learning in which VGs can make contributions. Instances of these areas - together with the specific contributions associated with each one of them - are reflected in *Table 3*.

Virtual Games in Action: What TYPES OF Learning and Skills are Embodied in Such Games?

This section of the chapter examines how VGs help gamers leverage multi-skills and multi-literacies while engaging in social learning, situated learning

Table 3. Areas of learning in which virtual games can contribute (Based on Gros, 2007)

Areas	Aspects video games can contribute
Personal and social development	Provide interest and motivation to learn, maintain attention and concentration.
Language and literacy	Encourage children to explain what is happening; use talk to organize, sequence and clarify thinking, ideas, feelings and events.
Mathematical development	Use everyday words to describe position.
Creative development	Respond in a variety of ways; use their imagination in art and design, music and stories.
Knowledge and understanding of the world	Use early control software to investigate direction and control
Physical development	Fine motor control can be developed with the increased refinement in using a mouse for navigation and selection objects.

and problem based learning. It also highlights how VGs help facilitate meta-gaming, meta-literacies and multi-tasking on the part of gamers.

Social Learning and Social Skills: MMORPGs

Massively multiplayer online role-playing games (MMORPGs) serve as an ideal socialisation and learning platform for a community of gamers (CoGs). Thus, they are capable of leveraging social learning and social skills. Social learning, in this instance, is learning based on the socio-cultural approach and which views learning as part of social interaction (see Mitchell & Savill-Smith, 2004). It is also a form of learning tapping into gamers' social experiences.

One case study highlighting how MMORPGs can help harness social learning and social skills and promote socialisation is Ducheneaut and Moore's (2005) work. This study examined *Everquest Online Adventures* (*EQOA*) which is a MMORPG based on a medieval fantasy genre. The game is set five centuries ago and takes place on a single continent, Tunaria, in Norrath. In this game players select a 'race' (e.g., human, elf, dwarf, etc.) and a 'class' (e.g., wizard and warrior) both of which affect their attributes and abilities. Players then take control of avatars or virtual bodies in a 3D space, where they battle various creatures and accomplish quests so as to both progress in the game and develop their characters (Ducheneaut & Moore, 2005).

The study reports initial findings related to player-to-player interactions in *EQOA*. In particular, it documents players' cultural practices and how the process of socialisation into CoGs is an important source of learning. Its findings focus on three major areas: player self-organisation, instrumental interactions, and sociability. The study involved participant observation and consisted of two classes of players - a combat-oriented class and a combat-assist class. Besides this, it had 100 hours of game play.

The study yielded findings some of which are relevant to this chapter. First, it appeared that *EQOA*'s quests are too difficult for a single player as only a coordinated and complementary group of players are needed to accomplish them. Thus, players have to do much more than just accumulate *experience points* (xp): they need to leverage their social capital within the game's society. This means that in addition to learning the game commands, players also have to be socialised into the game community. Moreover, players must learn the *lingo* of the game - and have to engage in the game's multi-tasks - for them to be recognised as good players (see Ducheneaut & Moore, 2005).

Second, is situated learning that results in social learning. In *EQOA*, players are confronted with entities, concepts, lingo and practices that they have to learn. Some of these practices evolve from and are based on multi-user dungeons (MUDs), Internet relay chat (IRC), and instant messaging (IM). Examples are *brb* (be right back), *afk* (away from keyboard), and *lol* (laugh out aloud). As a result, both situated learning and social learning are an integral part of *EQOA* and of many other MMORPGs such as *Ultimate Online*, *Star War Galaxies* and *World of Warcraft*. They occur as a normal feature of participation or social interactions in a CoGs (Ducheneaut & Moore, 2005).

Third, there are four modes of social learning – which involve multi-tasking - through which situated learning occurs in *EQOA* as pointed out by Ducheneaut and Moore (2005):

- *In-game, in-context discussions*: *EQOA* allows players to engage in a textual chat system and to exchange information contextually on demand and just-in-time.
- *Out-game, out-of-context discussions*: Communication between players flows beyond the game into websites and social forums.
- *Observation*: Most game's activities are accomplished in full view of other players culminating in peripheral participation or meta-learning.
- *In-situ teaching: EQOA* leads to on-the-site teaching in which players teach one another (see Mitchell & Savill-Smith, 2004).

Fourth, three types of social interaction play a vital role in *EQOA*: self-organisation, instrumental coordination, and sociability. These three types of social interaction facilitate the learning and acquisition of social skills (such as interpersonal and intercultural communication skills) on the part of players as highlighted below:

- *Self-organisation:* MMORPGs like *EQOA* encourage players to team up with each other in small groups and help players meet each other and socialise accordingly. Group activities entail group formation (see *Figure 2*), group maintenance, and group disbandment.
- *Instrumental coordination:* This covers moments in the game when players need to work together as a team to accomplish the objectives of the game. It also includes coordinating and cooperating with others. Here the ability to perform a given role reliably is a sign of a player's social competence.
- *Sociability:* This involves social features such as humour (or its absence), small talk, and players *catching up* with each other. Sociability is central to social cohesion (Ducheneaut & Moore, 2005; see Mitchell & Savill-Smith, 2004).

Problem Based Learning (PBL) and MRGs

An instance of a case study employing multiplayer role games (MRGs) for leveraging problem based learning (PBL) is Sancho, Gómez and Fernández-Manjón's (2008) project. Delivered through Moodle, the project employs *NUCLEO* as a system for offering PBL within MRGs to Spanish students. It is applied to three different subjects for computer programming (two of which in a university context, and the third one in intermediate teaching). Its purpose is to enable students to collaborate in small groups to reach a solution for real-world, open-ended, ill-structured problems as they would in conventional problem based learning scenarios.

NUCLEO is a virtual game universe inhabited by three races - the *Evians*, the *Ruks* and the *Exters* (see *Figure 3*) - in the form of artificial intelligences (AIs) who belong to the *NUCLEO* civilisation. The *Evians* are especially qualified AIs, have powerful minds trained in strategies and logics, and inhabit *NUCLEO*'s metropolis.

Figure 2. EQOA's interface (above, players are forming a group) (Source: Ducheneaut & Moore, 2005)

The *Ruks* are an itinerant native tribe inhabiting *NUCLEO*'s peripheral regions. They are mainly made up of pirates and mercenaries. On the other hand, the *Exters* are strange and unpredictable AIs who survive in extreme conditions. They are mutants who have developed odd forms and strange powers that are difficult to control.

NUCLEO's civilisation is threatened by extinction stemming from a mysterious virus (the *Marsh*) that destroys the entire virtual world. To confront this menace, the *Arcanes* (*NUCLEO*'s superior council comprising the wisest and oldest AIs) decide to train specially qualified citizens in the weapons of knowledge. The training simulates a real attack from the enemy in the form of a mission which trainees have to thwart clustered in small combat units constituting crews of symbiotic spaceships. The crews consist of 3 or 4 members. Students' avatars play the roles of champions and their types of participation, duties, and skills in the crews are determined by their roles. The different crews then compete among themselves to get the best solution. At the end of the training session, only the best crew reaches the status of *Paladines* to fight in the real war against the *Marsh* (Sancho et al., 2008).

Based on the preceding information, the project strives to blend problem solving and game based learning. So, for players to progress through the game, they need to solve the problems and engage in the multiple tasks immersed in the narrative of the game. This methodology ties in with PBL. The game is structured around three strategies. The first is aimed at promoting social bonds among

Figure 3. The three different races in NUCLEO (From left to right: Evians, Ruks, and Exters) (Adapted from Sancho et al., 2008)

students; the second is to form heterogeneous groups; and the third is using functional roles to structure collaboration among team members so as to maximise group dynamics.

There are benefits flowing from this project as reported by Sancho et al. (2008) that need highlighting here:

- This type of game based learning (GBL) lends itself well to problem based learning (PBL).
- The game narrative has a positive influence on students' motivation to learn.
- The game helps students and tutors reach the learning objectives as set out in the course.
- Using functional roles as a means to structure collaboration among teams improves team work performance.
- Competition serves as an incentive and helps increase students' motivation.
- Immersing students in a virtual world in which they are represented by their avatars helps form social bonds among students and facilitates an effective collaborative learning process.

Complex Problem Solving with *Homicide*

A case study focusing on the use of *Homicide* for complex problem solving is Magnussen's (2005) experiment. *Homicide* is a cross-disciplinary role-playing forensic investigation game developed at Learning Lab Denmark for science education. In this game, players play forensic experts solving four different murder cases. Its main goal is to use the game media in order to simulate an authentic science practice. Overall, *Homicide* takes place in the fictional town of Melved and is meant for grade 7 to grade 10 pupils or for pupils aged between 13 and 16. It is one form of GBL structured around simulated situated learning.

Briefly, *Homicide* immerses players in multiple tasks. Thus, it involves dividing players into four investigation groups each assigned its own case for a week. Groups have to meet and share information about their individual cases, and are encouraged to set goals for their investigation cases. They also hold press and status meetings. During the investigation, investigators analyse the evidence obtained from relevant sources through forensic laboratory tests. Examples here include: DNA analysis; fingerprint and footprint analysis; blood spatter analysis; soil analysis; wet chromatography; phone record analysis; gunshot residue tests; and autopsy. At the end of the game, groups present their theories/views to others and write indictments based on the evidence and testimonies gathered from suspects and witnesses (Magnussen, 2005; see Larsen, n.d.).

In the current case study, two week-long experiments were conducted to two grade 8 classes belonging to two schools. The classes played the full version of the game and the latter was initiated by science and language teachers. In both schools, video observations were conducted and the investigation practices of each class documented. Pupils who participated in the game were monitored in relation to the following aspects:

- Their actions/behaviours at the different stages of the investigation process
- How they had formulated their cases
- The tools they had used in analysing the data (samples of evidence) they had gathered
- The argumentation they had used in formulating their final theory (Magnussen, 2005).

In all, the following are some of the preliminary findings of these two *Homicide* experiments:

- The pupils were able to handle large amounts of data and redesign the game tools to formulate their own hypotheses and theories
- Thus, they managed to operate at a meta-methodological level as they were in a

position to evaluate tools and methods and adjust them to the game's challenges
- In solving the tasks of the game, the pupils worked together thereby engaging in collaborative skills
- The game facilitated cooperation among the groups - e.g., sharing information - and thus minimised competition
- The game immersed the pupils in simulated situated learning, project-based learning and role-playing
- It also helped the pupils engage in collaborative complex problem solving (Magnussen, 2005).

Scientific Argumentation Skills and *Mad City Mystery*

Squire and Jan's (2007) study focuses on the use of augmented reality (AR) games as a platform to immerse students in authentic scientific inquiry and adult scientific discourses. The study took place in the spring and fall of 2005 and involved three groups of students (roughly 28 students). It employed an AR game, *Mad City Mystery* (*MCM*), to facilitate learning in environmental science. It set out to investigate the following: (a) whether AR games on handhelds could be used to engage students in scientific thinking (especially argumentation skills); (b) how game structures affected students' thinking; (c) the impact of role playing on learning; and (d) the role of the physical environment in shaping learning.

MCM is a place-based (location-based) AR game for Earth science students and has been played by students ranging from 4th and 5th graders to adults. It takes place on the University of Wisconsin-Madison campus (near Lake Mendota Madison). The game's duration is about 90 to 120 minutes, depending on the group dynamics involved. Based on this, some of the questions the study sought to answer included the following:

- What types of discourse emerge from game play, and how do these compare with school and science-based discourses?
- What form does students' argumentation take, and does students' argumentation meet the criteria for quality described in educational standards?
- Do groups with more robust scientific understandings engage in more complex forms of argumentation?
- Does playing the game in the physical environment trigger prior knowledge?

Moreover, the game was designed in line with contemporary game theory to:

- Encourage players to inhabit professional roles with specific professional perspectives and identities
- Challenge players through multiple layers of narratives and tasks – through multi-narratives and multi-tasks
- Situate the contested game space in a local/physical place where the meaning of a place is understood from professional perspectives
- Scaffold learning through multimodal representations
- Create social interactions that promote collaboration, competition, and reflection-in-action (Squire & Jan, 2007).

Three groups of school classes participated in the study: 18 4th graders, 3 middle school students, and 7 high school students. Each group studied played *MCM* for 2-3 hours. Included in this time were briefing, game play and debriefing. The game begins with the revelation of Ivan Ilyich's mysterious death at a nearby lake. Students role-play doctors, environmental scientists, and government officials. They race against time to provide the police investigator (played by a real person) sufficient data to open an investigation into the causes of the death. The cause of death is unknown. However, mercury found in fish, TCE (trichloroethane) in the factory where Ivan worked, and PCBs (polychlorinated biphenyls) found in ground water and fish are potential causes. From there, players must interview virtual characters, gather quantitative data samples, probe government documents describing chemicals, and conduct forensic tests to piece together some explanations. Players work in teams that may or may not compete with each other.

The game's educational goals are to help students develop investigation and inquiry skills, especially scientific argumentation skills through virtual investigation. Above all, the game play requires students to do some of the following tasks: (1) observe events in their environment and relate them to underlying scientific processes and phenomena; (2) engage in formulating hypotheses for scientific argumentation, revising those hypotheses based on evidence, and formulating a theory together with its rationale; and (3) develop conceptual understandings of geochemical water cycles, particularly, how chemicals move through the water system (Squire & Jan, 2007).

The following are some of the findings of this study which are vital to this chapter:

- The game play managed to engage the students in the practice of scientific argumentation - thus, it served as a platform for developing scientific literacy.
- All the groups engaged in argumentation cycles akin to those advocated by science educators.
- The younger students more readily formulated and abandoned hypotheses based on new forms of evidence, displaying an inclination towards relatively simple causal models.
- On the contrary, the high school students accepted fewer hypotheses, clinging to their hypotheses until counter evidence was found.
- The high school students in particular engaged in a series of conversations that helped them raise and reject hypotheses, and provide evidence and counter evidence, thereby slowly and iteratively building a body of theory.
- The game play encouraged collaboration and served as a scaffolding for reading.
- The students readily assumed roles, valued the experience of being in those roles, and showed some evidence of orienting to the game from within these roles.
- In addition, the students developed a logical coherence for the game, devised plausible theories, and yet held one another's arguments to a standard of plausibility (Squire & Jan 2007).

MMOGaming as a Series of Literacy Practices

One of the case studies exploring MMOGaming (massively multiplayer online gaming) as a series of literacy practices is Steinkuehler's (2007) work. MMOGaming includes games such as *Ultimate Online*, *World of Warcraft* (*WoW*), and *Lineage* (*I* and *II*). Carried out in 2005, the project investigated *Lineage* - in its two incarnations - as an instance of both a MMOGame and a virtual world exemplifying a persistent and material world. Within the game, members of different races (e.g., humans, dwarfs, elves, dark elves, and orcas) and classes (e.g., crafters, fighters, mages, etc.) join forces in the form of guilds to compete for the control of the castle in battles and sieges. In both versions, the *Lineage* clan system is closely tied to both the guiding narrative of the game and the virtual world's economic system. This gives rise to a complex social space of affiliations and disaffiliations based on shared - albeit disparate - social and material practices.

The project was a two-year ethnographic study drawing on a socio-cultural perspective whose goal was to explicate: the types of social and intellectual activities in which gamers engage; individual and collaborative problem-solving; joint negotiation of meaning and values; the coordination of people, tools and artifacts; and multiple forms of texts. It employed cognitive ethnography as its primary research methodology. In particular, it had the following as its procedural features: participant observation of the game; several thousand lines of recorded and transcribed observations of naturally occurring game play; collections of game-related player communication (e.g., discussion board posts, chat room and instant message conversations, and emails); community documents (e.g., fan websites, community-authored game fictions, community- and company-written player manuals and guidebooks; and structured and unstructured interviews). It then analysed the *Lineage* game play as a constellation of literacy practices (Steinkuehler, 2007).

Two definitions of literacy underscore the *Lineage* game play. The first is literacy as *sense making* within a socially situated multimodal space. This means that a MMOGame such as *Lineage* entails fluency and participation in a thoroughly literate virtual space of icons, gestures, action, pictorial representations, and text. Accordingly, gamers have to continually *read* and *write* meaning within this complex semiotic domain since every successful move requires participants to recognise and produce meaning from an array of multimedia and multimodal resources making up the game. Thus, based on this definition, a case can be made that playing a MMOGame is in itself a literacy activity. The second is literacy as the ability to *read* and *write* print text in a restricted sense. According to this definition, MMOGames are a constellation of literacy practices. For instance, when kids play MMOGames, they read and write enormous amounts of print text. All these literacy practices collectively constitute *Lineagese* (Steinkuehler, 2007).

Based on the preceding pointers, some of the literacy practices constituting a constellation within the *Lineage* game world, include the following:

In-Game Text Talk
: This relates to specialised linguistic practices (or a closed code) with a lot of cross-references that take the form of hybrid writing. It is fraught with *abbreviations* (e.g., *g2g - got to go*); *truncations* (e.g., *regen - regenerate*); *typographical forms* (e.g., *ot - to*); *grammatical errors* (e.g., *too* in place of *to*; *syntactic erosions* (e.g., the omitted initial string *I have* from the construction *[I have] g2g*); and *specialised vocabulary* (e.g., *poms* for *potions of mana*) (Steinkuehler, 2007). This is very much like the language of mobile short messaging service (SMS) or instant messaging (IM).

In-Game "Orally Delivered" Narratives and Poetry
: These are a form of a literacy practice that MMOGamers engage in when playing. It entails producing and consuming *orally delivered* narratives and poetry. They are performances in which players adopt and adapt designed-in elements of the game narratives to craft their oral story telling performances.

In-Game Written Letters
: Within the *Lineage* game world, players read and write letters (see *Figure 4*) to one another - or to the whole guilds - as a means of an asynchronous communication. This serves different functions, ranging from very informal (e.g., personal accounts of absences from the game, and playful bantering among friends) to very formal (e.g., invitations to alliance or guild meetings, and orders from leaders to the troops).

Figure 4. Two sample letters produced within Lineage (Steinkuehler, 2007)

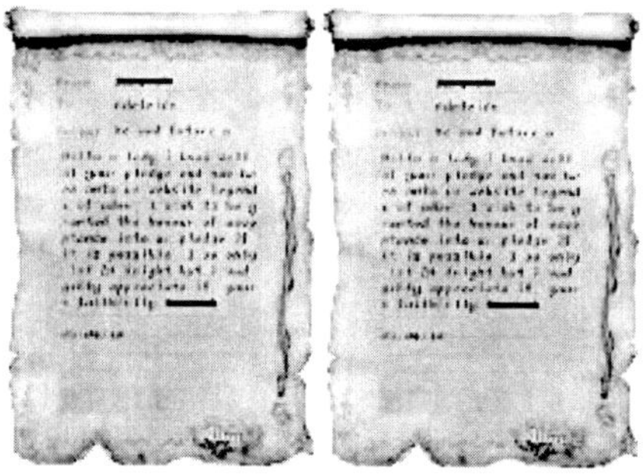

Meta-Gaming Practices

Meta-gaming is a literacy practice in which players theorise their own game both within the virtual game world and outside it in the online fandom space - e.g., websites, discussion forums, chatrooms, blogs, wikis, etc. - embodying the game itself. As a literacy practice, meta-gaming shifts seamlessly from in-game conversations to out-game online interactions and back again. Examples of meta-gaming practices are strategy development for group or guild endeavours (e.g., the creation of research documents about a given location of interest and planning documents), or the development of game *exploits* (e.g., the construction, evaluation, and revision of mathematical models of game mechanics based on data collected in-game) (Steinkuehler, 2007).

Most significantly, at the macro level, participating in MMOGames involves being immersed in the game's virtual environment and producing and consuming online fandom content in the form of discussion boards, website contributions and story writing. At the micro level, participating in a game play means moving across multiple attentional spaces and engaging in multiple tasks. In this way, the literacy practices comprising *Lineage* are not detached and autonomous but, instead, interconnected in complex and mutually defining ways (Steinkuehler, 2007).

Virtual Gaming and 21st Century Skills

The affordances provided by VGaming in leveraging certain skills and literacies are evident in the case studies discussed above. VGaming - and game based learning (GBL) in general - is seen as contributing to the acquisition of 21st century skills and as harnessing these skills on the part of learners (Galarneau & Zibit, 2006; Spires, 2008; Spires, Lee & Lester, 2008). Loosely stated, 21st century skills are skills necessary for citizens to fully participate and adequately survive in the 21st century knowledge economy.

Currently, there are at least four key scholarly perspectives influencing the theorisation and formulation of the 21st century skills. These are the Partnership for 21st Century Skills (P21) (2004); the enGuage 21st Century Skills paradigm (Burkhardt, Monsour, Valdez, Gunn, Dawson, Lemke et al., 2003), the new media literacies perspective (Jenkins, 2006); and the *whole new mind* movement (Pink, 2005). The P21 frames core content and skills deemed crucial for 21st century learners according to an information/media, cognitive and social skills classification. Likewise - albeit slightly differently - the enGuage 21st Century Skills paradigm represents the 21st century skills in terms of technical, cognitive and social skills dimensions. In contrast, the new media

Table 4. An integrated framework of some of the 21st century skills (Adapted fromBurkhardt et al., 2003; Jenkins, 2006Partnership for 21st century skills, 2004,Pink, 2005&Spires, 2008)

Skill types	Descriptions
Digital/Technological literacy	Basic, scientific, economic and technological literacy skills
Information, media and visual literacy	Analysing, accesing, managing, integrating, evaluating and creating information in a variety of forms and media
Trans-media navigation	Ability to follow the flow of stories and information across multiple modalities
Effective communication	Understanding, managing and creating effective oral, written and multimedia communication in a variety of forms and contexts
Inventive systems and critical thinking	Exercising sound reasoning in understanding and making complex choices, understanding the interconnections among systems. This includes creative and innovative thinking, strategic thinking, lateral thinking, higher-order thinking and risk taking
Problem identification, formulation and solution	Ability to frame, analyse and solve problems
Multitasking, parallel processing and simultaneous attention	Ability to carry out several tasks/duties, process information, process information from diverse sources and pay attention to many things simultaneously
High productivity	Prioritizing, planning and managing for results and ability to produce relevant, high quality products
Performance and design	Ability to adopt alternative identities for improvisation and discovery and to create something aesthetically appealing or emotionally engaging
Symphony	Ability to put together different pieces; to synthesise rather than analyse; to see relationships in unrelated fields; to detect patterns;to invent something new by combining elements nobody else thought to pair
Simulation	Ability to interpret and construct dynamic models of real-world processes
Play	Capacity to experiment with one's surroundings as a form of problem solving
Distributed cognition	Ability to interact meaningfully with tools that expand mental capacities
Collective intelligence	Ability to pool knowledge and compare notes to others toward a common goal
Interpersonal, collaborative, negotiating and social skills	Demonstrating teamwork and leadership; adapting to varied roles and responsibilities; working productively with others; exercising empathy; respecting diverse perspectives; and forming networks

literacies perspective delineates these skills with a strong emphasis on their cognitive and social attributes. For its part, the whole new mind movement lays emphasis on certain global right-brain conceptual skills and attributes essential for the conceptual age (see Pink, 2005; Spires, 2008).

There are three aspects worth noting about these skills. First, most of them are not new skills as they have existed before in the form of *soft skills*. Second, these skills build on the prevailing literacy, cognitive, technical and social skills. Third, they are mostly embodied in skill sets. Thus, in this chapter some of the 21st century skills that VGaming - and the GBL paradigm in general - stands to both facilitate and develop in learners are summarised in *Table 4* where they are presented in an integrated framework.

Future Trends

Nowhere else do trends matter more than in the area of VGaming. Here trends are social, commercial and aesthetic currents flowing through the present trajectories to the future trajectories of gaming. Given this scenario, six trends are likely to influence developments in VGaming. These are: digitisation; simulated living; experience economy; consumerisation; convergence; and the conceptual age.

Digitisation as a trend is about three related gaming processes. The first is that virtual games (VGs) will get more digitised while at the same time their virtualisation will increase. The second is that the platforms for VGs (e.g., game consoles, handhelds, mobile phones, etc.) will become more digitised and miniaturised so they are better interoperable with the VGs for which they serve as delivery devices. The third is chunking. This entails presenting information or concepts in *chunks* (small quanta) so as to make for easier and faster reading and understanding of the self-same information or concepts. Simulated living, for its part, relates to simulation and augmented reality (AR) games and MMOGames, leading to simulated lifestyles by players. That is, the more individuals embrace simulation and AR games and MMOGames, the more they will privilege simulated living at the expense of real world living.

The notion of experience economy has to do with experience being a key driver in the gaming economy. This encompasses many related processes: experiential learning; learning through experience; learning by doing; learning by actions; and action learning. In all, it is a view that values the economics of experience in the fields of gaming and learning. In this context, consumerisation refers to technologies such as VGs being adopted first by consumers and, then, being adopted later by the corporate and business world. It is about the corporate and business sectors embracing and leveraging VGs based on the viral effect VGs have on and their successful adoption by consumers.

Convergence refers to the different VGs being offered on convergent platforms and not on different platforms functioning as non-interoperable isolated silos. It entails seamless convergent offerings for VGs as on: the Internet, consoles, handhelds, and mobile phones. Finally, the conceptual age is related to Pink's (2005) view of the self-same notion. In this case, it refers specifically to the fact that conceptual skills tend to play an increasingly vital role in the world of gaming as part of the 21st century skills. Regarded as the right-brain concepts, these conceptual skills include, design, symphony, empathy and play. As such, they tend to balance out the traditional left-brain reasoning skills in the 21st century skills equation.

CONCLUSION

This chapter has argued that virtual gaming (VGaming) serves as an ideal platform for leveraging multi-skills and multi-literacies on the part of gamers (learners). In addition, it has framed the argument that VGaming enables gamers to engage not only in social learning, situated learning and problem based learning, but also in meta-gaming, meta-literacies and multi-tasking. In this context, it has presented five case studies showcasing how virtual games (VGs) help leverage multi-skills and multi-literacies and help promote social learning, situated learning, problem based learning, meta-gaming, meta-literacies and multi-tasking in varying degrees. For instance, it has demonstrated how a massively multiplayer online role-playing game (MMORPG) such as *Everquest Online Adventures* (*EQOA*) enables gamers to engage in social learning, socialisation and meta-learning, thereby helping them acquire social skills.

Similarly, it has highlighted how multiplayer role games (MRGs) (e.g., *NUCLEO*) and a game like *Homicide* facilitate problem solving and complex problem solving skills respectively. The latter also immerses gamers in simulated situated learning. It further exposes them to a combination of cognitive and meta-cognitive skills: hypothesis and theory formulation skills; meta-methodological skills; and collaborative and information sharing skills. Moreover, the chapter has outlined how an augmented reality (AR) game like *Mad City Mystery* and a MMOGame such as *Lineage* expose gamers to scientific argumentation skills and a constellation of literacy practices, respectively. *Lineage*, in particular, enables gamers to engage in: in-game text talk; in-game oral narration and poetry; in-game letter writing; and meta-gaming practices (e.g., theorising about one's game both within and outside the game world). Above all, all the five game case studies investigated in this chapter expose gamers (learners) to multi-tasks in varying degrees.

Most significantly, the chapter has made an argument that VGaming is an ideal medium for the acquisition and harnessing of the 21st century skills. To this effect, it has mapped out an integrated framework for the 21st century skills drawn from four scholarly traditions that seem to have gained currency in the domain of 21st century learning and skills. Lastly, the chapter has briefly outlined the future trends for VGaming, highlighting especially, the following: digitisation; simulated living; experience economy; consumerisation; convergence; and the conceptual age.

REFERENCES

Burkhardt, G., Monsour, M., Valdez, G., Gunn, C., Dawson, M., Lemke, C., et al. (2003). *enGauge 21st century skills: Literacy in the digital age*. Retrieved November 22, 2007, from http://www.grec.ky.gov/SLC_grant/Engauge21st_Century_Skills.pdf

Claro, M. (2007). *OECD background papers for OECD-ENLACES expert meeting: Video games and education*. Retrieved March 16, 2009, from http://www.oecd.org/dataoecd/14/60/39548100.pdf

Ducheneaut, N., & Moore, R. J. (2005). *More than just 'XP': Learning social skills in massively multiplayer online games*. Retrieved February 27, 2009, from http://www2.parc.com/csl/members/nicolas/documents/ITSE.pdf

Egenfeldt-Nielsen, S. (2005). *Beyond edutainment*. Unpublished Doctoral dissertation, IT-University of Copenhagen, Denmark. Retrieved March 22, 2006, from http://www.it-c.dk/people/sen/egenfeldt.pdf

Egenfeldt-Nielsen, S. (2006). *Overview of research on the educational use of video games*. Retrieved March 16, 2009, from http://www.itu.dk/people/sen/papers/game-overview.pdf

Galarneau, L., & Zibit, M. (2006). *Online games for 21st century skills*. Retrieved October 15, 2007, from http://lisa.socialstudygames.com/Galarneau_Zibit_OnlineGames.pdf

Gros, B. (2007). *Digital games in education: The design of games-based learning environments*. Retrieved March 13, 2009, from http://www.iste.org/Content/ NavigationMenu/EducatorResources/YourLearningJourney/InnovateLearningTechnologies/digital_games.pdf

Jenkins, H. (2006). *Confronting the challenges of participatory culture: Media education for the 21st century*. Retrieved December 13, 2007, from http://www.projectnml.org/files/working/NMLWhitePaper.pdf

Kirriemuir, J., & McFarlane, A. (2004). *Literature review in games and learning*. Retrieved March 18, 2009, from http://www.futurelab.org.uk/resources/documents/lit_reviews/Games_Review.pdf

Klastrup, L. (2003). *A poetics of virtual worlds*. Retrieved January 21, 2009, from http://hypertext.rmit.edu.au/dac/papers/Klastrup.pdf

Klopfer, E., Osterweil, S., Salen, K., Haas, J., Groff, J., & Roy, D. (2009). *Moving learning games forward: Obstacles, opportunities & openness*. Retrieved February 27, 2009, from http://education.mit.edu/papers/MovingLearningGamesForward_EdArcade.pdf

Krotoski, A., Ellis, H., Heppell, S., Kirriemuir, J., & McFarlane, A. (2006). *Unlimited learning: Computer and video games in the learning landscape*. Retrieved August 8, 2007, from http://www.elspa.com/assets/files/0/20070308110513566_359.pdf

Larsen, S. A. (n.d.). *Homicide - Forensic learning game*. Retrieved March 23, 2009, from http://www.his.se/PageFiles/10488/LLD_Svend_Ask_Larsen.pdf?epslanguage=sv

Magnussen, R. (2005). *Learning games as a platform for simulated science practice*. Retrieved March 13, 2008, from http://www.digra.org/dl/db/06278.37511.pdf

Mitchell, A., & Savill-Smith, C. (2004). *The use of computer and video games for learning: A review of the literature*. Retrieved March 13, 2009, from http://lsda.org.uk/files/PDF/1529.pdf

Partnership for 21st Century Skills. (2004). *21st century skills*. Retrieved November 22, 2007, from http://www.21stcenturyskills.org/images/stories/matrices/ictmap_english.pdf

Pink, D. H. (2005). *A whole new mind: Moving from the information age to the conceptual age*. New York: Riverhead Books.

Prensky, M. (2001). *Digital game-based learning*. New York: McGraw-Hill.

Sancho, P., Gómez, P. P., & Fernández-Manjón, B. (2008). *Multiplayer role games applied to problem based learning*. Retrieved December 10, 2008, from http://www.e-ucm.es/drafts/e-UCM_draft_101.pdf

Shaffer, D. W., Squire, K. R., Halverson, R., & Gee, J. P. (2004). *Video games and the future of learning*. Retrieved February 27, 2009, from http://www.academiccolab.org/resources/gappspaper1.pdf

Spires, H. A. (2008). *21st century skills and serious games: Preparing the N generation*. Retrieved March 13, 2009, from http://www.fi.ncsu.edu/assets/research_papers/crystal-island-5/21st-century-skills-and-serious-games-preparing-the-n-generation.pdf

Spires, H. A., Lee, J. K., & Lester, J. (2008). *The twenty-first century learner and game-based learning*. Retrieved February 16, 2009, from http://www.ncsu.edu/meridian/win2008/21st/print.html

Squire, K. (2008). *Video game-based learning: An emerging paradigm for instruction*. Retrieved March 13, 2009, from http://website.education.wisc.edu/kdsquire/tenure-files/09-PIQ-Squire-submitted.pdf

Squire, K. D., & Jan, M. (2007). *Mad City Mystery: Developing scientific argumentation skills with a place-based augmented reality game on handheld computers*. Retrieved March 13, 2009, from http://website.education.wisc.edu/kdsquire/manuscripts/madcity-squire-jan-final.pdf

Steinkuehler, C. (2007). Massively multiplayer online gaming as a constellation of literacy practices. In B. E. Shelton & D. Wiley (Eds.), *The design and use of simulation computer games in education* (pp. 187-212). Rotterdam, The Netherlands: Sense Publishers. Retrieved October 22, 2008, from http://inst.usu.edu/~bshelton/simcompgames/steinkuehler_187-212.pdf

Thomas, D., & Brown, J. S. (2009). *Why virtual worlds can matter*. Retrieved February 3, 2009 from http://www.johnseelybrown.com/needvirtualworlds.pdf

KEY TERMS AND DEFINITIONS

Augmented Reality Games: These are games played in the real world with the support of digital devices (e.g., personal digital assistants (PDAs) or mobile phones) that create a fictional layer on top of the real world context.

Cognitive Ethnography: In this context, cognitive ethnography refers to the description of specific cultures in respect of cognitive practices, their basis, and their consequences (see Steinkuehler, 2007).

Constructionism: Also known as social constructivism, constructionism refers to learning as a result of active participation in a community where new meanings are co-constructed by the learner and his/her community of practice and knowledge is the result of consensus.

Constructivism: In this context, this term refers to learning as the construction of new meanings (knowledge) by the learner.

Edutainment: A term consisting of a blend between education and entertainment, edutainment is often used to describe products in which play, fun and game design assume a secondary role.

Guilds: A term referring to a group of characters working together towards a common goal.

Lineagese: This refers to the language and literacy practices (including rituals, behaviors, and social activities) related to the virtual game, Lineage.

Multi-Literacies: A term used to refer to multiple literacies gamers acquire and learn within a gaming universe.

Multi-Skills: Like multi-literacies, multi-skills is a term referring to multiple skills gamers acquire and learn within a gaming universe.

Chapter 16
Designing Game-Based Learning Activities in Virtual Worlds:
Experiences from Undergraduate Medicine

Maria Toro-Troconis
Imperial College London, UK

Martyn R. Partridge
Imperial College London, UK

ABSTRACT

In view of the current interest taking place in the area of education and virtual worlds, such as Second Life®, many educationalists have began to explore the benefits of applying game-based learning in these environments. In this chapter, the authors attempt to explore the elements associated with game-based learning in virtual worlds, focusing on the design process and how effective game-based learning activities can be achieved following pedagogic frameworks. The authors view learning in games as a form of driving learners' motivations and this is reflected in the design and development of the virtual respiratory ward at Imperial College virtual hospital explained in this chapter.

INTRODUCTION

Computer games have been developed and embedded in academic settings since the first arrival of computers in the classroom. As Veugen and de Lange (2007) pointed out, one of the key factors for using computer games in education is the power to motivate. The British Educational Communications and Technology Agency (BECTA) highlighted the following statement:

"A striking feature of games software is its power to motivate. Motivation or the will to continue the use of the software is the end product of a mixture of psychological effects" (BECTA, 2001, pp.2).

Malone (1981) and Malone and Lepper (1987) identified four features that motivate persistence and enjoyment of games: challenge, control, curiosity and fantasy. At the same time, Flow Theory has become very significant in explaining the feelings of enjoyment including playing computer games (Sherry, 2004). According to this theory, arousal

DOI: 10.4018/978-1-61520-713-8.ch016

will increase as a task becomes more challenging but performance and enjoyment will depend on the level of skills. Flow is achieved when a gamer reaches an optimal match between his/her skills and the challenges presented by the game (Boyle and Connolly, 2008). Video game designers create these emotions by balancing a number of game components, such as character traits, game rewards, obstacles, game narrative, competition and opportunities for collaboration (Squire, 2003).

The theories described above contribute to our understanding of player enjoyment in computer games. However, games that over-emphasize educational requirements in some cases undermine the potential of play, game and story for creating memorable experiences (Hirumi and Stapleton, 2008). Therefore, the right balance between educational requirements and motivational factors should be achieved in order to ensure an enjoyable and effective game-based learning experience.

Learners, usually in their 20s, are native speakers of the digital language of computer, video games, DVD players, mobile phones, iPods and the internet (Holloway, 2003). According to Prensky (2001), they are "*digital natives*". The "gamer generation" has a cognitive style characterised by multi-tasking while learning, short attention span during learning, and an exploratory and discovery approach to learning (Asakawa & Gilbert, 2003; Bain & Newton, 2003; Prensky, 2005).

Virtual worlds present rich interactive 3D collaborative spaces in which users can meet and interact (Livingstone, 2007). These virtual worlds can be used by many different users at the same time and for a range of different applications, including cultural, business, tourism and education (De Freitas, 2008). According to the Federation of American Scientists (FAS) and De Freitas (2008), virtual worlds have the following characteristics:

- "Learner control: learners control and interact through the creation of a virtual representation of themselves, called "avatars"" (De Freitas, 2008, pp. 8).
- "Collaboration: emphasis upon collaboration and community building". (De Freitas, 2008, pp. 8).
- "Persistence: persistence of the world leads to the capacity for immediacy and synchronous use of the world" (De Freitas, 2008, pp.8).
- "Inclusion of shareable and user generated digital content." (De Freitas, 2008, pp. 8).
- "Immersion and interactivity: the user feels immersed in the environment and fully engaged with the activities being undertaken." (De Freitas, 2008, pp.8).

As De Freitas pointed out, it is worth noting that

"the lines between virtual worlds, games and social networking are blurring significantly leading to the assertion that over the next five years the majority of young people under 18 coming into tertiary education will have avatars and will be using this kind of applications daily and therefore have different expectations about how education may be delivered to them." (De Freitas, 2008, pp.8).

Virtual worlds have been around for a very long time starting with the popular Multi-User Dimensions/Dungeons (MUDs) and Multi-Object Oriented MUDs (MOOs), developed in the early 1970s. Multi-User Dungeon also known to former players on CompuServe as British Legends was developed in 1975. It is the world's oldest virtual world which can still be played (British Legends, 2005). These environments had the characteristics of modern virtual worlds except they were text-based. They provided the foundations for the development of modern online communities that are supported by 3D spaces. Following these social text-based communities emerged the first virtual world which used graphics and avatars. Lucasfilm's Habitat, came out in 1985 and supported its online community for six years. Habitat was able to:

"support a population of thousands of users in a single shared cyberspace. It presented its users with a real-time animated view into an online simulated world in which users can communicate, play games, go on adventures, fall in love, get married, get divorced, start businesses, found religions, wage wars, protest against them, and experiment with self-government. The Habitat project proved to be a rich source of insights into the nitty-gritty reality of actually implementing a serious, commercially viable cyberspace environment" (Morningstart & Farmer, 1993, pp.1).

The key factors that have made the transition between those virtual worlds developed in the 1970s and 1980s and the current virtual worlds, are the increased broadband and graphics capabilities and higher specifications available in personal computing. Currently Massively Multiplayer Online Role Playing Games (MMORPGs), or Massively Multiplayer Online Games (MMOGs), have been used and are the most widely used examples of 3D environments. These 3D environments are not designed or used for supporting formal education. However, some studies have indicated the use of these leisure games for educational purposes (De Freitas, 2008). Some examples of these include: Everquest, Guild Wars, Lineage, Lineage 2 and World of Warcraft.

According to De Freitas (2008), open-ended social virtual worlds have also been very popular among educators. Examples of these worlds include Second Life®, Active Worlds Educational Universe and There.com. Other examples of popular social worlds are: Cyworld which has been very popular in Korea, Habbo (formely Habbo Hotel) or Gaia Online which are targeted at children. The social element found in these worlds clearly has some synergies with the process of learning needing further exploration (De Freitas 2006).

The distinction between multiplayer virtual worlds such as Everquest and World of Warcrat and the open-ended social virtual worlds such as Second Life® are difficult to establish. Some do not classify Second Life® as a game, because of its lack of predefined goals (Livingstone 2007). The problem of adapting social virtual worlds and developing new game-based learning activities, as described by De Freitas et al, (2006) would become easier if systematic frameworks and toolkits were developed which ease the implementation and integration of game-based learning activities in the curriculum.

"The main challenge for game designers when combining motivational and instructional features is in managing superfluous mental load so that the game challenge, fantasy and control elements do not undermine learning" (Clark and Mayer, 2007).

However, educators, instructional designers and learning technologists may know in most of the cases little about game design and game developers may know little about education and instructional design (Hirumi & Stapleton, 2008). Therefore, in order to support educators, instructional designers and learning technologist in the development of game-based learning activities in virtual worlds, it is important to develop frameworks, approaches and models.

Large corporations have also been producing their own in-house virtual worlds as is the case of Project Wonderland, developed by Sun Microsystems using the Project Darkstar platform and IBM Innovative Quick Internal Metaverse Project. It is worth pointing out that one of the main differences between social and working worlds is cost.

SECOND LIFE®

Social worlds offer exciting new ways of collaboration and educational opportunities. A large number of educational institutions are already exploring ways of making use of these new virtual environments. According to Eduserv Spring 2009

Snapshot of Virtual World use in UK Higher and Further Education, many universities in the UK are studying the use of virtual worlds –mainly Second Life®- in education. In this study, a range of different uses of social worlds in UK higher and further education were identified with learning and teaching activities predominating, as well as simulations, the visualisation of complex structures and safety role-play.

Second Life® users are represented by avatars and can be moved in the environment using mouse and keyboard controls. Users can communicate using instant messages, voice chat or text-based 'notecards'. There has been increasing investigation and trialling of the potential of Second Life® for learning (Helmer 2007). Second Life® has common community and collaborative features with recent contemporary developments such as Facebook, YouTube, Wikipedia, Sloodle and Flickr, which places it in the Web 2.0 spectrum.

Some of the advantages identified by the authors when using Second Life® as a learning environment are: the use of a pre-existing engine makes the development of game-based learning activities easier, especially when the engine has built-in authoring tools. Anonymity in Second Life® may help when training in sensitive subjects such as mental and sexual health. Second Life® is a 'safe place to fail', students can interact with virtual patients, trying different treatments and investigations.

On the other hand, some of the disadvantages highlighted by the authors when using Second Life® as a learning environment are: Second Life® interface is very different to any other browsing facility interface. Therefore, basic orientation takes more than 4 hours; mastery of the environment may take far longer; the multimedia rich environment in Second Life® requires high bandwidth demands; a high-spec computer with good graphics card may be required. (Toro-Troconis et al, 2010)

GAMES IN EDUCATIONAL CONTEXTS

There is little agreement among educational technologists on why games should be embedded for educational purposes, how they should be designed to support learning, or in what instructional situations learners are most likely to benefit from them (Gredler 1996). According to Squire (2002), different key factors that cover gaming within the instructional context, such as game conceptualisation, constructivist learning activities embedded in game play, as well as the nature of debriefing – are all critically important elements of the gaming experience.

According to De Freitas (2006), learning in immersive worlds is beginning to have a wider range of uses and applications. The Second Life® community is clearly demonstrating how interactions and collaborations are opening up new opportunities for learning. This provides novel challenges and opportunities to explore ways to create innovative approaches to learning. Games provide a meaningful and relevant context in which learning activities can be delivered. Good games have clear goals and "explicit information both on-demand and just in time when the learner needs it" (Gee, 2003).

"The term game-based learning has emerged as a generic name for the use of games for learning or educational purposes. It has also been termed 'serious games', and includes fully immersive environments (or 'metaverses'), in which learners can take on virtual presence in virtual worlds" (Joint Information Systems Committee 2007).

Game-based learning implementations in virtual worlds may provide the means to deliver guided and engaging teaching and learning experiences more suited to the 'digital natives' generation within virtual worlds.

Classification of Learning Types

Different learning types are identified and discussed by Helmer (2007). These learning types provide some guidelines for the design of immersed learning experiences in virtual worlds:

- **"Demonstrations**: this type of learning involves the least interaction and is most closely aligned with traditional educational experiences in which the virtual world is used to demonstrate activities and situations that can also be delivered in traditional face to face settings". Helmer (2007).
- **"Experiential learning** involves a higher level of engagement, providing a more immersive, time-based experience than a demonstration." Helmer (2007).
- **"Diagnostic Activity**: this category involves interaction with a simulated environment, designed to promote inquiry, analysis and identification."
- **"Role play** should cover engagements that have embedded learning objectives. It is already one of the primary activities in Second Life®." Helmer (2007).
- **"Constructive Learning:** this type of learning involves giving learners the opportunity to create or 'build' elements within the environment." Helmer (2007).

Murray (1997) also discussed three potential influential factors of emergent narrative that might allow the learner feel their interactions have real consequences.

- **"Emergent Narrative: linear content**: the progress of the story is defined and influenced by the choices the learner makes" (Murray, 1997). The navigational pathways in Second Life® will be enriched by the 'metaverse'. Introductions in the form of audio, video and 'notecards' allow the learner to progress through a scenario.
- **"The responsive environment**: the learner will expect the environment to respond to his/her input. These expectations will not be limited to one path in Second Life®" (Murray, 1997). Learners will be able to follow different routes and move from different areas. Different activities can be triggered and results be released to learners depending on their choices, using Scaffolding information in the form of audio, video and 'notecards'. Some forms of Assessment using multiple choice questions could also be provided.
- **"The psycho-social moratorium: cyclical content**: successive attempts can be made to achieve the main objective of the activity". Each attempt will be increasingly informed by knowledge acquired in previous attempts. Learners will be encouraged to return and try again. Cyclical content can be implemented when: - timing is critical (doing the same things too early or too late) - incremental signs inform the learner when things are going well or badly - magnitude is important – the instances where doing the same thing a bit more or a bit less matters. (Murray, 1997).

In addition to the learning types described by Helmer (2007), and the different aspects of emergent narrative described by Murray (1997), the four-dimensional framework described by De Freitas and Martin (2006), has also provided the basis for the design of game-based learning activities for virtual patients in Second Life® (Toro-Troconis et al, 2010).

VIRTUAL PATIENTS DESIGN IN SECOND LIFE®

The Faculty of Medicine at Imperial College London has developed a Respiratory Ward in Second Life® with a series of virtual patients'

Figure 1. Virtual patient at the respiratory ward – Imperial College London region in Second Life® (http://www.elearningimperial.com/).

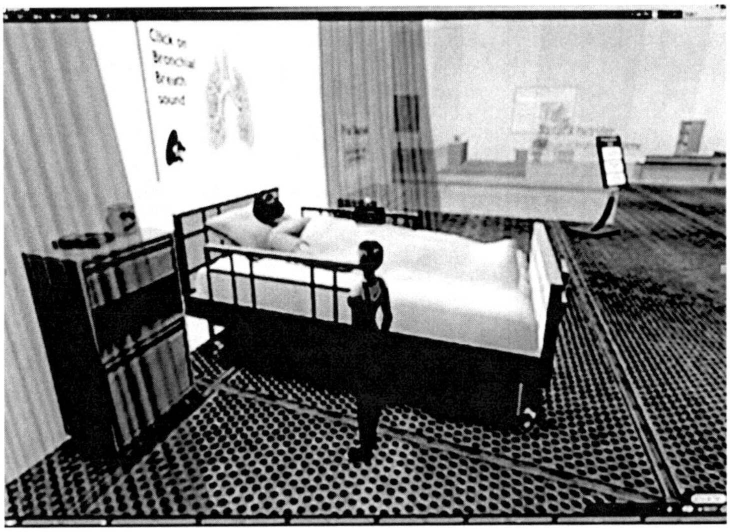

activities following a game-based learning model (Figure 1). The game-based learning activities aim to drive experiential, diagnostic and role-play learning activities within the 3-D world, aiming to support students as they select investigations and make diagnoses. The Respiratory Ward was developed with five virtual patients, each with a different diagnosis, and each includes elements of medical history, differential diagnosis, investigations, working diagnosis and production of a management plan.

The game-based learning process covers a wide range of activities and phases which should be followed in order to ensure a pedagogically sound game-based learning implementation. The game-based learning process described bellow has been developed following the game development process described by Hirumi and Stapleton (2008) (Figure 2).

Concept Development Phase

This phase started when the idea of game-based learning for virtual patients was conceived in 2007 (Toro-Troconis & Partridge, 2007). The main learning outcomes of the activities were determined. The framework for evaluating games and simulation-based education developed by De Freitas and Martin (2006) were also utilised in this research (Toro-Troconis et al, 2010).

Draft paper prototypes were created and a Concept Document was produced covering the following:

- High Concept. This looks at what makes the game-based learning experience different from other similar activities.
- Player Motivation. This section identifies the key motivational factors across the target population.
- Game Play. This looks at what the learner will do while playing the game, including rules, rewards and tools.
- Story. The story identifies the main events, characters and setting in which the learning experience takes place.
- Target Audience.
- Game Genre.
- Target Platform and hardware requirements.
- Competitive analysis.

Figure 2. Game-based learning – development process. Adapted from Hirumi & Stapleton (2008)

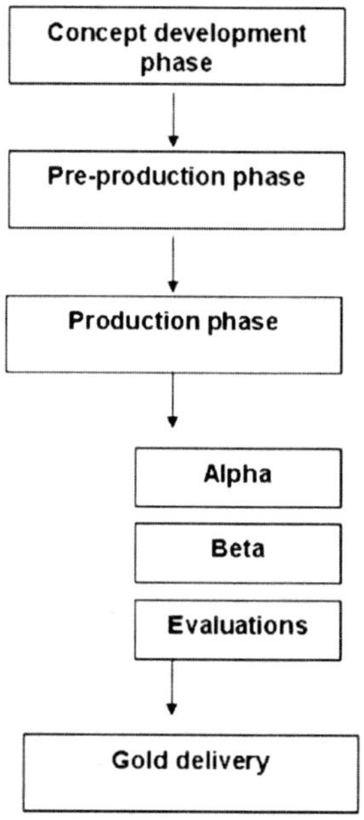

The role of a game designer or learning technologist is crucial at this stage. They all have to work together to come out with a clear idea about: learning outcomes, learner characteristics, important contextual factors, and the desired instructional approach to be followed.

The game should be identified within a specific instructional strategy or theory addressing the right instructional design model to be applied. For example, Case-Based Reasoning (Aamodt and Plaza, 1994), Learning by Doing (Schank, Berman & Macpherson, 1999) or Problem-Based Learning (Barrows, 1985). The selection of the right instructional design principle will determine the nature of the game-based learning activity, guiding the game narrative, interactions and game activity.

The instructional strategy selected for the design of game-based learning activities for the delivery of virtual patients was a constructivist approach. In this case the "story" presents the learners with a virtual patient scenario and the "game play" requires the learners to interact with different tools and dialogue messages to access content information and construct their own knowledge on how to work their way through the virtual patient cases.

This particular activity focused upon common respiratory emergencies (for example patients presenting with pneumonia or a collapsed lung) and learners were required to assimilate the clinical story, construct a possible diagnosis and learn the value of different investigations in helping them to make a correct diagnosis. The format had additional educational advantages in that it was easy to design the program to prevent the trainee from approaching the virtual patient without first washing their hands!

User controls and interfaces were designed to accommodate to the Second Life® capabilities. The use of notecards and on-screen text messages were used as the main user communication interface (Figure 3). A Heads-up display (HUD) was designed in order to keep the learner informed of his/her performance. HUD elements are identified when developing the Concept Document (Game

Figure 3. Virtual patient user controls and interface.

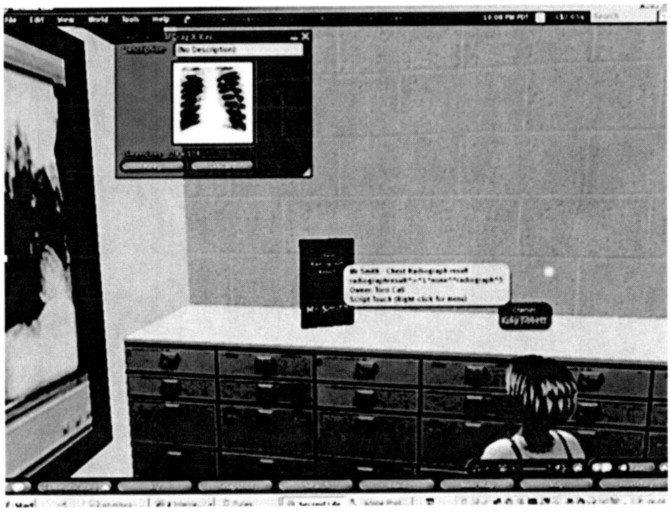

Play); these elements indicate player/learner status showing which direction the player/learner is going or where the player/learner ranks in the game (Figure 4).

The HUD is a very good method for conveying information to the player/learner during the game. The main elements the HUD displays have been classified under different categories following the main reasons for playing games identified by Lucas and Sherry (2004): competition, challenge, social interaction, diversion, fantasy and arousal. The main categories are the following:

- Activities attempted
- Activities status
- User's score
- Highest score per activity (all users)

Pre-Production Phase

Once the game concept has been produced after completion of the concept development phase, the development team starts planning the pre-production phase. This phase aims to identify the following:

- Story (nature of characters, activities and events the learners will interact with when playing the game-based learning activity).
- Game goals.
- User controls.
- User interface.
- Game levels.
- Media assets (audio, video, art design and technical issues).
- Production details.

During the pre-production phase for the Respiratory Ward the main activity of the virtual patient characters were identified as well as the levels of interaction within the environment. It was decided to keep the game-based learning experience to a single-player, although multiple players can communicate in a Problem-Based Learning (PBL) approach when accessing the virtual patients.

Production Phase

The production phase began once the prototype was approved. The production phase was broken down into Alpha and Beta versions and the final

Figure 4. Heads up display (HUD) - virtual patients

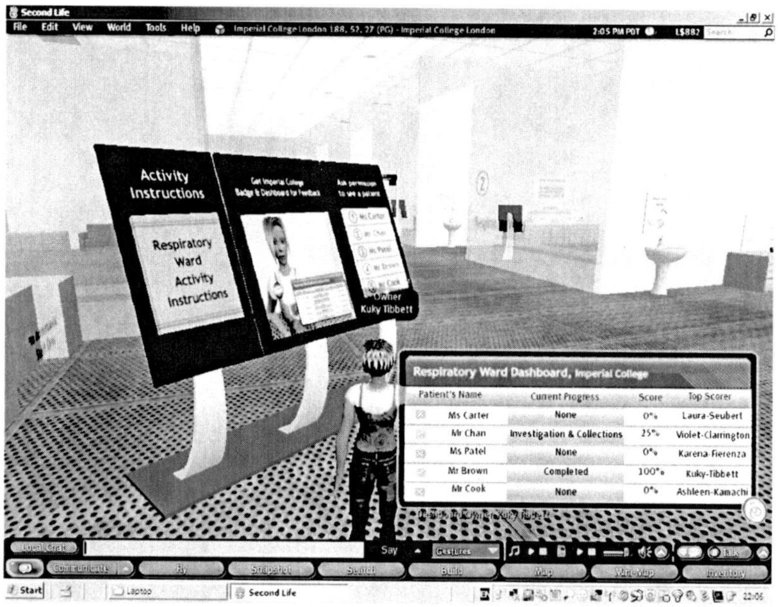

"Gold" version was delivered once the Alpha and Beta versions were fully tested. Once the game-based learning activity passed satisfactorily Beta testing, evaluations were carried out in order to identify any potential user interface and/or navigational or educational issues. Usability tests are normally performed during this evaluation phase incorporating the use of verbal protocols, surveys and focus groups. The final Gold version is delivered once all the changes identified during the evaluation phase are incorporated.

CONCLUSION

This chapter is written to help educators realise the potential of game-based learning or "serious games" when implemented within virtual worlds. It provides an overview of the game development steps identifying key design phases and tasks carried out during the process. This chapter also discusses motivational and institutional theories related to game-based learning design. It clearly suggests how the game design process requires a large number of resources and disciplines to be integrated in order to drive instruction design and game design activities in a creative and systematic way.

Although very exciting projects are currently being undertaken in this area, it is important to highlight the lack of support currently provided by social virtual worlds, such as Second Life® for authoring game-based learning activities. Their current authoring environments are mainly focused on the provision of design authoring tools which currently offer very user-friendly and effective features. However, social virtual worlds do not yet offer design tools and features for authoring game-based learning activities.

Game-based learning authoring tools ought to provide easy to use tools by which learning technologists and educators may be able to design game narratives avoiding the development of open-ended activities. Game narratives may be developed by incorporating design tools and features within an authoring environment identifying activators, triggers, actions and scaffolding activities guiding how narratives unfold. At the same time, Game Play elements may be available within the authoring tool allowing the introduction of different variables such as rewards.

The incorporation of game-based learning authoring tools within social virtual worlds would be a big step forward in the effective implementation and delivery of game-based learning at a large scale within educational institutions. The provision of game-based learning authoring tools within social virtual worlds may result in a greater proportion of cost-effective game-based learning activities being developed and delivered via social virtual worlds. This may represent a challenge for social virtual world companies and developers. However, it would indeed represent a very important step forward in the development and implementation of game-based learning across social virtual worlds.

REFERENCES

Aamodt, A., & Plaza, E. (1994). Case-Based Reasoning: Foundational Issues, Methodological Variations and Systems Approaches. *Artificial Intelligence Communications*, *7*(1), 39–59.

Asakawa, T., & Gilbert, N. (2003). Synthesizing Experiences: Lessons To Be Learned from Internet-Mediated Simulation Games. *Simulation & Gaming*, *34*(1), 10–22. doi:10.1177/1046878102250455

Bain, C., & Newton, C. (2003). Art Games: Pre-Service Art Educators Construct Learning Experiences for the Elementary Art Classroom. *Art Education*, *56*(5), 33–40.

Barrows, H. S. (1985). *How to Design a Problem-Based Curriculum for the Preclinical Years*. New York: Springer Publishing Co.

BECTA. (2001). *Computer Games in Education Project: Report*. Retrieved August 19, 2009, from http://partners.becta.org.uk/index.php?section=rh&rid=13595

Boyle, E., & Connolly, T. M. (2008). Gamer for Learning: Does Gender Make a Difference? In Connolly, T. M., Stansfield, M. H., & Boyle, E. (Eds.), *Games-based Learning Advancement for Multisensory Human Computer Interface Techniques and Effective Practices*. Hershey, PA: Idea-Group Publishing.

British Legends. (2005). *Multi-User Dugeon (MUD)*. Retrieved August 19, 2009, from http://www.jisc.ac.uk/media/documents/publications/seriousvirtualworldsv1.pdf

Clark, R. C., & Mayer, R. E. (2007). e-Learning and the Science of Instruction (2nd Ed.). San Francisco: Pfeiffer.

De Freitas, S. (2008). *Serious Virtual Worlds: a scoping study*. Prepared for the JISC e-Learning Programme. Retrieved August 19, 2009, from http://www.jisc.ac.uk/media/documents/publications/seriousvirtualworldsv1.pdf

De Freitas, S., & Martin, O. (2006). How can exploratory learning with games and simulations within the curriculum be most effectively evaluated? *Computers & Education*, *46*(3), 249–264. doi:10.1016/j.compedu.2005.11.007

Gee, J. P. (2003). *What video games have to teach us about learning and literacy*. New York: Palgrave/ St. Martin's.

Gredler, M. E. (1996). Educational games and simulations: A technology in search of a research paradigm. In Jonassen, D. H. (Ed.), *Handbook of research for educational communications and technology* (pp. 521–539). New York: MacMillan.

Helmer, J. (2007). Second Life and virtual worlds. *Learning Light Limited*. Retrieved August 19, 2009, from http://www.epic.co.uk/content/news/nov_07/Second_Life_and_Virtual_Worlds_JH.pdf

Hirumi, A., & Stapleton, C. (2008). *Games: Purpose and Potential in Education*. New York: Springer.

Holloway, S. L., & Valentine, G. (2003). *Cyberkids: children in the information age*. London: Routledge.

Joint Information Systems Committee. (2007). Game-based learning. *E-learning innovation programme*. Retrieved August 19, 2009, from http://www.jisc.ac.uk/publications/publications/pub_gamebasedlearningBP.aspx

Livingstone, D. (2007). Learning support in multi-user virtual environments. In *Proceedings of the European Conference on Game-Based Learning*, University of Paisley, Scotland, 25–26 October.

Lucas, K., & Sherry, J. L. (2004). Sex Differences in Video Game Play: A Communication-Based Explanation. *Communication Research, 31*, 499–523. doi:10.1177/0093650204267930

Malone, T. (1981). Toward a theory of intrinsically motivating instruction. *Cognitive Science, 4*, 333–369.

Malone, T. W., & Lepper, M. R. (1987). Making Learning Fun: A Taxonomy of Intrinsic Motivations for Learning. In Snow, R. E., & Farr, M. J. (Eds.), *Aptitute, Learning and Instruction: III. Cognitive and affective process analyses* (pp. 223–253). Hilsdale, NJ: Erlbaum.

Morningstar, C., & Farmer, R. (2008). The Lessons of Lucasfilms's Habitat. *Journal of Virtual Worlds Research, 1*(1), 1-21. Retrieved August 19, 2009, from http://journals.tdl.org/jvwr/article/viewFile/287/241

Murray, J. (1997). *Hamlet on the holodeck: the future of narrative in cyberspace*. Cambridge, MA: MIT Press.

Prensky, M. (2001). *Digital game-based learning*. St Paul, MN: Paragon House.

Prensky, M. (2005). Adopt and Adapt. 21st-Century Schools Need 21st-Century Technology. *Edutopia*. Retrieved June 9, 2009, from http://www.digitaldivide.net/articles/view.php?ArticleID=786

Schank, R. C., Berman, T. R., Bransford, T. R., & Macpherson, K. A. (1999). Learning by doing. In Reigeluth, C. M. (Ed.), *Instructional Design Theories and Models: A New Paradigm of Instructional Theory* (pp. 161–179). Hillsdale, NJ: Lawrence Erlbaum Associates.

Sherry, J. L. (2004). Flow and media enjoyment. *Communication Theory, 14*, 392–410. doi:10.1111/j.1468-2885.2004.tb00318.x

Squire, K. (2002). Cultural framing of computer/video games. *The International Journal of Computer Game Research, 2*(1). Retrieved August 19, 2009, from http://www.gamestudies.org/0102/squire/

Squire, K. (2003). Video games in education. *International Journal of Intelligent Simulations and Gaming, 2*(1). Retrieved June 5, 2009, from http://website.education.wisc.edu/kdsquire/tenure-files/39-squire-IJIS.pdf

Toro-Troconis, M., & Partridge, M. (2007). Designing a 3D Teaching Hospital in Second Life to support clinical skills development. In *Proceedings of the Association for Medical Education in Europe (AMEE)*, NTNU Norwegian University of Science and Technology, Trondheim, Norway, 25-29 August.

Toro-Troconis, M., Partridge, M., Mellstrom, U., Meeran, K., & Higham, J. (2010). Design and Delivery of game-based learning for virtual patients in Second Life®: initial findings. In Peachey, A., Gillen, J., Livingstone, D., & Robbins, S. (Eds.), *Researching Learning in Virtual Worlds*. London: Springer. doi:10.1007/978-1-84996-047-2_7

Veugen, C., & de Lange, M. (2007). Learning can't be fun, can it. In Siebehhanddl, K., Wagner, M., & Zauchner, S. (Eds.), *Gender in E-learning and Educational Games* (pp. 239–260). Innsbruck, Austria: Studienverlag.

Epilogue
Principles of Educational Digital Game Structure for Classroom Settings

Youngkyun Baek
Korea National University of Education, Korea

ABSTRACT

The scope of learning with games is determined by their genre, characteristics and scenarios, or content. Therefore, the frame of a game containing its type and content somewhat confines the activities of players to learn and to play. Game-based learning adopts much of the same interactional techniques that have been used in traditional instruction. Learning with games includes activities such as 'learning by practice and feedback', 'learning by doing', 'learning by making mistakes', 'learning by discovery', and 'learning by role playing'. Games are adopted for classroom based learning to motivate students, to support main curricular activities, to strengthen what is learned, and to summarize and evaluate what is learned. There is no straightforward guideline on how to use a game effectively in classroom settings. However, the instruction for teaching and learning with games needs to be designed before any other actions are taken.

INTRODUCTION

In order to use games for learning, the game structure and activities of players need to be given careful consideration. Among many characteristics of gaming, context, immersion, and interaction are the main factors which educators must focus on when using games in classrooms.

DOI: 10.4018/978-1-61520-713-8.ch017

The situation or context in which a game resides is an environment in which learning and gaming happens simultaneously. It provides players with a sense of reality for their activities. Immersion leads players to experience "flow" in gaming. Thus it contributes toward a player's active learning. Also, it empowers learners by motivating them to learn. Interaction is an important factor because it is fundamental to gaming as well as to learning. Meaningful learning with a game is possible based on interactions just as learning in general is made possible through effective interactions. Learning with games, which is characterized by combining fun and learning, thus tries to achieve given objectives based on immersion, interaction, and context.

Games are not a shortcut for inducing effective learning. Rather, games require the creativity of teachers and learners to find the best usage for their current situation. To find out what kinds of application types and game activities are meaningful in classroom settings, the internal structures of games and the activities of players learning with games must be explored as those are what affect the learning processes of game based activities.

Internal Structures of Game

The scope of learning with games is determined by their genre, characteristics and scenarios, or content. Therefore, the frame of a game containing its type and content somewhat confines the activities of players to learn and to play.

1. **Intrinsic versus Extrinsic.** The distinction between intrinsic and extrinsic games is whether the learning scenario and the game scenario are separate or integrated. Malone (1980) asserted that learning games are categorized as either intrinsic or extrinsic. He contends that the learning content of an intrinsic game is integrated with the framework of the game. Most simulation games are examples of intrinsic games. On the other hand, an extrinsic game has a separate or less integrated scenario with the learning content. In this type of game, learning and gaming are independent activities and gaming remains unchanged when the learning content is replaced.

In sum, these two types of games have their own values. For certain topics of learning, intrinsic games are more effective than extrinsic games. On the other hand, extrinsic games are economical in that they can be developed separately and maintained with ease because their learning content can be replaced without modifying the game framework.

2. **Template versus Custom Designed.** This distinction is based on the game framework. A template-based game is composed of several steps or assembled modules. Most games of this type are developed using authoring tools. On the other hand, custom designed games are developed as a whole unit. This distinction is not based on the development method but on the structure of a game. A game structured into compartments supports various activities and topics of learning. Each module of the game can have a distinctive objective of learning which support various or stepwise activities. A custom designed game is more tightly interwoven and supports comparatively long term objectives of learning. In a sense, instructors can control more of the content in the learning path for the players in a template based game, while it is very difficult for the instructors to control the content and learning paths in a custom-built internally interwoven game.
3. **Reflection versus Action.** For teaching and learning with games, the scope of a player's reflective thinking should be taken into consideration as an important indicator of a player's quality of learning. The player's thinking and tactics are important internal processes of learning, and some games require less thinking than action. Action games, for example, require less reflective thinking than role playing, adventure, and simulation games. However, this does not mean that action games are necessarily less important in learning. Some hand-eye coordination learning, for example, would be best addressed through an action-oriented game. In short, one of the issues in game

based learning is to balance the goals of the game play with those of learning and to select a game of action or reflection according to learning objectives.

4. **Synchronous versus Asynchronous.** Most real-time or synchronous games do not allow players to pause to think, nor do they allow players to get involved in other activities simultaneously. Whether players are involved in gaming or not, the game continues. In such cases, players often lose the game due to take a long pause from the game play. But in an asynchronous game such as a chess game between the computer and a player, the computer waits for the player's input unless a time limit has been set. The synchronous/asynchronous distinction also makes a difference in multi-user games. Multi-user synchronous games such as combat games or business simulations can add higher levels of interest and fun for players. Players can perform significant activities only when they react in real time in the same space. However, multi-user asynchronous games generate reactions from players only when they input responses. Thus, this type of game cannot provide the same level of immediacy as a synchronous game. This fact requires that asynchronous games contain other ways to involve and immerse players in the in gaming and learning, such as giving timed tasks for certain intervals.
5. **One-user versus Multi-user.** Most game-based learning has been pursued in an independent manner in "one user" situations. Today, network and internet technology has made it possible to play multi-user network games allowing multiple players to solve problems effectively and efficiently together over distances. This is a good example of the co-construction of knowledge and cooperative learning.
6. **Session versus Persistent.** A session game is opened and closed by the player. This kind of game exists only when players want to continue playing. If the game can be temporarily stopped by any player, then the rest of the players have to stop the game. On the other hand, persistent games continue like the daily life of players. Players can pause anytime and restart the game at will. Players can accumulate their knowledge and skills over time. This kind of game can make significant progress on long-term objectives of learning.
7. **Story versus Twitch.** Each story in a game can have various lengths and depth of detail. A movie is an example of a long story. A twitch game concentrates on just a series of actions. If the learning objective is rather long-term, then adopting stories is the best alternative. However, twitch games like 'Tetris' can induce player's involvements and achieve short-term objectives by increasing the level of difficulty. Stories and characters in a game affect the affective domain and recall of players whereas a twitch game is effective in generating prompt responses and in stimulating quick memorization for tasks such as language learning. In this domain of knowledge, a twitch game can constitute effective and interesting experiences for players by providing clues and generating quick responses.

Activities in Learning with Games

Game-based learning adopts much of the same interactional techniques that have been used in traditional instruction. However, some traditional techniques are modified to fit digital forms. Those interaction techniques accelerate game usage for learning.

1. **Learning by Practice and Feedback**

In the early days of computer-based instruction, drill and practice was one of the most common techniques used. This interaction type has been blamed for being overly simplistic and not requiring thinking in the process. This was apparently an effective use but not that much fun. Even though adaptive functions have been added to this initial type of interaction, it is still recognized as a primitive interaction. However, it has been widely used until now, especially to reinforce already obtained knowledge and skills.

My Word Coach is a video game from Ubisoft for the Nintendo DS, Wii and iPhone OS. Players of this game type in the word equivalent to the given explanation.

Evaluation record of a player's score with spent time subtracted is displayed after playing. There are six training exercises for each player which focuses on word selection and improving memorization. Activities include word recognition, spelling, and definitions.

2. **Learning by Doing**

Learning by doing in game-based learning is a type of experiential learning. Learners develop their skills, attitudes, and thinking based on doing and experiencing in gaming. In gaming, players create and renew their knowledge by solving problems. Experiential learning applies to recognizing a problem to solve, generating ideas, testing them, observing the results, and lastly identifying or changing previous concepts. This ongoing process of trial and error makes cognitive reconstruction happen and leads to meaningful learning. This "hands-on, minds-on" process includes all activities of active participation, motivation to learn, and learner-centered knowledge construction.

X-Plane is a flight simulator for personal computers, offering a complete flight simulation environment. It is capable of modeling fairly complex aircraft designs, including helicopters, rockets, rotor craft, and tilt-rotor craft.

Players acquire the skills for operating an aircraft in an environment equipped with the necessary concepts and controls.

3. **Learning by Making Mistakes**

Making mistakes is a big part of game play. It represents one of the most common activities. Players relentlessly proceed toward the goal of the game and get feedback from the game. They repeat trials and errors. Finally, they learn what

Figure 1. My word coach (http://ubisoftcoach.uk.ubi.com/games/my-word-coach-ds/1)

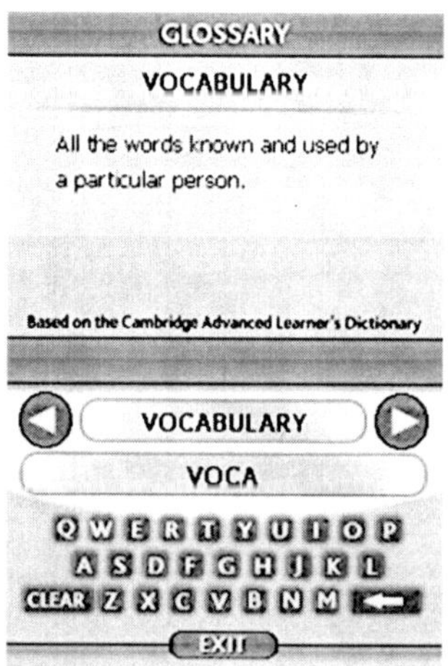

Figure 2. X-plane (http://www.x-plane.com/pg_instructions_mobile.html)

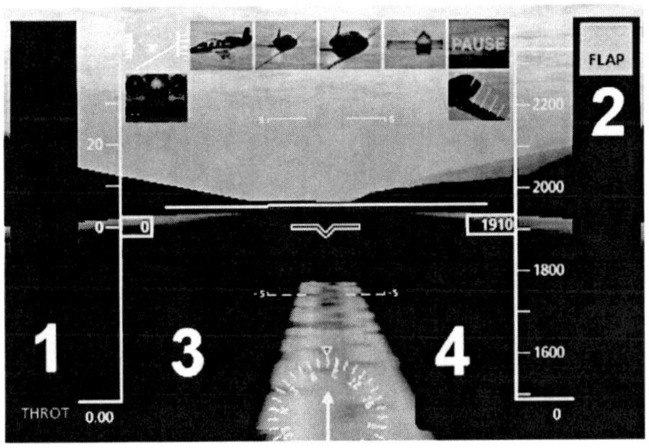

was wrong and what was right. Gaming fits into this process because players are highly motivated to continue. So making mistakes is a starting point for learning with games and then feedback directs the players to proceed in gaming. If the feedback gives the player internal motivation and satisfaction, learning becomes more effective.

In Crazy Machines, players select the necessary tools needed for the experiment. Players try to answer a given question such as, 'how can you operate the balloon with a vacuum machine?' Players select the most efficient process and result for the experiment and this trial and error is denoted as a score. Making mistakes promotes logical thinking and stimulates the imagination of players. Thus, they can design the next experiment in an improved manner.

4. **Learning by Discovery**

Participants learn more when they discover facts, rules, and knowledge by themselves than when knowledge is pre-packaged and delivered to them. Discovering happens when learners find clues or pieces leading to solving problems. Thus, learning by discovering may happen when players are asked to organize learning content. In this process, they relate and classify each learning object,

Figure 3. Crazy Machines 2 (http://www.mathlove.co.kr/crazy/introduce2.php)

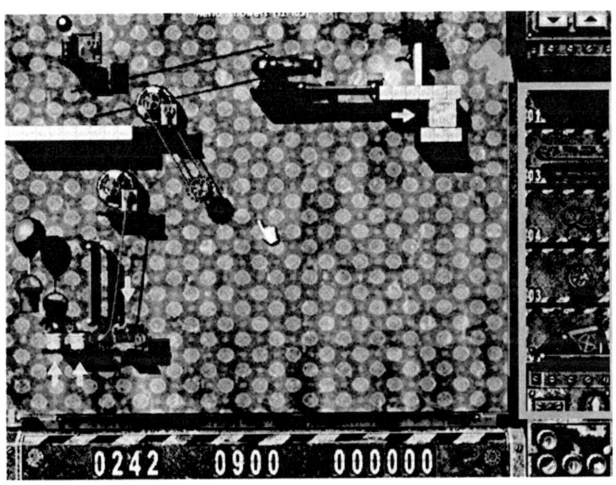

finding commonality and relationships between events and objects using given information.

Food Force is an educational game published by the United Nations World Food Programme (WFP) in 2005. Players take on missions to distribute food in a famine-affected country and to help it to recover and become self-sufficient again. At the same time they learn about hunger in the real world and the WFP's work to prevent it.

The game takes place on the fictional island of Sheylan in the Indian Ocean, which is suffering from both drought and civil war. The player's character is a rookie who has joined a team of UN experts, including a nutritionist, a logistics officer, a pilot, an appeals officer, and the director of food purchasing. Most of the game play is arcade oriented, with time-limited sequences. All missions can be played through in under an hour, though players might replay individual missions as their high scores can be uploaded online for worldwide comparison with other players.

5. **Learning by Role Playing**

Through taking specific roles and playing them in games, players can understand the problems, causes, and effects caused by social interaction taking place around them.

In the Game of Luminary, the goal of all characters is to learn about players' character and the weapons that are provided, join a town community and guild community where players will interact with other players. A character is elected by fellow players to guide everyone and do the job of the King.

Players learn politics, distribution of scarcity value, and formation of social strata by playing their roles in this virtual society.

TYPES OF APPLICATION

This section will summarize how and when a game can be used in the classroom.

To Motivate

It is well known that gaming improves motivation. In general, games can motivate learners and maintain high suspense and challenge. So in the beginning of learning, a game can be used to make learners curious, maintain their concerns,

Figure 4. Food Force (http://www.educational-freeware.com/freeware/food-force.aspx)

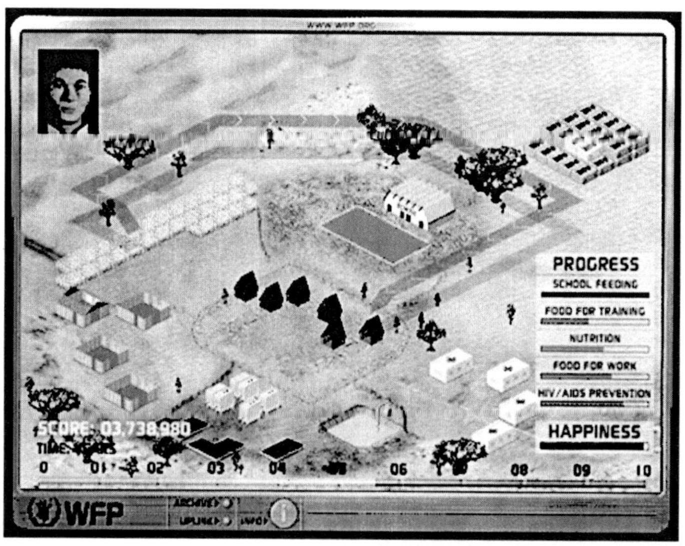

and challenge them to learn the topics to come. A well-selected game can provide learners with more intrinsic motivation to start than many other instructional strategies (Lepper and Chabay, 1985). If teachers introduce or talk about games which learners are already familiar with, it can be a good start for learners to participate in their class with immersion and curiosity.

In the Wild Weather Adventure game, the player's weather research blimp explores Earth and its weather. With luck, skill, and strategy, players race other weather research blimps to be the first to travel all the way around the world and win the game. It can be played with friends or by oneself with a computer opponent.

Players learn about air movements based on their previous conception of movement. As shown, movements are like chess, which the players may be familiar with, to match the air flow with a world map.

To support main curricula activities, below are students' main activities when they are in the midst of learning with games.

- **Problem solving/Exploring.** In many cases, games used in teaching and learning processes such as puzzle games are explorative not competitive (Brown, 1995). To solve problems, a creative thinking process is needed. When the learning objective is to solve given problems, a game should lead players to define the problems by themselves, and build problem solving strategies by offering new problem circumstances. Through this process, learners can develop higher order thinking abilities such as reasoning, logical thinking, and critical thinking by exercising their skills and strategies during problem solving. Games supporting problem solving vary in length and openness. If a game consists of a small set of problems, it can be used in a short period of teaching. However, a problem that takes longer to solve requires multiple teaching sessions. Also, depending on the type of problem, a game can be played in groups.
- **Memorizing/Practicing.** In certain areas of Math and Language Arts, memorization can be effective. Games used in this area are often used to acquire new facts and to store them in long-term memory. The main procedures of memorizing/practicing games are presenting a question or problem circumstance requiring learner's immediate response, collecting the answer, and giving direct feedback. For example, teachers can use games such as puzzles or quizzes for quick and easy memorization.
- **Absorbing/Obtaining.** Even a simple and

Figure 5. Luminary (http://luminary.aeriagames.com/overview/features)

Figure 6. Wild weather adventure (http://spaceplace.nasa.gov/en/kids/goes/wwa/index.shtml#)

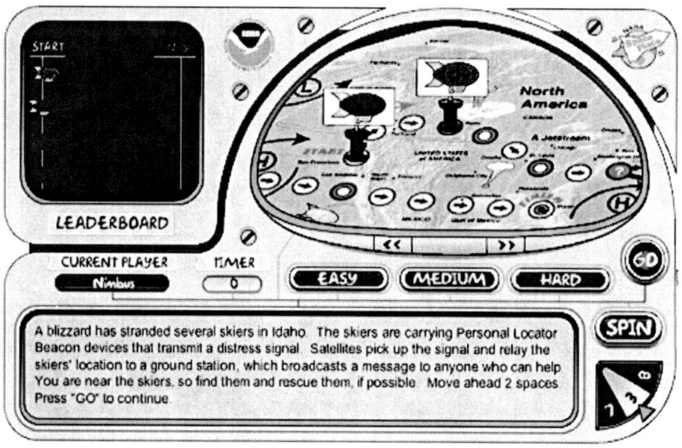

short game can deliver new facts and rules. In addition to facts and rules, complex and long games aim to deliver specific procedures and complex relationships to players. Playing complex games such as adventure, RPG, and simulation games can support obtaining knowledge from simple to higher order skills. To use games in class for teaching new concepts, teachers need to map the goals of a game to the objectives of their curriculum in order to insert the game most effectively into designed learning activities.

- **Manipulating and Observing.** When the learning objective is to explore the relationship between variables and to get acquainted with the real world, a simulation game is recommended. Most simulation games aim for transfer to real life with a savings of space and cost. In classroom teaching, teachers can use simulation games for scientific exploration as well as indirect real-life experiences.

In Buzz Lightyear, astronauts experiment with a variety of toys on the International Space Station to help students understand microgravity.

In this activity, players write about how a certain toy behaves on Earth; then they predict how that same toy will behave in the microgravity environment of space. The players can watch footage from space showing astronauts using the toys to determine if the predictions are correct. Thus, players research facts about astronomy, space exploration, space exploration history, space vehicles, or another space-related subject. Then, they create a board or card game that they can play with friends or classmates.

To Strengthen What is Learned

For a game to be used for this purpose, the learning content of a game should be open and divergent. This means that the game should carry various topics related to what players have learned. Therefore, the game should emphasize closely related inter-subjects and be adapted to the needs and interests of individual players. The game should hold content for interpretation, understanding, and generalization rather than presenting detailed concepts and facts. So the game has to present further and successive studies for players.

Civilization is used to deliver understanding about a particular subject or content area. Players learn about history in detail through playing Civilization. When games are used this way, students must be provided with opportunities for reflection on and discussion of the content

Figure 7. Buzz Lightyear (http://www.nasa.gov/externalflash/Buzz_Lightyear/web/)

in spaces external to the game in order to allow students to see the game as part of a larger body of knowledge on that subject (Klopfer, Osterweil, & Salen, 2009).

Civilization is a turn-based game in which the player builds an empire from very limited initial resources. All standard full-length games begin in 4,000 BC with a settler who builds a single city. From there, the player expands an empire while contending with rival nations, using the geography, developing infrastructure, and encouraging scientific and cultural progress. By default, players can win the game by accomplishing one of five goals: conquering all other civilizations, controlling a supermajority of the world's land and population, being the first to land a sleeper ship in the Alpha Centauri star system, increasing the Culture ratings of three different cities to "legendary" levels, or by being declared "World Leader" by winning a popularity election through

Figure 8. Civilization 4 (http://www.2kgames.com/civ4/)

the United Nations. If the game's clock runs out (by default in the year 2050 AD) with none of these goals fulfilled by any nation, the nation with the highest score is declared the winner (http://en.wikipedia.org/wiki/Civilization_IV).

To Summarize and Evaluate What is Learned

Games can be used effectively to summarize what is learned by presenting a clear summary with fascinating elements such as simulations and animations. A player's achievement can also be evaluated using a simple puzzle and/or quiz embedded in an adventure game or a role playing game. At the end of gaming, players are given feedback which will be used as a clue for deciding the subsequent learning path.

SGLL ProjectX is to be used to supplement class-work and consolidate what students have already learned, including reading, aural comprehension, and written responses.

The approach used in this project is to use a series of mini-games linked by a common theme. Each mini-game maps to the curriculum.

Obstacles/Solutions for Using Games in Classrooms

Previous surveys revealed that there are some obstacles to using games in classroom settings. Aside from technical and financial limitations, frequently mentioned obstacles are the limited time span of individual classes, lack of verification, a lack of support materials, a lack of time to familiarize, curriculum unsuitability, and loss of learning momentum (Kirriemuir and McFarlane, 2003; De Freitas, 2006; Gros, 2007; Sandford, Ulicsak, Facer, and Rudd, 2006).

The limited time span of individual classes makes it hard to insert a game into the curriculum plan; this situation favors games where the student is immediately learning. The teacher has to be aware of the time that is likely to be spent on learning complex controls, playing through irrelevant content, or watching videos unrelated to learning. Teachers also have to be aware that frequently "learning momentum" is lost because some games are closed environments in which there are no options to continue or explore further. In addition, the content of a game should be accurate and appropriate in order to be used in the class.

Figure 9. SGLL ProjectX: European language learning game (http://sgllprojectx.blogspot.com/)

To address these kinds of challenges, support materials for teachers need to be provided. These materials include descriptions of scenarios that can be enacted through the game, methods of evaluating the player's performance, and cases or exercises for the players to work through. Teachers need much time to familiarize themselves with the educational components of the game. Games can be used appropriately in the class when they fit into ongoing curriculum activities. Thus, versions of games need to be tailored to the curriculum so that they can be mapped onto it.

Suggestion: Design First, Above All

There is no straightforward guideline on how to use a game effectively in classroom settings. This is because teachers should reflect on their behaviors and do formative evaluation on their teaching with games when they are trying to use a game in their classroom. They need to keep indicators of good teaching and learning with games in mind such as:

- Did the game provide players with fun?
- Did the participants think of themselves as learners/trainees or players?
- Were they enthusiastic?
- Would the players recommend the game to their colleagues?
- Did the game allow players to reflect?

Those indicators assume that learning with games places fun first and learning next. Strictly speaking, fun should precede learning. That is, fun should be emphasized more than learning and teaching with games. This is because players avoid those games which are not fun and therefore learning never happens in that case. The following diagram (Figure 10) is suggested as an instructional design for teaching with games in classroom settings.

For designing instruction that includes games, first of all, instructors should define learning objectives and map game characteristics to those. This mapping process can help instructors review the learning objectives and the target game's characteristics appropriate to their classes. Topics of learning, activities of learners, and time spans of the topic to be covered should be considered at this initial stage. Based on the objectives, instructors should also consider instructional variables

Figure 10. Instructional design for teaching with games in classroom settings

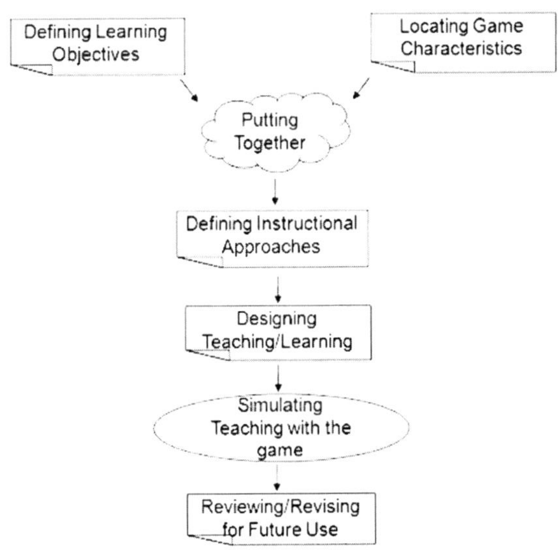

such as the motivational status of learners, summary and evaluation methods, as well as game characteristics such as internal structures, types of application, learner's activities with games, length of game, and number of players. Ideally, the designed teaching session is then simulated in order to find the advantages and disadvantages in implementing the planned game-based learning. In the last stage, self-reflection and colleague's reviews of the simulation are considered to alter the design of the game-based learning experience.

These suggested steps can help instructors determine the expected functions of the game and where the game will be used in the process of learning. In sum, in order to apply games in classroom settings, instructors need to take teaching, learning, and gaming conditions all into consideration.

REFERENCES

Brown, E. (1995). *That's Edutainment!* New York: Osborne McGraw-Hill.

De Freitas, S. (2006). *JISC Learning in Immersive worlds: a review of game based learning. A Report*. Retrieved July 31, 2006, from http://www.jisc.ac.uk/media/documents/programmes/elearning_innovation/gaming report_v3.3.pdf

Gros, B. (2007). Digital Games in Education: The Design of Game-Based Learning Environments. *Journal of Research on Technology in Education*, *40*(1), 23–38.

Kirriemuir, J., & McFarlane, A. (2003 November). Use of Computer and Video Games in the Classroom. In *Proceedings of 2003 Level Up Conference*. Retrieved October 6, 2007, from http://digra.org:8080/Plone/dl/db/05150.28025.pdf

Klopfer, E., Osterweil, S., & Salen, K. (2009). *Moving learning games forward*. The Education Arcade, Massachusetts Institute of Technology.

Lepper, M. R., & Chabay, R. W. (1985). Intrinsic motivation and instruction: Conflicting views on the role of motivational processes in computer-based education. *Educational Psychologist*, *20*, 217–231. doi:10.1207/s15326985ep2004_6

Malone, T. W. (1981). Toward a theory of intrinsically motivating instruction. *Cognitive Science*, *4*, 333–369.

Prensky, M. (2001). *Digital Game-Based Learning*. New York: McGraw-Hill.

Sandford, R., Ulicsak, M., Facer, K., & Rudd, T. (2006). *Teaching with Games: Using commercial off-the-shelf computer games in formal education*. Bristol, UK: Futurelab. Retrieved October 7, 2007, from http://www.futurelab.org.uk/resources/documents/project_reports/teaching_with_games/TWG_report.pdf

Wikipedia. (n.d.). *Civilization 4*. Retrieved from http://en.wikipedia.org/wiki/Civilization_IV

KEY TERMS AND DEFINITIONS

Intrinsic Game: An intrinsic game is a game in which learning content is integrated within the framework of the game. In this type of game, learning and gaming are closely related and both happen simultaneously.

Extrinsic Game: An extrinsic game is a game in which the scenario is separate or less integrated within the learning content. In this type of game, learning and gaming are independent activities.

Compilation of References

Aamodt, A., & Plaza, E. (1994). Case-Based Reasoning: Foundational Issues, Methodological Variations and Systems Approaches. *Artificial Intelligence Communications*, 7(1), 39–59.

Abdullah, M., et al. (2008). *Motivating Factors Associated with Adult Participation in Distance Learning Program*. Retrieved on August 28, 2009, from http://ccsenet.org/journal/index.php/ies/article/viewFile/629/604

Ainsworth, S. (2008). How do animations influence learning? In Robinson, D., & Schraw, G. (Eds.), *Current Perspectives on Cognition, Learning, and Instruction: Recent Innovations in Educational Technology that Facilitate Student Learning* (pp. 37–67). Charlotte, NC: Information Age Publishing.

Ajjan, H., & Hartshorne, R. (2008). Investigating faculty decisions to adopt Web 2.0 technologies: Theory and empirical tests. *The Internet and Higher Education*, *11*(2), 71–80. doi:10.1016/j.iheduc.2008.05.002

Akcan, S. (2005). Supporting Oral Second Language Use: A Learning Experience in a First Grade German Immersion Class. *Early Childhood Education Journal*, *32*(6), 359–364. doi:10.1007/s10643-005-0005-7

Aldrich, C. (2004). *Simulations and the future of learning*. San Francisco: Pfeiffer.

Aleburu, J. O. (2008). *Design and utilization of ICT-based instructional delivery system and students' learning outcomes in computer application course in Colleges of Education in Lagos*. Unpublished Ph.D. dissertation, University of Ibadan, Nigeria.

Alexander, P. A., Murphy, P. K., Woods, B. S., Duhon, K. E., & Parker, D. (1997). College instruction and concomitant changes in students' knowledge, interest, and strategy use: A study of domain learning. *Contemporary Educational Psychology*, *22*, 125–146. doi:10.1006/ceps.1997.0927

Alkan, C. (1995).Eğtim teknolojisi. Ankara, Atilla: Kitapevi.

Allen, S. (2005). *The Missing Link in Alternative Certification: Teacher Identity Formation*. Retrieved January 20, 2009, from http://www.umbc.edu/llc/llcreview/2005/Vol5_No1_Fall2005.pdf#page=3

Amory, A. (2007). Game object model version II: a theoretical framework for educational game development. *Etr& D-Educational Technology Research and Development*, *55*(1), 51–77. doi:10.1007/s11423-006-9001-x

Anderson, J. R., Conrad, F. G., & Corbett, A. T. (1989). Skill acquisition and the LISP tutor. *Cognitive Science*, *13*, 467–505.

Anderson, J. R., Corbett, A. T., Koedinger, K., & Pelletier, R. (1995). Cognitive tutors: Lessons learned. *Journal of the Learning Sciences*, *4*, 167–207. doi:10.1207/s15327809jls0402_2

Anderson, L. W., & Krathwohl, D. R. (Eds.). (2001). A taxonomy for learning, teaching and Assessing: A Revision of Bloom's Taxonomy of Educational Objectives: Complete Ed. New York: Longman.

Andrieu, B., & Bourgeois, I. (2003). Interaction enseignant-élèves au cours des TPE, les dynamiques du processus de structuration des connaissances [Teacher-student interaction during independent study projects: Dynamics in the process of structuring knowledge]. In C. Larcher & A. Crindal (Eds.), Structuration des connaissances et nouveaux dispositifs d'enseignement (pp. 40-45). Paris: Institut national de recherche pédagogique.

Appelman, R., & Goldsworthy, R. (1999). *The Juncture of Game & Instructional Design: Can Fun be Learning?* Paper presented at the Association for Educational Communications and Technology, Houston, TX.

APQC. (n.d.). Retrieved August 28, 2009, from http://www.apqc.org/portal/apqc/site.

Aremu, A. (2004). Knowledge of the Educational Implications of Computer Games by some student Teachers in Southwest Nigeria. *The Nigerian Journal of Guidance & Counselling, 9*(1), 16–24.

Aremu, A. (2008). Why are games effective? A look at the interaction patterns in a game based Mathematics classroom in Nigeria. In Gómez Chova, L., Martí Belenguer, D., & Candel Torres, I. (Eds.), *INTED 2008 conference proceedings*. Valencia, Spain: International Association of Technology, Education and Development IATED.

Aremu, A. (2008b). The Acquisition of Environmental Knowledge through the Development of Games in a Higher Degree Course in Nigeria. *The International Journal of Learning, 15*(5), 299–306.

Aremu, A., & Adefelu, J. A. (2005). Computer Assisted Instruction and Achievement of Girls in Integrated Science. *African Development Review, 1*(1&2), 34–37.

Aremu, A., & Ekine, F. (2003, October). *Parental Perception ofThe Educational Values ofToys in school processes*. Paper presented at the 2nd National Conference of the Active Learning and Leisure Libraries. Stellenbosch, Cape Town, South Africa.

Artino, A. R., Jr. (2008). *A brief analysis of research on problem-based learning*. Online submission. Retrieved April 12, 2009, from http://eric.ed.gov/ERICWebPortal/contentdelivery/servlet/ERICServlet?accno=ED501593

Asakawa, T., & Gilbert, N. (2003). Synthesizing Experiences: Lessons To Be Learned from Internet-Mediated Simulation Games. *Simulation & Gaming, 34*(1), 10–22. doi:10.1177/1046878102250455

Atkinson, R. (2002). Optimizing learning from example using animated pedagogical agents. *Journal of Educational Psychology, 94*, 416–427. doi:10.1037/0022-0663.94.2.416

Attwell. (2004). *E-Learning and Sustainability*. Retrieved on August 28, 2009, from http://lefo.net/lefo_sustainability_graham.htm.

Ausubel, D. P. (1968). *Educational Psychology: A Cognitive View*. New York: Holt, Rinehart & Winston.

Azevedo, R. (2005). Using hypermedia as a metacognitive tool for enhancing student learning? The role of self-regulated learning. *Educational Psychologist, 40*, 199–209. doi:10.1207/s15326985ep4004_2

Azevedo, R., & Bernard, R. M. (1995). A meta-analysis of the effect of feedback in computer-based instruction. *Journal of Educational Computing Research, 13*, 109–125.

Azevedo, R., & Cromley, J. G. (2004). Does training on self-regulated learning facilitate students' learning with hypermedia? *Journal of Educational Psychology, 96*, 523–535. doi:10.1037/0022-0663.96.3.523

Bachman, L. (1990). *Fundamental considerations in language testing*. New York: Oxford University Press.

Bachman, L., & Palmer, A. (1996). *Language teaching in practice*. New York: Oxford University Press.

Bacigalupa, C. (2005, August). The Use of Video Games by Kindergartners in a Family Child Care Setting. *Early Childhood Education Journal, 33*(1), 25–30. doi:10.1007/s10643-005-0016-4

Baek, Y. K. (2008). What hinders teachers in using computer and video games in the classroom? exploring factors inhibiting the uptake of computer and video games. *Cyberpsychology & Behavior, 11*(6), 665–671. doi:10.1089/cpb.2008.0127

Bain, C., & Newton, C. (2003). Art Games: Pre-Service Art Educators Construct Learning Experiences for the Elementary Art Classroom. *Art Education, 56*(5), 33–40.

Baker, A., Oh Navarro, E., & Van Der Hoek, A. (2004). An experimental card game for teaching software engineering processes. *Journal of Systems and Software*, *75*, 3–16. doi:10.1016/j.jss.2004.02.033

Baker, E. L., & Mayer, R. E. (1999). Computer-based assessment of problem solving. *Computers in Human Behavior*, *15*, 269–282. doi:10.1016/S0747-5632(99)00023-0

Baldaro, B., Tuozzi, G., Codispoti, M., & Montebarocci, O. (2004). Aggressive and non-violent videogames: short-term psychological and cardiovascular effects on habitual players. *Stress and Health*, *20*, 203–208. doi:10.1002/smi.1015

Bandura, A. (1986). *Social Foundations of Thought and Action.: A Social cognitive Theory*. Englewood Cliffs, NJ: Prentice Hall.

Bandura, A. (1997). *Self-efficacy: The exercise of control*. New York: W.H. Freeman.

Bandura, A. (2000). Self-efficacy: The foundation of agency. In Perig, W., & Grob, A. (Eds.), *Control of human behavior, mental processes, and consciousness: Essays in honor of the 60th birthday of August Flammer* (pp. 17–33). Mahwah, NJ: Erlbaum.

Barab, S., Thomas, M., Dodge, T., Carteaux, R., & Tuzun, H. (2005). Making Learning Fun: Quest Atlantis, A Game Without Guns. *ETR & D-Educational Technology Research and Development*, *53*(1), 86–107. doi:10.1007/BF02504859

Barnett, D. J., Everly, G. S. Jr, Parker, C. L., & Links, J. M. (2005). Applying educational gaming to public health workforce emergency preparedness. *American Journal of Preventive Medicine*, *28*(4), 490–495. doi:10.1016/j.amepre.2005.01.001

Barrows, H. S. (1985). *How to Design a Problem-Based Curriculum for the Preclinical Years*. New York: Springer Publishing Co.

Bartholow, B. D., Sestir, M. A., & Davis, E. B. (2005). Correlates and consequences of exposure to video game violence: hostile personality, empathy, and aggressive behavior. *Personality and Social Psychology Bulletin*, *31*(11), 1573–1586. doi:10.1177/0146167205277205

Barton, M. D. (2004, March). Gay characters in videogames. *Armchair Arcade*. Retrieved April 10, 2008, from http://www.armchairarcade.com/neo/node/305

Bastruk, R. (2005). The effectiveness of Computer-assisted Instruction in teaching Introductory Statistics. *Educational Technology & Society*, *8*(2), 170–178.

Batson, L., & Feinberg, S. (2006). Game Designs that Enhance Motivation and Learning for Teenagers. *Electronic Journal for the Integration of Technology in Education*, *5*, 34–43.

Baylor, A. L., & Kim, Y. (2005). Simulating instructional roles through pedagogical agents. *International Journal of Artificial Intelligence in Education*, *15*, 95–115.

Becker, K. (2005). How Are Games Educational? Learning Theories Embodied in Games. *Proceedings of DIGRA 2005 Conference: Changing Views – Worlds in Play*.

Becker, K., & Parker, J. R. (2005, Oct 13-15). *All I ever needed to know about programming, I learned from re-writing classic arcade games*. Paper presented at the Future Play: The International Conference on the Future of Game Design and Technology, East Lansing, MI.

Becta. (2001). *Computer Games in Education Project: Findings Report*. Retrieved July 2008, from http://partners.becta.org.uk/index.php?section=rh&rid=13595

BECTA. (2001). *Computer Games in Education Project: Report*. Retrieved August 19, 2009, from http://partners.becta.org.uk/index.php?section=rh&rid=13595

Bennett, W. L. (2008). Changing citizenship in the digital age. In Bennett, W. L. (Ed.), *Civic life online: Learning how digital media can engage youth* (pp. 1–24). Cambridge, MA: The MIT Press.

Benyon, D., Turner, P., & Turner, S. (2005). *Designing Interactive Systems*. Harlow, UK: Addison Wesley.

Bereiter, C., & Bird, M. (1985). Use of thinking aloud in identification and teaching of reading comprehension strategies. *Cognition and Instruction*, *2*, 131–156. doi:10.1207/s1532690xci0202_2

Bereiter, C., & Scardamalia, M. (1985). Cognitive coping strategies and the problem of 'inert knowledge. In Chipman, S. F., Segal, J. W., & Glaser, R. (Eds.), *Thinking and learning skills: Current research and open questions* (pp. 65–80). Hillsdale, NJ: Lawrence Erlbaum Associates.

Berger, A. (2006, January 31). Neverwinter Nights in the Classroom. *University of Minnesota News*. Retrieved April 30, 2008, from http://www1.umn.edu/umnnews/Feature_Stories/22Neverwinter_Nights22_in_the_classroom.html

Bergmann, W., & Hüther, G. (2006). *Computersüchtig. Kinder im Sog der modernen Medien*. Düsseldorf: Walter Verlag.

Bers, M. U. (2008). Civic identities, online technologies: From designing civic curriculum to supporting civic experiences. In Bennett, W. L. (Ed.), *Civic Life Online: Learning How Digital Media Can Engage Youth* (pp. 139–160). Cambridge, MA: The MIT Press.

Biggs, W. D. (1978). A comparison of ranking and relational grading procedures in a general management simulation. *Simulation & Games*, *9*(2), 185–200. doi:10.1177/104687817800900204

Birgin, O., Çathoğlu, H., Coştu, S., & Aydin, S. (2009). The investigation of the views of student mathematics teachers towards computer assisted mathematics instruction. *Procedia Social and Behavioural Sciences*, *1*, 676–680. doi:10.1016/j.sbspro.2009.01.118

Birnbaum, R. (1982). Games and simulations in higher education. *Simulation & Games*, *13*(1), 3–11. doi:10.1177/104687818201300101

Biswas, G., Leelawong, K., Belynne, K., & Adebiyi, B. (2005). Case studies in learning by teaching behavioral differences in directed versus guided learning. In *Proceedings of the 27th Annual Conference of the Cognitive Science Society*, Stresa, Italy (pp. 828-833).

Björk, S., & Holopainen, J. (2004 October). Describing games: an interaction-centric structural framework. In M. Copier & J. Raessens (Eds.), *Level Up – CD-ROM Proceedings of Digital Games Research Conference 2003*. Retrieved from http://www.playresearch.com/publications/2003/structuralframework.pdf

Blejec, A. (n.d.). *Teaching statistics by using simulations on the Internet*. Retrieved August 15, 2008, from http://www.ph-ludwigsburg.de/iase/proceedings/Invited%20Papers%20refereed/Blejec.pdf

Bliss, J., & Ogborn, J. (1989). Tools for Exploratory Learning. A Research Programme. *Journal of Computer Assisted Learning*, *5*, 37–50. doi:10.1111/j.1365-2729.1989.tb00196.x

Blizzard Entertainment. (2008a). *Intro to WoW*. Retrieved September 29, 2008 from http://www.worldofwarcraft.com/info/beginners/index.html

Blizzard Entertainment. (2008b). Joining guilds. Retrieved September 29, 2008 from http://www.worldofwarcraft.com/info/basics/joiningguilds.html

Blizzard Entertainment. (2009c). What's a guild? Retrieved April 7, 2009 from http://www.worldofwarcraft.com/info/basics/guilds.html

Blizzard Entertainment. (2009d). Create guild rules. Retrieved April 7, 2009 from http://www.worldofwarcraft.com/info/basics/guildleadership.html

Bloom, B. S. (1956). *Taxonomy of educational objectives: The classification of educational goals, Handbook 1: Cognitive domain*. New York: McKay.

Bloom, B., & Krathwohl, D. R. (1956). *Taxonomy of educational objectives: the classification of educational goals, by a Committee of College and University Examiners. Handbook 1: Cognitive Domain*. New York: Longmans, Green.

Blouin, M., & Bergeron, C. (1997). Dictionnaire de la réadaptation, tome 2: termes d'intervention et d'aides techniques. Québec: Les Publications du Québec.

Blum, H. T., & Yocom, D. J. (1996). A fun alternative: Using instructional games to foster student learning. *Teaching Exceptional Children*, *29*(2), 80–63.

Blumberg, F. C., & Sokol, L. M. (2004). Boys and girls use of cognitive strategy when learning to play video games. *The Journal of General Psychology*, *131*(2), 151–158. doi:10.3200/GENP.131.2.151-158

Boekaerts, M., Pintrich, P., & Zeidner, M. (2000). *Handbook of self-regulation*. San Diego, CA: Academic Press.

Borsook, T. K., & Higginbotham-Wheat, N. (1991). Interactivity: What is it and what can it do for computer-based instruction. *Educational Technology, 31*(10), 11–17.

Boseman, G., & Schellenberger, R. (1974). Business gaming: An empirical appraisal. *Simulation & Games, 5*(4), 383–402. doi:10.1177/104687817400500403

Boyle, E., & Connolly, T. M. (2008). Gamer for Learning: Does Gender Make a Difference? In Connolly, T. M., Stansfield, M. H., & Boyle, E. (Eds.), *Games-based Learning Advancement for Multisensory Human Computer Interface Techniques and Effective Practices*. Hershey, PA: Idea-Group Publishing.

Bransford, J. D., Brown, A. L., & Cocking, R. R. (2000). *How people learn*. Washington, DC: National Academy Press.

Braskamp, L. A., & Hodgetts, R. (1971). The Role of an Objective Evaluation Model in Simulation Gaming. *Simulation & Games, 2*(2), 197–212. doi:10.1177/003755007122005

Bredemeier, M., & Greenblat, C. (1981). The educational effectiveness of simulation games. *Simulation & Games, 12*(3), 307–332. doi:10.1177/104687818101200304

Brenenstuhl, D. (1975). Cognitive versus affective gains in computer simulations. *Simulation & Games, 6*(3), 303–311. doi:10.1177/003755007563004

Brenenstuhl, D. C., & Blalack, R. O. (1978). Role preference and vested interest in a bargaining environment. *Simulation & Games, 9*(1), 53–64. doi:10.1177/003755007891004

Brien, R. (1994). *Science cognitive et formation*. Québec, Canada: Presses de l'Université du Québec.

British Educational Communications and Technology Agency (BECTA). (2001). *Computer Games in Education Project*. Retrieved December 30, 2008, from http://www.becta.org.uk

British Legends. (2005). *Multi-User Dugeon (MUD)*. Retrieved August 19, 2009, from http://www.jisc.ac.uk/media/documents/publications/seriousvirtualworldsv1.pdf

Brown, D. (2007). *Principles of Language Learning and Teaching* (5th ed.). New York: Pearson Longman.

Brown, E. (1995). *That's Edutainment!* New York: Osborne McGraw-Hill.

Bruner, J. (1986). *Actual minds, possible words*. Cambridge, MA: Harvard University.

Bruner, J. S. (1966). *Toward a Theory of Instruction*. Oxford, UK: Oxford University Press.

Brunning, R., Schraw, G., Norby, M., & Ronning, R. (2004). *Cognitive psychology and instruction*. Upper Saddle River, NJ: Prentice Hall.

Buckley, K. E., & Anderson, C. A. (2006). A Theoretical Model of the Effects and Consequences of Playing Video Games. In Vonderer, P., & Bryant, J. (Eds.), *Playing Video Games - Motives, Responses, and Consequences* (pp. 363–378). Mahwah, NJ: LEA.

Burgos, D., & Specht, M. (2006). Adaptive e-learning methods and IMS Learning Design. An integrated approach. In Proceedings of ICALT2006, Kerkrade, Holland.

Burkhardt, G., Monsour, M., Valdez, G., Gunn, C., Dawson, M., Lemke, C., et al. (2003). *enGauge 21st century skills: Literacy in the digital age*. Retrieved November 22, 2007, from http://www.grec.ky.gov/SLC_grant/Engauge21st_Century_Skills.pdf

Burstein, J. (2003). The *e-rater* scoring engine: Automated essay scoring with natural language processing. In Shermis, M. D., & Burstein, J. (Eds.), *Automated essay scoring: A cross-disciplinary perspective* (pp. 113–124). Hillsdale, NJ: Erlbaum.

Byers, C. (2009). Digital simulations for improving education. In Gibson, D., & Baek, Y. K. (Eds.), *Digital simulations for improving education: Learning through artificial teaching environments*. Hershey, PA: Information Science Reference.

Byrne, B. (1998). *The foundations of literacy: The child's acquisition of the alphabetic principle.* Hove, UK: Psychology Press.

Cadotte, E. (1995). Business Simulations: The Next Step in Management Training. Selections, Graduate Management Admission Council, (Autumn), 8-19.

California State Board of Education. (n.d.). *Kindergarten English-language arts content standards.* Retrieved June 19, 2009, from http://www.cde.ca.gov/be/st/ss/documents/elacontentstnds.pdf

Can, G., & Cagiltay, K. (2006). Turkish Prospective Teachers' Perceptions Regarding the Use of Computer Games with Educational Features. *Educational Technology & Society, 9*(1), 308–321.

Cantin, F., Delage, M., Sauvé, L., Renaud, L., & Gauvin, M. (2006). *Le jeu ITS: Stopper la transmission [STIs: Stopping the transmission Game].* Québec: SAVIE - Carrefour Virtuel de Jeux Éducatifs. Retrieved from http://www.savie.qc.ca/CarrefourJeux2/Site/Jeux/ Parchesi/infoParchesi.Asp?NoPartie=255.

Caravolas, M., Hulme, C., & Snowling, M. G. (2001). The foundations of spelling ability: Evidence from a 3-year longitudinal study. *Journal of Memory and Language, 45*, 751–774. doi:10.1006/jmla.2000.2785

Carbonaro, M., Cutumisu, M., McNaughton, M., Onuczko, C., Roy, T., Schaeffer, J., et al. (2005). *Interactive story writing in the classroom: Using computer games.* Paper presented at the DiGRA 2005 Conference, Vancouver, Canada.

Cassell, J., & Jenkins, H. (Eds.). (1998). *From Barbie to Mortal Kombat.* Boston: The MIT Press.

Castronova, E. (2005). On the research value of large games: Natural experiments in Norrath and Camelot. *CESifo Working Paper Series No. 1621.* Retrieved June 26, 2009 from http://ssrn.com/abstract=875571

Center for Civic Education. (1994). *National standards for civics and government.* Calabasas, CA: Author.

Cesarone, B. (1998). *Video Games: Research, ratings, recommendations.* Chiago: ERIC Clearinghouse on Elementary and Early Childhood Education.

Chapman, K. J., & Sorge, C. (1999 March). Can a Simulation Help Achieve Course Objectives? An Exploratory Study Investigating Differences Among Instructional Tools. *Journal of Business Education*, 225-230.

Chen, S., & Michael, D. (2005). Proof of Learning: Assessment in Serious Games. *Gamasutra.* Retrieved December 20, 2008, from http://www.gamasutra.com/features/20051019/chen_01.shtml

Cheong, Y., & Young, R. M. (2006). A Computational model of Narrative Generation for Suspense. *Proceedings of AAAI 2006 Workshop on Computational Aesthetics.*

Chickering, A. W., Ehrmann, S. E. (1996). Implementing the seven principles: Technology as lever. *AAHE Bulletin*, October, 3-6.

Childress, M. D., & Braswell, R. (2006). Using massively multiplayer online role-playing games for online learning. *Distance Education, 27*(2), 187–196. doi:10.1080/01587910600789522

Clark, L., Lawrence, A. J., Astley-Jones, F., & Gray, N. (2009). Gambling near-misses enhance motivation to gamble and recruit win-related brain circuitry. *Neuron, 61*(3), 481–490. doi:10.1016/j.neuron.2008.12.031

Clark, R. (2003). *Building expertise.* Silver Spring, MD: International Society for Performance Improvement.

Clark, R. C., & Mayer, R. E. (2007). e-Learning and the Science of Instruction (2nd Ed.). San Francisco: Pfeiffer.

Clark, R., Ngyuyen, F., & Sweller, J. (2006). *Efficiency in learning: Evidence-based guidelines to manage cognitive load.* New York: John Wiley & Sons.

Claro, M. (2007). *OECD background papers for OECD-ENLACES expert meeting: Video games and education.* Retrieved March 16, 2009, from http://www.oecd.org/dataoecd/14/60/39548100.pdf

Cole, H., & Griffiths, M. D. (2007). Social interactions in massively multiplayer online role-playing gamers. *Cyberpsychology & Behavior, 10*(4), 575–583. doi:10.1089/cpb.2007.9988

Cole, R. V. S., Pellom, B., Hacioglu, K., Ma, J., Movellan, J., & Schwartz, S. (2003). Perceptive animated interfaces: first steps toward a new paradigm for human-computer interaction. *Proceedings of the IEEEE: Special Issue on Human-Computer Multimodal Interface, 91*(9), 1391–1405.

Collins, A. (1991). Cognitive apprenticeship and instructional technology. In Idol, L., & Jones, B. F. (Eds.), *Educational values and cognitive instructions: Implications for reform*. Hillsdale, NJ: Erlbaum.

Combs, S. (2008). Current trends in the media industry: File production, television commercials and video games. *The Current and Potential Economic and Fiscal Impacts of Texas' Moving Media Industry*. Texas Controller of Public Account report.

Conati, C. (2002). Probabilistic assessment of user's emotions in educational games. *Journal of Applied Artificial Intelligence, 16*, 555–575. doi:10.1080/08839510290030390

Corbett, A. T. (2001). Cognitive computer tutors: Solving the two-sigma problem. *User modeling: Proceedings of the 8th International Conference* (pp. 137-147). Berlin: Springer.

Corbett, A. T., & Anderson, J. R. (1990). The effect of feedback control on learning to program with the lisp tutor. In *Proceedings of the Twelfth Annual Conference of the Cognitive Science Society* (pp. 796-803). Austin, TX: Cognitive Society.

Corbett, A. T., & Anderson, J. R. (2001). Locus of feedback control in computer-based tutoring: Impact on learning rate, achievement and attitudes. In *Conference on Human Factors in Computing Systems* (pp. 245-252). New York: ACM Press.

Cordova, D. I., & Lepper, M. R. (1996). Intrinsic motivation and the process of learning: Beneficial effects of contextualization, personalization, and choice. *Journal of Educational Psychology, 88*, 715–730. doi:10.1037/0022-0663.88.4.715

Coventry Evening Telegraph. (2002). *Computer games can help children develop*. Retrieved March 26, 2009, from http://www.highbeam.com/doc/1G1-84164174.html

Craig, S., Graesser, A. C., Sullins, J., & Gholson, B. (2004). Affect and learning: An exploratory look into the role of affect in learning. *Journal of Educational Media, 29*, 241–250.

Cranton, C. (1994). *Understanding and Promoting Transformative Learning* (pp. 3–21). San Francisco: Jossey-Bass.

Cranton, P. (1994). Self-directed and transformative instructional development. *The Journal of Higher Education, 65*(6), 726–744. doi:10.2307/2943826

Crawford, C. (2003). *Chris Crawford on Game Design*. Carmel, IN: New Riders Publishing.

Crawford, C. (2004, July 14). *A-Ritzer-Encyclopedia*. Retrieved September 28, 2009, from http://www.sagepub.com/upm-data/5222_Ritzer__Entries_beginning_with_A__%5B1%5D.pdf.

Crookall, D. (1986). Human and computer involvement in simulation. *Simulation & Games, 17*(3), 345–375. doi:10.1177/0037550086173005

Csikszentmihaly, M. (1990). *Flow, the psychology of optimal experience*. New York: Harper Collins.

Csikszentmihalyi, M. (1991). *Flow: The Psychology of Optimal Experience*. New York: Harper Perennial.

Csikszentmihalyi, M. (1992). *Flow: the Psychology of Happiness*. London: Random House.

Cuban, L. (2001). *Oversold and overused: computers in the classroom*. Cambridge, MA: Harvard University Press.

D'Mello, S. K., Taylor, R., & Graesser, A. C. (2007). Monitoring affective trajectories during complex learning. In D. S. McNamara & J. G. Trafton (Eds.), *Proceedings of the 29th Annual Cognitive Science Society* (pp. 203-208). Austin, TX: Cognitive Science Society.

Davidson, C., & Goldberg, D. (2009). *The Future of Learning Institutions in a Digital Age*. Chicago, IL: John D. & Catherine T. MacArthur Foundation.

De Freitas, S. (2006). *JISC Learning in Immersive worlds: a review of game based learning. A Report.* Retrieved July 31, 2006, from http://www.jisc.ac.uk/media/documents/programmes/elearning_innovation/gaming report_v3.3.pdf

De Freitas, S. (2008). *Serious Virtual Worlds: a scoping study.* Prepared for the JISC e-Learning Programme. Retrieved August 19, 2009, from http://www.jisc.ac.uk/media/documents/publications/seriousvirtualworldsv1.pdf

De Freitas, S., & Martin, O. (2006). How can exploratory learning with games and simulations within the curriculum be most effectively evaluated? *Computers & Education, 46*(3), 249–264. doi:10.1016/j.compedu.2005.11.007

De Grandmont, N. (2005) *Pédagogie du jeu...philosophie du ludique* [Game pedagogy... ludic philosophy]. Retrieved from http://cf.geocities.com/ndegrandmont/index.htm.

De la Cruz, R. E., Cage, C. E., & Lian, M.-G. J. (2000). Let's play mancala and sungka! *Teaching Exceptional Children, 32*(2), 38–42.

Dede, C. (1995). 21st Century. In *Committee on Science and Committee on Economics and Educational Opportunities* (pp. 1–10). Testimony to the U.S Congress, House of Representatives, Joint Hearing on Educational Technology in the.

DeKanter, N. (2004). Gaming redefines interactivity for learning. *TechTrends, 29*(3), 26–31. doi:10.1007/BF02763644

deKanter, N. (2007, July). *A guild-ed future: Lessons in leadership from massively multiplayer on-line games.* Paper presented at the 2nd James F. Ackerman Colloquium on Technology and Citizenship Education, W. Lafayette, IN.

Delwiche, A. (2006). Massively multiplayer online games (MMOS)) in the new media classroom. *Educational Technology & Society, 9*(3), 160–172.

Dena, C. (2008). *ARG Stats.* Retrieved November 9, 2008, from http://www.christydena.com/online-essays/arg-stats/

Detweiler, R. (2004, July 9). At last, we can replace lectures. *The Chronicle Review.*

Dewey, J. (1938). *Experience and education.* New York: The Macmillan Company.

Dexter, S. (2006). Educational theory into practice software. In Gibson, D., Aldrich, C., & Prensky, M. (Eds.), *Games and simulations in online learning: Research & development frameworks.* Hershey, PA: Idea Group.

Dey, A. K., Abowd, G. D., & Salber, D. (2001). A conceptual framework and a toolkit for supporting the rapid prototyping of context-aware applications. *Human-Computer Interaction, 16*(2-4), 97–166. doi:10.1207/S15327051HCI16234_02

Dick, W., & Carey, L. (1996). *The systematic design of instruction* (4th ed.). New York: Harper Collins College Publishers.

Dictionary.com. (2008). *Citizenship* definition. Retrieved on February 8, 2008, from http://dictionary.reference.com/browse/citizenship

Dijkstra, S. (1991). Instructional design models and the representation of knowledge and skills. *Educational Technology, 31*(6), 19–26.

Dodds, P., & Fletcher, J. D. (2004). Opportunities for new 'smart' learning environments enabled by next-generation web capabilities. *Journal of Educational Multimedia and Hypermedia, 13*, 391–404.

Donahue, D., Daane, M., & Grigg, W. (2003). *The Nation's Report Card: Reading Highlights 2003 (NCES 2004-452). U.S. Department of Education, National Center for Education Statistics.* Washington, DC: U.S. Government Printing Office.

Douglass, J. (2007). *Command lines: Aesthetics and technique in interactive fiction and new media.* Dissertation, University of California, Santa Barbara.

Dreyfus, H. (2004). *A Phenomenoloy of Skill Acquisition as the basis for a Merleau-Pontian Non-representationalist Cognitive Science.* Retrieved May 2006 from http://socrates.berkeley.edu/~hdreyfus/html/papers.html

Droge, c., & Spreng, R. (1996). Enhancing involvement and skills with a student-led method of case analysis. *Journal of Marketing Education, 18, 25-34.*

Ducheneaut, N., & Moore, R. J. (2005). *More than just 'XP': Learning social skills in massively multiplayer online games.* Retrieved February 27, 2009, from http://www2.parc.com/csl/members/nicolas/documents/ITSE.pdf

Dufeu, B. (1994). *Teaching myself.* Oxford: Oxford University Press.

Duke, C. R., & Reese, R. M. (1995). A case study in curriculum evaluation using strategic and tactical assessments. *Journal of Education for Business, 70*, 344–353.

Duke, R. D., & Kemeny, N. (1989). Keeping Score, One Score Later: Two decades of the Simulation & Games Journal. *Simulation & Games, 20*(2), 165–183. doi:10.1177/104687818902000204

Dukes, R., & Mattley, C. (1986). The effects of social structure and mobility on attitudes and behavior in a simulated society. *Simulation & Games, 17*(3), 467–484. doi:10.1177/0037550086174005

Durkin, K., & Barber, B. (2002). Not so doomed: Computer game play and positive adolescent development. *Journal of Applied Developmental Psychology, 23*, 373–392. doi:10.1016/S0193-3973(02)00124-7

Dynarski, M., Agodini, R., Heaviside, S., Novak, T., Carey, N., & Campuzano, L. (2007). *Effectiveness of reading and mathematics software products: Findings from the first student cohort.* Washington, DC: U.S. Department of Education, Institute of Education Sciences.

Eckersley, C., Richards, C., & Schofield, N. (2004). Evaluation of a Learning Object. *World Conference on Educational Multimedia, Hypermedia and Telecommunications,* 1, 3718-3720.

Egenfeldt-Nielsen, S. (2005). *Beyond edutainment.* Unpublished Doctoral dissertation, IT-University of Copenhagen, Denmark. Retrieved March 22, 2006, from http://www.it-c.dk/people/sen/egenfeldt.pdf

Egenfeldt-Nielsen, S. (2006). *Overview of research on the educational use of video games.* Retrieved March 16, 2009, from http://www.itu.dk/people/sen/papers/game-overview.pdf

Egunjobi, A. O. (2002). *The Relative Effectiveness of Computer assisted Instructional modes on student's learning outcomes in Geography.* Unpublished Ph.D. dissertation, University of Ibadan, Nigeria.

Ehri, L. (1998). Learning to read and learning to spell are one and the same, almost. In Perfetti, C., Rieben, L., & Fayol, M. (Eds.), *Learning to spell* (pp. 237–269). Mahwah, NJ: Lawrence Erlbaum.

Ellis, R. (1985). Teacher-pupil interaction in second-language development. In Gass, S. M., & Madden, C. (Eds.), *Input in second language acquisition* (pp. 69–85). Rowley, MA: Newbury House.

Engle, S., & Ochoa, A. (1988). *Education for democratic citizenship: Decision making in the social studies.* New York: Teachers College Press.

Entertainment Software (ESA). (2004). *ESA'S 2004 Essentials facts about the computer and video game industry.* Retrieved April 9, 2005, from http://www.theesa.com/files/EFBrochure.pdf

ESA. (2008). *Essential facts about the computer and video game industry.* Washington, DC: Entertainment Software Association. Retrieved August 1, 2008, from http://www.theesa.com/facts/pdfs/ESA_EF_2008.pdf

ESA. (2009). *Essential facts about the computer and video game industry.* Washington, DC: Entertainment Software Association. Retrieved August 1, 2009, from http://www.theesa.com/facts/pdfs/ESA_EF_2009.pdf

Evreinova, T., Evreinova, G, & Raisamo, R. (2006). An alternative approach to strengthening tactile memory for sensory disabled people. *Universal Access in the Information Society*, 1-10.

Facer, K. (2001). *Children's Out of School Uses of Computers. A Report for the InterActive Education Project.* Retrieved December 30, 2008, from http://www.interactiveeducation.ac.uk/school.pdf

Faria, A. J. (1987). A survey of the use of business games in academia and business. *Simulation & Games*, *18*(2), 207–224.

FAS. (2006). Harnessing the power of video games for learning. In *Summit on Educational Games 2006*. Retrieved July 2008, from http://fas.org/gamesummit/Resources/Summit%20on%20Educational%20Games.pdf

Ferdig, R. E. (Ed.). (2009). *Handbook of research on effective electronic gaming in education*. Hershey, PA: Idea Group.

Fernandes, R., & Simon, H. A. (1999). A study of how individuals solve complex and ill-structured problems. *Policy Sciences*, *32*(3), 225–244. doi:10.1023/A:1004668303848

Ferry, B., Kervin, L., Cambourne, B., Turbill, J., Hedberg, J., & Jonassen, D. (2005). Incorporating real experience into the development of a classroom-based simulation. *Journal of Learning Design*, *1*(1), 22–32.

Flanagan, C. A., Syvertsen, A. K., & Stout, M. D. (2007) Civic Measurement Models: Tapping Adolescents' Civic Engagement. *Circle Working Paper 55*. Retrieved June 26, 2009 from http://www.eric.ed.gov/ERICWebPortal/contentdelivery/servlet/ERICServlet?accno=ED497602

Fletcher, J. D. (2003). Evidence for learning from technology-assisted instruction. In O'Neil, H. F. Jr, & Perez, R. (Eds.), *Technology applications in education: A learning view* (pp. 79–99). Hillsdale, NJ: Lawrence Erlbaum Associates.

Fletcher, J. D., & Tobias, S. (2007). What research has to say about designing computer games for learning. *Educational Technology Magazine*, *47*, 20–29.

Foltz, P. W., Gilliam, S., & Kendall, S. (2000). Supporting content-based feedback in online writing evaluation with LSA. *Interactive Learning Environments*, *8*, 111–129. doi:10.1076/1049-4820(200008)8:2;1-B;FT111

Fournier, M., Vincent, S., Brougère, G. et al. (2004). À quoi sert le jeu? [What use are games?] *Sciences humaines*, 152, 19-45.

France, W., & McClure, J. (1972 June). Building a Child Care Staff Learning Game. *Simulation and Game*, 189-202.

Frean, A., & Woolcock, N. (2007, December 6). Overhaul of primary schools as progress in 3Rs grinds to a halt. *Times Online*. Retrieved December 2007, from http://www.timesonline.co.uk/tol/life_and_style/education/article3007334.ece

Frété, C. (2002). *Le potentiel du jeu vidéo pour l'éducation. Mémoire de maîtrise. Université de Genève Faculté de Psychologie et des Sciences de l'Education, TECFA*. Technologies de la Formation et de l'Apprentissage.

Friedman, A. M. (2006). State standards and digital primary sources: A divergence. *Contemporary Issues in Technology & Teacher Education*, *6*(3). Retrieved from http://www.citejournal.org/vol6/iss3/socialstudies/article1.cfm.

Friedman, T. L. (2005). *The world is flat: A brief history of the twenty-first century*. New York: Farrar, Straus, and Giroux.

Fukuchi, S. G., Offutt, L. A., Sacks, J., & Mann, B. D. (2000). Teaching a Multidisciplinary Approach to Cancer Treatment during Surgical Clerkship via an Interactive Board Game, Association for Surgical Education. *American Journal of Surgery*, *179*, 337–340. doi:10.1016/S0002-9610(00)00339-1

Gagne, R. (1977). *The Conditions of Learning*. New York: Holt.

Gagne, R. M., & Briggs, L. J. (1974). *Principles of instructional design*. New York: Holt, Rinehart, and Winston, Inc.

Gagné, R. M., Wager, W. W., Golas, K. C., & Keller, J. M. (2005). *Principles of Instructional Design* (5th ed.). Orlando, FL: Harcourt Brace.

Galarneau, L. (2005). Spontaneous Communities of Learning: Learning Ecosystems in Massively Multiplayer Online Gaming Environments. *Paper for Digra Conference*. Retrieved October 2, 2008 from http://www.digra.org/dl/db/06278.10422.pdf

Galarneau, L., & Zibit, M. (2006). *Online games for 21st century skills*. Retrieved October 15, 2007, from http://lisa.socialstudygames.com/Galarneau_Zibit_OnlineGames.pdf

Gallager, W. (2009). *Rapt: attention and the focused life.* New York: Penguin Publishers.

Gamson, W., & Stambaugh, R. (1978). The model underlying Simsoc. *Simulation & Games, 9*(2), 131–157. doi:10.1177/104687817800900201

Garner, R., Alexander, P. A., Gillingham, M. G., & Brown, R. (1991). Interest and learning from text. *American Educational Research Journal, 28*, 643–659.

Garner, R., Gillingham, M., & White, C. (1989). Effects of seductive details on macroprocessing and microprocessing in adults and children. *Cognition and Instruction, 6*, 41–57. doi:10.1207/s1532690xci0601_2

Gass, S. M. (1997). *Input, interaction and the second language learners.* Mahwah, NJ: Lawrence Erlbaum Associates.

Gass, S. M., Mackey, A., & Pica, T. (1998). The role of input and interaction in second language acquisition: Introduction to the special issue. *Modern Language Journal, 82*(3), 299–305.

Gee, J. P. (2003). *What video games have to teach us about learning.* New York: Palgrave.

Gee, J. P. (2004). *Game-Like Learning: An Example of situation Learning and Implications for Opportunity to Learn.* Retrieved May 2008, from http://www.academiccolab.org/ resources/documents/Game-Like%20 Learning.rev.pdf

Gee, J. P. (2004). *Learning by design: Games as learning machines.* Paper presented at the Game Developers Conference, San Jose, CA, March 22-26. Retrieved April 29, 2005 from http://www.gamasutra.com/gdc2004/ features/20040324/gee_01.shtml

Gee, J. P. (2004). *What videogames have to teach us about learning and literacy.* New York: Palgrave-MacMillan.

Gee, J. P. (2005). Learning by design: good video games as learning machines. *e-learning, 2*(1), 5–16. doi:10.2304/ elea.2005.2.1.5

Gee, J. P. (2008). Learning and Games. In Salen, K. (Ed.), *The ecology of games: Connecting youth, games, and learning* (pp. 21–40). Cambridge, MA: The MIT Press.

Gibson, D. (2008). Make it a two-way connection: A response to Connecting informal and formal learning experiences in gthe age of participatory media. *Contemporary Issues in Technology & Teacher Education, 8*(4).

Gibson, D., & Grasso, S. (2007 November). The global challenge: Saving the earth on their way to college. *Leading and Learning with Technology*, 12-16.

Gibson, D., & Grasso, S. (2008). An enterprise simulation platform for education: Building a world game for pre-college students with Microsoft ESP. *Innovate, 4*(6).

Gibson, D., & Halverson, B. (2004). SimSchool: Preparing tomorrow's teachers to improve student results. In *Society for Information Technology in Teacher Education Annual Conference*, March 2 – 4, 2004. Atlanta, GA: SITE.

Giumelli, K. (2008). *Cognition and learning with special needs students. Research proposal presentation.* NSW, Australia: University of Wollongong.

Glazer, S. (2006). Video games: Do they have educational value? *CQ Researcher, 16*(4), 939–949.

Godwin-Jones, B. (2005). Skype and podcasting: Disruptive technologies for language learning. *Language Learning & Technology, 9*(3), 9–12.

Gorniak, P., & Roy, D. (2005). *Speaking with your sidekick: Understanding situated speech in computer role playing games.* Paper presented at the 1st Artificial Intelligence and Interactive Digital Entertainment Conference (AIIDE). Retrieved April 10, 2008, from http://petergorniak.org/papers/AIIDE05GorniakSituatedSpeech.pdf

Gottfried, A. E., Fleming, J. S., & Gottfried, A. W. (2001). Continuity of academic intrinsic motivation from childhood through late adolescence: A longitudinal study. *Journal of Educational Psychology, 93*, 3–13. doi:10.1037/0022-0663.93.1.3

Government of Quebec, Ministry of Education. (2001) *Quebec Education Program: Approved Version.* Retrieved March 27, 2009 from http://www.mels.gouv.qc.ca/DGFJ/dp/programme_de_formation/primaire/ educprg2001h.htm

Grabe, M., & Grabe, C. (2007). *Integrating Technology for meaningful Learning*. Boston: Houghton Mifflin Company.

Graeme, D. (2003). *Board Games for learning*. Retrieved September 22, 2007, from http://magazines.fasfind.com/wwwtools/magazines.cfm?rid=210

Graesser, A. C., & King, B. (2008). Technology-based training. In Blascovich, J. J., & Hartel, C. H. (Eds.), *Human behavior in military contexts* (pp. 127–149). Washington, DC: National Academy of Sciences.

Graesser, A. C., & Ottati, V. (1995). Why stories? Some evidence, questions, and challenges. In R. S. Wyer Jr. (Ed.), Knowledge and memory: The real story. Vol. 8, Advances in social cognition (pp. 121-132). Hillsdale, NJ: Lawrence Erlbaum Associates, Inc.

Graesser, A. C., Chipman, P., Haynes, B. C., & Olney, A. (2005). AutoTutor: An intelligent tutoring system with mixed-initiative dialogue. *IEEE Transactions on Education*, *48*, 612–618. doi:10.1109/TE.2005.856149

Graesser, A. C., Chipman, P., Leeming, F., & Biedenbach, S. (2009). Deep learning and emotion in serious games. In Ritterfield, U., Cody, M., & Vorderer, P. (Eds.), *Serious games: Mechanisms and effects* (pp. 81–100). Mahwah, NJ: Routledge, Taylor, and Francis.

Graesser, A. C., Jackson, G. T., & McDaniel, B. (2007). AutoTutor holds conversations with learners that are responsive to their cognitive and emotional states. *Educational Technology*, *47*, 19–22.

Graesser, A. C., Jackson, G. T., Mathews, E. C., Mitchell, H. H., Olney, A., Ventura, M., Chipman, P., Franceschetti, D., Hu, X., Louwerse, M. M., Person, N. K., & TRG. (2003). Why AutoTutor: A test of learning gains from a physics tutor with natural language dialogue. In R. Alterman & D. Hirsh (Eds.), *Proceedings of the 25th Annual Conference of the Cognitive Science Society* (pp. 1–6). Mahwah, NJ: Erlbaum.

Graesser, A. C., Leon, J. A., & Otero, J. C. (2002). Introduction to the psychology of science text comprehension. In Otero, J., Leon, J. A., & Graesser, A. C. (Eds.), *The psychology of science text comprehension* (pp. 1–5). Mahwah, NJ: Erlbaum.

Graesser, A. C., Lu, S., Jackson, G. T., Mitchell, H., Ventura, M., Olney, A., & Louwerse, M. M. (2004). AutoTutor: A tutor with dialogue in natural language. *Behavior Research Methods, Instruments, & Computers*, *36*, 180–193.

Graesser, A. C., Person, N. K., & Magliano, J. P. (1995). Collaborative dialogue patterns in naturalistic one-on-one tutoring. *Applied Cognitive Psychology*, *9*, 495–522. doi:10.1002/acp.2350090604

Graesser, A. C., Singer, M., & Trabasso, T. (1994). Constructing inferences during narrative text comprehension. *Psychological Review*, *101*, 371–395. doi:10.1037/0033-295X.101.3.371

Gredler, M. (1992). *Designing and Evaluating Games and Simulations – a Process Approach*. London: Kogan Page.

Gredler, M. E. (1996). Educational games and simulations: a technology in search of a research paradigm. In Jonassen, D. H. (Ed.), *Handbook of research for educational communications and technology* (pp. 521–540). New York: Simon & Schuster Macmillan.

Gredler, M. E. (2004). Games and simulations and their relationships to learning. In Jonassen, D. H. (Ed.), *Handbook of research on educational communications and technology* (pp. 571–582). Mahwah, NJ: Lawrence Erlbaum Associates.

Green, D. A. (2002). Last one standing: creative, cooperative problem solving. *Teaching Children Mathematics*, *9*(3), 134–139.

Greenblat, C. (1989). Introduction: Special Issue 20th Anniversary. *Simulation & Games*, *20*(2), 123–129. doi:10.1177/104687818902000201

Greene, J. A., & Azevedo, R. (2007). Adolescents' use of self-regulatory processes and their relation to qualitative mental model shifts while using hypermedia. *Journal of Educational Computing Research*, *36*, 125–148. doi:10.2190/G7M1-2734-3JRR-8033

Greenlaw, P., & Wyman, P. (1973). The teaching effectiveness of games in collegiate business courses. *Simulation & Games*, *4*(3), 259–294. doi:10.1177/003755007343001

Gros, B. (2003 July). The impact of digital games in education. *First Monday*, *8*(7). Retrieved February 19, 2005, from http://www.firstmonday.dk/issues/ issue8_7/ xyzgros/

Gros, B. (2007). *Digital games in education: The design of games-based learning environments*. Retrieved March 13, 2009, from http://www.iste.org/Content/ NavigationMenu/EducatorResources/YourLearningJourney/ InnovateLearningTechnologies/digital_games.pdf

Guillot, B. (2004). La psychothérapie assistée par ordinateur PsyaO. *Adolescence*, *22*(1), 53–58.

Gunter, G., Kenny, R., & Vick, E. H. (2006). *A Case for a Formal Design Paradigm for Serious Games*. Retrieved May 2008, from http://www.units.muohio.edu/ codeconference/ papers/papers/Gunter%20Kenny%20 Vick%20 paper.pdf

Haas, J. P., Quiros, D., Hyman, S. R., & Larson, E. L. (2006). Use of an Innovative Game To Teach and Reinforce Hand Hygiene Compliance among Healthcare Workers. *American Journal of Infection Control*, *34*(5), E52–E53. doi:10.1016/j.ajic.2006.05.109

Hall, J. K., & Verplaetse, L. S. (2000). Language learning through classroom interaction. In Hall, J. K., & Verplatse, L. S. (Eds.), *Second and foreign language learning through classroom interaction* (pp. 1–20). Mahwah, NJ: Lawrence Erlbaum.

Hamalainen, R. (2008). Designing and evaluating collaboration in a virtual game environment for vocational learning. *Computers & Education*, *50*(1), 98–109. doi:10.1016/j.compedu.2006.04.001

Hamalainen, R., Manninen, T., Jarvela, S., & Hakkinen, P. (2006). Learning to collaborate: Designing collaboration in a 3-D game environment. *The Internet and Higher Education*, *9*(1), 47–61. doi:10.1016/j.iheduc.2005.12.004

Hannafin, M. J., & Land, S. M. (1997). The foundations and assumptions of technology-enhanced student-centered learning environments. *Instructional Science*, *25*, 167–202. doi:10.1023/A:1002997414652

Harper, B., Squires, D., & McDougall, A. (2000). Constructivist simulation: A new design paradigm. *Journal of Educational Multimedia and Hypermedia*, *9*(2), 115–130.

Helmer, J. (2007). Second Life and virtual worlds. *Learning Light Limited*. Retrieved August 19, 2009, from http://www.epic.co.uk/content/news/nov_07/Second_Life_and_Virtual_Worlds_JH.pdf

Herring, D. F., Notar, C., & Wilson, J. (2005). Multimedia software evaluation form for teachers. *Education*. Retrieved March 26, 2009, from http://www.highbeam.com/doc/1G1-136846796.html

Heyde, A. (1979). *The relationship between self-esteem and the oral production of a second language*. Unpublished doctoral dissertation, University of Michigan, MI.

Hidi, S. (1990). Interest and its contribution as a mental resource for learning. *Review of Educational Research*, *60*, 549–571.

Higgins, M. M., & Barkley, M. C. (2004). Improving effectiveness of nutrition education resources for older adults. *Journal of Nutrition for the Elderly*, *23*(3), 19–54. doi:10.1300/J052v23n03_03

Hingston, P., Combes, B., & Masek, M. (2006). Teaching an undergraduate AI course with Games and simulation. *Lecture Notes in Computer Science*, *3942*, 494–506. doi:10.1007/11736639_61

Hirumi, A., & Stapleton, C. (2008). *Games: Purpose and Potential in Education*. New York: Springer.

Hollander, P. A. (1977). The uses of simulation in teaching law and lawyering skills. *Simulation & Games*, *8*(3), 319–340. doi:10.1177/003755007783002

Holloway, S. L., & Valentine, G. (2003). *Cyberkids: children in the information age*. London: Routledge.

Holton, D., Ahmed, A., Williams, H., & Hill, C. (2001). On the importance of mathematical play. *International Journal of Mathematical Education in Science and Technology*, *32*, 401–415. doi:10.1080/00207390010022158

Honebein, P. C. (1996). Seven goals for the design of constructivist learning environments. In Wilson, B. G. (Ed.), *Constructivist Learning Environments: Case Studies in Instructional Design*. Englewood Cliffs, NJ: Educational Technology Publications.

Huang, Z. Y., & Cappel, J. J. (2005). Assessment of a web-based learning game in an information systems course. *Journal of Computer Information Systems*, *45*(4), 42–49.

Hughes, B. (2005). Indentifying attitudes and deterring factors toward continuing education among certified athletic trainers. *The Internet Journal of Allied Health Sciences and Practice, 3*(1). Retrieved on August 28, 2009, from http://ijahsp.nova.edu/articles/vol3num1/HUGHES.pdf

Ibode, O. F. (2004). *Relative effects of Computer-Assisted and Videotape Instruction methods on students' achievement in and attitude to English Language*. Unpublished Ph.D Dissertation. Institute of Education, University of Ibadan, Nigeria.

Illovsky, M. E. (1994). Counseling, Artificial Intelligence and Expert Systems. *Simulation & Gaming, 25*(1), 88–98. doi:10.1177/1046878194251009

Interactive, D. I. S. T. I. L. (2009). *Learning with Digital Game Based Learning (DGBL)*. Retrieved July 19, 2008, from http://www.distilinteractive.com/approach/learning_with_dgbl.php

IOP. (2001). *Physics-Building a flourishing Future. Report of the Inquiry into Undergraduate Phyiscs*. Institute of Physics, London. Retrieved August 29, 2006, from http://policy.iop.org/UPI/index.html

Jackson, G. T., & Graesser, A. C. (2007). Content Matters: An investigation of feedback categories within an ITS. In Luckin, R., Koedinger, K., & Greer, J. (Eds.), *Artificial Intelligence in Education: Building technology rich learning contexts that work* (pp. 127–134). Amsterdam, The Netherlands: IOS Press.

Jackson, G. T., Olney, A., Graesser, A. C., & Kim, H. J. (2006). AutoTutor 3-D Simulations: Analyzing user's actions and learning trends. In R. Son (Ed.), *Proceedings of the 28th Annual Meetings of the Cognitive Science Society* (pp. 1557-1562). Mahwah, NJ: Erlbaum.

Jenkins, H. (2006). *Confronting the challenges of participatory culture: Media education for the 21st century*. Retrieved December 13, 2007, from http://www.project-nml.org/files/working/NMLWhitePaper.pdf

Jenkins, H., Purushotma, R., Clinton, K., Weigel, M., & Robison, A. (n.d.). Confronting the challenges of participatory culture: Media education for the 21st Century [Electronic Version]. *New Media Literacies Project*, 72. Retrieved April 5, 2009, from http://www.newmedialiteracies.org/files/working/NMLWhitePaper.pdf

Jensen, J., Sims, J., & Reventos, L. (2004). Jeux vidéo: la nouvelle pop culture. *Courrier international*, 709, 40-46.

Jenson, J., & De Castell, S. (2006). You're going to die: gender, performance and digital game play. In V. Uskov (Eds.), *Proceedings of the International conference on computer and advanced technology in Education*, Lima, Peru.

JISC. (2004). Effective Practice with e-Learning - A good practice guide in designing for learning. Retrieved Sept. 2008, from http://www.jisc.ac.uk/elearning_pedagogy.html

Johnson, W. L. (2001). Pedagogical Agent Research at CARTE. *AI Magazine*, *22*, 85–94.

Johnson, W. L., Kole, S., Shaw, E., & Pain, H. (2003). Socially intelligent learner-agent interaction tactics. *Proceedings of the 11th International Conference on Artificial Intelligence in Education (AIED)*. Amsterdam: IOS Press.

Joint Information Systems Committee. (2007). Game-based learning. *E-learning innovation programme*. Retrieved August 19, 2009, from http://www.jisc.ac.uk/publications/publications/pub_gamebasedlearningBP.aspx

Jonassen, D. (1995). Constructivism and computer-mediated communication in distance education. *American Journal of Distance Education*, *9*(2), 7–26. doi:10.1080/08923649509526885

Jonassen, D. H. (1996). *Computers in the classroom: Mindtools for critical thinking*. Englewood Cliffs, NJ: Merrill.

Jonassen, D. H. (1997). Instructional design model for well-structured and ill-structured problem-solving learning outcomes. *Educational Technology Research and Development, 45*(1), 65–95. doi:10.1007/BF02299613

Jonassen, D. H. (1999). Designing constructivist learning environments. In Reigeluth, C. M. (Ed.), *Instructional Design Theories and Models: Their Current State of the Art*. Mahwah, NJ: Lawrence Erlbaum Associates.

Jonassen, D. H. (2000). Toward a design theory of problem solving. *Etr& D-Educational Technology Research and Development, 48*(4), 63–85. doi:10.1007/BF02300500

Jonassen, D. H. (2004). *Learning to solve problems: an instructional design guide*. San Francisco: Pfeiffer.

Jonassen, D. H., & Wang, S. (1993). Acquiring Structural Knowledge from Semantically Structured Hypertext. *Journal of Computer-Based Instruction, 20*(1).

Jones, T. S., & Richey, R. C. (2000). Rapid prototyping methodology in action: A developmental study. *Educational Technology Research and Development, 48*(2), 63–80. doi:10.1007/BF02313401

Kadakia, M. (2005). Increasing student engagement by using Morrowind to analyze choices and consequences. *TechTrends, 49*(5), 29–32. doi:10.1007/BF02763687

Kafai, Y. B. (1994). Electronic play worlds: Children's construction of video games. In Kafai, Y. B., & Resnick, M. (Eds.), *Constructionism in practice: Rethinking the roles of technology in learning* (pp. 97–123). Mahwah, NJ: Lawrence Erlbaum Associates.

Kafai, Y. B. (1996). Electronic play worlds: gender differences in children's construction of video games. In Kafai, Y., & Resnick, M. (Eds.), *Constructivism in practice: Designing, thinking, and learning in a digital world* (pp. 97–123). Mahwah, NJ: Erlbaum.

Kafai, Y. B. (1998). Video game designs by girls and boys: Variability and consistency of gender differences. In Cassell, J., & Jenkins, H. (Eds.), *From Barbie to Mortal Kombat: Gender and computer games* (pp. 90–117). Cambridge, MA: MIT Press.

Kafai, Y. B. (2001). *The Educational Potential of Electronic Games: From Games–To–Teach to Games–To–Learn*. Presented in the Playing by the Rules Conference, Chicago, October 26.-27. Retrieved November 5, 2004, from http://culturalpolicy.uchicago.edu/conf2001/papers/kafai.html

Kafai, Y. B. (2006). Playing and making games for learning: Instructionist and constructionist perspectives for game studies. *Games and Culture, 1*(1), 36–40. doi:10.1177/1555412005281767

Kafai, Y. B., & Resnick, M. (Eds.). (1996). *Constructionism in practice: Designing, thinking, and learning in a digital world*. Mahwah, NJ: Lawrence Erlbaum Associates.

Kahne, J. (2007). Is Digital Media Good for Democracy? *Spotlight: Digital Media and Learning*. Retrieved October 2, 2008 from http://spotlight.macfound.org/main/entry/joe_kahne_digital_media_democracy/

Kahne, J., & Westheimer, J. (2006). The limits of political efficacy: Educating citizens for a democratic society. *PS: Political Science and Politics, 39*(2), 289–296.

Kahne, J., Middaugh, E., & Croddy, M. (2005). *The California Survey of Civic Education. Report to Educating of Democracy: California Campaign for the Civic Mission of Schools*. Constitutional Rights Foundation. Retrieved October 5, 2008 from http://www.cms-ca.org/civic_survey_final.pdf

Karlsen, F. (2008). Quests in context: A comparative analysis of Discworld and World of Warcraft. *Game Studies, 8*(1).

Keeffe, M. J., Dyson, D. A., & Edwards, R. R. (1993). Strategic Management Simulations: A Current Assessment. *Simulation & Games, 24*(3), 363–368. doi:10.1177/1046878193243008

Keegan, M. (1995). *Scenario educational software: Design and development of discovery learning*. Englewood Cliffs, NJ: Educational Technology Publications.

Keller, J. M. (1987). Development and use of the ARCS model of motivational design. *Journal of Instructional Development, 10*(3), 2–10. doi:10.1007/BF02905780

Kelly, H. (2005). Games, Cookies, and the Future of Education. *Issues in Science and Technology, 21*(4), 33–40.

Kennedy, M. I. (1973). Theoretical Framework for the use of urban simulation games in education and urban planning. *Simulation & Games, 4*(3), 331–339. doi:10.1177/003755007343005

Khoo, A., & Gentile, D. A. (2007). Problem based Learning in the World of Digital Games. In Tan, O.-S. (Ed.), *Problem-based Learning in eLearning Breakthroughs* (pp. 97–129). Singapore: Thompson Learning.

KidSmart. (2007). Retrieved March 13, 2009, from http://www.kidsmartearlylearning.org/

Kim, B., Hyun, E., & Han, S. (2008). A Study on the effects of students' sociality level on self-efficacy and academic achievement in on-line game-based Learning. *Journal of Learner-Centered Curriculum and Instruction, 8*(2), 49–75.

Kintsch, E., Caccamise, D., Franzke, M., Johnson, N., & Dooley, S. (2007). Summary street: LSA-based software for comprehension and writing. In Landauer, T., McNamara, D. S., Dennis, S., & Kintsch, W. (Eds.), *Handbook of latent semantic analysis.* Mahwah, NJ: Erlbaum.

Kintsch, W. (1998). *Comprehension: A paradigm for cognition.* Cambridge, MA: Cambridge University Press.

Kirkpatrick, D. L. (1994). *Evaluating training programs: The four levels.* San Francisco: Berrett-Koehler.

Kirriemuir, J., & McFarlane, A. (2003 November). Use of Computer and Video Games in the Classroom. In *Proceedings of 2003 Level Up Conference.* Retrieved October 6, 2007, from http://digra.org:8080/Plone/dl/db/05150.28025.pdf

Kirriemur, J., & McFarlane, C. A. (2004). *Literature Review in Games and Learning, A Report for NESTA Futurelab.* Retrieved November 5, 2004, from http://www.nestafuturelab.org/ research/ reviews/08_01.htm

Kirschner, P. A., Sweller, J., & Clark, R. E. (2006). Why minimal guidance during instruction does not work: An analysis of the failure of constructivist, discovery, problem-based, experiential, and inquiry-based teaching. *Educational Psychologist, 41*(2), 75–86. doi:10.1207/s15326985ep4102_1

Klastrup, L. (2003). *A poetics of virtual worlds.* Retrieved January 21, 2009, from http://hypertext.rmit.edu.au/dac/papers/Klastrup.pdf

Klopfer, E., Osterweil, S., & Salen, K. (2009). *Moving learning games forward.* The Education Arcade, Massachusetts Institute of Technology.

Klopfer, E., Osterweil, S., Salen, K., Haas, J., Groff, J., & Roy, D. (2009). *Moving learning games forward: Obstacles, opportunities & openness.* Retrieved February 27, 2009, from http://education.mit.edu/papers/MovingLearningGamesForward_EdArcade.pdf

Knezek, G., & Vandersall, K. (2008). simMentoring Results. *simZine, 3*

Kochan, B., & Schröter, E. (2006). Abschlussbericht über die Studie zur Microsoft Bildungsinitiative. *Schlaumäuse – Kinder entdecken Sprache.* ComputerLernWerkstatt an der Technischen Universität Berlin. Retrieved March 13, 2009, from http://www.schlaumaeuse.de/Informationen/Seiten/Mediathek.aspx

Koedinger, K. R., Anderson, J. R., Hadley, W. H., & Mark, M. A. (1997). Intelligent tutoring goes to school in the big city. *International Journal of Artificial Intelligence in Education, 8*, 30–43.

Kolb, D. A. (1985). *Experiential Learning: Experience as the Source of Learning and Development.* Upper Saddle River, NJ: Prentice-Hall.

Krajewsky, P. R., & Piroli, V. B. (2002). Something Old, Something New, Something Borrowed, Something Blue: Active Learning in the Classroom. *Journal of Library Administration, 36*(1-2), 177–194.

Kraus, W. H. (1982). The Use of Problem-Solving Heuristics in the Playing of Games involving Mathematics. *Journal for Research in Mathematics Education, 13*(3), 172–182. doi:10.2307/748554

Kraut, R. E., & Fussell, S. R. (2002). Understanding effects of proximity on collaboration: Implications for technologies to support remote collaborative work. In

Hinds, P. J., & Kiesler, S. (Eds.), *Distributed Work*. Cambridge, MA: The MIT Press.

Kreimeier, B. (2002, March 13). The Case for Game Design Patterns. *Gamasutra*. Retrieved April 12, 2009, from http://www.gamasutra.com/features/20020313/kreimeier_03.htm

Kress, G. (1998). *Before Writing: rethinking the paths to literacy*. London: Routledge.

Krotoski, A., Ellis, H., Heppell, S., Kirriemuir, J., & McFarlane, A. (2006). *Unlimited learning: Computer and video games in the learning landscape*. Retrieved August 8, 2007, from http://www.elspa.com/assets/files/0/20070308110513566_359.pdf

Kuhn, H. W. (2003). *Lectures on the theory of games*. Princeton, NJ: Princeton University Press.

Kutner, L. A., Olson, C. K., Warner, D. E., & Hertzog, S. M. (2008). Parents' and sons' perspectives on video game play - a qualitative study. *Journal of Adolescent Research, 23*(1), 76–96. doi:10.1177/0743558407310721

Lakoff, G. (1987). *Women, Fire and Dangerous Things: What Categories reveal about the Mind*. Chicago: Il., University of Chicago Press.

Lamy, C. (2004). NetAdos 2004 - Sondage réalisé auprès des ados québécois & de leurs parents [Poll of Québécois adolescents and their parents]. Québec: CEFRIO. Retrieved October 6, 2007, from http://www.cefrio.qc.ca/rapports/NetAdos_ 2004_rapport.pdf.

Lancy, D. F., & Hayes, B. L. (1986). Building an Anthology of "Interactive Fiction." *Report: ED275991*.

Lancy, D. F., & Hayes, B. L. (1988). Interactive Fiction and the Reluctant Reader. *English Journal, 77*(7), 42-66. Retrieved March 26, 2009, from http://www.jstor.org/stable/818936

Larsen, S. A. (n.d.). *Homicide - Forensic learning game*. Retrieved March 23, 2009, from http://www.his.se/PageFiles/10488/LLD_Svend_Ask_Larsen.pdf?epslanguage=sv

Laughlin, D., Roper, M., & Howell, K. (2007). NASA eEducation Roadmap: Research Challenges in the Design of Massively Multiplayer Games for Education & Training. Retrieved Nov. 2008, from http://www.fas.org/programs/ ltp/publications/roadmaps/_docs/NASA%20eEd ucation%20Roadmap.pdf

Lave, J., & Wenger, E. (1991). *Situated Learning. Legitimate Peripheral Participation*. Cambridge: University of Cambridge.

Lee, K. M., & Peng, W. (2006). What do we know about social and psychological effects of computer games? A comprehensive review of the current literature. In Vorderer, P., & Bryant, J. (Eds.), *Playing video games, motives, responses, and consequences* (pp. 327–345). Hillsdale, NJ: Lawrence Erlbaum.

Lee, M. S., Ko, Y. H., Song, H. S., Kwon, K. H., Lee, H. S., & Nam, M. (2007). Characteristics of internet use in relation to game genre in korean adolescents. *Cyberpsychology & Behavior, 10*(2), 278–285. doi:10.1089/cpb.2006.9958

Lenhart, A., Kahne, J., Middaugh, E., & Macgill, A. Evans, C., & Vitak, J. (2008). *Teens, video games, and civics: Teens' gaming experiences are diverse and include significant social interaction and civic engagement*. Washington, DC: PEW Internet and American Life Project. Retrieved on October 5, 2008 from http://www.pewinternet.org/report_display.asp?r=263

Lenhart, A., Madden, M., & Hitlin, P. (2005). *Teens and technology: Youth are leading the transition to a fully wired and mobile nation*. Washington, DC: Pew Internet and American Life Project. Retrieved on February 9, 2007 from http://www.pewinternet.org/pdfs/PIP_Teens_Tech_July2005web.pdf

Lennon, J. L., & Coombs, D. W. (2006). Child-invented health education games: A case study for dengue fever. *Simulation & Gaming, 37*(1), 88–97. doi:10.1177/1046878105285550

Lepper, M. R., & Chabay, R. W. (1985). Intrinsic motivation and instruction: Conflicting views on the role of motivational processes in computer-based education. *Educational Psychologist, 20*, 217–231. doi:10.1207/s15326985ep2004_6

Lepper, M. R., & Malone, T. W. (1987). Intrinsic motivation and instructional effectiveness in computer-based education. In Snow, R., & Farr, M. (Eds.), *Aptitude, Learning and Instruction, III: Cognitive and Affective Process Analysis*. Hillside, NJ: Lawrence Erlbaum Associates.

Lepper, M. R., & Woolverton, M. (2002). The wisdom of practice: Lessons learned from the study of highly effective tutors. In Aronson, J. (Ed.), *Improving academic achievement: Impact of psychological factors on education* (pp. 135–158). San Diego, CA: Academic Press. doi:10.1016/B978-012064455-1/50010-5

Lepper, M. R., Aspinwall, L. G., Mumme, D. L., & Chabay, R. W. (1990). Self-perception and social-perception processes in tutoring: Subtle social control strategies of expert tutors. In Olson, J. M., & Zanna, M. P. (Eds.), *Self-inference processes: The Ontario symposium* (pp. 217–237). Hillsdale, NJ: Erlbaum.

Lepper, M. R., Drake, M., & O'Donnell-Johnson, T. (1997). Scaffolding techniques of expert human tutors. In Hogan, K., & Pressley, M. (Eds.), *Scaffolding student learning: Instructional approaches and issues. Advances in learning and teaching* (pp. 108–144). Cambridge, MA: Brookline Books.

Lesgold, A., Lajoie, S., Bunzo, M., & Eggan, G. (1992). SHERLOCK: A Coached Practice Environment for an Electronics Troubleshooting Job. In Larkin, J. H., & Chabay, R. W. (Eds.), *Computer assisted instruction and intelligent tutoring systems* (pp. 201–238). Hillsdale, NJ: Lawrence Erlbaum.

Leshin, C. B., Pollock, J., & Reigeluth, C. M. (1992). *Instructional design strategies and tactics*. Englewood Cliffs, NJ: Education Technology Publications.

Lester, J., Callaway, C., Gregoire, J., Stelling, G., Towns, S., & Zettlemoyer, L. (2001). Animated Pedagogical Agents in Knowledge-Based Learning Environments. In Forbus, K., & Feltovich, P. (Eds.), *Smart machines in education: The coming revolution in educational technology* (pp. 269–298). Menlo Park, NJ: AAAI/MIT Press.

Leuckefeld, K. (2006). Der Erwerb sprachlicher Strukturen. In K. Jampert, K. Leuckefeld, A. Zehnbauer, & P. Best (Eds.), Sprachliche Förderung in der Kita. Wie viel Sprache steckt in Musik, Bewegung, Naturwissenschaften und Medien? (pp. 28-48). Berlin: Verlag das netz, Weimar.

Levin, D. E., & Rosenquest, B. (2001). The Increasing Role of Electronic Toys in the Lives of Infants and Toddlers: should we be concerned? *Contemporary Issues in Early Childhood, 2*(2), 242–246. doi:10.2304/ciec.2001.2.2.9

Levin, D., & Arafeh, S. (2002). *The digital disconnect: The widening gap between Internet-savvy students and their schools*. Pew Internet and American Life Project. Retrieved on February 22, 2008 from http://www.pewinternet.org/pdfs/PIP_Schools_Internet_Report.pdf

Levin, I. (2007). The role of Hebrew letter names in early literacy: The case of multiphonemic acrophonic names. *Journal of Experimental Child Psychology, 98*, 193–216.

Levin, I., Shatil-Carmon, S., & Asif-Rave, O. (2006). Learning of letter names and sounds and their contribution to word recognition. *Journal of Experimental Child Psychology, 93*, 139–165. doi:10.1016/j.jecp.2005.08.002

Liao, Y. C. (2007). Effects of computer-assisted instruction on student's achievement in Taiwan: A meta analysis. *Computers & Education, 48*(2), 216–233. doi:10.1016/j.compedu.2004.12.005

Lieberman, D. A. (1998). *Health education video games for children and adolescents: Theory, design, and research findings*. Paper presented at the annual meeting of the International Communication Association, Jerusalem.

Lieberman, D. A. (2001). Management of chronic pediatric diseases with interactive health games: theory and research findings. *The Journal of Ambulatory Care Management, 24*(1), 26–38.

Lim, C.-I., Maxwell, K. L., Able-Boone, H., & Zimmer, C. R. (2009). Cultural and linguistic diversity in early childhood teacher preparation: The impact of contextual characteristics on coursework and practica. *Early Childhood Research Quarterly, 24*, 64–76. doi:10.1016/j.ecresq.2008.10.003

Lisowski, M. (2007). Le jeu: gadget ou innovation pédagogique? *Inffo Flash, 708, 16 au 30 septembre*. Retrieved February 2, 2008, from http://www.centre-inffo.fr/Le-jeu-gadget-ou-innovation.html

Livingstone, D. (2007). Learning support in multi-user virtual environments. In *Proceedings of the European Conference on Game-Based Learning*, University of Paisley, Scotland, 25–26 October.

Loh, C. S., & Byun, J. H. (2009). Modding Neverwinter Nights into serious games. In Gibson, D., & Baek, Y. K. (Eds.), *Digital simulations for improving education: Learning through artificial teaching environments* (pp. 408–426). Hershey, PA: Information Science Reference.

Loh, C. S., Anantachai, A., Byun, J., & Lenox, J. (2007). Assessing what players learned in serious games: *in situ* data collection, information trails, and quantitative analysis. In Mehdi, Q. (Ed.), *Computer games: AI, animation, mobile, educational & serious games (CGAMES)*. Wolverhampton, UK: University of Wolverhampton.

Lohnman, M. C. (2000). Environmental inhibitors to informal learning in the workplace: a case study of public school teachers. *Adult Education Quarterly, 50*(2), 83–101. doi:10.1177/07417130022086928

Low, M., Venkataraman, S., & Zrivatsan, V. (1994). Developing and Entrepreneurship Game for Teaching and Research. *Simulation & Gaming, 25*(3), 383–401. doi:10.1177/1046878194253006

Lowood, H. (2008). Found technology: Players as innovators in the making of machinima. In McPherson, T. (Ed.), *Digital Youth, Innovation, and the Unexpected* (pp. 165–196). Cambridge, MA: The MIT Press.

Lucas, K., & Sherry, J. L. (2004). Sex Differences in Video Game Play: A Communication-Based Explanation. *Communication Research, 31*, 499–523. doi:10.1177/0093650204267930

Macfarlane, A., Sparrowhawk, A., & Heald, Y. (2002). *Report on the educational use of video games: An exploration by TEEM (Teachers Evaluating Educational Multimedia) of the contribution which games can make to the education process.* Retrieved August 23, 2003, from http://www.teem.org.uk/publications/teem_gamesined_full.pdf

Magnussen, R. (2005). *Learning games as a platform for simulated science practice*. Retrieved March 13, 2008, from http://www.digra.org/dl/db/06278.37511.pdf

Malik, D., & Howard, B. (1996). How do we know where we're going if we don't know where we've been? A review of business simulation research. *Development in Business Simulation and Experiential Exercises, 232*, 29–53.

Malone, M. D. (2008). The Efficacy of Personal Learning Plans in Early Childhood Teacher Preparation. *Early Childhood Education Journal, 36*, 47–56. doi:10.1007/s10643-008-0238-3

Malone, T. (1980). *What makes things fun to learn? A study of intrinsically motivating computer games*. Technical Report CIS-7, Xerox Parc.

Malone, T. W. (1981). Toward a theory of intrinsically motivating instruction. *Cognitive Science, 4*, 333–369.

Malone, T. W., & Lepper, M. R. (1987). Making Learning Fun: A Taxonomy of Intrinsic Motivations for Learning. In Snow, R. E., & Farr, M. J. (Eds.), *Aptitude, Learning and Instruction* (*Vol. 3*). Lawrence Erlbaum Associates.

Markey, C., Power, D., & Booker, G. (2003). Using structured games to teach early fraction concepts to students who are deaf or hard of hearing. [from http://www.gallaudet.edu/~ossweb/annals/]. *American Annals of the Deaf, 148*(3), 251–258. Retrieved November 5, 2004. doi:10.1353/aad.2003.0021

Marsch, J. (2002). Electronic Toys: why should we be concerned? A Response to Levin & Rosenquest (2001). *Contemporary Issues in Early Childhood, 3*(1), 132–138. doi:10.2304/ciec.2002.3.1.3

Martens, R. L., Gulikers, J., & Bastiaens, T. (2004). The impact of intrinsic motivation on e-learning in authentic computer tasks. *Journal of Computer Assisted Learning, 20*(5), 368–376. doi:10.1111/j.1365-2729.2004.00096.x

Maslow, A. (1943). A theory of human motivation. *Psychological Review, 50*, 370–396. doi:10.1037/h0054346

Mayer, R. E. (2001). *Multimedia Learning.* New York: Cambridge University Press.

Mayra, F. (2008). *Games & Social Media - SoPlay.* Retrieved September 9, 2008, from http://www.sombiz.net/content/games-social-media-soplay

McGonigal, J. (2008). Alternate Realities: Jane McGonigal Keynote. *South by Southwest World.* Retrieved from http://www.slideshare.net/avantgame/alternate-realities-jane-mcgonigal-keynote-sxsw-2008

McLeroy, C. (2008, September). History of Military Gaming. *Soldiers, 63*, 4–6.

McNamara, D. S., & Shapiro, A. M. (2005). Multimedia and hypermedia solutions for promoting metacognitive engagement, coherence, and learning. *Journal of Educational Computing Research, 33*, 1–29. doi:10.2190/7N6R-PCJL-UMHK-RYPJ

McNamara, D. S., Boonthum, C., Levinstein, I. B., & Millis, K. (2007). Evaluating self-explanations in iSTART: Comparing word-based and LSA analysis. In Landauer, T., McNamara, D. S., Dennis, S., & Kintsch, W. (Eds.), *Handbook of latent semantic analysis* (pp. 227–242). Mahwah, NJ: Erlbaum.

McNamara, D. S., Levinstein, I. B., & Boonthum, C. (2004). iSTART: Interactive strategy trainer for active reading and thinking. *Behavior Research Methods, Instruments, & Computers, 36*, 222–233.

McNamara, D. S., O'Reilly, T., Rowe, M., Boonthum, C., & Levinstein, I. B. (2007). iSTART: A web-based tutor that teaches self-explanation and metacognitive reading strategies. In D. S. McNamara (Ed.), Reading comprehension strategies: Theories, interventions, and technologies (pp. 397-421). Mahwah, NJ: Erlbaum.

Merrill, D. C., Reiser, B. J., Ranney, M., & Trafton, J. G. (1992). Effective tutoring techniques: a comparison of human tutors and intelligent tutoring systems. *Journal of the Learning Sciences, 2*, 277–306. doi:10.1207/s15327809Jls0203_2

Meskill, C. (2005). Triadic Scaffolds: Tools for Teaching English Language Learners with Computers. *Language Learning & Technology, 8*(4), 46–59.

Milech, D., Kirsner, K., Roy, G., & Waters, B. (1993). Applications of Psychology to Computer-Based Tutoring Systems. *International Journal of Human-Computer Interaction, 5*(1), 23–40. doi:10.1080/10447319309526054

Miller, C. S., Lehman, J. F., & Koedinger, K. R. (1999). Goals and Learning in Microworlds. *Cognitive Science, 23*(3), 305–336.

Millis, K., Cai, Z., Graesser, A., Halpern, D., & Wallace, P. (2009). Learning scientific inquiry by asking questions in an educational game. In T. Bastiaens et al. (Eds.), *Proceedings of World Conference on E-Learning in Corporate, Government, Healthcare, and Higher Education* (pp. 2951-2956). Chesapeake, VA: AACE.

Mishra, P., & Koehler, M. (2006). Technological pedagogical content knowledge: A new framework for teacher knowledge. *Teachers College Record, 108*(6), 1017–1054. doi:10.1111/j.1467-9620.2006.00684.x

Mitchell, A., & Savill-Smith, C. (2004). *The use of computer and video games for learning. A review of the literature. Learning and skills development* Agency. Ultralab. Retrieved November 5, 2004, from http://www.lsda.org.uk/files/PDF/1529.pdf

Mitrovic, A., Suraweera, P., Martin, B., & Weerasinghe, A. (2004). DB-suite: Experiences with three intelligent web-based database tutors. *Journal of Interactive Learning Research, 15*, 409–432.

Modelski, G. (1970). Simulations, "Realities," and International Relations Theory. *Simulation & Games, 1*(2), 111–134.

Moisy, M. (2004). EN-JEUX. *Adolescence, 22*(1), 77–89.

Mondozzi, M. A., & Harper, M. A. (2001). In search of effective education in burn and fire prevention. *The Journal of Burn Care & Rehabilitation, 22*(4), 277–281. doi:10.1097/00004630-200107000-00006

Montfort, N. (2003). *Twisty Little Passages: An Approach to Interactive Fiction.* Cambridge, MA: MIT Press.

Moore, J. S., & Price, C. B. (2009) Development of an Educational Immersive Environment for Primary School Literacy Education (To appear, *European Conference on Games Based Learning*, 2009).

Moreno, R., & Duran, R. (2004). Do multiple representations need explanations? The role of verbal guidance and individual differences in multimedia mathematics learning. *Journal of Educational Psychology, 96*(3), 492–503. doi:10.1037/0022-0663.96.3.492

Moreno, R., & Mayer, R. E. (2004). Personalized messages that promote science learning in virtual environments. *Journal of Educational Psychology, 96*, 165–173. doi:10.1037/0022-0663.96.1.165

Moreno, R., & Mayer, R. E. (2005). Role of guidance, reflection, and interactivity in an agent-based multimedia game. *Journal of Educational Psychology, 97*, 117–128. doi:10.1037/0022-0663.97.1.117

Morgan, M. (1984). Reward-induced decrements and increments in intrinsic motivation. *Review of Educational Research, 54*, 5–30.

Morningstar, C., & Farmer, R. (2008). The Lessons of Lucasfilms's Habitat. *Journal of Virtual Worlds Research, 1*(1), 1-21. Retrieved August 19, 2009, from http://journals.tdl.org/jvwr/article/viewFile/287/241

Morris, P. E., Fritz, C. O., & Buck, S. (2004). The Name Game: Acceptability, Bonus Information and Group Size. *Applied Cognitive Psychology, 18*, 89–104. doi:10.1002/acp.948

Morrison, J. L., & Aldrich, A. (2003). *Simulation and the learning revolution: An interview with Clark Aldrich. Vision*. September/October.

Moshirnia, A. (2007). The educational potential of modified video games. *Issues in Informing Science and Information Technology, 4*, 511–521.

Moyer, P. S., & Bolyard, J. J. (2003). Classify and Capture: Using Venn Diagrams and Tangrams To Develop Abilities in Mathematical Reasoning and Proof. *Mathematics Teaching in the Middle School, 8*(6), 325–330.

Murphy, K. P., & Alexander, P. A. (2000). A motivated exploration of motivation terminology. *Contemporary Educational Psychology, 25*, 3–53. doi:10.1006/ceps.1999.1019

Murray, J. (1997). *Hamlet on the holodeck: the future of narrative in cyberspace*. Cambridge, MA: MIT Press.

NAE. (2004). *The Engineer of 2020*. Retrieved from http://www.nap.edu/catalog/10999.html

National Center for Education Statistics. (2001). *The nation's report card: Science highlights 2000 (NCES 2002-452). U.S. Department of Education, National Center for Education Statistics*. Washington, DC: U.S. Government Printing Office.

National Center for Education Statistics. (2006). *The nation's report card: Science highlights 2005 (NCES 2006-466) U.S. Department of Education, National Center for Education Statistics*. Washington, DC: U.S. Government Printing Office.

National Council for the Social Studies. (1994). *Expectations for excellence: Curriculum standards for social studies*. Washington, DC: National Council for the Social Studies.

National Council for the Social Studies. (2001). *Creating effective citizens*. Retrieved June 27, 2007, from http://www.socialstudies.org/positions/effectivecitizens/

National Endowment for Science. Technology and the Arts (NESTA) Futurelab. (2004). *Literature Review in Games and Learning*. Retrieved December 30, 2008, from http://www.futurelab.org.uk/resources/publications_reports_articles/literature_reviews/Literature_Review378

Nelson, G. (2008). *Inform 7 – A Design System for Interactive Fiction Based on Natural Language*. Retrieved from http://www.inform-fiction.org/I7/Welcome.html

Nguyen, T. T. H., & Khuat, T. T. N. (2003). The effectiveness of learning vocabulary through games, *Asian EFL Journal Quarterly,* 5(4). Retrieved April 25, 2009, from http://www.asian-efl-journal.com/dec_03_vn.pdf

Norris, D., & Niebuhr, R. (1980). Group variables and gaming success. *Simulation & Games, 11*(3), 301–312. doi:10.1177/104687818001100303

Novak, J. D., & Musonda, D. (1991). A twelve-year longitudinal study of science concept learning. *American Educational Research Journal, 28*(1).

Nuyen, N. T. T., & Nga, K. T. T. 2003. The effectiveness of learning vocabulary through games. *Asian EFL Journal* 5. Retrieved April 20, 2009 from http://www.asian-efl-journal.com/dec_03_sub.Vn.html

O'Leary, A. (1971). Attitude and personality effects of a three-day simulation. *Simulation & Games, 2*(3), 308–347.

O'Neil, H. F., & Fisher, Y. C. (2004). A technology to support leader development: Computer games. In Day, D. V., Zaccaro, S. J., & Halpin, S. M. (Eds.), *Leader development for transforming organizations* (pp. 99–121). Mahwah, NJ: Lawrence Erlbaum Associates.

O'Neil, H. F., & Perez, R. (2003). *Technology Applications in Education: A Learning View*. Hillsdale, NJ: Lawrence Erlbaum Associates.

O'Neil, H. F., Wainess, R., & Baker, E. L. (2005). Classification of learning outcomes: Evidence from the computer games literature. *Curriculum Journal, 16*, 455–474. doi:10.1080/09585170500384529

Orbach, E. (1977). Some theoretical considerations in the evaluation of instructional simulation games. *Simulation & Games, 8*(3), 341–360. doi:10.1177/003755007783003

Overbaugh, R. C., & Lin, S. (2004). Student characteristics, sense of community, and cognitive achievement in web-based and lab-based learning environments. *Journal of Research on Technology in Education, 39*(2), 205–223.

P2CS. (2008). *Partnership for 21st Century Skills*. Retrieved September 9, 2008, from http://www.21stcenturyskills.org/

Packard, E. B. (1987, October). Interactive Fiction for Children: Boon or Bane? *School Library Journal*, , 40–41.

Padgett, L. S., Strickland, D., & Coles, C. D. (2005, April). Case Study: Using a Virtual Reality Computer Game to Teach Fire Safety Skills to Children Diagnosed with Fetal Alcohol Syndrome. *Journal of Pediatric Psychology*, •••, 1–6.

Page, D., & Roberts, R. M. (1992). Executive evaluation of college student learning via 'The Looking Glass Inc.' simulation. *Simulation & Gaming, 23*(4), 499–506. doi:10.1177/1046878192234010

Pajares, F. (1996). Self-efficacy beliefs in academic settings. *Review of Educational Research, 66*, 543–578.

Papert, S. (1980). *Mindstorms*. New York: Basic Books.

Papert, S. (1993). *The Children's Machine*. New York: Basic Books.

Parette, H. P., Hourcade, J. J., Dinelli, J. M., & Boeckmann, N. M. (2009). Using Clicker 5 to Enhance Emergent Literacy in Young Learners. *Early Childhood Education Journal, 36*, 355–363. doi:10.1007/s10643-008-0288-6

Partnership for 21st Century Skills. (2004). *21st century skills*. Retrieved November 22, 2007, from http://www.21stcenturyskills.org/images/stories/matrices/ictmap_english.pdf

Partnership for 21st Century Skills. (2006). *Results that matter: 21st century skills and high school reform*. Tucson, AZ: Partnership for 21st Century Skills.

Partnership for 21st Century Skills. (2007). *Core subjects and 21st century themes*. Retrieved October 17, 2008 from http://www.21stcenturyskills.org/route21/index.php?option=com_content&view=article&id=6&Itemid=3

Pashler, H., Bain, P. M., Bottge, B. A., Graesser, A., Koedinger, K., McDaniel, M., & Metcalke, J. (2007). *Organizing instruction and study to improve student learning. IES Practice Guide, NCER 2007-2004*. Washington, DC: US Department of Education.

Paton, G. (2007) England slides down world literacy league http://www.telegraph.co.uk/news/main.jhtml?xml=/news/2007/11/29/nliterate129.xml (accessed Jan. 2009)

Paul, N., Hansen, K., & Taylor, M. (2005). *Modding Neverwinter Nights: A simulation for reinforcing information seeking concepts for Mass Communication students*. Paper presented at the DiGRA 2005 Conference, Vancouver, Canada.

Pcmag.com. (2009). *MMORPG definition*. Retrieved April 7, 2009 from http://www.pcmag.com/encyclopedia_term/0,2542,t=MMORPG&i=56863,00.asp

Perrien, C. (2008). *Web 2.0: from publishing to participation.* Retrieved January 20, 2009, from http://www.issi.at/index.php?id=5

Petranek, C. F., Corey, S., & Black, R. (1992). Three levels of learning in simulations: Participating, debriefing and journal writing. *Simulation & Gaming, 23*(2), 174–185. doi:10.1177/1046878192232005

Pew. (2008). Teens, Video Games and Civics. *Pew Internet and American Life Project.* Retrieved January 20, 2009, from http://www.pewinternet.org/PPF/r/263/report_display.asp

Piaget, J. (1992). *Einführung in die genetische Erkenntnistheorie* (5th ed.). Frankfurt am Main: Suhrkamp Taschenbuch Wissenschaft.

Piette, J. (2005). *Conférence de Jacques Piette lors du congrès de la FADBEN à Nice.* Médias communication TICE académie de Nice, avril.

Pils, E., & Pils, M. (2005). Blended Learning im Kindergarten. In Auinger, A. (Ed.), *Oesterreichische Computer GesellschaftWorkshop-Proceedings der 5. fachübergreifenden Konferenz Mensch und Computer 2005* (*Vol. 197*, pp. 119–126).

Pink, D. H. (2005). *A whole new mind: Moving from the information age to the conceptual age.* New York: Riverhead Books.

Pintrich, P. R. (2000). Multiple goals, multiple pathways: The role of goal orientation in learning and achievement. *Journal of Educational Psychology, 92*, 544–555. doi:10.1037/0022-0663.92.3.544

PISA. (2006). Science competencies for tomorrow's world: volume 1 Analysis. New York: OECD publishing.

Pratt, D. (1998). *Five perspectives on teaching in adult and higher education.* Malabar, Florida: Krieger Publishing Co.

Prensky, M. (2001). *Digital Game based Learning.* Boston: McGraw-Hill.

Prensky, M. (2001). Digital natives, digital immigrants. *Horizon, 9*(5), 1–6. doi:10.1108/10748120110424816 http://www.marcprensky.com/writing/Prensky%20-%20Digital%20Natives,%20Digital%20Immigrants%20-%20Part1.pdf accessed Jan. 2009.

Prensky, M. (2005). Adopt and Adapt. 21st-Century Schools Need 21st-Century Technology. *Edutopia.* Retrieved June 9, 2009, from http://www.digitaldivide.net/articles/view.php?ArticleID=786

Prensky, M. (2005). Engage me or Enrage me What today's learners demand. *EDUCAUSE Review, 40*(5), 60–65.

Prensky, M. (2006). *Don't bother me mom – I'm learning!*St. Paul, MN: Paragon House.

Prensky, M. (2008). Students as designers and creators of educational computer games: Who else? *British Journal of Educational Technology, 39*(6), 1004–1019. doi:10.1111/j.1467-8535.2008.00823_2.x

Price, C. B. (2006). A Crisis in Physics Education: Games to the Rescue! (2006) *ITALICS* 5(3), http://www.ics.heacademy.ac.uk/italics/vol5iss3.htm (accessed Jan. 2009)

Price, C. B. (2008). Learning Physics with the Unreal Tournament engine. *Physics Education, 43*(3). doi:10.1088/0031-9120/43/3/006

Price, C. B. (2009). The Path from Pedagogy to Technology: Establishing a Theoretical Basis for the Development of Educational Game Environments. In Conolly, T., Stansfield, M., & Boyle, L. (Eds.), *Games-Based Learning Advancements for Multi-Sensory Human Computer Interfaces: Techniques and Effective Practices. Information Science Reference, Salen, K., & Zimmerman, E. (2003). Rules of Play: Game Design Fundamentals.* Cambridge, MA: The MIT Press.

Purushotma, R. (2005). Commentary: you're not studying, you're just. *Language Learning & Technology, 9*(1), 80–96.

Puto, C. (2004). The next best thing. *BizEd*, May/June, 44-49.

Raizen, S. (1994). Learning and work: The research base. In VOTEC for youth: Policy Educational Practice, Paris: OECD. pp. 69-113.

Ramsey, G. (2000). *Quality Matters Revitalising teaching: Critical times, critical choices. Review of Teacher Education in NSW.* Sydney, Australia: NSW Department of Education and Training.

Randel, J., Morris, B. A., Wetzel, C. D., & Whitehill, B. V. (1992). The Effectiveness of Games for Educational Purposes: A Review of Recent Research. *Simulation & Gaming, 23*(3), 261–276. doi:10.1177/1046878192233001

Rassin, M., Gutman, Y., & Silner, D. (2004). Developing a computer game to prepare children for surgery. *AORN Journal, 80*(6), 1099–1102. doi:10.1016/S0001-2092(06)60689-3

Ravenscroft, A. (2007). Promoting thinking and conceptual change with digital dialogue games. *Journal of Computer Assisted Learning, 23*(6), 453–465. doi:10.1111/j.1365-2729.2007.00232.x

Ravenscroft, A., & Matheson, M. P. (2002). Developing and evaluating dialogue games for collaborative e-learning. *Journal of Computer Assisted Learning, 18*(1), 93–101. doi:10.1046/j.0266-4909.2001.00215.x

Raynes-Goldie, K., & Walker, L. (2008). Our space: Online Civic engagement tools for youth. In Bennett, W. L. (Ed.), *Civic life online: Learning how digital media can engage youth* (pp. 161–188). Cambridge, MA: The MIT Press.

Read, S. J., & Miller, L. C. (1995). Stories are fundamental to meaning and memory: For social creatures, could it be otherwise. In Wyer, R. S., Abelson, R. P., & Schank, R. C. (Eds.), *Knowledge and Memory: The Real Story* (pp. 139–152). Hillsale, NJ: Erlbaum.

Reese, D. D. (2007, March 23-27). *Designing Selene: Theory-based game design and data-mining.* Paper presented at the Serious Games Summit, San Francisco, CA.

Reese, D. D. (2008). Engineering instructional metaphors within virtual environments to enhance visualization. In Gilbert, J. K., Reiner, M., & Nakhleh, M. (Eds.), *Visualization: Theory and practice in science education* (*Vol. 3*, pp. 133–153). Amsterdam: Springer Netherlands. doi:10.1007/978-1-4020-5267-5_7

Reeves, B., & Nass, C. (1996). *The media equation: How people treat computers, television, and new media like real people and places.* New York: Cambridge University Press.

Reynolds, C. (2006). Videogame windows. *Maclean's, 119*, 42.

Rice, J. W. (2007). Assessing higher order thinking in video games. *Journal of Technology and Teacher Education, 15*(1), 87–100.

Rieber, L. P. (1996). Seriously considering play: Designing interactive learning environments based on the blending of microworlds, simulations, and games. *Educational Technology Research and Development, 44*(2), 43–58. doi:10.1007/BF02300540

Rieber, L. P. (2005). Multimedia learning in games, simulations and microworlds. In Mayer, R. E. (Ed.), *The Cambridge Handbook of Multimedia Learning.* New York: Cambridge University Press.

Roberts, D. F., Foehr, U. G., Rideout, V. J., & Brodie, M. (1999). *Kids and media at the new milennium: A comprehensive national analysis of children's media use.* Menlo Park, CA: Kaiser Family Foundation.

Roberts, L. D., Smith, L. M., & Pollock, C. M. (2000). U r a lot bolder on the net. In Ray Crozier, W. (Ed.), *Shyness: Development, consolidation and change.* New York: Routledge.

Roberts, M. J. (2006) *TADS – Text Adventure Development System.* Retrieved March 27, 2009, from http://www.tads.org

Robertson, J., & Good, J. (2005). Story creation in virtual game worlds. *Communications of the ACM, 48*(1), 61–65. doi:10.1145/1039539.1039571

Rodrigo, M. M. T., Baker, R. S. J. D., Lagud, M. C. V., Lim, S. A. L., Macapanpan, A. F., Pascua, S. A. M. S., et al. (2007). Affect and usage choices in simulation problem solving environments. In R. Luckin, K. R. Koedinger & J. Greer (Eds.), *Proceedings of the 13th International Conference on Artificial Intelligence in Education* (pp. 145-152). Amsterdam: IOS Press.

Roed, J. (2003). Language learner behavior in a virtual environment. *Computer Assisted Language Learning, 16*, 155–172. doi:10.1076/call.16.2.155.15880

Rogers, E. M. (1983). *Diffusion of innovations*. New York: Free Press.

Rosas, R., Nussbaum, M., Cumsille, P., Marianov, V., Correa, M., & Flores, P. A. (2003). Beyond Nintendo: Design and Assessment of Educational Video Games for First and Second Grade Students. *Computers & Education, 40*(1), 71–94. doi:10.1016/S0360-1315(02)00099-4

Rus, V., McCarthy, P. M., McNamara, D. S., & Graesser, A. C. (2008). A study of textual entailment. *International Journal of Artificial Intelligence Tools, 17*, 659–685. doi:10.1142/S0218213008004096

Sachs, J. (1999). *Teacher Professional Identity: Competing Discourses, and Competing Outcomes*. Paper Presented at the AARE Annual Conference Melbourne November 27-30

Salen, K., & Zimmerman, E. (2005). *The game design reader*. Cambridge, MA: MIT Press.

Sancho, P., Gómez, P. P., & Fernández-Manjón, B. (2008). *Multiplayer role games applied to problem based learning*. Retrieved December 10, 2008, from http://www.e-ucm.es/drafts/e-UCM_draft_101.pdf

Sandford, R., Ulicsak, M., Facer, K., & Rudd, T. (2006). *Teaching with Games: Using commercial off-the-shelf computer games in formal education*. Bristol, UK: Futurelab. Retrieved October 7, 2007, from http://www.futurelab.org.uk/resources/documents/project_reports/teaching_with_games/TWG_report.pdf

Saunders, P. M. (1997). Experiential learning, cases, and simulations in business communication. *Business Communication Quarterly, 60*, 97–114. doi:10.1177/108056999706000108

Sauvé, L., & Chamberland, G. (2006). Jeux, jeux de simulation et jeux de rôle: une analyse exploratoire et pédagogique. [Games, simulation games and role-playing games: An exploratory pedogical analysis] Cours TEC 1280: Environnement d'apprentissage multimédia sur l'inforoute. Québec, Canada: Télé-université.

Sauvé, L., Kaufman, D., & Renaud, L. (2007). A Systematic Review of the Impact of Games and Simulations on Learning. In *ED-MEDIA 2007- World Conference on Educational Multimedia, Hypermedia & Telecommunications*, Vancouver, Canada, June 25-29, 10 pages.

Sauvé, L., Renaud, L., & Hanca, (2008). *Étude de cas auprès des élèves du secondaire: apprentissage des ITS à l'aide d'un jeu éducatif en ligne*. Québec, Canada: Rapport de recherche, mars.

Sauvé, L., Renaud, L., Kaufman, D., & Sibomana, F. (2008). Revue systématique des écrits (1998-2007) sur les impacts du jeu, de la simulation et du jeu de simulation sur l'apprentissage. Rapport final [Systematic review on the impact of games, simulations, and simulation games on learning: Final report]. Québec: SAGE et SAVIE, mars.

Savery, J. R., & Duffy, T. M. (1995). Problem based learning: an instructional model and its constructivist framework. *Educational Technology, 35*, 31–38.

Schacter, J., Herl, H. E., Chung, G. K. W. K., Dennis, R. A., & O'Neil, H. F. (1999). Computer-based performance assessments: a solution to the narrow measurement and reporting of problem-solving. *Computers in Human Behavior, 15*(3-4), 403–418. doi:10.1016/S0747-5632(99)00029-1

Schank, R. C., & Abelson, R. P. (1995). Knowledge and memory: The real story. In Wyer, R. S. (Ed.), *Knowledge and memory: The real story* (pp. 1–85). Hillsdale, NJ: Lawrence Erlbaum Associates.

Schank, R. C., Berman, T. R., Bransford, T. R., & Macpherson, K. A. (1999). Learning by doing. In Reigeluth, C. M. (Ed.), *Instructional Design Theories and Models: A New Paradigmof Instructional Theory* (pp. 161–179). Hillsdale, NJ: Lawrence Erlbaum Associates.

Schiefele, U. (1991). Interest, learning, and motivation. *Educational Psychologist, 26*, 299–323. doi:10.1207/s15326985ep2603&4_5

Schlaumäuse. (2009). *Österrreichisches Schlaumäuse-Kompetenzzentrum*. Retrieved March 13, 2009, from http://www.idv.edu/schlau/schlau1.ssi

Schrader, P. G., & Lawless, K. A. (in press). The hidden literacies of massively multiplayer online games. In Pullen, D. L., Baguley, M., & Gitsaki, C. (Eds.), *Technoliteracy, Discourse and Social Practice: Frameworks and Applications in the Digital Age*. Hershey, PA: Information Science Reference.

Schrader, P. G., & McCreery, M. (2007). The acquisition of skill and expertise in massively multiplayer online games. *Educational Technology Research & Development, 56*(5-6), 557–574. Retrieved October 10, 2007, from http://www.springerlink.com/content/n2496u376825u512/

Schrader, P. G., Lawless, K. A., & McCreery, M. (2009). Intertextuality in massively multiplayer online games. In Ferdig, R. E. (Ed.), *Handbook of Research on Effective Electronic Gaming in Education* (*Vol. 3*, pp. 791–807). Hershey, PA: Information Science Reference.

Schunk, D. H., & Pajares, F. (2001). The development of academic self-efficacy. In Wigfield, A., & Eccles, J. (Eds.), *Development of achievement motivation.* San Diego, CA: American Press.

Sfard, A. (2008). *Thinking as Communicating: Human development, the growth of discourses and mathematizing.* Cambridge: CUP. doi:10.1017/CBO9780511499944

Shaffer, D. (2007). *Epistemic games.* Innovate.

Shaffer, D. W. (2004). When computer-supported collaboration means computer-supported competition: Professional mediation as a model for collaborative learning. *Journal of Interactive Learning Research, 15*, 101–115.

Shaffer, D. W. (2007). *How Computer Games Help Children Learn.* New York: Palgrave.

Shaffer, D. W., & Gee, J. (2005). *Before every child is left behind: How epistemic games can solve the coming crisis in education.* Department of Educational Psychology, University of Wisconsin-Madison, WI. Retrieved January 20, 2009, from http://66.102.1.104/scholar?hl=en&lr=&q=cache:TrtOVvs0SUQJ:www.discoverproject.net/greece/images/learning_crisis.pdf+shaffer++and+gee

Shaffer, D. W., Squire, K. R., Halverson, R., & Gee, J. P. (2004). *Video games and the future of learning.* Retrieved February 27, 2009, from http://www.academiccolab.org/resources/gappspaper1.pdf

Shaftel, J., Pass, L., & Schnabel, S. (2005). Math Games for Adolescents. *Teaching Exceptional Children, 37*(3), 27–33.

Sharrock, W. W., & Watson, D. R. (1987). Power and realism in simulations and gaming: Some pedagogic and analytic observations. In Crookall, D., Greenblat, C., Coote, A., Klabbers, J., & Watson, D. (Eds.), *Simulation-gaming in the late 1980's* (pp. 35–42). Oxford, UK: Pergamon.

Shaw, E., LaBore, C., Chiu, Y. C., & Johnson, W. L. (2004). Animating 2D Digital Puppets with Limited Autonomy. *Proc. of the Smart Graphics 4th Int'l Symposium, SG 2004.*

Sherry, J. L. (2004). Flow and media enjoyment. *Communication Theory, 14*, 392–410. doi:10.1111/j.1468-2885.2004.tb00318.x

Shimai, S., Masuda, K., & Kishimoto, Y. (1990). Influence of TV games on physical and psychological development of Japanese kindergarten children. *Perceptual and Motor Skills, 70*, 771–776. doi:10.2466/PMS.70.3.771-776

Shin, B. (2007). *The effect of the interaction patterns on the task commitment according to sociality level of the students in Educational game.* Unpublished master's thesis. Korea National University of Education.

Shirky, C. (2008a). *Gin, Television, and Social Surplus.* Retrieved January 20, 2009, from http://www.shirky.com/herecomeseverybody/2008/04/looking-for-the-mouse.html

Shirky, C. (2008b). *Here comes everybody: The power of organizing without organizations.* New York: Penguin Press.

Shirts, R. G. (1989). The second revolution. *Simulation & Games, 20*(2), 130–143. doi:10.1177/104687818902000202

Shreve, J. (2005). Let the Games Begin. Video Games, Once Confiscated in Class, Are Now a Key Teaching Tool. If They're Done Right. *George Lucas Educational Foundation.* (Eric Document Reproduction Service No. ED 484 766).

Shubik, M. (1989). Gaming: Theory and Practice, Past and Future. *Simulation & Games*, *20*(2), 184–189. doi:10.1177/104687818902000205

Shute, V. (2006). *Focus on formative feedback*. Unpublished manuscript. Princeton, NJ: Educational Testing Service.

Shute, V., & Psotka, J. (1996). Intelligent tutoring systems: Past, present, and future. In Jonassen, D. H. (Ed.), *Handbook of research for educational communications and technology* (pp. 570–600). New York: Macmillan Library Reference USA.

Silverman, B. G., Holmes, J., Kimmel, S., & Branas, C. (2002). Computer games may be good for your health. *Journal of Healthcare Information Management*, *16*(2), 80–85.

Smith, A., & Rainie, L. (2008). *The Internet and the 2008 election*. Washington, DC: Pew Internet and American Life Project. Retrieved July 17, 2008, from http://www.pewinternet.org/pdfs/PIP_2008_election.pdf

Smithers, A., & Robinson, P. (2005). *Physics in Schools and Colleges: Teacher Deployment and Student Outcomes*. Buckingham, UK: Carmichael Press, University of Buckingham.

Smithers, A., & Robinson, P. (2006). *Physics in Schools and Universities: Patterns and Policies*. Buckingham, UK: Carmichael Press, University of Buckingham.

Smyth, J. M. (2007). Beyond self-selection in video game play: an experimental examination of the consequences of massively multiplayer online role-playing game play. *Cyberpsychology & Behavior*, *10*, 717–721. doi:10.1089/cpb.2007.9963

Snow, C. E. (2002). *Reading for understanding: Toward an R&D program in reading comprehension*. Santa Monica, CA: Rand Education.

Snyder, T. D. (2009). *Mini-Digest of Education Statistics, 2008 (NCES 2009-021). National Center for Education Statistics, Institute of Education Sciences, U.* Washington, DC: S. Department of Education.

Spires, H. A. (2008). *21st century skills and serious games: Preparing the N generation*. Retrieved March 13, 2009, from http://www.fi.ncsu.edu/assets/research_papers/crystal-island-5/21st-century-skills-and-serious-games-preparing-the-n-generation.pdf

Spires, H. A., Lee, J. K., & Lester, J. (2008). *The twenty-first century learner and game-based learning*. Retrieved February 16, 2009, from http://www.ncsu.edu/meridian/win2008/21st/print.html

Sprecht, L., & Sandlin, P. (1991). The differential effects of experiential learning activities and traditional lecture classes in accounting. *Simulation & Gaming*, *22*(2), 196–210. doi:10.1177/1046878191222003

Springer, C. W., & Borthick, A. F. (2004). Business simulation to stage critical thinking in introductory accounting: Rationale, design, and implementation. *Issues in Accounting Education*, *19*(3), 277–303. doi:10.2308/iace.2004.19.3.277

Squire, K. (2002). Cultural framing of computer/video games. *The International Journal of Computer Game Research*, *2*(1). Retrieved August 19, 2009, from http://www.gamestudies.org/0102/squire/

Squire, K. (2003). Video games in education. *International Journal of Intelligent Simulations and Gaming*, *2*(1). Retrieved June 5, 2009, from http://website.education.wisc.edu/kdsquire/tenure-files/39-squire-IJIS.pdf

Squire, K. (2004). *Replaying history: Learning world history through playing Civilization III.* Unpublished Doctoral Dissertation, Indiana University, Bloomington, IN.

Squire, K. (2006). From Content to Context: Videogames as Designed Experience. *Educational Researcher*, *35*(8), 19–29. doi:10.3102/0013189X035008019

Squire, K. (2008). *Video game-based learning: An emerging paradigm for instruction*. Retrieved March 13, 2009, from http://website.education.wisc.edu/kdsquire/tenure-files/09-PIQ-Squire-submitted.pdf

Squire, K. D. (2006). From content to context: videogames as designed experience. *Educational Researcher*, *35*(8), 19–29. doi:10.3102/0013189X035008019

Squire, K. D., & Jan, M. (2007). *Mad City Mystery: Developing scientific argumentation skills with a place-based augmented reality game on handheld computers.* Retrieved March 13, 2009, from http://website.education.wisc.edu/kdsquire/manuscripts/madcity-squire-jan-final.pdf

Steiner, B., Kaplan, N., & Moulthrop, S. (2006). *When play works: Turning game-playing into learning.* Paper presented at the 2006 Conference on Interaction Design and Children, Tampere, Finland.

Steinkuehler, C. (2006). Games as a highly visible medium for the study of distributed, situated cognition. In S.A. Barab, K.E. Hay, N.B. Songer, & D.T. Hickey (Eds.), *Proceedings of the International Conference of the Learning Sciences* (pp. 1048-1049). Mahwah, NJ: Erlbuam.

Steinkuehler, C. (2007). Massively multiplayer online gaming as a constellation of literacy practices. In B. E. Shelton & D. Wiley (Eds.), *The design and use of simulation computer games in education* (pp. 187-212). Rotterdam, The Netherlands: Sense Publishers. Retrieved October 22, 2008, from http://inst.usu.edu/~bshelton/simcompgames/steinkuehler_187-212.pdf

Steinkuehler, C. A. (2004). Learning in massively multiplayer online games. In Y. B. Kafai, W. A. Sandoval, N. Enyedy, A. S. Nixon, & F. Herrera (Eds.), *Proceedings of the Sixth International Conference of the Learning Sciences* (pp.521–528). Mahwah, NJ: Erlbaum.

Steinkuehler, C. A. (2006). Why game (culture) studies now? *Games and Culture, 1*, 1–6. doi:10.1177/1555412005281911

Steinkuehler, C., & Chmiel, M. (2006). Fostering scientific habits of mind in the context of online play. In S. A. Barab, K. E. Hay, N. B. Songer & D. T. Hickey (Eds.), *Proceedings of the International Conference of the Learning Sciences* (pp. 723-729). Mahwah, NJ: Erlbaum.

Steinkuehler, C., & Johnson, B. Z. (2009). Computational Literacy in Online Games: The Social Life of Mods. *International Journal of Gaming and Computer-Mediated Simulations, 1*(1), 53–65.

Steinkuehler, C., & Williams, D. (2006). Where everybody knows your (screen) name: Online games as third places. *Journal of Computer-Mediated Communication, 11*(4). Retrieved June 26, 2009, from http://jcmc.indiana.edu/vol11/issue4/steinkuehler.html doi:10.1111/j.1083-6101.2006.00300.x

Steinman, R. A., & Blastos, M. T. (2002). A trading-card game teaching about host defence. *Medical Education, 36*(12), 1201–1208. doi:10.1046/j.1365-2923.2002.01384.x

Stembler, W. A. (1975). Cognitive effects of a programmed simulation. *Simulation & Games, 6*(4), 392–403. doi:10.1177/003755007500600403

Stephen, C., McPake, J., Plowman, L., & Berch-Heyman, S. (2008). Learning from the children: exploring preschool children's encounters with ICT at home. *Journal of Early Childhood Research, 6*, 99–117. doi:10.1177/1476718X08088673

Stewart, S. (2008). *Alternate reality games.* Retrieved from http://www.seanstewart.org/interactive/args/

Strogatz, S. (2004). *Sync: The Emerging Science of Spontaneous Order.* New York: Hyperion.

Subrahmanyam, K., & Greenfield, P. M. (1998). Computer games for girls: What makes them play? In Cassell, J., & Jenkins, H. (Eds.), *From Barbie to Mortal Combat: Gender and computer games.* Cambridge, MA: MIT Press.

Subrahmanyam, K., Greenfield, P. M., Kraut, P. M., & Gross, E. (2001). The Impact of computer use on children's development. *Journal of Applied Developmental Psychology, 22*, 7–30. doi:10.1016/S0193-3973(00)00063-0

Suppes, P. (1990). Three current tutoring systems and future needs. In Frasson, C., & Gauthier, G. (Eds.), *Intelligent Tutoring Systems: At the Crossroads of Artificial Intelligence and Education* (pp. 251–265). Norwood, NJ: Ablex Publishing.

Swaak, J., & de Jong, T. (2001). Discovery simulations and the assessment of intuitive knowledge. *Journal of Computer Assisted Learning, 17*, 284. doi:10.1046/j.0266-4909.2001.00183.x

Tang, S., Hanneghan, M., & El-Rhalibi, A. (2007). *Pedagogy Elements, Components and Structures for Serious Games Authoring Environment.* Paper presented at the 5th International Game Design and Technology Workshop (GDTW 2007), Liverpool, UK.

Tansey, P. J. (1970). Simulation techniques in training of teachers. *Simulation & Games*, *1*(3), 281–303. doi:10.1177/104687817000100303

Technorati. (2008). *State of the Blogosphere 2008.* Retrieved April 5, 2009, from http://technorati.com/blogging/state-of-the-blogosphere/

TEEM. (2002). *Report on the Educational Use of Games – An Exploration by TEEM of the contribution which games can make to the education process.* Retrieved December 28, 2008, from http://www.teem.org.uk/publications/teem_gamesined_full.pdf.

Tergan, S.-O. (1998). Checklists for the evaluation of educational software: Critical review and prospects. *Innovations in Education and Training International.* Retrieved March 26, 2009 from http://www.highbeam.com/doc/1P3-29781007.html

Thatcher, D. (1990). Promoting learning through games and simulations. *Simulation & Gaming*, *21*(2), 196–210.

The Week. (2007, February 16). Living in a virtual world. *The Week: The Best of the U.S. & International Media.*

Thomas, D., & Brown, J. S. (2009). *Why virtual worlds can matter.* Retrieved February 3, 2009 from http://www.johnseelybrown.com/needvirtualworlds.pdf

Tobias, S. (1994). Interest, prior knowledge, and learning. *Review of Educational Research*, *64*, 37–54.

Tomorrow Project. (2007). *Speak Up Survey 2007.* Retrieved January 20, 2009, from http://www.tomorrow.org/speakup/speakup_reports.html

Toro-Troconis, M., & Partridge, M. (2007). Designing a 3D Teaching Hospital in Second Life to support clinical skills development. In *Proceedings of the Association for Medical Education in Europe (AMEE)*, NTNU Norwegian University of Science and Technology, Trondheim, Norway, 25-29 August.

Toro-Troconis, M., Partridge, M., Mellstrom, U., Meeran, K., & Higham, J. (2010). Design and Delivery of game-based learning for virtual patients in Second Life®: initial findings. In Peachey, A., Gillen, J., Livingstone, D., & Robbins, S. (Eds.), *Researching Learning in Virtual Worlds.* London: Springer. doi:10.1007/978-1-84996-047-2_7

TPCK. (2008). *TPCK - Technological Pedagogical Content Knowledge.* Retrieved September 9, 2008, from http://www.tpck.org/tpck/index.php?title=Main_Page

Tutak, T., & Birgin, O. (2008). The effect of computer assisted instruction on the students' achievement in geometry. *International Educational Technology Conference Proceedings* (pp.1062-1065). Ankara, Turkey: Nobel Yayin Dağtum

Udousoro, U. J. (2000). *The relative effect of computer and text- assisted programmed instruction on student's learning outcomes in mathematics.* Unpublished Ph.D. Dissertation. University of Ibadan,Nigeria.

Ulrich, M. (1997). Links Between Experiential Learning and Simulation & Gaming. In J. Geurts, C. Joldersma, & E. Roelofs (Eds.), *Gaming/Simulation for Policy Development and Organizational Change.* Proceedings of the 28th Annual International Conference of the International Simulation and Gaming Association (ISAGA) July 1997, Tilburg, the Netherlands (pp. 269-275).

Union Européenne en Éducation des médias. (2006). *The appropriation of New Media by Youth.* A European Research Project, Mediappro.

United States Census Bureau. (2005). *Voting and registration in the election of November 2004.* Retrieved June 19, 2007, from http://www.census.gov/population/www/socdemo/voting/cps2004.html

Vail, K. (1997). Girlware. *The American School Board Journal*, *184*, A18–A21.

Vale, C. M., & Leder, G. C. (2004). Student Views of Computer-Based Mathematics in the Middle Years: Does Gender Make a Difference? *Educational Studies in Mathematics*, *56*(2/3), 287–312. doi:10.1023/B:EDUC.0000040411.94890.56

Van Eck, R. (2006, March/April). Digital Game-Based Learning: It's Not Just the Digital Natives Who Are Restless. *EDUCAUSE Review, 41*(2), 16–30.

Van Eck, R. (2007). Building Intelligent Learning Games. In Gibson, D., Aldrich, C., & Prensky, M. (Eds.), *Games and Simulations in Online Learning Research & Development Frameworks*. Hershey, PA: Idea Group.

Van Lehn, K., Graesser, A. C., Jackson, G. T., Jordan, P., Olney, A., & Rose, C. P. (2007). When are tutorial dialogues more effective than reading? *Cognitive Science Journal, 31*, 3–62.

Van Lehn, K., Lynch, C., Schulze, K., Shapiro, J. A., Shelby, R., & Taylor, L. (2005). The Andes Physics Tutoring System: Lessons Learned. *International Journal of Artificial Intelligence in Education, 15*, 147–204.

Vandeventer, S. S., & White, J. A. (2002). Expert Behavior in Children's Video Game Play. *Simulation & Gaming, 33*(1), 28–48. doi:10.1177/1046878102033001002

VanFossen, P. (1999-2000). An analysis of the use of the Internet and World Wide Web by secondary social studies teachers in Indiana. *The International Journal of Social Education, 14*(2), 87–109.

VanFossen, P. J., Friedman, A. M., & Hartshorne, R. (2008). The emerging role of synthetic worlds and massively-multiplayer online role-playing games (MMORPGs) in social studies and citizenship education. In Ferdig, R. (Ed.), *Handbook of research on effective electronic gaming in education* (pp. 235–250). Hershey, PA: IGI Publishing.

Varela, F., Thompson, E., & Rosch, E. (1991). *The embodied mind.* Cambridge, MA: The MIT Press.

Veugen, C., & de Lange, M. (2007). Learning can't be fun, can it. In Siebehhanddl, K., Wagner, M., & Zauchner, S. (Eds.), *Gender in E-learning and Educational Games* (pp. 239–260). Innsbruck, Austria: Studienverlag.

Virtual reality. (2009). Merriam-Webster Online Dictionary. Retrieved August 26, 2009, from http://www.merriam-webster.com/dictionary/virtual reality

Virvou, M., Katsionis, G., & Manos, K. (2005). Combining Software Games with Education: Evaluation of its Educational Effectiveness. *Educational Technology & Society, 8*(2), 54–65.

Vorderer, P., & Bryant, J. (2006). *Playing computer games – Motives, responses, and consequences.* Mahwah, NJ: Lawrence Erlbaum Associates.

Vorderer, P., Klimmt, C., & Ritterfeld, U. (2004). Enjoyment: At the heart of media entertainment. *Communication Theory, 14*, 388–408. doi:10.1111/j.1468-2885.2004.tb00321.x

Vorderer, P., Wulff, H. J., & Friedrichsen, M. (1996). *Suspense: Conceptualizations, theoretical analyses, and empirical explorations.* Mahwah, NJ: Erlbaum.

Wang, S. K., & Reeves, T. C. (2007). The effects of a web-based learning environment on student motivation in a high school earth science course. *Educational Technology Research and Development, 55*(2), 169–192. doi:10.1007/s11423-006-9016-3

Ward, A. K., & O'Brien, H. L. (2005). A gaming adventure. *Journal for Nurses in Staff Development, 21*(1), 37–41. doi:10.1097/00124645-200501000-00009

Wasserman, L. H. (2007, June). The Correlation Between Brain Development, Language Acquisition, and Cognition. *Early Childhood Education Journal, 34*(6), 415–418. doi:10.1007/s10643-007-0155-x

Westheimer, J., & Kahne, J. (2004). What kind of citizen? The politics of educating for democracy. *American Educational Research Journal, 41*(2), 237–269. doi:10.3102/00028312041002237

Wiggins, G. (1992). Creating tests worth taking. *Educational Leadership, 49*(8), 26–33.

Wikipedia. (n.d.). *Civilization 4.* Retrieved from http://en.wikipedia.org/wiki/Civilization_IV

Wild, C. (2008). *ADRIFT – Adventure Development and Runner – Interactive Fiction Toolkit.* Retrieved from http://www.adrift.org.uk

Williamson, B., & Facer, K. (2004). More than 'just a game': the implications for schools of children's computer games communities. *Education Communication and Information*, *4*(2/3), 255. doi:10.1080/14636310412331304708

Winne, P. H. (2001). Self-regulated learning viewed from models of information processing. In Zimmerman, B. J., & Schunk, D. H. (Eds.), *Self-regulated learning and academic achievement: Theoretical perspectives*. Mahwah, NJ: Erlbaum.

Winne, P. H., & Hadwin, A. F. (2008). The weave of motivation and self-regulated learning. In Schunk, D. H., & Zimmerman, B. J. (Eds.), *Motivation and self-regulated learning: Theory, research, and applications* (pp. 297–314). Mahwah, NJ: Lawrence Erlbaum Associates.

Wisher, R. A., & Fletcher, J. D. (2004). The case for advanced distributed learning, information, and security. *International Journal (Toronto, Ont.)*, *14*, 17–25.

Wissmann, J. L., & Tankel, K. (2001). Nursing student's use of a psychopharmacology game for client empowerment. *Journal of Professional Nursing*, *17*(2), 101–106. doi:10.1053/jpnu.2001.22274

Wong, W. (2007 May). Gaming In Education. *Ed Tech Magazine*. Retrieved April 10, 2008, from http://www.edtechmag.com/higher/may-june-2007/gaming-in-education.html

Wood, D. (2001). In search of fluency: What is it and how can we teach it? *Canadian Modern Language Review*, *57*, 573–589.

Woodcock, B. S. (2008a). *MMOGCHART.COM*. Retrieved on October 2, 2008, from http://www.mmogchart.com/category/charts/

Woodcock, B. S. (2008b). *MMOG Subscriptions Market Share – April 2008*. Retrieved on October 2, 2008, from http://www.mmogchart.com/Chart7.html

Woolf, B. (1990). 20 Years in the Trenches: What have we learned? In Frasson, C., & Gauthier, G. (Eds.), *Intelligent Tutoring Systems: At the Crossroads of Artificial Intelligence and Education* (pp. 234–250). Norwood, NJ: Ablex Publishing.

Woolf, B. P. (2009). *Building intelligent interactive tutors*. Burlington, MA: Morgan Kaufmann Publishers.

Xenos, M., & Foot, K. (2008). Not your father's Internet: The generation gap in online politics. In Bennett, W. L. (Ed.), *Civic life online: Learning how digital media can engage youth* (pp. 51–70). Cambridge, MA: The MIT Press.

Yang, H. L., & Wang, C. S. (2008). Product placement of computer games in cyberspace. *Cyberpsychology & Behavior*, *11*(4), 399–404. doi:10.1089/cpb.2007.0099

Yee, N. (2006). Motivations for play in online games. *Cyberpsychology & Behavior*, *9*(6), 772–775. doi:10.1089/cpb.2006.9.772

Yee, N. (2006). The Demographics, Motivations and Derived Experiences of Users of Massively-Multiuser Online Graphical Environments. *Presence (Cambridge, Mass.)*, *15*, 309–329. doi:10.1162/pres.15.3.309

Yee, N. (2007). *The Daedalus Project*. Additional player demographics. Retrieved on October 9, 2008, from http://www.nickyee.com/daedalus/archives/001556.php

Yip, F. W. M., & Kwan, A. C. M. (2006). Online vocabulary games as a tool for teaching and learning English vocabulary. *Educational Media International*, *43*(3), 233–249. doi:10.1080/09523980600641445

Young, M. E., & Nguyen, N. (2009). The problem of delayed causation in a video game: Constant, varied, and filled delays. *Learning and Motivation*, *40*(3), 298–312. doi:10.1016/j.lmot.2009.02.002

Young, M. F., Schrader, P. G., & Zheng, D. P. (2006). MMOGs as Learning environments: an ecological journey into Quest Atlantis and the Sims Online. *Innovate*, *2*(4). Retrieved March 20, 2006, http://www.innovateonline.info/index.php?view=article&id=66

Young, R. M. (2006). *Story and discourse: A bipartite model of narrative generation in virtual worlds*. Interaction Studies.

Zimmerman, B. J., & Kitsantas, A. (1997). Developmental phases in self-regulation: Shifting from process goals to outcome goals. *Journal of Educational Psychology, 89*, 29–36. doi:10.1037/0022-0663.89.1.29

Zimmerman, B. J., & Schunk, D. H. (2001). Reflections on theories of self- regulated learning and academic achievement. In Zimmerman, B. J., & Schunk, D. H. (Eds.), *Self-regulated learning and academic achievement: Theoretical perspectives* (pp. 289–307). Mahwah, NJ: Erlbaum.

Zyda, M., Hiles, J., Mayberry, A., Wardynski, C., Capps, M., & Osborm, M. (2003). *Entertainment R&D for Defense*. IEEE Comp.Graphics and Applications.

Zyda, M., Mayberry, A., McCree, J., & Davis, M. (2005). From Viz-Sim to VR to Games: How We Built a Hit Game-Based Simulation. In Rouse, W. B., & Boff, K. R. (Eds.), *Organizational Simulation: From Modeling & Simulation to Games & Entertainment*. New York: Wiley Press.

About the Contributors

Youngkyun Baek Ph.D., has been teaching at Korea National University of Education since 1991. His research interests are on educational games, simulation, and mobile devices in education. He has presented several papers at SITE and NECC on gaming and simulations. He published three books on educational games and wrote two books chapters: "Design of an adaptive mobile learning management system based on student learning styles" in Handbook of Research on User Interface Design and Evaluation For Mobile Technology; "Revealing New Hidden Curriculum of Digital Games" in Handbook of Research on Effective Electronic Gaming in Education (IGI Global). He is co-author of the book entitled "Digital Simulations for Improving Education: Learning Through Artificial Teaching Environments" by IGI Global. Now he is authoring the book, "Gaming for Classroom-Based Learning: Digital Role Playing as a Motivator of Study". He developed the Virtual English Adventure in Second Life recently.

* * *

Ayotola Aremu has a B.Sc in Electrical and Electronics Engineering , M.Ed and Ph. D in Educational Technology. A Senior Lecturer in the Department of Teacher Education, University of Ibadan, Nigeria, she teaches courses on the integration of technologies into teaching and learning processes at both the undergraduate and post-graduate levels. Her research interests (in which areas she has published severally) include the design and development of mathematics teaching and learning resources which are developmentally appropriate and culturally relevant particularly for girls.

Brian Bauer is the founder and Managing Partner at Étape Partners LLC / OnTrack Technology, and is responsible for business development and overall company strategy. Brian is committed to designing innovative technology solutions for collaboration, learning and communication. With customers including the largest public-education system in the country and other Fortune 25 companies, Brian's expertise has made him an in-demand speaker/author on the topic of 3D virtual learning.

Lisa Carrington is a PhD candidate in the Faculty of Education, University of Wollongong. Lisa's PhD utilises a comparative case study approach focusing on the experiences of first and final year pre-service teachers enrolled in an undergraduate education degree who engaged with a virtual learning environment provided by an online classroom simulation (ClassSim). Lisa Carrington expects to submit her PhD thesis late 2009. Lisa is currently teaching in the area of ICT education and research methods and is completing a Graduate Certificate in Research Commercialisation at the University of Wollongong.

Chaka Chaka is a senior lecturer in the Department of English at Walter Sisulu University (Eastern Cape, South Africa). His research interests include: collaborative learning (CL); concept mapping; computer-mediated communication (CMC); electronic learning (e-learning); computer assisted language learning (CALL); mobile learning (m-learning); mobile assisted language learning (MALL); Web 2.0 learning/Mobile Web 2.0 learning; Web 3.0/Mobile Web 3.0 learning; Semantic Web/Mobile Semantic Web; game based learning (GBL); online genre and discourse analysis; online/digital and virtual identities; knowledge management (KM); and learning organisation (LO).

Brian Ferry is a Professor in the Faculty of Education, University of Wollongong. His research interests focus on pre-service teacher education and the use simulations and games as authentic learning environments. He teaches science and ICT education and currently supervises nine PhD students. Outside of university he is interested in travel and golf.

Adam M. Friedman is an Assistant Professor, Director of Social Studies Education, and Director of Secondary Education in the Department of Education at Wake Forest University. He teaches undergraduate and graduate secondary social studies methods, undergraduate elementary social studies methods, a course in descriptive research in social studies, and conducts student teaching supervision. Among his research interests is to scrutinize the potential effect and impact of the Internet (particularly MMORPGs and other Web 2.0 tools) on citizenship education within the field of social studies. Dr. Friedman has published his research in various social studies and technology journals and book chapters. He was formerly the co-chair of the technology committee of the National Council for the Social Studies, and is currently the Treasurer of the North Carolina Council of Professors of Social Studies Education.

David Gibson is Associate Research Professor of Education at the Fulton Institute and Graduate School of Education at Arizona State University. He conducts research at the Equity Alliance at ASU (http://www.equityallianceatasu.org/) and is Executive Director of The Global Challenge Award (www.globalchallengeaward.org), a team and project-based learning and scholarship program for high school students that engages small teams in studying science, technology, engineering and mathematics in order to solve global problems. Dr. Gibson's research and publications include work on complex systems analysis and modeling of education, Web applications and the future of learning, the use of technology to personalize education, and the potential for games and simulation-based learning. He is creator of simSchool (www.simschool.org), a classroom flight simulator for training teachers, currently funded by the US Department of Education FIPSE program and eFolio, an online performance assessment system. His business, CURVESHIFT, is an educational technology company (www.curveshift.com) that assists in the acquisition, implementation and continuing design of games and simulations, e-portfolio systems, data-driven decision making tools, and emerging technologies.

Art Graesser is a professor in the Department of Psychology, adjunct professor in Computer Science, and co-director of the Institute of Intelligent Systems at the University of Memphis. He received his Ph.D. in psychology from the University of California at San Diego. His primary research interests are in cognitive science, discourse processing, and the learning sciences. More specific interests include knowledge representation, question asking and answering, tutoring, text comprehension, inference generation, conversation, reading, education, memory, artificial intelligence, and human-computer interaction. He served as editor of the journal Discourse Processes (1996–2005), is the current editor of

Journal of Educational Psychology, is president of the Society for Text and Discourse, and was recent president of Artificial Intelligence in Education. He and his research team has designed, developed, and tested intelligent software in learning, language, and discourse technologies, including AutoTutor, Coh-Metrix, HURA Advisor, SEEK Web Tutor, MetaTutor, Operation ARIES!, Question Understanding Aid, QUEST, and Point&Query.

Shawn Graham is an Adjunct Professor of History with Grand Canyon University in Phoenix Arizona. He specializes in the use of digital media for learning and research in archaeology and history. He is also a Faculty Specialist in the Department of Faculty Training and Development at GCU, where he supports quality assurance and training for GCU's online faculty. He trained at the University of Reading, and prior to working with Grand Canyon, held posts at the University of Manitoba, Brock University, Roehampton University, and Birkbeck College University of London. He has written extensively on agent-based simulations for studying antiquity, and produces historically-themed mods for Civilization IV.

Richard Hartshorne is an Assistant Professor of Instructional Systems Technology at the University of North Carolina at Charlotte. He earned his Ph.D. in Curriculum and Instruction from the University of Florida. At the University of North Carolina at Charlotte, his teaching focuses on the integration of technology into the educational landscape, as well as instructional design and development. His research interests primarily involve the production and effective integration of instructional technology into the teaching and learning environment. The major areas of his research interest are rooted in online teaching and learning, technology and teacher education, and the integration of emerging technology into the k-post-secondary curriculum.

G. Tanner Jackson is a Postdoctoral Research Fellow in the Department of Psychology at the University of Memphis. His academic background includes a B.A. in Psychology (2001, Rhodes College), a M.S. in Cognitive Psychology (2004, University of Memphis), and a Ph.D. in Cognitive Psychology (2007, University of Memphis). His research focus is in cognitive science and specific interests include human-computer interaction, intelligent tutoring systems, serious games, and pedagogical design. These interests have led him to collaborate on numerous learning environments (AutoTutor, AutoTutor-3D, HURAA, iSTART, Writing Pal) which span multiple funding agencies (NSF, IES, ONR, DoD, IDA, SBIRs). He has also served as a reviewer for several publication outlets (Journal of Educational Psychology, Discourse Processes, Journal of Media Psychology), and recently won the Cognition and Student Learning Prize at the 2009 Cognitive Science Society Conference.

Regina Kaplan-Rakowski has a strong background in foreign languages, which allows her to combine expertise in applied linguistics with the research opportunities that are available using modern instructional technology. Kaplan-Rakowski's education includes B.Ed. in TESL, M.Ed. in European Studies, and M.A. in Foreign Languages and Literatures. Presently, she is pursuing a doctorate in Curriculum & Instruction (Instructional Technology & Design) at Southern Illinois University, Carbondale. Her current focus is research on the educational possibilities of teaching foreign languages in virtual environments, especially through virtual worlds and digital games. Nevertheless, she has also accumulated detailed research interests in second language acquisition, especially in bilingualism/multilingualism, code-switching, and the application of mnemonics in language acquisition and instruction.

Elisabeth Katzlinger-Felhofer is research assistant and lecturer at the Department of Data Processing in Social Sciences, Economics and Business, Johannes Kepler University Linz, Austria. She has degrees in business administration and business education. She received her doctorate in business administration from the Johannes Kepler University Linz, Austria. Her research focus is in business education and technology enhanced learning. Early childhood education and game-based learning is another research interest. She teaches information processing, e-tutoring and business and internet, it is an introductory course to e-business.

Kevin Kee is the Canada Research Chair of Humanities Computing, and an Associate Professor of History, at Brock University in St. Catharines, Ontario. He researches best practices for the design, development and use of computer simulations and serious games for history. He has written extensively on history computing and has developed history Web sites, simulations and games. He also specializes in Canadian cultural history. Before arriving to Brock in 2005, he was a Director and Project Director at the National Film Board of Canada (1999-2002), and an Assistant Professor at McGill University (2002-2005).

Lisa Kervin is a lecturer in the Faculty of Education, University of Wollongong. She has taught across the primary grades and has been employed in consultancy roles within New South Wales education systems. She graduated in July 2004 with her PhD and her thesis was focused on the professional development of teachers in literacy. Lisa Kervin's current research interests are related to the literacy development of children, the use of technology to support student learning and teacher professional development.

Hoe Kyeung Kim Ph.D. is an Assistant Professor of TESOL program, Department of Teacher Education at Cleveland State University, Ohio. At Cleveland State University, she teaches master's and undergraduate courses of second language acquisition, TESOL methods and materials, assessment and evaluation for ESL/Bilingual class, and TESOL practicum. She received her Ph.D. in Foreign and Second Language Education with a certificate in Advanced Educational Technology from the University at Buffalo. She is currently working on ESL/EFL learners' participation patterns in online discussions. Her research interests focus on second language acquisition, educational technology and teacher education. Since 2000, she has presented her research on language teaching and computer use at numerous national and international professional conferences, including TESOL, AERA, CALICO and SITE. She is a co-editor of Research in Second Language Learning in the 2011 volume. Her articles are published in peer-reviewed journals including Foreign Language Annals and Calico Journal.

Christian Sebastian Loh is an Assistant Professor of Instructional Design Technology and one of the coordinators for the /Collaboratory for Interactive Learning Research/ (CILR) at the Southern Illinois University, Carbondale. He also serves as President (2008-2009) for the Multimedia Production Division (MPD) of the Association for Educational Communications and Technology (AECT), reviews journal papers as an associate editor for the International Journal of Games and Computer-Mediated Simulation (IJGCMS), and judges professional serious game competitions. His publications include journal articles and book chapters on and about serious games, assessment, music education, and emerging technology. Currently, he is pioneering the research on "Information Trails": a user behavior analysis framework for performance assessment within multi-user virtual environment, including serious games and virtual worlds.

Hélder Fanha Martins is currently writing his PhD thesis on information systems applied to education and training and has written several articles on the topic of virtual teams. His experience in the fields of technology extends to the project management sector as well. Hélder Fanha Martins is lecturer of business management at the Lisbon School of Accounting and Administration (Lisbon Polytechnic). He is currently teaching a Business Simulation course as well as a Principles of Management course.

Danielle S. McNamara is a professor in the Department of Psychology and the Director of the Institute for Intelligent Systems at the University of Memphis. Her academic background includes a Linguistics B.A. (1982), a Clinical Psychology M.S. (1989), and a Ph.D. in Cognitive Psychology (1992; UC-Boulder). Her current research ranges a variety of topics including text comprehension, writing strategies, building tutoring technologies, serious games, and developing natural language algorithms. The goal of her research is to further our theoretical understanding of cognition and to apply that understanding to educational practice by creating and testing educational technologies (e.g., Coh-Metrix, iSTART, Writing Pal). She has served on the editorial boards of Discourse Processes, Memory & Cognition, and JEP:LMC and currently serves as Associate Editor for three journals (topiCS, the Cognitive Science Journal, the Journal of Educational Psychology). She has served on numerous review panels for funding agencies and on society governing boards.

June Moore is currently employed as a Research Assistant at the University of Worcester on a joint project between the Department of Psychology and Computing at the Worcester Business School. Her expertise lies in education theories and instructional design principles. Her research interests involve the mapping of these theories and principles onto the design and development of serious games. June has developed and evaluated serious games for the teaching of Literacy and Numeracy in Primary Schools in the UK. Central to her research is a close iterative involvement with both teachers and pupils.

Daniel W. O'Brien is a doctoral student in Educational Psychology with a focus on Cognition and Instruction at the University of Illinois at Chicago. He received a M.Ed. in Educational Psychology with a concentration in MESA (Measurement, Evaluation, Statistics, and Assessment) from UIC. He is a former middle-school Language Arts teacher and received a B.A. in Creative Writing from San Francisco State University. His research interests include the assessment of ill-structured problem solving, the use of computer games in problem-based learning and applications of Rasch models. His curriculum vita is available at dwobrien.wordpress.com.

Martyn R. Partridge is Professor of Respiratory Medicine in Imperial College London, NHLI Division based at the Charing Cross Hospital, and Honorary Consultant Physician to Imperial College Healthcare NHS Trust. He is Lead Director of the North West London Comprehensive Local Research Network. His academic interests are in evaluating the delivery of respiratory health care. Prof. Partridge is Immediate Past President of the British Thoracic Society. For two decades he was (Honorary) Chief Medical Advisor to Asthma UK (previously known as the National Asthma Campaign) and was involved in the production and dissemination of the British Asthma Guidelines from 1990 to 2008.He currently chairs the UK Department of Health Asthma Steering Group. He is an elected member of the Council of the Royal College of Physicians, Final Year Undergraduate Coordinator for the Faculty of Medicine, Imperial College London and on the Clinical Steering Committee of London Ambulance Service .

Collin Price started his career teaching physics at the British School of Brussels, Belgium for some six years. After obtaining a Ph.D in electronic engineering from the Catholic University of Leuven in Belgium, he joined the University staff and taught physics to first year undergraduates. He is currently Principal Lecturer in Computing at the University of Worcester where he teaches computer game development, Java programming and concepts and philosophy of computing. His research interests involve computer science education, theory and application of serious games, and self-organising pattern forming systems in biophysics. He collaborates in teaching and research with Moscow State University.

Louise Sauvé Professor at Télé-université, Quebec's distance education institution, received her doctorate in Educational Technology from the University of Montreal in 1985. She is Director of the Center for Expertise and Research in Lifelong Learning (SAVIE) for which she has obtained many major research grants and contracts. Dr. Sauvé has received numerous awards, notably the medal of the National Assembly of Quebec and the Special Prize of the Quebec Minister of Education, and has presented more than 250 scientific papers and workshops in North America, Europe, Asia, Central and South America, North Africa, and Australia. She has directed 20 university-level distance education courses and produced more than 60 research reports. Dr. Sauvé has published more than 160 research papers, review articles and book chapters. She also serves as a reviewer for several funding agencies and journals. Dr. Sauvé and her colleague Dr. Kaufman recently completed a $3 million, five-year project entitled Simulation and Advanced Gaming Environments (SAGE) for Learning. They currently hold an SSHRC research grant and are continuing their work in this area.

Maria Toro-Troconis is a senior learning technologist at the Faculty of Medicine, Imperial College London. Her main role is to support the development and delivery of the Faculty's e-learning strategy. Maria's background is in Computer Science and Human Factors. Maria is currently undertaking research in the area of game-based learning in virtual worlds. She initiated the Imperial College London Second Life region. She is also currently the technical lead and manager of this project. Her key skills include instructional design, coordination across distributed teams, business analysis and project management. She also has an in depth knowledge of International Learning Standards and their implementation across platforms.

Phillip J. VanFossen is the James F. Ackerman Professor of Social Studies Education and Director of the Ackerman Center for Democratic Citizenship in the College of Education at Purdue University. He is also the Associate Director of the Purdue University Center for Economic Education (and holds a courtesy appointment in the Krannert School of Management at Purdue) where he teaches introductory economics courses for the Economics department. He is the program author for the high school economics text Economics Alive! The Power to Choose (Teachers Curriculum Institute, 2009) His research interests include how social studies teachers use the Internet and digital media in their teaching and in 2008, he co-edited The Electronic Republic?: The Impact of Technology on Citizenship Education (Purdue University Press). Recently, this research interest has led him to explore the potential of virtual worlds (e.g., MMORPGs such as World of Warcraft) for social studies and citizenship education.

Tamara Vaughan is a teacher with the Western Quebec School Board, and a designer and teacher with LearnQuebec, the Leading English Education and Resource Network, which provides curricular materials and online learning to high school students across the province. She was educated at the University of Maine, McMaster University, and the University of Manitoba.

Index

D

E

I

K

L

M

N

O

P

Q

R

S

Y

Z